Contents

Dear Student,

On behalf of Center for Student Opportunity, thank you for picking up this copy of the *College Access & Opportunity Guide*.

We developed the Guide to help students like you get to college and succeed. In fact, with help from the Walmart Foundation last year, we traveled across the country to get feedback from students who helped make this year's Guide even better.

If you feel overwhelmed by the college process, don't worry! There are specific steps you need to take during the college-going process. With help from our friends at KnowHow2GO, the Guide will turn your college dreams into action-oriented goals and simplify the steps to college so you know what to do next.

It's your responsibility to find out which school is right for you. Asking the right questions and knowing what information to seek out is important. To help you get started, the Guide profiles 284 colleges and universities that are committed to helping students like you thrive in college.

Remember too that you are not alone on the college journey. In the Guide, you will read inspiring stories of students who have overcome many obstacles in their life to become first in their family to go to college. They, along with others, share great advice on how you too can become a college student.

We wish you the best of luck on this journey to college and hope you find the *College Access & Opportunity Guide* to be valuable along the way.

Joe Tavares
Program Director, *College Access & Opportunity Guide*

The Most Costly Education Is the One Not Begun. College Doesn't Just Happen!

KnowHow2GO

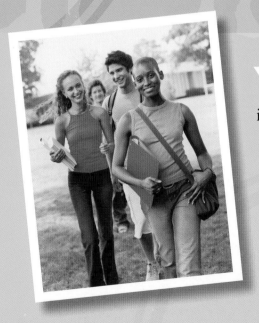

You have big plans. Big dreams. You know college is where to start. But a dream is not enough. College doesn't just happen; you have to work to make it a reality. Most people know **why** to go to college. We're here to tell you **how**. There are specific steps you need to take, and remember, it's never too early—or too late—to start on the road to college.

College is the first step in pursuing a successful and fulfilling career. It's not only where you explore different career options, but also where you learn essential job skills. "But college is so far off," you may be thinking. "It's too early to start preparing now." Think again!

Planning for college takes time. There are lots of things you need to know and do. Now is exactly when you need to think about what you want to do after high school. The choices you make today will determine you life tomorrow.

THE 4 STEPS TO COLLEGE

1. **Be a Pain.** Let everyone know that you're going to college and need their help!

2. **Push yourself.** Working a little harder today will make for a smoother road to college.

3. **Find the right fit.** Find out what kind of school is the best match for you and your goals.

4. **Put your hands on some cash.** If you think you can't afford college—think again. There is lots of aid out there.

About KnowHow2GO

Young people in all socio-economic groups have college aspirations. In fact, eight out of 10 expect to attain a bachelor's degree or higher, according to the U.S. Department of Education. But despite their aspirations, low-income students and those who are the first in their families to pursue higher education are severely underrepresented on college campuses. Studies show these students often lack the guidance they need to prepare for postsecondary education.

In order to turn these students' college dreams into action-oriented goals, the **American Council on Education, Lumina Foundation for Education and the Ad Council** launched the KnowHow2GO campaign in January 2007. This multi-year, multimedia effort includes television, radio, outdoor public service advertisements (PSAs), an interactive website KnowHow2GO.org—and now collaboration with **Center for Student Opportunity's** *College Access & Opportunity Guide*—to encourage students to prepare for college using four simple steps.

1 BE A PAIN (in a good way)

Find an adult who can help you with the steps to college. Let everyone know you want to go to college. And don't stop until you find an adult who will help you.

1 How2 BE A PAIN

• **Never say no.** Don't ever take that "no" in your head for an answer!

• **Find family support.** So what if your parents didn't go to college? Your folks may well have real experience and knowledge that can help you on your way.

• **Call on coaches.** Ask your teachers and coaches for advice on college–it's their job to help you succeed.

• **Gain experience.** Track down places outside school where you can get real-world experience from adults who can show you how it's done.

• **Seek advice.** If you can't talk with your school counselor, check your local community college or community center and meet with the counselors there.

• **Make connections.** Connect with family, friends, or neighbors who have been to college and ask them how they got there.

Why College

With everything you need to do to get ready for college, you may wonder if it's all worth it. Here are four quick (but very important) reasons why:

REASON **#1** Every bit of education you get after high school increases the chances you'll earn good pay. Most college graduates earn a lot more money during their working years than people who stop their education at high school.

REASON **#2** The more education you get, the more likely it is you will always have a job. According to one estimate, by the year 2028 there will be 19 million more jobs for educated workers than there are qualified people to fill them.

REASON **#3** Continuing education after high school is much more important for your generation than it was for your parents' generation. Today most good jobs require more than a high school diploma. Businesses want to hire people who know how to think and solve problems.

REASON **#4** Education beyond high school gives you a lot of other benefits, including meeting new people, taking part in new opportunities to explore your interests, and experiencing success.

ARE YOU READY FOR COLLEGE Quiz

Ninety percent of teens want to go to college, regardless of their income level.

⟶ TRUE   ⟶ FALSE

TRUE Unfortunately not all of these students have access to adult mentors who can guide them through the college preparation process.

Get the conversation started!

Planning for college isn't something you do by yourself—it's really a team effort. But it's up to you to put together your team. **And that means talking to the adults in your life who can help—from your parents, guardian, or other family members to your teachers, coaches, guidance counselor, or religious leader.**

YOUR PARENTS

The best way to communicate with parents, or any adult, is to keep talking to them, no matter what. Strong relationships really depend on keeping the lines of communication open. Here are some ways to approach your parents (or any adult) with a specific topic:

Plan what to say.

Think over what you want to say in advance, and write down the two or three most important points you want to make.

Be direct.

Let them know directly that there's something you'd like to discuss. Be sure you have their full attention and be direct in your language. Say, "There's something important I want to talk to you about" instead of "Hey, when you have a moment I'd like to talk."

Pick a good time to talk.

Try to approach them at a time when you know they'll be less busy and more able to focus on you. You may even want to ask if they could talk at a particular time so that you know you have their attention.

Write it down first.

Some people find it easier to put their ideas into a letter. Let the other person read it and then have your discussion.

Disagree without disrespect.

Parents are only human, and they can feel offended when their views are challenged. Using respectful language and behavior is important. Resist the temptation to use sarcasm, yell, or put down your parents and you'll have a much better chance of getting what you want.

OTHER ADULTS

No matter how good your relationship is with your parents or guardian, there will be times when you'll feel more comfortable confiding in other adults. Even if you'd rather talk to friends about certain things, an adult may have more experience, be able to contact the right person, or find the best resources to get help.

Ask for their word.

Most adults will keep your conversations confidential if you ask them to, unless they fear that your health or well-being may be in danger.

Other adults.

Other adults who may be able to help include teachers, your school guidance counselor, or other family members such as an aunt, uncle, or older sibling. Parents of a close friend may also be able to help.

Spiritual leaders.

If you're involved in a church group or belong to a synagogue or mosque, your spiritual or youth group leader may also be a good source of advice.

Extracurricular leaders.

If you're involved in an extracurricular activity, such as sports or drama, you may feel close enough to your coach or advisor to ask him or her about more personal stuff.

ARE YOU READY FOR COLLEGE Quiz

Parents are always the best people to talk to about preparing for college.

⟶ TRUE   ⟶ FALSE

FALSE
If your parents didn't go to college, chances are there's an adult in your life who did — and would be happy to help you prepare for college.

YOUR SCHOOL COUNSELOR

Your school counselor, or guidance counselor, may be one of your best resources as you plan for college. She or he has information about admission tests, college preparation, and your education and career options. Here are some basic questions to help get you started:

Questions to ask your school counselor

- Do you have any information to help me start exploring my interests and related careers?

- What are the required and recommended courses—for graduation and for college prep?

- How should I plan my schedule so I'll complete these courses?

- Do you have any after-school or evening sessions available for college planning?

- Do you have college handbooks or other guides that I can browse or borrow?

- What activities can I do at home and over the summer to get ready for college?

- What kinds of grades do different colleges require?

- Where do other kids from this school attend college?

- What are the requirements or standards for the honor society?

- How does our school compare to others, in terms of test scores and reputation?

- Which elective courses do you recommend?

- Which AP courses are available?

- When is the PSAT/NMSQT going to be given here?

- Is this school a testing center for standardized tests, or will I need to go somewhere nearby?

- Are there any college fairs at this school or nearby?

- Can you put me in touch with recent graduates who are going to the colleges on my list?

- If my colleges need a recommendation from you, how can I help you know me better so it can be more personal?

- Are there any special scholarships or awards I should know about now so I can work toward them?

- Can I see my transcript as it stands now to see if everything is as I think it should be?

- Do you have any forms I need to apply for financial aid?

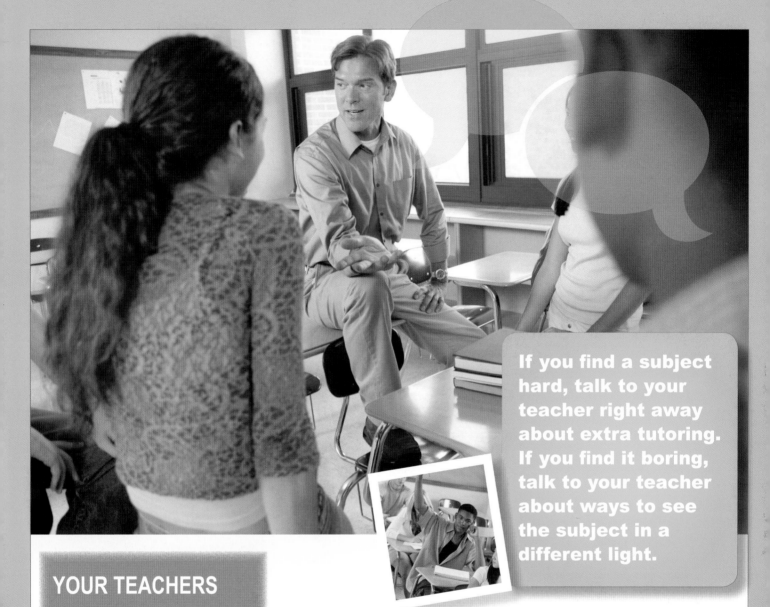

If you find a subject hard, talk to your teacher right away about extra tutoring. If you find it boring, talk to your teacher about ways to see the subject in a different light.

YOUR TEACHERS

OK, so it may be hard to think of your teachers as real people. But they eat pizza, watch movies, and enjoy sports on the weekends just like you. And they know about more than just their subject matter. Given the chance they can offer you the kind of advice and support that might change your life forever. Here's how to build a connection:

Show some interest.

Obviously, your teachers are really interested in their subjects. Showing the teacher that you care—even if you're not a math whiz or fluent in French—sends the message that you are a dedicated student.

Schedule a conference.

Schedule a private conference during a teacher's free period to get extra help, ask questions, inquire about a career in the subject, or talk about your progress in class. You may be surprised to learn that your teacher is a bit more relaxed one-on-one than when lecturing in front of the whole class.

Be yourself.

Teachers can sense when your only motivation for trying to be a "favorite student" is to get special treatment or a good grade. Just be yourself and forget about trying to show off.

Deal with study problems.

If you find a subject hard, talk to your teacher right away about extra tutoring. If you find it boring, talk to your teacher about ways to see the subject in a different light. For example, you may hate math, but learning how to calculate averages and percentages can help you in everything from sports to leaving a tip.

Show some respect.

Just as teachers need to be fair and treat everyone equally, students have responsibilities too. You don't have to like your teacher or agree with what he or she says, but it is necessary to be polite.

2 PUSH YOURSELF

Colleges require you to take certain classes in high school.
Find out which classes and sign up!

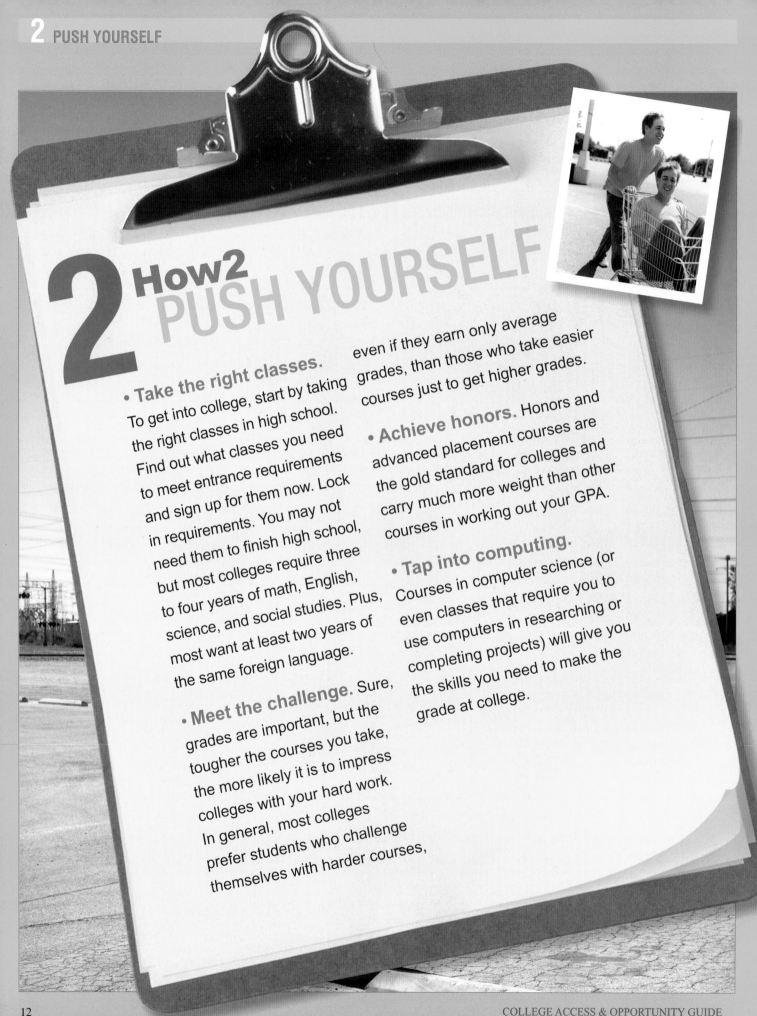

2 How2 PUSH YOURSELF

- **Take the right classes.** To get into college, start by taking the right classes in high school. Find out what classes you need to meet entrance requirements and sign up for them now. Lock in requirements. You may not need them to finish high school, but most colleges require three to four years of math, English, science, and social studies. Plus, most want at least two years of the same foreign language.

- **Meet the challenge.** Sure, grades are important, but the tougher the courses you take, the more likely it is to impress colleges with your hard work. In general, most colleges prefer students who challenge themselves with harder courses, even if they earn only average grades, than those who take easier courses just to get higher grades.

- **Achieve honors.** Honors and advanced placement courses are the gold standard for colleges and carry much more weight than other courses in working out your GPA.

- **Tap into computing.** Courses in computer science (or even classes that require you to use computers in researching or completing projects) will give you the skills you need to make the grade at college.

There's an old Chinese saying that goes, "The journey of a thousand miles begins with a single step." But no matter how unsure you feel taking that first step, every single one after that will be a little easier. Here's some helpful tips to get you started.

Plan out a challenging program of classes.

PLAN OUT YOUR **CLASSES**

○ Colleges care about which courses you're taking in high school. Remember, you will have more options if you start planning now for college and do your best to earn good grades.

○ The courses you take in high school show colleges what kind of goals you set for yourself. Are you signing up for advanced classes, honors sections, or accelerated sequences? Are you choosing electives that really stretch your mind and help you develop new abilities? Or are you doing just enough to get by?

○ Colleges will be more impressed by respectable grades in challenging courses than by outstanding grades in easy ones.

○ Do your high school course selections match what most colleges expect you to know? For example, many colleges require two to four years of foreign language study.

○ Your schedule should consist of at least 4 college preparatory classes per year.

FILE YOUR IMPORTANT DOCUMENTS

Create a file of important documents and notes.

○ Copies of report cards.

○ Lists of awards and honors.

○ Lists of school and community activities in which you are involved, including both paid and volunteer work, and descriptions of what you do.

FIND OUT ABOUT WHICH COLLEGES **TO ATTEND**

Start thinking about the colleges you want to attend.

○ Create list of colleges and universities in which you are interested.

○ Discuss the list with your school counselor and narrow it down to your top few.

○ Start visiting the campuses.

TAKE HONOR-LEVEL CLASSES

Find out about honors-level courses at your school.

○ Ask if AP or other honors courses are available.

○ See if you are eligible for the honors classes you want to take.

○ Stay active in clubs, activities, and sports that you enjoy.

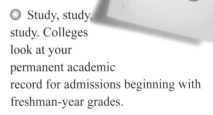

OTHER TOP **TIPS**

○ Study, study, study. Colleges look at your permanent academic record for admissions beginning with freshman-year grades.

○ Think about an after school or summer job to start saving for college.

STUDY SMARTER

Think class work and homework are a waste of your time? Well, listen up—studies show that the more math courses you take in high school, the more likely you are to graduate from college. And that's just for starters. Learning how to study smarter can give you a real edge by the time you get to college. And it's not hard if you make these habits a part of your school life:

Focus

Find a quiet, organized space—maybe a study table at the library. And turn off anything that could possibly distract you.

Plan ahead

If you have a big test or paper coming up, set aside plenty of time so that you aren't cramming. Manage your time and study your most important assignments first.

Pay attention

If you are actively contributing and listening in class, your studying will be easier and more interesting.

Check your work

Studying can tire you out—but after you've completed an assignment take a few minutes to look it over for any mistakes. You never want to turn in anything but your best effort.

Don't go it alone

Find a classmate, mentor, coach, tutor, or study buddy to help keep you going.

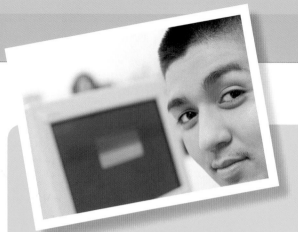

STAY IN SCHOOL

Over a lifetime, a high school dropout working full-time will earn $300,000 less than a high school graduate, and more than $1 million less than a college graduate. It's easy to see that if you want to do well, graduating is what you've got to do first. Here are a few more good reasons why you should stay in school:

R E A S O N **# 1** High school dropouts are four times more likely than college graduates to be unemployed.

R E A S O N **# 2** Graduating from high school will most likely determine how well you live for the rest of your life.

R E A S O N **# 3** On average, high school graduates earn $175 more per week than high school dropouts. College graduates earn $368 more per week than high school graduates.

THE BIG LESSON HERE?

You've got a lot to lose by giving up, and everything to gain by being serious about school.

Myth—A lot of extracurricular activities will make up for poor grades.

Reality—Although colleges consider extracurricular activities such as athletics, student government and the arts when they review an application, they assess academic performance first. Lots of extracurricular activities are great, but first you have to do the work.

ARE YOU READY FOR COLLEGE Quiz

Colleges require you to take three years of English classes (grammar, composition, literature, etc.) during high school.

⇢ TRUE   ⇢ FALSE

FALSE Since reading and writing are so important to success in college, most schools require four or more years of English classes.

REQUIRED COURSES

The chart below gives you a good overview on what courses you need to take in high school to meet standard college entrance requirements. Of course, every college has its own requirements—check with the ones you're interested in to see what they recommend.

SUBJECT	NUMBER OF YEARS	COURSES
English	four or more years	grammar, composition, literature, etc.
Mathematics	three or more years	algebra I and higher—does not include general math, business math, or consumer math
Natural Sciences	three or more years	earth science, biology, chemistry, physics, etc.
Social Sciences	three or more years	history, economics, geography, civics, psychology, etc.
Additional Courses (Some colleges and universities require other classes as prerequisites for admission)	two or more years	foreign language
	one or more year	visual arts, music, theater, drama, dance, computer science, etc.

FACT
Studies show that the more math courses students take in high school, the more likely they are to graduate from college.[4]

[4] *Clifford Adelman, "Mathematics Equals Opportunity" (U.S. Department of Education, 1997).*

STANDARDIZED TESTS

Their names can sometimes sound like alphabet soup, but the standardized tests you will take in high school are important for college. Some schools require different tests, so you want to make sure to check with each one about their requirements. Here are the four main tests you may have to take if you want to apply to most colleges:

PLAN

The PLAN is the pre-ACT test taken to help students estimate how well they will do on the ACT. This test is very important, and in some cases can have bearing or implications on scholarship opportunities and possible college placement. It is a comprehensive guidance resource that helps students measure their current academic development, explore career/training options, and make plans for the remaining years of high school and post-graduation years.

When do I take the test?
The PLAN is taken during the tenth grade.

How do I register?
The PLAN is administered in-school, so check with your high school counselor to register.

What is the test's structure?
PLAN is a four part multiple-choice test structured very similarly to the ACT with sections covering English, mathematics, reading and science.

For more information about PLAN, talk to your high school counselor or visit www.actstudent.org/plan/.

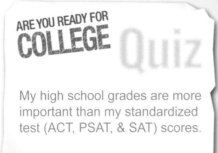

ARE YOU READY FOR COLLEGE Quiz

My high school grades are more important than my standardized test (ACT, PSAT, & SAT) scores.

⇢ TRUE ⇢ FALSE

ACT

This standardized test is designed to assess high school students' general educational development and their ability to complete college-level work. It often is used for college admission decisions, and virtually all U.S. colleges and universities accept ACT results.

When do I take the test?
The ACT is offered usually six times during a given school year. Students generally take the test during their junior year or during the fall of their senior year.

When and how do I register?
A registration packet should be available at your high school, but you may also register online at www.actstudent.org. Be mindful of the registration deadlines for each test, as they are generally one month in advance, but it is suggested that you register at least six weeks prior to the test. Fee waivers are available for students who qualify for financial assistance, so inquire with the ACT directly.

What is the test's structure?
The ACT consists of four multiple-choice tests in English, mathematics, reading, and science, as well as an optional writing test.

How is it scored?
Each subject is scored 1-36 for a composite score, the highest being a 36 overall.

All pertinent ACT testing date information, fee information, registration information and all other questions can be answered by visiting www.actstudent.org.

Free practice tests and questions are also available online. Be sure to familiarize yourself with the test and sample questions before taking the real thing.

TRUE Colleges know that your performance in high school is a better predictor of college success than the standardized tests. That does not mean that most colleges will ignore your test scores.

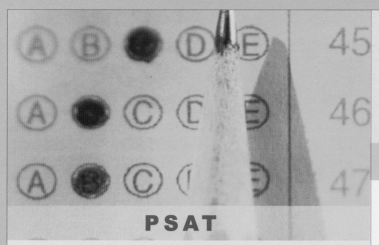

PSAT

The PSAT (Preliminary SAT) is a two-part, exam that is very similar to the SAT. Not to be taken lightly, the PSAT is generally the first indicator colleges and universities use for scholarship purposes and placement.

When do I take the test?

Most people take the PSAT in the fall of their junior year in high school. Some students choose to take it during their sophomore year, which is strongly encouraged. However, scores on the PSAT during your junior year are used to determine National Merit Scholars, students who qualify for merit-based scholarships distributed throughout the United States. Talk to your high school counselor for more information.

How do I register?

You must sign up for the PSAT at your high school. The PSAT is administered during October of every school year. There is a fee associated with taking the PSAT, but there are fee waiver opportunities for certain students. See your high school counselor for more information about fee waivers.

What is the test's structure?

The PSAT consists of two 25-minute verbal sections, two 25-minute math sections, and one 30-minute writing skills section.

For more information on the PSAT, ask your school counselor or visit www.collegeboard.com.

STANDARDIZED TESTS

SAT

The SAT is one of two standardized tests used by colleges as part of their admissions requirements. The SAT I is a three-hour exam that measures verbal, written, and math reasoning skills used for admission at most colleges. The SAT Subject Tests (formerly SAT II) consists of more than 20 subject areas, or achievement tests designed to measure subject-area knowledge. Many colleges use the Subject Tests for admissions, for course placement, and to advise students about course selection, but only some require them.

When do I take the test?

The SAT and SAT II are administered every October, November, December, February, March, May and June of each school year. Most students take the SAT during the second semester of their junior year or the first semester of the senior year.

When and how do I register?

A registration packet should be available at your high school, but you may also register online at www.collegeboard.com. Keep in mind the registration deadlines for each test, as they are generally one month in advance, but it is suggested that you register at least six weeks prior to the test. While there are costs associated with taking the test, students who require financial assistance may qualify for fee waivers. See your high school counselor for more information about fee waivers.

What's the test's structure?

The SAT is a ten-section exam consisting of critical reading, math, writing, and one experimental. The experimental section is masked to look like a regular section.

How is it scored?

Scores on each section range from 200-800 points. The scores from each section are combined, and the highest possible combined score is 2400.

All pertinent SAT testing date information, fee information, registration information and all other questions can be answered by visiting www.collegeboard.com.

Free practice tests and questions are also available online. Be sure to familiarize yourself with the test and sample questions before taking the real thing.

ALGEBRA II

FOREIGN LANGUAGES

BIOLOGY

TAKE ON THE TOUGH CLASSES

THEY PREPARE YOU FOR COLLEGE

KnowHow2GO.org

3 FIND THE RIGHT FIT

Think about interests and activities that you enjoy.
Explore colleges with programs that suit your interest.

3 How2 FIND THE RIGHT FIT

- **What's the right match?** The kind of college you choose to attend should reflect your goals and your personality. Whether you choose a public, private, community, technical, trade, or even online college, make sure it's the best match for you.

- **Big or small?** Do you want to attend a big university with a greater choice of studies and social activities, but also larger lecture classes? Or would you like fewer choices but more personal attention and a greater chance to stand out? You decide.

- **Home or Away?** Attending a local college versus living in a dorm—what's better? It depends. For some, residence hall life is an important part of the college experience—but commuting from home is less expensive.

- **Which major works?** Figuring out what you like doing most, plus what you're best at, can point to the careers you should consider—and what majors will help you reach your career goal.

- **Do extras matter?** Getting into extracurricular activities outside of class—band, science club, the school newspaper, or drama—or even volunteering at local organizations helps you discover what your real interests are—and where you're heading.

ARE YOU READY FOR COLLEGE Quiz

Big colleges are best if I haven't decided on a major field.

⫸ TRUE   ⫸ FALSE

FALSE
If you are undecided, the best college is one that has core requirements or distribution requirements that ensure you will explore new areas and fields.

EXPLORE YOUR INTERESTS

What are you good at? Do you have something you love to do? Whether it's playing sports, building models, or playing an instrument, your interests today say a lot about what career you might have tomorrow. To get there, follow these ten steps. And be sure to discuss them with your school counselor and your parents or guardian:

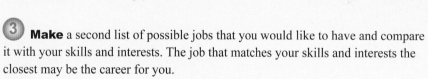

1 **Make** a list of your skills and interests. Think hard about what you enjoy and what you are good at.

2 **Find** out more about the kinds of the jobs that interest you, along with their educational requirements, salary, working conditions, future outlook, and anything else that can help you decide what's best.

3 **Make** a second list of possible jobs that you would like to have and compare it with your skills and interests. The job that matches your skills and interests the closest may be the career for you.

4 **Consider** your career goal. Once you've decided what occupation matches up best with you, then you can begin developing a plan to reach your career goal.

5 **Begin** a career plan. Think about what you want to do and find out more about the kind of training, education, and skills you will need to achieve your career goal.

6 **Find** schools that offer a college degree or training program that best meets your career goal and financial needs.

7 **Find** out about financial aid to help support you in obtaining your career goal.

8 **Learn** about job hunting tips as you prepare to graduate or move into the job market.

9 **Prepare** your resume, and practice job interviewing techniques.

10 **Go** to your career guidance center at school or local library for information and help on career planning.

MAKING A SAMPLE CAREER PLAN

Making a career plan is a matter of matching your skills and interests to an occupation to create a career goal, and then deciding the steps you need to take to reach that goal. Here's a sample:

My Career Plan

Career Goal:

To become a civil engineer. To design, plan, and supervise the construction of buildings, highways, and rapid transit systems.

Requirements:

- Bachelor's degree in engineering
- Ability to work as part of a team
- Creativity
- Analytical mind
- Capacity for detail
- Presentation skills
- Writing skills
- Knowledge of physical sciences and mathematics
- Accreditation by Licensing Board

Current Skills and Interests:

- Summer worker for Smith Construction Co.
- High School mathematics courses
- High School science courses
- Experience working as a team
- Attended high school writing courses
- Gave presentations in high school courses

Plan To Reach Career Goal:

- Bachelor's Degree
- Attend an accredited engineering school
- Job Experience
- Continue working for Smith Construction Co.
- Seek internships through the university career placement office
- Networking
- Join campus organizations for engineering students

Courtesy of Mapping Your Future.org / http://mapping-your-future.org/planning/careersa.htm

Myth—You need to decide on a career before you can choose a college.

Reality—College is a time to explore. Many students discover their ideal field while taking a course they didn't expect to like. If you aren't ready to decide on a major or a career, choose a college that allows you to keep your options open. Take your time.

VISIT THE CAMPUS

No matter how many brochures you read or websites you visit, nothing tells you more about a college than visiting its campus in person. Plus, you can learn a lot more just by asking questions. Here's a list to get you started:

Ask your college host:

- What activities and services are available to help students get settled (academically and socially) during their first year?

- How big are the classes?

- What is the total cost of attending the college?

- What types of financial aid does the college offer and how do I apply?

- Are all freshmen assigned to an academic advisor?

- Where do most freshmen live?

- Can I take a tour?

- What activities are available for students?

- Who teaches the courses for first-year students?

- How successful are the college's graduates in finding jobs?

- What services (such as transportation and shopping) are available locally?

Ask any students you meet:

- How easy is it to meet with faculty?

- Are you able to register for the classes you want?

- What is there to do on weekends? Do most students stay or leave campus on weekends?

Can't get to a campus? Go online:

- Visiting a college's website is an invaluable tool to learn everything you need to know about a school. You can find answers to many of the questions above and some college websites even offer a virtual tour for you to get familiar with the campus.

- KnowHow2GO-U—accessible at **www.KnowHow2GO.org/campustour**— is a virtual pre-college tour that replicates the experience of being on a real college campus and is designed to help you learn what to expect. By visiting various campus buildings—Admissions, Financial Aid, Academics, Career Center, Student Center, Library, Dormitories, Quad, and the Athletic Complex—you'll learn about the college environment and what it takes to get there.

Myth—If you haven't heard of a particular college or university, it can't be very good.

Reality—Televised athletic games are how some colleges are known, but many great colleges do not get that kind of exposure. Some of the nation's finest colleges don't field big-time sports teams. Learn about colleges by looking at college guides in the library or your counselor's office or "visit" them on the Internet.

KH2G
KnowHow2GO University

APPLYING

Completing college applications can take a lot of time. So you want to make sure that you get it right and not make mistakes. Here are some tips to guide you through the process:

Know the guidelines.

Before you start applying to schools, find out the application deadline and fees for each school you are considering.

Plan ahead.

It takes time to get standardized test scores tabulated and mailed, and it takes time for school counselors and others providing references to gather information.

Follow the instructions and proofread.

The application is often a college admission committee's first contact with you. Make a good impression with a neat application free of spelling and grammatical errors. Ask a friend, relative, or mentor to read and provide feedback on your materials.

Work with your high school to send all records and test scores.

Go to your high school's guidance office for help getting all necessary transcripts (grade history), records, test scores, and applications sent to prospective schools. If you decide to apply to schools that have not already received your test scores, you can ask to send your scores to that college.

Make the most of personal references.

Ask people who know you well, and give the best impression of you to your school. Prepare a neat and legible reference form and give your references plenty of time to respond.

Write an outstanding essay.

Most college applications require an essay, so spend time developing a good one. While a great essay probably won't get you into college if you don't meet the other academic requirements, it could move you as a "maybe" up the list.

Be ready to interview, audition, or submit a portfolio.

Some colleges also require a personal interview or examples of work in special areas such as art or music.

Keep a copy of all your application materials. You never know when you might need them!

ARE YOU READY FOR
COLLEGE Quiz

I will have a better chance of getting into law or medical school if I go to a university that offers those graduate programs.

⋯> TRUE   ⋯> FALSE

FALSE
Very few universities give their students special preference for graduate study, and those that do reserve it for only the very best students.

4 PUT YOUR HANDS ON SOME CASH

There's money out there to help you pay for college. Apply for it.

4 How2 PUT YOUR HANDS ON SOME CASH

• Who gets financial aid?

Many more students than you might think. Financial aid is awarded by need or on merit—academic achievement, athletics, or other talents. But you have to apply for aid to find out.

• What kind of money?

Grants, scholarships, work-study, student loans—there are a lot of different types of financial aid out there and you need to find out which kind or combination works best for your needs.

• Where do you look?

Colleges expect you and your parents to pay what you can—but schools, state and federal governments, and private businesses and organizations are also all great sources for financial aid.

• Is it free money?

Not likely—most financial aid packages are a mixture of grants that don't need to be paid back and loans that do, but not until after you graduate from college.

• How to apply?

Your school guidance counselor can help you, including how to file a Free Application for Federal Student Aid (FAFSA), which makes you a candidate for all federal student aid. For help online, go to http://www.fafsa.ed.gov/ or http://www.collegegoalsundayusa.org/

• Do deadlines matter?

Absolutely. College financial aid goes fast. The earlier you can get in your FAFSA application and all the other info that a college asks for, the sooner you'll receive your financial aid package.

Myth—Only the very best students receive financial aid from colleges.

Reality—Although high-ability students or students with special talents may receive merit-based scholarships, many scholarships are based on financial need—colleges generally want students they've admitted to be able to attend, and will help them find the resources to do so.

ARE YOU READY FOR
COLLEGE Quiz

Colleges want to help students get financial aid.

⤏ TRUE   ⤏ FALSE

TRUE
The job of a college's financial aid officer is to make it possible for all admitted students to attend their college while staying within the federal guidelines.

COSTS AND FINANCIAL AID

There's no escaping the fact that college costs are rising. According to recently released reports, most students and their families can expect to pay, on average, from $112 to $1,190 more than last year for this year's tuition and fees, depending on the type of college.

Still, there is good news. There is more financial aid available than ever before—over $135 billion. And, despite all of these college cost increases, a college education remains an affordable choice for most families.

"Sticker Price" vs. Affordability

Although some of the college price tags you hear about can be discouraging—$30,000 or more for yearly tuition and fees—most colleges are more affordable than you might think. For example, did you know that about 60 percent of students attending four-year schools pay less than $6,000 for tuition and fees? After grants are taken into consideration, the net price the average undergraduate pays for a college education is significantly lower than the published tuition and fees. And remember, financial aid will further reduce the amount your family will actually pay.

Financial Aid Makes College Affordable for You

Financial aid is intended to make up the difference between what your family can afford to pay and what college costs. Nearly two-thirds of the students currently enrolled in college receive some sort of financial aid to help pay college costs.

The financial aid system is based on the goal of equal access—that anyone should be able to attend college, regardless of financial circumstances. Here's how the system works:

Students and their families are expected to contribute to the cost of college to the extent that they're able. If a family is unable to contribute the entire cost, financial aid is available to bridge the gap.

EFC Works in Your Favor

The amount your family is able to contribute is frequently referred to as the Expected Family Contribution, or EFC. The figure is determined by whoever is awarding the aid —usually the federal government or individual colleges and universities.

The federal government and financial aid offices use "need formulas" that analyze your family's financial circumstances (things like income, assets, and family size) and compare them proportionally with other families' financial circumstances.

Most families can't just pay the EFC out of current income alone. But, not to worry— the formulas assume that families will meet their contribution through a combination of savings, current income, and borrowing.

Second, financial aid is limited. The formulas therefore measure a particular family's ability to pay against other families' ability to pay.

Don't Rule Out Colleges with Higher Costs

Say your EFC is $5,000. At a college with a total cost of $8,000, you'd be eligible for up to $3,000 in financial aid. At a college with a total cost of $25,000, you'd be eligible for up to $20,000 in aid. In other words, your family would be asked to contribute the same amount at both colleges.

Current Average College Costs

Average College Costs Per Year 2007-2008

Public, two-year: $2,361

Public, four-year: $6,185

Private, four-year: $23,712

Did you know that...

• About 60% of students attending public four-year colleges pay less than $6,000 for tuition and fees per year.

• 44% of all students attend two-year colleges. The average two-year public college student receives grant aid that reduces the average tuition to about $400.

• A record $135 billion in financial aid is available to students and their families.

• About 60% of all college students receive grant aid. In 2004-05 grant aid averaged $1,800 per student at two-year public colleges, $3,300 at four-year public colleges, and $9,600 at private four-year colleges.

ARE YOU READY FOR COLLEGE Quiz

If my parents saved for college, we can still qualify for aid.

⋯▷ **TRUE** ⋯▷ **FALSE**

TRUE Saving for college is almost always a good idea. Since a lot of financial aid comes in the form of loans, the aid you are likely to receive will need to be repaid.

FINANCIAL AID: LOTS OF OPTIONS

Financial aid is any type of assistance used to pay college costs that is based on financial need. There are three main types:

Grants and Scholarships

Also called gift aid, grants don't have to be re-paid and you don't need to work to earn them. Grant aid comes from federal and state governments and from individual colleges. Scholarships are usually awarded based on merit. To search for scholarships, visit **www.fastweb.com.**

Work

Student employment and work-study aid helps students pay for education costs such as books, supplies, and personal expenses. Work-study is a federal program which provides students with part-time employment to help meet their financial needs and gives them work experience while serving their campuses and surrounding communities.

Loans

Most financial aid (54%) comes in the form of loans to students or parents— aid that must be re-paid. Most loans that are awarded based on financial need are low-interest loans sponsored by the federal government. These loans are subsidized by the government so no interest accrues until you begin repayment after you graduate.

MORE ABOUT LOANS

There are many different types of loans, both for students and for parents to take on behalf of their student. Read on for the basics.

Federal Student Loans

Perkins Loans

Perkins Loans are need-based loans and are awarded by the financial aid office to students with the highest need. The interest rate is very low—5 percent—and you don't make any loan payments while in school.

Subsidized Stafford or Direct Loans

Subsidized Stafford Loans are need-based loans with interest rates in the 4-6 percent range. The federal government pays the yearly interest while you're in school. This is why they're called "subsidized" loans.

Unsubsidized Stafford or Direct Loans

Unsubsidized Stafford Loans aren't based on financial need and can be used to help pay the family share of costs. You're responsible for paying interest on the loan while in school. You may choose to capitalize the interest. The advantage of doing this is that no interest payments are required. The disadvantage is that the interest is added to the loan, meaning that you will repay more money to the lender.

Grad PLUS Loans

This is a student loan for graduate students sponsored by the federal government that is unrelated to need. Generally, students can borrow Grad PLUS loans up to the total cost of education, minus any aid received. The advantage of this loan is that it allows for greater borrowing capacity. However, we recommend that students consider lower-interest loans, such as the Subsidized Stafford or Unsubsidized loans prior to taking out a Grad PLUS loan.

Parent Loans

Federal PLUS loans

The PLUS Loan program is the largest source of parent loans. Parents can borrow up to the full cost of attendance minus any aid received, and repayment starts 60 days after money is paid to college.

Private parent loans

A number of lenders and other financial institutions offer private education loans for parents. These loans usually carry a higher interest rate than PLUS Loans.

College-sponsored loans

A small number of colleges offer their own parent loans, usually at a better rate than PLUS. Check each college's aid materials to see if such loans are available.

Other Student Loan Options

Private student loans

A number of lenders and other financial institutions offer private education loans to students. These loans are not subsidized and usually carry a higher interest rate than the federal need-based loans. The College Board private loan program is an example of a private education loan for students.

College-sponsored loans

Some colleges have their own loan funds. Interest rates may be lower than federal student loans. Read the college's financial aid information.

Other loans

Besides setting up scholarships, some private organizations and foundations have loan programs as well. Borrowing terms may be quite favorable. You can use Scholarship Search to find these.

HIGH SCHOOL TIMELINES

The college planning process can be daunting for everyone. It's best to plan ahead and allow plenty of time. It also helps if you have a plan to follow from your freshman year through your senior year—and here it is.

FRESHMEN TIMELINE

START HERE FRESHMEN

FALL

❑ Make sure you enroll in geometry or algebra. Colleges require that you take rigorous math courses in high schools.

❑ Create a college information folder that you can take with you through high school.

❑ Start the school year off right by getting organized and practicing good study habits.

❑ Meet new people by signing up for extracurricular activities and trying something new!

❑ Explore careers on the Web on your home computer or at the library.

❑ Find job shadowing opportunities in the community, where you can spend a day shadowing someone at work and watching what he or she does.

SPRING

❑ Start to plan your sophomore year.

❑ Talk with your parents and counselor about summer vacation. Explore summer programs or camps to attend at local colleges and universities. Look for volunteer or service opportunities in the community. Some may be sponsored by a local church, synagogue or mosque.

SOPHOMORE TIMELINE

SOPHOMORE TIMELINE

FALL

❑ Polish your study skills. If you need to improve in some subjects, this is the time to do it. Colleges and future employers look at high school transcripts and are impressed with regular attendance and improving grades.

❑ Have you taken a career interest inventory? Ask your counselor or guidance office to give you one. These tests help assess your strengths and weaknesses and can help guide your college search and long-term career plans.

❑ Take the Preliminary Scholastic Aptitude test PSAT—the preliminary version of the SAT—or the PLAN, the preliminary version of the ACT. Taking the PSAT now is practice for the PSAT test in junior year which allows your student to be considered for a National Merit Scholarship. Find dates and more information about the PSAT from your high school's guidance office.

❑ Surf the Web to check out colleges, technical schools and apprenticeship opportunities.

❑ Consider job shadowing to get some work experience and test possible careers.

SPRING

❑ Begin exploring financial aid and scholarships options.

❑ Use the Internet to explore different careers.

❑ Select five to ten colleges to contact for brochures and applications.

❑ Visit your school or community Career Center.

❑ Plan a productive summer. The summer before 11th grade is a good time to have a part-time job to prepare for a future career.

❑ Choose a summer camp or find volunteer service program to jumpstart your skills.

❑ Remember to sign up for the most challenging classes for next year.

ARE YOU READY FOR COLLEGE Quiz

The best time to visit colleges is before I have been admitted.

⋗ TRUE   ⋗ FALSE

TRUE Many students find that none of the colleges to which they were admitted "felt" right when they visited. If possible, visit before you apply and again after you have been admitted.

JUNIOR YEAR TIMELINE

August:

❑ Start your year off right: Talk with your guidance counselor about your options and your plans. Be sure to ask about test dates for the PSAT, ACT, and SAT. You'll need to register up to six weeks ahead of time.

❑ Sign up for courses with your eyes on the prize: college and money to pay for it! A tougher course load may pay off with scholarships and may get you a better chance to get admitted to the school of your choice.

❑ Start investigating private and public sources for financial aid. Take note of scholarship deadlines and plan accordingly.

❑ Sign up for activities to boost your college applications.

September:

❑ Find out about schools you are interested in attending. Treat your school selection process like a research paper: Make a file and gather information about schools, financial aid, and campus life to put in it. Go to college fairs and open houses and learn as much as you can from the Internet about schools.

❑ Begin planning college visits. Fall, winter, and spring break are good times because you can observe a campus when classes are going on.

October:

❑ Take the PSAT. You'll get the results by Christmas.

❑ Sign up for ACT or SAT prep courses.

❑ Do your top college picks require essays or recommendations? Now is the time to begin planning your essays and choosing whom you'd like to ask for a recommendation.

November:

❑ Sign up for the ACT and SAT, if you haven't already.

December:

❑ Begin the application process for service academies (West Point, Annapolis, etc.)

❑ Decide if you should take AP exams in May. Investigate the College-Level Examination Program® or CLEP, which grants college credit for achievement in exams covering many different college-level subjects.

January:

❑ Meet with your guidance counselor again to develop your senior schedule.

❑ Organize your Individual Graduation Plan.

February:

❑ Think about lining up a summer job, internship, or co-op.

❑ Plan campus visits for spring break.

❑ Memorize your Social Security number if you haven't already. It will be your identity on campus.

March/April:

❑ Get ready for AP exams next month.

❑ Write a résumé.

SENIOR YEAR TIMELINE

August

❑ Sign up for the ACT and/or SAT if you didn't take it as a junior, or if you aren't satisfied with your score.

❑ Review ACT and/or SAT test results and retest if necessary.

August to December

❑ Visit with your school counselor to make sure you are on track to graduate and fulfill college admission requirements. Consider taking courses at a local university or community college.

❑ Keep working hard all year; second semester grades can affect scholarship eligibility.

❑ Ask for personal references from teachers, school counselors, or employers early in the year or at least two weeks before application deadline.

❑ Follow your school's procedure for requesting recommendations.

❑ Visit with admissions counselors who come to your high school.

❑ Attend a college fair.

❑ Begin your college essay(s).

❑ Apply for admission at the colleges you've chosen.

❑ Avoid common college application mistakes.

❑ Find out if you qualify for scholarships at each college where you have applied.

❑ Start the financial aid application process.

❑ See your school counselor for help finding financial aid and scholarships.

January to May

❑ If you need it, get help completing the FAFSA (Free Application for Federal Student Aid).

❑ Ask your guidance office in January to send first semester transcripts to schools where you applied. In May, they will need to send final transcripts to the college you will attend.

❑ Visit colleges that have invited you to enroll.

❑ Decide which college to attend, and notify the school of your decision.

❑ Keep track of and observe deadlines for sending in all required fees and paperwork.

❑ Notify schools you will not attend of your decision.

❑ Continue to look for scholarship opportunities.

❑ Keep track of important financial aid and scholarship deadlines.

❑ Watch the mail for your Student Aid Report (SAR)—it should arrive four weeks after the FAFSA is filed.

❑ Compare financial aid packages from different schools.

❑ Sign and send in a promissory note if you are borrowing money.

❑ Notify your college about any outside scholarships you received.

June to August

❑ Make sure your final transcript is sent to the school you will be attending.

❑ Getting a summer job can help pay some of your college expenses.

❑ Make a list of what you will need to take with you for your dorm room.

❑ If you haven't met your roommate, call, write, or e-mail to get acquainted in advance.

❑ Make sure housing documentation is quickly accessible when you move into the dorm.

❑ Learn how to get around at your new school. Review a campus map.

❑ Wait until after your first class meeting to buy your books and supplies.

KnowHow2GO State Partners

KnowHow2GO supports a strong grassroots network of state partners to ensure that students and adult mentors can easily find real-time, on-the-ground assistance. Whether you need information on counseling, academics or financial aid, these organizations and Web sites can help.

California
www.knowhow2gocalifornia.org   **KnowHow2GOCalifornia**

Partners:

California State University, www.calstate.edu

Campaign for College Opportunity, www.collegecampaign.org

Cash for College, www.lacashforcollege.org

Community College League of California, www.ccleague.org

CaliforniaColleges.edu

La Opinión

Los Angeles Area Chamber of Commerce

Southern California College Access Network Unite L.A.

Univision (San Francisco & Los Angeles)

Campaign Highlights:

• KnowHow2GO2College Forums at churches, community centers, and schools provide an opportunity for students and their families to be inspired and informed about the path to college and student success. During the forums, participants listen to guest speakers with important messages about attending college and are provided information and materials to help make their college planning easier.

• In collaboration with the Los Angeles Public Library's Youth Librarian section, kits including materials and resources that help increase college awareness and financial aid opportunities for young people were disseminated to every youth librarian in the city's library branches during the fall of 2009.

• In February 2010, in collaboration with La Opinión, the largest Spanish language daily newspaper in the U.S. with a daily circulation of nearly 125,000 persons, a bilingual insert to the Sunday paper called—The Road to College (Camino a la Universidad)—featured vital information that students need to know in order to get into college and succeed.

• KnowHow2GOCalifornia's website continues to be a reliable source of current information for students and their families, including a listing of current events, conferences, and activities throughout the state, as well as links to scholarships and financial aid.

California (Los Angeles)
www.knowhow2gocalifornia.org   **KnowHow2GOCalifornia**

Partners:

Southern California College Access Network, www.socalcollaborative.org

Visit our website for a complete listing of SoCal CAN members

Campaign Highlights:

• More than 150 KnowHow2GO events have taken place in Southern California. Learn about upcoming programs and resources in your neighborhood by visiting KnowHow2GOCalifornia.org.

• Interested in talking with friends about college? Join the team of 100+ KnowHow2GO Ambassadors who are spreading college knowledge on middle and high schools campuses in Los Angeles County.

• Looking for guidance on how to prepare for and pay for college? Check out our bilingual publication on the KnowHow2GOCalifornia.org home page. More than 400,000 copies have been distributed to students, parents, teachers and mentors in the state.

Connecticut

www.knowhow2goconnecticut.org

Partners:

CT Department of Education, www.sde.ct.gov

CT Department of Higher Education, www.ctdhe.org

CT African-American Affairs Commission, www.cga.ct.gov/aaac Unite L.A.

Campaign Highlights:

• With funding from the Lumina Foundation for Education, KnowHow2GOConnecticut awarded Education Connection (Litchfield), The Boys and Girls Clubs (Hartford), Eastern Connecticut State University (Windham), Wesleyan University - Public School Collaborative (Middletown), University of Bridgeport, (Bridgeport), Manchester Community College (Manchester), and North End Action Team (Middletown) grants for programs designed to increase access and success to post-secondary educational opportunities for traditionally underserved students.

• The KnowHow2GOConnecticut Network received a $19,000 grant from National Council for Community and Education Partnerships to promote the expansion and development of the Local college access and success networks throughout the state in collaboration with the GEAR UP Project in Bridgeport and New Haven.

• A statewide symposium on Network Building for college access and success programs was held on May 11, 2010 at the Burroughs Community Center in Bridgeport. Paul Vandeventer, the author of the book Networks that Work, facilitated and a panel included representatives from community foundations, community organizations and educators.

• KnowHow2GOConnecticut awarded the second of three rounds of re-granting to non-profit organizations in late May/early June 2010 through a grant from the Lumina Foundation for Education.

Florida

www.knowhow2goflorida.org

Partners:

ENLACE Florida, enlacefl.usf.edu

University of South Florida, www.usf.edu

Campaign Highlights:

• ENLACE Florida received approval in 2010 for a statewide expansion of KnowHow2GO from KnowHow2GOTampa Bay to KnowHow2GOFlorida. The expansion is expected to be implemented through 2012.

• In 2009, ENLACE Florida conducted focus group meetings with community-based organizations and school district officials in Gainesville, Orlando, and Miami as part of the statewide expansion planning process.

• ENLACE Florida will be incorporating a Haitian initiative component to KnowHow2GO in South Florida.

Idaho

www.knowhow2goidaho.org

Partners:

J. A. & Kathryn Albertson Foundation, www.jkaf.org

Campaign Highlights:

• The J.A. and Kathryn Albertson Foundation completed a soft launch of the KnowHow2GOIdaho.org web site and has initiated work on the air campaign and ground campaign for KnowHow2GO in Idaho.

• Fifteen originating members met on March 30, 2010 to brainstorm what will become the Idaho College Access Network. Among the next steps are the creation of a steering committee and development of a mission, vision, and goals statement.

• Plans for an official launch of the KnowHow2GOIdaho.org site and special events are in the works, and many more partners are anticipated as efforts ramp up to help more Idahoans move from awareness to action through the KnowHow2GO campaign.

Illinois

www.knowhow2goillinois.org

KnowHow2GOIllinois

Partners:

Illinois Student Assistance Commission,
www.collegezone.com

Illinois College Access Network,
www.illinoiscan.org

Chicago Public Schools,
www.postsecondary.cps.k12.il.us

Campaign Highlights:

• Since September 2009, approximately 60 Illinois Student Assistance Corps (ISACorps) members—recent college graduates recruited from the undergraduate class of 2009—have established strong relationships within their communities to promote college planning and preparation among high school students and their families utilizing KnowHow2GO as their primary outreach tool, philosophy and strategy. Their efforts have included organizing and offering outreach events, career counseling, test preparation, FAFSA completion workshops for students and parents, college selection and application assistance, and knowledge and assistance about applying for financial aid.

• ISACorps members support the work of the 10 KnowHow2GO Illinois Vertical Teams throughout the state by tapping into organic and local social networks in and between area high schools and community-based organizations. They build partnerships with local schools, businesses and nonprofits in order to deliver free career and college planning and preparation services to students from families with no prior college-going experience.

Indiana

www.knowhow2goindiana.org

KnowHow2GOIndiana

Partners:

Learn More Indiana,
www.learnmoreindiana.org

Central Indiana Community Foundation

Boys & Girls Clubs

Independent Colleges of Indiana

Indiana Black Expo

Indiana Youth Institute

College Goal Sunday

Indiana's College Choice 529

Starfish Initiative

Indiana's Twenty-first Century Scholars Program

United Ways

Work One/Workforce Development Services

YWCA

Campaign Highlights:

• Leveraging Indiana's College Success Coalition members and state programs like Indiana's Twenty-first Century Scholars, KnowHow2GOIndiana Week provides families an opportunity to visit a college campus, participate in their choice of workshops, and take advantage of other opportunities based on the campaign's four steps.

• Held at the beginning of the academic year, College GO! Week encourages every high school student to take practical, grade-specific steps in preparation for college. Schools are provided with the tools needed to run a successful event, and partners across the state are encouraged to reach out in a variety of ways to help inspire and motivate students.

• The Cash for College promotion includes practical, grade-specific steps to help students prepare to pay for college, all leading up to the annual March 10 deadline for students to complete the Free Application for Federal Student Aid (FAFSA).

• Learn More Indiana sponsors two FAFSA Friday broadcasts that feature interactive online webinars led by state financial aid experts.

Iowa

www.knowhow2goiowa.org

KnowHow2GOIowa

Partners:

Iowa College Access Network, www.icansucceed.org

Iowa College Student Aid Commission

Iowa Department of Education

College Savings Iowa

Des Moines Public Library

GEAR UP

Iowa TRIO – Educational Talent Search

Campaign Highlights:

• Awarded $140,000 to ten Iowa education programs enabling these organizations to expand college access in their local communities.

• Partnered with GEAR UP Iowa to provide a KnowHow2GO Training Workshop for grant recipients. Attendees left the workshop armed with a KnowHow2GO toolkit and increased knowledge for expanding the campaign to their regions of the state of Iowa.

• Integrated the KnowHow2GO campaign into the ICAN High School Success presentation for eighth and ninth grade students. More than 50 programs were held throughout the state reaching just over 2,000 students.

• Featured the KnowHow2GO campaign and Algebra II at the Iowa State Fair. Algebra II posed for pictures with students of all ages and introduced fair-goers to the four steps of going to college.

Kentucky

www.knowhow2gokentucky.org

KnowHow2GOKentucky

Partners:

Council on Postsecondary Education, www.cpe.ky.gov

GEAR UP Kentucky, www.gohigherky.org/GearUp/

GEAR UP Alliance

Kentucky College Access Network, www.kentuckycan.org

Kentucky Higher Education Assistance Authority

Kentucky Department of Education

Kentucky Family Resource and Youth Service Centers

Kentucky Department of Juvenile Justice

Kentucky TRIO & Upward Bound

Metro Louisville United Way

Bluegrass United Way

Project Graduate

Graduate Kentucky

Governor Steve Brashear

Center for Teaching & Learning

Prichard Committee for Academic Excellence

Lumina Foundation for Excellence

Kentucky Adult Education

Kentucky's Public Colleges & Universities

Association of Independent Kentucky Colleges & Universities

Kentucky Broadcaster's Association

Kentucky Chamber of Commerce

Campaign Highlights:

• In partnerships with the Kentucky College Access Network, KnowHow2GOKentucky holds "rallies" across the state with speeches and testimonials from policy-makers (congressmen, mayors, university presidents and educational leaders), teachers, students, and mentors.

• KnowHow2GOKentucky created Price is Right game sets that are loaned—along with themed props and music—to any college access organization in the Commonwealth. Following the structure of the TV game show, students are invited to "come on down," competing with three other students to answer college-related questions. Prizes range from KnowHow2GO goodies to iPods. Any organization can call and reserve this great interactive college-access tool.

• Partnering with GEAR UP and the two state-wide daily papers through Newspapers in Education, KnowHow2GOKentucky activities and the associated messages are featured at least eight times annually in a 4-full page color spread that is distributed to all GEAR UP schools and included in all delivered and newsstand copies.

• An 8-page full-color Exploring College publication is available to college-access programs across the Commonwealth.

Louisiana

www.knowhow2golouisiana.org

KnowHow2GOLouisiana

Partners:

Louisiana Board of Regents, www.regents.state.la.us

Louisiana GEAR UP, www.lasip.org/lagearup/rfs.asp

Louisiana Office of Student Financial Assistance, www.osfa.la.gov

Campaign Highlights:

• Louisiana officially kicked off its KnowHow2GO campaign on April 16, 2010 in coordination with a statewide meeting of the GEAR UP Explorer Club Conference.

• More than 500 8th to 12th grade students from across the state attended the conference, along with more than 100 parents and educators.

• The festivities included motivational speakers, training sessions, a "stomp the yard" celebration, formal dinner and prom style dance.

Michigan

www.KnowHow2GOMichigan.org

KnowHow2GOMichigan

Partners:

Michigan College Access Network, www.micollegeaccess.org

Office of the Governor, www.michigan.gov/gov

Michigan Department of Treasury, Student Financial Services Bureau, www.michigan.gov/mistudentaid

King Chavez Parks Initiative (GEAR UP)

The Imagine Fund, www.theimaginefund.com

The Kresge Foundation, www.kresge.org/

Muskegon Opportunity, www.muskegonopportunity.com

KnowHow2GOSt.Clair, www.stclairfoundation.org/knowhow2go

Bay Commitment, www.bayfoundation.org/bay_commitment.htm

Campaign Highlights:

• Michigan College Access Network has awarded more than $250,000 to help Michigan communities establish local college access networks, including incorporation of the statewide initiatives, KnowHow2GO and the Michigan College Access Portal (MiCAP)

• Michigan College Access Portal (MiCAP), a one-stop-shop web portal that will help students plan, apply and pay for college, is currently in the development phase for the 2010-2011 school year

• The KnowHow2GOMichigan website has been officially launched and KnowHow2GOMichigan materials will be incorporated into local events across the state, such as the Muskegon Opportunity KnowHow2GO College Road Show, premiering in April 2010.

Montana

www.knowhow2gomontana.org

KnowHow2GOMontana

Partners:

MT GEAR UP, www.gearup.montana.edu

Student Assistance Foundation (SAF), www.safmt.org

Campaign Highlights:

• With the assistance of a grant from Lumina Foundation for Education, SAF offers funds to Montana community organizations, colleges and other groups with education-related missions to host KnowHow2GO Week, a week of events geared to helping students get to college. Activities are based on the KnowHow2GO campaign's four steps.

• Montana College Access Network was created to provide a coordinated network of mentors, counselors, and other individuals to help students with the postsecondary process, financial aid awareness, and career development. The network facilitates educational calls/Webinars, the sharing of resources (KnowHow2GO materials) that expand services and support for Montana students, and more.

• National Training for Counselors and Mentors (NT4CM) offers counselors, educators and other professionals working with college-bound youth the opportunity to learn about current financial aid practices through free training sessions.

• At www.KnowHow2GOMontana.org, students and parents can learn the four steps to get to college, in addition to find out about Montana programs designed to help them achieve their goals.

Nebraska

www.knowhow2gonebraska.org

KnowHow2GONebraska

Partners:

EducationQuest Foundation

Foundation for Lincoln Public Schools

Office of the Governor

Nebraska P-16 Initiative

Nebraska Department of Education

University of Nebraska System

Nebraska State College System

Association of Independent Colleges and Universities of Nebraska

Nebraska Community College Association

Nebraska's Coordinating Commission for Postsecondary Education

Nebraska State Education Association

Nebraska Council of School Administrators

Nebraska Association of School Boards

Bright Futures Foundation

Foundation for Lincoln Public Schools

Mexican American Commission

Nebraska Children and Families Foundation

Western Nebraska Community College

TeamMates Mentoring Program

Westfield Gateway Mall

Statewide School Districts

Statewide Community Agencies

Campaign Highlights:

• Each fall, KnowHow2GONebraska distributes over 65,000 copies of Exploring College, an eight-page publication that covers the four KnowHow2GO steps to Nebraska middle schools and high schools

• EducationQuest provides the KnowHow2GONebraska Partner Playbook to guidance counselors, educators and community agency personnel to help them promote KnowHow2GO to their students and clients.

• Produced a 10-minute video "College Doesn't Just Happen" that is based on the four KnowHow2GO steps.

• Created a KnowHow2GONebraska Ambassador Program in which college students present KnowHow2GO information to younger students and share how they made college possible.

Ohio

KnowHow2GOOhio

Partners:

Ohio Department of Education,
www.ode.state.oh.us

Ohio College Access Network,
www.ohiocan.org

Ohio Board of Regents,
www.regents.ohio.gov

GEAR UP

Ohio TRiO

AmeriCorps Ohio College Guides Program

KnowledgeWorks Foundation

Business Alliance for Higher Education

The Ohio State University Economic Access
Initiative

Ohio Association of Student Financial Aid
Administrators

Ohio Association for College Admissions
Counseling

Campaign Highlights:

• The Ohio College Access Network (OCAN) enlisted Ohio's governor in early 2007 to launch the KnowHow2GO campaign in early 2007. Since then, OCAN and KnowHow2GOOhio have created a one-stop, student-friendly website, secured 300 donated billboards and produced and distributed nearly one million pieces of KnowHow2GO collateral material to students. In conjunction with the Ad Council, OCAN and KnowHow2GOOhio secured millions of dollars worth of donated TV and radio airtime for public service announcements over nearly two years.

• OCAN and KnowHow2GOOhio have awarded college access programs over $300,000. Grantees have held local launch events, created college clubs, integrated KnowHow2GO into classroom activities and much more.

• OCAN's membership includes 36 college access programs that serve nearly 200 of Ohio's school districts in 51 counties touching nearly 200,000 students annually. High schools with OCAN member programs have an average 4.5% higher graduation rate. In 2009, the college access communities raised nearly $18 million in private funding to provide services to students in Ohio; OCAN and its members helped secure $90 million for students in the form of financial aid and awarded more than 6,000 scholarships to college students that totaled nearly $7.5 million.

Tennessee

KnowHow2GOTennessee

Partners:

TN Higher Education Commission,
www.tn.gov/thec/

GEAR UP,
www.CollegeforTN.org/Home/Gear_Up/_
default.aspx

Campaign Highlights:

• Tennessee's public awareness campaign, "Higher Education...Put Your Mind to It," has received awards at both the national and regional level, winning three MarCom Awards and Memphis PRSA's highest honor, the Vox Grandis.

• Through a partnership with the Tennessee Association of Broadcasters, the campaign has received over $1 million in free radio and television air time.

• Over 950,000 trayliners displaying the campaign's message to "Put Your Mind to It" were distributed in McDonald's restaurants across Tennessee.

• Using social media, the campaign engages and shares important college-going messages with nearly 10,000 Tennessee students.

Washington

Partners:

Northwest Education Loan Association, www.nela.net

College Success Foundation, www.collegesuccessfoundation.org

Alliance for Education, www.alliance4ed.org

Campaign Highlights:

• More than 52,000 students signed up for the College Bound Scholarship! The College Bound Scholarship provides hope and incentive for low-income 7th and 8th grade students and families who otherwise might not consider college as an option because of its cost. Learn more at www.hecb.wa.gov

• College Goal Sunday and KnowHow2GOWashington partner to provide college planning information and FAFSA completion support to over 3,500 students and families. Learn more at www.collegegoalsundaywa.org

• Washington College Access Network (WCAN) launched in March 2010! This collaboration promotes and supports the use of best practices, leverages training opportunities and supports public policies to ensure all students have the opportunity and tools to succeed in higher education. Learn more at www.collegesuccessfoundation.org/wcan

• The Alliance for Education convened the Seattle College Access Network (SCAN) in March 2009 to help increase the number of students who apply for, attend, and graduate from college. This 40 member network includes public schools, two-year and four-year colleges, the Washington Higher Education Coordinating Board, education advocacy non-profits, and the funding community.

Wisconsin

Partners:

University of Wisconsin System, www.wisconsin.edu

Wisconsin Covenant, www.wisconsincovenant.wi.gov/

Wisconsin Department of Public Instruction, www.dpi.state.wi.us/vm-student.html

Wisconsin Association of Independent Colleges & Universities, www.waicu.org

Wisconsin Technical Colleges, www.witechcolleges.org

Wisconsin Higher Educational Aids Board, www.heab.state.wi.us

UW Help, www.uwhelp.wisconsin.edu

Campaign Highlights:

• In 2009, KnowHow2GOWisconsin added test preparation to its repertoire of pre-college preparation activities and partners have been working on establishing a state-wide College Access Network.

• KnowHow2GOWisconsin has been working on establishing a peer-based KnowHow2Go Ambassadors Program where college students can provide guidance and information to students who have begun or are in the midst of the college search process.

KNOWitALL

Real advice from real students.

Preparing for college is tough, but teens across the country are making their dreams a reality. Visit the KnowItAll library and click on the questions you have about preparing for college. Then, watch videos of real students who went on to be successful there.

www.KnowHow2GO.org/knowitall

COLLEGE ACCESS & OPPORTUNITY GUIDE

2 0 1 1 E D I T I O N

Insider Advice from College Students and Other Experts

You're in the right place to find the help and information

you need to make your college dreams a reality! In the following pages you'll find insight and advice from college students and other experts to set you on the path to college. However, this book is just the beginning.

You can continue your research and college prep on the web!

www.CSOcollegecenter.org

Designed to accompany the *College Access & Opportunity Guide*, **www.CSOCollegeCenter.org** is a FREE website for students like you. You can find even more information about the hundreds of colleges featured in this book and send them your information to get an inside edge in the admissions process.

And better yet, students who use **www.CSOCollegeCenter.org** are given the special title of Opportunity Scholar and receive free college search guidance, support, and scholarships.

Opportunity Scholars

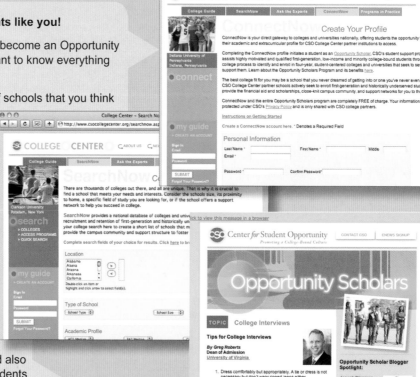

Connect with colleges recruiting students like you!

Get started by creating a student profile to become an Opportunity Scholar. Be prepared to brag—colleges want to know everything that is great about you.

Then search the colleges and save a list of schools that you think would be a "good fit!"

You can also send your profile to colleges you're interested in. They want to hear from you and will give special consideration to Opportunity Scholars in the admissions process.

Get College Admissions Guidance and Support!

Have a question about the college search or application process?

Just Ask the Experts on **www.CSOCollegeCenter.org**. Submit your questions any time of day or night and also be sure to check out more articles from students and professionals offering their expert advice.

You will also begin to receive monthly Opportunity Scholars e-newsletters!

Opportunity Scholarship

Apply for the $1,000 Opportunity Scholarship!

At the end of your senior year—when you've decided where you're going to college—apply for the Opportunity Scholarship.

Not only do scholarship winners receive $1,000 for each of their four years of college, they are also given the opportunity to blog about their college experiences and offer advice to college-bound students like you.

Our past scholarship winners show that where you come from doesn't mean you can't go to college. Check out their posts on the Opportunity Scholars blog at **www.CSOCollegeCenter.org.**

HOMELESSNESS and COLLEGE EDUCATION aren't often discussed in the same sentence, and it is rarely positive.

Khadijah Williams
College: Harvard University
Hometown: Los Angeles, CA

For low-income students like us, it's enough of a challenge to get through high school. Being homeless presents its own crazy challenges. Your transcript reads like the CIA's most wanted, except, instead of moving from country to country, you move from city to city, county to county, or even state to state, often within the span of weeks or days. How is education even in the cards?! You don't even have steady food or shelter.

I don't remember even participating in the first grade, or finishing the second grade, 5th grade is a blur, 6th grade was a one month stint, 7th grade was speckled with absences, tardies, and unsatisfactories for late work or no work. In middle school, teachers thought I could care less about my education, and I let them believe that. I didn't want them to know I was homeless. But I wanted to learn, I loved to learn, I needed to learn.

But there was hope. It's not as easy as going "I'm homeless, let me in your college." I had to fight feelings of insecurity and anxiety, not to mention not knowing what the college process entailed. I didn't know where and how to apply. I applied to two colleges without knowing what the heck I was doing. I didn't know what kind of recommendations I needed, or if my teachers who only knew me a couple of semesters, knew enough about me. I didn't have a computer to apply to college! Often, it was the lack of these few resources that made my college process suffer.

It can be done though. The key is to seek help. You DO NOT have to do the college application process alone. Seek programs and resources designed to help low income kids. Ask your school about college prep programs. Upward Bound is a great programs that you can apply to as early as 9th grade. Find people who you admire, who went to college, and ask for their help. You wouldn't believe how helpful people can be once they know you want to go to college. I got where I am today because of two things—my inner drive and the help from caring adults who I looked up to as role models. Good, caring people will want to see you succeed, and they'll go out of their way to help you if you let it be known that you will do whatever it takes to succeed.

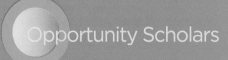
Opportunity Scholars

KHADIJAH WILLIAMS is a 2009-2010 Opportunity Scholarship winner and is writing about her college experiences and offering advice on the Opportunity Scholars blog.

Visit www.CSOCollegeCenter.org to read the blog, become an Opportunity Scholar, and have the chance to be a future Opportunity Scholarship winner and blogger yourself.

By Theresa Atta

Finding and Building Your Network: Are You Connected?

Become "networked" by looking around you.

Who are your friends? Who are the ones that also want to go to college and want to see you achieve the same dream? Learn to distinguish who is in your corner and who wants you to succeed.

The college application process is a rewarding one, but it is not easy. A lot of hard work and time must be invested to find the right college for you. At this point, you probably have a lot of questions and, perhaps, a few doubts. "Can I really do this? Do I have the grades for college? Will I be able to afford my dream school? And once I get to college, do I have what it takes to compete with everyone else?" Believe it or not, asking these questions is a signal that you are on the right track.

The most important thing to remember, however, is that you do not have to go it alone. There are plenty of resources, like this guidebook, to help you along the path. But your network – the people with whom you connect for advice, support, encouragement, and a helping hand – is even better than any publication or Web site available. As with any computer or cell phone, your abilities are limited if you are not connected to a good network!

How do you become "networked?" Just start by looking around you. Who are your friends? Who are the ones that also want to go to college and want to see you achieve the same dream? Learn to distinguish who is in your corner and who wants you to succeed.

If your dream is to go to college, and you are hanging out with people who skip class, then it is time for a new set of friends.

I remember when I was applying to college, and I grew complacent after completing five out of six college applications. As the submission deadline approached, I was uninspired about completing that last application – five schools were good enough, right? Wrong. One of my friends, who also had the same application due, dragged me into the computer lab with her and said, "We are not leaving until we are both finished with this application." Well, that last school was the only college to offer me a full scholarship! What a missed opportunity that would have been were it not for my friend.

I have spent many years working for and with community organizations that assist traditionally underserved students with the college process. These students are sometimes also referred to as "underrepresented" or "at-risk". From my point of view, one of the best ways to help bridge the "opportunity gap" between this population and their more affluent or "connected" counterparts is to emphasize the importance of finding and building a strong network. At Collegiate Directions, Inc., we do just that, in addition to helping students complete

applications, improve testing and study skills, and develop leadership and self-advocacy skills.

If you belong to a similar college support program, take full advantage of the assistance offered. Be sure to take the initiative in reaching out to your high school counselors, teachers, coaches, or people in your neighborhood and/or church group. Making smart connections can help you get to college; it will also help you survive once you get there. Rather than dealing with challenges on your own, be sure to reach out to professors, advisors and classmates, which may mean stepping out of your comfort zone. When you demonstrate your passion towards a particular goal – in this case going to college – you will be amazed at how many people will line up to join your network. ■

BIO *Theresa Atta is Executive Director of Collegiate Directions, Inc. (CDI), a non-profit organization committed to closing the education gap by providing comprehensive college counseling services and ongoing support – beginning in high school and continuing through college graduation – to a target population of low-income, first-generation-to-college students.*

By Tomika Ferguson

Ask People for Help!

I didn't see asking for help as a sign of weakness, but rather getting advice was the most important step in following my dream.

When I was younger, I had aspirations to attend the University of Virginia. Despite not having a strong college going culture in my hometown, opportunities existed for me to accomplish my goals.

Every semester during high school, I signed up for classes that challenged me. I did not always get straight A's, but I did gain skills that prepared me for college. I was not the valedictorian of my high school class, but I was a risk taker.

My parents and I did not understand all of the specifics about applying to college since I was first in our family to do so. I took a personal risk and asked people for advice about the college application process. I didn't see asking for help as a sign of weakness, but rather getting advice was the most important step in following my dream to being accepted to the University of Virginia.

Here are a few people who helped me throughout my college journey.

• **My English teacher** was the best writer I knew, and she helped me to organize my thoughts. I felt very confident in the essays I submitted with my college applications.

• **An older cousin** helped me craft a résumé, and it paid off big time! High school activities demonstrated my capacity for leadership and interests beyond academics.

• **My parents** didn't understand how to fill out the Free Application for Federal Student Aid (FAFSA) but with the help of my guidance counselor, we completed it well before the deadline.

As a high school student, you are surrounded by teachers, college counselors, family members and friends who want you to become successful. They will do everything they can to help you reach your goals.

It is hard to admit when you need help, but you have to be brave and take the first step and find people who have the answers you need. Without asking for help, I never would have accomplished my goal of graduating from the University of Virginia. ■

BIO *Tomika Ferguson is a doctoral candidate in the Higher Education & Student Affairs (HESA) program at Indiana University-Bloomington (IUB). Previously, she was a member of the National College Advising Corps (NCAC), a program that places recent college graduates in high schools with low college attendance in an attempt to reduce barriers to college access.*

By Johnavae Quinn

Finding a College Access Program

College Access Programs Can Help

You're not alone if you feel overwhelmed by the prospect of going to college. Fortunately, there is help for students and families through college access programs that exist in communities across the country to assist students and families in planning for their future.

These programs come in all different shapes and sizes, and most offer one-on-one college counseling, assistance filling out the necessary financial aid forms, mentorship, academic tutoring, college visits, scholarships, parental support groups and internship opportunities.

Here's a list of several web-based resources to help research programs.

When you've found a program that fits your needs, call or visit their office. These programs exist to serve students and will be happy to give you the help and information you need.

Programs in Practice on www.CSOCollegeCenter.org
www.csocollegecenter.org/programnp.aspx

www.CSOCollegeCenter.org is an online college search tool for first-generation and underserved college-bound students. The Programs in Practice portal is a searchable database with spotlight profiles promoting the good work of leading college access programs, community-based organizations, educational resources centers, and scholarship foundations from across the nation.

The National College Access Program Directory
www.collegeaccess.org/accessprogramdirectory/default.aspx

Developed by the National College Access Network (NCAN) and the Pathways to College Network (PCN), the National College Access Program Directory is a searchable online set of profiles of college access programs across the United States that help underserved students prepare, plan and pay for college.

National Partnership for Educational Access (NPEA)
www.educational-access.org

NPEA is a membership organization for programs working to provide underrepresented students with academic preparation, placement services and counseling, and ongoing support to ensure enrollment at and graduation from four-year colleges. Visit their website to learn about their over 140 member organizations in 27 states.

KnowHow2GO
www.knowhow2go.org

KnowHow2GO's "Find Help" page offers visitors a searchable map to help you connect with local resources.

Directory of TRIO and GEAR UP Programs
www.coenet.us

The Council for Opportunity in Education works in conjunction with colleges, universities, and agencies that host TRIO Programs to specifically help low-income students enter college and graduate and offers a directory of all TRIO and GEAR UP programs by state and institution.

BIO *Johnavae Quinn is the former Deputy Director of College Goal Sunday, a volunteer-run program that provides free expert advice about financial aid and filling out the Free Application for Federal Student Aid (FAFSA) in 37 states every January, February and March.*

REALITY CHANGERS SAVED MY LIFE.

Jesse Sanchez
College: Harvard University
Hometown: San Diego, CA

It took me away from the environment I was used to and placed me in an environment where students from all over San Diego who face the same obstacles I face were working towards the same goal—college. I didn't feel alone in the struggle anymore. I felt like I was working towards something that actually mattered. Reality Changers helped me realize the importance of working hard, the importance of determination, and the importance of a higher education.

Reality Changers also gave me hope. I can't count how many times I was told that I wasn't going to amount to anything because of where I came from, where I grew up, or how I looked. After hearing this for so long, I really began to believe it. I felt that I could never amount to anything because of my background. No one else in my family went to college, why should I? Reality Changers helped me realize that I could actually make something of myself. It gave me the tools necessary to succeed and helped me move closer to realizing my full potential. Reality Changers helped me learn to believe in myself.

Reality Changers helps you believe by giving you the chance to prove yourself. If you get a 3.5 gpa or above, you earn a scholarship to UCSD Academic Connections where you can take a college course for college credit before even graduating from high school. This is an opportunity that I would have never had if it were not for Reality Changers. Because

I was able to succeed at Academic Connections, I was that much more confident in my ability to make it to college. It made me feel like I was worthy of a college education, and that it was actually possible for me to go to college.

Reality Changers puts you in an environment where the students are driven and ready to do whatever it takes to get to college. It makes you feel like you are a part of a family, and helps you stay driven. Whenever I feel like just giving up, I think back to all my friends at Reality Changers and how hard they're working and how they are counting on me to work just as hard.

We are fighting an unfair fight and Reality Changers helps us make the fight a little more even.

Opportunity Scholars

JESSE SANCHEZ is a 2009-2010 Opportunity Scholarship winner and is writing about his college experiences and offering advice on the Opportunity Scholars blog.

Visit www.CSOCollegeCenter.org to read the blog, become an Opportunity Scholar, and have the chance to be a future Opportunity Scholarship winner and blogger yourself.

Find a TRIO program in your community

TRIO is a set of federally-funded college opportunity programs that motivate and support students from disadvantaged backgrounds in their pursuit of a college degree. Over 850,000 low-income, first-generation students and students with disabilities—from sixth grade through college graduation—are served by more than 2,800 programs nationally.

The TRIO programs have been successfully assisting students prepare for, attend and graduate from college in every state and territory in America since 1965.

TRIO programs provide:

- academic tutoring
- personal counseling
- mentoring
- financial aid and scholarship assistance
- summer programs opportunities
- cultural enrichment and educational trips
- opportunities to visit colleges
- other supports to help you enter college be successful once enrolled

Famous TRIO students

Patrick Ewing, basketball hall of famer

Angela Bassett, Oscar nominated actress

Viola Davis, Oscar nominated actress

John Quinones, award-winning journalist

Gwendolynne Moore, U.S. Member of Congress

Shelley Berkley, U.S. Member of Congress

Ronald E. McNair, astronaut who died in the 1996 space-shuttle tragedy

TRiO EDUCATIONAL OPPORTUNITY CENTERS

Programs at a Glance

Upward Bound helps youth prepare for higher education. Participants receive instruction in literature, composition, mathematics, and science on college campuses after school, on Saturdays and during the summer. Currently, 964 projects are in operation throughout the United States.

Upward Bound Math & Science helps students from low-income families to strengthen math and science skills. In addition, students learn computer technology as well as English, foreign language and study skills. Currently, 117 projects are serving students throughout the country.

Talent Search projects serve young people in grades six through 12. In addition to counseling, participants receive information about college admissions requirements, scholarships and various student financial aid programs. More than 363,000 students from families with incomes under $33,075 (where neither parent graduated from college) are enrolled in 466 Talent Search TRIO projects to better understand their educational opportunities and options.

Student Support Services projects work to enable low-income students to stay in college until they earn their baccalaureate degrees. Participants receive tutoring, counseling and remedial instruction. Students are now being served at 947 colleges and universities nationwide.

The **Ronald E. McNair Postbaccalaureate Achievement** program, named in honor of the astronaut who died in the 1986 space-shuttle explosion, is designed to encourage low-income students and minority undergraduates to consider careers in college teaching as well as prepare for doctoral study. Students who participate in this program are provided with research opportunities and faculty mentors.

The Council for Opportunity in Education can help you find a TRIO program in your community and join the over three million who have already completed their college degree with the help of TRIO. Visit www.coenet.us for more information and check out a directory of all TRIO programs by state and institution.

By Karin Elliot

Starting Early on the Path to College

One of the best resources to help you achieve your goal of attending college is an *educational access program.* Found all across the country, these programs give you academic support after-school, academic enrichment during the summer and will start working with you during middle school.

College-Prep Programs

Do you want to take academic and elective classes, participate in leadership activities, and community service? If so you might want to learn about college-prep programs that can help you get ready for college—either after school or during the summer.

EXAMPLES:

Breakthrough Collaborative—With 35 sites across the country serving 2,700 students. Breakthrough's core belief is that it is "cool to be smart," and the program attempts to establish this belief in its student participants by setting high standards and supporting their educational goals. Students begin in Breakthrough programs as early as 5th grade and commit to involvement for a minimum of two years.

Aim High—With 12 sites in California serving more than 1,000 students, Aim High supports students starting after their 5th or 6th grade year, and students must commit to a minimum of three summers. Aim High prepares students for success in school and ensures they have an appreciation for community and an awareness of issues that affect their lives.

Placement Programs

Do you need scholarship assistance in order to attend a high-quality independent high school? If so you might want to learn about placement programs that can connect you with very generous financial aid packages and support your enrollment at competitive college-preparatory high schools.

EXAMPLES:

The Steppingstone Academy—Students in the Boston Public School system can get support from to apply to the best high schools in the city. Students who apply must demonstrate a commitment to their education and show academic promise. Steppingstone also supports students and their families as they navigate the process of choosing and applying to these rigorous schools. The Steppingstone Foundation has affiliate sites in Hartford and Philadelphia.

Daniel Murphy Scholarship Fund (DMSF)—This placement program in Chicago provides four-year high school scholarships and educational support, and has a number of core activities such as tutoring, mentoring, and summer opportunities.

Things to remember about education access programs:

• No matter where you live, you can find one that will meet your needs

• They are free, but require a significant time commitment

• Programs start as early as 5th grade and will continue to support you in high school

• During the application process, you will describe your goals and share why you think accessing quality education is important for your future

How to find programs:

• Talk to your school counselor or advisor and explain what you are looking for

• Talk with your parents or guardian about the difference a program could make in your life

• Visit the National Partnership for Educational Access website at **www.educational-access.org** and search the programs that are members of this group

NATIONAL PARTNERSHIP FOR EDUCATIONAL ACCESS

BIO *Karin Elliott is director of the National Partnership for Educational Access (NPEA), a membership organization for programs working in collaboration with independent and public college preparatory schools to provide underrepresented students with academic preparation, placement services and counseling and ongoing support to ensure enrollment at four-year colleges.*

By Mary Lee Hoganson

HOW TO Use your High School Counselor

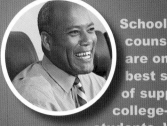

School counselors are one of the best sources of support for college-bound students. Whatever grade you are in, now is the time to start helping your counselor get to know you and your college dreams.

Introduce yourself and state clearly that it is your definite goal to attend college. Let your counselor know that, regardless of your test scores or grades to date, you are highly motivated.

Also, make sure to tell your counselor about yourself: your interests, activities, college and career goals and family background — including what your parents do and whether or not anyone in your family has attended college. With this initial meeting as a good starting point, your counselor can help you plot a successful course for college.

Top 10 items to cover with your counselor:

1) Plan classes that will prepare you for college.

2) Review your academic record and suggest areas that need improvement.

3) Identify the questions you should be asking, like Do I want to stay near home? Does the college have my major? How important is size?

4) Get information about specific colleges and universities.

5) Identify opportunities like college fairs, weekend or summer programs on college campuses (often free for first-generation or low-income students), internships, or community college classes open to high school students.

6) Register for college admission tests and get fee waivers if your family can't afford to pay for tests.

7) Write a letter of recommendation to colleges or universities.

8) Complete and submit college applications carefully and on time and ask colleges to waive application fees.

9) Figure out how to pay for college.

10) Compare offers of admission and financial aid from all of your colleges.

There are a few other very important things to remember about working with your school counselor:

• Most school counselors have many, many students who they want to help. So make appointments early, show up on time and submit forms that require counselor completion well in advance of due dates.

• Make backup copies of everything you mail or give to your counselor.

• Make sure that you keep your counselor "in the loop" in terms of what you are hearing from colleges. If there are any problems which arise, your counselor can act as your direct advocate with colleges.

• If you think it would be helpful, try to schedule a meeting with your counselor AND your parent(s). There are parts of the college process for which you will need a lot of help from them, such as completing the financial aid applications.

• Be sure to thank your counselor for assistance given. When you have made it successfully through the college selection and admission process, thank your counselor with a handwritten note (as well as any teachers who helped).

BIO *Mary Lee Hoganson has over 35 years experience as a high school counselor, 25 of those years focused on college counseling. She served as President of the National Association for College Admission Counseling in 2007.*

By Joyce Smith

A DAY AT THE FAIR

With about 4,000 colleges and universities in this country alone, choosing one that's the right match for you may be challenging! The good news is that there is a venue where you can talk directly to many colleges at once—NACAC National College Fairs.

The fairs are free to students and parents, and packed with booths that colleges have set up so they can talk to you face-to-face. The college admission representatives know almost everything about their schools—from majors, to accommodations, to scholarships. All you have to do is bring your questions!

Visit the NACAC National College Fair Website at www.nationalcolleg-efairs.org to investigate fair locations, which colleges will be attending, how to navigate a fair, directions, and other important details.

It's also important to bring your parents or guardians with you if you can—they will have questions too, most likely concerning things like cost of tuition, financial aid and campus safety. Where you spend the next four years of your life is ultimately your decision, but an adult perspective is helpful.

Also build in some extra time. You may need to visit the Counseling and Resource Center for questions about the admission process, and it never hurts to visit one last booth. Who knows? It may be the college of your dreams!

You may want to schedule a meeting with your school counselor before you attend a fair. They can help you narrow your search and suggest ways to research colleges, ensuring that you spend quality time at each booth, rather than rushing through the fair.

The **National Association for College Admission Counseling (NACAC)**, founded in 1937, is an organization of more than 11,000 professionals from around the world dedicated to serving students as they make choices about pursuing postsecondary education.

NACAC is committed to maintaining high standards that foster ethical and social responsibility among those involved in the transition process, as outlined in the NACAC Statement of Principles of Good Practices (SPGP).

National Association for College Admission Counseling

BIO *Joyce Smith is CEO of the National Association for College Admission Counseling (NACAC).*

By Bob Craves

Money and Mentors: Essentials to the College Process

If you want to be prepared for whatever may lie ahead, college is the first step and you should do all you can to get scholarship money, find a mentor and make sure you're taking the right steps to graduate.

So where do I start finding money and mentors?

COLLEGE SUCCESS FOUNDATION

Look everywhere for scholarship money

College is expensive. But you must look at it as an investment in yourself. In your search to afford college, look everywhere you can for financial aid.

There are several kinds of financial aid, scholarships being one of them. Think of scholarships (and grants) as free money – money you don't have to pay back. A person or organization has chosen to invest in you and is paying you to go to school, learn all you can, and graduate with a degree.

You don't need to be a world-class athlete or have a 4.0 grade point average. If you come from a low-income family, you could be eligible for many need-based scholarships that have very little to do with your performance in high school. You automatically qualify because of your family's financial situation. The largest of

all is the Pell Grant which is a government program that could award you over $5,000 a year for every year you are in college.

Don't forget the colleges and universities to which you want to attend. Contact financial aid offices at the schools you are interested in and ask about financial aid opportunities and how to qualify/apply for them. Be sure they recognize you as a face or a voice on the phone, and not just a piece of paper in a pile of many.

Find a mentor

You've heard the expression "don't go it alone." Well, that couldn't be truer during your college search and application process. A mentor can provide you with a safety net for when the college-going process gets tough.

Find someone who knows about the college process so you have a "go to" person when you have questions. And you will have questions – many of them! If you are having trouble finding the right mentor,

try asking teachers, coaches, employers, and your contacts at youth and faith-based organizations to which you belong.

My wife and I have mentored young people going to college, and have known others who have found mentoring to be very helpful. In fact, in my life, I have had the good fortune of having a mentor myself. I have learned as much from the students I've mentored, as they have learned from me.

College is a growing experience that sets the stage for the rest of your life. Enjoy it! ■

BIO *Bob Craves is the co-founder, chairman, and CEO of the College Success Foundation, an organization providing college scholarships and mentoring to low-income, high-potential students in Washington State and the District of Columbia. Prior to CSF, Bob was one of the founding officers of the Costco Wholesale Corporation.*

By Rachel Brody

Being the FIRST

First things first.

Everyone loves the first.

The first man on the moon, the first African-American president, and the first in flight. First kisses, first impressions, first place.

What is it about the first?

In many ways, it is easier for students who have siblings or parents who took on the big firsts. When it comes to college, students with parents who attended college have a better chance of attending college themselves.

So what does that mean for students who don't have a family history of higher education? These students who enroll in colleges and universities are called first-generation college students.

Yes, being the first can be lonely. Everything feels strange and different the first time. You might worry how your friends and family will see you, the first. "He thinks he is so special because he is first."

But don't hold back on being first. The great thing about being the first one is that it doesn't mean that you will be the last one. By being the first in your family to graduate from college, you open the door for younger siblings, for your children, and their children. College will not be an intimidating unknown because you went first.

OK, maybe the betterment of your imaginary grandchildren isn't the most convincing reason to take on being the first in college. So, think of yourself. College is four years that are all about you. Your discoveries, your achievements, and your firsts. People who attend college live longer, make more money, and vote more often. You will have more opportunities in your lifetime if you go to college.

Although it can be daunting, being the first is an accomplishment. It will make you a stronger and happier person. And that is what really matters. ■

BIO *Rachel Brody is an adviser with the National College Advising Corps (NCAC), a national program that places recent college graduates in high schools with low college attendance in an attempt to reduce barriers to college access.*

CHANGE YOUR LIFE IN ONE SUMMER

Lysa Vola
College: Williams College
Hometown: Jensen Beach, FL

You've just made it through a year of high school. So, what are your plans for this summer? What about going to college? Every summer there are programs held at college campuses across the country. They range by various interests, activities, and academic areas. Some are science programs, while others enhance artistic ability or musicality, but all of them are right at your fingertips.

So, now you might be thinking, how can I afford to go to a summer program, I don't have the money? Many summer programs such as MITES (Minority Introduction to Engineering and Science) and Quest Bridge affiliated summer programs offer full scholarships for all students accepted into their programs. You could attend a program the summer following your junior or even sophomore year of high school for free!

While these programs may not sound like the most exciting thing to do over your summer, let me share my experience with you.

As a high school junior, I applied to the MITES program on the campus of MIT. It is a seven week program in Science and Engineering that is aimed towards helping disadvantaged minorities and/or students from low-income backgrounds excel in the field of science. While at MIT, I was given the chance to complete research in genomics at the Broad Institute of MIT and Harvard. My research team dealt with Single Nucleotide Polymorphisms in genetic disorders such as Cystic Fibrosis and early onset Breast Cancer. Prior to the summer, I had no idea what that even meant!

Besides doing work and taking courses, I also explored the city of Boston on weekends, went to theme parks, dances, and dinners. I spent that summer at MIT living on my own and learned how to balance my time. I got a chance to experience what college might be like before actually getting into college.

My point is not that all of you should apply to the MITES program, but rather, that you should consider finding out more information about summer programs like MITES.

Summer programs provide you with opportunities to discover what it's like to be in a college setting prior to actually applying to or attending college. Summer programs also offer high school students an edge in the college admissions process. They are looked highly upon, because many of them are a lot of work, and prove your dedication and skill. Completing the program successfully makes you stand out from amongst thousands of high school college applicants who didn't take the opportunity to explore, learn, or take their summer seriously. Most are only a few weeks long, so you will still have time to be home and relax with friends before school starts!

So before you turn away an application to spend your summer away studying, consider how it might change your life, the new adventures you might be able to take, and the people you may meet. Never turn down an opportunity, because they are just that, something that you either take or leave, but ultimately can never be replaced!

Opportunity Scholars

LYSA VOLA is a 2009-2010 Opportunity Scholarship winner and is writing about her college experiences and offering advice on the Opportunity Scholars blog.

Visit www.CSOCollegeCenter.org to read the blog, become an Opportunity Scholar, and have the chance to be a future Opportunity Scholarship winner and blogger yourself.

By Alma Powell

AMERICA'S PROMISE ALLIANCE

LITTLE RED WAGON

On behalf of the America's Promise Alliance, congratulations on being the first in your family to pursue higher education. You are right to seek a college degree; 80% of the new jobs in our 21st century economy require the higher skills and creative thinking that are hallmark of a college education. What you learn in college, about your courses and yourself, will serve you throughout your life.

Alma Powell is the chairman of the board of America's Promise Alliance, an organization founded by her husband, former Secretary of State General Colin Powell.

Finding your way across a new landscape of college will be as challenging as your first days in elementary school, or your transition to middle school and high school. But it is also an exciting experience you can shape with your energy and creativity like nothing you have encountered before. The knowledge and discipline that helped you earn a high school diploma will be compasses that enable you to successfully navigate this new world and set your course for even higher things.

I am proud to serve as chair of America's Promise Alliance, a coalition founded by my husband, Colin, on the principle that all young people need five fundamental resources to fulfill their potential. Just as surely as plants need water and sunshine, every child needs caring adults, safe places for learning and growing, a healthy start, an effective education, and, not least, the opportunity to help others and learn the critical importance of service. Experience and research confirm that, when young people receive these "promises," the odds of success swing strongly in their favor. We call them the "Five Promises" because that is what they must be: promises we keep to our children.

For our Alliance, the Little Red Wagon has always been a symbol of childhood and the hopes and dreams that propel us into adulthood. In the beginning, adults pull you along, support you, and nurture you. Soon, you will support yourselves, proudly and independently.

Think about the people who pulled your little red wagon along your way: the parents who came to this country or worked two or even three jobs so you would have a better life; the mentors, tutors and coaches who saw your potential and helped you see it, too; the teachers and guidance counselors who believed you could graduate and go on to college. These are people who kept the Promises for you, and equipped you so you could keep them for others, leading by example and pulling together to meet society's challenges.

Even as adults, we still carry our red wagons of hopes and dreams. When you feel uncertain, ill prepared, or torn between school, community and family obligations, find rapport and mutual support from your professors and peers. Be a pest if you must but keep looking for allies.

Whatever your aspirations may be, getting a higher education is the key to achieving them. You are up to the challenge. Some people may tell you differently. Don't believe them. Don't be afraid to dream big. Never give up. And just as caring adults helped pull you this far, keep the Promise for the children who need a hand in getting to their own hopes and dreams. ■

BIO *Alma Powell is the chairman of the board of America's Promise Alliance, an organization founded by her husband, former Secretary of State General Colin Powell. America's Promise Alliance serves a mission to mobilize people from every sector of American life to build the character and competence of youth.*

By Tally Hart

The Importance of Your "Real Life" in Scholarships and Admissions

The days when scholarships or admissions applications relied just on grades are long past. Although grades are still important, many colleges and universities want students that bring varying backgrounds into the classroom and campus community. In fact, colleges understand that they must bring the real world into the classroom, which means recruiting students from a wide range of backgrounds so that a campus community best reflects the real world.

Since a diverse student body is so important to a college, certain aspects of your life that were once overlooked in the college application process suddenly become important indicators of future success in college. You can describe family commitments—caring for a grandparent or younger siblings, for example—on a scholarship and admission application because this dedication to the family's needs shows your efforts extend outside the classroom.

Work experience is another good example of what colleges think is important in a prospective student. You might be the primary financial support for your family, and that commitment and the time it takes to work and still stay a good student is a desirable skill set.

But here's the catch – colleges and scholarship providers need to know about these parts of your "real life" to be able to consider you in the selection process. Don't be afraid of talking about your job or even difficult situations you've solved at work when you write essays for these applications. ■

BIO *Tally Hart has served students seeking access to higher education throughout her career and presently serves as Senior Advisor for Economic Access at Ohio State University.*

I Wish — Lessons Learned Through the Admissions & Financial Aid Process

By Desireé Johnson, Ohio State University, '09

The financial aid process is pretty overwhelming for a high school student, and there are a few things I would like to share with you before you begin the process.

I wish I had known the importance of applying for aid early. Coming from a family where no member had ever gone to college, I was in the dark about the college-going process until my senior year of high school. That was too late. There are many scholarships you can apply for long before then—even your freshman year.

I wish I had met priority deadlines. I barely submitted my FAFSA on time, and unfortunately, I missed certain award opportunities. For example, I did not find out about The Ohio State University's merit scholarships until after numerous deadlines had passed.

I wish I had prepared for the SAT-ACT. I had to take the ACT twice. Also, I was not aware that schools often offer full- or partial-fee waivers to cover the test costs, and that an improvement of a point or two is so crucial in opening additional doors for aid.

I wish I would have known more about loans and loan options. I made assumptions about loans, and I avoided them. Truthfully, I was intimidated by the idea of putting myself in debt, and I relied on money I saved from over-working myself in jobs during high school and my federal-work study program in college. This has been extremely stressful, not to mention a hindrance in getting involved on campus.

I wish I knew that scholarships can't always be combined. Aside from my lack of knowledge about the financial process, I had another setback in getting aid. I received a scholarship from a university program that I was not able to use since I had been awarded another university-administered scholarship. This restriction was a definite setback as I had been counting on that additional funding.

I Did — Looking back, however, there were steps I followed that I am so grateful I did, and would recommend to others.

I did approach my high school guidance counselor to ask for scholarship applications. He turned out to be very helpful in providing me with scholarships he had seen previously and contacting me when he learned of new scholarships.

I did online searches for available scholarships. Besides checking out www.scholarships.com, additionally, I researched scholarships through my community library. I checked out books that had information on available money and tips on how to go about applying for it.

I did go to financial aid events. If your school or city puts on a financial aid event, go to it and encourage your parents to attend. I can't stress enough how important it is to be informed and knowledgeable about financial aid.

I did fill out each and every application I found and met the qualifications for. The more applications you fill out, the more you increase your chances of being awarded aid. Some of my scholarships, which have shown to be among the most helpful, include those which I thought there was little-to-no-chance of me getting.

I did take the application process seriously. Think every response through thoroughly and do not get lazy or intimidated by lengthy forms or multiple essays. That extra time and effort can result in more money to fund your *future*.

IN ALL HONESTY MY LIFE HAS BEEN A WAR.

Every day I have to fight. I have to fight my parents, my past, my own insecurities, and feelings of stagnation. I still struggle to make sense of things and I carry my war wounds with me everywhere I go. From having a part-time job, traveling to two different high schools, to Hurricane Katrina, my journey to pursue college has been full of many obstacles.

Living in New Orleans during my teenage years was certainly a struggle. I can honestly say that the culture of my city has shaped my life. I've lived in the Lower Ninth Ward in New Orleans all my life on the same street in the same home. My parents did not have much money to support my four siblings and me, which led me to take on a part-time job after-school and on the weekends. I wanted to set an example for my younger siblings by making my way through our financial obstacles and getting to college. My mother would tell me that getting an education was the only way out and a way to build independence.

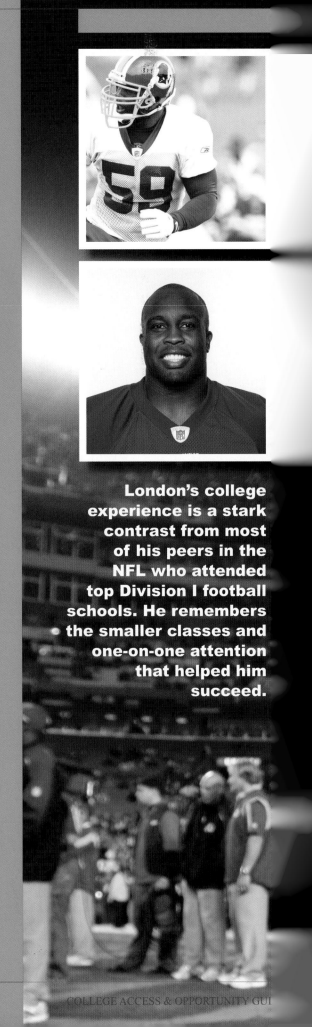

Angelica Robinson
College: Dillard University
Hometown: New Orleans, LA

When Hurricane Katrina hit New Orleans, I returned to my home in New Orleans with no running water, no electricity, no schools and no friends. Having to rebuild my home and my life at age 15 due to Hurricane Katrina, gave me the strength to crash through any barricade, leap over any hurdle. I was taught as a youth that an individual is strengthened and defined by their struggles; an achievement isn't worth anything if it is placed into your palm. I wasn't going to let anything—not even a natural disaster—stand in the way of me going to college.

I am now attending Dillard University, an HBCU in New Orleans, where I am pursuing my passion for writing. Attending a Historically Black College or University has always been my dream and I am thankful for the opportunities that my university can provide. I am living my dream thanks to hard work and perseverance. I've been blessed with the opportunity to further my education and my writing career—I am truly thankful for this. I hope my writing will inspire and give others the strength to overcome their obstacles and to find the courage to open up their world. One should never forget their struggles, but when I cross The Avenue of the Oaks to receive my diploma, I will have a smile on my face and strength etched in my heart.

London's college experience is a stark contrast from most of his peers in the NFL who attended top Division I football schools. He remembers the smaller classes and one-on-one attention that helped him succeed.

Opportunity Scholars

ANGELICA ROBINSON is a 2009-2010 Opportunity Scholarship winner and is writing about her college experiences and offering advice on the Opportunity Scholars blog.

Visit **www.CSOCollegeCenter.org** to read the blog, become an Opportunity Scholar, and have the chance to be a future Opportunity Scholarship winner and blogger yourself.

Building a Bridge to College

Yes, he's a Pro Bowler and Super Bowl Champion. But London Fletcher did not take your typical path to the National Football League. London admits that sports were his reason to go to college, but he wasn't an All-American destined for a career in professional sports.

London was 11 when his sister was murdered and that despair led his mother to drug addiction. London found solace at the E.J. Kovacic Recreation Center, a building he and his friends call "the Rec," and a mentor in the Rec's director, Tim Isaac.

Mr. Issac taught London, a boy so strong that his family called him "Bam" after "Bamm-Bamm" on "The Flintstones," that guns and drugs would not validate him, but an education and sports could.

London's first love was basketball and after two state championships in high school, he accepted a scholarship to Saint Francis University, a small Division I school in rural Pennsylvania, becoming the first in his family to go to college. He spent one and a half years there before transferring to John Carroll University back home in Cleveland.

It was at John Carroll that London excelled in football and committed himself in the classroom.

"You don't go to John Carroll thinking you'll make it to the NFL," London said about the NCAA Division III school that doesn't offer athletic scholarships. "I focused on academics and attaining my degree to make my mother and family proud."

London's college experience is a stark contrast from most of his peers in the NFL who attended top Division I football schools. He remembers the smaller classes and one-on-one attention that helped him succeed.

"John Carroll has such a great academic reputation and I had to adjust to the academic rigor," said London, who earned a degree in sociology. "But the campus is small and I was not lost in the shuffle."

For London, making it to the NFL was icing on the cake. Despite being the NCAA Division III defensive player of the year his senior year, the NFL passed him by in the draft. While he got his shot as a rookie free agent with the St. Louis Rams and now plays for the Washington Redskins where he earned his first Pro Bowl selection in 2010, London doesn't forget that education is the key to a better future.

Through London's Bridge Foundation, he is helping students in Cleveland, OH, Washington, DC, and Charlotte, NC with mentoring, test preparation and college scholarships.

"Often times first-generation college students don't know the route to college," London explained. "I started the foundation out of a desire to help others and to bridge that gap to college." ■

Peer Leader Tim Spicer Introduces President for Historic Speech on Education

Every single one of you has something that you're good at. Every single one of you has something to offer. And you have a responsibility to yourself to discover what that is. That's the opportunity an education can provide.

–President Obama

On September 8, 2009 President Barack Obama delivered an inspirational back to school speech to the nation's students at Wakefield High School in Arlington, VA. He was skillfully introduced by Timothy Spicer, a Peer Leader who completed a College Summit workshop at the University of Richmond in July 2009. Thanks in part to the college list he generated at the workshop, in chatting with the President before his remarks, Tim was able to provide a solid answer to President Obama's question, "So, are you thinking about college?" Tim rattled off names from his college list, including Morehouse, North Carolina A&T, James Madison University, Hampton and Temple.

"My current personal goals came straight out of the workshop," Timothy said in reflecting on the President's call to action for students to set personal goals. "I want to get my college applications done by November, and I want to challenge myself to do better on the SAT next month." ■

College Summit is a national nonprofit organization that partners with schools and districts to strengthen college-going culture and increase college enrollment rates, so that all students graduate career and college-ready.

Throughout the summer, College Summit runs four-day workshops guiding 40-50 low-income high school seniors through the college transition process to:

- Complete a college common application

- Craft a personal statement

- Gain insight about the financial aid process

- Talk one-on-one with a college counselor

- Learn how to positively influence their peers outside of the workshop

Learn more at www.collegesummit.org

Thank you, Secretary Duncan.

Good Morning. I would like to extend a warm welcome to President Barack Obama, Secretary of Education, Arne Duncan, White House Staff, School Board Members, County Board Members, Superintendent, Dr. Patrick Murphy, Senior Staff, Principal Doris Jackson, Wakefield Faculty and my fellow classmates.

I am honored to have been chosen to speak before my classmates as well as the students across America today! Over the past three years I have taken advantage of every academic, extracurricular and community opportunity that has been presented to me. As I reflect, a scholar expressed disappointment within my writing and challenged me to do better. Being reassigned to another class wasn't an option. After that experience I was determined to excel. Therefore, I managed to succeed within the advanced placement class by maintaining focus along with using a setback as constructive energy. As I stand before my peers today, I want you to know that excellent educational opportunities may be handed to us, but as students we must all take responsibility for our future. We may be taught, but we must take ownership of our learning. As Senior Class President, I encourage all of our freshmen to take advantage of the opportunities that Wakefield High School has to offer.

Along with the inspiration I have taken from President Obama, I would not be standing HERE before you, to introduce the President of the United States, if I had not been HERE at Wakefield High School, in Arlington, VA pursuing my education. Just as we are fortunate to have President Obama come here to Wakefield today to speak to us, we are also

fortunate that after he leaves, we will continue to have the opportunities and support that Wakefield gives to all of us.

At this time it is with great honor and pride that I ask everyone to stand, to welcome the man who proved that Yes, We Can – ladies and gentlemen, please join me in welcoming the President of the United States of America, Barack Obama!

By Roy Jones

Simple Recipe for Success

I have worked my entire life as an educator, and I often find myself working with students who remind me of myself at 18 years old. My story and pathway to success were hardly a result of a strategic plan. I didn't graduate high school with honors, nor did I take AP courses or receive high SAT scores.

In fact, college was hardly on the radar for me. When I was growing up, I never set foot on a college campus, and although my parents worked hard, I felt they didn't have the kind of money it would have taken to support me in college.

Luckily for me, a dedicated group of university educators and community leaders recruited me and a few of my friends to attend our local state university and offered us significant financial support. My life would be forever changed!

Although I stumbled into college, I became committed to education, social justice, activism and learned a few things along the way.
So, here is my simple success recipe:

Recipe for Success

Master the fundamentals

Mastering the fundamentals of reading, writing, language skills, parts of speech and arithmetic is essential. Building a strong knowledge of physical and biological sciences, along with a foreign language is vital. Success with challenging courses will help improve your scores on standardized tests, which are required for college admission and financial aid opportunities. Testing is a way of life, so get used to it!

Think outside the box

It is a myth that having athletic talent is the only pathway to access and afford college. The majority of college students are not highly recruited point guards or running backs! It is important to be able to identify your unique gifts and abilities, as every person has genius and greatness within them, but the challenge is to figure out exactly what yours is and how to apply it. Here's a hint: try volunteering in your community to help stimulate your curiosity and interests.

Be assertive

You should know colleges are aggressively trying to identify and compete for students who want to pursue careers in education, science, math, technology, and health-related fields, but you need to be assertive, open to suggestions, and demonstrate an interest in your future. If you do all that, people will come out of the woodwork to assist you.

Develop positive relationships

All successful people have mentors. Learning how to build and develop positive relationships with elders is one of the most important skills you can have. The person serving as your mentor is typically not a family member, but rather it's somebody with a proven and demonstrated track record doing what you aspire to do. Find that person, tell them your story, explain where you desire to go with your life, and ask them to work with you. ∎

Want to be a teacher?

The mission of the Call Me MISTER (acronym for Mentors Instructing Students Toward Effective Role Models) Initiative is to increase the pool of available teachers from a broader more diverse background among the lowest performing elementary schools. Student participants are largely selected from among under-served, socio-economically disadvantaged and educationally at-risk communities.

Call Me MISTER provides:

• Tuition assistance through Loan Forgiveness programs for admitted students pursuing approved programs of study in teacher education at participating colleges

• An academic support system to help assure their success

• A cohort system for social and cultural support

For more information about Call Me MISTER, please contact MISTER@clemson.edu or call 1-800-640-2657.

Participating Colleges

Anderson University (SC)*
Benedict College (SC)
Cheyney University (PA)
Claflin University (SC)*
Clemson University (SC)
College of Charleston (SC)*
Coastal Carolina University (SC)
Eastern Kentucky University
Greenville Technical College (SC)
Longwood University (VA)
Metropolitan Community College (MO)
Midlands Technical College (SC)
Morris College (SC)
South Carolina State University (SC)
The North East Florida Educational Consortium
Tri-County Technical College (SC)
Trident Technical College (SC)
University of South Carolina – Beaufort

*Colleges featured in the *College Access & Opportunity Guide*

BIO *Dr. Roy Jones is lecturer and executive director for the Eugene T. Moore School of Education's Call Me MISTER Program at Clemson University.*

By Karen Gross

What Size College is "Right" for You

Think about what makes you most comfortable, what energizes you . . .

How can you know whether you are better suited to a larger university or a small liberal arts college? Well, instead of looking at size as the central dividing line among colleges, think instead about who you are (and who you will become) – as a person and as a learner. Think about what makes you most comfortable, what energizes you, what environment will enable you to thrive over the next four years.

Let me share with you three prominent myths about college size.

MYTH ONE: YOU MUST GO TO A COLLEGE THAT IS BIGGER THAN YOUR HIGH SCHOOL. FALSE!

The critically important differences between college and high school are NOT based on size. Colleges, whatever their size, are engaged in a different enterprise than high school. At colleges, the number and breadth of courses is vast and unlike most high school curricula. You will have lots of opportunities over your college career to select among the courses and to specialize in what most interests you.

At college, you get to focus on what most interests you, what most captures your imagination. This can happen in many academic settings, large or small.

MYTH TWO: STUDENTS GET LOST AT LARGE UNIVERSITIES AND BECOME A NUMBER NOT A NAME. FALSE!

All colleges, regardless of size, work very hard to help their students find niches within their communities. For some students, that "small" feel comes from athletics where student-athletes bond with each other and with the coaching staff. For other students, closeness comes through clubs and organizations. For some, it appears through shared academic interests where students connect with others in courses and projects.

Rather than the size of a college, the more important thing is for you to find ways to connect – to other students, to faculty members, to the community. You can do that at all colleges, large and small.

MYTH THREE: SMALL COLLEGES OFFER LIMITED OPPORTUNITIES. FALSE!

Small colleges and large universities all offer amazing opportunities—more opportunities than one student could experience fully in four years. What is important in assessing the opportunities on a college or university campus is not size but the philosophy and vision of the college and its leadership.

So, visit campuses. Walk around without an admissions guide for a while. Make sure you sit in on a class or two. Speak with students in the halls and in the dining facilities. Listen to what is happening when students interact with faculty and staff. Meet coaches. See if you can sense and feel the college's ambition and goals.

... what environment will enable you to thrive

Conclusion

Think about selecting the size of a college this way: If you were shopping for clothing, it is likely that there are many choices, many things that fit at many prices, with many styles, in many colors. But, some of the items selected will just feel right to you. They may not feel right to your friends or parents. But, you will find something you can see yourself wearing.

The same is true for colleges. There are many, many choices. The goal is to choose the places that feel right to you. ■

BIO *Karen Gross is the President of Southern Vermont College, a small private liberal arts college located in Bennington, Vermont.*

SIZE QUIZ ✔

WHAT SIZE COLLEGE IS OPTIMAL FOR YOU

Of course, some students will be happy and thrive in any academic setting. But this quiz will help you determine if you are best suited to small colleges (1,500 or fewer students) or larger universities (over 15,000 students).

There are two truisms about the choices confronting college-aged students: No one school is right for every student (even a stellar place), and there is always more than one right school for each student. So, use this quiz as a way of thinking about college size.

1. Are you one who has experienced freedom at home and in school and can handle it well, avoiding peer pressure and bad choices when confronted with limited oversight and supervision?

☐ YES ☐ NO ☐ MAYBE

2. Are you one for whom structure and personal contact will be beneficial and appealing because you thrive in a situation where you want and appreciate support from teachers, coaches, close friends, and mentors?

☐ YES ☐ NO ☐ MAYBE

3. Are you one who can make decisions easily (courses, athletics, after-school activities) and enjoys the decision making process without parental or institutional oversight and steering?

☐ YES ☐ NO ☐ MAYBE

4. Are you one for whom choosing among options takes time, requires advice or feedback from third parties to reach a decision, and for whom second-guessing or indecision is a common trait?

☐ YES ☐ NO ☐ MAYBE

5. Are you able to advocate for yourself, ask the right questions (and have experience doing this in school and in the community), identify problems and then get the right answers and solutions?

☐ YES ☐ NO ☐ MAYBE

6. Are you shy, laid-back or re-active, a person who accepts results and situations even if they are not optimal?

☐ YES ☐ NO ☐ MAYBE

7. Are you someone who can easily engage and find opportunities, friendships and adult relationships within their school and community, most particularly if you are younger than those around them?

☐ YES ☐ NO ☐ MAYBE

8. Are you one who prefers deep engagement in one activity to find your sense of place or for whom engagement (with people and opportunities) takes more time and does not come naturally?

☐ YES ☐ NO ☐ MAYBE

How to score the results:

There are no right or wrong answers to this quiz. Your preference to one environment is not a value judgment about you; instead, it is an assessment of how you function and what might optimize your college success and happiness.

QUESTIONS 1, 3, 5 and 7

"Yes" answers suggest you are likely suited to larger colleges and universities.

"No" answers suggest you may be better suited to smaller colleges and universities.

"Maybe" answers suggest you take a deeper look at whether a large college or university will be a comfortable fit for you—it probably is.

QUESTIONS 2, 4, 6 and 8

"Yes" answers suggest you will likely be well suited to smaller colleges and universities.

"No" answers suggest you may be better suited to larger colleges and universities.

"Maybe" answers suggest you take a deeper look at whether a smaller college or university will be a comfortable fit for you—it probably is.

A combination of answers suggests you think about your personality and how it might relate to different college size to determine the right fit for you.

By Michelle D. Gilliard, Ph.D.

get engaged in finding the right fit

What you learn depends on the educational opportunities your college provides and how you take advantage of them.

So how do you begin to find a college that is a good fit?

Don't let size fool you!

Smaller colleges, medium-sized universities and large institutions alike are capable of providing students with high-quality learning experiences in which students are required to become actively engaged in their learning. Instead of college size, you should think about which school environment will best develop your ability to reason, to solve complex problems, and to perform at higher levels. Finding the right fit requires you to identify the type of learning environment where you will be successful.

Review curricular offerings

A careful review of an institution's course requirements in both major concentration and general education courses is a good way to decide if the institution provides an active learning environment. By reading an institution's course catalogue, you'll see if you are required to complete a certain number of hours of community service in order to graduate, or if you are provided the opportunity to pursue internships at businesses, government entities and community agencies.

Get to know the institution

The final, and perhaps, most important step to finding a "right fit" institution is to connect with the institution directly. If visiting the campus is possible, go! Talk to students, talk to faculty, take a tour from the admissions

---

By Dr. Larry D. Shinn

FINDING A FIT: A TWO-WAY STREET

"Which is the right college for me?" "Where will I find the major I want to study?" "What college will be the right fit?" With colleges asking similar questions about the students who apply, you will find that your "fit" with a college is a two-way street.

What should you be looking for?

Surprisingly, more than half of college students who declare a major when they arrive as freshmen change their major one or more times before they graduate! So, selecting a college that has the major you want to study is not a sufficient reason when deciding the best college fit.

There is one consideration that all students should make in deciding the "fit" of a college: its capacity to provide an educational environment that promotes life-long learning. Even if the colleges that you are considering have programs specialized for a specific career path (e.g. fashion design, civil engineering, architecture, or teaching), every one of those professions will require continued learning beyond college.

The best fit is ultimately the college whose learning environment is diverse and where you are challenged to think and grow beyond your current interests. From internships to undergraduate research and study abroad programs, your college experience should expand your abilities and horizons in ways you cannot do yourself.

What are colleges looking for?

Again, "fit" is a two-way street. An important ingredient to your fit for a college is what that college is looking for in the students it seeks to admit.

When you are trying to decide what college best fits you, you need to ask what that college is seeking in the students it admits. Some colleges focus more on academic qualifications than others. Some colleges use standardized tests scores like the SAT or ACT as an initial screen and others don't require such scores at all. Some colleges focus more on mathematically and scientifically talented students (e.g. engineering and technical colleges) while others seek well-rounded students who want to study a discipline or major in a broader educational context (e.g., liberal arts colleges).

office, sit in on a class, ask to spend the night in a residence hall, visit the library and the student union. Do anything and everything to learn about the school, its students and the academic and social environment.

If visiting the campus is not an option, go on-line and watch a video tour of the campus. Send questions and consider the answers.

Get started!

Finding an institution that provides the right fit works best when you take the time to develop a short list of institutions that (1) offer majors in the student's areas of interest, (2) provide you with multiple opportunities to become actively engaged in their own learning, and (3) are focused on creating an environment where students from a variety of backgrounds and experiences are successful.

Ultimately, finding the right college fit is also about taking time to think about why you want a college education and what you hope to do with your life. Selecting a college that both challenges and supports your educational and social development is the type of college that will lead to your success.

BIO *Michelle D. Gilliard, Ph.D. is Senior Director for Workforce Development and Education at the Walmart Foundation.*

How do your life experiences and aspirations, previous academic studies and accomplishments, and career interests and life-long learning needs "fit" with the mission, academic programs, and learning environment of the colleges you are considering? These are the questions that both you and the colleges to which you apply will be asking to decide your mutual fit.

Conclusion

In the end, the "fit" between you and a college you are considering is about maximizing the learning you will receive. Regardless of the college or university you attend or what your major or your chosen career is, you should graduate having the ability to think, speak, and to act well—an education of your total person.

BIO *Dr. Larry D. Shinn is president of Berea College, a liberal arts college in Berea, Kentucky that provides every admitted student a four-year tuition scholarship and the opportunity to work on campus to assist with costs of room and board.*

I MUST SAY FROM THE GET-GO

Duylam Nguyen-Ngo
College: Babson College
Hometown: Richmond, VA

that I never really had a "mentor" or someone who helped me through the college process. And this is true for many first-generation students. We just don't have anyone who takes our hands and shows us the ins and outs of looking for colleges or helps us fill out financial aid or any of that.

As a son of immigrant parents, I am my family's "golden child". My family has sacrificed their own comfort just so I can live unchained by the limitations of Vietnam. Guess what? I'm just one out of thousands of kids with the same story. Your life could be based off the same platform as mine—a family who believes in their seed. I understand what it's like to have a family who believes in you, and I understand that you sometimes feel like Atlas carrying the weight of the world.

The weight that is put on your shoulders is a weight that many first-generation students feel. I dare not call it a burden, but rather a 1,000 ton brick on your back. And that is why we do what we do. Because we love our families, because they expect so much from us, because we expect so much from ourselves, as the forerunners for wealth in future generations. This is what fuels our passion.

College really opens a lot of doors for you, but this mainly depends on how you spin college. Some people just go to class, go back to their dorm, and just chill out, work, or whatever. Honestly, I think the only limit on what college offers is the extent of your wanting to do things and the imagination you have.

There will be many resources and opportunities offered and you won't be able to capitalize on all of them. Do as much as you can. I know that, for many of us, money can be an issue, but I think you should definitely take whatever it is that comes your way. Hey, I went to New York to meet 700+ entrepreneurial people—no, I didn't really meet that many—and I had the chance to present my business concept at the New York Stock Exchange. Not that bad, right?

And that's what college has given me so far. In a nutshell, amazing people, even better connections, and a mind blowing experience in Boston.

Opportunity Scholars

DUYLAM NGUYEN-NGO is a 2009-2010 Opportunity Scholarship winner and is writing about his college experiences and offering advice on the Opportunity Scholars blog.

Visit **www.CSOCollegeCenter.org** to read the blog, become an Opportunity Scholar, and have the chance to be a future Opportunity Scholarship winner and blogger yourself.

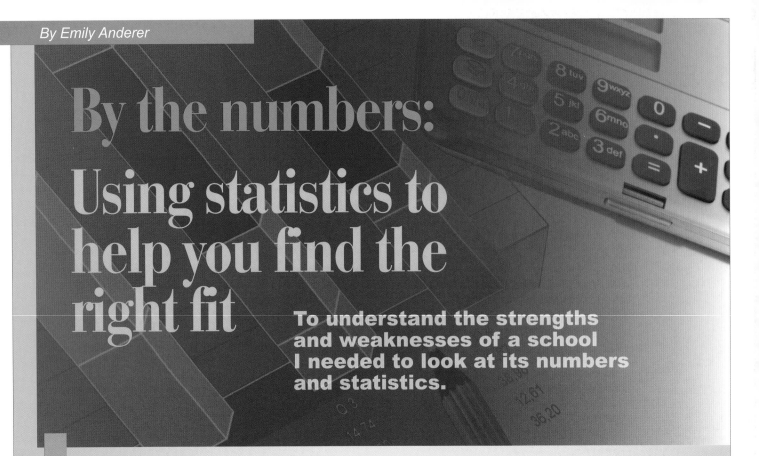

By Emily Anderer

By the numbers: Using statistics to help you find the right fit

To understand the strengths and weaknesses of a school I needed to look at its numbers and statistics.

was woefully uninformed when I began my college search process. Living in Utah, I knew about most of the universities in my state but very little about schools elsewhere. I didn't know the difference between a public and a private college, what a liberal arts school was, and I don't think I was even clear on the difference between undergraduate and graduate school. The most difficult part of my college search was struggling to determine the quality of colleges I had never heard about previously.

Eventually, I realized to understand the strengths and weaknesses of a school I needed to look at its numbers and statistics. This wasn't the most fun part of my college process, but good solid research helped me to make informed decisions.

Here are guidelines I followed to identify and interpret college numbers and statistics:

Admissions rate - The smaller a school's admission rate, the more competitive the school is considered to be. For example, Harvard's admissions rate is around 7%—only one out of 14 students who apply will be admitted. It's good to aim high and apply to some schools where the odds are you may not be admitted, but also apply to some schools where the admissions rate is in your favor.

SAT and ACT range - Looking at the standardized test scores of admitted applicants is a good way to evaluate the academic ability of the student body. Compare your test scores to the school's median test scores—the 25th to 75th percentile of admitted students—to get the best idea of your admissibility.

Financial aid - Financial aid is money you get to make up the difference between the cost of attending a college and your family's ability to pay. Look for schools that have need-blind admissions, by which students are admitted regardless of their ability to pay for tuition.

Merit scholarships - Schools give merit scholarships to reward academic accomplishment, particularly when a student's grades or test scores may be competitive enough to be admitted at a more selective institution. You may have a good chance of being offered a merit scholarship if you apply to a school where your grades or test scores are above their average students.

First-year retention rate - This percentage describes the number of enrolled freshmen who re-enroll as sophomores the following year. Be wary if a large percentage of the student body doesn't return for their second year. Clearly, the school is not providing students something they want or need.

Six-year graduation rate - Whether students failed to graduate from a school because they transferred, dropped out, or failed to complete requirements, this is one of the most important clues to understand the quality of a school. If this percentage is low, the school is not adequately supporting students to ensure graduation.

Don't just fall into a college because you didn't do enough research. I'm enormously thankful that I put in the time and hard work to research, identify and gain admittance to my dream school—a liberal arts college in upstate New York that none of my family or friends had ever heard of but which was perfect for me. Don't settle on your college just because you are unaware of what else is out there.

Use the numbers to help you find a college that fits your interests and needs. You won't regret it! ■

BIO *Emily Anderer attends Hamilton College in Clinton, New York and interned with Center for Student Opportunity.*

The Incredible Journey of Antoine Tate

I never expected that a young, African American male like me would enter a new environment and experience a sensational program that I would never forget. I had the privilege of participating in the College Summit workshop at Howard University in July 2007. My experience there has helped me mold my future.

I, Antoine Tate, have embarked on an incredible journey. The summer of 2007 was unquestionably a defining time in my life. I became a College Summit Peer Leader as a high school junior entering my senior year. While attending the program, I met many people with whom I continue to have strong relationships.

I was introduced to Sarah Rimer, a *New York Times* reporter who was eager to write an article about my life and experiences at the College Summit. A personal statement I wrote during the program about black stereotypes was of great interest to her.

On July 27, 2007, the article was published, and I must admit, I felt like a celebrity. Friends and family texted me, emailed me, contacted me on Myspace and Facebook, and called to congratulate me on the article. My life only got better when I received a phone call from Tom Harrison of College Summit explaining that a great man named Raymond Kurlak had offered to pay for my tuition for college. Can you say, "amazing"?

When I returned to Crossland High School in Prince George's County Maryland for my senior year, things got better. I created a relationship with the principal as well as the other staff members. I received support and feedback for the article, and to my surprise, not only was I featured in the *New York Times*, but I managed to grace the *Dallas Morning News* as well. My words went from Washington, DC, to New York and then to Texas. The article traveled all over the country!

My freshmen year at Penn State was dynamic as well! I became actively involved on my campus and am working towards a degree in Communications. I joined the Black Student Union, the Multicultural Recruitment Team, the Debate Team, the Chancellor's Special Program, and became an official member of Kappa Alpha Psi Fraternity. College is definitely the place for me.

I've always thought that I was destined for great things, but College Summit has definitely helped me BELIEVE that I am destined for great things. My experience as a Peer Leader was so rewarding while I was in high school that I decided to return as an Alumni Leader and give back to College Summit what it gave to me: knowledge and success.

So here I am, back at Penn State, waiting for a new phase in my life. Until then, I'll wait patiently, while continuing to make a difference on my campus. So far, I think I'm headed in the right direction. ■

College Summit is a national nonprofit organization that partners with schools and districts to strengthen college-going culture and increase college enrollment rates, so that all students graduate career and college-ready.

Throughout the summer, College Summit runs four-day workshops guiding 40-50 low-income high school seniors through the college transition process to:

• Complete a college common application

• Craft a personal statement

• Gain insight about the financial aid process

• Talk one-on-one with a college counselor

• Learn how to positively influence their peers outside of the workshop

**Learn more at
www.collegesummit.org**

college summit
connect to your future

NEWS

By John Emerson

College Success for Students from Foster Care

Graduating from college meant that I won. Most of all, it meant that I would gain the knowledge to use my experience in foster care to help other people. College meant freedom from my past and the ability to choose my future.

—Maria, 2007 college graduate

Graduating from college provides lifelong benefits such as increased earning power, health benefits, career satisfaction, and a large supportive network of friends, mentors and professors. And for students raised in foster care, college is often an essential step toward a better life. As Niki, a current college sophomore formerly raised in foster care, reflects, "College offered me the opportunity to break the negative cycle of my upbringing and make a better life for myself. I can take a negative experience and turn it into something positive with all the opportunities in front of me."

So why do so few young adults from foster care ever enroll in or graduate from college? The reasons are varied, but the following factors are all too common:

• *Students don't dream about or plan for college, as they have experienced so much disappointment and trauma in their lives.*

• *They don't know who to ask for advice or who to turn to for support.*

• *They rarely have a stable educational advocate, mentor or "college coach" on their side to guide and encourage them to succeed.*

• *They change schools frequently; which results in lost records, credit deficiencies, repeated classes, and inconsistent high school and college advising.*

• *Colleges are usually unaware of the students' unique support needs and of the various issues they face.*

• *They don't know how or where to get enough financial aid to pay for their college careers.*

But this trend seems to be changing. More and more students from foster care are now attending college and finding success. "Coming from the system is no excuse to do poorly in school," says Orlando, a college junior. "We have to break the cycle of living in poverty. Forget about the statistics against you and make something out of your lives. College is the only thing in your life that cannot be taken from you." A growing number of colleges are reaching out to this underserved population, and welcoming them into their programs.

On-campus support services that address their housing, academic, health, and career development needs are increasing.

And financial aid resources from a variety of public and private sources are now making it possible for students coming from foster care to attend college without overwhelming loan obligations. Some states also offer good educational benefits for students who choose to stay in foster care until age 21.

Advice for Students in Foster Care

What can you do to successfully prepare for college? Here are a few tips from successful college students who were formerly in foster care:

While in high school:

"Talk to your counselor to make sure you have the classes needed for the college you want to attend." *Malcolm*

"Sign up for college visits, financial aid events, and whatever else you can find. Become friendly with the person who runs the college office. Begin visiting colleges as soon as you can, because things really start piling up your junior and senior years, and you want to have time to fill out applications and write essays for scholarships." *Renee*

"Have a calendar or binder where you keep all of your college information in chronological order; that way everything will go smoothly." *Candice*

"When I learned that there was a section on college applications where you could write about "extenuating circumstances", it changed everything. Use this area of the application to talk about the difficulties and challenges you faced growing up in the foster care system." *Margaret*

BIO *John Emerson is the Postsecondary Education Advisor at Casey Family Programs. Casey Family Programs is the nation's largest operating foundation entirely focused on foster care.*

Free Online Resources

Orphan Foundation of America (OFA)
www.orphan.org
OFA provides scholarships for college and post-secondary education, as well as internships, virtual mentoring, care packages, and critical resources to guide foster teens to success.

Foster Care Alumni of America (FCAA)
www.fostercarealumni.org
Founded and led by alumni of the foster care system, FCAA connects the alumni community and transforms foster care policy and practice, ensuring opportunity for people in and from foster care.

Foster Club: The National Network for Young People in Foster Care
www.fosterclub.com
Foster Club has chapters and resources available in most states that can assist you and help provide a network of support. Just click on the "State-by-State" tab.

California Youth Connection (CYC)
www.calyouthconn.org/site/cyc
Guided, focused and driven by current and former foster youth with the assistance of other committed community members, CYC promotes the participation of foster youth in policy development and legislative change to improve the foster care system. CYC has chapters in counties throughout California.

California College Pathways
www.cacollegepathways.org
The goal of the California College Pathways is to increase the number of foster youth in California who enter higher education and achieve an academic or training outcome by expanding access to campus support programs. You can find out about resources, supports and college preparation opportunities.

College Goal Sunday
www.collegegoalsundayusa.org
College Goal Sunday provides free professional assistance filling out the FAFSA (Free Application for Federal Student Aid). Check out their special section on questions about the FAFSA for Foster Youth or Wards of the Court, along with information regarding state-wide student services, financial aid resources, admission requirements, and more! ∎

GROWING UP, THE IDEA OF COLLEGE WAS MORE OF A DREAM

Ashley Roberts
College: Illinois Wesleyan
Hometown: St. Peters, MO

than it was a goal. I grew up in a broken home to say the least. At the age of 11 I was put in foster care, and although I was only there for 6 months, it is something that still impacts me today.

The pressure of going through "the system" was that I was seen as a statistic. According to the officials I am supposed to be just like my mom, but my need to succeed and show that I am my own person is what keeps me going.

Neither of my parents graduated from high school, let alone went to college, and before foster care, that was the path I was on. In foster care I learned that I did not have to have the same life my parents had. I was always smart, but it was in foster care that I started putting forth the effort to do my work and make the grades.

After foster care, I was put in the care of my aunt and uncle. By this time I knew I wanted to go to college. I didn't know much else about it, but I was determined to go. I knew I wanted to help kids like me.

When it came to looking at schools I had no idea what I was doing. I had every kind of article, pamphlet, and brochure that told me how to find a school, but my biggest fear was how I was going to pay for school.

In high school I participated in a program that guaranteed I would receive two free years at a 2 year institution of my choice in my state. Although it was a blessing, I chose to attend a four-year university to increase my opportunities. I had learned that if a school wanted you, they would meet your needs. Every school I applied to gave me wonderful financial aid packages. Since I had that worry out of the way, I could focus on the other aspects I was looking for in a school to make it the school of my dreams.

I want a better life for myself and college is just a stop on the road to my goal.

Opportunity Scholars

ASHLEY ROBERTS is a 2009-2010 Opportunity Scholarship winner and is writing about her college experiences and offering advice on the Opportunity Scholars blog.

Visit **www.CSOCollegeCenter.org** to read the blog, become an Opportunity Scholar, and have the chance to be a future Opportunity Scholarship winner and blogger yourself.

By Keisha L. Brown

What HBCUs offer 21st Century Students

Many students—African Americans and non-blacks alike—are choosing HBCUs for the unique educational experience.

Historically Black Colleges and Universities (HBCUs) have played a crucial role in America's higher education system by educating African Americans who were denied access to white institutions of higher learning in the late nineteenth and early twentieth centuries.

Today, African American students have access to a wide range of post-secondary institutions, especially since an increasing number of schools are actively recruiting minority students. But despite having more options for higher education than ever before, many students—African Americans and non-blacks alike—are choosing HBCUs for the unique educational experience they offer.

Ethnic and Racial Diversity

In the 21st century, HBCUs aren't just for black students anymore. Colleges know that in order to be competitive and train students who are prepared to succeed in the global community, they need diversity. More and more HBCUs, especially public HBCUs, are recruiting white and Hispanic students to add to their campus' rich ethnic diversity.

Even schools whose student body is totally African American exhibit remarkable diversity as students from all over the country bring a bit of their regional culture to the campus mix. Some HBCUs boast an impressive international student population too, with students hailing from Africa, the Caribbean, South America and in some cases as far away as the Middle East.

A Legacy of Academic Excellence and Success

While HBCUs represent only 3% of American institutions of higher learning, they graduate nearly 25% of all African Americans who earn Bachelor's degrees. HBCUs are leaders in training young professionals—especially in the arts, business and the sciences—who are prepared to address the unique needs of the African American community.

HBCUs also provide African American and minority students the opportunity to work with mentors who share the same cultural background as students and are successful in their respective fields. The extensive support networks available at HBCUs help students excel in academically rigorous programs. Furthermore, a substantial number of HBCU graduates go on to pursue advanced degrees, often being recruited by elite schools seeking to diversify their graduate programs.

Opportunities for Real World Experience

Every year, numerous national organizations partner with HBCUs to create programs that increase minority, particularly African American, participation in underrepresented fields such as engineering, business, and medicine among others. Businesses and corporations that are committed to increasing diversity often look first to students enrolled in HBCUs to fill internships and part-time positions that offer real world experience and develop leadership skills.

Also, many HBCUs offer students the opportunity to spend a semester or two at other leading universities through domestic exchange programs, which allow students to experience a different academic environment and network with distinguished professionals in a different region of the country.

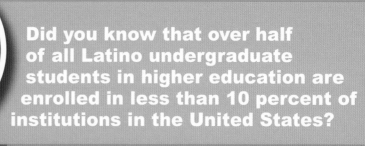

Choosing between a HBCU or a TWI

Many students struggle with the decision to attend either a HBCU or a traditionally white institution (TWI). While both HBCUs and TWIs provide academically challenging and personally rewarding collegiate experiences, the social dynamics of HBCUs and TWIs are markedly different.

Your college experience can provide you excellent opportunities to break outside of your comfort zone and to grow and adapt in a new environment. Students who went to predominantly white high schools can benefit from the cultural exposure of an HBCU. Also, some HBCUs can be cheaper to attend than TWIs in the same region but still offer students the same solid academic instruction.

You will be spending the next four years of your life at the college you attend, so put the time, effort and research into finding the school that's right for YOU. The decision you make can result in one of the most rewarding experiences of your life.

HBCUs in the *College Access & Opportunity Guide*

Bowie State University (MD)
Claflin University (SC)
Dillard University (LA)
Jarvis Christian College (TX)
Johnson C. Smith University (NC)
Lincoln University (MO)
Morehouse College (GA)
Norfolk State University (VA)
Prairie View A&M University (TX)
Spelman College (GA)
Winston-Salem State University (NC)

Check out the **United Negro College Fund (UNCF) at www.uncf.org** to learn about all Historically Black Colleges and Universities (HBCUs) and the many scholarships available to African American students.

BIO *Keisha L. Brown is a graduate of Howard University ('09) and interned with Center for Student Opportunity.*

Did you know that over half of all Latino undergraduate students in higher education are enrolled in less than 10 percent of institutions in the United States?

This concentration of Latino enrollment in higher education gave way to a Federal program designed to assist colleges or universities in the United States that attempt to assist first generation, majority low-income Hispanic students, now known as **Hispanic-Serving Institutions (HSIs).**

What defines HSIs is not necessarily their mission, but their Hispanic enrollment. Under federal law, HSIs are accredited and degree-granting public or private nonprofit institutions of higher education with 25% or more total undergraduate Hispanic enrollment.

The opportunities for Latino students at HSIs have never been greater. The Department of Education offers large grants to institutions defined as HSI which are to be used for the development and improvement of academic programs, endowment funds, academic tutoring, counseling programs, student support services and more.

HSIs in the *College Access & Opportunity Guide*

Barry University (FL)
California State University, San Bernardino
Heritage University (WA)
Mount St. Mary's College (CA)
New Mexico Highlands University
Notre Dame de Namur University (CA)
Nova Southeastern University (FL)
Occidental College (CA)
Saint Peter's College (NJ)
Texas State University, San Marcos
University of the Incarnate Word
University of New Mexico
University of St. Thomas (TX)
University of Texas at El Paso
University of Texas at San Antonio
Whittier College (CA)

Because there is no official list of Hispanic-serving Institutions (HSIs), the above list reflects HSI members of the **Hispanic Association of Colleges and Universities (HACU).** Check out HACU at **www.hacu.net** to learn about all Hispanic-Serving Institutions.

Looking for scholarships, resources, and mentoring?

Check out the Hispanic Scholarship Fund at www.hsf.net and Hispanic College Fund at www.hispanicfund.org

Check out ¡Excelencia!

in Education at www.edexcelencia.org to learn about their work to accelerate higher education success for Latino students by identifying programs that positively impact Latino college enrollment and graduation.

By Jarrid Whitney

Dancing the Circle

An Indigenous Perspective on College Admissions

As a first-generation Native American raised in upstate New York, I never really considered attending college until my senior year. Now reflecting back after working in college admissions for the last 15 years, I often make the analogy that applying to college is like a dance since it is an important form of expression for many American Indians, and most teenagers in general.

First Steps

To this day, I distinctly remember attending my first Iroquois Social Dance and feeling like I didn't belong. It seemed that everyone already knew all the right moves, which only made me feel that much more intimidated to enter the dance ring.

Similarly, many Native American and first-generation high school graduates are scared off by college. And if they do apply, they stick with what's familiar—applying only to local colleges or those that are very well known. I'm not suggesting you apply to more than 15 colleges, but it is wise to apply to a range of schools that offer varying programs and opportunities. Don't let fear hold you back.

Learning the Beat

Before I first started dancing, I needed time to listen carefully to the beat so I could coordinate my steps appropriately. Once a high school student gets over the fear of applying to a range of colleges, the next step is understanding how to interpret the beat.

Prospective applicants must research each school they are interested in and keep track of each school's application process and deadlines. Some may even offer early action or early decision programs with deadlines during the fall semester of senior year.

Other schools offer rolling admission or open enrollment opportunities. But if a college offers such a program, it is still best to apply as early as possible, as on-campus housing or scholarship opportunities can sometimes be limited and are often awarded on a first-come, first-serve basis.

Expressing Uniqueness

Just like most Native American dances, especially competitive powwows, there is always room for individualized self-expression.

Once a student knows which colleges they want to apply to, the next step is actually filling out the applications. Prospective students need to understand that although they have to follow the application guidelines, they should also take some liberty in expressing their identity.

The best way students can showcase their special talents, culture and heritage is through the personal essays, extracurricular lists, and even letters of recommendation. Even though ceremonial dances or writing pottery are not high school functions, they can still be noted as extracurricular activities and expressed in an essay. Colleges seek to maintain a diverse student body and value those who are willing to share their life experiences with others.

Selecting Your Dance Partner

Once you have mustered up the courage to enter the dance ring, the most fun part is finding the right dance partner. But choosing a dance partner is a two-way street. To successfully dance with someone, the person you ask to dance must accept your invitation first.

Similarly, in the college admissions process, an applicant won't be able to fully control who a college will admit. But if your application and essays are representative of the best of your abilities, there will still be plenty of options.

When picking the right school to attend, it really does come down to personal fit. Each student and their family has to evaluate the academic offerings, location, size, support programs, and especially financial aid opportunities before a final "partner" can be chosen. Always try to visit before making the final decision. Often times, colleges offer specialized fly-in or open house programs for underserved populations.

Completing the Circle

Entering the dance circle of college admissions will not be easy but the outcome of a college education far outweighs any challenges. My advice to students is to enjoy the experience but never forget your roots. ■

Adapted from original article published in Winds of Change 15th Annual College Guide, 2008-09

BIO *Jarrid Whitney, Six Nations Cayuga, is Senior Associate Dean of Undergraduate Admission at Santa Clara University.*

Charles Barry/SCU

By Carmen Lopez

College Pride, Native Pride

When selecting a college to attend, Native American, Alaska Native, and Native Hawaiian students have more choices than ever. There are over 300 colleges and universities that offer academic, social, cultural, and community services, programs, and student spaces to support and enhance the unique needs of Native students on campus.

Finding the right fit is especially important for Native students who bring a unique perspective and indigenous experience to feel comfortable in the place they will live, study, and grow in for 4 years. As a Native student you don't want to just survive college, you want to thrive—so make sure the college you attend provides the support an environment that will help you succeed as a student AND as a Native student.

Be proud of yourself for getting into college and show your Native Pride in college too!

Did you know that there are colleges out there that are excited to work with Native students and have created programs to attract them to their schools? College Horizons partners with over 50 colleges that have made a commitment to recruiting Native students and meeting their full demonstrated financial need.

Learn more at www.collegehorizons.org

Questions to Ask a College

- What is the Native student enrollment?
- What percentage of Native students graduate in 4 years and in 5 years?
- What student support services do you offer Native students?
- Are there academic programs on Native Studies or Indigenous Studies?
- How many faculty teach courses in Native Studies?
- Are there any Native faculty or Native staff at the college?
- Are Native alumni active with the college?
- What percentage of Native students go onto graduate school?

COLLEGE HORIZONS

2010 College Horizons College & University Participants

BBard College at Simon's Rock (MA)*
Brown University (RI)*
Carleton College (MN)*
Columbia University (NY)*
Colorado State University*
Connecticut College
Cornell University (NY)*
Dartmouth College (NH)*
Duke University (NC)
Fort Lewis College (CO)
Grinnell College (IA)*
Hamline University (MN)
Haverford University (PA)*
Johns Hopkins University (MD)
Kenyon College (OH)
Lawrence University (WI)*
Linfield College (OR)*
Macalester College (MN)
New York University
Naropa University (CO)
Oberlin College (OH)*
Occidental College (CA)*
Princeton University (NJ)*
Reed College (OR)
Rice University (TX)
Smith College (MA)*
Stanford University (CA)*
St. John's College Santa Fe (NM)
St. Lawrence University (NY)*
Swarthmore College (PA)*
Texas Christian University
Union College (NY)*
University of Colorado at Boulder
University of Hawai'i Hilo
University of Notre Dame (IN)
University of Pennsylvania*
University of Portland (OR)
University of Puget Sound (WA)*
University of Rochester (NY)*
University of Southern California*
US Air Force Academy (CO)*
Wellesley College (MA)
Wesleyan College (CT)*
Whitman College (WA)*
Whittier College (CA)*

*Colleges featured in the *College Access & Opportunity Guide*

BIO *Carmen Lopez is Executive Director of College Horizons, a pre-college program for Native American high school students open to sophomores and juniors. Each summer students work with college admissions officers, college counselors, essay specialists, and other educators in a five-day "crash course" on the college application process.*

By Janice Ferebee

Advice for Girls:
How to Prepare for the Female Leadership Pipeline

If you are a girl who is going to compete and succeed in the future, you need to believe you are worthy of the opportunity to attend college. Learning needs to become a lifestyle choice – beginning with realizing that college is valuable, accessible and some of the best days of your life!

Pursuing a college education will seem very discouraging at times, and you might face challenges that threaten your future and sidetrack dreams of success, including neglect or abuse; drugs, alcohol, gangs and violence; early sexual activity and teen pregnancy; or even the absence of positive role models and spiritual guidance. That said, all obstacles can be overcome with the right attitude and resources. Life is 10% what happens – 90% what you do about it.

Here are some tips for getting and staying in the Female Leadership Pipeline headed toward college:

1. Develop an "I am enough!" spirit. Don't ever be ashamed of your past. Learn to use your life experiences as a testimony to your strength and resiliency. Learn from mistakes, become aware of your strengths and weaknesses, and be proud and accepting of the wonderful girl you already are – just the way you are! No matter what life has dealt you, know that you are valuable and worthy of a college education and a great future.

2. Create a "Dream Team" of friends and women (or men) you admire. People are heavily influenced by who they choose to hang out with, so don't let just anyone in the "front row" of your life. Once you've decided that college is for you, make sure your peers have the same goals for their lives. Look for people who are doing what you want to do and invite them to be on your dream team. Their presence in your life will help guide your dream to attend college.

3. Establish "Goals and Guidelines." Use your sense of determination and your team of role models to set your sights on specific goals for your future. Become consistent, disciplined,

Life is 10% what happens– 90% what you do about it.

focused and obedient to that goal. Don't let the "haters" derail your dream for a college education.

4. Build a "Bridge" to help connect your friends and family to the resources they need to pursue a college education and leadership opportunities. By sharing your experience with others, you can help them begin the same journey into the "pipeline."

With college as a natural and attainable life experience open to all girls, the *Female Leadership Pipeline* is a valuable path through which every girl has the opportunity to travel on her journey to greatness. Don't miss your chance to join the movement! □

BIO *Janice Ferebee is the Director of the Bethune Program Development Center at the National Council of Negro Women, Inc. (NCNW), where she is responsible for community-based and national programs for women and girls of African descent.*

By Susan E. Lennon

A Women's College Might be for You

"Women not only see things differently from men, but they see different things."
–Ret. Lt. Gen. Claudia J. Kennedy

Why does this matter in your education and in your college search? Finding the right fit in a college is all about *you*. Why might a women's college be the right fit for you? Take a look at what matters in college—because what matters *in* college matters *after* college. And it matters in the college selection process.

Women's colleges are focused on you—your dreams and aspirations, your education, your personal and professional development for the many different roles you will assume in life, and your advancement in the ever-changing global economy.

What women's college have in common is an unequivocal commitment to your education and advancement.

Research shows that a women's college education:

- Enables students to engage with top faculty and resources.
- Creates leaders, communicators, and persuaders.
- Develops critical skills for life and career.
- Proves its value over a lifetime.

Take a look at women's colleges—they're about you!

Women's Colleges in the *College Access & Opportunity Guide*

Bay Path College (MA)
Bryn Mawr College (PA)
Hollins University (VA)
Meredith College (NC)
Mills College (CA)
Mount Holyoke College (MA)
Mount St. Mary's College (CA)
Pine Manor College (MA)
Saint Mary-of-the-Woods College (IN)
Saint Mary's College (IN)
Smith College (MA)
Spelman College (GA)
Sweet Briar College (VA)
Trinity Washington University (DC)
Wellesley College (MA)
Wesleyan College (GA)

Check out the Women's College Coalition and learn more about other women's colleges at **www.womenscolleges.org**.

BIO *Susan E. Lennon is the President of the Women's College Coalition, an association of women's colleges and universities – public and private, independent and church-related, two- and four-year – in the United States and Canada whose primary mission is the education and advancement of women.*

Did you know that several colleges offer special housing and educational programs for single parents?

The **Higher Education Alliance of Residential Single Parent Programs (HEARSPP)** is a coalition of colleges and universities that offer residential degree programs for single parents. The Alliance assists single-parent families as they make decisions about higher education.

Higher Education Alliance
For Residential Single Parent Programs

HEARSPP Member Institutions:

Baldwin-Wallace College (OH)*
Berea College (KY)*
College of Saint Mary (NE)
Endicott College (MA)
Misericordia University (PA)
Saint Paul's College (VA)
Wilson College (PA)

*Colleges featured in *College Access & Opportunity Guide*

For more information, visit
www.singleparentcollegeprograms.org/

Wilson College also houses the **National Clearinghouse for Single Mothers in Higher Education**, a clearinghouse of information to assist single parent women in the process of becoming successful college students, as well as mothers.

For more information, visit
www.wilson.edu/nationalclearinghouse

I AM A SINGLE TEEN MOM AND I AM ENROLLED FULL-TIME AT COLLEGE WHILE WORKING FULL-TIME.

Tereza Ponce de Leon
College: Augsburg College
Hometown: Saint Paul, MN

That is a statement that you do not hear often. As most already know, when you get pregnant in high school everyone automatically assumes that you are not going to graduate high school, let alone go on to college. I am proud to say that I am still pursing my dreams and going to college.

In my opinion, getting pregnant does not prevent you from doing anything. I can take the same road as everyone else does; my road is just a little bumpier than everyone else. Is it hard? Yes, it is hard, but it is worth it.

Since my mom did not go to college and my father did not even finish high school, I came from a place where my parents struggled with money every day to raise my brother and me. I do not want that type of life for my son. I want him to be able to have a better life than I had and have more opportunities available than I had. I know that none of that can be possible if I do not go to college to get an education to better myself. Once you have a child everything you do affects your child too, and I know that bettering myself is what is best for him.

To be able to go to college full-time, work full-time, and be a mom full-time takes a lot of time management skills. Basically every minute of every day I am busy doing something. At times, it can be a bit stressful, but I just have to keep thinking about the reward at the end. To be less stressed you have to try your best to not procrastinate and keep up with your school work. If you let your school work pile up on you then it will add stress to your life that you do not need.

I hope that more teen moms realize that they can still go to college because it is not an impossible dream. It just takes hard work and determination, and in the end, it will benefit you and your child more than you know.

Opportunity Scholars

TEREZA PONCE DE LEON is a 2009-2010 Opportunity Scholarship winner and is writing about her college experiences and offering advice on the Opportunity Scholars blog.

Visit www.CSOCollegeCenter.org to read the blog, become an Opportunity Scholar, and have the chance to be a future Opportunity Scholarship winner and blogger yourself.

WE ADMIT... GUIDANCE FROM THOSE WHO DO

Applying to college does not have to be overwhelming! The following principles and guidelines can help make the college admission process more manageable and more productive.

Student Guidelines

An admission decision, test score, or GPA is not a measure of your self-worth. And, most students are admitted to colleges they want to attend. Knowing this, we encourage you to:

• **Be confident!** Take responsibility for your college admission process. The more you do for yourself, the better the results will be.

• **Be deliberate!** Applying to college involves thoughtful research to determine distinctions among colleges, as well as careful self-examination to identify your interests, learning style and other criteria. Plan to make well-considered applications to the most suitable colleges. This is often referred to as "making good matches."

• **Be realistic and trust your instincts!** Choosing a college is an important process, but not a life or death decision. Since there are limits to what you can know about colleges and about yourself, you should allow yourself to do educated guesswork.

• **Be open-minded!** Resist the notion that there is one perfect college. Great education happens in many places.

• **Use a variety of resources for gathering information.** Seek advice from those people who know you, care about you, and are willing to help.

• **Be honest; be yourself!** Do not try to game the system.

• **Resist taking** any standardized test numerous times (twice is usually sufficient).

• **Limit your applications** to a well-researched and reasonable number. No more than six should be sufficient, except in special cases.

• **Know that what you do** in college is a better predictor of future success and happiness than where you go to college.

Visit **www.educationconservancy.org** to learn more.

THE EDUCATION CONSERVANCY

BIO *After nearly twenty-eight years in the college admission and college counseling professions, Lloyd Thacker established The Education Conservancy in 2004 to help students, colleges and high schools calm the frenzy and hype that plague contemporary college admissions.*

By Bob Schaeffer

TEST-OPTIONAL ADMISSIONS

Did you know that there are a growing number of "test-optional" colleges and universities that are creating more opportunities for first-generation, low-income and minority applicants seeking higher education?

There are 850 accredited, bachelor-degree granting schools that do not require all or many applicants to submit SAT or ACT results before making admissions decisions recognize that students are "more than their test scores." Instead, they want to recruit young people with skills and talents that are not measured well by filling in multiple-choice bubbles.

They recognize that teenagers who are from low-income backgrounds or are among the first in their families to consider college often have solid academic records, but not super-high exam scores. Whether the reason is test bias, lack of access to high-priced coaching courses, or simply not testing well, these schools are worth considering in your college search.

Beware of one wrinkle. Some colleges and universities, including a number that are test-optional for admission, do require test scores for some "merit" scholarships. But many make meeting your financial need their top priority.

If a particular school interests you, always look at the admissions and financial aid details on its web pages. With nearly 850 test-optional institutions in the U.S., you are sure to find at least several that meet your needs and interests.

Test-optional admissions can open additional doors to college and beyond. It's up to you to take advantage of these great opportunities! ■

Schools of all sorts—from all parts of the country—now offer test-optional admission. The range of types—with a few examples from each—includes:

• National liberal arts colleges committed to diversity—Bates (ME), Mt. Holyoke (MA), Lake Forest (IL), Pitzer (CA), Agnes Scott (GA), and Lawrence (WI) (all told 33 of the "top 100," according to U.S. News & World Report)

• Large public and private universities— University of Arizona (AZ), Wake Forest University (NC), and Worcester Polytechnic Institute (MA)

• Colleges whose religious traditions emphasizes access and opportunity—Holy Cross (MA), Baptist Bible (MO), Loyola (MD), Providence (RI), and Rabbinical (NY)

• Top-notch regional schools—Fairfield (CT), Rollins (FL), Baldwin-Wallace (OH), and Whitworth (WA)

• Visual and performing arts institutes— Berklee College of Music (MA), San Francisco Art Institute (CA), and Ringling College of Art and Design (FL)

• Trade or occupation-oriented institutions— Fashion Institute of Technology (NY), Johnson & Wales (RI, NC, and FL), and New School of Architecture (CA)

To see the full variety of choices available to you in the test-optional universe, check out http://www.fairtest.org/university/optional. There, you can view free lists of colleges and universities that do not need to see your SAT/ACT scores listed in alphabetical, state-by-state, and printable formats.

Be careful to follow the footnotes. Some programs require students to meet requirements, such as ranking in the top quarter of their high school class, posting "B" average grades, or submitting a graded writing project, to qualify for test-optional consideration.

FairTest
The National Center for Fair and Open Testing

BIO *Bob Schaeffer is the Public Education Director of the National Center for Fair & Open Testing (FairTest). He is coauthor of Standing Up to the SAT and Test Scores Do Not Equal Merit: Enhancing Equity & Excellence in College Admissions by Deemphasizing SAT and ACT Results.*

By William Fitzsimmons

Colleges Value Your Experience

Many colleges, including Harvard, have embarked on new efforts to meet students' aspirations and ensure that talented students from all economic backgrounds can attend.

Even though my Catholic high school was only fifteen miles from Harvard, I had never set foot on the campus. Harvard was not well regarded in our blue-collar community, as it seemed an exclusive, unapproachable place where people like us would not be welcome.

Eventually, my curiosity got the better of me and I went for an interview and an overnight visit. I had a wonderful talk with my interviewer and all of the students with whom I stayed (some of them rich but not snobs) were friendly and interesting.

When I finally decided to go to Harvard in April, one of my recommenders, a brilliant history teacher, gave me a framed copy of a Latin phrase: "Illegitimis non Carborundum" – don't let the "punks" grind you down. He exhorted me to share my background – both religious and economic – with my Harvard classmates. "You'll learn a lot there," he said, "but you can teach them a thing or two."

Today, there has never been so much opportunity for students to pursue the college of their dreams and share their backgrounds in the process. Many colleges, including Harvard, have embarked on new efforts to meet students' aspirations and ensure that talented students from all economic backgrounds can attend.

Harvard's new financial aid program that requires no family contribution from families with under a $60,000 annual income (and a greatly reduced contribution from families with incomes up to $180,000 as well as a policy that eliminates any loan requirement) has met with great success. And many other schools are following suit, with similar financial aid programs and no debt/no loan promises to ensure access and success for all.

Colleges recognize that students from modest income backgrounds add to a dynamic college campus. In the classroom, discussions about unemployment, welfare reform, health care for the uninsured, public housing, mass transportation, and a wide range of issues take on meaning if there are people present who have been personally affected by the topics. I'd like to think I added to my college classmates' education by giving them a reality check, especially the occasional "clueless"

rich kid who had no idea that most people had to worry about making ends meet on a day-to-day basis.

It is encouraging to observe how Harvard and many other institutions have become, over the years, much more inclusive of women, minority students and those from the other side of the tracks. It has been an exciting time and the changes have been stunning – leaving America in a much better position to realize the full talents of all its citizens. ☐

Adapted from "Getting to Harvard," National Association for College Admission Counseling *Journal of College Admission*, Fall 2006

BIO *One of the country's most respected and well-known experts on undergraduate education and financial aid, William R. Fitzsimmons has been the Dean of Admissions and Financial Aid at Harvard College since 1986. He grew up in the Boston area and earned his A.B. ('67), Master's ('69), and Doctorate ('71) degrees from Harvard.*

By Jaye Fenderson

Writing a Great College Esssay

Not all colleges require an essay – some require more than one, but if you're like most students, the idea of having to write an essay for the college application can be overwhelming or a complete turn-off. But before you let 500 words stand in the way of applying to the school of your dreams, here's why the essay is so important and how you can write one that will leave a great impression with the college admissions office.

Why an Essay?

Believe it or not, the colleges that ask you to write an essay are actually interested in more than just your grades and test scores. They want to get to know you - your story, how you see the world, and what you have to say - and one of the best means of getting your voice heard is by writing an essay. It should give an admissions officer a glimpse into your personality and character, and it's also a chance to discuss aspects of yourself that may not show up elsewhere in your application, like a story about your family, neighborhood or community in which you grew up or a unique experience that has had an impact on your life.

here's why the essay is so important and how you can write one that will leave a great impression

Write to Stand Out

Follow these tips to write a memorable college essay:

Start Early— Allow yourself enough time to brainstorm ideas, write a couple drafts, and proofread the final essays. That means starting the essay writing process at least one month before the application deadline, but working on your essays the summer before your senior year is a great way to get comfortable with the 500 word format and makes for one less thing you have to worry about during the fall application season.

Keep it personal— The essay is your chance to say things that test scores and grades can't communicate, so you want to give a college a sense of your personality and character. Are you funny? Caring? Serious? Courageous? Creative? Motivated? Tell stories that showcase your strengths, and let your personality shine through in your writing style. Remember that every question asked in the application is an opportunity to talk about yourself. It may feel uncomfortable at first to write so openly (especially to complete strangers!), but rest assured that colleges want to know about your background and the experiences that have shaped you.

Show, Don't Tell— It's important to not just say you're interested in a particular field but to show how your experiences have shaped your interests. That means illustrating how events, books, magazines, people, and moments have inspired you to pursue your educational and life goals. Show how you continue to cultivate your interests and talents at school, home and in your community.

Proofread— Keep in mind that the college essay is first and foremost a writing exercise to demonstrate your knowledge of the English language as well as your ability to organize your thoughts to make a statement. The biggest essay buzz-kills are spelling mistakes, grammatical errors, and typos. So don't just rely on your computer's spell-check. Have someone you trust read your essay to look for anything out of place.

Topics to Avoid

Remember that the college essay is a chance to share a part of yourself, so the cool thing about that is that there are no wrong answers! However, you'll want to steer clear of these overused and inappropriate essay topics:

Don't use an old homework assignment or report as your essay.

Don't tackle a topic that cannot be done justice in 500 words or less, like how you would achieve world peace.

Don't use the essay to make excuses for poor grades.

Don't write about other people's experiences; keep it personal!

Don't use the essay space as résumé for accomplishments and activities previously mentioned in the application.

Do write what you know, be yourself, add descriptive details, and don't forget to proofread!

An awesome essay can be the tipping point that pushes a good application into the acceptance bin, so take some time to think about what sets you apart and how you can best share your unique story in the admissions essay. ◼

BIO *Jaye Fenderson is the author of Seventeen's Guide to Getting Into College and the producer of First Generation, a documentary about students who are first in their families to go to college.*

By Dr. DeAngela Burns-Wallace

Polish Your Admissions Application

by Following Some Do's and Don'ts

Filling out applications can be a time-consuming and arduous process, but you can also make it really creative and exhilarating. It's a way for you to show an admissions office who you really are and what you are passionate about. It is also an opportunity to reflect on all that you have accomplished and experienced in high school.

Have fun with the application. Yes, I said "fun" in the same sentence as "application." Have fun, and when you click the "submit" button or seal the envelope, feel confident that the application is a true and polished reflection of who you are as a student.

To help you through the process, here are a few do's and don'ts:

Do

- Proofread you entire application (not just the essays) for spelling errors or grammatical mistakes.

- Include an e-mail address that is appropriate and professional. If your personal e-mail address is a little too casual, then you can create a new one for free using any number of popular e-mail providers. You can then use this account just for college communication.

- Infuse your application with your own voice, beliefs, and unique reflections.

- Do your research on the opportunities available at a specific school before you answer at the question, "Why do you want to go to _____ College?"

- Pay attention to word, character, and space limits.

- Write essays that will reflect your voice and your unique perspective. Write about things that interest you.

- Be specific when describing your activities. Remember that activities include things you do both inside and outside of school. Work, church involvement, caring for siblings, and caring for family members are all things that count as activities, and we want to hear about them.

- Brag about yourself. Tell us everything you have accomplished, and don't spare us the details. We want to hear it all.

- Write meaty essays within the word, character, or space limits.

Don't

- Leave words misspelled or write in texting shorthand;

- Forget to change the name of a school in an essay when you are using the same essay to apply to multiple schools.

- Use your personal e-mail address if it is inappropriate. Often time, your e-mail address in one of the first things an admissions officer will see. You might not want hotstuffxoxo@email.com to make that first impression.

- Treat you application like a Facebook profile. Your application should be a vivid portrait of you, but not a casual one.

- Copy and paste the same answer to the question, "Why do you want to go to _____College?" for every college you apply to.

- Write more than the word limit, character limit, or space will allow. Any words written beyond this limit will be lost in application outer space.

- Write essays that you think will please or impress an admissions officer.

- Assume we will know what an acronym means or will know that you were a leader in a club/group if you don't tell us. If you can't fit an appropriate explanation into the activities chart of an application, you can use the additional information section to elaborate.

- Be too humble and feel embarrassed about detailing your achievements, awards, honors, and leadership opportunities.

- Write only one or two sentences and call it an essay.

BIO *Dr. DeAngela Burns-Wallace is Director of Access Initiatives at University of Missouri.*

By Scott Anderson

Don't ask yourself what colleges want to hear. Ask yourself what you want them to know.

Tell your story in the application

If you are getting ready to apply to college, chances are you're about to make a mistake. It's not something that any amount of proofreading will catch, but it is something that you can avoid. At some point between now and the day you hit the submit button on your application, you are probably going to ask yourself, "What do colleges want me to tell them?" It's a good question. The problem is it's the wrong question.

It makes sense that you would try to figure out what colleges want to hear from you. After all, you are about to ask a group of people you've never met to decide whether or not you can join their community—a decision that will be based on a few pieces of paper containing a few hundred words that describe you. But believe it or not, you have more control over this process than you think.

Applying to college and asking what admission counselors want to hear is kind of like going to a restaurant and asking the chef what he feels like cooking. Think of the application as your menu. It gives you some boundaries to work within (you're not going to be able to get an egg roll at Pizza Hut), but it also gives you tremendous freedom to

make the choices that feel right to you, to share your joys and your interests, your background and your obligations, your successes and your failures, your goals and your dreams—in other words, your story. And that is the key to the question—the right question. Don't ask yourself what colleges want to hear. Ask yourself what you want them to know.

Too many applicants try to package themselves as the students that they think colleges will want to admit. There are two problems with this plan. First, it's hard. It's hard to use a thesaurus when simple English would be much more effective. It's hard to strategize about which extracurricular activity sounds most impressive. It's hard to pretend that you care deeply about an issue that doesn't

really interest you. Applying to college is difficult enough. Why make it tougher by pretending to be someone you're not?

That brings us to the second problem: it's inauthentic. Of all the qualities that admission counselors find appealing, authenticity tops the list. Let them know what is important to you, whether it's student government or theater or basketball or a part-time job or even taking care of your younger siblings while your parents are at work. If it matters to you, tell them about it, because in the end, the whole purpose of your college search is to find the place that will help you to be more successful that you can possibly imagine. And that success starts with a simple plan: Be yourself.

THE COMMON APPLICATION
For Undergraduate College Admission

BIO *Scott Anderson is Director of Outreach for The Common Application, Inc., a membership organization of nearly 400 institutions that provides a common, standardized application in both online and print for First-year and Transfer Applications.*

By Joe Tavares

Visiting College FOR FREE!

See about fly-in and special visit programs where schools pay for prospective students with limited financial resources to visit campus.

The biggest question you need to answer before choosing your future college home is "what would it really be like for me at this school?" No matter how much research you do, how many pictures you see, or how many people you speak with, the only way you can find out what it would be like at a school is to spend a few days there.

If you're thinking about going to school away from home, you should be familiar with fly-in and special visit programs where schools pay for prospective students with limited financial resources to visit campus. These programs can give you a unique opportunity to not only visit campus, but to spend a few days there, sit in on classes, and interact with students who may very well be your peers for the next four years.

Where do you start?

You can find out about fly-in and special visit programs by using guidebooks like this, websites like www.CSOCollegeCenter.org, and checking out schools' websites for information about visiting campus.

Does the school offer tours, on-campus interviews, and overnight stays? Do they have special events for low-income or multicultural students? If you're not sure,

call up the school's Admissions Office and let them know who you are, when you want to visit and if your family has financial difficulties. They may have special programs or transportation stipends for you and your family to visit campus.

Preparing for your visit

Make sure you write down all the questions you have about a school before you go. If you're attending a special visit program, review the agenda beforehand to see if there's anything not included that you want to see or do.

Being on Campus

Make sure you speak with students and professors, look around the library, eat in a dining hall, visit a dorm, and pick up the school newspaper.

How would you fit in at the school? What would you bring to the campus community? Would you feel safe? Is this an environment you would thrive in? Are support services and professors easily accessible?

Campus visits will have a big impact on your college choice, so take advantage of special visit opportunities and fly-in programs that are available for you! ■

BIO *Joe Tavares is Program Director for Center for Student Opportunity and volunteers as a CollegeBound mentor in Washington, DC.*

Check out these programs hosted by schools featured in the *College Access & Opportunity Guide:*

Dartmouth College
Hanover, NH
Native American Fly-In Program
Dartmouth hosts an annual Native American Fly-In Program, which is usually held during the summer and/or fall after students' junior year of high school. Other students with limited financial resources may qualify for complimentary transportation expense coverage for fly-in and other extended campus-visit programs. An application for the Fly-In program is required.

Lewis & Clark College
Portland, OR
Lewis & Clark Fly-In Program
Each year, Lewis & Clark College invites approximately 50 newly admitted students to visit campus at the expense of the college. These selected students of color and first-generation college-goers learn about life and academics at Lewis & Clark through a series of activities. They attend classes, meet faculty and staff, spend time with current students and experience life in the residence halls.

Ohio Wesleyan University
Delaware, OH
Campus Visit Cost Assistance
To enable multicultural and first-generation students to visit campus, Ohio Wesleyan assists with transportation arrangements and costs.

Saint Vincent College
Latrobe, PA
Subsidized Campus Visits
In keeping with its dedication to multicul-turalism and diversity, Saint Vincent College subsidizes travel expenses incurred in a visit to the college. Saint Vincent provides this assistance to low-income minority students who have been accepted to the college, thereby supporting informed matriculation decisions.

Vanderbilt University
Nashville, TN
MOSAIC Weekend
Held in mid-March, Vanderbilt University's MOSAIC Weekend invites minority students admitted to Vanderbilt to campus for four days. The weekend features academic sessions, student activities and performances and tickets to the annual Vanderbilt Step Show. The Office of Admissions offers financial assistance for travel to students in need.

Williams College
Williamstown, MA
Windows on Williams
Windows on Williams (WoW) is a visiting program specifically for students who are low-income or the first in their family to go to college. It is an all-expenses-paid, three-day trip that allows students to sit in on classes, meet professors and students and try Williams on for size. Applications for this program are available at the beginning of each summer.

The Posse Foundation

is a college access and youth leadership development program that identifies, recruits and selects student leaders from public high schools and sends them in groups called Posses to some of the top colleges and universities in the country. A Posse is a multicultural team made up of 10 students, which acts as a support system to ensure that each Posse Scholar succeeds and graduates from college. Posse Scholars receive four-year, full-tuition leadership scholarships from Posse partner colleges and universities.

To date, **The Posse Foundation** has recruited 3,110 Posse Scholars who have won over $329 million in scholarship dollars.

The Posse Foundation partners with 37 partner colleges and universities in 17 states.

The Posse Foundation is a national initiative with sites in Atlanta, Boston, Chicago, Los Angeles, Miami, New York City, and Washington, D.C.

To be eligible, a high school senior MUST:

• Be nominated by their high school or a community-based organization.

• Be in the first term of their senior year in high school. Depending on the Posse city, nominations are often taken between the spring and early August before the new school year begins.

• Demonstrate leadership within their high school, community or family.

• Demonstrate academic potential.

Application and nomination for Posse Scholarships begin in August.

Check out **www.possefoundation.org** and contact your local Posse office to learn more.

University Partners

Babson College (MA)*
Bard College (NY)
Brandeis University (MA)
Bryn Mawr College (PA)*
Bucknell University (PA)*
Carleton College (MN)*
Centre College (KY)*
Claremont McKenna College (CA)*
Colby College (ME)*
Denison University (OH)*
DePauw University (IN)
Dickinson College (PA)*
Franklin and Marshall College (PA)
Grinnell College (IA)*
Hamilton College (NY)*
Kalamazoo College (MI)*
Lafayette College (PA)*
Lawrence University (WI)*
Middlebury College (VT)*
Oberlin College (OH)*
Pepperdine University (CA)
Pomona College (CA)*
Sewanee: The University of the South (TN)
Trinity College (CT)*
Tulane University (LA)
Union College (NY)*
University of California, Berkeley
University of California, Los Angeles
University of Illinois at Urbana-Champaign*
University of Pennsylvania*
University of Wisconsin at Madison
Vanderbilt University (TN)*
Wheaton College (MA)*

*Colleges featured in the *College Access & Opportunity Guide*

THE **POSSE** FOUNDATION, INC.

By Ed Pacchetti

By Bob Giannino-Racine

Don't let "sticker price" scare you

How much $ and how?

Congratulations, you've been accepted to college! Now comes the hard part of figuring out how much college is going to cost and how to pay for it. Below are some tips to help you understand your financial aid package and make the decision about how to pay.

One of the most heartbreaking scenarios that unfolds all too often is one in which a low-income, first-generation student logs onto a college or university website, looks at the "sticker price" for tuition and fees, determines they and their families cannot afford it, logs off of the website and gives up on the dream of going to college.

This scenario would happen with less frequency if low-income and first-generation students and their families knew just a few things about financial aid.

1) Your family's credit history will not affect your ability to get federal student aid. The amount of financial aid that you are eligible to receive is based on many factors, such as family size and the cost of the institution that you will be attending, but it has nothing to do with credit history.

2) State aid deadlines are often earlier than federal aid deadlines. File the FAFSA as soon after January 1 of your senior year as you can. As soon as you have tax information available, you should be completing the FAFSA. Your FAFSA report will tell you what "federal aid" you qualify for, but it will not include state aid or institutional aid from the college or university you attend. The combination of federal aid, state aid and institutional aid can provide a substantial portion of your college expenses.

3) Federal aid is available to full-time and part-time students, so even if you only plan to attend college part-time, you should still fill out the FAFSA to determine what kind of federal aid you are entitled to receive.

4) Indicate on the FAFSA that you are interested in a work-study job. Answering "Yes" to this question does not obligate you to have a work-study job when you're in college. You can always turn it down later. However, if you answer "No" to that question and decide later that you need a work-study job, all of the work-study funds at your school may have been used up.

5) Don't assume that you will pay the "sticker price" that a college or university advertises. In fact, very few students pay the "full sticker price" of attending college. This price is most often discounted, and especially for students who demonstrate financial need.

Understanding Award Letters. When analyzing your award letters, consider two key categories of information – Gift Aid vs. Self-Help Aid and the Full Cost of Attendance. Gift Aid is money from the government (federal or state), the college, or other sources that do ***not*** need to be paid back. Self-Help Aid is money that either needs to be paid back or earned through work study. By comparing these two categories – on a school-by-school basis – you will find how much of the final bill you and your family will be required to foot. The second aspect of your award letter is the Full Cost of Attendance, which includes tuition, fees, room, board, books, transportation, and any miscellaneous charges.

Calculating Need. After figuring out how much school will cost and how much financial aid you'll receive, you can determine the unmet need or gap that will have to pay. To find your need, take the Full Cost of Attendance and subtract the total amount of aid offered (both Gift Aid and Self-Help Aid). All schools don't cost the same and every financial aid package is different, so it's important to follow this exercise for every one of the colleges you get in to.

Making a Decision. Finances are the number one reason cited by students for not finishing college, so it's very important that you carefully consider cost when choosing a school. Be mindful of how much debt you'll have at graduation because it can impact major life decisions like buying a home or what jobs you can accept. Once you've decided which school is the right fit academically and financially – in the short and long term – then you're ready to decide.

Final Tips.

1. Don't hesitate to call a school's financial aid office if you don't understand your award letter.

2. Remember that the offer you're considering – unless it says differently – is ***only*** for the first year, not for all four years!

3. Consider living at home if your college is close by, even for just a year or two. It can save you a lot of money!

4. Search for outside scholarships to help bring down your tuition.

5. A tuition payment plan can help break down your unmet need into small, manageable payments that are interest free! ∎

BIO *Ed Pacchetti is Deputy Director for the U.S. Department of Education Office of Postsecondary Education (OPE). OPE formulates federal postsecondary education policy and administers programs that address critical national needs in support of increased access to quality postsecondary education. Learn more at www.ed.gov.*

BIO *Bob Giannino-Racine is the Executive Director of ACCESS (The Action Center for Educational Services and Scholarships), the leading provider of financial aid advising and scholarships for Boston Public School Students.*

Questions about the **FAFSA** (Free Application for Federal Student Aid) and financial aid:

What is the FAFSA?

Students use this application to apply for federal student grants, work-study money, and loans to assist them in funding their college education. They also may use this application to apply for most state and some private financial aid.

When should I complete the FAFSA?

You should apply as soon as possible after January 1. If your college has a deadline earlier than when your parents will have their taxes done, go ahead and estimate and meet the college's deadline. You can always correct the information later.

My parents are separated or divorced. Which parent fills out the FAFSA?

The parent you lived with most during the last 12 months. If you didn't live with either parent, or if you lived with each parent an equal number of days, use the parent who provided most of the support to you in the most recent calendar year.

Does my step-parent's income and assets have to be reported on the FASFA?

If the parent whose information you are reporting on the FASFA has married or remarried, you must include information about your step-parent (even if they were not married for the entire year).

What if I don't have a Social Security number or don't want to report it on the FAFSA?

You must enter your Social Security number on the FAFSA. If you don't submit your social security number, the form will be returned unprocessed and you will not be considered for federal student aid. Additionally, at least one parent has to include his/her social security number however, if neither parent has one the FAFSA instructs those parents to put 0's instead of a social security number.

The FAFSA asks about last year's income. My parent now is unemployed and our income is significantly less. What should we do?

Go ahead and fill out the FAFSA using last year's income. However, when you get your Student Aid Report (SAR) back, you need to see or write the Financial Aid Administrator at the school(s) you want to attend. Explain the situation documenting the decrease in income. Financial Aid Administrators might use professional judgment to adjust your need if it is warranted and can be documented sufficiently to meet federal guidelines.

Can my parents and I fill out the FAFSA over the internet?

Yes, you can fill out the FAFSA online. It is recommended that you and your parents get PIN codes first so you can sign the FAFSA electronically and not have to print out, sign and send in a paper signature page. Here are the web addresses:

www.pin.ed.gov

www.fafsa.ed.gov

This information furnished by College Goal Sunday, a statewide volunteer program that provides free information and assistance to students and families who are applying for financial aid for post secondary education.
Find us online at **www.collegegoalsundayusa.org**

Questions about College Goal Sunday:

Why is College Goal Sunday important?

College Goal Sunday provides assistance in applying for financial aid to families who need it. By delivering help to families in their own communities, College Goal Sunday helps ensure that students get the help they need crossing the paper barrier to qualify for financial aid.

When and where is College Goal Sunday?

The College Goal Sunday program usually is offered on a Sunday afternoon, most often between 2 and 4 p.m. at several locations in each state. Find where you can get help at www.collegegoalsundayusa.org

Who participates in College Goal Sunday?

College Goal Sunday is open to all college-bound students regardless of age. Whether a traditional student right out of high school or an adult who is returning or pursuing higher education for the first time, College Goal Sunday will help you complete the FAFSA, accurately and on time. Dependent students (those under 24) should bring a parent or legal guardian. Independent students (24 or over) will not require a parent's income information.

By Amy Weinstein

Tips for Finding Scholarships to Help Pay for Your College Education

search and find all kinds of scholarships . . . start early and look everywhere

Did you know scholarships can help you pay for your college education? In fact, the more scholarship money you get, the less you will have to borrow to pay for tuition, room and board, books, and other expenses. Most importantly, unlike loans, scholarships do not need to be repaid and need to be an important part of your financial aid package.

You can find scholarships that are industry specific – those that have to do with science, technology, engineering, the arts or mathematics. Additionally, there are scholarships if you have overcome challenging life obstacles. There are a number of scholarships available for students who are gifted academically, artistically, athletically, or musically.

Members from the National Scholarship Providers Association (NSPA) give scholarships and are committed to access, choice and success. They offered the following tips for finding and applying for scholarships:

Start Early

"If you're a freshmen and sophomore in high school, you should be looking at scholarship applications early on, in order to see what kind of information scholarship providers request. It is overwhelming for many students who begin looking at applications late in their junior year, only to realize that they could have been a bit more proactive in their level of involvement both in their school and in their community." *Patti Ross, Coca-Cola Scholars Foundation*

Look Everywhere

"Remember to look for scholarships at your local community foundation! Other sources include high schools, libraries, employers, civic groups, community organizations, private foundations, and online searches. It's worth spending time to complete these applications. Two hours spent completing applications that can get you a $500 scholarship is like getting $250 per hour for your efforts!" *Dawn Lapierre, Community Foundation of Western Mass.*

"Applying for scholarships is like applying for college. The process is lengthy, and takes commitment on your part to find the best options available. Check with your local area merchants, guidance counselors and librarians for information on possible opportunities. Search the web. Adhere to all deadlines and information requirements. Applying late or sending incomplete information is not the message you want to send to scholarship providers." *Vanessa Evans, Ron Brown Scholar Program*

"Don't Give Up. You might be able to find scholarships your freshman year in college to fund the next year. Some scholarships are renewable each year (provided you meet certain requirements). Register on Scholarships.com while you are in high school, the earlier the better." *Kevin Ladd, Scholarships.com*

Be Thorough

"When searching for scholarships using an online matching service like FastWeb.com, try to complete the profile as thoroughly as possible. Students who answer all of the optional questions on average will match twice as many scholarships as students who answer only the required questions. If you have to pay money to get money, it's probably a scam. Never invest more than a postage stamp to obtain information about scholarships or to apply for scholarships." *Mark Kantrowitz, Publisher of FinAid.org and FastWeb.com*

"Earn it. Scholarships are free, but they require effort on your part. Write the topically specific essays first and see if you can "recycle" some of the language for the general essays. Be thorough and polite. Once you begin applying, make sure to read, understand and follow the rules. If you don't follow the rules you could be disqualified." *Kevin Ladd, Scholarships.com* ■

BIO *Amy Weinstein is Executive Director of the National Scholarship Providers Association (NSPA), the only national organization dedicated solely to supporting the needs of professionals administering scholarships in colleges and universities, non-profits and foundations.*

Getting free money for college

Now is the time for you to prepare for applying to competitive scholarship programs. **Consider these steps:**

1 Set goals. Develop short- and long-term goals for your college years and beyond. Scholarship programs want you to have goals to work toward. They lay a foundation for your future.

2 Make the grades. It is important to do well academically. Scholarship programs are looking for students who do well in school. Strong study and note taking skills are keys to academic achievement.

3 Be a leader. Engage in leadership and extracurricular activities. You do not have to limit yourself to being an officer in an established organization. You can also create opportunities for leadership, such as identifying a cause that interests you and develop and implement a plan.

4 Make a difference. Community service can benefit those you serve and can make you competitive for scholarships. Giving back is a way to enhance your leadership skills, make a difference in the lives of others and support your community.

5 Keep a log. Document your leadership and community service activities. Most scholarship applications require you to provide information from 9th through 12th grade that details the date, activity and number of hours of your engagement in your activity. Include a description that measures your activities. A good example, "I coordinated a project that provided clothing for over 200 homeless people." Versus, "I participated in a clothing drive effort."

6 Build relationships. A teacher or other educator is often required to support your scholarship application. It is important to start developing relationships early with individuals who know your academic and/or personal achievements.

7 Use your resources. Family members, teachers and community organizations are all a part of your resources. Ask for their assistance in reviewing your work, reading essays for scholarships and providing tips for success.

8 Make a commitment to succeed. Most scholarship applications have some question(s) that determine your ability to meet challenges. Make the choice to never give up and use those experiences when you are successful to tell your story.

Did you know that the **Gates Millennium Scholars Program (GMS)** is the nation's largest private scholarship program?

Initially funded by a $1 billion grant from the Bill & Melinda Gates Foundation, the goal of GMS is to promote academic excellence and to provide an opportunity for outstanding minority students with significant financial need to reach their highest potential.

Learn more and apply at **www.gmsp.org**.

BIO *Mary Williams is Director of Communications & Administration for the Gates Millennium Scholars Program.*

SHOW ME THE MONEY!

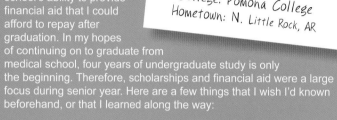

Seanna Leath
College: Pomona College
Hometown: N. Little Rock, AR

For many low-income, first-generation students, scholarships and financial aid are crucially important in the college choice process. Personally, one of my top priorities in choosing a college relied on the school's ability to provide financial aid that I could afford to repay after graduation. In my hopes of continuing on to graduate from medical school, four years of undergraduate study is only the beginning. Therefore, scholarships and financial aid were a large focus during senior year. Here are a few things that I wish I'd known beforehand, or that I learned along the way:

1. It is a process. Pursuing scholarships and financial aid does not happen overnight. Rome was not built in a day, and only on very rare occasions will a student acquire all of the funds necessary to support a college education through one source. Instead, students should plan on looking at a variety of sources for financial support, including community, school, and corporation scholarships. Many colleges have available grant money or special scholarships given annually to a select number of students. Also, just as in any process, generous amounts of time should be devoted to seeking and completing scholarship applications. Although some applications may only require demographic information, many require recommendations and essays, all of which require time, attention, and effort.

2. Just do it! Searching for scholarships is an active process of trial and error. Although there are millions of scholarship opportunities out there, many apply to a limited number of people (students born on an Indian reservation or students whose parents work at Wal-Mart). Although a great number might apply to you, there is still the process of weeding out those that don't. Using scholarship search engines can be a great way to find hundreds of opportunities that seem to fit your criteria, but you must still zone in on those that suit you best. Procrastinating is one of the worst things that can be done during this process. Start early and remain diligent.

3. Collaborate and Synthesize Although every scholarship deserves your undivided attention, the reality of being able to write new essays for every application is impractical and could potentially add extra, unnecessary stress to your senior year. Instead, determine if a certain spectacular essay can be applied to more than one scholarship. If three different applications ask about your aspirations for after college, consider writing one original and creative essay to satisfy all three. It is always beneficial to manage time wisely!

"He is able who thinks he is able" ~Gautama Siddharta

SEANNA LEATH is a 2009-2010 Opportunity Scholarship winner and is writing about her college experiences and offering advice on the Opportunity Scholars blog.

Visit **www.CSOCollegeCenter.org** to read the blog, become an Opportunity Scholar, and have the chance to be a future Opportunity Scholarship winner and blogger yourself.

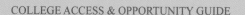

By Ann Coles

Smart Borrowing for College

Paying for college can be very intimidating, but smart borrowing ensures your investment in your education will pay off. Here are some tips to help make going to college affordable.

STUDENT LOAN APPLICATION

Applicants Name

1. Use scholarships, grants, savings, and work-study earnings before taking out loans

• Grants and scholarships are gift money that you never have to repay. Work-study requires you to earn the money awarded.

• Complete the FAFSA (Free Application for Federal Student Aid) before March 1 of the year you plan to go to college. Some colleges also require you to complete the CSS PROFILE. If your family has limited income, you may be eligible for a fee waiver.

• Search scholarships in online databases and talk to high school counselors, public librarians, community organization and church staff, parents' employers and college financial aid officers.

• Save as much money for college as you can from after-school and summer jobs.

• Talk to a financial aid officer at the college you want to attend if your family has special financial circumstances that make it difficult for them to help you with college costs.

2. Reduce borrowing by using other options

• Use an interest-free monthly payment plan that allows you to spread the cost of paying for college over the school year. Your college financial aid office can recommend a plan.

• Work part-time but preferably not more than 15 hours a week so that you will have enough time to do well in your studies.

• Consider going to a college that has eliminated or limited loans for most students.

3. Borrow wisely

• Borrow only what you need because loans need to be repaid—even if you don't finish college. Never use student loans to pay off other bills or buy things you may want but don't need.

• Carefully compare your financial aid award letters from different colleges. If you don't understand an award letter, call the financial aid office and ask someone to explain it to you.

• Borrow federal student loans first. Federal loans (Perkins and Stafford Loans for students, PLUS loans for parents) have low fixed interest rates and flexible repayment plans. Apply for a private student loan only if federal loans are not enough.

• Consider options for having your student loans forgiven, such as volunteer service (participating in the Peace Corps, VISTA, or AmeriCorps).

4. Never use credit cards to pay for your education

• Credit cards are the most expensive source of funds. If you must borrow, exhaust all federal loan options first and then consider private education loans to pay for expenses.

• If you have an emergency, talk to a financial aid advisor to see if your college has an emergency loan fund or can help you in some other way.

Useful Web Sites

> Federal Student Aid: **www.federalstudentaid.ed.gov** provides information about federal grants and loans. You also can complete the FASFA online.

> FinAid! Calculators: **www.finaid.org/calculators** has calculators you can use to estimate your college costs, compare your financial aid awards from different colleges, compare the cost of borrowing different types of loans, and determine how much to borrow.

> Project on Student Debt: **www.projectonstudentdebt. org** features advice to borrowers and a listing of colleges and universities that have decided to eliminate or limit loans from their financial aid award packages for many students.

> Simple Tuition: **www.simpletuition.com** allows users to compare student loans from over 90 sources. Remember, featured lenders may not necessarily be the best alternative for you.

Important Student Loan Terms

- **APR (Annual Percentage Rate):** the total cost of a loan, including the interest rate and fees, expressed as the percentage of the amount borrowed that you have to pay each year. It is a good way to compare loans from different lenders.

- **Co-borrower or co-signer:** A person who agrees to pay the loan if the primary borrower can not or does not pay. Some lenders require students to get a co-borrower with good credit before they will make a loan.

- **Cost of Attendance:** The total cost of attending a particular college for a year, including tuition and fees, housing costs, food, books and supplies, transportation, and other necessary expenses such as a personal computer and health care.

- **Credit:** Indicates a person's financial strength, which includes a history of having paid bills and the demonstrated ability to repay a future loan.

- **Discount:** A reduction in the interest rate or the fees charged on a loan.

- **Interest:** The money or price paid by the borrower to use someone else's funds. Interest is stated as a percentage of the original amount borrowed.

- **Promissory Note or Credit Agreement:** A legal contract the borrower signs with the lender that details the terms of the loan including how and when it must be repaid.

BIO *Ann Coles has been working on college readiness since the 1960s and currently serves as College Access Senior Fellow at ACCESS, an organization that works to ensure that all young people in Boston have the financial information and resources necessary to achieve their dream of a higher education.*

Angelica Robinson
College: Dillard University
Hometown: New Orleans, LA

Ashley Roberts
College: Illinois Wesleyan
Hometown: St. Peters, MO

DaLonn Pearson
College: St. John's University
Hometown: New Haven, CT

Duylam Nguyen-Ngo
College: Babson College
Hometown: Richmond, VA

Jesse Sanchez
College: Harvard University
Hometown: San Diego, CA

Joseph Dingman
College: Occidental College
Hometown: Pueblo, CO

2009-2010
Opportunity
Scholarship

winners

Learn how they made it to college and get their advice on how you can too.

blog

www.CSOcollegecenter.org

FREE services
for students

- Connect with colleges recruiting first-generation, low-income, minority students

- Monthly newsletters, college admissions guidance and support

- Apply for CSO's $1,000 Opportunity Scholarships at the end of your senior year for your chance to become a student blogger on the Opportunity Scholars blog

Khadijah Williams
College: Harvard University
Hometown: Los Angeles, CA

Lysa Vola
College: Williams College
Hometown: Jensen Beach, FL

Seanna Leath
College: Pomona College
Hometown: N. Little Rock, AR

Tereza Ponce de Leon
College: Augsburg College
Hometown: Saint Paul, MN

 Center for Student Opportunity
www.CSOpportunity.org

Opportunity Scholars

MENTORS

Listen
Encourage
Let go

Whether you're a parent, guardian, teacher, mentor, or other caring adult, chances are there's a teen in your life who wants to go to college. You can help your teen succeed by taking time to learn about college planning and financing. Together, you and the teen you care about can share this important goal and achieve it.

MENTORS: Why College?

"Why should I get a college degree?" Has the teen in your life ever asked you this question? Whether you're a parent, guardian, or other caring adult, you need convincing, practical answers to share with your teen. Here they are:

"You'll gain greater understanding and skills to help you be successful in our complex world."

College enables you to:

- Expand your knowledge and skills.
- Express your thoughts clearly in speech and in writing.
- Grasp abstract concepts and theories.
- Increase your understanding of the world and your community.
- Gain more financial security.

"You'll find a greater range and a number of job opportunities."

In our changing world, more and more jobs require education beyond high school. College graduates have more jobs to choose from than those who don't pursue education beyond high school.

"You'll earn more money—a lot more."

A person who goes to college usually earns more than a person who doesn't. According to the U.S. Census Bureau, on average, someone with a bachelor's degree earns $51,206—almost double the $27,915 earned annually by someone with only a high school diploma.

Planning for College: Ten Steps

10

Step One

Save money as early as possible to help pay for your teen's education.

Step Two

Encourage your teen to make high school count, preparing academically for higher education.

Step Three

Discuss with your teen his or her skills and interests, career options and schools he or she is interested in attending.

Step Four

Meet with the high school guidance counselor to determine what schools match your teen's academic abilities.

Step Five

Gather information about the schools your teen is interested in attending, including information on financial aid.

Step Six

Take your teen to visit a college campus and ask the right questions.

Step Seven

Help your teen apply for admission. To apply for financial aid, help your child complete the FAFSA.

Step Eight

Consider scholarships, grants, and work-study programs. Complete any necessary applications or forms and submit them before the deadline.

Step Nine

Consider the loan programs available to you and your child.

Step Ten

Learn more about tax credits, deductions, and other considerations for education expenses.

Talking to Your Teen

It may not always be easy to talk with your teen. But it's important that you support your teen throughout their college planning— help them organize the process, meet deadlines, and talk with the right people. Here are a few tips to consider:

Listen.
Be receptive to and listen when your teen wants to discuss career and/or college plans.

Explore.
Have your teen explore career and college options and collect as much information as possible.

Encourage.
Encourage them to capture their ideas on paper. One idea is to create a scrapbook of their plans for career and college.

Be aware.
Be aware of various deadlines for applications to colleges and financial aid. Put them on a calendar that both you and your teen can look at.

Step in.
Suggest that your teen meet with a school counselor at least once a year, beginning in the 10th grade, to learn more about college and career planning.

Step out.
Give your teen the space *and* support to set some goals and take steps to reach them.

Be supportive.
Be supportive of your teen, and meet with their counselor if you sense that he or she needs additional help.

Connect to career.
Encourage your teen by helping them see the connection between college and career. Emphasize the importance of selecting a major that helps them prepare for a career.

Research.
If your teen is undecided about a career direction, do not try to fix it. Let them look into all the possibilities.

Conversation-Starters

We know that it is often difficult to break the ice with students and get them talking about the steps they need to take to go to college. Think about asking your student the following questions to encourage him or her to turn college dreams into a college plan.

Which adults in your life do you know who went to college?

What excites you about going to college?

What are the reasons you want to go?

Which adults do you turn to for help when you have a problem you need to solve?

I know you want to go to college. Who else have you told about your college plans?

STEP 1 BE A PAIN

Students know that colleges require certain courses, but they often don't know which ones or find out too late into high school to take them all. Get your student thinking about the courses required for college admission by asking some of the following questions:

What courses are you taking this year?

Which courses do you find easiest?

Which do you find the hardest?

Have you thought about which courses are required for certain majors or careers?

Does your high school offer Advanced Placement courses?

How can you sign up?

STEP 2 PUSH YOURSELF

Conversation-Starters

It is often hard for students to visualize the many postsecondary options available to them. But finding the right fit is an important factor in ensuring a student enjoys and completes college. Use the following questions to get your student thinking about the type of school that's right for him or her.

When you think about college …

Do you have thoughts on what you'd like to study?

Are you interested in going away to school or going to school close to home?

Do you like the idea of a big campus with a lot of students or a smaller campus?

Are you interested in participating in activities like sports? Music? Community service?

Would you like to be in an urban environment or somewhere more rural?

Do you want to live in a campus dorm or commute from home?

STEP 3 FIND THE RIGHT FIT

It's hard to talk about money, especially with middle or high school students who may not understand their family's financial situation. Here are some ways to start the conversation and get your student thinking about preparing financially for college.

What courses are you taking this year?

Do you know that the government provides loans to students who can't afford college?

Have you talked with your parents about how you might pay for college?

Do you have questions about how much college costs?

Where would you look first for information about loans and scholarships? Is there an adult at school who would know where to look?

STEP 4 PUT YOUR HANDS ON SOME CASH

By Jaye Fenderson

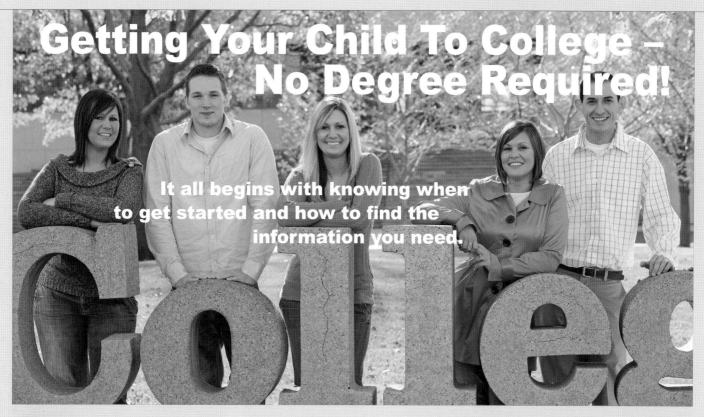

Getting Your Child To College – No Degree Required!

It all begins with knowing when to get started and how to find the information you need.

For many parents the idea of their son or daughter going to college is exciting but also overwhelming.

There's a lot to think about and plan for even if you're a parent that graduated from college. But the good news is that there is a wealth of information about how to prepare and apply for college, so even if this is your first time going through the process, rest assured that there are resources to help you and your teenager find the best college fit at an affordable price.

It all begins with knowing when to get started and how to find the information you need.

Start Early – Get a College Mindset

Many students wait until senior year before they start thinking about their college plans, but the truth is that students should actually start planning for college in middle school or junior high. Why so early, you might ask? Well, that's because colleges take into consideration all four years of high school (9th-12th) including the classes a student takes, his or her GPA, as well as any activities, leadership or awards received.

Get Organized

You'll soon receive a flood of information in the form of college brochures, scholarship and financial aid forms, and notifications from your child's guidance office. If you don't have a way to organize all this information, it can be overwhelming or worse yet, you might end up losing track of important papers.

So help your teen create a simple filing system with dividers labeled for college brochures, scholarships, financial aid, as well as one for your child's awards and accomplishments. By the time senior year rolls around, you'll easily be able to access the information you need to help your teen apply for college. You should get in the habit of keeping a calendar on the refrigerator or in your teen's bedroom that lists important college admission dates and deadlines.

Know Where to Look

Visit the high school's college and career center—this is the most important resource where you'll find information about financial aid, local scholarships, and college deadlines

and requirements—and meet with your teen's counselor at the beginning of high school.

Attend a college night or college fair—most school districts will typically hold some kind of college information session where admission representatives from schools across the country will attend to share information about their programs and how to apply.

Don't Be Afraid to Ask

One of the best resources you have is the power of asking. If you're unsure about an admissions requirement, the cost of applying, or how to fill out the college or financial aid forms, talk to your teen's college counselor, call the college admissions or financial aid office, or find someone—another parent or a current college student—who has recently been through the college admissions process and may be able to answer your question.

So don't be afraid to ask for help – and once you've been through the process yourself, you'll be able to lend a hand to another family. ■

BIO *Jaye Fenderson is the author of Seventeen's* Guide to Getting Into College *and the producer of First Generation, a documentary about students who are first in their families to go to college.*

Visit the Campus

The best reason to visit a college campus is to get a personal feeling for the quality of education being offered there. While on a campus visit, you and your teen should ask questions that will reveal a school's commitment to providing the best educational environment. The questions that follow can help:

Level of academic challenge?

Challenging intellectual and creative work is central to maintaining a quality learning environment.

• To what degree is studying and spending time on academic work emphasized?

• Do faculty hold students to high standards?

• How much time do students spend on homework each week?

• How much writing is expected?

• How much reading is expected?

Active and collaborative learning?

Students learn more when they are directly involved in their education and have opportunities to collaborate with others in solving problems or mastering difficult material.

• How often do students discuss ideas in class?

• How often are topics from class discussed outside of the classroom?

• Do students work together on projects—inside and outside of class?

• How often do students make class presentations?

• How many students participate in community-based projects in regular courses?

• How many students apply their classroom learning to real life through internships or off-campus field experiences?

• Do students have opportunities to tutor or teach other students?

Student-faculty interaction?

In general, the more contact students have with their teachers, the better. Working with a professor on a research project or serving with faculty members on a college committee or community organization lets students see first-hand how experts identify and solve practical problems.

• Are faculty members accessible and supportive?

• How many students work on research projects with faculty?

• Do students receive prompt feedback on academic performance?

• How often do students talk with their teachers about what they are learning in class?

• How often do students talk with advisors or faculty members about their career plans?

• Do students and faculty members work together on committees and projects outside of course work?

Enriching educational experiences?

Educationally superior colleges offer a variety of learning opportunities inside and outside the classroom that compliment the goals of the academic program. One of the most important is exposure to students and faculty from diverse backgrounds.

• What types of honors courses, learning communities, and other distinctive programs are offered?

• In what ways do faculty use technology in their classes?

• How often do students interact with peers with different social, political, or religious views?

• How often do students interact with peers from different racial or ethnic backgrounds?

• How many students study in other countries?

• Do students participate in activities that enhance their spirituality?

• What percentage of students do community service?

• What kinds of activities are students involved in outside of the classroom?

• What kinds of events does the campus sponsor?

• Is a culminating senior year experience required?

Supportive campus environment?

Students perform better and are more satisfied at colleges that are committed to their success—and that cultivate positive working and social relationships among different groups on campus.

• How well do students get along with other students?

• Are students satisfied with their overall educational experience?

• How much time do students devote to co-curricular activities?

• How well do students get along with administrators and staff?

• To what extent does the school help students deal with their academic and social needs?

/ант

You've probably heard, and might believe, some of these common **MYTHS** about college. Read on for the **REALITIES**.

MYTH: Anyone can get into a public university, but it's hard to get into a private college.

REALITY: Some public universities are among the most competitive to get into, while other public universities are required to take nearly all applicants. It's true that some private colleges are very selective, but others take students who wouldn't even be admitted to a home state public university. Check with the colleges you are considering to learn more about the average academic credentials of its students and its admission policies.

MYTH: My teen can make a good living without a college education.

REALITY: There is no doubt that some people have done well without a college degree. However, a college graduate will earn on average about a million dollars more than a high school graduate in his/her lifetime. For most people, college pays.

MYTH: To make it in today's world you need a four-year college degree.

REALITY: Someone with a four-year degree may have more career options, but there are many satisfying and good-paying jobs that are possible with certain technical or two-year degrees. Your teen should start with the fields that are of interest to him and learn what kind of education is required and what the job opportunities are in those areas. Then get the degree he needs for the type of career he wants.

MYTH: Courses and grades in the spring of senior year aren't important because students already have been accepted by a college by the time those courses are done.

REALITY: Most colleges make statements in their admissions materials that they will look at a senior's spring grades. If the student's academic performance has dropped off substantially, colleges have been known to cancel an offer of admission.

MYTH: The college with the lowest price will be the most affordable.

REALITY: Not necessarily! Some of the colleges with a high "sticker price" have raised significant amounts of money for scholarships from their graduates and friends. As a result, they have more money to give to students in the form of scholarships, which reduces the "sticker price." After taking financial aid into consideration, a seemingly more expensive college may be more affordable than a college with a lower list price. Tip: Find out what kinds of scholarship options are available at the colleges you are considering.

MYTH: I don't have the money and my teen can't afford to take out loans to pay for college, even if she wanted to go.

REALITY: Almost all students today can get low-rate education loans to help them pay for college, and education loans typically don't have to be paid back until a student is out of school. The average loan debt of undergraduate students today is roughly $20,000 – that's less than the cost of most new cars! A car lasts a few years. A college education lasts a lifetime.

myth?

MYTH: You need to start planning for college during your junior year of high school.

REALITY: While some students may wait this late to do certain things like visiting potential colleges or taking the SAT's, there are other things that should never wait this long. For example, high school course selections and grades represent the single most important consideration in most colleges' admissions decisions. High school course decisions are made sometimes as early as the middle school years. Financial planning, saving for college, and finding out which colleges will be affordable also should be done well before the junior year.

MYTH: It really doesn't matter if I wait a year or two to go to college.

REALITY: Many students who don't go to college right after high school never get around to it. Others bring great experience to the college when they enroll because of what they did with the time off from school. It is wise for a student to apply to colleges of interest during senior year just like any other student. She can then ask a college to defer enrollment for a year or two, if the student needs the time away. Most colleges will hold the offer of admission, especially if the student has plans that will ultimately make the student even more interesting or valuable as a member of the campus community.

Caution: If the student works during this time away, the income of the student (if substantial) may hinder her/his need-based financial aid eligibility when s/he goes back to school. Because the student will in many cases still qualify as a dependent student, only a small amount of income will be protected under the federal formula. Amounts beyond that can hurt financial aid eligibility.

MYTH: No one in my family has gone to college – why should my teen be the first?

REALITY: After high school, your teen may have 40 or 50 years of employment ahead. Many changes will occur in the job market during this time. A college education will certainly give him more options for the long term. Many of today's jobs which require only a high school diploma may no longer exist a few years from now. His education should prepare him for the job market of the future, not the present.

MYTH: Students today have so much loan debt that it doesn't make sense to pay a lot to go to college.

REALITY: Most students who have huge loan debt usually have either done a poor job of finding a college where their family's financial aid works well, or they made a conscious decision to take on that kind of loan debt so they can attend a particular college. (Remember, the average loan debt of undergraduate students today is roughly $20,000 – that's less than the cost of most new cars!) The goal for most families is to find in advance schools that will be financially reasonable for them, usually by using a published financial aid estimator to understand where they stand under the federal formula for financial aid.

MYTH: There isn't a lot of financial aid available, and what is available only goes to a few of the very best students.

REALITY: During the 2002-03 academic year, over $105 billion dollars in financial aid was awarded. The vast majority of this money was doled out by the federal government through grant, loan and work-study programs, while colleges' own grants and scholarships accounted for almost 20% of all financial aid. States helped too by contributing over $5.5 billion to the pot. That's a lot of money for a lot of students. In fact, over 70% of students nationally receive some kind of financial aid.

Be a Safety Net

How to Support Your Child During the College Application Process

Remember the feeling you had when you dropped your child off for the first day of school? I was surprised when that feeling came back years later as I helped my son and daughter navigate the college application process.

Even though they were a lot older, the experience was just as momentous. Going to college is one of the most significant transitions in a young person's life. The ultimate decision about which college is the best fit belongs to him or her, but your support as parents is critical during this complex journey.

It is important to familiarize yourself with the steps your child must take to complete the application process successfully. Serious preparation for college begins in 9th grade as students move into high school. Things really heat up in their junior and senior years. Speaking as a parent of two children who are currently in college, and as a professional in the college-readiness field, I'd like to share a few valuable tips and strategies that got me through this daunting and intense time.

THE RIGHT FIT – Be involved!

• **Get your child thinking.** The more research your child does during junior year, the more informed a decision he or she will be able to make. Ask your child questions about possible majors and career interests. What colleges would be best for those? What about college size and location?

• **Read college handbooks.** Many print resources are available to assist with the college search. Congratulations for reading one right now!

• **Do Internet research.** Websites offer many options to assist students in narrowing down their college choices. You can sort and arrange by campus type, majors, size, and setting. The CSO College Center at www. csocollegecenter.org will get you started.

• **Visit campuses.** April vacation of the junior year is a great time to tour campuses with your child. College visits allow young people to feel the energy of a school and determine if it is a good match. It's an opportunity to explore, evaluate, and get firsthand information.

• **Check academic entrance requirements.** Be sure your child is on track to meet all college/university requirements before applying: college entrance exams, GPA, required high school course load, and so on.

THE TOOLS - Be organized!

• **Get a school year planner.** Have your child record all deadlines (application and financial aid) in a planner. It's a great visual tool!

• **Use an accordion file folder.** Assign one pocket for each application.

• **Stock up on stamps and envelopes.** Your child must supply a self-addressed stamped envelope with every request for a recommendation from teachers and guidance counselors.

THE DEADLINES - Be ahead of the curve!

• **Request applications early in the senior year.** Most colleges and universities have an online application system. Your child can also receive applications by postal mail.

• **Be considerate of busy educators.** Give teachers and guidance counselors enough time to provide recommendations and transcripts. Encourage your child to request appointments with school staff as soon as possible in senior year to get the ball rolling.

• **Help your child prepare a résumé.** Colleges want to know about your child's extracurricular activities because it helps them see what kind of person he or she is. Make a list together of everything noteworthy: work experience, honors and achievements, major responsibilities (even babysitting), and hobbies.

• **Set a schedule for essay writing.** Many students find the personal essay section of the application a difficult task and are tempted to procrastinate. Don't let your child wait to get started till the day before the application is due. And remind him or her to proofread! An English teacher is often happy to help.

• **Organize your income taxes in December.** The federal financial aid form, or FAFSA, can be completed after January 1. Have your taxes prepared early, so your child won't have to file an updated FAFSA later on.

THE EMOTIONS - Be calm!

• **Be prepared for tears.** Your child may not always appreciate it when you pester him or her about deadlines. It's natural reaction. Just keep the communication open.

• **Stand back but stand by.** Remember that many decisions in this journey belong to your child. Learn how to let go. Know your role, and be a safety net. All the hard work will be worth it when those college acceptances arrive in the mail! ■

BIO *Maria Carvalho is High School Manager for The College Crusade of Rhode Island, where she oversees high school college-readiness programs and manages a team of full-time Advisors who interact daily with hundreds of students in the state's urban high schools.*

Concerns About College

For teens, going off to college represents a huge change in their lives. But this change can affect the parents and guardians just as much. While you are proud and excited about their accomplishments, there can also be a feeling of loss and separation. Dealing with these mixed emotions can be difficult, but are normal. Handling these changes can be easier if you keep these tips in mind:

Stay connected.

There can be some truth to "absence makes the heart grow fonder" but parents or guardians may worry that "out of sight means out of mind." So you and your student need to determine ways to stay involved in each other's lives and remember to say and do the little things that matter. Cards sent home, care packages sent to school, pictures of events that were missed, and email and phone calls do provide a way to stay connected and involved.

Adjust to a new relationship.

As you play a new role in your teen's life, try to adjust to the new adult-to-adult aspect of the parent-child relationship. Children always need parents, but the relationship may become more peer-like.

Expect ups and downs.

One minute college students are the models of independence, the next they call in tears. This back and forth is natural and expected, as both students and parents become more comfortable and confident in the ability of students to handle situations on their own.

Redirect your time and energy to new activities.

With your parenting time now free time, taking stock of personal interests and assets will reveal areas of your life that may have been neglected. It can be time to develop, reawaken, and pursue old and new hobbies, leisure activities, and careers.

Allow for mistakes.

You should encourage and accept the child's ability to make independent decisions. Both the college student and the parents must realize mistakes will be made along the way—it's called life. Learning from mistakes is just another type of learning.

Guide rather than pressure.

Communicating educational goals and expectations should be done in a manner respectful of your student's own style and interests. College students need to pursue their own passions. Although parental input can be useful, children should not be expected to live out their parents' dreams.

Tips from the NYU Child Study Center, www.aboutourkids.org

MENTORES

Eschucar
Animar
Deje van

Ya sea usted padre, tutor, maestro, mentor u otro adulto afectuoso, es probable que en su vida haya un adolescente que desea ir a la universidad. Puede ayudarlo a triunfar si toma el tiempo para aprender sobre la planificación y el financiamiento de la educación superior. Juntos, usted y el adolescente por el que se interesa pueden compartir esta importante meta y alcanzarla.

"¿Para que ir la Universidad?"

¿Le ha hecho alguna vez el adolescente en su vida esta pregunta? Ya sea usted padre, tutor u otro adulto a cargo, necesita respuestas convincentes y prácticas para compartir con su adolescente. Aquí las tiene:

"Vas a lograr un mayor entendimiento y habilidades que te ayudarán a triunfar en este mundo complejo".

La educación superior te permite:

• Ampliar tus conocimientos y habilidades.

• Expresar claramente tus pensamientos, en forma oral y escrita.

• Captar conceptos y teorías abstractas.

• Aumentar tu comprensión del mundo y de tu comunidad.

• Obtener más seguridad financiera.

"Vas a encontrar mayor variedad y cantidad de oportunidades de trabajo".

En nuestro mundo cambiante, más y más trabajos requieren una educación posterior a la de la escuela secundaria. Los graduados de una institución de nivel superior tienen más trabajos para elegir que los que no continúan con su educación luego de la secundaria.

"Ganarás más dinero, mucho más".

La gente con educación superior generalmente gana más que la que no la tiene. Según la Oficina de Censos de los EE. UU., como promedio, la persona con un título universitario gana $51,206, casi el doble que los $27,915 que gana por año la persona que sólo tiene el título de secundaria.

Planificación para la Universidad: Diez Pasos

10

Paso Uno

Comience a ahorrar dinero lo más pronto posible para ayudar al pago de la educación de su adolescente.

Paso Dos

Aliente a su adolescente a darle importancia a la escuela secundaria, preparándose desde el punto de vista académico para la educación superior.

Paso Tres

Analice con su adolescente sus aptitudes e intereses, sus opciones de carreras e instituciones educativas a las que le interesa asistir.

Paso Quatro

Reúnase con el consejero de orientación de la escuela secundaria para determinar qué instituciones se ajustan a las capacidades académicas de su adolescente.

Paso Cinco

Recopile información sobre aquellas a las que su adolescente tiene interés en asistir, incluso información sobre asistencia financiera.

Paso Seis

Lleve a su adolescente a visitar un campus y formule las preguntas adecuadas.

Paso Siete

Ayúdelo a solicitar la admisión. Para solicitar asistencia financiera, ayude a su hijo a completar la Solicitud Gratuita de Ayuda Financiera (Free Application for Federal Student Aid, FAFSA).

Paso Ocho

Considere becas, subsidios y programas de estudio-trabajo. Complete todas las solicitudes o formularios necesarios y preséntelos antes de la fecha límite.

Paso Nueve

Considere programas de préstamos disponibles para usted y su hijo.

Paso Diez

Obtenga más información sobre créditos fiscales, deducciones y otros factores para gastos de educación.

Como hablar con su adolescente

No siempre es fácil hablar con su adolescente. Pero es importante que lo respalde a lo largo de su planificación para la universidad: ayúdelo a organizar el proceso, a cumplir con las fechas y a hablar con las personas adecuadas. Aquí presentamos algunos consejos para considerar:

• Sea receptivo y escúchelo cuando su adolescente desee analizar planes de carrera o de educación superior.

• Hágalo que explore opciones de carrera e institución educativa superior y que recopile toda la información posible.

• Anímelo a que registre sus ideas en papel. Por ejemplo, puede hacer un libro de recortes con sus planes de carrera y de educación superior.

• Esté consciente de las diversas fechas límites para presentar las solicitudes de admisión a las instituciones educativas y para asistencia financiera. Póngalas en un calendario que tanto usted como su hijo puedan mirar.

• Sugiérale que se reúna con un consejero escolar al menos una vez al año, a partir del 10mo grado, para aprender más sobre la educación superior y la planificación de su carrera.

• Bríndele su apoyo y reúnase con su consejero si le parece que su hijo necesita ayuda adicional.

• Anime a su adolescente ayudándole a ver la conexión entre la educación superior y la carrera. Enfatice la importancia de seleccionar una asignatura principal (un "major") que lo ayude a prepararse para una carrera.

• Si el joven está indeciso sobre la orientación de su carrera, no trate de decidir por él. Déjelo que explore todas las posibilidades.

Probablemente haya oído, y tal vez crea, algunos de estos MITOS comunes sobre la educación superior. Siga leyendo para ver cuál es la REALIDAD.

MITO: cualquiera puede entrar a una universidad pública, pero entrar a una institución superior privada es muy difícil.

REALIDAD: algunas universidades públicas están entre las más competitivas en términos de admisión, mientras que otras están obligadas a aceptar prácticamente a todos los solicitantes. Es verdad que algunas instituciones educativas privadas son muy selectivas, pero otras aceptan a estudiantes que ni siquiera serían aceptados en la universidad pública de su estado. Verifique con las instituciones que esté analizando, para saber más sobre los rendimientos académicos promedio de sus estudiantes y sus políticas de admisión.

MITO: la institución educativa de menor precio será la más accesible.

REALIDAD: no necesariamente. Ciertas instituciones educativas de mayor costo han recolectado sumas de dinero significativas para becas de sus graduados y amigos. Como consecuencia, cuentan con más dinero para ofrecer a los estudiantes en la forma de becas, lo que reduce ese precio. Tras tomar en cuenta la asistencia financiera, es posible que la institución aparentemente más costosa sea más accesible que otra con un menor precio de lista. Consejo: averigüe qué tipos de opciones de becas hay disponibles en las instituciones educativas que estén analizando.

MITO: mi adolescente puede tener buenos ingresos sin educación superior.

REALIDAD: sin dudas a algunas personas les ha ido bien sin un título de grado. Sin embargo, en el curso de su vida la persona con un título de grado en promedio ganará un millón de dólares más que un graduado de secundaria. Para la mayoría de la gente, la educación superior paga.

MITO: los cursos y las notas del período de primavera del último año no son importantes porque a los estudiantes ya los han aceptado en alguna institución superior para la época en que esos cursos se llevan a cabo.

REALIDAD: la mayoría de las instituciones de educación superior incluyen notas en sus materiales de admisión donde manifiestan que tomarán en cuenta las notas de primavera del estudiante de último año. Si el rendimiento académico del estudiante muestra una caída sustancial, se sabe de instituciones que han cancelado la oferta de admisión.

MITO: no tengo el dinero y mi adolescente no puede permitirse tomar préstamos para pagar la universidad, incluso si quisiera ir.

REALIDAD: actualmente casi todos los estudiantes pueden conseguir préstamos a tasas bajas para ayudarlos a pagar la educación superior y los préstamos para educación típicamente no deben reembolsarse hasta que el estudiante no se haya graduado. El préstamo promedio de un estudiante de grado actualmente es de alrededor de $20,000; menos que el costo de la mayoría de los autos nuevos. Un auto dura unos años. La educación superior dura toda la vida.

MITO: para subsistir en el mundo actual se necesita un título de grado de cuatro años.

REALIDAD: la persona con un título de cuatro años puede tener más opciones de carrera, pero existen muchos trabajos satisfactorios y bien pagos que pueden obtenerse con ciertos títulos técnicos o de dos años. Su adolescente debe comenzar en las áreas que sean de su interés, y averiguar qué tipo de educación se requiere y cuáles son las oportunidades laborales en esas áreas. Y luego procurar el título que necesite para el tipo de carrera a la que aspira.

MITO: en realidad no importa si espero uno o dos años para ir a la universidad.

REALIDAD: muchos estudiantes que no van a la universidad inmediatamente después de la secundaria nunca se deciden a hacerlo. Otros llevan consigo una gran experiencia cuando se inscriben, gracias a lo que hicieron en el tiempo en que no estudiaron. Es sensato que el estudiante se postule a las instituciones educativas que le interesan durante el último año, como cualquier otro. Luego puede pedirle a la institución que posponga su inscripción por un año o dos, si el estudiante necesita el tiempo. La mayoría de las instituciones de educación superior acepta mantener la oferta de admisión en suspenso, en especial si el estudiante tiene planes que en definitiva lo harán más interesante o valioso como miembro de la comunidad del campus.

Precaución: si el estudiante trabaja durante ese tiempo, sus ingresos (si son grandes) pueden deteriorar su elegibilidad para asistencia financiera en función de la necesidad al retomar los estudios. Como el estudiante en muchos casos todavía calificará como estudiante dependiente, sólo un pequeño monto de ingresos estarán protegidos por la fórmula federal. Los montos que la excedan pueden afectar su elegibilidad para asistencia financiera.

MITO: se debe empezar a planificar para la universidad durante el penúltimo año de secundaria.

REALIDAD: si bien algunos estudiantes pueden esperar hasta este punto para hacer ciertas cosas como visitar las posibles instituciones educativas o tomar el SAT, hay otras que jamás deben dejarse para tan tarde. Por ejemplo, las selecciones y notas de los cursos de secundaria representan la consideración individual más importante en las decisiones de admisión de la mayoría de las instituciones de educación superior. Las decisiones de los cursos de secundaria se toman mucho antes, incluso en los años de escuela media. La planificación financiera, el ahorro para la educación superior y averiguar qué instituciones educativas se podrán costear son actividades que también deben llevarse a cabo antes del penúltimo año.

MITO: los estudiantes hoy en día tienen tanta deuda por los préstamos que no tiene sentido pagar mucho para ir a la universidad.

REALIDAD: la mayoría de los estudiantes con deudas inmensas normalmente no hicieron un buen trabajo al buscar una institución de educación superior donde la asistencia financiera de su familia funcionara bien o tomaron una decisión consciente de asumir ese tipo de deuda a fin de poder asistir a una universidad en particular. (Recuerde, la deuda promedio de los estudiantes de grado actualmente es de alrededor de $20,000; menos que el costo de la mayoría de los autos nuevos). La meta para la mayoría de las familias es encontrar por anticipado las instituciones educativas que sean razonables para ellas desde el punto de vista financiero, normalmente mediante el uso de un estimador de asistencia financiera publicado a fin de entender cuál es su posición según la fórmula federal para asistencia financiera.

MITO: la asistencia financiera disponible no es mucha, y la que hay va a unos pocos de los mejores estudiantes.

REALIDAD: durante el año académico 2002-2003, se otorgaron más de $105,000 millones de dólares en asistencia financiera. La mayor parte de este dinero fue entregado por el gobierno federal a través de subsidios, préstamos y programas de estudio y trabajo, en tanto los subsidios y becas propios de las instituciones de educación superior totalizaron casi el 20% de toda la asistencia financiera. Los estados aportaron lo suyo, contribuyendo con más de $5,500 millones al pozo. Esto es mucho dinero, para muchos estudiantes. De hecho, más del 70% de los estudiantes de todo el país reciben algún tipo de asistencia financiera.

MITO: nadie de mi familia ha ido a la universidad; ¿por qué mi hijo debería ser el primero?

REALIDAD: al terminar la secundaria, su adolescente puede tener 40 ó 50 años de trabajo por delante. Durante ese tiempo pueden ocurrir muchos cambios en el mercado laboral. Una educación superior ciertamente le dará más opciones en el largo plazo. Es posible que muchos de los trabajos actuales que sólo exigen un diploma de secundaria ya no existan en unos pocos años. Su educación lo preparará para el mercado laboral del futuro, no el actual.

Preguntas para su visita al campus

El mejor motivo para visitar el campus de una institución de educación superior es tener una impresión personal de la calidad de educación que allí se ofrece. Durante la visita al campus, usted y su adolescente deben hacer preguntas que revelen el compromiso de la institución para brindar un ambiente educativo óptimo. Las siguientes preguntas pueden ser útiles:

¿Nivel de exigencia académica?

Un trabajo creativo e intelectual exigente es fundamental para mantener un ambiente educativo de calidad.

- ¿Hasta qué punto se enfatiza el estudio y la dedicación de tiempo al trabajo académico?
- ¿El cuerpo de profesores impone parámetros elevados a los estudiantes?
- ¿Cuánto tiempo dedican los estudiantes a las tareas cada semana?
- ¿Cuánto se espera que escriban?
- ¿Cuánto se espera que lean?

¿El aprendizaje es activo y cooperativo?

Los estudiantes aprenden más cuando participan en forma directa en su educación y tienen oportunidades de colaborar con otros para resolver problemas o dominar materiales difíciles.

- ¿Con qué frecuencia los estudiantes discuten ideas en clase?
- ¿Con qué frecuencia los temas de la clase se discuten fuera de ella?
- ¿Los estudiantes trabajan en grupo en proyectos, dentro y fuera de la clase?
- ¿Con qué frecuencia los estudiantes hacen presentaciones ante la clase?
- ¿Cuántos estudiantes participan en proyectos de base comunitaria en cursos regulares?
- ¿Cuántos estudiantes aplican lo aprendido en clase a la vida real, a través de pasantías o experiencias de campo fuera del campus?
- ¿Tienen los estudiantes oportunidades de actuar como tutores o de enseñar a otros estudiantes?

¿Hay interacción entre profesores y estudiantes?

En general, mientras más contacto tienen los estudiantes con sus profesores, mejor. Trabajar con un profesor en un proyecto de investigación o trabajar junto con los miembros del cuerpo de profesores en un comité universitario u organización comunitaria permite que los estudiantes vean de forma directa cómo los expertos identifican y resuelven problemas prácticos.

- ¿Son los miembros del cuerpo de profesores accesibles y alentadores?
- ¿Cuántos estudiantes trabajan en proyectos de investigación con profesores?

- ¿Reciben los estudiantes comentarios inmediatos sobre su desempeño académico?

- ¿Con qué frecuencia hablan los estudiantes con sus profesores sobre lo que aprenden en clase?

- ¿Con qué frecuencia hablan los estudiantes con consejeros o miembros del cuerpo de profesores sobre sus planes de carrera?

- ¿Trabajan juntos los profesores y estudiantes en comités y proyectos fuera del trabajo académico?

¿Hay experiencias educativas enriquecedoras?

Las instituciones que son superiores desde el punto de vista educativo ofrecen diversas oportunidades de aprendizaje dentro y fuera del aula, que complementan las metas del programa académico. Una de las más importantes es la exposición a estudiantes y profesores de diversos orígenes.

- ¿Qué tipos de cursos honorarios, comunidades de aprendizaje y otros programas distintivos se ofrecen?

- ¿De qué forma los profesores utilizan la tecnología en clase?

- ¿Con qué frecuencia interactúan los estudiantes con pares de distintas opiniones sociales, políticas o religiosas?

- ¿Con qué frecuencia interactúan los estudiantes con pares de distintos orígenes raciales o étnicos?

- ¿Cuántos estudiantes estudian en otros países?

- ¿Participan los estudiantes en actividades que aumentan su espiritualidad?

- ¿Qué porcentaje de estudiantes prestan servicios comunitarios?

- ¿En qué tipo de actividades participan los estudiantes fuera del aula?

- ¿Qué tipo de eventos auspicia el campus?

- ¿Se requiere una experiencia de culminación del último año?

¿Hay un ambiente de apoyo en el campus?

Los estudiantes rinden más y están más satisfechos en las instituciones educativas que se comprometen con su éxito y que cultivan relaciones laborales y sociales positivas entre los distintos grupos del campus.

- ¿Qué tan bien se llevan los estudiantes unos con otros?

- ¿Están los estudiantes satisfechos con su experiencia educativa en general?

- ¿Cuánto tiempo dedican los estudiantes a actividades cocurriculares?

- ¿Qué tal se llevan los estudiantes con los administradores y el personal?

- ¿En qué medida la institución ayuda a los estudiantes a manejar sus necesidades académicas y sociales?

Costos Ayuda Financiera

No hay forma de escapar al hecho de que los costos de la educación superior están creciendo. Según los últimos informes divulgados, la mayoría de los estudiantes y sus familias pueden esperar pagar, en promedio, de $112 a $1,190 más que el año pasado en concepto de matricula y costos este año, de acuerdo al tipo de institución educativa.

Sin embargo, hay buenas noticias. La asistencia financiera disponible es más alta que nunca: más de $135,000 millones. Y a pesar de todos los aumentos en los costos, la educación superior sigue siendo una opción accesible para la mayoría de las familias. Haga clic en los signos de "más" para ver más información:

"Precio de lista" vs. Accesibilidad

Si bien los precios de algunas de las instituciones de educación superior que se oyen pueden ser desalentadores ($30,000 anuales o más por matricula y costos), la mayoría de ellas cuesta mucho menos. Por ejemplo, ¿sabía usted que alrededor del 60 por ciento de los estudiantes que asisten a instituciones de grado de cuatro años pagan menos de $6,000 en concepto de matricula y costos? Luego de tomar en cuenta los subsidios, el precio neto que el estudiante de grado promedio paga por su educación es significativamente menor que la cifra publicada para matricula y costos. Y recuerde, la asistencia financiera puede reducir aún más el monto que su familia pagará en realidad.

La asistencia financiera hace que la universidad le resulte más accesible

La asistencia financiera pretende compensar la diferencia entre lo que su familia puede costear y el costo de la universidad. Más de la mitad de los estudiantes actualmente inscritos en instituciones de educación superior reciben algún tipo de asistencia financiera para ayudar a pagar sus costos.

El sistema de asistencia financiera se basa en la meta del acceso igualitario: que todos puedan tener educación superior, independientemente de sus circunstancias financieras. El sistema funciona así:

• Se espera que el esudiante y su familia contribuyan al costo de la educacion superior en la medida de sus posibilidades.

• Si la familia no puede aportar la totalidad del costo, hay asistencia financiera disponible para cerrar la brecha.

La contribución familiar esperada lo favorece a usted

El monto que su familia puede contribuir es comúnmente conocido como "contribución familiar esperada" (Expected Family Contribution, EFC). La cifra la determina quien quiera que otorga la asistencia; en general, el gobierno federal o cada universidad o institución de educación superior.

El gobierno federal y las oficinas de asistencia financiera utilizan "fórmulas de necesidad" para analizar las condiciones financieras de su familia (elementos como ingresos, activos y tamaño de familia) y las compara en términos de proporción con las condiciones financieras de otras familias.

La mayoría de las familias simplemente no pueden afrontar la EFC sólo con sus ingresos corrientes. Las fórmulas asumen que las familias cumplirán con su contribución a través de una combinación de ahorros, ingresos corrientes y préstamos. Verifique con las instituciones educativas para averiguar de qué modo se espera que satisfaga la EFC.

No descarte a las instituciones de educación superior de mayor costo

Por ejemplo su EFC es de $5,000. En una institución educativa con un costo total de $8,000, usted sería elegible para un máximo de $3,000 en asistencia financiera. En otra institución educativa con un costo total de $25,000, usted sería elegible para un máximo de $20,000 en asistencia financiera. En otras palabras, su familia deberá aportar la misma suma en ambas.

Costos Promedio de La Educación Superior

Costos promedio de la educación superior para el año 2007-2008

Institución pública, dos años: $2,361

Institución pública, cuatro años: $6,185

Institución privada, cuatro años: $23,712

¿Sabía usted...?

• Alrededor del 60% de los estudiantes que asisten a instituciones públicas de educación superior de cuatro años pagan menos de $6,000 anuales por matricula y costos.

• 44% de todos los estudiantes asisten a instituciones de educación superior de dos años. El estudiante promedio en una institución de educación superior pública de dos años recibe un subsidio de asistencia financiera que reduce los costos de matricula promedio a alrededor de $400.

• Hay un monto récord de $135,000 millones en asistencia financiera disponible para los estudiantes y su familia.

• Alrededor del 60% de todos los estudiantes universitarios reciben asistencia financiera. En 2004-05 la asistencia promedio por estudiante fue de $1,800 en las instituciones públicas de dos años, de $3,300 en las públicas de cuatro años, y de $9,600 en las privadas de cuatro años.

Conocimientos básicos de asistencia financiera

La asistencia financiera es cualquier tipo de asistencia que se utilice para pagar los costos de la educación superior y que se base en necesidad financiera. Hay tres tipos principales:

Subsidios y becas

También denominada donación para asistencia, los subsidios no deben reintegrarse y no se debe trabajar para ganarlos. Los subsidios provienen del gobierno federal y estatal y de las instituciones de educación superior individuales. Las becas en general se otorgan en función del mérito. Para buscar becas, visitewww.fastweb.com.

Trabajo

El empleo estudiantil y la asistencia de trabajo y estudio ayuda a que el estudiante pague por costos educativos como libros, insumos y gastos personales. El programa de trabajo y estudio es un programa federal que proporciona empleos de tiempo parcial a los estudiantes, de modo de ayudarlos a cubrir sus necesidades financieras, y les brinda experiencia laboral a la vez que atienden a sus campus y a las comunidades circundantes.

Préstamos

La mayor parte de la asistencia financiera (54%) se presenta en forma de préstamos a los estudiantes o padres y es una asistencia que debe reembolsarse. La mayoría de los préstamos otorgados en función de las necesidades financieras son préstamos de bajo interés, patrocinados por el gobierno federal. Estos préstamos están subsidiados por el gobierno, de modo que no se acumula interés hasta que comienzan a ser reembolsados, una vez que el estudiante se ha graduado.

Más información sobre préstamos

Hay distinto tipos de préstamos, para estudiantes y para padres que los toman en nombre de sus hijos. Siga leyendo para conocer la información básica.

Préstamos para padres

Préstamos federales PLUS

El programa de préstamos PLUS es la mayor fuente de préstamos para padres. Los padres pueden tomar hasta el costo total de asistencia menos cualquier asistencia recibida y el reembolso comienza a los 60 días de haber pagado el dinero a la institución educativa.

Préstamos privados para padres

Algunas instituciones financieras y de préstamos ofrecen préstamos privados para educación para padres. Estos préstamos en general tienen una tasa de interés más alta que los préstamos del programa PLUS.

Préstamos patrocinados por las instituciones educativas

Un pequeño número de instituciones de educación superior ofrecen sus propios préstamos para padres, en general con una mejor tasa de interés que el programa PLUS. Verifique los materiales sobre asistencia de cada institución educativa para ver si cuentan con ese tipo de préstamos.

Préstamos federales para estudiantes

Préstamos Perkins

Los préstamos Perkins son préstamos en función de la necesidad, que son otorgados por la oficina de asistencia financiera a aquellos estudiantes que más lo necesitan. La tasa de interés es muy baja (5%) y no se hace ningún pago durante el curso de los estudios.

Préstamos directos o Stafford subsidiados

Los préstamos Stafford subsidiados son préstamos en función de la necesidad, con tasas de interés en el orden del 4-6 por ciento. El gobierno federal paga los intereses durante el curso de los estudios. Por eso se los llama préstamos "subsidiados".

Préstamos directos o Stafford no subsidiados

Los préstamos Stafford no subsidiados no surgen de la necesidad financiera y pueden utilizarse para ayudar a pagar la porción de costos a cargo de la familia. Usted es responsable del pago de los intereses durante el curso de los estudios. Puede optar por capitalizar los intereses. La ventaja de hacerlo es que no se requiere ningún pago de intereses. La desventaja es que los intereses se suman al préstamo, lo que implica que debe reintegrarle más dinero al acreedor.

Préstamos Grad PLUS

Se trata de préstamos para estudiantes graduados, patrocinados por el gobierno federal, que no están vinculados a la necesidad. En general, los estudiantes pueden solicitar préstamos Grad PLUS por el costo total de la educación, menos cualquier asistencia recibida. La ventaja de este préstamo es que permite una mayor capacidad de endeudamiento. Sin embargo, recomendamos que los estudiantes consideren los préstamos de bajo interés, como los Stafford subsidiados o no subsidiados antes de tomar un préstamo Grad PLUS.

Otras opciones de préstamos para estudiantes

Préstamos privados para estudiantes

Algunas instituciones financieras y de préstamos ofrecen préstamos privados para educación para los estudiantes. Estos préstamos no están subsidiados y en general conllevan una mayor tasa de interés que los préstamos federales en función de las necesidades. El programa de préstamos privados del College Board es un ejemplo de préstamos educativos privados para estudiantes.

Préstamos patrocinados por las instituciones educativas

Ciertas instituciones de educación superior cuentan con sus propios fondos para préstamos. Las tasas de interés pueden ser menores que las de los préstamos federales para estudiantes. Lea la información sobre asistencia financiera de la institución.

Otros préstamos

Además de establecer becas, ciertas organizaciones y fundaciones privadas también cuentan con programas de préstamos. Los términos del endeudamiento pueden ser muy favorables. Puede utilizar Búsqueda de Becas para encontrarlos.

Desafios

Para los adolescentes, la ida a la universidad representa un enorme cambio en sus vidas. Pero este cambio puede afectar en la misma medida a los padres y tutores.

Si bien con seguridad usted está orgulloso y entusiasmado con sus logros, también puede aparecer un sentimiento creciente de pérdida y separación. Afrontar esta mezcla de emociones puede ser difícil, pero son normales.

El manejo de estos cambios puede hacerse más fácil si tiene en cuenta estos consejos:

Manténgase en contacto.

Puede haber algo de verdad en el dicho de que la distancia aviva los sentimientos, pero los padres o tutores tal vez se preocupen de que "ojos que no ven, corazón que no siente". De modo que usted y su estudiante deben acordar las formas de seguir participando en las vidas del otro y recordar decir y hacer esas pequeñas cosas importantes. El envío de tarjetas a casa, los paquetes que se envían a la universidad, las fotos de los eventos a los que no se pudo asistir y las llamadas de teléfono y mensajes de correo electrónico son ciertamente un modo de mantenerse en contacto y participar.

Amóldese a una nueva relación.

A medida que juega un nuevo papel en la vida de su adolescente, trate de amoldarse al nuevo aspecto de adulto a adulto en la relación padre e hijo. Los hijos siempre necesitan a los padres, pero la relación puede transformarse más en una entre pares.

Espere altos y bajos.

Un día los estudiantes son un modelo de independencia y al día siguiente llaman entre llantos. Este ida y vuelta es natural y esperable, a medida que tanto estudiantes como padres se sienten más cómodos y van tomando confianza en la capacidad de los estudiantes de manejar las situaciones por sí mismos.

Reoriente su tiempo y energía hacia nuevas actividades.

Ahora que su tiempo de paternidad se ha transformado en tiempo libre, hacer un inventario de sus intereses y activos personales le revelará áreas de su vida que tal vez tenía descuidadas. Puede ser el momento de desarrollar, volver a despertar y atender viejas y nuevas aficiones, actividades placenteras y carreras.

Contemple que se cometerán errores.

Debe apoyar y aceptar la capacidad de su hijo para tomar decisiones independientes. Tanto el estudiante como los padres deben aceptar que se cometerán errores en el camino; eso es la vida. Aprender de los errores es simplemente otro tipo de aprendizaje.

Guíe sin presionar.

La comunicación de las metas y expectativas educativas debe hacerse de una manera respetuosa hacia el propio estilo e intereses de su estudiante. Los estudiantes deben perseguir sus propias pasiones. Si bien la opinión de los padres puede ser útil, no se debe esperar que los hijos hagan realidad los sueños de los padres.

Consejos del Centro de Estudios sobre los Hijos (Child Study Center) de la Universidad de Nueva York, www.aboutourkids.org

Pasos para la Universidad

El proceso de planificación para los estudios superiores puede ser atemorizante para cualquiera, de modo que es mejor planificar por adelantado y contemplar mucho tiempo. De hecho, es una buena idea comenzar las conversaciones sobre la educación superior cuando el adolescente está aun en la escuela media.

Ayude a orientar al joven a través del proceso de planificación para la educación superior. Haga clic en los signos de "más" a continuación para ver los pasos básicos en cada grado. También le recomendamos leer los consejos específicos para estudiantes haciendo clic en los niveles de grado (por ej., Primer año) en la barra de navegación principal y luego en "Pasos hacia la universidad".

CRONOGRAMA: 9NO GRADO

OTOÑO

❑ Consulte al consejero escolar para asegurarse que el estudiante esté asistiendo a los cursos preparatorios para la universidad, comenzando por álgebra.

❑ Ayude al joven a crear una carpeta de información para su educación superior.

❑ Comience el año escolar correctamente ayudando al joven a organizarse y a poner en práctica buenos hábitos de estudio.

❑ Aliente al estudiante a conocer gente nueva mediante la inscripción en actividades extracurriculares e intentando algo nuevo.

❑ Explore carreras por Internet, en la computadora de su casa o en la biblioteca.

❑ Ayude a su adolescente a encontrar oportunidades de aprendizaje por observación del trabajo en la comunidad, donde pasan el día siguiendo de cerca a una persona mientras trabaja y observan lo que la persona hace.

PRIMAVERA

❑ Siéntese con su estudiante para planificar el segundo año.

❑ Hable sobre las vacaciones de verano. Explore los programas o campamentos de verano a los que puede asistir en universidades e instituciones de educación superior locales. Busque oportunidades de servicio o voluntarias en la comunidad. Algunas pueden ser patrocinadas por una iglesia, sinagoga o mezquita local.

CRONOGRAMA: 10MO GRADO

OTOÑO

❑ Apoye a su estudiante para que se prepare y tome todos los exámenes necesarios para completar los requisitos de graduación de la escuela secundaria.

❑ Haga que su estudiante comience el segundo año puliendo sus aptitudes de estudio. Aconseje a su hijo o hija que si necesita mejorar en ciertos temas, éste es el momento de hacerlo. Refuerce la idea de que las universidades y los futuros empleadores se fijan en certificados analíticos de la escuela secundaria y se impresionan con asistencia regular y mejoras en las calificaciones.

❑ Aliente al joven a hacer un inventario de intereses de carrera.

❑ Los estudiantes deben tomar el examen de Prueba Preliminar de Aptitud Escolar (Preliminary Scholastic Aptitude, PSTA), la versión preliminar del Examen de Aptitud Escolástica (Scholastic Aptitude Test, SAT) o el PLAN, versión preliminar del Examen Estadounidense para la Universidad (American College Test, ACT). Dar el PSAT ahora es práctica para el PSAT del penúltimo año, que permite que a su estudiante se lo considere para una beca nacional de mérito. Obtenga las fechas e información adicional sobre el PSAT en la oficina de orientación de su escuela secundaria.

❑ Navegue por Internet junto con el estudiante para investigar oportunidades de universidades, escuelas técnicas y aprendizajes.

❑ Anime al estudiante a comenzar o a seguir aprendiendo sobre carreras.

PRIMAVERA

❑ Comience a explorar las opciones de asistencia financiera y becas.

❑ Anime a su estudiante a preguntar a sus amigos, colegas y líderes de la comunidad sobre distintas carreras o use Internet para explorar distintas carreras.

❑ Ayude al estudiante a seleccionar de cinco a diez instituciones de educación superior a las cuales pedir folletos y solicitudes de ingreso.

❑ Arregle con él para visitar un centro de carreras en la zona.

❑ Planifique un verano productivo para su adolescente. Si todavía no tiene un trabajo en el verano anterior al 11mogrado, es un buen momento de buscar uno que lo ayude a prepararse para una futura carrera.

❑ Elija un campamento de verano o ayúdelo a encontrar programas de servicio voluntario para incentivar las aptitudes de su adolescente.

❑ Recuerde a su adolescente que se inscriba en las clases más exigentes para el próximo año.

CRONOGRAMA: 11MO GRADO

11MO GRADO
CRONOGRAMA

OTOÑO

❏ Verifique que su estudiante esté encaminado hacia la educación superior y tómese tiempo para analizar intereses universitarios.

❏ Anime a su estudiante a comenzar una carpeta de información sobre instituciones educativas de nivel superior.

❏ Durante el receso de otoño, visiten universidades.

❏ Aliente a su adolescente a tomar el examen PSAT para prepararse para el SAT y calificar para el programa de becas nacional de mérito.

❏ Participe en noches universitarias y ferias universitarias en la escuela o centros comunitarios locales.

❏ Durante el receso de invierno, sugiera reuniones con amigos que estén de regreso de la universidad y arregle visitas a campus.

PRIMAVERA

❏ Vuelva a verificar que su adolescente esté inscrito para dar el SAT o ACT. Busque libros para ayudarlo a prepararse. Considere qué universidades deben recibir los puntajes. Reúnase con el consejero escolar de su estudiante para saber qué universidades y becas están disponible según los resultados del examen.

❏ Comience una búsqueda activa de becas y asistencia financiera.

❏ Continúe animando a su estudiante para que mantenga el rumbo a fin de completar todos los cursos necesarios para la graduación, más cualquier otro curso requerido para la admisión a la universidad.

❏ Anímelo a hacer más visitas a universidades durante el verano y hable con los consejeros de admisión con respecto a lo que puede hacerse para aumentar las posibilidades de ser admitido.

❏ Si no puede viajar, los sitios web de las universidades e instituciones educativas de nivel superior pueden proporcionarle gran cantidad de información y recorridos en línea.

❏ Para adquirir una impresión de la vida universitaria y explorar posibles carreras, anímelo a participar en un programa de verano preuniversitario.

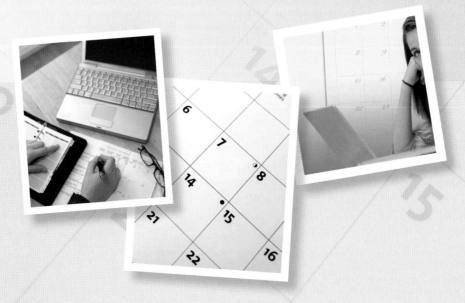

CRONOGRAMA: 12VO GRADO

OTOÑO

❏ Si los hay disponibles, aliente al estudiante a inscribirse en cursos que ofrezcan créditos para la universidad, como los denominados "Advance Placement" o "AP" (equivalencia universitaria) y "Dual Enrollment" (matrícula doble).

❏ Ayúdelo a ir reduciendo el abanico de posibilidades de instituciones educativas y a recopilar las correspondientes solicitudes. Haga una lista de verificación con los requisitos de admisión, certificados analíticos, costos de la solicitud, puntajes de los exámenes, cartas de recomendación, ensayos y solicitudes de asistencia financiera.

❏ Haga que su estudiante de último año prepare una lista de todos sus servicios escolares y comunitarios junto con sus clases y premios de la secundaria. Esta lista lo ayudará al momento de comenzar a llenar las solicitudes de admisión.

❏ Haga que su estudiante practique el llenado del formulario y la escritura del ensayo de admisión a la universidad. Procure recomendaciones para las admisiones y becas universitarias.

❏ Visite las instituciones educativas que su estudiante esté considerando. Llame por anticipado para fijar citas con los funcionarios de admisión y de asistencia financiera.

❏ Lleve un control de las fechas límite para las solicitudes.

❏ Trabaje junto al estudiante a fin de completar las solicitudes aproximadamente dos semanas antes de la fecha límite. Ofrézcase a revisarlas. Verifique que la oficina de orientación escolar esté enviando los certificados analíticos y los puntajes de los exámenes a las instituciones educativas que su estudiante haya elegido.

❏ Si el joven no está satisfecho con los puntajes del SAT, sugiérale que tome el SAT o el ACT por segunda vez. Verifique las políticas de cada institución educativa. Muchas oficinas de admisión se concentran sólo en los mejores puntajes.

❏ Asista a todas las ferias universitarias y talleres de asistencia financiera que pueda.

❏ Ayude a su adolescente a buscar becas e información general sobre temas de asistencia financiera por Internet.

INVIERNO

❏ Ayude a su estudiante a llenar la Solicitud Gratuita de Asistencia Federal para Estudiantes (Free Application for Federal Student Aid, FAFSA), que se requiere a todos los solicitantes de asistencia financiera. Este formulario determinará su elegibilidad para subsidios y préstamos con miras a ayudar a cubrir los costos universitarios.

PRIMAVERA

❏ Verifique que se envíen las notas de mediados de año, de ser necesario, a las instituciones educativas seleccionadas. Pídale al consejero escolar del estudiante que las envíe.

❏ Festeje las cartas de aceptación junto a su estudiante, y empiece los planes para su primer año. Recuérdele mantener buenas notas y asistencia.

❏ Minimice las cartas de rechazo, y anímelo a concentrarse en la meta real: ir a la universidad.

❏ Repase y evalúe las ofertas de asistencia financiera. Una vez que el estudiante tome la decisión definitiva con respecto a la selección de institución educativa, verifique las fechas límites para el envío del depósito, la solicitud de alojamiento y todos los demás elementos que ésta exija. Notifique a las otras instituciones que su hijo o hija no asistirá a ellas.

❏ Ayude a su adolescente a empezar a buscar un trabajo para el verano.

VERANO

❏ Verifique que se envíen las notas finales de su estudiante a la institución educativa seleccionada.

❏ Ayúdelo a planificar el próximo año en la universidad, haciendo un presupuesto, un horario y una lista de números telefónicos de servicios y apoyos importantes.

Notes

Notes

log on

www.CSOcollegecenter.org

FREE services for students

- Connect with colleges recruiting first-generation, low-income, minority students

- Monthly newsletters, college admissions guidance and support

- Apply for CSO's $1,000 Opportunity Scholarships

COLLEGE ACCESS & OPPORTUNITY GUIDE

2 0 1 1 E D I T I O N

College Profiles

College Profiles

In the following pages, you'll find comprehensive profiles of several hundred colleges and universities committed to serving and supporting first-generation, low-income, and minority students on their campus and in their community.

The section is organized by state, with schools presented alphabetically within each state. You are encouraged to continue your research and to connect with the colleges and universities profiled here at www.CSOCollegeCenter.org, a free online college search tool. First-generation college, low-income, and minority students can sign up on the site to become a CSO **Opportunity Scholar** and receive free college search guidance, support, and scholarships.

Criteria for Inclusion

The colleges and universities profiled here do not reflect each and every—or the only—schools that serve first-generation, low-income, and/or minority students. Still, the colleges and universities that are included exemplify the many four-year schools committed to college access and retention and are profiled in light of the programs and opportunities they present for first-generation, low-income, and minority students.

Profiled colleges and universities partner with Center for Student Opportunity to build awareness of their institution and its college access programs, recruit qualified and motivated first-generation college and other traditionally underserved college-bound students, and improve outreach, recruitment and retention efforts aimed to serve and support first-generation college, underserved students on their campuses.

Explaining the College Profile

The information and data represented in the college profiles were developed by Center for Student Opportunity staff in collaboration with and approved by the schools themselves. Because of this close editorial process, we believe the information presented in the profiles to be accurate and up-to-date. If a college did not supply a certain piece of data requested, the information either does not appear or is marked as "n/a" for "not available." We still encourage you to check with a college or university of interest to verify important information on programs, application deadlines, tuition and fees, and other necessary data.

Explaining the College Profile

We believe that the best way to research and select your college is not just by the numbers, but by the important programs and services that will support you academically, socially and financially through your college education and help you persist to graduation.

Learn more about the colleges profiled in this book and send them your information at **www.CSOCollegeCenter.org**, a FREE website to research and connect with colleges. Students who use **www.CSOCollegeCenter.org** are given the special title of **Opportunity Scholar** and receive free college search guidance, support, and scholarships.

www.csocollegecenter.org/astate

Arkansas State University–Jonesboro
P. O. Box 1630
State University, AR 72467

ARKANSAS

Arkansas State University

With a population of more than 12,000 students and more than 200 degree programs, Arkansas State University provides an affordable and accessible, quality education to a diverse and dynamic array of students. The University treats each individual as an equal and important member of its community and offers more than 300 student organizations, valuing community involvement outside of the classroom as part of students' core education.

"I decided to attend ASU after attending Senior Preview Day. I enjoyed the campus environment and felt like the campus was a home away from home. The people I met were extremely nice and made every student visiting the campus feel special and welcomed. Also, ASU was close enough to my home town, but far enough that I was able to experience something different."
– Adrian E., '12
McGehee, AR
Chemistry, Education

ACCESS **Discover Div**

Discover Diversity is a leadership program designed to give student

ACCESS programs serve pre-college students beyond a college's own gates. These programs include partnerships with underserved schools and organizations and efforts that leverage administration, faculty, and student bodies to assist college-bound students with academic enrichment, mentoring, college preparation, and college guidance.

ACCESS **"Back to School" Day**

"Back to School" Day provides an educational venue for students of color and first generation high school students and their parents in preparation for the start of a new academic year. Topics covered include self-esteem, importance of the ACT test, reasons to avoid the legal system, and a question and answer session for parents. The goal is to reduce the number of incidents in the schools and improve the students' motivation to succeed.

ACCESS **Discover Diversity**

Discover Diversity is a leadership development program designed to give students of color and first generation college students a closer look into their future by exposing them to college life through academic workshops, class lectures, financial aid presentations, and much more. Students who meet the requirements are selected by their high school counselors to participate in this program. During this program, students have the opportunity to get to know faculty, staff, alumni, and current ASU students.

OPPORTUNITY **Thompson Minority Scholarship**

The Thompson Minority Scholarship program awards scholarships to incoming African-American freshmen and currently enrolled African-American students. This scholarship was developed to increase the enrollment of entering African-American freshmen and the retention rates of currently enrolled students by honoring academic achievement and eliminating financial barriers.

SUCCESS **First Year Experience Program (FYE)**

The First Year Experience Program provides incoming students with the information and skills needed to meet the expectations of college faculty, develop effective study skills, and become familiar with college policies and procedures. Topical coverage includes decision making, goal setting, planning, time management, and group team building skills.

SUCCESS **Student Support Services (SSS)**

Student Support Services is a comprehensive program designed to promote retention and academic success in college. It provides participants with academic and support services in a caring environment that seeks to ensure their successful completion of a baccalaureate degree at Arkansas State University. These services are offered free of charge to participants and include tutoring, academic and financial advising, counseling, mentoring, workshops, and cultural enrichment trips. Participants must demonstrate financial need, documentation of a disability, or be first-generation college students.

SUCCESS **Summer Bridge Program**

The Summer Bridge Program, supported by Student Support Services, is designed to introduce incoming or nontraditional students to the resources needed for success in college. Students demonstrate academic or financial need, or documentation of a disability, and have been weeks prior to the start

OPPORTUNITY **Thomps**

The Thompson Minority Scholars freshmen and currently enrolled

OPPORTUNITY programs serve prospective students in getting to know a college and providing financial incentives for admitted students. These programs include scholarships, financial aid initiatives, visit and open house programs, and fly-in programs that in most cases cater specifically to first-generation, low-income, and minority students.

SUCCESS **Student Sup**

Student Support Services is a comp academic success in college. It pro caring environment that seeks to e

SUCCESS programs are academic assistance, student support services, and retention initiatives that help students persist to graduation. These programs exist both in and out of the classroom and include pre-orientation/orientation, first-year programs, academic advising, mentoring, living learning communities, and student organizations and clubs.

Arkansas State University–Jonesboro
P. O. Box 1630
State University, AR 72467
Ph: (870) 972-3024
admissions@astate.edu
www.astate.edu

F A S T   F A C T S

STUDENT PROFILE
# of degree-seeking undergraduates	9,200
% male/female	41/59
% African American	18
% American Indian or Alaska Native	<1
% Asian or Pacific Islander	<1
% Hispanic	
% White	
% International	
% Pell grant recipients	

First-generation
Mike Beebe, governor, state of Arkansas; Maj. Gen. Elder Granger, former deputy director of the Department of Defense's TRICARE Management, former Commander, Task Force 44th Medical Command and Command Surgeon for Multinational Corps-Iraq in Baghdad, Iraq; Dr. Thomas Hill, Vice President for Student Affairs at Iowa State University, Olympic bronze medalist; The Hon. James Pardew, former U. S. ambassador to Bulgaria, former deputy assistant secretary general for NATO International; Dr. Kathy Brittain White, former chief information officer for Cardinal Health, founder and president of Rural Sourcing, Inc.

ACADEMICS
full-time faculty	461
full-time minority faculty	76
student-faculty ratio	18:1
average class size	28
% first-year retention rate	68.3
% graduation rate (6 years)	38.6

Popular majors Business, Nursing, Early Childhood Education

CAMPUS LIFE
% live on campus (% fresh.)	23 (54)

Multicultural student clubs and organizations
Black Student Association, N.A.A.C.P., International Student Association, Indian Student Association, Spanish and Latino Student Association, Chinese Student Association, Nepali Student Association, Common Ground
Athletics NCAA Division I, Sunbelt Conference

ADMISSIONS
# of applicants	4,288
% accepted	82
# of first-year students enrolled	1,902
SAT Critical Reading range	460-520
SAT Math range	480-580
SAT Writing range	410-490
ACT range	18-24
average HS GPA	3.13

Deadlines
regular decision	rolling
application fee (online)	$15 ($15)
fee waiver for applicants with financial need	no

COST & AID
tuition	in-state $4,890; out-of-state $12,810
room & board	$5,056
	$9,500,000
	97
	100
	96
	28
	$18,750

Fast Facts

I met were extremely nice and made every student visiting the campus feel special and welcomed. Also, ASU was close enough to my home town, but enough that I was experience something different."
– Adrian E., '12
McGehee, AR
Chemistry, Education

...Y GUIDE

Most profiles feature a quote from a current student about how they have benefited from an ACCESS, OPPORTUNITY, or SUCCESS program at their college.

FAST FACTS

The information and data presented here gives a snap-shot of the school's vital statistics. In addition to the program information, this data will help determine if a school is the right fit for you.

Arkansas State University–Jonesboro
P. O. Box 1630
State University, AR 72467
Ph: (870) 972-3024
admissions@astate.edu
www.astate.edu

STUDENT PROFILE

How many students go here? Is it a diverse student body? Does the school serve many students from low-income backgrounds?

The data here includes number of undergraduate students, male and female percentage, the racial/ethnic breakdown of the student body, percentage of Pell grant recipients—federal grant aid given to students with the greatest financial need—and a list of distinguished alumni that happen to be first-generation college graduates or from low-income, minority backgrounds.

STUDENT PROFILE
# of degree-seeking undergraduates
% male/female
% African American
% American Indian or Alaska Native

ACADEMICS

Will you be in small or large classes? Will you know your professors? How many students drop out or do most graduate?

The data here includes number of full-time faculty, student-faculty ratio, average class size, first-year retention percentage—students returning for their sophomore year—six year graduation rate, and a short list of popular majors.

ACADEMICS
full-time faculty
full-time minority faculty
student-faculty ratio
average class size

CAMPUS LIFE

Is it a residential campus, meaning the majority of students live on campus? What opportunities exist to get involved with student organizations, clubs, or athletic programs?

The data here includes percentage of students living on campus, a list of multicultural student organizations and clubs, and an overview of the athletics program.

CAMPUS LIFE
% live on campus (% fresh.)
Multicultural student clubs and organiza
Black Student Association, N.A.A.C.P., Int
Student Association, Indian Student Ass

ADMISSIONS

How many students apply and how many get in? How do I compare to most students academically? When are the application deadlines?

The data here includes number of applicants, percentage of applicants accepted, median SAT and ACT scores of admitted students, average high school GPA of admitted students, application types, deadlines, fees, and fee waiver availability.

ADMISSIONS
# of applicants
% accepted
# of first-year students enrolled
SAT Critical Reading range

COST AND AID

What are the "sticker price" costs of attendance—similar to buying a car, it is rarely the case that a student pays the full amount? How many students receive financial aid and what kinds? Do students tend to graduate from a school with high loan debt that will need to be repaid?

The data here includes tuition and room and board, percentage of students receiving financial aid, percentage of students receiving need-based scholarship or grant aid—money you do not have to pay back—percentage of students whose need was fully met, average financial aid package in dollars, and the average student loan debt upon graduation.

COST & AID
tuition   in-state $4,890; out-of-sta
room & board
total need-based institutional

FAST FACTS

STUDENT PROFILE

# of degree-seeking undergraduates	9,200
% male/female	41/59
% African American	18
% American Indian or Alaska Native	<1
% Asian or Pacific Islander	1
% Hispanic	1
% White	71
% International	7
% Pell grant recipients	53

First-generation and minority alumni The Hon. Mike Beebe, governor, state of Arkansas; Maj. Gen. Elder Granger, former deputy director of the Department of Defense's TRICARE Management, former Commander, Task Force 44th Medical Command and Command Surgeon for Multinational Corps-Iraq in Baghdad, Iraq; Dr. Thomas Hill, Vice President for Student Affairs at Iowa State University, Olympic bronze medalist; The Hon. James Pardew, former U. S. ambassador to Bulgaria, former deputy assistant secretary general for NATO International; Dr. Kathy Brittain White, former chief information officer for Cardinal Health, founder and president of Rural Sourcing, Inc.

ACADEMICS

full-time faculty	461
full-time minority faculty	76
student-faculty ratio	18:1
average class size	28
% first-year retention rate	68.3
% graduation rate (6 years)	38.6

Popular majors Business, Nursing, Early Childhood Education

CAMPUS LIFE

% live on campus (% fresh.)	23 (54)

Multicultural student clubs and organizations Black Student Association, N.A.A.C.P., International Student Association, Indian Student Association, Spanish and Latino Student Association, Chinese Student Association, Nepali Student Association, Common Ground

Athletics NCAA Division I, Sunbelt Conference

ADMISSIONS

# of applicants	4,288
% accepted	82
# of first-year students enrolled	1,902
SAT Critical Reading range	460-520
SAT Math range	480-580
SAT Writing range	410-490
ACT range	18-24
average HS GPA	3.13

Deadlines

regular decision	rolling
application fee (online)	$15 ($15)
fee waiver for applicants with financial need	no

COST & AID

tuition	in-state $4,890; out-of-state $12,810
room & board	$5,056
total need-based institutional scholarships/grants	$9,500,000
% of students apply for need-based aid	97
% of students receive aid	100
% receiving need-based scholarship or grant aid	96
% receiving aid whose need was fully met	28
average student loan debt upon graduation	$18,750

College Profile List by **Name**

College Profile List by **State**

University of Montevallo

University of Montevallo
Station 6030
Montevallo, AL 35115-6030
Ph: (800) 292-4349 / (205) 665-6030
admissions@montevallo.edu
www.montevallo.edu

One of only 21 public liberal arts universities in the United States, the University of Montevallo offers students from Alabama (and elsewhere) an affordable, liberal arts education. Located in the town of Montevallo, 35 miles south of Birmingham, the university is spread out across a 160-acre main campus, surrounded by lawns, groves, and flower beds. The university's famed architecture and landscaping — particularly the work of the famed Olmstead Brothers — draws many to its campus. In fact, 28 campus structures and sites are listed on the National Register of Historic Places. Undergraduate programs are offered in more than 70 academic areas, and the full-time student-to-faculty ratio is roughly 16:1. Members of the faculty come from prestigious institutions from across the United States, with a large percentage holding terminal degrees in their respective academic disciplines. High achieving students can take advantage of the University of Montevallo's Honors program, which confers special benefits and recognition upon these students.

> ACCESS Upward Bound

Upward Bound is a federally funded program that provides academic support, counseling, tutorial services, career mentoring, cultural exposure, and community service opportunities necessary for potential first-generation college students and/or economically disadvantaged youth to complete both high school and college. The University of Montevallo Upward Bound Program, in particular, provides academic and cultural enrichment opportunities for high school students in Shelby, Bibb and Chilton counties. Students meet about every other week from September to May to attend seminar-style academic classes that emphasize a particular skill or concept. These sessions are designed to resemble college classes as closely as possible to give the students an opportunity to experience the college setting. All services are provided at no cost to program participants and their parents.

> OPPORTUNITY Minority Scholarships

Scholarships at the University of Montevallo are primarily awarded based upon ACT/SAT scores, grades, and in many cases, financial need. Minority students at Montevallo, however, are also eligible for three specific scholarship programs – the Minority Academic Recognition Scholarship, the Martin Luther King, Jr. Scholarship and the Minority Teachers Scholarship Program. The first two of these programs are open to students of all disciplines, while the latter awards scholarships to those seeking a degree that will lead to teacher certification.

> SUCCESS Student Support Services

Student Support Services (SSS) is a U.S. Department of Education TRIO program that provides free academic, career, and counseling support to eligible college students. Student Support Services can help students adjust to higher education by providing academic and personal advising/counseling, tutoring, academic success seminars, access to a computer lab equipped with Mathematics and Study Skills software, cultural enrichment activities, and study skills handouts. The program also provides referrals to appropriate university and other resources that would be beneficial for students. The goal is to deliver services and resources that will provide support for students; resulting in students having a positive experience at University of Montevallo and graduation.

FAST FACTS

STUDENT PROFILE
# of degree-seeking undergraduates	2,558
% male/female	32/68
% African-American	12
% American Indian or Alaska Native	<1
% Asian or Pacific Islander	3
% Hispanic	2
% White	76
% International	2
% Pell grant recipients	26

ACADEMICS
full-time faculty	140
full-time minority faculty	15
student-faculty ratio	16:1
average class size	35
% first-year retention rate	73
% graduation rate (6 years)	51

Popular majors Art/Art Studies, Biology, Business, Elementary Education and Teaching, English Language and Literature

CAMPUS LIFE
% live on campus (% freshmen)	n/a

Multicultural student clubs and organizations African-American Society, Feminine Majority Leadership Alliance, German Club, International Students Association

Athletics NCAA Division II, East Division of the Gulf South Conference

ADMISSIONS
# of applicants	1,543
% accepted	69
# of first-year students enrolled	825
SAT Critical Reading range	n/a
SAT Math range	n/a
SAT Writing range	n/a
ACT range	20-25
average HS GPA	3.3

Deadlines
regular decision	8/1
application fee (online)	$25 ($25)
fee waiver for applicants with financial need	yes

COST & AID
tuition	in-state: $7,100; out-of-state: $13,610
room & board	$4,440
total need-based institutional scholarships/grants	n/a
% of students apply for need-based aid	63
% of students receive aid	48
% receiving need-based scholarship or grant aid	80
% receiving aid whose need was fully met	30
average aid package	$7,926
average student loan debt upon graduation	$19,674

University of Alaska Anchorage

East Hall

University of Alaska Anchorage
3901 Old Seward Highway
Anchorage, Alaska 99503
Ph: (907) 786-1480
enroll@uaa.alaska.edu
www.uaa.alaska.edu

The University of Alaska Anchorage is the state's largest post-secondary institution. Located in the heart of Alaska's largest city, the campus is nestled in the middle of a greenbelt, surrounded by lakes, ponds and wildlife, and is connected to a city-wide trail system perfect for students' active lifestyles. The University offers many career pathway programs in more than 150 major study areas, including arts, sciences, business, education, human services and health sciences. Through UAA's comprehensive curriculum, students learn practical job skills and develop a strong educational foundation that prepares them for graduate of professional schools and the workplace.

> ACCESS Junior Academy

Junior Academy is a program aimed at pre-college students who are between their junior and senior years in high school. Junior Academy students live on the UAA campus for six weeks while attending classes in biology, physics, trigonometry, chemistry and introduction to engineering. Students who successfully complete Junior Academy are awarded $2,000 scholarships toward furthering their education at any University of Alaska campus.

> OPPORTUNITY Seawolf Opportunities Scholarship

The Seawolf Opportunities Scholarship is a four-year renewable scholarship providing financial assistance for tuition and other education expenses, including housing and licensed childcare, to degree-seeking students at the University of Alaska Anchorage who are first-generation college students and first-time freshmen.

> OPPORTUNITY Commit to Success Scholarship

Commit to Success Scholarship is four-year renewable and provides financial assistance for tuition and other educational expenses to a full-time student from Alaska public high school, who may otherwise not likely be able to obtain a four-year college degree. Preference shall be given to first generation college students.

> OPPORTUNITY UAA First Generation Student Scholarship

First Generation Student Scholarship provides scholarships to students who are the first in their family to complete a college education. Award amount is a minimum $2000 per academic year.

> SUCCESS Native Early Transition (NET) Program

NET is an exciting program which involves both rural and Native high school seniors who will be attending fall UAA classes. The program ensures their transition from rural villages to the UAA campus and the city of Anchorage be made as easy as possible.

> SUCCESS AHAINA Stars Peer Mentor Program

This program assists freshmen and sophomore students in transitioning into the collegiate experience by providing monthly meetings that address pertinent issues and develop skills related to academic success. Peer Mentors are upperclassmen whose experiences along with specialized training provide a support network of information and resources.

> SUCCESS Native Student Services (NSS)

Native Student Services provide quality support services to Native and rural students which promotes their scholastic achievement, student retention, and personal success. NSS foster academic excellence, career development, leadership skills, personal growth, college-transitioning, a sense of belonging, and the attainment of one's scholastic and life goals.

F A S T   F A C T S

STUDENT PROFILE
# of degree-seeking undergraduates	15,762
% male/female	41/59
% African American	3
% American Indian or Alaska Native	9
% Asian or Pacific Islander	7
% Hispanic	4
% White	61
% International	1
% Pell grant recipients	24

ACADEMICS
full-time faculty	515
full-time minority faculty	71
student-faculty ratio	18:1
average class size	17
% first-year retention rate	70
% graduation rate (6 years)	24

Popular majors Elementary Education, Psychology, Nursing, Accounting, Business Administration

CAMPUS LIFE
% live on campus	n/a

Multicultural student clubs and organizations
AHAINA Student Programs, Native Student Services, Alaska Native/American Indian Science and Engineering Society (AISES), Chinese Language, Diversity Pre-Health Club, German Culture Club, ANIME, Hip Hop Club, International Student Association, International Youth Fellowship, Japanese Culture Club (Nihon Bunka), Polynesian College Council, Russian Club (Russki Klub), Spanish Club (La Tertulia), Students for Social Equality, The Alaska Native Oratory Society (AkNOS)

Athletics NCAA Division II, Great Northwest Athletic Conference, Hockey Division I

ADMISSIONS
# of applicants	10,241
% accepted	70.2
# of first-year students enrolled	60
SAT Critical Reading range	430-540
SAT Math range	420-560
SAT Writing range	n/a
ACT range	17-24
average HS GPA	n/a

Deadlines
regular decision	7/1
application fee (online)	$50 ($50)
fee waiver for applicants with financial need	yes

COST & AID
tuition	in-state: $4,320; out-of state $14,130
room & board	$8,605
total need-based institutional scholarships/grants	$1,818,289
% of students apply for need-based aid	57
% of students receive aid	57
% receiving need-based scholarship or grant aid	43
% receiving aid whose need was fully met	73
average aid package	$10,055
average student loan debt upon graduation	$22,043

Arizona State University

As one of the largest public universities in the country, Arizona State University offers an unparalleled number of programs and opportunities for students. Arizona State boasts a record-high number of minority students and one of the highest numbers of Native American faculty of any national university. The nationally recognized Barrett, the honors college, offers resources supported

by a $10 million endowment. When not involved in academic pursuits, Arizona State University students can cheer on the Sun Devils in PAC-10 sports or participate in one of the more than 625 clubs and student organizations.

> ACCESS Hispanic Mother Daughter Program (HMDP)

Hispanic Mother Daughter Program raises educational and career aspirations of Hispanic women by involving mothers in the education of their daughters. One-on-one mentoring opportunities and monthly on-campus workshops provide participants the opportunity to plan their academic and professional careers. The program begins when students are in eighth grade and continues through the completion of a university degree. Outstanding participants may be eligible for Arizona State scholarships.

> ACCESS African American Men of Arizona State University Program

The African American Men of Arizona State University Program is designed to positively impact the recruitment, persistence and graduation of male African-American college students. The program brings high school juniors and seniors — and their parents — to campus to prepare them for university enrollment, retention and graduation. The program provides a critical connection to Arizona State for potential and current university students. Events such as the Fall Leadership Conference, the Carter G. Woodson lecture series and various spoken-word performances serve as an invaluable complement to the academic rigor of workshops.

> OPPORTUNITY President Barack Obama Scholars Program

As a commitment to President Obama's challenge to enhance college accessibility, ASU expanded its most important financial aid program (ASU Advantage) and renamed it the President Barack Obama Scholars Program. Through a combination of aid sources, the program will provide funding for direct costs to all academically qualified Arizona freshmen from families that earn less than $60,000. Covered costs include tuition, fees, books, and room and board. Obama Scholars are encouraged to have a work-study job on-campus and participate in a one-on-one mentoring program. For fall 2009, 1,100 students are expected to benefit from this program.

> OPPORTUNITY ASU Advantage

ASU Advantage offers qualifying Arizona residents and low-income students a combination of financial aid resources that do not require repayment. This financial aid covers eight semesters of tuition, room, board and books for full-time enrollment. Since its inception in Fall 2005, nearly 1,000 freshmen have benefited from this program.

> SUCCESS LINK @ ASU

LINK @ ASU is a one-week, transitional summer program which introduces incoming college freshmen to the first year ASU experience. With a focus on the multicultural experience, participants meet with student leaders and become familiar with student resources and services, organizations and university traditions.

"I am the first person in my family to attend college. I chose ASU because it has lots of opportunities and majors. I have been successful because of great professors and my personal determination to get an education. Without financial aid I would not have had this opportunity."

– Gideon H., '12
Dewey, AZ
Urban Planning

Arizona State University
P.O. Box 870112
Tempe, AZ 85287
Ph: (480) 965-7788
ugrading@asu.edu
www.asu.edu

F A S T   F A C T S

STUDENT PROFILE
# of degree-seeking undergraduates	52,883
% male/female	48/52
% African American	5
% American Indian or Alaska Native	2
% Asian or Pacific Islander	6
% Hispanic	15
% White	65
% International	2
% Pell grant recipients	30.4

First-generation and minority alumni
Christine Yaro Devine, news anchor, Fox Network (LA affiliate); Albert Hale, Arizona senator, former president, Navajo Nation; Reggie Jackson, inductee, Baseball Hall of Fame; Barry Bonds, professional baseball player; Vada Manager, director of Global Issues Management, Nike, Inc.

ACADEMICS
full-time faculty	2,520
full-time minority faculty	530
student-faculty ratio	22:1
average class size	10-19
% first-year retention rate	80
% graduation rate (6 years)	56

Popular majors Journalism, Business, Engineering

CAMPUS LIFE
% live on campus (% freshmen)	14 (57)

Multicultural student clubs and organizations
Seventeen ethnic and multicultural fraternities and sororities, Asian/Asian Pacific American Students' Coalition, Philippine American Student Association, Aguila Leadership and Mentoring Association, Upward Bound Alumni Association, Arab Students' Association, American Indian Council, Native Americans Taking Initiative ON Success, Students Identifying Multiracial and Biracial at ASU, Hispanic Honor Society/Latino Students Union, Movimiento Estudiantil Chicana/o de Aztlan

Athletics NCAA Division I, Pacific-10 Conference

ADMISSIONS
# of applicants	27,089
% accepted	90
# of first-year students enrolled	9,707
SAT Critical Reading range	470-600
SAT Math range	480-610
SAT Writing range	n/a
ACT range	20-26
average HS GPA	3.41

Deadlines
regular decision	rolling
application fee (online)	$25 ($25) in-state
	$50 ($50) out-of-state
fee waiver for applicants with financial need	no

COST & AID
tuition	$6,334 in-state; $18,919 out-of-state
room & board	$9,210
total need-based institutional scholarships/grants	$48,853,033
% of students apply for need-based aid	54
% of students receive aid	100
% receiving need-based scholarship or grant aid	88
% receiving aid whose need was fully met	22
average aid package	$10,062
average student loan debt upon graduation	$17,732

Northern Arizona University

Northern Arizona University (NAU) is a diverse, comprehensive public university that provides students with a quality, affordable education in two major cities. Founded in 1899, the university promotes a learning community where students are prepared to contribute to the social, economic, and environmental needs of a changing world. From its inception, NAU has implemented innovative and accountable teaching practices, including the effective use of technology. With nearly 22,500 students from 48 states and 65 countries. Students at NAU become active citizens, leaders, and problem solvers with an understanding of global issues.

> ACCESS **Nizhoni Academy**

Nizhoni Academy is a pre-college program designed to encourage Native American students to seriously prepare for scholastic achievement in secondary and post-secondary education. The Academy emphasizes a rigorous academic discipline to provide students a clear understanding of the demands of college studies and the requirements of academic study skills necessary to be successful in college.

> ACCESS **Four Corners**

The Four Corners Upward Bound Math and Science Program is a year-round academic program that begins with a Summer Academy on the NAU campus, followed by an academic year component that students participate in from their high schools. The Four Corners Program is for freshmen and sophomore high school students interested in math and science careers who qualify as low-income or first-generation.

> ACCESS **Upward Bound**

Upward Bound is a year-round program providing educational services and college preparatory assistance to Northern Arizona high school students who attend either Williams, Coconino, Hopi or Winslow high schools. There is also a 5-week summer academy held every year.

> SUCCESS **Successful Transition and Academic Readiness (STAR)**

The STAR experience is a five-week summer bridge program used in conjunction with NAU's advisor program. STAR is offered to a selected group of incoming freshmen from underrepresented backgrounds from various areas in Arizona as well as the nation. This program helps these students with the academic processes of the university that are vital to their success.

> SUCCESS **LEADS Center**

The Leadership, Engagement, Achievement, Diversity and Service (LEADS) Center encompasses three campus departments to bring the best in advising, mentoring and cultural celebrations. It encompasses the Multicultural Student Center (Peer Advisor Program, clubs and organizations, newsletter, local scholarships in addition to counseling and a resource library); Native American Support Services (culturally-sensitive support services to Native American and Alaskan Native students); and Student Support Services (a federal TRIO program designed to help low-income, first generation students adjust to campus life and the rigors of academic study).

"The STAR program was very beneficial because it not only helped me adjust to the college lifestyle, but it also taught me how to become more of an independent person and experience life on my own. During STAR, I met such a diverse group of people; many of which became some of my closest friends. I'm so happy that I was a part of the program!"

– Kristina R., '12
Gilbert, AZ
Biology Major

Northern Arizona University
Undergraduate Admissions
P.O. Box 4084
Flagstaff, AZ 86011-4084
Ph: (888) 628-2968 / (298) 523-5511
undergraduate.admissions@nau.edu
www.nau.edu

F A S T   F A C T S

STUDENT PROFILE

# of degree-seeking undergraduates	16,787
% male/female	41/59
% African American	3
% American Indian or Alaska Native	6
% Asian or Pacific Islander	3
% Hispanic	13
% Pell grant recipients	32

First-generation and minority alumni Kevin Chase ('01), NAU Program Coordinator for Student Support Services; Claudia Clark ('08), NAU Graduate Student; Cecilia Estudillo ('09), Elementary School Teacher

ACADEMICS

full-time faculty	809
full-time minority faculty	85
student-faculty ratio	17:1
average class size	28
% first-year retention rate	69
% graduation rate (6 years)	53

Popular majors Elementary Education, Hotel and Restaurant Management, Biology, Nursing, Management

CAMPUS LIFE

% live on campus (% fresh.)	40 (89)

Multicultural student clubs and organizations Black Student Union, Hispanic Honor Society, MEChA-Native Americans United, National Society of Minorities in Hospitality, Native American Business Association, American Indian Science and Engineering Society, Club STAR

Athletics NCAA Division I, Big Sky Conference

ADMISSIONS

# of applicants	20,109
% accepted	74
# of first-year students enrolled	3,588
SAT Critical Reading range	470-580
SAT Math range	470-590
SAT Writing range	450-560
ACT range	21-25
average HS GPA	3.4

Deadlines

regular decision	rolling
priority application	3/15
application fee (online)	$25 ($25)
fee waiver for applicants with financial need	yes

COST & AID

tuition	in-state: $5,145; out-of-state: $16,242
room & board	$7,086
total need-based institutional scholarships/grants	$36,056,554
% of students apply for need-based aid	68
% of students receive aid	73
% receiving need-based scholarship or grant aid	70
% receiving aid whose need was fully met	21
average aid package	$8,589
average student loan debt upon graduation	$14,714

Arkansas State University

With a population of more than 12,000 students and more than 200 degree programs, Arkansas State University provides an affordable and accessible, quality education to a diverse and dynamic array of students. The University treats each individual as an equal and important member of its community and offers more than 300 student organizations, valuing community involvement outside of the classroom as part of students' core education.

> ACCESS "Back to School" Day

"Back to School" Day provides an educational venue for students of color and first generation high school students and their parents in preparation for the start of a new academic year. Topics covered include self-esteem, importance of the ACT test, reasons to avoid the legal system, and a question and answer session for parents. The goal is to reduce the number of incidents in the schools and improve the students' motivation to succeed.

> ACCESS Discover Diversity

Discover Diversity is a leadership development program designed to give students of color and first generation college students a closer look into their future by exposing them to college life through academic workshops, class lectures, financial aid presentations, and much more. Students who meet the requirements are selected by their high school counselors to participate in this event. During this program, students have the opportunity to get to know faculty, staff, alumni, and current ASU students.

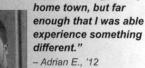

"I decided to attend ASU after attending Senior Preview Day. I enjoyed the campus environment and felt like the campus was a home away from home. The people I met were extremely nice and made every student visiting the campus feel special and welcomed. Also, ASU was close enough to my home town, but far enough that I was able experience something different."

– Adrian E., '12
McGehee, AR
Chemistry, Education

> OPPORUNITY Thompson Minority Scholarship

The Thompson Minority Scholarship program awards scholarships to incoming African-American freshmen and currently enrolled African-American students. This scholarship was developed to increase the enrollment of entering African-American freshmen and the retention rates of currently enrolled students by honoring academic achievement and eliminating financial barriers.

> SUCCESS First Year Experience Program (FYE)

The First Year Experience Program provides incoming students with the information and skills needed to meet the expectations of college faculty, develop effective study skills, and become familiar with college policies and procedures. Topical coverage includes decision making, goal setting, planning, time management, and group team building skills.

> SUCCESS Student Support Services (SSS)

Student Support Services is a comprehensive program designed to promote retention and academic success in college. It provides participants with academic and support services in a caring environment that seeks to ensure their successful completion of a baccalaureate degree at Arkansas State University. These services are offered free of charge to participants and include tutoring, academic and financial advising, counseling, mentoring, workshops, and cultural enrichment trips. Participants must demonstrate financial need, documentation of a disability, or be first-generation college students.

> SUCCESS Summer Bridge Program

The Summer Bridge Program, supported by Student Support Services, is designed to introduce incoming or nontraditional students to the resources needed for success in college. Students must demonstrate academic or financial need, or documentation of a disability, and have been accepted into Student Support Services. The program takes place during a week prior to the start of the academic year and is offered free of charge.

Arkansas State University–Jonesboro
P. O. Box 1630
State University, AR 72467
Ph: (870) 972-3024
admissions@astate.edu
www.astate.edu

FAST FACTS

STUDENT PROFILE

# of degree-seeking undergraduates	9,200
% male/female	41/59
% African American	18
% American Indian or Alaska Native	<1
% Asian or Pacific Islander	1
% Hispanic	1
% White	71
% International	7
% Pell grant recipients	53

First-generation and minority alumni The Hon. Mike Beebe, governor, state of Arkansas; Maj. Gen. Elder Granger, former deputy director of the Department of Defense's TRICARE Management, former Commander, Task Force 44th Medical Command and Command Surgeon for Multinational Corps-Iraq in Baghdad, Iraq; Dr. Thomas Hill, Vice President for Student Affairs at Iowa State University, Olympic bronze medalist; The Hon. James Pardew, former U. S. ambassador to Bulgaria, former deputy assistant secretary general for NATO International; Dr. Kathy Brittain White, former chief information officer for Cardinal Health, founder and president of Rural Sourcing, Inc.

ACADEMICS

full-time faculty	461
full-time minority faculty	76
student-faculty ratio	18:1
average class size	28
% first-year retention rate	68.3
% graduation rate (6 years)	38.6

Popular majors Business, Nursing, Early Childhood Education

CAMPUS LIFE

% live on campus (% fresh.)	23 (54)

Multicultural student clubs and organizations Black Student Association, N.A.A.C.P., International Student Association, Indian Student Association, Spanish and Latino Student Association, Chinese Student Association, Nepali Student Association, Common Ground

Athletics NCAA Division I, Sunbelt Conference

ADMISSIONS

# of applicants	4,288
% accepted	82
# of first-year students enrolled	1,902
SAT Critical Reading range	460-520
SAT Math range	480-580
SAT Writing range	410-490
ACT range	18-24
average HS GPA	3.13

Deadlines

regular decision	rolling
application fee (online)	$15 ($15)
fee waiver for applicants with financial need	no

COST & AID

tuition	in-state $4,890; out-of-state $12,810
room & board	$5,056
total need-based institutional scholarships/grants	$9,500,000
% of students apply for need-based aid	97
% of students receive aid	100
% receiving need-based scholarship or grant aid	96
% receiving aid whose need was fully met	28
average student loan debt upon graduation	$18,750

Hendrix College

As a leader in engaged liberal arts and sciences education, Hendrix provides a demanding yet supportive environment where tomorrow's leaders learn to combine critical thought with action. A private, undergraduate institution of the liberal arts founded in 1876 and related to the United Methodist Church, Hendrix offers distinguished academic programs in a residential setting. "Your Hendrix Odyssey: Engaging in Active Learning" is an exciting and unique component of the curriculum that guarantees that each Hendrix student will participate in at least three engaging, hands-on learning experiences before graduating. In addition to the Odyssey Program, Hendrix stands apart from other colleges for its small participatory classes, close relationships between faculty and students, and its welcoming community, which is enhanced by the belief that diversity in the student body enhances the intellectual experience.

> *"I'm most proud to call myself a Hendrix Warrior because of how alluring Hendrix's atmosphere is. People here are open-minded, welcoming, generally relaxed, but still ambitious, goal-oriented, and fun. It feels like a small vibrant village. I hate long breaks away from Hendrix because this is easily my second home!"*
>
> *– Dominique K., '11*
> *Little Rock, AR*
> *Art*

> ACCESS **Mentoring Programs**

Hendrix students take time to call high school students in order to familiarize them with the College as well as answer any questions they might have. In addition to working with the Upward Bound program, Hendrix students serve as mentors in a local "All-Stars" program that aims to help minority and low-income students with the college application process.

> OPPORTUNITY **Scholarships and Financial Aid**

The availability of academic and extracurricular scholarships as well as federally funded need-based financial aid allows Hendrix to develop personalized financial aid packages, and 100 percent of enrolled students receive some form of achievement-based and/or need-based state, federal, or institutional assistance. The Robert and Ruby Priddy Scholarships are awarded to students from middle-income families who do not qualify for larger merit-based scholarships or federal grants but who show exceptional promise for leadership, service, and success.

> SUCCESS **Office of Multicultural and International Student Services**

The Office of Multicultural and International Student Services (MISS) provides students with opportunities to engage in cross-cultural reflection and promotes appreciation of diversity, service, and leadership. The services that MISS provides range in scope from student programming activities to diversity and leadership training to support. Its Cultural Connection Committee collaborates with student organizations on diversity-related issues and develops an annual outreach plan to enhance the diversity on the Hendrix campus. MISS also promotes cultural heritage immersions through programs, which include hosting speakers and organizing field trips and film screenings.

> SUCCESS **Campus-Wide Retention Initiatives**

All incoming students are assigned a faculty adviser as well as an academic peer mentor who helps them adjust to academic and social life at Hendrix. The Office of Academic Support Services provides services to promote academic success, including peer tutoring in most subjects, one-on-one academic counseling and encouragement, and academic discussion and workshops in areas such as time management and test anxiety.

Hendrix College
1600 Washington Avenue
Conway, AR 72032-3080
Ph: (501) 450-1362
adm@hendrix.edu
www.hendrix.edu

FAST FACTS

STUDENT PROFILE

# of degree-seeking undergraduates	1,456
% male/female	44/56
% African American	3
% American Indian or Alaska Native	1
% Asian or Pacific Islander	3
% Hispanic	4
% White	79
% International	3
% Pell grant recipients	18.6

First-generation and minority alumni Theodore Bunting, Jr., senior vice president and chief accounting officer, Entergy Corporation; the Honorable Linda Pondexter Chesterfield, former president, Arkansas Education Association, and former state representative, Arkansas; Walter Pryor, principal, Podesta Group, and former deputy director and managing attorney, National Association of Attorneys General; T.J. Ticey, vice president of member services, Evangelical Lutheran Church in America Board of Pensions

ACADEMICS

full-time faculty	102
full-time minority faculty	10
student-faculty ratio	13:1
average class size	19
% first-year retention rate	88
% graduation rate (6 years)	66

Popular majors Biochemisty/Molecular Biology, Biology, English, Psychology, and Sociology/Anthropology

CAMPUS LIFE

% live on campus (% fresh.)	86 (99)

Multicultural student clubs and organizations Asian Culture Club, Cultural Connection Committee, Hillel, International Club, Multicultural Development Committee, Students for Black Culture, Students for Latin and Iberian Culture, UNITY
Athletics NCAA Division III, Southern Collegiate Athletic Conference (SCAC)

ADMISSIONS

# of applicants	1,572
% accepted	81
# of first-year students enrolled	412
SAT Critical Reading range	580-700
SAT Math range	560-680
ACT range	27-32
average HS GPA	3.82

Deadlines

decision	rolling to 4/1
application fee (online)	$40 ($0)
fee waived for applicants with financial need	yes

COST & AID

tuition	$31,740
room & board	$9,086
total need-based institutional scholarships/grants	$13,068,520
% of students apply for need-based aid	82
% of students receive aid	100
% receiving need-based scholarship or grant aid	61
% receiving aid whose need was fully met	43
average aid package	$22,104
average student loan debt upon graduation	$17,641

Azusa Pacific University

Azusa Pacific University is a mid-size, private, comprehensive Christian university. The school is located in Azusa, Calif., approximately 30 minutes northeast of Los Angeles. Azusa Pacific's approach to higher education is built on four cornerstones: Christ, Scholarship, Community and Service. This foundation impacts the university's students from the moment they enter the school as freshmen and throughout their lives as Azusa Pacific students, as they remain a close-knit community through the school's alumni association. Azusa Pacific is devoted to its students' Christian worldview and is known for its academic excellence. The university maintains a large Hispanic population and is dedicated to outreach and service in the greater Los Angeles region.

> ACCESS College Headed and Mighty Proud (CHAMP)

The CHAMP Program is a partnership between Azusa Pacific University and the Azusa Unified School District that sends college mentors to local at-risk fourth grade students. APU student mentors encourage young students to seek higher education through the semester-long CHAMP Program. CHAMP students practice filling out college applications, discuss career options and receive a diploma at the end of the program for all their hard work. CHAMP students and their families stay connected to the program through the CHAMP Alumni Association, which provides continued information about higher education.

> OPPORTUNITY Multi-Ethnic Leadership Scholarship

Azusa Pacific's Multi-Ethnic Leadership Scholarship is part of a leadership development program that challenges diverse students to serve as leaders and promote ethnic diversity and multicultural awareness on campus. Twelve students are awarded a renewable $4,500 per year scholarship based on their applications. Students must be active advocates for ethnic diversity, racial reconciliation and multicultural awareness and meet academic and other requirements.

> OPPORTUNITY Connection Preview Day

Each year, prospective college students from urban communities are invited along with their parents to visit the Azusa Pacific campus. Connection Preview Day educates under-served populations in the greater Los Angeles area about Azusa Pacific University and college admissions in general. The all-day event focuses on diversity at Azusa Pacific and promotes the school's inclusive atmosphere.

> SUCCESS Omega Program

The Omega Program is a transition program designed to meet the needs of Azusa Pacific's graduating seniors. Students meet and network with university alumni, receive financial planning information, attend an etiquette dinner and learn about graduate school. The Omega Program aims to meet graduating students' most challenging questions about life after college.

> SUCCESS Office of Multi-Ethnic Programs (MEP)/Multi-Ethnic Student Alliance (MESA)

MEP promotes student development through ethnic organizations (AMIGOS, Black Student Awareness, and the Pacific Islander Organization) and the general values of ethnic diversity. The MEP staff advises the Multi-Ethnic Student Alliance (MESA), a student-led organization. MESA's mission is to "embody Christian values by promoting sensitivity and awareness, while welcoming and celebrating cultural diversity." MESA seeks to be a safe place where students can challenge themselves, build friendships, share each other's culture, and learn to identify with one another.

Azusa Pacific University
901 East Alosta Avenue
Azusa, CA 91702-7000
Ph: (626) 812-3016
admissions@apu.edu
www.apu.edu

FAST FACTS

STUDENT PROFILE
# of degree-seeking undergraduates	4,858
% male/female	36/64
% African American	5
% American Indian or Alaska Native	<1
% Asian or Pacific Islander	8
% Hispanic	15
% White	62
% International	2
% Pell grant recipients	21.2

ACADEMICS
full-time faculty	315
full-time minority faculty	79
student-faculty ratio	13:1
average class size	12-15
% first-year retention rate	82
% graduation rate (6 years)	65

Popular majors Business Administration, Liberal Studies, Nursing

CAMPUS LIFE
% live on campus (% freshmen)	58 (93)

Multicultural student clubs and organizations AMIGOS, Black Men's Fellowship, Black Student Awareness, Chinese Campus Fellowship, Faith and Culture, Hawaiian Club, International Justice Mission, Japanese Christian Fellowship, Pacific Islanders

Athletics NAIA, Golden State Athletic Conference

ADMISSIONS
# of applicants	4,441
% accepted	63
# of first-year students enrolled	1,090
SAT Critical Reading range	490-590
SAT Math range	490-600
SAT Writing range	n/a
ACT range	21-26
average HS GPA	3.63

Deadlines
early action	12/1
regular decision	rolling to 6/1
application fee (online)	$45 ($45)
fee waiver for applicants with financial need	yes

COST & AID
tuition	$25,840
room & board	$7,842
total need-based institutional scholarships/grants	$12,520,053
% of students apply for need-based aid	100
% of students receive aid	99
% receiving need-based scholarship or grant aid	90
% receiving aid whose need was fully met	13
average aid package	$11,874
average student loan debt upon graduation	n/a

California Lutheran University

California Lutheran University
60 West Olsen Road # 1350
Thousand Oaks, CA 91360
Ph: (805) 493-3135
admissions@callutheran.edu
www.callutheran.edu

Founded in 1959, California Lutheran University is a diverse, scholarly, co-educational, private university dedicated to excellence in the liberal arts and professional studies. Rooted in the Lutheran tradition of Christian faith, the university encourages critical inquiry into matters of both faith and reason. California Lutheran University's mission is to educate leaders for a global society who are strong in character and judgment, confident in their identity and vocation and committed to service and justice.

"Through SSS (Student Support Services), SOAR, and events such as the Multicultural Night you learn how much you matter and how you can change the lives of others. CLU shares opportunities in all areas of life. There is nothing you can't do!"
– Rachel M., '10 Liberal Studies

> ACCESS Upward Bound

The Upward Bound program is dedicated to providing quality academic and personal development services to high school students from low-income and/or first-generation families. Beyond increasing the rate at which high school graduates pursue post secondary education, the California Lutheran University Upward Bound program strives to increase participants' competency in English, mathematics, science, social science and foreign language. Participants receive tutoring, counseling and mentoring, as well as the opportunity to attend cultural enrichment events.

> OPPORTUNITY InCLUsive Overnight Scholars Program

The InCLUsive Overnight Scholars Program was established to increase diversity within the student body and to foster a campus climate that encourages inclusive, cross-cultural interaction, respect and appreciation of diversity and global awareness. The program gives admitted high school students the opportunity to visit California Lutheran University. Participants learn what student life is like by staying in a residence hall, making connections with faculty, staff and student leaders, meeting other prospective students and interacting with current students who make California Lutheran University their home. InCLUsive participants have the opportunity to be selected for designated scholarships offered through a special InCLUsive Program essay competition.

> SUCCESS FOCUS Mentoring Program

Freshmen and transfer students from traditionally underrepresented backgrounds are encouraged to sign up for a mentor. New students are assigned a faculty member or administrator to act as their personal mentor during their first year at California Lutheran University. The program provides scheduled activities, but more important are the relationships students form with their mentors.

> SUCCESS Summer Orientation to Academic Resources Program

Incoming first-generation college freshmen are invited to attend this orientation program. The program gives participants an orientation to the college environment and provides them with opportunities to connect with other first-generation students. In addition, the program assists participants in the process of academic exploration by introducing them to relevant resources, challenging them to examine their values and interests and facilitating their transition to California Lutheran University. During the academic year, students participate in the Student Support Services program that offers a holistic range of services including academic counseling and personal support to assist first-generation students to successfully complete their degree.

FAST FACTS

STUDENT PROFILE

# of degree-seeking undergraduates	2,352
% male/female	38/62
% African American	3.6
% American Indian or Alaska Native	.9
% Asian or Pacific Islander	5.5
% Hispanic	16.4
% White	60.8
% International	6.7
% Pell grant recipients	19.9

ACADEMICS

full-time faculty	144
full-time minority faculty	24
student-faculty ratio	15:1
average class size	22
% first-year retention rate	80
% graduation rate (6 years)	63

Popular majors Business Administration, Liberal Studies, Exercise Science, Psychology, Biology

CAMPUS LIFE

% live on campus (% fresh.)	63 (88)

Multicultural student clubs and organizations Asian Club and Friends, Brothers & Sisters United, Latin American Student Organization, United Students of the World, Chinese Students Association

Athletics NCAA Division III, Southern California Intercollegiate Athletic Conference

ADMISSIONS

# of applicants	3,665
% accepted	62
# of first-year students enrolled	464
SAT Critical Reading range	490-580
SAT Math range	510-610
SAT Writing range	490-590
ACT range	20-28
average HS GPA	3.6

Deadlines

early action	11/15
regular decision I	1/5
regular decision II	3/15
application fee (online)	$45 ($25)
fee waiver for applicants with financial need	yes

COST & AID

tuition	$30,750
room & board	$10,580
total need-based institutional scholarships/grants	$17,763,100
% of students apply for need-based aid	88
% of students receive aid	93
% receiving need-based scholarship or grant aid	64
% receiving aid whose need was fully met	13
average aid package	$22,500
average student loan debt upon graduation	$16,000

California State University, Chico

California State University, Chico
400 West First Street
Chico, CA 95929-0722
Ph: (800) 542-4426
info@csuchico.edu
www.csuchico.edu

California State University, Chico ("Chico State"), founded in 1887, is a residential campus located in Northern California. With Little Chico Creek winding through the center of campus, CSU, Chico is known for its beauty. CSU, Chico offers more than 100 undergraduate majors and options, and maintains one of the highest graduation rates in the 23 campus CSU system. Chico is committed to its diversity, students who are the first in their family to attend college and the success of its students. CSU, Chico was recognized as a top 100 school by Hispanic Outlook in Higher Education for the number of Hispanic students who graduate. They have earned marks as high as 99 percent from graduating seniors when asked if they were satisfied with CSU, Chico as a whole.

> OPPORTUNITY MESA Schools Program

The MESA (Mathematics, Engineering, Science Achievement) Schools Program is an academic preparation program of the University of California, working through schools and colleges throughout the state. It is designed to strengthen the academic skills needed for students to pursue mathematics and science based courses of study in college and to provide support for them to go on to careers in technology-based industries. The program seeks to motivate, support, and prepare underrepresented and disadvantaged students in order to increase their number in undergraduate programs at four-year universities with an emphasis in these fields.

> OPPORTUNITY TRIO Upward Bound

Chico's TRIO Upward Bound programs are academic programs which assist a diverse population of motivated low-income and first-generation high school students to achieve their goals of reaching and succeeding in post-secondary education. These programs include Upward Bound Original, Upward Bound for ESL Learners, Upward Bound Math/Science, Student Support Services and Educational Talent Search.

"Choosing a college is scary, but picking Chico State was easy."
– Marques B., '11
Los Angeles, CA
Biology

> SUCCESS Educational Opportunity Program (EOP)

The Educational Opportunity Program office functions as the home base for all EOP students once they have been admitted to the University. EOP students are offered support services designed to assist them in overcoming the many obstacles that a new educational and social environment may present. Services include a computer lab, supplemental instruction, Summer Bridge Program, social activities and student job opportunities.

> SUCCESS Chico Student Success Center (CSSU)

The Chico Student Success Center is a collaborative, student development program with a decade of successful diversity recruitment and retention experiences. The CSSC serves low-income students in an effort to create and support a successful college experience while attending CSU, Chico. CSSC students use the facilities for individual and group projects, an opportunity to be around mentors and academic support, and sometimes simply to be in a comfortable environment that is focused on student achievement.

FAST FACTS

STUDENT PROFILE
# of degree-seeking undergraduates	15,617
% male/female	49/51
% African-American	2
% American Indian or Alaska Native	1
% Asian or Pacific Islander	6
% Hispanic	13
% White	68
% International	3
% Pell grant recipients	34

First-generation and minority alumni Mary J. Kight, '73, adjutant general of the CA National Guard; Lily Roberts '87, Ph.D., head of evaluation, CA Dept. of Education; Nhia Vang, MD '99, family practice physician; Dean N. Williams '85, senior research computer scientist, Lawrence Livermore National Laboratory

ACADEMICS
full-time faculty	501
full-time minority faculty	92
student-faculty ratio	23:1
average class size	27
% first-year retention rate	82
% graduation rate (6 yrs)	55

Popular majors Business, Liberal Studies (teaching), Psychology, Art & Art History, Computer Science and Animation

CAMPUS LIFE
% live on campus (% fresh.)	12 (64)

Multicultural student clubs and organizations American Indian club, Cross-Cultural Leadership Center, Filipino American Student Organization, Hmong Student Association, MEChA, Men of Honor, Multicultural Affairs Council, Multicultural Greek Council, Pacific Islanders Connection, Southeast Asian Student Association

Athletics NCAA Division II, California Collegiate Athletic Association

ADMISSIONS
# of applicants	12,881
% accepted	88
# of first-year students enrolled	2,505
SAT Critical Reading range	450-550
SAT Math range	460-570
SAT Writing range	n/a
ACT range	19-24
average HS GPA	3.12

Deadlines
regular decision	11/30
application fee (online)	$55 ($55)
fee waiver for applicants with financial need	yes

COST & AID
tuition	in-state: $5,336; out-of-state: $16,496
room & board	$9,404
total need-based institutional scholarships/grants	$24,171,640
% of students apply for need-based aid	56
% of those requesting need-based aid who receive aid	n/a
% receiving need-based scholarship/grant aid	58
% receiving aid whose need was fully met	7
average aid package	$13,803
average student loan debt upon graduation	$14,693

California State University, San Bernardino

California State University, San Bernardino is a vital public comprehensive university serving the San Bernardino and Riverside counties of Southern California. Founded in 1965, the university currently enrolls more than 17,000 students and employs more than 2,000 faculty and staff. The university offers more than 70 traditional baccalaureate and master's degree programs and education credential and certificate programs, as well as one of the first doctorate programs in the California State University. Every program that is eligible has earned national accreditation. Cal State San Bernardino's programs in business, public administration, geographic information and decision sciences, psychology, health, kinesiology, English, public administration, accounting and finance, teacher education, computer science and engineering and many others are all highly regarded.

> ACCESS Admissions and Student Recruitment

The Office of Admissions and Student Recruitment is the first point of contact for prospective domestic and international students interested in learning more about the university. The office provides pre-admission counseling sessions, visits to high schools and community colleges, guided campus tours and hosts on-campus events such as Open House and Transfer Day. These events are aimed at prospective high school and community college students considering attending Cal State San Bernardino in the future. Students are invited to get a first-hand look at the campus, meet faculty and staff members, and learn about the university, its programs and financial aid. In addition, students interact with representatives from student clubs and organizations on campus and meet with current students.

> OPPORTUNITY President's Academic Excellence Scholarship (PAES)

San Bernardino County high school students who rank in the top 1 percent of their graduating class are eligible to receive the President's Academic Excellence Scholarship at Cal State San Bernardino. PAES recipients receive an annual $5,000 scholarship to attend the university. The scholarship covers student fees (elsewhere known as tuition) and textbook costs and also provides a small stipend to cover other student expenses. The President's Academic Excellence Scholarship is renewable for up to four academic years — potentially a $20,000 total scholarship — as long as recipients are full-time students and maintain a 3.5 GPA. Nearly 20 percent of those students who were eligible in 2008 selected Cal State San Bernardino.

> SUCCESS SOAR 2 Success

SOAR 2 Success is an event designed to provide academic advising and class registration for first-time freshmen at Cal State San Bernardino. It is a two-phase program that will help first-time freshmen achieve a comfort level as they transition to college. The first phase of the program provides the earliest possible advising and enrollment for all new freshmen who have already been admitted. The second phase is a required two-day overnight orientation program designed to acclimate new students to the day-to-day life of a college student. Information from the departments of financial aid, bursar, housing and residential life is available for parents, along with tours of the campus and residence halls with a special session for Spanish-speaking parents.

> SUCCESS International Center

Cal State San Bernardino's International Center is the primary contact for newly admitted international students, including new immigrant and permanent resident students who are nationals of other countries. Upon arrival, international students are assisted in locating temporary and permanent housing. The center provides an orientation to the community and the campus, including information about academic requirements, immigration requirements, housing, health and support services available to the student. There are also programs and activities designed to help students with personal growth and development. Assistance and referrals are available for academic and personal counseling. The center coordinates the CSU International Programs, the Fulbright programs, and also houses the Phi Beta Delta Honor Society for international scholars. The center works closely with the international clubs and the various nationality organizations in bringing cultural events to campus.

California State University,
  San Bernardino
5500 University Parkway
San Bernadino, CA 92407
Ph: (909) 537-5188
moreinfo@mail.csusb.edu
www.csusb.edu

FAST FACTS

STUDENT PROFILE

# of degree-seeking undergraduates	13,947
% male/female	35/65
% African-American	12
% American Indian or Alaska Native	<1
% Asian or Pacific Islander	8
% Hispanic	39
% White	29
% International	3
% Pell grant recipients	51

ACADEMICS

full-time faculty	471
full-time minority faculty	135
student-faculty ratio	n/a
average class size	20-29
% first-year retention rate	78
% graduation rate (6 years)	41

CAMPUS LIFE

% live on campus (% freshmen)	10 (21)

Multicultural student clubs and organizations
Afrikan Student Alliance, Aikido Club, Association of Latin American Studies, Chinese Students Association, Flags, Golden Key International Honors Society, International Business Association, Japanese Student Association, Korean Student Association, Latino Business Student Association, Latter Day Saints Student Association, LOBOS Salsa Club, MPACT, Muslim Student Association, National Pan-Hellenic Council, Roman Catholic Newman Ministry, Student African American Brotherhood, Students for Justice in Palestine, Student International Knowledge, Taiwanese Student Association, Vietnamese Student Association

Athletics NCAA Division II, California Collegiate Athletic Association

ADMISSIONS

# of applicants	12,834
% accepted	28
# of first-year students enrolled	2,876
SAT Critical Reading range	390-500
SAT Math range	400-510
SAT Writing	370-480
ACT range	16-20
average HS GPA	3.07

Deadlines

priority decision	11/30
regular decision	12/15
application fee (online)	$55
fee waiver for applicants with financial need	yes

COST & AID

tuition	in-state: $3,779; out-of-state: $13,949
room & board	$9,624
total need-based institutional scholarships/grants	$41,351,993
% of students apply for need-based aid	78
% of students receive aid	80
% receiving need-based scholarship or grant aid	50
% receiving aid whose need was fully met	12
average aid package	$8,840
average student loan debt upon graduation	$17,946

Chapman University

CHAPMAN UNIVERSITY

Chapman University was the first private college or university in California to enroll students of all races and socio-economic backgrounds in the early part of the 20th century, a tradition to which the University firmly subscribes today. In addition to traditional need-based financial aid, merit, and talent-based scholarship programs, Chapman has historically offered funding for students who would be the first from their family to attend college in an effort to continue its legacy of enrolling a diverse student population.

> OPPORTUNITY Thurgood Marshall Scholarship

The Thurgood Marshall Scholars program is designated for admitted students who are the first from their immediate family to attend college. Recipients should display strong leadership and community service orientation. Scholarship amounts vary, but average approximately $8,000 annually, and are designed to complement a financial aid/scholarship package by alleviating gaps or loans.

> SUCCESS Human Diversity

As part of its General Education program, Chapman University requires all students to take a course focusing on human diversity and world cultures. Courses are designed to help students to address contemporary and historical issues that affect underrepresented groups, and to understand their implications and consequences.

> SUCCESS InsideTrack

Chapman University has a partnership with InsideTrack, an organization offering life and success coaching free of charge to freshman students in an effort to motivate, inspire and help sharpen time management and organizational skills.

> SUCCESS Center for Academic Success (CAS)

All Chapman students can take advantage of the Center for Academic Success, which oversees academic support programs including general academic advising, peer tutoring, advocacy, study strategies, and services for students with learning differences.

"I helped organize Chapman's inaugural Indian Festival. Through this, I realized the open-mindedness and willingness of Chapman students to integrate and learn about different cultures. After graduation, I plan to start my own non-profit organization helping underprivileged in India. I hope to make a difference by helping people improve their living conditions and health. The biggest thing I take from my Chapman experience is the development of my self-confidence and realization that I can reach high for myself and also help many others along the way."

– Ria S., '10
Mumbai, India
Public Relations

Chapman University
One University Drive
Orange, CA 92866
Ph: (714) 997-6711
admit@chapman.edu
www.chapman.edu

F A S T   F A C T S

STUDENT PROFILE

# of degree-seeking undergraduates	4,264
% male/female	42/58
% African-American	3
% American Indian or Alaska Native	<1
% Asian or Pacific Islander	9
% Hispanic	10
% White	67
% International	2
% Pell grant recipients	36.7

First-generation and minority alumni Emmitt Ashford, legendary Major League Baseball Umpire; Michel Bell, Tony Award nominated star of Broadway's Showboat; John Nuzzo, internationally acclaimed tenor, star of Vienna State Opera; Hon. George L. Argyros, philanthropist and former U.S. Ambassador to Spain; Hon. Loretta Sanchez, member, U.S. House of Representatives

ACADEMICS

full-time faculty	333
full-time minority faculty	48
student-faculty ratio	14:1
average class size	19
% first-year retention rate	86
% graduation rate (6 yrs)	67

Popular majors Film and Television Production, Business and Economics, Music, Theatre, Dance

CAMPUS LIFE

% live on campus (% fresh.)	37 (89)

Multicultural student clubs and organizations Amnesty International, Black Student Union (BSU), Pua I'kena Hawai'i Club, International Culture Club, Nihongo Japanese Club, M.E.Ch.A., Native American Club, South Asian Student Organization, Students for a Free Tibet

Athletics NCAA Division III Independent

ADMISSIONS

# of applicants	8,016
% accepted	40
# of first-year students enrolled	1,055
SAT Critical Reading range	548-666
SAT Math range	561-674
SAT Writing range	559-672
ACT range	25-29
average HS GPA	3.65

Deadlines

early action	11/15
regular decision	1/15
application fee (online)	$60 ($60)
fee waiver for applicants with financial need	yes

COST & AID

tuition	$37,500
room & board	$13,000
total need-based institutional scholarships/grants	$34,857,501
% of students apply for need-based aid	87
% of those requesting need-based aid who receive aid	100
% receiving need-based scholarship/grant aid	57
% receiving aid whose need was fully met	100
average aid package	$24,567
average student loan debt upon graduation	$22,955

Claremont McKenna College

Claremont McKenna College is a small, private liberal arts college located in Claremont, Calif., 35 miles east of Los Angeles. Claremont McKenna is committed to the well-being and success of all of its students, and offers specialized support services through the Asian American Resource Center, the Chicano/ Latino Student Affairs Center, the Office of Black Student Affairs and its many multicultural student organizations and clubs. Claremont McKenna is dedicated to offering an affordable college education —100 percent of students receiving aid have their need fully met and the college does not package students with loans. The college's 10 research institutes provide students with graduate-level research opportunities as they work alongside distinguished faculty members and participate in joint academic programs and cross-registration in courses with the other Claremont Colleges.

> ACCESS **Step Up to Leadership / Kravis Mentoring Program**

The Henry Kravis Leadership Institute sponsors Step Up To Leadership, a program that enables high school students to develop leadership competence and character. Participating students, nominated by their high school principals, engage in daily sessions on topics like communication skills, project planning, cultural diversity training, community service projects and outdoor leadership trips. The Henry Kravis Leadership Institute also sponsors the Kravis Mentoring Program at the college. Through a partnership with a local middle school, seventh graders and college students are brought together to form mutually meaningful relationships. These middle school students receive academic tutoring, encouragement to pursue higher education and personal mentoring from Claremont McKenna students, and partners attend group activities such as field trips and community service projects.

> OPPORTUNITY **Campus Visits**

During the fall, Claremont McKenna College hosts two On Campus Days. During these Saturdays, students can stay overnight on campus, speak with students and professors and get a good feel for what it means to attend Claremont McKenna. Additionally, the college is committed to providing admitted students from disadvantaged backgrounds the opportunity to visit campus.

> SUCCESS **Student Affairs Committees of The Claremont Colleges**

Students from all The Claremont Colleges come together under several joint student groups to support intercultural interests across campuses. Chicano/Latino Student Affairs maintains a strong commitment to the retention and graduation of Chicano/Latino students at The Claremont Colleges and provides support and resources to students and their families. The Office of Black Student Affairs hosts a variety of programs geared toward the success of African-American students on campus, including the Ujima Peer Mentoring Program, which provides mentoring for first year and transfer students of Pan African descent, and the Anansi Academic Advancement Program, which provides tutoring, academic programs and learning style and skills assessments that are particularly tailored for these students.

> SUCCESS **Summer Internship Funding**

Every summer, nearly 85 percent of students complete an internship in an area of interest. Internships are often developed by students themselves, but funding is available from various college sources for international, human rights, political, community service-based and science research-oriented internships. For summer 2009, Claremont McKenna awarded more than $300,000 for internships and student-research initiatives.

Claremont McKenna College
CMC Admission and Financial Aid
890 Columbia Avenue
Claremont, CA 91711-6425
Ph: (909) 621-8088
admission@claremontmckenna.edu
www.claremontmckenna.edu

F A S T   F A C T S

STUDENT PROFILE
# of degree-seeking undergraduates	1,200
% male/female	54/46
% African American	7
% American Indian or Alaska Native	1
% Asian or Pacific Islander	19
% Hispanic	15
% White	51
% International	13
% Pell grant recipients	12

ACADEMICS
full-time faculty	127
full-time minority faculty	24
student-faculty ratio	8:1
average class size	17
% first-year retention rate	97
% graduation rate (6 years)	92

Popular majors Government, Economics, History, Biology, Psychology, International Relations

CAMPUS LIFE
% live on campus (% fresh.) 98 (100)
Multicultural Student Clubs and Organizations Asian Pacific American Mentoring Program, Black Student Affairs, Cultural Affairs Committee, Chicano-Latino Student Affairs, Civitas, Hawaiian Club, International Club, Korean Student Association
Athletics Athletics NCAA Division III, Southern California Intercollegiate Athletic Conference, Western Water Polo Association

ADMISSIONS
# of applicants	4,264
% accepted	17
# of first-year students enrolled	300
SAT Critical Reading range	510-800
SAT Math range	520-800
SAT Writing range	n/a
ACT range	n/a
average HS GPA	n/a

Deadlines
early decision	11/15
regular decision	1/2
application fee (online)	$60 ($60)
fee waiver for applicants with financial need	yes

COST & AID
tuition	$40,230
room & board	$13,000
total need-based institutional scholarships/grants	$17,237,465
% of students apply for need-based aid	54
% of students receive aid	51
% receiving need-based scholarship or grant aid	51
% receiving aid whose need was fully met	100
average aid package	$34,900
average student loan debt upon graduation	$0

Harvey Mudd College

Harvey Mudd College
Office of Admission
301 Platt Boulevard
Claremont, CA 91711
Ph: (909) 621-8011
admission@hmc.edu
www.hmc.edu

Founded in 1955, Harvey Mudd is a private, co-educational institution and one of the premier math, science and engineering colleges in the nation. The college offers a rigorous scientific and technological education, paired with a strong emphasis on collaboration and research. Humanities and social sciences compose a third of the curriculum, as Harvey Mudd College believes that students well-versed in these fields will have a clearer understanding of the impact of their work on society. The faculty is dedicated to teaching undergraduates and mentoring student research.

> ACCESS Future Achievers in Science and Technology (FAST)

A weekend program held annually in the fall for high school seniors from underrepresented backgrounds as part of Harvey Mudd College's On-Campus Day, Future Achievers of Science and Technology includes workshops on selective college admission and financial aid, class visits, research lab tours, academic presentations and other events. Travel expenses, meals, and accommodation on campus are provided. Participants also receive a Harvey Mudd College application fee waiver.

> OPPORTUNITY President's Scholar Program (PSP)

This four-year, full tuition scholarship is designated for students who are first in their families to attend college or are from traditionally underrepresented gender or race backgrounds at Harvey Mudd. President's Scholars have an intellectual curiosity and a willingness to advance the college's diversity efforts and are poised to become future leaders in engineering, science, mathematics and technology. Approximately eight first-year students are accepted into the program annually. In addition to tuition assistance, students have opportunities for summer internships, research fellowships and ongoing academic and professional development support.

> SUCCESS Office of Institutional Diversity

Harvey Mudd works to ensure the promotion of campus-wide diversity while providing support for the academic mission of the college. Staff prepare students to take responsibility for creating an environment where diversity is valued and to engage others in exploring diversity themselves. The office promotes programs and resources designed to foster the College's diversity mission by providing a forum for dialogue, as well as opportunities to celebrate the diverse individuals at Harvey Mudd College.

> SUCCESS Summer Institute (SI)

About 25 to 30 incoming first year students are invited to participate in this program, designed to ensure their academic and personal success, each August. The program runs two and a half weeks prior to Freshman Orientation and targets students who are underrepresented in the fields of science, technology, engineering and mathematics. It includes room and board, and students get an early feel for the campus, classes, professors, workload, lingo, folklore, independence and self-responsibility of Harvey Mudd. Most importantly, program participants develop a long-lasting bond with other students and mentors prior to the commencement of the school year.

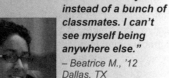

"Coming to Mudd was one of the best decisions I've ever made. Even though it's small, it's really easy to find a place to fit in, and the community starts to feel like an eccentric extended family instead of a bunch of classmates. I can't see myself being anywhere else."
– Beatrice M., '12
Dallas, TX
Computer Science

FAST FACTS

STUDENT PROFILE

# of degree-seeking undergraduates	757
% male/female	64/36
% African American	1
% American Indian or Alaska Native	1
% Asian or Pacific Islander	19
% Hispanic	7
% White	57
% International	3
% Pell grant recipients	13.3

ACADEMICS

full-time faculty	83
full-time minority faculty	24
student-faculty ratio	9:1
average class size	20-30
% first-year retention rate	91
% graduation rate (6 years)	91

Popular majors Engineering, Physics, Mathematics, Computer Science, Chemistry

CAMPUS LIFE

% live on campus (% fresh.)	98 (100)

Multicultural Student Clubs and Organizations Asian Pacific Islander Support Program at Mudd (API SPAM), International Place, National Society of Black Engineers (NSBE), The Society for the Advancement of Latino Scientific Achievement (SALSA), Society of Hispanic Professional Engineers, Students for the Middle Eastern Cultural Promotion (SMECP)

Athletics NCAA Division III, Southern California Intercollegiate Athletic Conference

ADMISSIONS

# of applicants	2,340
% accepted	32
# of first-year students enrolled	208

Middle 50%

SAT Critical Reading	680-770
SAT Math	740-790
SAT Writing	665-750
ACT Average Composite	32-35
average HS GPA	n/a

Deadlines

early decision	11/15
early decision II	1/3
regular decision	1/3
application fee (online)	$60 ($60)
fee waiver for applicants with financial need	yes

COST & AID

tuition	$38,467
room & board	$12,570
total need-based institutional scholarships/grants	$9,108,984
% of students apply for need-based aid	63
% of students receive aid	83
% receiving need-based scholarship or grant aid	52
% receiving aid whose need was fully met	100
average aid package	$30,891
average student loan debt upon graduation	$21,018

Mills College

Nestled on 135 lush acres in the heart of the San Francisco Bay Area, Mills College offers women the opportunity to study and grow in a dynamic environment that embraces diversity, supports intellectual exploration, and prepares students for excellence in their careers and graduate education. Working closely with renowned faculty members and diverse students in intimate, collaborative classes, Mills women think critically, debate intelligently, and ask questions—both inside and outside the classroom. Students can choose from more than 350 course titles and 40 undergraduate majors. Mills is committed to empowering women to overcome social barriers that have excluded them from educational and career opportunities and actively works to extend access to women from diverse backgrounds of every kind. Located in the foothills of Oakland, California, Mills provides a beautiful home with convenient access to the thriving cultural, artistic, social and professional worlds of the San Francisco Bay Area.

 ACCESS Upward Bound

Local high school students who come from low-income families in which neither parent holds a bachelor's degree can benefit from Mills College's Upward Bound, a pre-college program that provides students with the right tools to pursue their dreams of earning a college degree. During the academic year, students benefit from weekly tutoring, field trips and workshops at Mills.

 ACCESS METS Program

The Mills Educational Talent Search Program (METS) reaches out to low-income, first-generation college-bound students aged 11–27. METS academic advisers go out into the community, visiting local schools and offering personalized academic advising and college planning, services for students who plan to re-enter high school or college, educational workshops, campus visits, access to computer labs, and referrals to additional community services.

"I was accepted by Mills and another college, but the strong Mills financial aid package won out. Without the merit and need-based scholarships and work-study aid, I couldn't have gone to college. Now I'm active in the Black Women's Collective and plan to earn my MBA at Mills too."

– Amber W., '10 Suisun, CA Political, Legal, and Economic Analysis

> **OPPORTUNITY Financial Aid**

Ninety-one percent of Mills students receive some portion of their aid directly from the college, with scholarship amounts ranging from $1,000 per year to full tuition. Mills strives to provide financial aid to all students who demonstrate need and offers merit and need-based scholarships specifically for first-generation and minority students.

> **SUCCESS Summer Academic Workshop (SAW)**

For 20 years, Mills has prepared first-generation students and students of color for success in college with the Summer Academic Workshop, an intensive four-week residential program for entering first-year students from disadvantaged communities. Every summer, approximately 20 students live in the Mills residence halls with peer counselors and tutors studying English, math, sociology, and social justice. Participants also learn additional writing, study, and leadership skills. More than 90 percent of women who have completed the SAW program have gone on to graduate from college.

> **SUCCESS Women of Color Resource Center (WCRC)**

The WCRC was founded by Mills students, faculty, and alumnae of color. The center is run by and for women of color and works with the Ethnic Studies Department to provide a community for women of color at Mills and in the wider community. The WCRC is dedicated to the elimination of racism, the development of leadership by young women of color, and the creation of coalitions between women of diverse ethnic origins. Activities include leadership training for young women, coalition building and networking between ethnic groups, sponsorship for academic research, and conferences.

Mills College
5000 MacArthur Blvd
Oakland, CA 94613
Ph: (510) 430-2135
admission@mills.edu
www.mills.edu/undergrad

F A S T   F A C T S

STUDENT PROFILE

# of degree-seeking undergraduates	956
% male/female	0/100
% African American	9
% American Indian or Alaska Native	1
% Asian or Pacific Islander	8
% Hispanic	14
% White	44
% International	3
% Pell grant recipients	43.3

First-generation and minority alumni Barbara Lee, U.S. congresswoman; Thoraya Ahmed Obaid, executive director, United Nations Population Fund, United Nations under-secretary general; Patricia Piñeda, Toyota Motor North America, Inc. group vice president, national philanthropy and the Toyota USA Foundation; Renel Brooks-Moon, voice of the San Francisco Giants, first African-American baseball announcer; Jade Snow Wong, renowned author, ceramicist

ACADEMICS

full-time faculty	96
full-time minority faculty	25
student-faculty ratio	11:1
average class size	16
% first-year retention rate	74
% graduation rate (6 years)	57

Popular majors English; Psychology; Political, Legal, and Economic Analysis (PLEA); Anthropology and Sociology; Biology

CAMPUS LIFE

% live on campus (% fresh.)	56 (96)

Multicultural student clubs and organizations Asian Pacific Islander Sisterhood Alliance, Barakat Foundation, Black Women's Collective, Jewish Student Union, Movimiento Estudiantil Chicano de Aztlan, Mujeres Unidas, Muslim Students Association, Native American Student Alliance, Queer Melanin, South Asian & Middle Eastern Cultural Awareness Organization
Athletics NCAA Division III, California Pacific Conference

ADMISSIONS

# of applicants	1,177
% accepted	66
# of first-year students enrolled	205
SAT Critical Reading range	520-650
SAT Math range	490-590
SAT Writing range	520-620
ACT range	20-27
average HS GPA	3.65

Deadlines

early action	11/15
regular decision	3/1
application fee (online)	$50 ($50)
fee waiver for applicants with financial need	yes

COST & AID

tuition	$35,196
room & board	$11,480
total need-based institutional scholarships/grants	$13,886,475
% of students apply for need-based aid	92
% of students receive aid	100
% receiving need-based scholarship or grant aid	100
% receiving aid whose need was fully met	46
average aid package	$30,184
average student loan debt upon graduation	$24,255

Mount St. Mary's College

Mount St. Mary's College is an independent, Catholic, liberal arts college primarily for women that provides a values-based undergraduate education and innovative programs for professional men and women on two historic campuses in Los Angeles. Founded in 1925 by the Sisters of St. Joseph of Carondelet, Mount St. Mary's College offers a traditional baccalaureate degree program from its Chalon campus and graduate degree programs, the associate in arts program, the education credential program and the Weekend College, which offers a baccalaureate degree program to working adults from its Doheny Campus. At both campuses, the college provides a superior education enhanced by an emphasis on building leadership skills and fostering a spirit to serve others.

> ACCESS Student Ambassador Program

Mount St. Mary's College's Student Ambassador Program motivates high school students to complete high school and aspire to a college education. Through the program, College Student Ambassadors work with high school students, answering questions that pertain to the college application process, preparation for college, college life, and financial aid, and provide assistance to the high school counselors. Each ambassador is assigned to a high school or site and is expected to work on a weekly basis. A key to the effectiveness of the Student Ambassador Program is the aspect of peer counseling and role modeling. Many of the Student Ambassadors come from backgrounds similar to those of the individuals and/or communities they assist — and if possible, the college sends ambassadors back to the high schools from which they graduated.

> OPPORTUNITY Minority Access to Research Careers (MARC)

The biology department at Mount St. Mary's College is a recipient of the National Institutes of Health (NIH) Minority Access to Research Careers undergraduate training grant. This grant supports twelve student research assistant fellowships for juniors and seniors each year. Each student trainee receives a grant to pay for over half of their tuition and a stipend for the work they conduct in the research laboratory. This is an outstanding program that teaches expertise in biomedical research fields, and it allows students to network with researchers across the country.

> SUCCESS Institute for Student Academic Enrichment (ISAE)

Mount St. Mary's College's Institute for Student Academic Enrichment is a federally funded TRIO program under the Department of Education. ISAE participants receive assistance with financial aid applications and in academic, career and life planning and counseling. The institute also offers free tutoring services, and students may sign up for Learning Assistance Programs workshops, take advantage of the laptop loan program and are eligible to participate in the Peer Adviser Program. Peer advisers help ISAE students acclimate to college life, including monitoring the need for academic support and educate them about campus and ISAE services and activities.

Mount St. Mary's College
Office of Admissions
12001 Chalon Road
Los Angeles, CA 90049
Ph: (800) 999-9893 / (310) 954-4000
admissions@msmc.la.edu
www.msmc.la.edu

FAST FACTS

STUDENT PROFILE
# of degree-seeking undergraduates	1,883
% male/female	5/95
% African-American	8.7
% American Indian or Alaska Native	<1
% Asian or Pacific Islander	22.2
% Hispanic	45.9
% White	12.9
% International	<1
% Pell grant recipients	18

ACADEMICS
full-time faculty	84
full-time minority faculty	n/a
student-faculty ratio	13:1
average class size	18
% first-year retention rate	85
% graduation rate (6 years)	67

Popular majors Biology/Biological Sciences, Liberal Arts and Sciences/Liberal Studies, Nursing

CAMPUS LIFE
% live on campus (% freshmen)	51 (76)

Multicultural student clubs and organizations African American Council of Women, Latinas Unidas, Le Club Français, Na Pua O Ka 'Aina (Hawaiian club), Pangkat Pilipino, Vietnamese Student Association

Athletics No varsity athletics; intramurals

ADMISSIONS
# of applicants	992
% accepted	84
# of first-year students enrolled	n/a
SAT Critical Reading range	470-560
SAT Math range	450-550
SAT Writing	470-560
ACT range	19-23
average HS GPA	3.47

Deadlines
regular decision	2/15
application fee (online)	$40 (reduced)
fee waiver for applicants with financial need	yes

COST & AID
tuition	$27,840
room & board	$9,820
total need-based institutional scholarships/grants	n/a
% of students apply for need-based aid	63.1
% of students receive aid	60.6
% receiving need-based scholarship or grant aid	n/a
% receiving aid whose need was fully met	n/a
average aid package	$18,171
average student loan debt upon graduation	$28,156

Notre Dame de Namur University

Commitment to diversity is just one of the many features of Notre Dame de Namur, a private, catholic-affiliated, co-educational university. Founded in 1851, the university also offers students an intimate learning experience — fewer than 1,000 undergraduates attend, enabling students to meet their classmates, know faculty members and form lasting relationships easily, and smaller

classes give more personal attention. Notre Dame de Namur is located in the pristine community of Belmont, Calif., located between San Francisco (30 minutes to the north) and San Jose, and close to major highways and transportation as well as the ocean and mountains. The university is made up of three schools, the College of Arts and Sciences, School of Business and Management and School of Education and Leadership, and there are more than 20 student organizations reflecting academic, cultural, professional, social and service groups, as well as athletics and a lively arts and entertainment scene.

> OPPORTUNITY Grant Programs

Full-time Notre Dame de Namur students may qualify for school grants, which range in value from $500 to $17,000. The university has also recently announced that it will match students' Cal Grants, which come from the state of California and are valued around $9,700 for the 2009-2010 school year. Also, students who intend to teach and have a GPA of 3.25 or higher can qualify for federal TEACH grants, which revert to loans if recipients fail to fulfill career requirements.

> OPPORTUNITY Merit Scholarships

Students with significant academic and extra-curricular achievements may qualify for the Belmont, Presidential and Provost scholarships, all of which are merit-based. These awards, which range in value from $2,500 to $24,000 yearly, are renewable provided recipients uphold themselves to Notre Dame de Namur's academic standards.

> SUCCESS Center for Spirituality and Social Change

Under the auspices of the Center for Spirituality and Social Change, Notre Dame de Namur offers a number of opportunities for service, including a Learn and Serve grant program for students interested in community service, a resource center for community service and community-based learning and immersion programs in community service and social justice.

> SUCCESS Office of Mission and Diversity

Responsible for working with all constituencies of Notre Dame de Namur to strengthen and deepen the university's commitment to diversity, social justice and global peace, the Office of Mission and Diversity oversees a number of studies and programs designed to understand and address issues of diversity. Under the guidance of this office, an anti-racism team called Seeking Transformation toward Anti-Racist Systems (STARS) was formed, made up of people from across the campus and wider communities.

> SUCCESS Academic Success Center

The Academic Success Center is a major resource for first-generation students. Its staff members work to help students become independent and effective learners by offering them individualized assessments of their learning strengths and then recommending learning strategies based on those strengths. Highly trained faculty, staff and tutors in the facility's Tutorial Center assist students in their learning and offer study skills workshops and courses.

> SUCCESS Writing Center

The Writing Center is also a resource frequently used by first-generation students, helping them to develop as writers by focusing on the writing process: brainstorming, clustering, outlining, free-writing, editing and revising. The center offers individual tutoring in grammar, research and essay organization and revision.

Notre Dame de Namur University
1500 Ralston Ave.
Belmont, CA 94002
Ph: (650) 508-3600
admiss@ndnu.edu
www.ndnu.edu

FAST FACTS

STUDENT PROFILE
# of degree-seeking undergraduates	801
% male/female	34/66
% African-American	8
% American Indian or Alaska Native	<1
% Asian or Pacific Islander	14.5
% Hispanic	24.6
% White	31.8
% International	2.3
% Pell grant recipients	32

ACADEMICS
full-time faculty	54
full-time minority faculty	14
student-faculty ratio	11:1
average class size	14
% first-year retention rate	71
% graduation rate (6 years)	56

Popular majors Business Administration, Human Services, Psychology, Biology, Liberal Studies

CAMPUS LIFE
% live on campus (% fresh.)	92

Multicultural student clubs and organizations Black Student Union, Hawaiian Club, International Club, Isang Lahi Club, Latinos Unidos
Athletics NCAA Division II, Pacific West Conference

ADMISSIONS
# of applicants	998
% accepted	79
# of first-year students enrolled	116
SAT Critical Reading range	390-520
SAT Math range	400-510
SAT Writing range	410-510
ACT range	16-21
average HS GPA	2.85

Deadlines
regular decision	rolling
application fee (online)	$50 ($50)
fee waiver for applicants with financial need	yes

COST & AID
tuition	$26,830
room & board	$11,210
total need-based institutional scholarships/grants	$5,285,866
% of students apply for need-based aid	79
% of students receive aid	95
% receiving need-based scholarship or grant aid	74
% receiving aid whose need was fully met	10
average aid package	$24,693
average student loan debt upon graduation	$23,877

Occidental College

Founded in 1887, Occidental College (a.k.a. Oxy) is one of the oldest liberal arts colleges in the West and one of few liberal arts colleges located in an urban area. Its beautiful green campus, designed by celebrated architect Myron Hunt, is nestled 10 minutes north of downtown in the Eagle Rock neighborhood of Los Angeles. Within this scenic setting thrives a long tradition of academic rigor and community action. Over 15 percent of students are first-generation, and many choose Occidental because of its rich history, dedication to diversity, and culture of collaborative, hands-on learning.

> ## OPPORTUNITY **Multicultural Visit Program (MVP)**

Each fall, Occidental College's Admission staff selects and brings to campus a group of 40 outstanding high school seniors of underrepresented backgrounds for a 2-day visit at no cost to them or their families. While on campus, MVP students stay overnight in a residence hall, participate in classes, interact with current students and professors, attend information sessions on admissions and financial aid, and interview with an admission officer. The purpose of the fall program is to enable MVP students to fully explore Oxy as a college option and to encourage them to apply for admission. Interested high school seniors can request MVP application materials from Occidental's Office of Admission in the month of August. The MVP is also offered in the spring to all underrepresented students who have been admitted, but have not had a previous opportunity to visit campus on their own.

> ## OPPORTUNITY **Need-Based Scholarships**

While there are no scholarships specifically geared towards minority populations and first-generation students, Occidental College is committed to meeting the full demonstrated need of all enrolled students. While a portion of need is met with loans and work programs, need-based scholarships meet the majority of need for most students. These scholarships differ from merit awards, as they are not linked to academic promise, but rather to an individual family's financial situation.

> ## SUCCESS **The Multicultural Summer Institute (MSI)**

Occidental College chooses 50 admitted students each year to participate in a co-curricular program called the Multicultural Summer Institute. A four-week summer program taking place before students begin their first year at Occidental, the institute prepares students for their academic career by acquainting them with the campus experience. In preparing participants for college life, students participate in academic courses, community service, diversity training and other programs.

> ## SUCCESS **Intercultural Community Center**

The Intercultural Community Center is the co-curricular resource for diversity education and social justice programming. The center fosters an inclusive, democratic community, so that socially responsible and diverse leaders can improve both leadership and communication skills. The center collaborates with student organizations, academic departments, residence halls and members of the surrounding community to sponsor programs that examine, celebrate and appreciate identity, pluralism and democracy.

"Oxy's scenery and students are what distinguish it from any other institution. Oxy has a very welcoming campus. It has so much energy and the students are passionate about what they're doing and what their classmates are doing. Everybody is really supportive of one another. It is academically challenging while, at the same time, students have time for social activities and interactions. The curriculum is less about memorization and more about understanding material and applying it to your life. Oxy nurtures well-balanced people."
– Yelka K., '12
Jackson Heights, NY
Diplomacy, World Affairs

Occidental College
1600 Campus Road
Los Angeles, CA 90041
Ph: (323) 259-2700
admission@oxy.edu
www.oxy.edu

F A S T   F A C T S

STUDENT PROFILE
# of degree-seeking undergraduates	1,989
% male/female	44/56
% African American	6
% American Indian or Alaska Native	1
% Caucasian	57
% Asian or Pacific Islander	16
% Hispani	13
% Pell grant recipients	19

First generation and minority alumni Barack Obama '83, President of the United States; Roger Guenveur Smith '81, Actor, Writer, and Director; Sammy Lee '43, Doctor and 2-time Olympic Gold Medalist in Diving

ACADEMICS
full-time faculty	163
full-time minority faculty	n/a
student-faculty ratio	10:1
average class size	15
% first-year retention rate	91
% graduation rate (6 years)	86

Popular majors Diplomacy & World Affairs (DWA), Economics, English & Comparative Literary Studies (ECLS), Politics, Psychology

CAMPUS LIFE
% live on campus (% fresh.)	80 (100)

Multicultural student clubs and organizations Asian Pacific Islander Association, Black Student Alliance, First Nations, MEChA/ALAS, Oxy PAUS (Promoting Achievement in Underrepresented Students), Pilipino United Students Organization, Queer Straight Alliance, Rebirth: Students Rebuilding New Orleans, Sista Talk, White Students Against White Supremacy

Athletics NNCAA Division III, Southern California Intercollegiate Athletic Conference

ADMISSIONS
# of applicants	6,013
% accepted	43
# of first-year students enrolled	541
first-year retention rate	94
SAT Critical Reading median	650
SAT Math median	650
SAT Writing median	660
ACT median	30
average HS GPA	3.6

Deadlines
early decision	11/15
regular decision	1/10
application fee (online)	$60 ($60)
fee waiver for applicants with financial need	yes

COST & AID
tuition	$39,870
room & board	$11,360
% students receiving assistance	78
% receiving need-based institutional scholarships/grants	n/a
% of students apply for need-based aid	60
% of students receive aid	53
% receiving need-based scholarship or grant aid	50
% receiving aid whose need was fully met	100
average aid package	$29,180
average student loan debt upon graduation	$17,561

Pitzer College

Pitzer College, one of seven schools in the Claremont Colleges consortium, is ranked as the fifth most diverse, private, co-educational, liberal arts college in the top tier. Its graduates and alumni consistently achieve recognition for their academic accomplishments: 14 graduates of the 2006 class and four alums received Fulbright scholarships in 2006-2007 alone. Pitzer stresses an interdisciplinary approach to coursework, and, unlike in many other schools, Pitzer favors educational objectives that guide students in making registration choices rather than traditional requirements. Pitzer has the distinction of having one of the highest participation rates of study abroad programs in the nation. Indicative of the college's dedication to social responsibility, Pitzer houses the Center for California Cultural and Social Issues, which supports research and education that contributes to the understanding of critical community issues and enhances the resources of community organizations.

> **ACCESS Claremont College Scholars Program (CCSP)**

First-generation and minority high school juniors from selected Los Angeles and Inland Empire schools are eligible to participate in this program. Students attend workshops designed to educate them on the unique opportunities offered by a small, liberal arts and sciences college experience, and to answer questions regarding the admission and financial aid process.

> **ACCESS Targeted Admissions Partnership**

The admissions staff visits California high schools with particularly high rates of minority student enrollment. The staff also collaborates with a significant number of community agencies (such as The Fulfillment Fund, Bright Prospect, Cristo Rey Schools, Hispanic Scholarship Fund, College Match, One Voice, Young Scholars and AVID) that assist first-generation and underrepresented students who are considering applying to college.

> **OPPORTUNITY Diversity Program**

In encouraging minority students to visit, apply, and enroll at the college, Pitzer invites approximately 50 high school seniors from these backgrounds for a three-day paid visit during the fall and spring semesters. The fall program is for prospective applicants and the spring program is for admitted students. During each program, students stay with an overnight host in a residence hall, attend classes and meet members of the Pitzer community, admission and financial aid staff. The fall program helps prospective applicants learn about the selection process and how to apply for financial aid. In the spring, an emphasis is placed on learning more about student life. During both programs, participants may also interview with an admissions officer or representative.

> **SUCCESS Student Affairs Committee of the Claremont Colleges**

Students from all Claremont Colleges come together under several joint student groups to support inter-cultural interests across campuses. The Chicano/Latino Student Affairs Center maintains a strong commitment to the retention and graduation of Chicano/Latino students and provides support and resources to students and their families. The Office of Black Student Affairs hosts a variety of programs geared toward the success of African-American students on campus, including the Ujima Peer Mentoring Program and the Anansi Academic Advancement Program, which provide mentoring, tutoring, academic programs and learning style and skills assessments. The Center for Asian Pacific American Students (CAPAS) serves as an advocate for the Asian and Pacific Islander community and promotes an educational dialogue that embraces the unique experiences of ethnic communities, the cultural fabric of the institution.

Pitzer College
1050 North Mills Avenue
Claremont, CA 91711
Ph: (909) 621-8000
admission@pitzer.edu
www.pitzer.edu

F A S T   F A C T S

STUDENT PROFILE
# of degree-seeking undergraduates	911
% male/female	42/58
% African-American	6
% American Indian or Alaska Native	<1
% Asian or Pacific Islander	9
% Hispanic	15
% Pell grant recipients	14

First-generation and minority alumni Fabian Nuñez, speaker, California State Assembly; Debra W. Yang, former U.S. Attorney

ACADEMICS
full-time faculty	68
full-time minority faculty	12
student-faculty ratio	12:1
average class size	13
% first-year retention rate	92
% graduation rate (6 years)	70

Popular majors Psychology, English & World Literature, Sociology

CAMPUS LIFE
% live on campus (% freshmen)	73 (97)

Multicultural student clubs and organizations Center for Asian Pacific American Students, Chicano/Latino Student Affairs Center, Office of Black Student Affairs, Black Student Union, Latino Student Union, Center for California Cultural and Social Issues, Community-Based Spanish Program, Jumpstart

Athletics NCAA Division III, Southern California Intercollegiate Athletic Conference

ADMISSIONS
# of applicants	4,031
% accepted	22
# of first-year students enrolled	264
SAT Critical Reading range	570-680
SAT Math range	550-650
SAT Writing range	n/a
ACT range	n/a
average HS GPA	3.7

Deadlines
early decision	11/15
regular decision	1/1
application fee (online)	$50 ($50)
fee waiver for applicants with financial need	yes

COST & AID
tuition	$39,332
room & board	$11,438
total need-based institutional scholarships/grants	$8,892,382
% of students apply for need-based aid	44
% of students receive aid	37
% receiving need-based scholarship or grant aid	98
% receiving aid whose need was fully met	100
average aid package	$33,940
average student loan debt upon graduation	$21,044

Pomona College

Pomona College
333 N. College Way
Claremont, CA 91711
Ph: (909) 621-8000
admissions@pomona.edu
www.pomona.edu

The founding member of the seven schools in the Claremont University Consortium, Pomona College is considered among the most prestigious liberal arts colleges in the country. Pomona prides itself in its small classes and in its comprehensive liberal arts curriculum, which begins with a freshman seminar designed to help students develop critical thinking, analysis, and writing skills. The college is in close proximity to Los Angeles, as well as to famous beaches and ski resorts.

"In every class I've taken, professors have always taken the time if you need help. Whether it was on a weekend, lunch, by e-mail, phone, they're there."
– Carlos A., '09 Southgate, CA Neuroscience

> ACCESS **Pomona Partners**

Pomona Partners is a Friday afternoon program in which Pomona College students serve as activities coordinators at Fremont Middle School in South Pomona, and at times at Garey High School. On a typical Friday, 15 Pomona students will be at Fremont leading students in college-planning activities, workshops, arts related sessions, understanding current events, fieldtrips, etc.

> ACCESS **Pomona Academy for Youth Success (PAYS)**

The Pomona College Academy for Youth Success (PAYS) is an intensive 4-week academic program that serves rising sophomores through rising seniors from groups traditionally under-represented in higher education-students who are first in their family to attend college, those from low income families and those who are African American or Latina/o. The program enrolls up to 90 participants from the Los Angeles area and the Inland Valley. PAYS participants live in Pomona's residence halls from Sunday night thru Friday evening.

> OPPORTUNITY **Student Affairs Committees of The Claremont Colleges**

Students from all Claremont Colleges come together under several joint student groups to support intercultural interests across campuses. Chicano/Latino Student Affairs maintains a strong commitment to the retention and graduation of Chicano/Latino students at the Claremont Colleges and provides support and resources to students and their families while the Office of Black Student Affairs hosts a variety of programs geared toward the success of African-American students on campus.

> SUCCESS **Asian American Resource Center (AARC)**

The Asian American Resource Center helps Asian Pacific American students develop academically and personally. Central to all programs is the value of developing leadership skills among APA students. Working in conjunction with the Intercollegiate Department of Asian American Studies, the AARC raises awareness of issues affecting Asian Americans and Pacific Islanders.

> SUCCESS **Office of Black Student Affairs (OBSA)**

The Office of Black Student Affairs addresses the educational needs of students of African descent through its cultural programs and academic services. The Office seeks to create a supportive environment for students pursuing their undergraduate and graduate degrees and to help students develop emotional autonomy, a positive ethnic identity, and an education and career path. Programs and services are open to all students of The Claremont Colleges.

FAST FACTS

STUDENT PROFILE

# of degree-seeking undergraduates	1,550
% male/female	50/50
% African-American	9
% American Indian or Alaska Native	>1
% Asian or Pacific Islander	14
% Hispanic	11
% White	45.3
% International	4
% Race/ ethnicity unknown	15.5

First-generation and minority alumni George Wolfe, Tony Award-winner, actor, director, producer at The Public Theater; Cruz Reynoso, former justice, California Supreme Court; Merlie Evers-Williams, civil rights leader; John Payton, president, NAACP Legal Defense Fund; Maria Luz Garcia, Ford Foundation Pre-Doctoral Fellowship for Minorities recipient; Cuc Vu, director of the national immigration program, Service Employees International Union

ACADEMICS

full-time faculty	178
full-time minority faculty	46
student-faculty ratio	8:1
average class size	15
% first-year retention rate	97
% graduation rate (6 years)	95

Popular majors Economics, Politics, Media Studies, Molecular Biology, English

CAMPUS LIFE

% live on campus (% freshmen)	98 (100)

Multicultural student clubs and organizations Asian Pacific Islander Awareness Committee, Asian American Students Association, Chinese Student Association, Hui Laule'a, International Club, International/Intercultural Association, Korean Students Association, Movimiento Estudiantil Chicano de Aztlan (MEChA), Pan-African Students Association, Unidos, Vietnamese American Student Association, World Youth Network

Athletics NCAA Division III, Southern California Intercollegiate Athletic Conference

ADMISSIONS (FALL 2009)

# of applicants	6,150
% accepted	15.5
# of first-year students enrolled	390

Middle 50%:

SAT Critical Reading range	710-780
SAT Math range	690-770
SAT Writing range	690-770
ACT range	31-34
average HS GPA	n/a

Deadlines

early decision	11/15
regular decision	1/2
application fee (online)	$65($65)
fee waiver for applicants with financial need	yes

COST & AID

tuition	$38,087
room & board	$12,936
total need-based institutional scholarships/ grants	$29,020,589
% of students apply for need-based aid	66
% of students receive aid	54
% receiving need-based scholarship or grant aid	100
% receiving aid whose need was fully met	100
average aid package	$35,976
average student loan debt upon graduation	$0*

*Pomona has replaced loans with grants in their financial aid packages

Saint Mary's College of California

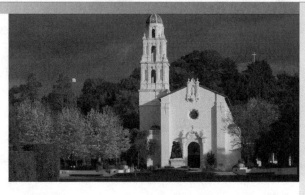

Rooted in the tradition of Saint John Baptist de la Salle, founder of the Christian Brothers and the patron saint of teachers, Saint Mary's College of California is a private liberal arts institution situated in the rolling hills of the Moraga Valley, 20 miles east of San Francisco. Now in its second century of providing education in the liberal arts, the sciences, business administration and economics, Saint Mary's is one of the oldest colleges in the West. At Saint Mary's, students are encouraged to embrace complexity, contemplate their place and purpose in the world and undertake a searching examination of self, spirit and society.

> OPPORTUNITY **High Potential Program**

The High Potential Program at Saint Mary's College has been dedicated to provide support services for first-generation, college bound students for the past 32 years. The program is geared toward students who have overcome social, economic, educational and personal factors due to racial and/or socio-economic background. The program is designed to support students who may have average high school performance as indicated by overall academic GPA, college prep course work and SAT or ACT scores, but have the potential to succeed at Saint Mary's College. The High Potential experience begins in the summer before the start of the student's freshman year at Saint Mary's College. Students in the program learn essential college success skills and are paired with a mentor for extra guidance and support.

> SUCCESS **The Office of Black Student Programs**

Founded in 1972, the Office of Black Student Programs recognizes distinct African and African-American descended cultures and identities in the college community. The office fosters a supportive environment for academic and personal development through peer mentoring, comprehensive academic assessment and planning for field of study and post-baccalaureate degrees. Ongoing activities and services include orientation, opportunities for intercultural learning, and intellectual and social development activities.

> SUCCESS **The Office of Latino Student Programs**

The Office of Latino Student Programs develops and implements programs and services designed to make college a culturally relevant experience for Latino students. Services include academic advising, referrals to on-campus resources and bilingual (English/Spanish) information to students and their families. In collaboration with the Latino student organizations, the office also supports celebrations for traditional Latino holidays.

> SUCCESS **The Foundation Generation**

Students who are the first in their families to attend college in the United States are valued members of the Saint Mary's community. First-generation students make up approximately 40 percent of the incoming class of 2009 at the college. The Foundation Generation helps to support this community of students by organizing a Foundation Generation Conference, holding classes and providing avenues of communication for first generation students. Additionally, Saint Mary's created The Foundation Generation Web site, which chronicles first-generation students' challenges and success in college, as well as their family history. Each individual research project was developed and collected in an academically rigorous way and complied into a shared collection to honor the legacy of the Foundation Generation as they pave the way for future generations of college students.

"The Saint Mary's College High Potential Program offered great insight to the college and the academic expectations of the school. I was able to meet fellow classmates and faculty members during our three week academic boot camp prior to the school year starting. This was advantageous as it gave me a familiarity with the campus before the rest of the school arrived. Having this program made my transition to college easier and prepared me for all the academic work and social aspects of Saint Mary's College."
– Jacqueline G., '11
Madera, CA

Saint Mary's College of California
PO Box 4800
Moraga, CA 94575-4800
Ph: (800) 800-4SMC / (925) 631-4224
smcadmit@stmarys-ca.edu
www.smcadmit.com

FAST FACTS

STUDENT PROFILE
# of degree-seeking undergraduates	2,539
% male/female	35/65
% African American	7
% American Indian	1
% Asian	11
% Caucasian	48
% Hispanic	20
% Pell grant recipients	25

First-generation and minority alumni Joseph Alioto, former mayor, San Francisco; Laura Garcia Cannon, news anchor, NBC-11; Shirley Griffin, executive vice president, Wells Fargo Bank; James Guyette, president and CEO, Rolls-Royce of North America, Inc; Jack Henning, California labor leader; John Henry Johnson, Pro Football Hall of Fame; Tom Lyons, activist, Catholic Relief Services; John Macken, scientist and inventor with numerous patents; Dr. Carl Wu, distinguished cancer researcher, National Institutes of Health

ACADEMICS
full-time faculty	202
student-faculty ratio	12:1
average class size	20
% first-year retention rate	82
% graduation rate (6 years)	68

Popular majors Business, Communication, Liberal & Civic Studies/Integral, Psychology

CAMPUS LIFE
% live on campus (% freshmen)	85 (97)

Multicultural student clubs and organizations Asian-Pacific American Association, Black Student Union, HAPA Club, Gay-Straight Alliance, Japanese-Pop Culture Club, Latin-American Student Association, Pulses Step Team

Athletics NCAA Division I, West Coast Conference

ADMISSIONS
# of applicants	3,241
% accepted	78
# of first-year students enrolled	572
SAT Critical Reading range	490-590
SAT Math range	490-600
ACT range	n/a
average HS GPA	3.4

Deadlines
early action	11/15
regular decision	2/1
application fee	$55
fee waiver for applicants with financial need	yes

COST & AID
tuition	$33,760
room & board	$11,940
% of students receiving aid	73
% receiving need-based scholarship or grant aid	57
average aid package	$29,750
average federal loan indebt upon graduating seniors	$18,140

Santa Clara University

As a Jesuit, Catholic university, Santa Clara seeks to provide students with both a strong academic experience, and one that underscores the importance of ethics and justice. To this end, the University offers a myriad of service opportunities for students through the Santa Clara Community Action Program, a clearinghouse for service endeavors and other student programs. The University also houses the Arrupe Center, which serves the marginalized and poor, and the Markkula Center for Applied Ethics, which is one of the most prominent forums for discussion and research on the topic of ethics nationwide. The Center for Science, Technology and Society also promotes the common good of society by providing an independent forum for public dialogue and interdisciplinary inquiry into the social and cultural dimensions of technological change in today's society.

"Santa Clara showed me a world without limitations, where minority student success is possible and necessary to create a promising future. When one minority student succeeds, the dreams and aspirations of a family, and of a community, are fulfilled."

– Claudia F., '12
San Jose, CA
Public Health, Individual Studies

> ACCESS Future Teachers Program (FTP)

SCU's Future Teachers Program is a long-term effort designed to recruit and retain students throughout the San Francisco Bay Area who want to teach in urban and underserved communities. FTP aims to provide students with the skills needed to effectively pursue their teaching career in urban and underserved settings. Each year, six students from urban or underserved schools throughout the Bay Area are selected for the FTP Scholarship. Students receive awards for four years of undergraduate study and a fifth-year teaching credential at SCU. This scholarship must be coordinated with any other financial aid awarded, including state or federal aid. If the student demonstrates financial need, a selected student will receive an award varied in amounts. Potential candidates are generally identified by the FTP during their junior or senior years of high school.

> OPPORTUNITY Hurtado Scholars Program

The Hurtado Scholars Program provides scholarships for Santa Clara University students who have extraordinary life circumstances and needs. The Hurtado Scholars Program enables select students to attend Santa Clara University and gain valuable study, community, and research experiences as students on campus. They may interact with the Office for Multicultural Learning and other departments, colleges, centers and community organizations. This is a very competitive scholarship and is granted on a yearly basis depending on funds donated to the pool. On average, three to four scholarships are available each year.

> SUCCESS LEAD Scholars Program / First-Generation Orientation

The Leadership Excellence and Academic Development Scholars Program assists first-generation college students and their families in the student's journey at SCU. Participation in the program is by invitation only. Students are selected based on their being awarded a grant or scholarship by SCU and the distinction of being among the first members of their families to attend college. The LEAD Scholars Program is among those administered by the University Honors Program, and offers a variety of opportunities and services that promote success in a student's educational pursuits. The LEAD Scholars Program is a community of peers and faculty committed to scholarship, community engagement, and service. The program begins in the freshman year to ensure a student's smooth transition from high school to college, and it lasts through the senior year by connecting students with internships, graduate school preparation, and leadership opportunities.

Santa Clara University
500 El Camino Real
Santa Clara, CA 95053
Ph: (408) 554-4000
admissions@scu.edu
www.scu.edu

F A S T   F A C T S

STUDENT PROFILE (as of Sept. 2009)
# of degree-seeking undergraduates	5,200
% male/female	47/53
% African American	5
% Asian	15
% Native American	0.3
% Hawaiian/Other Pacific Islander	0.5
% Hispanic/Latino	15
% Caucasian	38
% Multiethnic	9
% International	3
% Pell grant recipients	16

First-generation and minority alumni Reza Aslan '95, writer, scholar, CBS analyst, NPR commentator; Khaled Hosseini '88, author, *The Kite Runner*, *A Thousand Splendid Suns*; Randy Winn '96, outfielder, San Francisco Giants; Noelle Lopez '09, Rhodes Scholar

ACADEMICS
full-time faculty	449
full-time minority faculty	82
student-faculty ratio	13:1
average class size	25
% first-year retention rate	93
% graduation rate (6 years)	85

Popular majors Biology, Communications and Media Studies, Engineering, Finance, Psychology

CAMPUS LIFE
% live on campus (% freshmen)	48 (95)

Multicultural student clubs and organizations Arab Cultural Society, Asian-Pacific Islander Student Union, Association of South East Asian Students, Barkada, Chicanos & Latinos in Engineering & Sciences, Chinese Student Association, Igwebuike, Intandesh, Iranian Student Organization, Japanese Student Association, Ka Mana'o O Hawaii, Latino Business Student Association, Vietnamese Student Association

Athletics NCAA Division I, West Coast

ADMISSIONS (Class of 2013)
# of applicants	10,226
% accepted	59
# of first-year students enrolled	1,085
SAT Critical Reading (mean)	624
SAT Math (mean)	643
ACT (mean)	28
average HS GPA (unweighted)	3.63

Deadlines
early action	11/1
regular decision	1/7
application fee	$55
fee waiver for applicants with financial need	yes

COST & AID
tuition	$37,368
room & board	$11,742
total need-based institutional scholarships/grants	$25,759,344
% of students apply for need-based aid	59
% of students receive aid	78
% receiving need-based scholarship or grant aid	67
% receiving aid whose need was fully met	80
average aid package	$23,859
average student loan debt upon graduation	$23,909

Soka University of America

Soka University of America provides students with an international and personalized college experience. Founded as part of the Soka schools of the Soka Gakkai International, an educational society that is among the world's largest lay Buddhist organizations, Soka which means "to create value," has established a tradition of humanistic scholarship and growth. The University offers study abroad for all students with expenses built into the tuition, and the campus serves international and U.S. students alike. A recently implemented program will waive tuition for admitted B.A. students whose family's annual income is $60,000 or less.

> **ACCESS Advance Via Individual Determination (AVID) tours**

Special tours are arranged for Advance Via Individual Determination classes, which serve secondary students who will often be the first in their families to attend college and who hope to realize their academic potential. These students have opportunities to talk to college admission counselors during these tours at Soka University of America.

> **ACCESS Soka Club Outreach**

Soka University of America has over 35 clubs devoted to arts, dance, music, sports and community outreach. Club members visit local elementary, middle and high schools to share international cultures and to discuss the college experience.

> **OPPORTUNITY Free Tuition Policy**

Students admitted into the liberal arts program at Soka University of America do not have to pay tuition if their family's annual income is $60,000 or less and if they have neither graduated from college nor completed more than 3/4 of their required coursework towards their first undergraduate degree at the time of application to the University. Soka is one of the few private schools in California able to offer this opportunity to both American and international students.

"I will be the first in my family to graduate from a university in the United States. I chose Soka University due to its captivating mission. I always knew I wanted to create a peaceful change for the world. At Soka I have learned about the many contributions I can offer and have met students that share a common goal."

*– Astrid D., '11
San Diego, CA
Liberal Arts,
concentrating in
International Studies*

> **OPPORTUNITY First-Generation and Minority Scholarships**

Various other scholarships are available to first-generation and minority students who do not qualify for free tuition. These include the Hispanic Educational Endowment Fund, which offers two scholarships of $1,500 to first-generation Latino students from Orange County, and one Makiguchi Scholarship to an international applicant who has graduated from high school in an African Nation.

> **SUCCESS Opportunities for Multicultural Study**

Fifty percent of Soka University of America's students are international, hailing from more than 40 countries. All undergraduate students study a non-native language and every student participates in a semester abroad during his or her junior year. In addition to its undergraduate concentrations in environmental studies, humanities, international studies and social and behavioral sciences, Soka also offers a master's program in second and foreign language education.

Soka University of America
1 University Drive
Aliso Viejo, CA 92656
Ph: (949) 480-4150
admission@soka.edu
www.soka.edu

FAST FACTS

STUDENT PROFILE

# of degree-seeking undergraduates	431
% male/female	36/64
% African-American	4
% American Indian or Alaska Native	0
% Asian or Pacific Islander	24
% Hispanic	9.5
% White	13
% International	44
% Pell grant recipients	23

First generation and minority alumni SUA's first undergraduate class graduated in 2005. Alumni are already working for the United Nations, World Development Bank, the Peace Corps and the education department in Venezuela.

ACADEMICS

full-time faculty	51
full-time minority faculty	15
student-faculty ratio	9:1
average class size	13
% first-year retention rate	96
% graduation rate (6 years)	87

Popular areas of study Liberal Arts, concentrating in: Environmental Studies, Humanities, Social and Behavioral Sciences, International Studies

CAMPUS LIFE

% of fresh. live on campus	99

Multicultural student clubs and organizations Chinese Club, Corea Club, Ghungroo (Indian Dance), Humanism in Action, Josho Daiko Club (Taiko drums), Kapilina Ho'olokahi (Hawaiian dance), Kendo Club, Sualseros (Salsa dance), World Bridgers, Break Dancers, Rhythmission (Hip Hop)

Athletics NAIA, California Collegiate Athletic Association (CCAA)

ADMISSIONS

# of applicants	504
% accepted	25
# of first-year students enrolled	125
SAT Critical Reading range	410-800
SAT Math range	420-800
SAT Writing range	410-800
ACT range	20-33
average HS GPA	3.85

Deadlines

early decision	10/15
regular decision	1/15
online application fee	$30
fee waiver for applicants with financial need	no

COST & AID

tuition	$26,294
room & board	$10,122
total need-based institutional scholarships/grants	n/a
% of students apply for need-based aid	89
% of students receive aid	100
% receiving need-based scholarship or grant aid	55
% receiving aid whose need was fully met	90
average aid package	$30,621
average student loan debt upon graduationn	$22,000

Stanford University

Stanford University
Undergraduate Admission, Montag Hall
Stanford, CA 94305-6106
Ph: (650)723-2091
admission@stanford.edu
www.stanford.edu

Stanford University, located on more than 8,000 acres in northern California, is one of the most selective private institutions in the world. As a respected leader in both the sciences and the humanities, Stanford brings together extraordinary faculty members and students in the pursuit of excellence. At the heart of Stanford's mission is scholarly inquiry, innovation and investigation. Opportunities for discovery begin in the classroom and extend into the rich research life of campus laboratories, libraries, studios and beyond. Stanford encourages undergraduates to join with faculty in the search for new knowledge and new artistic creation. Learning outside the classroom is supported by a vibrant residential system that emphasizes service and community. Students may choose to participate in a vast array of educational opportunities, including freshman and sophomore seminars, undergraduate research programs, 11 overseas study centers and department honors programs. Stanford has a strong commitment to diversity — more than half of the graduating class of 2013 is made up of students of color.

"I decided to attend Stanford because of the tremendous diversity within the undergraduate student population. Never before have I seen such a diverse grouping of my peers, hailing from all parts of the country and the world, from every background imaginable. In addition, all of these groups are given the ability to express themselves via the university's resources."

– Bernard F., '10
Mishawaka, IN
Political Science
and Linguistics

> ACCESS Youth Mentorship Programs

Through sponsored programs such as Upward Bound, which provides academic support, tutoring and college application support to high school students, and Ravenswood Reads, which provides one-to-one literacy tutoring to young elementary school students, Stanford offers a number of opportunities for its students to mentor and connect with youth in the surrounding areas. Also particularly successful is Stanford's East Palo Alto Tennis and Tutoring Program, which serves approximately 100 students who receive both tennis instruction and academic tutoring.

> ACCESS Office of Undergraduate Admissions

Partnering with numerous local and regional community-based organizations, such as Foundation for a College Education, College Match, College Summit and College Track, the Office of Undergraduate Admissions provides guided campus tours, college information sessions and essay-writing workshops designed to help students think about and prepare for the transition to higher education.

> SUCCESS Expanded Advising Programs (EAP) / Ethnic Centers

In addition to the faculty advisers that the Undergraduate Advising and Research (UAR) department assigns all freshmen, the Expanded Advising Programs works in conjunction with campus community and ethnic centers. Stanford's four ethnic community centers, including the Asian American Activities Center, Black Community Services Center, El Centro Chicano and the Native American Cultural Center, can help students be successful by offering them additional resources and support networks. Stanford's ethnic-themed houses — Ujamaa (the African American themed dorm), Casa Zapata (the Latino themed dorm), Muwekmah-tah-ruk (the Native themed dorm) and Okada (the Asian American themed dorm) — all serve to further these networks as well.

FAST FACTS

STUDENT PROFILE

# of degree-seeking undergraduates	6,564
% male/female	51/49
% African American	10
% American Indian	3
% Asian	23
% Hispanic	12
% White	38
% International	7
% Pell grant recipients	13.1

First-generation and minority alumni David Henry Hwang, playwright; JuJu Chang, ABC correspondent; Maria Echaveste, White House Chief of Staff, Clinton Administration; March Kong Fong Eu, former Secretary of State, California; Cory Booker, mayor, Newark, N.J.

ACADEMICS

full-time faculty	1,008
full-time minority faculty	186
student-faculty ratio	6:1
average class size	15
% first-year retention rate	98
% graduation rate (6 years)	94

Popular majors Human Biology, International Relations, Economics, Political Science, Psychology

CAMPUS LIFE

% live on campus (% freshman)	94 (n/a)

Multicultural student clubs and organizations El Centro Chicano, Black Community Services Center, Asian American Activities Center, Native American Cultural Center, Women's Community Center, LGBT Community Resources Center
Athletics NCAA Division I

ADMISSIONS

# of applicants	30,429
% accepted	8
# of first-year students enrolled	1,694

Middle 50% Range:

SAT Critical Reading range	650-760
SAT Math range	680-780
SAT Writing range	670-760
ACT range	30-34
average HS GPA	n/a

Deadlines

regular decision	1/1
application fee	$90
fee waiver for applicants with financial need	yes

COST & AID

tuition	$37,380
room & board	$11,463
total need-based institutional scholarships/grants	$104,397,282
% of students apply for need-based aid	61
% receiving need-based scholarship or grant aid	99
% receiving aid whose need was fully met	77
average aid package	$38,037
average student loan debt upon graduation	$12,570

University of the Pacific

University of the Pacific
3601 Pacific Avenue
Stockton, CA 95211
Ph: (209) 946-2011
admission@pacific.edu
www.pacific.edu

The University of the Pacific is a mid-size, private, comprehensive university. The university is devoted to small class sizes and personalized attention from professors that emphasize student-centered learning and individual success. Pacific integrates liberal arts and professional education to prepare its students for career achievement after graduation. The university's diverse student body is supported by Pacific's many student resources, including the United Cultural Council, the Multicultural Greek Council and the PRIDE Resource Center. The United Cultural Council oversees all cultural organizations on campus, promotes cultural diversity and builds leadership skills. Pacific also offers leadership opportunities for minority students through Multicultural Leadership Retreats, the Martin Luther King, Jr. Celebration, the Celebrate Diversity Calendar and other events.

> ACCESS Bilingual Financial Aid Workshop

Pacific, in partnership with the Hispanic Chamber of Commerce of San Joaquin County, hosts the Bilingual Financial Aid Workshop each winter. This event draws several hundred participants each year; the program's objective is to lead high school seniors and their families through the process of completing the Free Application for Federal Student Aid (FAFSA). There are also workshops for junior high and younger high school students about financial aid opportunities and applying to college. This is a family event, and younger brothers and sisters come along to get a first taste of life on a college campus.

> OPPORTUNITY SUCCESS Grants

SUCCESS Grants are available through the University of the Pacific's Office of Financial Aid for students who are current Pell grant recipients to help meet any unmet financial need. To qualify for a SUCCESS Grant, students must participate in the program at the university and maintain a minimum 2.0 GPA. Participants must also meet the U.S. Department of Education's income criteria, be a first-generation college student or have a documented physical or learning disability. Approximately 50 grants are awarded each year up to the amount of $1,000.

> SUCCESS Successful Connections

The Successful Connections program assists Pacific students of underrepresented backgrounds (Latino/Hispanic, African-American and Native American) in making a successful transition to the university. Successful Connections provides academic and social support from fellow students, faculty and staff through multicultural events, academic tutoring and social opportunities. Peer mentors are Pacific student leaders of similar backgrounds who can guide incoming students and lead them to academic and personal success.

FAST FACTS

STUDENT PROFILE
# of degree-seeking undergraduates	3,501
% male/female	45/55
% African-American	4
% American Indian or Alaska Native	1
% Asian or Pacific Islander	35
% Hispanic	12
% White	35
% Pell grant recipients	31

First-generation and minority alumni Tom Flores, former NFL head coach, general manager; Jose Hernandez, NASA astronaut; Michael Olowokandi, professional basketball player; Judge Johnnie Rawlinson, first African-American woman to sit on the U.S. 9th Circuit Court of Appeals

ACADEMICS
full-time faculty	434
full-time minority faculty	n/a
student-faculty ratio	13:1
average class size	18
% first-year retention rate	85
% graduation rate (6 years)	64

Popular majors Business Administration/Management, Engineering

CAMPUS LIFE
% live on campus (% freshmen)	57 (90)

Multicultural student clubs and organizations African-American Student Union, Cambodian Student Association, Hmong Student Association, Kilusan Philipino, Korean Students Association, M.E.Ch.A., Middle Eastern Student Association, Muslim Student Association, Pakistan Student Association, Society of Hispanic Professional Engineers

Athletics NCAA Division I, Big West Conference, Mountain Pacific Sports Federation

ADMISSIONS
# of applicants	450
% accepted	69
# of first-year students enrolled	1,003
SAT Critical Reading range	500-620
SAT Math range	530-670
SAT Writing range	500-620
ACT range	22-28
average HS GPA	3.5

Deadlines
regular decision	rolling
application fee (online)	$0 ($0)

COST & AID
tuition	$28,980
room & board	$9,210
total need-based institutional scholarships/grants	n/a
% of students apply for need-based aid	75
% of students receive aid	67
% receiving need-based scholarship or grant aid	98
% receiving aid whose need was fully met	22
average aid package	$27,263
average student loan debt upon graduation	n/a

University of San Diego

The University of San Diego is a nationally ranked Roman Catholic institution committed to advancing academic excellence, expanding liberal and professional knowledge, creating a diverse and inclusive community and preparing leaders dedicated to ethical conduct and compassionate service. The university is a co-educational, residential university serving students of diverse backgrounds from across the country and around the world. The University of San Diego's President's Advisory Board on Inclusion and Diversity (PABID) believes academic excellence requires inclusive engagement with diverse groups and varying perspectives, and it recognizes that the benefits of a rich, diverse learning community are most likely realized when institutions demonstrate high levels of commitment to inclusion and diversity. The Board actively supports recruitment and retention of underrepresented students, staff, faculty and administrators in pursuit of the compositional diversity required to achieve excellence.

> ACCESS Upward Bound

The University of San Diego's Upward Bound program creates an academic, diverse learning community of low-income high school students who demonstrate the desire to pursue higher education. Upward Bound works with entire communities of students, parents, teachers and staff to teach academic foundations, values building and goal-setting. In turn, this foundation encourages academic and personal success from high school to college and beyond.

> OPPORTUNITY Diversity Circle of Excellence Scholarship

The Diversity Circle of Excellence Scholarship at the University of San Diego grants up to full-tuition awards to underrepresented students with financial need. Decisions are also based on superior academic achievement, standardized test scores, leadership, service, and other personal qualities.

> SUCCESS Lead@USD Program

The University of San Diego's Lead@USD Program enrolls qualifying students and provides resources, mentoring and support as they transition to college life. Lead@USD focuses on the learning that occurs inside and outside of the classroom. There is a strong emphasis on the development of leadership skills and how students can incorporate them into their major and professional career. Students in Lead@USD will receive specialized academic advising from the Director of the program.

> SUCCESS Student Support Services

Student Support Services is a federally funded grant by the US Department of Education to serve 160 eligible undergraduates at USD. The program provides opportunities for academic development, assists students with college requirements, and serves to retain and motivate students toward successful completion of their postsecondary education at USD. Services provided include: academic counseling/advising, tutoring, career counseling, personal counseling, faculty/student mentoring, cultural activities, grant aid, FAFSA assistance, Summer Bridge Program, time management techniques, note-taking techniques, test-taking techniques, essay writing improvement, reading strategies, and graduate school application assistance.

University of San Diego
Office of Undergraduate Admissions
5998 Alcala Park
San Diego, CA 92110
Ph: (619) 260-4506
admissions@sandiego.edu
www.sandiego.edu

FAST FACTS

STUDENT PROFILE
# of degree-seeking undergraduates	5,111
% male/female	42/58
% African American	3
% American Indian or Alaska Native	2
% Asian or Pacific Islander	11
% Hispanic	15
% White	63
% International	3
% Pell grant recipients	13.1

ACADEMICS
full-time faculty	381
full-time minority faculty	70
student-faculty ratio	15:1
average class size	15-25
% first-year retention rate	85
% graduation rate (6 years)	75

Popular majors Business Administration, Communication Studies, Psychology, Political Science, International Relations

CAMPUS LIFE
% live on campus (% freshmen)	49 (96)

Multicultural student clubs and organizations United Front Multicultural Center, Asian Student Association, Movimiento Estudiantil Chicano de Aztlan, Association of Chicana Activists, People of the Islands, Filipino Ugnayan Student Organization, 'Aikane O Hawaii, Brothers & Sisters United, Native American Student Union, PRIDE, International Student Organization and Jewish Student Union
Athletics NCAA Division I, Pacific Coast Softball Conference, Pioneer League Football

ADMISSIONS
# of applicants	11,000
% accepted	401
# of first-year students enrolled	1,082
SAT Critical Reading range	550-640
SAT Math range	565-660
SAT Writing range	550-650
ACT range	25-29
average HS GPA	3.84

Deadlines
early action	11/15
regular decision	1/15
application fee (online)	$55
fee waiver for applicants with financial need	yes

COST & AID
tuition	$36,950
room & board	$12,602
total need-based institutional scholarships/grants	$28,164,950
% of students apply for need-based aid	64
% of students receive aid	100
% receiving need-based scholarship or grant aid	93
% receiving aid whose need was fully met	19
average aid package	$26,809
average student loan debt upon graduation	$27,999

University of Southern California

The University of Southern California continues to be recognized as one of the most culturally diverse campuses in the United States. The Office of Admission actively recruits students from all backgrounds and socioeconomic statuses. This includes first-generation college-goers from lower income families who may need additional support as they continue on to college. The University partners with a number of organizations to ensure their students' continued academic success and that a top-tier education remains available and affordable to all students, regardless of background or ability to pay.

> ACCESS Neighborhood Academic Initiative Program

The USC Neighborhood Academic Initiative (NAI) offers a comprehensive college-preparation program for local middle-school students. Students also have the chance to earn a full scholarship to USC.

> ACCESS USC TRIO Programs

Support low-income and first-generation minority students as they progress from middle school to college. USC TRIO includes four Upward Bound programs, one Upward Bound Math-Science program and two Upward Bound Talent Search programs.

> ACCESS USC Family of Schools

Provides educational, cultural and developmental opportunities to more than 17,000 children in 15 schools surrounding the University Park and Health Sciences campuses. USC's partnership with the Family of Schools ensures that more families are engaged in their communities and that children are expected to attend college while receiving the necessary support from their parents.

> OPPORTUNITY Norman Topping Student Aid Fund

NTSAF offers financial support to students who demonstrate an extraordinary level of community awareness in their pursuit of higher education at USC. Primary consideration is given to applicants from neighborhoods surrounding the University Park and Health Science. For more information, please visit www.usc.edu/student-affairs/ntsaf/info_about.shtml.

> OPPORTUNITY USC Diversity Day

The Office of Admission invites high school juniors from diverse populations to participate in a day of application and financial aid workshops on the USC campus.

> OPPORTUNITY USC fly-in programs

The Office of Admission will fly in prospective students to admitted student programs. Students must demonstrate financial need, and each request is reviewed individually.

> SUCCESS Mexican American Alumni Association

One of the nation's leading Latino alumni associations devoted to the academic advancement and development of Latino students attending USC. MAAA is one of the few Latino alumni associations in the country with a $3 million endowment fund.

> SUCCESS Black Alumni Association

A primary alumni resource providing tuition assistance to African American students at USC, it was founded in 1976 by the late Reverend Dr. Thomas Kilgore, Jr., a peer of Martin Luther King, Jr., and special advisor to President John Hubbard. The BAA has provided over $1.7 million to 1600 USC students. BAA scholarships are awarded annually based on financial need and academic merit. BAA scholarship funds are matched 2:1 for undergraduate students.

"I grew up just north of the USC campus. I was familiar with Trojan pride. Soon after starting classes, I fell into my major and built a family with my fellow students. The USC experience has enriched my life and better prepared me academically, socially and culturally for the greater world."

– Ebonee R., '10
Los Angeles, CA
USC Annenberg School for Communication & Journalism

University of Southern California
700 Childs Way
Los Angeles, CA 90089-0911
213-740-1111
admitusc@usc.edu
www.usc.edu

FAST FACTS

STUDENT PROFILE

# of degree-seeking undergraduates	16,445
% male/female	50/50
% African-American	5
% American Indian or Alaska Native	1
% Asian or Pacific Islander	24
% Hispanic	13
% White	44
% International	11
% Pell grant recipients	18.3

First-generation and minority alumni Frank Cruz '69, USC Trustee, founder of Telemundo, chairman of Corporation for Public Broadcasting; Linda Johnson Rice '80, USC Trustee, President/CEO of Johnson Publishing; Brenda V. Castillo '85, Director, Government & Public Affairs, Western Region, BP America, Inc.; Paul Williams '19, First African American member of AIA; John Singleton '90, Director/Producer; Karime Sanchez Bradvica '80, Vice President, External Affairs, AT&T

ACADEMICS

full-time faculty	3,200
full-time minority faculty	217
student-faculty ratio	9:1
average class size	26
% first-year retention rate	88
% graduation rate (6 years)	96

Popular majors Cinematic Arts, Business, Music, Engineering, Communications

CAMPUS LIFE

% live on campus (% freshmen)	n/a

Multicultural student clubs and organizations Center for Black Cultural and Student Affairs, El Centro Chicano, Asian Pacific American Student Services, Black Student Assembly, Latino Student Assembly, M.E.Ch.A. de USC, 100 Black Men of USC, Vietnamese Student Association Athletics **Athletics** NCAA Division I, Pac-10 Conference

ADMISSIONS

# of applicants	35,753
% accepted	24
# of first-year students enrolled	2,869
SAT Critical Reading range	620-740
SAT Math range	650-740
SAT Writing range	640-730
ACT range	29-32
average HS GPA	3.7
Deadlines	
scholarship decision	12/1
regular decision	1/10
application fee	$65
fee waiver for applicants with financial need	yes

COST & AID

tuition	$39,184
room & board	$11,580
total need-based institutional scholarships/grants	$191,900,000
% of students apply for need-based aid	n/a
% receiving need-based scholarship or grant aid	60
% receiving aid whose need was fully met	100
average aid package	n/a
average student loan debt upon graduation	n/a

Whittier College

Founded in 1887 by the Religious Society of Friends, Whittier is a private, four-year liberal-arts college within close proximity to Los Angeles. Whittier is one of the most diverse liberal arts schools in the country, with a wide range of cultural and socio-economic backgrounds. Minority and international students constitute nearly half of the student body. In 2002, Whittier was awarded a $1.5 million development grant to support students on campus in accordance with the U.S. Department of Education's recognition of Whittier as a Hispanic Serving Institution. The college offers 31 majors and minors within 23 disciplines. Located on 75 acres, Whittier has more than 60 student-run organizations and a well-respected athletic program.

> ACCESS The Ortiz Programs

The Ortiz Programs, named after alumnus Martin Ortiz '48, seek to expand knowledge and awareness of Latino culture, language and history through a variety of events and activities. The Ortiz Programs provide academic and career resources, financial aid guidance, and overall emotional support, primarily to first-generation Latino students. The program serves as a liaison between Latino students, parents, alumni, community organizations and the Whittier College community.

> OPPORTUNITY Latino Opportunity Scholarship (LOS)

The Latino Opportunity Scholarship is a $1,000 scholarship offered to Latino students who are slated to attend Whittier. Selected students are sent an application during the month of May.

> SUCCESS Whittier Scholars Program (WSP)

The Whittier Scholars Program offers students a non-traditional curricular path. Students in the WSP design their own curriculum and can create their own interdisciplinary major. The WSP is not an honors program, but attracts those students who want to take responsibility for their education. Students work closely with faculty advisers and administrators in the WSP to ensure that each educational design has academic and intellectual integrity. Students in the WSP are also required to build an off-campus experience that complements their major, and must complete and publically present a senior project. Typically, 12 percent of a graduating class opts for the WSP.

> SUCCESS Center for Advising and Academic Success

The Center for Advising and Academic Success works with students to achieve their academic goals. Students, some of whom may be under-prepared in certain areas, are given opportunities to assess their strengths and weaknesses and are then provided the tools to help them reach their potential. Professional staff members, faculty and well-trained tutors are on-hand to support and guide students to advance to the next level.

> SUCCESS The Cultural Center

The Cultural Center seeks to create a campus community that appreciates and respects individuals of diverse identities and backgrounds. The center houses many programs and organizations seeking to enrich cultural interaction and dialogue throughout the Whittier campus. Heritage month celebrations, Diverse Identities Week, and diversity workshops are examples of programs, while events for underrepresented students include new student orientation receptions, graduation ceremonies and dinners. The Cultural Center collaborates with faculty to expand the understanding of cultural appreciation in the curriculum and connects underrepresented populations to academic services, career counseling and support networks.

> *"Being at Whittier College has allowed me to take my curriculum into my own hands and create a unique major that suits me through the Whittier Scholars Program. It has opened my mind to endless possibilities. Working with the Ortiz Programs has also allowed me to embrace my heritage more thoroughly."*
>
> *– Donna O., '11*
> *Gardena, CA*
> *Whittier Scholars—Immigration Rights and Policy*

Whittier College
13406 East Philadelphia St.
P.O. Box 634
Whittier, CA 90608-0634
Ph: (562) 907-4238
admission@whittier.edu
www.whittier.edu

FAST FACTS

STUDENT PROFILE

# of degree-seeking undergraduates	1,367
% male/female	47/53
% African-American	6
% American Indian or Alaska Native	1
% Asian or Pacific Islander	9
% Hispanic	29
% White	40
% International	2
% Pell grant recipients	30

First-generation and minority alumni Martin Ortiz, educator and activist, recipient of Distinguished Service Award from the U.S. Department of Education; J. Stanley Sanders, attorney, one of the first two African-Americans in more than a half-century to be awarded a Rhodes Scholarship; Darryl Walker, vice president for business affairs, Black Entertainment Television, Rhodes Scholar; Alma Martinez, stage, screen and television actress, director, and educator, Fulbright Award recipient for study in South America; Erin Clancy, Thomas R. Pickering Foreign Affairs Fellowship recipient; Malaika (Williams) Amneus, obstetrics/gynecology, Rhodes Scholar

ACADEMICS

full-time faculty	96
full-time minority faculty	26
student-faculty ratio	13:1
average class size	18
% first-year retention rate	79
% graduation rate (6 yrs)	61

Popular majors Business Administration, English, History, Political Science, Psychology

CAMPUS LIFE

% live on campus (% fresh.)	63 (78)

Multicultural student clubs and organizations Akwaaba, Black Student Union, Hispanic Student Association, Asian Student Association, M.E.Ch.A. **Athletics** NCAA Division III, Southern California Intercollegiate Athletic Conference

ADMISSIONS

# of applicants	2,263
% accepted	78
# of first-year students enrolled	358
SAT Critical Reading range	470-580
SAT Math Range	470-590
SAT Writing range	470-590
ACT Range	19-25
average HS GPA	3.4

Deadlines

early action	10/15, 12/1
regular decision	2/1
application fee (online)	$50($50)
fee waiver for applicants with financial need	yes

COST & AID

tuition	$33,868
room & board	$9,704
total need-based institutional scholarships/grants	n/a
% of students apply for need-based aid	80
% of students receive aid	85
% receiving need-based scholarship/grant aid	85
% receiving aid whose need was fully met	17
average aid package	$31,869
average student loan debt upon graduation	$40,862

Colorado State University

Colorado State University, one of the nation's premier research institutions, has never lost sight of its original land-grant mission to provide access to an exceptional, affordable college education. Colorado State believes that every qualified student should have a chance to gain the knowledge and skills he or she needs for a successful future. Countless students have taken advantage of the university's outstanding research and internship opportunities, not to mention its extensive support and career counseling services. Colorado State graduates have emerged as leaders in their respective fields, using their educations to improve lives and create change on a global scale.

"I want to make sure my little brother has someone to follow, because nobody in my family has graduated from college. All my professors have worked with me— Colorado State is a really nurturing environment. If you want a great education at an affordable price, this is the place to be."
– *Miguel G., '13*
Fort Lupton, CO
Environmental Health

> ACCESS Black Issues Forum (BIF)

BIF is a pre-collegiate leadership program that provides high school students with a vehicle to demonstrate their written and oral communication skills and to enhance their leadership. Participants meet in June after their junior year and interact with community leaders and Colorado State University faculty as they discuss and evaluate important issues that affect the black community at the local, state, national and global level. BIF participants spend significant time in the university's libraries researching pre-selected, current topics, then share their findings through presentations, debates or town meetings. In addition, BIF participants engage in social activities such as an evening of cultural expression, informal discussions and a recognition luncheon.

> ACCESS Lorenzo de Zavala (LDZ) Youth Legislative Session

Hispanic/Latino high school sophomores and juniors from across the nation flock to the CSU campus each June for the Lorenzo de Zavala Youth Legislative Session (LDZ). During mock state government sessions, students debate issues of special interest to the Hispanic/Latino community. Colorado State University is the only institution of higher education in Colorado and one of only five throughout the United States and Mexico to collaborate with the National Hispanic Institute in such a program.

> OPPORTUNITY First Generation Award

The First Generation Award was created 25 years ago to promote diversity within the University and to encourage first generation students to enroll at Colorado State. Colorado residents entering as freshmen or transfer students whose parents have not received a bachelor's degree and who demonstrate financial need are eligible to apply for these competitive awards.

> OPPORTUNITY Land Grant Award

As Colorado's only land-grant university, CSU is committed to keeping higher education within the reach of the state's citizens. The Land Grant Award helps Colorado-residents pay for their education at Colorado State, based on financial need.

> SUCCESS Key Communities

Freshmen and sophomores who participate in the Key Communities expand their opportunities for success through leadership, service, civic engagement and campus involvement. They forge personal connections with faculty and other students, while learning to appreciate cultural diversity, enriching their academic experience and exploring their career options.

Colorado State University
1062 Campus Delivery
Fort Collins, CO 80523-1062
Ph: (970) 491-6909
admissions@colostate.edu
www.admissions.colostate.edu

F A S T F A C T S

STUDENT PROFILE

# of degree-seeking undergraduates	21,204
% male/female	49/51
% African American	3
% American Indian or Alaska Native	2
% Asian or Pacific Islander	3
% Hispanic	7
% White	78
% International	2
% Pell grant recipients	22

First-generation and minority alumni John Mosley, Tuskegee Airman; Jusef Kommunyakaa, Pulitzer Prize-winning poet; Polly Baca, CEO of Latin American Research and Service Agency (LARASA) and former presidential advisor; Stan Matsunaka, former Colorado state senator; John Amos, actor; Mark Montano, designer and co-host of "While You Were Out."

ACADEMICS

full-time faculty	944
full-time minority faculty	119
student-faculty ratio	17:1
average class size	30
% first-year retention rate	83
% graduation rate (6 years)	63

Popular majors Business, Health and Exercise Science, Psychology, Biological Sciences, Construction Management

CAMPUS LIFE

% live on campus (% fresh.)	26 (96)

Multicultural student clubs and organizations American Indian Science & Engineering Society, Asian Fest Student Committee, Black Definition, Black Student Alliance, Hui 'O Hawai'i, Invisible Children: Schools for Schools, La Raza, Salam, Shades of CSU, Society for the Advancement of Chicanos & Native Americans, Students for Holocaust Awareness, United Men of Color, United Women of Color

Athletics NCAA Division I, Mountain West Conference

ADMISSIONS

# of applicants	15,253
% accepted	72
# of first-year students enrolled	4,285
SAT Critical Reading range	500-610
SAT Math range	510-640
SAT Writing range	490-600
ACT range	22-27
average HS GPA	3.6

Deadlines

regular decision	2/1
application fee (online)	$50 ($50)
fee waiver for applicants with financial need	yes

COST & AID

tuition	in-state $6,318; out-of-state $22,240
room & board	$8,378
total need-based institutional scholarships/grants	$11,785,653
% of students apply for need-based aid	63
% receiving need-based scholarship or grant aid	37
% receiving aid whose need was fully met	32
average aid package	$10,051
average student loan debt upon graduation	$20,432

United States Air Force Academy

United States Air Force Academy
2304 Cadet Drive, Suite 2400
USAF Academy, CO 80840-5025
Ph: (800) 443-9266
rr_webmail@usafa.edu
www.academyadmissions.com

The U.S. Air Force Academy is one of five military service academies that educates and trains young men and women in academics, leadership, character and athletics. The mission of the Academy is to educate, train and inspire men and women to become officers of character motivated to lead the United States Air Force in service to our nation. Graduates receive a Bachelor of Science degree in one of 31 majors and commission as a second lieutenant in the U.S. Air Force. The Academy has 27 NCAA Division I athletic teams. This institution offers many unique opportunities and programs, to include aviation programs, and about 50 percent of graduates are assigned an aviation career field. There are numerous other career fields the Air Force offers, ranging from engineering and acquisitions to intelligence and public affairs. The campus is located just north of Colorado Springs, Colorado, and 55 miles south of Denver.

> *"Becoming part of the 'Long Blue Line' is a life-changing decision that will open opportunities you never thought possible. The Academy will challenge you in many ways and teach you a lot about yourself while at the same time preparing you to lead the world's greatest air and space force."*
> *– Miguel M., '12*

> ACCESS The United States Air Force Academy Preparatory School

The United States Air Force Academy Prep School, better known as the "Prep School," is designed to academically, physically and militarily prepare qualified young men and women to enter the Academy. Successful completion of the Prep School improves chances for appointment as an Air Force Academy cadet, but does not guarantee one. In order to attend the tuition-free United States Air Force Prep School, students must complete the Pre-Candidate Questionnaire. The application can be completed as early as March 1 of the student's junior year, but no later than Dec. 31 of their senior year.

> ACCESS Summer Seminar

The USAFA Summer seminar allows high-performing high school students to spend one week at the United States Air Force Academy at the conclusion of their junior year. In addition to living on the Air Force Academy's campus, Summer Seminar features a week filled with numerous academic workshops (of the students' choice) and some intramural sports. Moreover, this experience allows students to take a Candidate Fitness Assessment, get some brief drill and ceremony exposure, attend a few informational admissions meetings and go through the "doolie for a day" program (freshmen at the Academy are frequently referred to as "doolies"). The Summer Seminar allows high school students to gain an insight to the numerous facets of the complex freshmen year at the Academy.

> SUCCESS Student Academic Affairs

The Student Academic Affairs office offers cadets self-improvement services, which include study skills, graduate school program assistance, and reading and writing assistance.

> SUCCESS Major's Night

During Major's Night, the dean of the faculty brings together 20 academic departments and staff agencies to provide a one-stop opportunity for undeclared cadets to learn about the 32 disciplinary academic majors, four divisional majors and two minors available at USAFA. Professionals from varied educational backgrounds and career fields unite as one military community with a common purpose: to share with cadets their collective knowledge and inspiration collected from years of academia and military experiences.

FAST FACTS

STUDENT PROFILE

# of degree-seeking undergraduates	4,527
% male/female	80/20
% African American	5
% American Indian or Alaska Native	1
% Asian or Pacific Islander	8
% Hispanic	8
% White	78
% International	1
% Pell grant recipients	n/a

First-generation and minority alumni Heather Wilson,'82, former Congresswoman, U.S. House of Representatives; Frederick Gregory,'64, former astronaut and NASA Deputy Administrator, NASA; William T Thompson,'73, President and CEO, Association of Graduates; Nicole Malachowski,'96, first female Thunderbird pilot, USAF; Chris Howard,'91, President, Hampden-Sydney College

ACADEMICS

full-time faculty	542
full-time minority faculty	n/a
student-faculty ratio	9:1
average class size	15-20
% first-year retention rate	87
% graduation rate (6 years)	75

Popular majors Aeronautical Engineering, Systems Engineering Management, Management, Civil Engineering, Social Sciences

CAMPUS LIFE

% live on campus	100

Multicultural student clubs and organizations National Society of Black Engineers, Way of Life, Los Padrinos, Native American Heritage Club, Tuskegee Airman, Pacific Rim, Society of Women Engineers, International Club, Prior Enlisted Cadet Assembly

Athletics NCAA Division I, Mountain West Conference

ADMISSIONS

# of applicants	9,898
% accepted	17
# of first-year students enrolled	1,368
SAT Critical Reading range	600-680
SAT Math range	630-690
SAT Writing range	n/a
ACT range	28-31
average HS GPA	3.86

Deadlines

regular decision	1/31
application fee	$0
fee waiver for applicants with financial need	yes

COST & AID

tuition	$0
room & board	$0
total need-based institutional scholarships/grants	n/a
% of students apply for need-based aid	n/a
% receiving need-based scholarship or grant aid	n/a
% receiving aid whose need was fully met	n/a
average aid package	n/a
average student loan debt upon graduation	$0

University of Denver

University of Denver
2199 South University Blvd.
Denver, CO 80208
Ph: (303) 871-2036
admission@du.edu
www.du.edu

The University of Denver offers a dynamic learning environment that prizes innovation, cross-disciplinary exploration, inclusive excellence, and adventurous learning partnerships between students and faculty. Students are groomed to excel in their life's work and to confront the great issues of the day. With a student-faculty ratio of 10:1, University of Denver students enjoy meaningful and sometimes life-changing interactions with faculty mentors. This rewarding relationship with professors continues through the undergraduate experience, with students collaborating with faculty members on research projects, fieldwork and creative endeavors. In addition, various student organizations offer leadership opportunities that give students a chance to catalyze and support positive change to campus and community. With the personal attention offered at a small liberal arts college and the resources of a large research institution, the University of Denver is the perfect choice for students looking to join other adventurous learners.

> ACCESS **Volunteers in Partnership**

Volunteers in Partnership collaborates with students, parents, faculty and staff from Denver West High School, Abraham Lincoln High School, Pinnacle Charter School, the Denver Center for International Studies, the Denver School of Science & Technology, and Rishel Middle School. Volunteers in Partnership are committed to the promotion of self-esteem in students, to encourage students to complete high school, and to assist with transition into higher education or career training.

> OPPORTUNITY **Cherrington Global Scholars Study Abroad Program**

Study and service abroad are an integral part of the University of Denver experience. Nearly 75 percent of students study abroad. Through the Cherrington Global Scholars program, eligible juniors and seniors can study abroad at no additional charge to the cost of studying at Denver.

> SUCCESS **Diversity Summit on Inclusive Excellence**

The University of Denver Diversity Summit on Inclusive Excellence is a power-packed day consisting of campus and nationally recognized scholars speaking on the topic of diversity.

> SUCCESS **The Lamont A. Sellers Diversity & Unity Retreat**

The Diversity & Unity Intergroup Relations Retreat is a two and a half day retreat that takes undergraduate and graduate students to the mountains of Colorado for self discovery and learning related to leadership and diversity.

> SUCCESS **The Center for Community Engagement and Service Learning (CCESL)**

University of Denver students are increasingly engaged in the world and the Center for Community Engagement and Service Learning offers an array of opportunities to become involved. The Center is committed to working with community partners to involve the campus community with opportunities in the Denver community.

> SUCCESS **Excelling Leaders Institute**

Excelling Leaders Institute students complete one week of on campus training focusing in the areas of academic preparation, interacting with faculty, learning the campus physical layout, meeting as many individuals and resources on campus as possible and most importantly, creating a tight knit community of support for themselves and other incoming students. Participants are also offered a wide range of benefits not offered to all students.

FAST FACTS

STUDENT PROFILE
# of degree-seeking undergraduates	4,913
% male/female	47/53
% African American	3
% American Indian or Alaska Native	1
% Asian or Pacific Islander	6
% Hispanic	6
% White	72
% International	6
% Pell grant recipients	12

First-generation and minority alumni
Condoleezza Rice, Former U.S. Secretary of State; Brad Anderson, former CEO, Best Buy; James Kennedy, chairman and CEO of Cox Enterprises

ACADEMICS
full-time faculty	576
full-time minority faculty	74
student-faculty ratio	10:1
average class size	20
% first-year retention rate	87
% graduation rate (6 years)	74

Popular majors Communication, Biology, Marketing, Engineering

CAMPUS LIFE
% live on campus (% freshmen)	42 (93)

Multicultural student clubs and organizations
AMIGOS, Black Men's Fellowship, Arab Student Association, Asian Student Alliance, Black Student Alliance, Graduate Leadership Association for Minorities & Allies, Japanese Student Association, Korean Student Association, Latino Student Alliance, Native Student Alliance, Saudi Student Club, Vietnamese Student Association

Athletics NCAA Division I, Sun Belt Conference

ADMISSIONS
# of applicants	8,395
% accepted	55
# of first-year students enrolled	1,474
SAT Critical Reading range	540-640
SAT Math range	540-660
SAT Writing range	n/a
ACT range	25-29
average HS GPA	3.7

Deadlines
early action	11/1
regular decision	1/15
application fee (online)	$50 ($50)
fee waiver for applicants with financial need	yes

COST & AID
tuition	$34,596
room & board	$9,496
total need-based institutional scholarships/grants	n/a
% of students apply for need-based aid	53
% of students receive aid	44
% receiving need-based scholarship or grant aid	99
% receiving aid whose need was fully met	23
average aid package	$26,599
average student loan debt upon graduation	$11,218

Eastern Connecticut State University

Part of the Connecticut State University system, Eastern Connecticut State University is a public, co-educational, liberal arts university. The university encourages intellectual and personal growth and development by offering a student-focused environment with small classes, personalized counseling and independent-study opportunities. The student body of 4,800 students is diverse ethnically, socio-economically and regionally, with students from 26 states and 34 foreign countries. Eastern Connecticut State University is located in Willimantic, a small city in eastern Connecticut, which is famous for its beautiful forests, rolling hills, state park areas and nature trails.

> ACCESS Summer Institute for Future Teachers (SIFT)

SIFT is a four-week residential program that allows local high school juniors and seniors to explore the teaching profession. The program aims to increase the number and diversity of Connecticut students who consider teaching as a career. Students are immersed in coursework and field trips. They work with pre-school, elementary and middle school children, and integrate educational theory with practical experiences. Participants gain three collegelevel credits and develop a professional portfolio.

> ACCESS Student Ambassador Program

The Student Ambassador Program organizes undergraduates to work in the recruitment of minority students. Ambassadors from multicultural organizations such as the Nubian Society, OLAS Club and West Indian Society serve as tour guides for the campus visitation program, visit high schools with large minority populations to inform and recruit prospective students, serve as representatives of Eastern Connecticut State University at multicultural college fairs and provide information via telephone to minority students and their parents.

"Since I came to Eastern I have been enlightened about various work fields and different societies. Eastern is a completely different world than the neighborhood where I grew up. It has changed me."
– Jose M., '09
Willimantic, CT

> OPPORTUNITY Summer Transition at Eastern Program / Contract Admission Program (STEP/CAP)

The Summer Transition at Eastern Program/Contract Admission Program at Eastern Connecticut State University targets highly motivated local high school students who may not have been admitted under traditional admissions criteria. For six weeks, these students work hard to demonstrate their academic readiness. Those who are successful are admitted for the fall semester. Students take credit courses in math and writing, and attend workshops in library research methods, public speaking, study skills and critical thinking skills.

> SUCCESS The Learning Center

Eastern Connecticut State's Academic Services Center provides tutoring, advising and other services that are available to all Eastern students. The Center also plays a critical role in supporting STEP/CAP students who have been admitted to the university following a successful experience in the summer portion of the program. Mathematics and writing tutoring are also offered at the center.

> SUCCESS Faculty Advising

Through this program, members of the university faculty and staff volunteer to be mentors to individual students, acting as confidants, role models and friends. Each student who chooses to participate is paired with a mentor, and together they agree on how they want the relationship to work. Going to lunch, getting together for coffee, exchanging e-mails and going to events together are some of the ways participants choose to meet.

Eastern Connecticut State University
Office of Admissions
83 Windham Street
Willimantic, CT 06226
Ph: (860) 465-5286
admission@easternct.edu
www.easternct.edu

F A S T   F A C T S

STUDENT PROFILE
# of degree-seeking undergraduates	4,896
% male/female	45/55
% African-American	8
% American Indian or Alaska Native	<1
% Asian or Pacific Islander	2
% Hispanic	6
% White	75
% International	1
% Pell grant recipients	20

First-generation and minority alumni
Chimamanda Ngozi Adiche '01, author; Marc Freeman '93, cancer researcher; Robb Nieto '96, TV producer; Francis Y. Falck Jr. '75, noted ophthalmologist; Edith Prague '65, Connecticut State Senator

ACADEMICS
full-time faculty	202
full-time minority faculty	52
student-faculty ratio	16:1
average class size	23
% first-year retention rate	74
% graduation rate (6 years)	46

Popular majors Psychology, Business Administration/Management, Sociology/Applied Social Relations, Communications, English

CAMPUS LIFE
% live on campus (% freshmen)	53 (91)

Multicultural student clubs and organizations
Organization of Latin American Students, P.O.W.E.R., Student Peace and Human Rights Organization, Unity Group, West Indian Society, Nubian Society, Turkish American Student Association

Athletics NCAA Division III, Little East Conference

ADMISSIONS
# of applicants	3,383
% accepted	63
# of first-year students enrolled	1,020
SAT Critical Reading range	460-540
SAT Math range	450-550
SAT Writing average	507
ACT range	n/a
average HS GPA	2.92

Deadlines
regular admission	5/1
application fee (online)	$50 ($50)
fee waiver for applicants with financial need	yes

COST & AID
tuition	in-state: $7,813; out-of-state: $17,505
room & board	$9,580
total need-based institutional scholarships/grants	$3,153,854
% of students apply for need-based aid	75
% of students receive aid	64
% receiving need-based scholarship or grant aid	39
% receiving aid whose need was fully met	11
average aid package	$9,341
average student loan debt upon graduation	$14,829

Fairfield University

Founded in 1942, Fairfield University is a private, coeducational institution that seeks to create a respectful, multicultural, multiethnic, and religiously inclusive community. Grounded in the values of Jesuit learning, the University respects the personal and academic freedom of all of its students, and is known for preparing them for leadership and service. Undergraduate students receive a general education in the traditional humanities to complement their selected majors, and emphasis is placed on both theoretical and applied learning. Located just within the New York metropolitan area, Fairfield provides students with many professional development, social, and cultural opportunities.

> ACCESS Cristo Rey Summer College Planning and Exploration Program

Fairfield University has partnered with the Cristo Rey Network to provide college enrollment information to students from Network high schools. This is a week-long residential program during which students partake in the annual Pre-College Workshop, including additional high school students and admission counselors from local colleges and universities. Students also visit other colleges throughout the area.

> OPPORTUNITY Horizons Weekend

Admitted students of color are invited to spend a weekend exploring Fairfield University and the many academic, cultural, spiritual, and social opportunities available. Students are hosted by current students who serve as their personal guide for the weekend. They participate in class visits, lunch with faculty, staff, and administrators, and an evening social event. While visiting during Horizons Weekend, admitted students are also given the opportunity to participate in the Admitted Student Open House.

"Challenge yourself. You're entering a community of people who care about you. If you take the first step, they'll help you go further than you thought you could."

– Peter O., '08 Englewood, NJ International Business, Finance

> SUCCESS Cura Personalis Mentoring Program

This mentorship program is open to all first-year students, with a special invitation going to first generation college students and students of color. The program helps students acclimate to college. They are paired with current students and faculty and staff members who serve as their mentors. Through regular one-on-one and group meetings, students receive valuable information and useful knowledge about the many resources available to the academic, career, spiritual, and support services available on campus.

> SUCCESS Academic Immersion Program

The Academic Immersion program is designed to assist admitted students from underrepresented populations with the college transition. The program focuses on the academic adjustments a student must make between high school and the first two years of college. Students are selected based on a combination of factors including first-generation to college, low-income, and race/ethnicity. It includes a four week, residential summer program during which students earn six credits completing an art history and philosophy course. Participants are provided with additional academic and personal support throughout the year.

Fairfield University
Office of Undergraduate Admission
1073 North Benson Road
Fairfield, CT 06824
Ph: (203) 254-4100
admis@fairfield.edu
www.fairfield.edu

FAST FACTS

STUDENT PROFILE
# of degree-seeking undergraduates	3,300
% male/ female	42/58
% African-American	4
% American Indian or Alaska Native	1
% Asian or Pacific Islander	3
% Hispanic	8
% White	70
% International	14
% Pell grant recipients	14.6

ACADEMICS
full-time faculty	253
full-time minority faculty 50 (31 excluding international)	
student-faculty ratio	13:1
average class size	23
% first-year retention rate	88
% graduation rate (6 years)	85

Popular majors Psychology, English, Finance, Nursing, Biology

CAMPUS LIFE
% live on campus (% fresh.)	79 (94)

Multicultural student clubs and organizations Asian Student Association, Spanish and Latino Student Association, Women of Color Forum, African American and Caribbean Student Association (Umoja), and Gay/Straight Alliance
Athletics NCAA Division I, Metro Atlantic Athletic Conference

ADMISSIONS
# of applicants	8,316
% accepted	65
# of first-year students enrolled	849
SAT Critical Reading range	550-640
SAT Math range	570-660
SAT Writing range	560-660
ACT range	23-27
average HS GPA	3.4

Deadlines
regular decision	1/15
application fee (online)	$60 ($60)
fee waiver for applicants with financial need	yes

COST & AID
tuition	$38,450
room & board	$11,740
total need-based institutional scholarships/grants	$31,222,924
% of students apply for need-based aid	73
% of students receive aid	99
% receiving need-based scholarship or grant aid	84
% receiving aid whose need was fully met	22
average aid package	$29,123
average student loan debt upon graduation	$35,161

Mitchell College

Founded in 1938, Mitchell College is a private, co-educational, residential institution offering associate and bachelor degree programs in the liberal arts and professional areas. Within a diverse and student-centered community and with an emphasis on holistic student development, Mitchell College supports individual learning differences, nurtures untapped academic potential and instills professional knowledge and skills necessary for students to contribute to an ever-changing world. Emphasizing student asset development rather than student deficit management, Mitchell College promotes programs that identify and cultivate each individual student's strengths.

> ACCESS Children's Learning Center

Mitchell College's Children's Learning Center is an early childhood educational program that encourages collaborative and cooperative learning experiences with and in the surrounding community. The center works with families to provide full-time, quality childcare and developmentally appropriate learning experiences for children between the ages of three and six years. Parents are encouraged to become actively involved in a child's early educational experiences. Distinguished by its close involvement with Mitchell College's Early Childhood and Human Development majors, the center provides them with opportunities to work with children and their families, assist special needs youngsters, develop and refine their teaching capacities, assist in conducting research and participate in program workshops and center-sponsored events.

> ACCESS English as a Second Language (ESL) Center

The English as a Second Language Center serves the needs of international students who must improve their command of English before pursuing coursework at an English-speaking institution. The ESL Program provides individualized instruction, college-credit ESL courses which can be taken simultaneously, preparation for the Test of English as a Second Language (TOEFL) and academic skills training with strong emphasis on preparation for college-level work. For students who need extensive support, Mitchell offers the Intensive English Language Program, 16-week course sessions whereby students receive a minimum of 20-instructional hours each week. If a student is qualified, permission may be granted to audit or take for credit a college course or courses as part of their program.

> SUCCESS Thames Academy

Thames Academy at Mitchell College is a pre-college transitional experience. It is a year of academic preparation that students take between the end of their secondary education and the start of their college studies. Unlike traditional post-graduate programs at independent or preparatory schools, the academy provides college-level courses for credit. Located on the Mitchell College campus, the Thames Academy provides a highly structured residential program within a collegiate environment and co-curricular interaction with two-year and four-year students. The academy helps students to improve study skills and board scores, strengthen their academic preparedness, adjust to living and studying away from home and develop increased confidence and maturity. Students can earn up to 18 college credits prior to full-time college study.

> SUCCESS Learning Resource Center (LRC)

Mitchell College's LRC is one of the nation's leading college support programs serving students with documented learning disabilities and/or AD/HD. Unique to the landscape of college learning disabilities programs, Mitchell College's LRC includes a staff of trained learning and writing specialists as well as three distinct Graduated Levels of Support. The LRC also provides adaptive technology, academic coaching for empowerment and trained educational faculty who are well-versed in the area of working with students who have different learning styles.

Mitchell College
Office of Admissions
437 Pequot Avenue
New London, CT 06320
Ph: (860) 701-5037
admissions@mitchell.edu
www.mitchell.edu

F A S T   F A C T S

STUDENT PROFILE
# of degree-seeking undergraduates	936
% male/female	45.7/54.3
% African-American	12.9
% American Indian or Alaska Native	2.2
% Asian or Pacific Islander	1
% Hispanic	6.6
% White	71.6
% International	<1
% Pell grant recipients	30

ACADEMICS
full-time faculty	31
full-time minority faculty	n/a
student-faculty ratio	n/a
average class size	12-18
% first-year retention rate	n/a
% graduation rate (6 years)	n/a

Popular majors Business/Management, Education, Criminal Justice

CAMPUS LIFE
% live on campus	85

Athletics NCAA Division III, New England Collegiate Conference

ADMISSIONS
# of applicants	1,500
% accepted	71
SAT Critical Reading range	460-550
SAT Math range	530-630
ACT range	n/a
average HS GPA	n/a

Deadlines
early decision	11/15
regular decision	rolling
application fee (online)	$30
fee waiver for applicants with financial need	yes

COST & AID
tuition	$25,627
room & board	$11,548
total need-based institutional scholarships/grants	n/a
% of students apply for need-based aid	80
% of students receive aid	100
% receiving need-based scholarship or grant aid	n/a
% receiving aid whose need was fully met	79
average aid package	$16,350
average student loan debt upon graduation	n/a

Quinnipiac University

On a campus of 500 acres in suburban Connecticut, just eight miles north of New Haven and midway between New York and Boston, Quinnipiac University offers students a range of opportunities, including access to Terry W. Goodwin '67 Financial Technology Center, a fully digital high-definition broadcast studio, and the nationally renowned Quinnipiac University Polling Institute. The school prides itself on its wide range of academic offerings, as well as its programs like Writing Across the Curriculum, which encourages students to use research methods to collaboratively improve their writing skills, thereby becoming critical thinkers. Founded in 1929, Quinnipiac is a private, comprehensive college offering 50 undergraduate majors and 19 graduate programs including Law. Quinnipiac is committed to offering programs of academic excellence, in a student-oriented environment on a campus with a sense of community, in Business, Education, Communications, Health Sciences, Arts and Sciences and Law.

> ACCESS Middle School Shadowing Program

Sponsored by the Office of Multicultural Affairs and Admissions, students from community middle schools are invited to the campus to spend part of a day shadowing Quinnipiac students and tour the campus. Quinnipiac has partnered with Betsy Ross Arts Magnet Middle School to identify outstanding students in grades 5-8. Students within the middle school who are identified as overall scholars are promised a $5,000 scholarship renewable for 4 years, to attend Quinnipiac.

> OPPORTUNITY Admissions Office Events

The Admissions Office hosts individual interviews, group information sessions, campus tours and Open House programs. See Quinnipiac's Web site, listed above, for dates and times.

> SUCCESS Quinnipiac 101

QU101, 201, and 301 are courses within the core curriculum. These courses examine the role of the individual in the local, national, and international community. All freshmen take QU 101 during the first semester. All students use a universal textbook that is discussed in class. This course thus provides a common ground for all students and assists them in the process of developing their role in society.

> SUCCESS SHADES / Student Diversity Board

Through the extensive Office of Multicultural Affairs, students at Quinnipiac can have a hands-on role in directing the multicultural services and events on campus. Participants in Students Helping & Advocating Diversity Education (SHADES) plan Multicultural Mondays programming, as well as an annual diversity conference and retreat. The Student Diversity Board gives students another opportunity for involvement, allowing them to promote diversity discussion though open forums, workshops and seminars.

> SUCCESS ALANA Mentoring Program

In order to support historically underrepresented students in their transition from high school to college, the university offers the ALANA Mentoring Program, which pairs new multicultural students with Quinnipiac staff and faculty and supplies them with additional support and resources. In so doing, the program provides students with a personal, direct link to the university and helps them to successfully complete their academic careers.

Quinnipiac University
275 Mount Carmel Ave
Hamden, CT 06518
Ph: (800) 462-1944 / (203) 582-8600
admissions@quinnipiac.edu
www.quinnipiac.edu

F A S T   F A C T S

STUDENT PROFILE
# of degree-seeking undergraduates	5,700
% male/female	39/61
% African American	3
% American Indian	0
% Asian	2
% Caucasian	79
% Hispanic	4
% Pell grant recipients	9

Distinguished first-generation and minority alums Eric Yutzy '02, sports anchor at WMGM

ACADEMICS
full-time faculty	297
student-faculty ratio	16:1
average class size	<25
% first-year retention rate	88
% graduation rate (6 years)	72

Popular majors Business Management, Finance, Physical Therapy, Psychology, Nursing, Public Relations, Journalism

CAMPUS LIFE
% live on campus (% freshmen)	75 (95)

Multicultural student clubs and organizations Association to Maximize Italian Cultural Influence, Asian & Pacific Islander Student Association, Black Student Union, Gay, Lesbian & Straight Supporters, International Club, Latino Cultural Society, Quinnipiac University Irish Club
Athletics NCAA Division I, Northeast Conference

ADMISSIONS
# of applicants	14,300
% accepted	60
SAT Critical Reading range	540-610
SAT Math range	560-630
ACT range	23-27
average HS GPA	3.4

Deadlines
physical therapy, nursing, physician asst.	11/1
regular admission	2/1

COST & AID (2010 - 2011)
tuition & fees	$34,250
room & board	$12,730
% of students receiving aid	70
% receiving need-based scholarship or grant aid	64
% receiving aid whose need was fully met	15
average aid package	$15,499
average student loan debt upon graduation	$34,621

Sacred Heart University

As the first Catholic university in the nation designed to be led and staffed by laypeople, Sacred Heart University prides itself on being "ahead of the curve," providing innovative programming and resources such as its fully wireless campus - indoors and out - and one of the largest Division I athletic programs in the country, with 31 varsity sports in addition to over 25 club sports. Stressing its triumvirate of values, 'Immersion, Innovation and Integrity,' Sacred Heart provides a comprehensive academic program that is rooted in service. Students can take advantage of Sacred Heart's many volunteer and service learning programs, creating an environment characterized by active, engaged learning.

 ### ACCESS **Young at Heart Day**

Sacred Heart University offers this annual program to bring hundreds of local school children from underrepresented communities to campus, where they participate in educational, artistic, and physical activities. Through these programs, which have included a Math/Spelling Egg Hunt and a Read-Aloud, students get a chance to connect with the University community and begin imagining themselves as college-bound. Sacred Heart freshmen, to whom the visiting students look as role models, are largely responsible for executing the event under the leadership of the University's Student Life program.

ACCESS **Upward Bound**

Local high school students who come from low-income families in which neither parent holds a bachelor's degree can benefit from Sacred Heart's Upward Bound, a pre-college program that provides a group of students with the right tools to pursue their dreams of earning a college degree. Students benefit from weekly tutoring, field trips, workshops, and a six-week summer enrichment program at the University.

ACCESS **College Search Assistance**

Sacred Heart University assists underrepresented students with the college search process through a variety of programs. Sacred Heart has hosted The National Hispanic College Fair for the southern Connecticut region, bringing hundreds of Hispanic high school students to campus, where they learn about the college search process, as well as about individual universities. Sacred Heart also hosts upwards of 200 students during its Gear Up Tour and Talent Search Tour programs, both of which offer tailored student programming and activities informative of the college search process.

OPPORTUNITY **Discovery Grant (Fairfield County Tuition-Free Plan for Low-Income Students)**

This plan offers full scholarships to graduating seniors who reside in Fairfield County, Connecticut, whose family income is at or below $50,000 and who have been admitted to Sacred Heart University as first-time, full-time, first-year students.

OPPORTUNITY **Foundation Scholars Program**

Founded in 1994, the GE Scholars Program, which has since accepted upwards of 150 undergraduate students, provides underrepresented students with annual scholarship assistance to help fund their Sacred Heart educations. Recipients — who must be full-time, low-income, minority students with a 3.0 GPA and show an interest in a quantitative-based field such as information technology, finance, economics, etc. — also develop a relationship with a GE executive who serves as a mentor to them, supporting their academic and career goals through a variety of workshops, professional and cultural events and individual meetings.

"The GE (Foundation Scholars) program has been phenomenal in providing a foundation for success both in the classroom and when the time comes; the real world. I have done and seen things that I otherwise would still be ignorant of to this day and for that I am truly grateful..."
– Charles C., '12 Frederick, MD Finance

Sacred Heart University
5151 Park Avenue
Fairfield, CT 06825
Ph: (203) 371-7880
enroll@sacredheart.edu
www.sacredheart.edu

FAST FACTS

STUDENT PROFILE
# of degree-seeking undergraduates	4,123
% male/female	40/60
% African American	5
% American Indian or Alaska Native	<1
% Asian or Pacific Islander	4
% Hispanic	7
% White	84
% International	1
% Pell grant recipients	13

ACADEMICS
full-time faculty	204
full-time minority faculty	25
student-faculty ratio	13:1
average class size	22
% first-year retention rate	82
% graduation rate (6 years)	66

Popular majors Business Administration, Finance, Kinesiology and Exercise Science, Psychology, Criminal Justice

CAMPUS LIFE
% live on campus (% fresh.)	65 (92)

Multicultural student clubs and organizations International Club, Gay/Straight Alliance, La Hispanidad
Athletics NCAA Division I, Northeast Conference (football I-AA); Atlantic Hockey Association; Colonial Athletic Association; Eastern Intercollegiate Volleyball Association

ADMISSIONS
# of applicants	7,343
% accepted	66
# of first-year students enrolled	909
SAT Critical Reading range	500-590
SAT Math range	490-560
SAT Writing	n/a
ACT range	n/a
average HS GPA	3.3

Deadlines
early decision	12/1
regular decision	rolling
application fee (online)	$50 ($50)
fee waiver for applicants with financial need	yes

COST & AID
tuition	$30,298
room & board	$11,860
total need-based institutional scholarships/grants	$23,766,215
% of students apply for need-based aid	84
% of students receive aid	84
% receiving need-based scholarship or grant aid	68
% receiving aid whose need was fully met	10
average aid package	$19,074
average student loan debt upon graduation	$18,819

Southern Connecticut State University

Southern Connecticut State University serves a significant number of first-generation and minority students (43 percent and 21 percent, respectively) and is positioned to meet their unique needs. The newly completed Strategic Plan has re-committed the university to core values of equity, diversity and access. The university is noted particularly for its education program, and future educators may benefit from a tuition waiver if they commit to remaining in neighboring New Haven to teach. Students also benefit from the university's metropolitan location, which provides easy access to Boston, New York and the Berkshires.

> ACCESS ConnCAP (Connecticut Collegiate Awareness and Preparation Program)

Southern Connecticut State's ConnCap program provides tutoring for middle and high school students in the New Haven system. Participants take a range of college preparatory classes after-school, on Saturdays and in the summer. As with programs like Upward Bound, ConnCAP also exposes participants to the possibility of higher education.

> OPPORTUNITY SEOP (Summer Educational Opportunity Program)

Southern offers SEOP, a five-week summer program which assists 50 students in refining their skills before being accepted into the university. All students live on campus, attend classes and explore campus life together. Resident advisers and peer counselors work with SEOP students and implement a variety of academic and recreational enrichment activities. SEOP participants receive a number of academic advantages, including individualized academic counseling, small classes and personal attention from faculty and staff.

> OPPORTUNITY Future Educator Scholarships

Through a partnership with the New Haven public school system, students who intend to become teachers, particularly in underserved disciplines such as math, science and special education, can receive free tuition if they commit to teach in New Haven schools upon graduation from the university.

> SUCCESS International Student Services

The International Student Services office assists international (temporary visa) and U.S. permanent resident students by handling questions pertaining to visas, employment, immigration and related matters. Students with concerns about their studies or everyday living are referred to other student services offices as appropriate.

> SUCCESS Academic Advisement / Office of Study Skills Enrichment

The Academic Advisement Center assists in the advisement of all returning full-time and part-time students with undeclared majors. The Academic Advisement Center serves as the first stop center where students' questions are readily and easily answered.

"My experience at SCSU is characterized by challenging coursework and profound, meaningful relationships with my peers. At Southern, diversity abounds. Southern's classrooms are filled with knowledgeable professors and engaging students. As reflected in the University's strategic plan, Southern is dedicated to maintaining a diverse student body, most notably through its acclaimed summer opportunity programs."

– Willie G., '11
Manchester, CT
Recreation and Leisure

Southern Connecticut State University
501 Crescent Street
New Haven, CT 06515
Ph: (888) 500-SCSU / (203) 392-5200
adminfo@southernct.edu
www.southernct.edu

F A S T   F A C T S

STUDENT PROFILE

# of degree-seeking undergraduates	8,594
% male/female	37/63
% African American	12.6
% American Indian	0.3
% Asian	2.4
% Caucasian	68.2
% Hispanic	6.2
% Pell grant recipients	27

First-generation and minority alumni Col. Adele E. Hodges '77, first woman to lead U.S. Marine Corps base Camp Lejeune; Juan Carlos Osorio '98, head coach, MLS' Red Bulls; Alexandria Earle Givan '93, won gold medal in track, 1994 Pan-American Games; Gary Highsmith '90, principal of Hamden High School, Hamden, Conn.

ACADEMICS

full-time faculty	407
student-faculty ratio	16:1
average class size	10-29
% first-year retention rate	79.7
% graduation rate (6 years)	42.3

Popular majors Business Administration, Education, Exercise Science, Nursing, Psychology

CAMPUS LIFE

% live on campus (% freshmen)	32 (53)

Multicultural student clubs and organizations African American Student Association, Asian Academic Society, Baka Chan's Anime Society, Black Student Union, Chinese Student Association, CIAO Italian Club, Cultural Affairs Club, Delta Mu Delta Zeta Nu Chapter, Hispanic Cultural Society, LGBTQI Prism, Muslim Student Association, NAACP, Organization of Latin American Students, South Asian Student Association, West Indian Academic Society, Women's Center

Athletics NCAA Division II, Northeast-10 Conference, Eastern College Athletic Conference (Division I Football)

ADMISSIONS

# of applicants	5,561
% accepted	69
SAT Critical Reading range	440-520
SAT Math range	430-530
ACT range	n/a
average HS GPA	n/a

Deadlines

regular admission	4/1
application fee	$50
fee waiver for applicants for financial need	yes

COST & AID

tuition	in-state $3,742; out-of-state $12,112
room & board	$9,469
% of students receiving aid	50
% receiving need-based scholarship or grant aid	40
% receiving aid whose need was fully met	22
average aid package	$8,709
average student loan debt upon graduation	$17,341

Trinity College

Founded in 1823, Trinity College brings the great tradition of the liberal arts into the 21st century with its dynamic living and learning community. The college's 2,300 students work closely with faculty, broaden their education through campus activities and organizations, engage with the city of Hartford through internships and community service, and explore the wider world through study abroad and international initiatives on campus. Together, these experiences prepare Trinity graduates for fulfilling lives.

> ACCESS Mentoring Programs

Trinity students mentor middle and high school students through programs such as Rising Stars and the Vision Academic Mentoring Program (VAMP). The college subsidizes and hosts the Dream Camp for more than 300 city youth and subsidizes and staffs the Trinity/Tom Johnson Boys & Girls Club. In addition, Trinity participates in the "5th Graders and 9th Graders Go to College" program sponsored by the Hartford Consortium for Higher Education.

> OPPORTUNITY Preview Weekend

This three-day fall program is designed to give high school seniors an opportunity to explore both the academic and social aspects of the Trinity community, with a focus on the experiences of minority students. The similar V.I.P. Days program exists in the spring for admitted students.

> OPPORTUNITY QuestBridge National College Match Program

The QuestBridge National College Match program provides students who have achieved academic excellence in the face of economic hardship with a free application to Trinity College. The application enables these students to highlight their academic achievements in light of their low-income background and provides them the chance to receive financial aid packages covering 100% of their demonstrated need.

> OPPORUNITY Posse Foundation

Trinity College participates in the Posse Foundation, a program that brings talented inner-city youth to campus to pursue their academics and to help promote cross-cultural communication. Posse students are nominated by their high school to the program and share a collaborative support system with a special mentor to adjust to campus and college life. Trinity's Posse Scholars hail from New York City and Chicago.

> SUCCESS Office of Multicultural Affairs

Trinity's Office of Multicultural Affairs offers advice and support regarding personal and academic concerns, as well as advising for student groups. The office brings speakers and programs to campus and encourages interaction between Trinity's students and alumni, and students, staff and faculty from other colleges.

"Trinity professors work hard to help you find, create, and excel within your own niche. Our tight-knit community has allowed me to confidently challenge myself and discover new possibilities for a future career in the arts."

– Jeanika B.S., '12 East Hartford, CT Studio Arts, Theater and Dance

> SUCCESS Gateway Courses

Trinity's efforts to raise academic performance include supplemental instruction in math and science "gateway" courses and TEAM (a small group of faculty and administrators who form a network of support for students at academic risk). The college also participates in CHAS (Consortium on High Achievement and Success), an organization initiated by Trinity with more than 30 other colleges that sponsors educational and networking workshops for faculty and staff, conducts research, and hosts several student-oriented conferences annually.

Trinity College
Admissions Office
300 Summit St.
Ph: (860) 297-2180
admissions.office@trincoll.edu
www.trincoll.edu

F A S T   F A C T S

STUDENT PROFILE

# of degree-seeking undergraduates	2,341
% male/female	50/50
% African-American	7
% American Indian or Alaska Native	<1
% Asian or Pacific Islander	6
% Hispanic	6
% White	64
% International	5
% Pell grant recipients	n/a

First-generation and minority alumni Robert Stepto, Ph.D., literary theorist, professor of African American Studies, English and American Studies, Yale University, author, *From Behind the Veil: A Study of Afro-American Narrative, Chant of Saints — A Gathering of Afro-American Literature, Art and Scholarship, Blue as the Lake: A Personal Geography;* Francisco Borges, first black president and managing partner, Landmark Partners, Inc.; Eddie Perez, first Latino mayor, Hartford, Conn.

ACADEMICS

full-time faculty	213
full-time minority faculty	45
student-faculty ratio	9:1
average class size	20
% first-year retention rate	91
% graduation rate (6 years)	86

Popular majors Political Science, Economics, English, History, Biology, Psychology

CAMPUS LIFE

% live on campus (% fresh.)	95(99)

Multicultural student clubs and organizations Asian-American Students Association, International Students Association, La Voz Latina, Men of Color Alliance, Caribbean Student Association, Trinity College Black Women's Organization

Athletics NCAA Division III, New England Small College Athletic Conference

ADMISSIONS

# of applicants	4,532
% accepted	41
# of first-year students enrolled	573
SAT Critical Reading range	590-680
SAT Math range	610-690
SAT Writing range	610-710
ACT range	26-30
average HS GPA	3.0

Deadlines

early decision	11/15
regular decision	1/1
application fee (online)	$60($60)
fee waiver for applicants with financial need	yes

COST & AID

tuition	$40,360
room & board	$10,960
total need-based institutional scholarships/grants	$27,902,749
% of students apply for need-based aid	49
% of students receive aid	43
% receiving need-based scholarship or grant aid	41
% receiving aid whose need was fully met	100
average aid package	$36,504
average student loan debt upon graduation	$13,492

Wesleyan University

Wesleyan is a highly selective private liberal-arts university that attracts a diverse student body from all over the world. It is dedicated to the outreach and support of underrepresented students in Connecticut and beyond, and approximately 30 percent of undergraduates are students of color and 12 percent are first-generation college students. The University is committed to fully meeting 100 percent of undergraduates' financial need. Located in the small New England city of Middletown, Conn., Wesleyan provides students the opportunity to attend a top-notch research university with the intimate intellectual and social community of a liberal arts college.

> ACCESS Wesleyan-Middletown Public Schools Collaborative

The Wesleyan-Middletown Public Schools Collaborative empowers and encourages upper-elementary and middle school students from first-generation and low-income backgrounds to achieve higher education. The program enhances students' academic performance, college preparation and career exploration through tutoring, special events and academic and cultural enrichment in the areas of math and science, art, foreign languages, college admissions and more.

> ACCESS Upward Bound

Local high school students who are from low-income families can benefit from the Wesleyan's Upward Bound program, a pre-college program that provides about 120 students in Middletown, Meriden and Portland with the right tools to pursue their goals of earning a college degree. Students benefit from weekly tutoring, field trips, workshops, and a summer enrichment program.

> OPPORTUNITY Subsidized Visits

To encourage first-generation, low-income and other underrepresented students to enroll in Wesleyan, the university arranges and subsidizes transportation for these students to attend fall open houses and the admitted student weekend, WesFest. Wesleyan admissions officers also offer workshops throughout the country to provide outreach and college preparation programs.

> SUCCESS Mellon Mays Undergraduate Fellowship

The Mellon Mays Undergraduate Fellowship is a mentoring program that supports students from underrepresented racial and ethnic groups interested in pursuing careers in academia. The program seeks to increase the number of minorities who will pursue doctoral degrees in core arts and sciences fields through mentoring, opportunities for independent research, skills development, and introduction to the academic life. Students are typically identified in their second year.

> SUCCESS The Ronald E. McNair Post-Baccalaureate Achievement Program

The Wesleyan McNair Program assists students from underrepresented backgrounds with strong academic potential, preparing them to pursue doctoral programs through involvement in research and other scholarly activities. Wesleyan provides support in and out of the classroom and financially as they complete their undergraduate and possibly graduate requirements.

"What struck me most about Wesleyan was its diverse and dynamic community, which truly makes me feel at home. Students willing to engage themselves will find that Wesleyan offers the opportunity to foster knowledge and encourage dialogue. Encouragement from faculty and my involvement with the Wesleyan community have helped me adjust to college. I've made long-lasting friendships and gained insight from amazing professors who have inspired me and opened my mind."
— Erik G., '09
Bronx, NY
Biology

Wesleyan University
70 Wyllys Ave.
Middletown, CT 06459
Ph: (860) 685-3000
admission@wesleyan.edu
www.wesleyan.edu

FAST FACTS

STUDENT PROFILE
# of degree-seeking undergraduates	2,774
% male/female	51/49
% African American	7
% American Indian	<1
% Asian or Pacific Islander	10
% White	58
% Hispanic	9
% International	7
% Pell grant recipients	13

First-generation and minority alumni
Majora Carter, founder and executive Director, Sustainable South Bronx (2006 MacArthur award winner); Lin-Manuel Miranda, Tony Award-winning composer and lyricist of the musical *In the Heights*; Michael S. Roth, president, Wesleyan University; Theodore M. Shaw, Columbia Law professor and former director-counsel and president, NAACP Legal Defense Fund; Michael Yamashita, photographer, National Geographic

ACADEMICS
full-time faculty	330
full-time minority faculty	58
student-faculty ratio	9:1
average class size	18
% first year retention rate	95
% graduation rate (6 years)	93

Popular majors English, Government, Psychology

CAMPUS LIFE
% live on campus (% fresh.)	99(100)

Multicultural student clubs and organizations
African Student's Association, Alliance of Progressive South Asians, Ajua Campos, Asian American Student Coalition, Black and Latino Brotherhood, Black Women's Collective, Chinese Adopted Sibs, Chinese Students Association, Fusion, Indonesian Society, Japan Society, Kol Israel, Korean Students' Association, Lac Viet, Nosotras, PADThai Culture and Society, Pangea, PINOY, Shakti, Students of Color Coalition, Taiwanese Cultural Society, Ujamaa, WesConnection, West Indian Student Association, Women of Color Collective

Athletics NCAA Division III, New England Small College Athletic Conference

ADMISSIONS
# of applicants	10,068
% accepted	22
# of first year students enrolled	745
SAT Critical Reading range	670-770
SAT Math range	670-760
ACT range	30-34
average HS GPA	3.95

Deadlines
early decision I, early decision II	11/15, 1/1
regular decision	1/1
application fee (online)	$55 ($55)
fee waiver for applicants with financial need	yes

COST & AID
tuition	$41,814
room & board	$11,794
total need-based institutional scholarships/grants	$31,295,000
% of students apply for need based aid	51
% of students receive aid	47
% receiving need-based scholarship or grant aid	48
% receiving aid whose need was fully met	100
average aid package	$34,488
average student loan debt upon graduation	$27,402

Yale University

Yale University
P.O. Box 208234
New Haven, CT 06520
Ph: (203) 432-9300
student.questions@yale.edu
www.yale.edu

As the third-oldest college in the United States, Yale University has educated a wide variety of leaders from all backgrounds. Today, Yale graduates can be found across the globe in every imaginable profession. Because the university is committed to opening up access to underrepresented minorities and students from lower socioeconomic backgrounds, financial need plays no role in the admissions process and the university meets 100 percent of admitted students' demonstrated need.

> ACCESS College Summit

Yale University recently entered into a partnership with College Summit, an organization that helps low-income students apply for and attend college. College Summit is a national non-profit organization that supports bright, low-income, mid-tier students and gives them the tools they need to be successful in the college admissions process during a four-day workshop, held on a college campus.

> ACCESS College Horizons / QuestBridge

Yale has worked with College Horizons since this non-profit was founded in 1996. College Horizons is a five-day pre-college workshop for Native American high school students. Participants work with college counselors and college admissions officers to help them navigate the college admission process. In addition, Yale entered into a partnership with QuestBridge in 2007, helping to link low-income high school students to the university.

> OPPORTUNITY Multicultural Open House / Fly-In Program

The Multicultural Open House introduces prospective students to Yale's academic programs, campus life, admissions process and financial aid resources. Admitted students who demonstrate significant financial need are provided with a travel stipend to visit the university.

> SUCCESS Residential College Dean

The primary academic adviser is a student's residential college dean. The dean is available for academic and personal advice. The college dean lives and has an office in the residential college where the students live.

> SUCCESS Freshman Counselor Program

Incoming students receive support from a senior counselor who lives nearby and serves as a mentor to ease the transition to college. Some freshman counselors also have special training in discussing issues of racial and ethnic identity.

> SUCCESS Science, Technology and Research Scholars (STARS)

STARS provides select freshmen through seniors with an integrated experience in research, course-based study and development of mentorship skills. STARS identifies and supports students from groups that are underrepresented in scientific and technological disciplines, along with students who come from disadvantaged circumstances, in any of Yale's natural sciences and engineering majors.

FAST FACTS

STUDENT PROFILE
# of degree-seeking undergraduates	5,256
% male/female	50/50
% African-American	9
% American Indian or Alaska Native	1
% Asian or Pacific Islander	14
% Hispanic	9
% White	45
% International	9
% Pell grant recipients	10.1

First-generation and minority alumni Clarence Thomas, Supreme Court Justice; Angela Bassett, actress; Wendell Mottley, Olympic runner; Prakazrel Samuel Michel, rapper; Michiko Kakutani, Pulitzer Prize-winning critic; Susan Choi, author; Fareed Zakaria, editor of *Newsweek International*

ACADEMICS
full-time faculty	1,100
full-time minority faculty	n/a
student-faculty ratio	7:1
average class size	10-19
% first-year retention rate	99
% graduation rate (6 yr.)	96

Popular majors Economics, History, Political Science, Psychology, and English

CAMPUS LIFE
% live on campus (% fresh.)	100(100)

Multicultural student clubs and organizations African Student Association, American Indian Science and Engineering Society, Asian American Students Association, Arab Students Association, Black Student Alliance, Chinese American Students' Organization, Cuban-American Undergraduate Student Association, Chinese Undergraduate Student Association, Despierta Boricua, Dominican Student Association, Eritrean and Ethiopian Students' Alliance, Foundations- Asian American Debriefing Project, Friends of Israel, Friends of Turkey, International Students Organization, Japanese American Students Union, The Filipino Club, Korean American Students of Yale (KASY), Latin American Student Organization, Model Arab League, The Persian Society, Taiwanese American Society, Vietnamese Student Association, West Indian Students' Organization

Athletics NCAA Division I, Eastern College Athletic Conference

ADMISSIONS
# of applicants	22,817
% accepted	9
# of first-year student enrolled	1,320
SAT Critical Reading range	700-800
SAT Math range	700-780
SAT Writing	700-790
ACT range	30-34
average HS GPA	n/a

Deadlines
early action	11/1
regular decision	12/31
application fee (online)	$75 ($75)
fee waiver for applicants with financial need	yes

COST & AID
tuition	$36,500
room & board	$11,000
total need-based institutional scholarships/ grants	$87,892,290
% of students apply for need-based aid	57
% of students receive aid	100
% receiving need-based scholarship or grant aid	100
% receiving aid whose need was fully met	100
average aid package	$37,223
average student loan debt upon graduation	$12,735

The George Washington University

The George Washington University attracts a multicultural, motivated, and active community, in which the leaders of today nurture the leaders of tomorrow. The University enrolls undergraduates from all 50 states, the District of Columbia, Puerto Rico, the Virgin Islands, and 125 countries worldwide. Committed to presenting multicultural points of view across the curriculum and University, it offers an array of classroom experiences, privileged access to academic resources on campus and in Washington, D.C., and a well-connected faculty. Students can create their own distinctive course of study to fit their individual needs and goals.

> **ACCESS GW's Summer Scholars Pre-College Programs**

A six-week Pre-College Program offers eleventh graders the opportunity to live on campus, take classes offered by the University's renowned faculty and to earn credits, and to explore Washington, D.C. The 10-day Mini-Courses Program provides ninth, tenth and eleventh graders with an opportunity to explore various career options through lectures, famous guest speakers, and visits to important institutions and sites unique to the nation's capitol. Need-based financial aid and merit scholarships are available to participants.

> **OPPORTUNITY Need-Based Scholarship and Grant Aid**

The University has initiated a fixed tuition rate for the duration of students' undergraduate studies and has made a commitment to those eligible for need-based financial assistance by guaranteeing them a tuition grant for up to ten consecutive semesters of undergraduate enrollment. The University offers various scholarships to students who demonstrate financial need, are eligible for Federal Pell Grants, and who are academically exceptional.

> **SUCCESS Colonial Inauguration and the Guide to Personal Success Program (GPS)**

The University offers this summer orientation program to incoming freshman, transfer and international students. It is a two and half day event led by the Colonial Cabinet, a diverse group of student leaders who introduce students to academic advisors and current students, help them learn about academic and extra-curricular opportunities, and help them get to know their fellow classmates. Additionally, programs are provided for parents, guardians and siblings. Once students arrive on campus in the fall, they are assigned a Guide to Personal Success (GPS), a knowledgeable George Washington University staff member who helps them navigate any personal, professional, or experiential issues, and connects them with University resources.

> **SUCCESS Multicultural Student Services Center**

The Center offers a variety of workshops, events, and programs each semester, including the Black Men's Initiative which offers activities to advance the mission of supporting the academic, social, intellectual, and spiritual growth of Black male students; C3, a cross cultural dialogue group; and The Jackie Robinson discussion series, which consists of a number of social and cultural activities to enhance multicultural ideals.

"One of the great things about GW is that our campus is integrated with the city. Often times you will find people venturing past the barriers of which they are accustomed befriending people of very different backgrounds. In addition there are a number of organizations on campus that raise awareness of the diverse city we have all chosen to call home. GW is a very diverse school with students from literally every corner of the world. So if I had to describe the "feel" of being on campus I would say that everyone is at home here."

*– Markus K., '10
Lawrenceville, NJ
International Affairs*

The George Washington University
2121 Eye Street, N.W. Suite 201
Washington, D.C. 20052
Ph: (800) 417-3765 / (202) 994-6040
gwadm@gwu.edu
www.gwu.edu

FAST FACTS

STUDENT PROFILE

# of degree-seeking undergraduates	10,291
% male/female	45/55
% African American	7
% American Indian or Alaska Native	<1
% Asian or Pacific Islander	10
% Hispanic	7
% White	58
% International	5
% Pell grant recipients	8

First-generation and minority alumni Colin Powell, former U.S. Secretary of State; Kerry Washington, actress; Warren Brown, Food Network host and owner of Cake Love; Gerardo I. Lopez, CEO and President of AMC Theaters

ACADEMICS

full-time faculty	861
full-time minority faculty	165
student/faculty ratio	13:1
average class size	20
% first year retention rate	91
% graduation rate (6 yr.)	81

Popular majors Biology, International Affairs, Political Science, Business Administration, Biomedical Engineering

CAMPUS LIFE

% live on campus (% fresh.)	66 (98)

Multicultural student clubs and organizations Black Student Union, George Washington Williams House, Asian Student Alliance, Organization of Latino American Students, Racially and Ethnically Mixed Student Association, Multicultural Greek Council, Organization of African Students, GW Raas, GW Bhangra

Athletics NCAA Division I, Atlantic 10

ADMISSIONS

# of applicants	19,430
% accepted	37
# of first-year students enrolled	2,461
SAT Critical Reading range	590-680
SAT Math range	600-690
SAT Writing range	600-690
ACT range	25-30
average HS GPA	n/a

Deadlines

early decision	11/10
regular decision	1/10
application fee (online)	$65 ($65)
fee waiver for applicants with financial need	yes

COST & AID

tuition	$41,610
room & board	$10,120
total need-based institutional scholarships and grants	$94,629,467
% students apply for need-based aid	48
% receiving need-based scholarship or grant aid	97
% receiving aid whose need fully met	82
average aid package	$37,252
average student loan debt upon graduation	$31,299

Trinity Washington University

Trinity Washington University
Office of Admissions
125 Michigan Avenue, NE
Washington, DC 20017
Ph: (800) 492-6882 / (202) 884-9400
admissions@trinitydc.edu
www.trinitydc.edu

Trinity Washington University, founded in 1897, is a private university in Washington, D.C. Trinity is committed to the academic success of D.C. students – nearly 50% of Trinity students are D.C. residents. Trinity is very affordable and was named "Best Value" among Washington, D.C., universities by Fox News. Trinity proudly enrolls more DC-TAG recipients than any other private institution in the region and in the nation.

Trinity prepares its students to become leaders of character — passionate intellectuals excited about their future. Trinity's College of Arts and Sciences is the university's undergraduate women's college, where there is a priority on the education of women, the development of women's leadership skills, and a focus on the academic and career success of women. Trinity's prestigious graduates include Speaker of the House of Representatives Nancy Pelosi and Secretary of Health and Human Services Kathleen Sebelius.

"Trinity, in Washington, D.C., has given me fantastic opportunities. I enjoy the small classes and a personal connection with my professors. The teachers know me and I know them."
– *Kamillah M., '12 Washington, DC Chemistry*

> ACCESS **Ensuring Smooth Transitions**

Trinity works closely with the DC College Success Foundation, the DC College Access Program (DC-CAP) and other programs to ensure a smooth transition from high school to college.

> OPPORTUNITY **Aspiring Leader Award**

Aspiring Leader awards are made to College of Arts and Sciences students who have demonstrated financial need and leadership potential.

> OPPORTUNITY **Trinity Scholarships and More**

In 2009-10, Trinity awarded more than $2.2 million in scholarships and grants to D.C. students. Full-time Trinity students are considered for a wide range of scholarships. The average student aid package is $17,000.

> SUCCESS **Student Support Services**

Trinity provides students with extensive academic support, including a Writing Center, tutoring services, disability support services, and workshops on transitioning to college. Trinity provides professional health care, mental health counseling and spiritual support.

> SUCCESS **First-Year Students Success Program**

First-year students at Trinity take part in a special curriculum in which students focus on a foundation of academic skills that ensures their success as a college student. Each student takes the Critical Reading Seminar which is also the student's Learning Community and the professor is her advisor. The Learning Community also fosters an academic and social support structure for the students in that class – they support each other as they make the transition from high school to college.

> SUCCESS **Internships in Washington, D.C.**

Internships prepare Trinity students for careers by giving them valuable work experience combined with academic training. The Washington, D.C., area offers amazing internship opportunities from Capitol Hill to the White House, Department of State, C-SPAN, *The Washington Post*, Black Entertainment Television (BET), and many corporate headquarters.

FAST FACTS

STUDENT PROFILE

# of degree-seeking undergraduates	1,386
% male/female	4/96
% African-American	66
% American Indian or Alaska Native	0
% Asian or Pacific Islander	1
% Hispanic	21
% White	6
% International	6
% Pell grant recipients	62

First-generation and minority alumni Perita Carpenter '02, journalist; Michelle Mitchell '06, lawyer at Hughes, Hubbard & Reed; Philonda Johnson '05, principal of KIPP DC school

ACADEMICS

full-time faculty	60
full-time minority faculty	13
student-faculty ratio	15:1
average class size	15
% first-year retention rate	70
% graduation rate (6 yr.)	52

Popular majors Nursing, Criminal Justice, Psychology, Business Administration, Education, Communication

CAMPUS LIFE

% live on campus (% fresh.)	28(35)

Multicultural student clubs and organizations Latin American and Caribbean American Student Association, International Student Association, Muslim Student Association, Minority Association of Pre-Health Students, NAACP
Athletics Division III, Independent

ADMISSIONS

# of applicants	1,284
% accepted	90
# of first-year student enrolled	293
SAT Critical Reading range	n/a
SAT Math range	n/a
SAT Writing	n/a
ACT range	n/a
average HS GPA	2.9
Deadlines	
regular decision	rolling
application fee (online)	$40 ($0)
fee waiver for applicants with financial need	yes

COST & AID

tuition	$19,360
room & board	$8,850
total need-based institutional scholarships/ grants	$3,830,962
% of students apply for need-based aid	96
% receiving need-based scholarship or grant aid	89
% receiving aid whose need was fully met	8
average aid package	$17,000
average student loan debt upon graduation	$17,000

Barry University

Barry University in Miami Shores, Florida, combines hands-on career preparation, a broad arts and sciences curriculum, and a diversity of cultures and faiths in a caring environment. *U.S. News & World Report* ranks Barry among the top 20 schools nationwide for campus diversity. It is the second-largest Catholic university in the Southeast. Barry offers more

than 60 undergraduate programs, including some that allow students to graduate in five years with both their bachelor's and master's degrees. With small classes, students receive personal attention from distinguished faculty. They also participate in internships and service learning to gain hands-on, professional experience before they graduate. The tropical, tree-lined campus is a few minutes from the dynamic city of Miami, and students can access recreational and cultural opportunities year-round. Founded in 1940, Barry is an independent, coed, Catholic-affiliated university. Through innovative programs, Barry promotes diversity, inclusion, and academic and personal growth.

> ACCESS High School Equivalency Program

The High School Equivalency Program helps migrant and seasonal farm workers earn their high school diploma or equivalent, so they can advance to college or other jobs. Participants are at least 16 years old and not currently enrolled in school. The program is federally funded by the U.S. Department of Education and is managed by Barry's School of Education.

> OPPORTUNITY Goizueta Foundation Scholarships

Since 2000, Barry University has been affiliated with the Goizueta Foundation for the promotion of social justice and community service. Barry has three Goizueta Foundation scholarships. The Minority Empowerment Scholarships promote and contribute to the education of minority women in the schools of Adult and Continuing Education, Arts and Sciences, Business, Education, Health Sciences, and Social Work. The Minority Science Scholarships focus on the education of successive generations of minority scientific leaders. The 2+2 Scholarships support future teachers enrolled in Barry University's Adrian Dominican School of Education.

> SUCCESS Orientation and Leadership

Barry's Division of Student Affairs sponsors both Orientation for first-year students and the Emerging Leaders Program. In Orientation, students get a head start on the academic year and the Barry experience through class registration and meet advisors, classmates, faculty, and staff. The Emerging Leaders Program helps students develop leadership skills through training and practical experience. Students gain skills in communication, time management, networking, and ethical decision-making while interacting with campus leaders and administrators.

"The small class size at Barry is the best environment for learning. It allows you to have a more personal relationship with the professor so that they can understand you and be able to help you better. This allows professors to become mentors, not only providers of information."
– Kelsa B., '10
San Fernando, Trinidad
Photography

> SUCCESS MARC U*STAR

The Minority Access to Research Careers – Undergraduate Student Training in Academic Research (MARC U*STAR) program is a federally funded effort to increase the representation of minority students in the biomedical field. Barry's program focuses on students majoring in biology, chemistry, computer science, math, or psychology. Selected students participate in on-campus research with faculty, summer research internships, and graduate school preparation. Students may also publish their research findings in scientific journals and attend national and international scientific meetings. Academic scholarships and funding for research and travel are also available through the program.

Barry University
11300 NE Second Avenue
Miami Shores, FL 33161-6695
Ph: (305) 899-3100
admissions@mail.barry.edu
www.barry.edu

F A S T   F A C T S

STUDENT PROFILE
# of degree-seeking undergraduates	4,963
% male/female	31/69
% African American	20
% American Indian or Alaska Native	1
% Asian or Pacific Islander	2
% Hispanic	28
% White	19
% International	5
% Pell grant recipients	40.2

ACADEMICS
full-time faculty	325
full-time minority faculty	92
student-faculty ratio	14:1
average class size	10-19
% first-year retention rate	64
% graduation rate (6 years)	39

Popular majors Biology, Education, Nursing, Management, Sport Management

CAMPUS LIFE
% freshmen who live on campus	63

Multicultural student clubs and organizations Black Student Union, Caribbean Student Association, Haitian Intercultural Association, Latin American Student Association, historically Black/Latino/multicultural fraternities and sororities
Athletics NCAA Division II, Sunshine State Conference

ADMISSIONS
# of applicants	3,660
% accepted	62
# of first-year students enrolled	586
SAT Critical Reading range	440-520
SAT Math range	420-520
SAT Writing range	n/a
ACT range	18-22
average HS GPA	n/a

Deadlines
early decision	n/a
regular decision	rolling
application fee (online)	$30 ($20)
fee waiver for applicants with financial need	yes

COST & AID
tuition	$27,200
room & board	$9,200
total need-based institutional scholarships/grants	$4,573,807
% of students apply for need-based aid	81
% of students receiving aid	76
% receiving need-based scholarship or grant aid	53
% receiving aid whose need was fully met	5
average aid package	$17,576
average student loan debt upon graduation	$31,469

Florida Atlantic University

Founded in 1964, Florida Atlantic University has consistently ranked among the top 50 four-year colleges in granting bachelor's degrees to Hispanic students, and is considered one of the most diverse campuses in the nation with students from all 50 states and over 130 countries. With a strong tradition of student success, service, and leadership, Florida Atlantic University values development in and out of the classroom and offers a variety of internship, study abroad, and scholarship opportunities, as well as more than 200 student organizations and 17 NCAA Division I sports. The Harriet L. Wilkes Honors College and University Scholars Program provide students with opportunities to challenge themselves academically while taking honors-level courses and participating in small seminars during their college careers.

> ACCESS The College Reach-Out Program (CROP)

The Office of Multicultural Affairs and Pre-College Programs offers a program for students in grades 6-12 to pursue and successfully complete post-secondary education by participating in Saturday tutoring, summer enrichment, and summer residence at Florida Atlantic University. Students also partake in community service and receive mentoring from the University.

> ACCESS Upward Bound

Local high school students who come from low-income families in which neither parent holds a bachelor's degree can benefit from Florida Atlantic University's Upward Bound, a pre-college program that provides a group of students with the right tools to pursue their dreams of earning a college degree. Students benefit from weekly tutoring, field trips, workshops, and a six-week summer enrichment program.

> OPPORTUNITY Southeastern Consortium for Minorities in Engineering, Inc. Scholarship

This $3,000 scholarship is awarded to a limited number of high school students in the Broward and Palm Beach counties in Florida who have met requirements for admission at Florida Atlantic University and have participated in the Southeastern Consortium for Minorities in Engineering Program. Applicants must have achieved a minimum score of 1450 on the SAT I or a score of 21 on the ACT, as well as submit two letters of reference and a personal essay.

> SUCCESS The Gateway Program

Florida Atlantic University provides support and encouragement for admitted students with SAT or ACT scores below the state-minimum requirements by encouraging these students to take on challenging college course work and to embark on a successful academic career. Students will enroll in an English course focusing on developing writing skills and another course offering an introduction to higher education and the resources the University has to offer. Students learn to develop time management, test-taking, and communication skills essential to the college experience.

> SUCCESS Passport to FAU

Held the first Saturday before fall classes begin, this is an annual conference to encourage freshmen and transfer student success. Topics include: Making a Successful Transition to Florida Atlantic University, Setting Goals for Success, Time Management, Stress Management, Exploring Learning Styles, Note Taking and Reading College Texts, Preparing for and Making Tests, and Financial Management.

"As a first-generation college student with limited resources, I sought the help of the Office of Multicultural Affairs at FAU. Their free tutoring and mentoring program provided me and other first-generation college students of different backgrounds with the individual attention I needed to succeed in reaching my goal of graduating."
– Pablo B., '09
North Lauderdale, FL
Political Science

Florida Atlantic University
Admissions Office
777 Glades Road
Boca Raton, FL 33431-0991
Ph: (561) 297-3040
admissions@fau.edu
www.fau.edu

F A S T   F A C T S

STUDENT PROFILE

# of degree-seeking undergraduates	20,946
% male/female	41/59
% African American	18
% American Indian	<1
% Asian	5
% Caucasian	55
% Hispanic	19
% International	3
% Pell grant recipients	28

ACADEMICS

full-time faculty	796
full-time minority faculty	172
student-faculty ratio	19:1
average class size	34
% first-year retention rate	75
% graduation rate (6 years)	39

Popular majors Area and Ethnic Studies, Business and Marketing, Education, Liberal Arts

CAMPUS LIFE

% live on campus (% fresh.)	13 (49)

Multicultural student clubs and organizations
Asian Student Union, Association of Latin American Students, Black Student Union and Multicultural Programming, Caribbean Students Association, Disciples of Nations, Helping International Students Ministry, Indian Students Association, International Student Union, Multicultural Café, National Society of Black Engineers, Pakistani Students Association, Palestinian American Organization, Students for Israel, Thai Student Association

Athetics NCAA Division I, Sun Belt Conference

ADMISSIONS

# of applicants	13,150
% accepted	49
SAT Critical Reading range	470-560
SAT Math range	480-570
ACT Range	22-25
average HS GPA	3.4

Deadlines

regular decision	rolling to 2/15
online application fee	$30
fee waiver for applicants with financial need	yes

COST & AID

tuition	in-state $3,662; out-of-state $17,389
room & board	$9,582
total need based institutional scholarships/grants	$6,423,961
% of students apply for need based aid	56
% of students receive aid	41
% receiving need-based scholarship or grant aid	32
% receiving aid whose need was fully met	12
average aid package	$6,568.50
average student loan debt upon graduation	n/a

Lynn University

Lynn University is a private, coeducational university awarding bachelor's and master's degrees in the liberal arts and sciences and professional education. Founded in 1962, Lynn offers a distinctive, innovative, and individualized approach to learning. Lynn has a remarkably international and diverse community with 2,400 students, representing forty states and eighty-four nations. Specialty programs include a Conservatory of Music, a School of Aeronautics, and the Institute for Achievement and Learning, which serves students with learning differences. Although grounded in liberal education, Lynn's programs are oriented toward emerging career opportunities, with an emphasis on real-world experience coupled with classroom study. The 16:1 student/faculty ratio provides a personalized environment with small classes and an innovative curriculum.

> ACCESS Open Houses and Campus Tours

Lynn University hosts five open houses per year; all programs are open to all interested students. Open houses give students an opportunity to meet the deans and degree program coordinators and talk to financial aid counselors. Campus tours are a great way for students to get a full taste of college life by eating lunch in the cafeteria and sitting in on a class. After the tour, admissions counselors are available to answer questions, address concerns and conduct an informational interview.

> OPPORTUNITY Lynn Scholarships and Financial Aid

Don't let cost prevent you from obtaining the college education of your dreams. Scholarships, grants, loans and other forms of financial assistance can make Lynn education more affordable than you ever imagined. In fact, for more than 62 percent of Lynn students receive some form of financial aid. Academic scholarships in the range from $6,000 to $12,000 are awarded on the basis of test scores and high school grades, in addition to need-based aid. A financial aid calculator is available on Lynn's website.

> SUCCESS Institute for Achievement and Learning

The Institute for Achievement and Learning is committed to the idea that each learner has a unique set of strengths and weaknesses and is dedicated to helping those individuals achieve their academic goals by maximizing the use of their strengths and minimizing the impact of their weaknesses. The Institute strives to help students understand their learning competencies and develop them during their time at the university. The Institute's current model incorporates services such as group and/or individual tutoring, specialized learning communities and group activities. Students are not only assisted in understanding specific course content but also, in each instance, strategies for planning, organizing and implementing their studies.

> *"Almost every single person I've met at Lynn is on financial aid. I am paying for school myself, and it's not rare here that students depend on some sort of aid to attend the school. The value of this place is just so entirely worth it. I wouldn't have gone anywhere else."*
>
> *– Jordan A., '12*
> *Hunterdon, NJ*
> *Film Major*

Lynn University
3601 North Military Trail
Boca Raton, Florida 33431
Ph: (800) 888-5966
admissions@lynn.edu
http://www.lynn.edu

F A S T   F A C T S

STUDENT PROFILE

# of degree-seeking undergraduates	1,786
% male/female	49/51
% African-American	3
% American Indian or Alaska Native	<1
% Asian or Pacific Islander	<1
% Hispanic	7
% White	47
% International	15
% Pell grant recipients	17

First-generation and minority alumni Jose Durate '98, Owner, Taranta restaurant, Boston; Tifany North '94, '97, PhD '03, education consultant; Maria Carrera '03, TV producer, Univision, San Antonio; Delsa Bush, '01, Chief of Police, West Palm Beach; Brandon Ackerman, '09, Vice President, Solar17 and Motionbrite

ACADEMICS

full-time faculty	103
full-time minority faculty	24
student-faculty ratio	16:1
average class size	17
% first-year retention rate	58
% graduation rate (6 years)	35

Popular majors Business and Management, Biology, Communications, Psychology, Hospitality

CAMPUS LIFE

% live on campus	83

Multicultural student clubs and organizations Caribbean Club, Black Student Union, Organization of Latin American Students (OLAS), International Affairs Society, Just About Kids, Students for the Poor, Interfaith Council, Gay-Straight Alliance
Athletics NCAA Division II, Sunshine State Conference

ADMISSIONS

# of applicants	2,454
% accepted	72
# of first-year students enrolled	477
SAT Critical Reading average	200-720
SAT Math average	200-800
SAT Writing average	n/a
ACT average	13-30
average HS GPA	2.8

Deadlines

regular decision	rolling
application fee	$35
fee waiver for applicants with financial need	yes

COST & AID

tuition	$28,600
room & board	$10,900
total need-based institutional scholarships/grants	n/a
% of students apply for need-based aid	68
% receiving need-based scholarship or grant aid	36
% receiving aid whose need was fully met	61
average aid package	$20,853
average student loan debt at graduation	$34,075

New College of Florida

Consistently rated as one of the country's top public liberal arts colleges, New College of Florida was founded in 1960 and is designated as Florida's state honors college for the arts and sciences. Located along the Gulf of Mexico in Sarasota, New College offers more than 30 academic programs in the humanities, social sciences and natural sciences. Plus, with the support of faculty, students may design individual concentrations to meet their personal academic interests. Uniquely, students at New College receive narrative evaluations from their professors, rather than letter grades — a system that provides constructive advice and challenges students to do their best work. New College students say that freedom and tolerance define social life on campus, and that respect for sexual orientation, political affiliation, freedom of speech, ethnic heritage and cultural associations are paramount. One hundred percent of New College's first-year students receive some form of financial aid, and more than 80 percent of New College graduates go on to earn advanced degrees.

"The financial aid I've received has helped me stay at New College and afforded me wonderful opportunities. I'm graduating with a double concentration in music and political science. While at New College, I've gotten to work with members of the Sarasota Orchestra, which is a rare and priceless benefit for a student composer."
– Alejandro C., '09
Tampa, FL
Political Science, Music

> **ACCESS PUSH/SUCCESS and Science Outreach for Students (SOS)**

New College collaborates with local schools to promote interest in the sciences, particularly among students from minority and underrepresented populations. The PUSH/SUCCESS summer program brings middle and high school students to campus for two weeks to learn science research and presentation methods. Through the college's Science Outreach for Students program, New College students get hands-on experience teaching middle and high school students about the sciences and designing educational programming at area parks and conservation areas.

> **OPPORTUNITY Guaranteed Scholarships**

All first-time-in-college students who enter New College in the fall are guaranteed a scholarship, so long as they completed the admission application by the scholarship deadline. New College gives special scholarship consideration for National Achievement Scholars; National Hispanic Scholars; National Merit Scholars; Ventures Scholars; Florida Education Fund National Achievers Society members; IB Diploma candidates; AICE Diploma candidates; students from member programs of the National Consortium for Specialized Secondary Schools for Mathematics, Science, and Technology; Intel Semifinalists and Finalists; and International Science and Engineering Fair Participants.

> **OPPORTUNITY First Generation Matching Grant**

Florida students who are the first in their family to attend college may be eligible for the First Generation Matching Grant for Florida Residents, a statewide grant program for students who demonstrate substantial financial need. Grant awards for this program range from $200 to the total cost of attendance.

> **SUCCESS Support Services and Activities**

The President's Office at New College champions cultural diversity and diversity of thought by organizing campus-wide diversity discussions, coordinating annual "Common Read" activities for incoming students, and attracting new minority faculty through the president's Hire of Opportunity program. Individual academic advising is provided to all students by faculty.

New College of Florida
5800 Bay Shore Road
Sarasota, FL 34243
Ph: (941) 487-5000
admissions@ncf.edu
www.ncf.edu

FAST FACTS

STUDENT PROFILE

# of degree-seeking undergraduates	785
% male/female	36/64
% African-American	2
% American Indian or Alaska Native	2
% Asian or Pacific Islander	2
% Hispanic	10
% White	76
% International	<1
% Pell grant recipients	18

First-generation and minority alumni Lincoln Díaz-Balart, U.S. Representative, Miami, Florida; Dr. Anita L. Allen, Henry R. Silverman Professor of Law and Philosophy, University of Pennsylvania; Jose Díaz-Balart, CBS News "This Morning" anchor and former Telemundo newscaster; Dr. David L. Smith, professor of English, Williams College; Natalie Arsenault, outreach coordinator, Lozano-Long Institute for Latin American Studies; Dr. Raymonda L. Burgman, assistant professor of economics and management, DePauw University

ACADEMICS

full-time faculty	73
full-time minority faculty	9
student-faculty ratio	10:1
average class size	18
% first-year retention rate	82
% graduation rate (6 years)	63

Popular majors Psychology, Biology, Political Science, Literature, Economics

CAMPUS LIFE

% live on campus	80 (99)

Multicultural student clubs and organizations Amnesty International, China Club, Hillel, Jesus Club, Multifaith Council, Multicultural Club, Sodalitas Catholica, Unitarian Universalist Club

Athletics No varsity athletics, but club sports and intramurals are available

ADMISSIONS

# of applicants	1,221
% accepted	58
# of first-year students enrolled	239
SAT Critical Reading range	630-730
SAT Math range	590-670
SAT Writing range	600-690
ACT range	27-31
average HS GPA	3.91

Deadlines

priority application	2/15
application fee (online)	$30 ($30)
fee waiver for applicants with financial need	yes

COST & AID

tuition	in-state: $4,784; out-of-state: $26,386
room & board	$7,783
total need-based institutional scholarships/grants	n/a
% of students apply for need-based aid	57.8
% of students receive aid	n/a
% receiving need-based scholarship or grant aid	39.2
% receiving aid whose need was fully met	71.8
average aid package	$12,911
average student loan debt upon graduation	$13,162

Nova Southeastern University

In 2007, Nova Southeastern University received the U.S. Department of Education's Title V Developing Hispanic-Serving Institutions program grant for $5.6 million to be funded over a 5 year period. It is the nation's sixth largest not-for-profit, independent university, offering the intimate class sizes of a small, private college, and the academic resources of a well-rounded university. Through the University's Dual Admission Program, qualified students can reserve a place in its graduate schools while completing an undergraduate degree, and through its Honors Program, qualified students access a challenging learning environment. According to Northwestern University's Medill School of Journalism, Nova Southeastern University ranks third in the nation of all private colleges in the percent of work study dollars it devotes to community service.

> OPPORTUNITY **Campus Visit Days**

Prospective undergraduate students can look forward to meeting with admissions counselors, touring the residence halls, and taking a golf cart driven tour of the campus with current NSU students. The university also has open houses on a regular basis.

> SUCCESS **Multicultural Affairs Programming**

The Multicultural Affairs Programming board has a number of different initiatives designed to provide support and a sense of belonging for diverse student populations. The board is run by current students who are interested in student inclusion. Programs include the Nova Southeastern University Diversity summit, an annual conference that promotes awareness, inclusion and social justice; the Cultural Coffeehouse, a bi-monthly event where the campus community can enjoy diverse cultural expression; and Unity Week, during which events educate students about diversity issues.

> SUCCESS **Title V Developing Hispanic-Serving Institutions Program**

In 2007, Nova Southeastern University was awarded the U.S. Department of Education's Title V Developing Hispanic-Serving Institutions Program grant for $5.6 million to be funded over a five year period. This federal grant assists Hispanic-serving institutions of higher education to expand their capacity to serve Hispanic and low-income students through the Title V office. The University assesses the best practices to achieve student engagement and retention, and in collaboration with the Title V Office of Undergraduate Studies and the Division of Student Affairs, provides Hispanic and low-income students with programs to increase their success, and to improve the overall success of students.

> SUCCESS **Dual Admission Program**

Highly motivated students with a focus on their career have the option to reserve a place in one of Nova Southeastern University's graduate or professional schools while completing their undergraduate course of study. Eligibility is determined at the time of students' acceptance into their undergraduate program.

Nova Southeastern University
3301 College Avenue
Fort Lauderdale, FL 33314
Ph: Ph: (800) 338-4723 / (954) 262-8000
admissions@nova.edu
www.nova.edu

F A S T F A C T S

STUDENT PROFILE
# of degree-seeking undergraduates	5,757
% male/female	34/66
% African-American	23.5
% American Indian or Alaska Native	.5
% Asian or Pacific Islander	7
% Hispanic	30
% White	30
% International	9
% Pell grant recipients	41.9

ACADEMICS
full-time faculty	678
full-time minority faculty	23
student-faculty ratio	22:1
average class size	22
% first-year retention rate	65
% graduation rate (6 yr)	46

Popular majors Biology, Business, Psychology, Legal Studies, and Marine Biology

CAMPUS LIFE
% live on campus	15

Multicultural student clubs and organizations Pan African Student Association (PASA), Minority Health Professions Association, Asian Student Association, Indian Student Association, Pakistani Student Association, Lambda Theta Alpha and Lambda Theta Phi (traditionally Hispanic Greek Sorority and Fraternity), Alpha Kappa Alpha, Zeta Phi Beta, and Phi Beta Sigma (traditionally African American Sororities and Fraternities).
Athletics NCAA Division II, Sunshine State Conference

ADMISSIONS
# of applicants	8,186
% accepted	52
# of first-year students enrolled	917
SAT Critical Reading average	523
SAT Math average	530
SAT Writing average	511
ACT average	22
average HS GPA	3.1

Deadlines
regular decision	rolling
application fee (online)	$50 ($50)
fee waiver for applicants with financial need	yes

COST & AID
tuition	$21,100
room & board	$8,634
total need-based institutional scholarships/grants	n/a
% of students apply for need-based aid	89.1
% of students receive aid	99.7
% receiving need-based scholarship or grant aid	63.2
% receiving aid whose need was fully met	8.3
average aid package	$15,305
average student loan debt at graduation	$35,789

University of Central Florida

As one of the fastest growing metropolitan research universities in the country, the University of Central Florida has a great deal to offer, including more than 200 bachelor's and master's degree programs and more than two dozen doctoral programs. The university enrolls the largest number of undergraduates in the state of Florida and the second-highest number of National Merit Scholars. For many students, Central Florida's campus and location are also particularly interesting — it is hard to dislike Orlando when winter rolls around.

> ACCESS Achievers Program

The University of Central Florida Achievers Program offers direct access to university-sponsored and community-based academic programs for high-achieving local students and their parents. Approximately 250 students are served annually. During the program's history at University of Central Florida, approximately 85 percent of participants have completed a post-secondary education.

> ACCESS Academic Based Service-Learning Initiative

Through the Academic Based Service-Learning Initiative, more than 13,000 Central Florida students participated in service-learning courses in 2006-2007. Many of these students provided Junior Achievement civic classes to schools, including the informally adopted Ivey Lane Elementary School, which is comprised of 95 percent minority students. Other single-class service-learning projects focus on underserved populations, providing health, counseling, administrative and communication services.

> OPPORTUNITY The Campus Visit Experience

The university provides year-round campus visits, including many Saturday open houses, for the benefit of prospective students. Updated event dates can be found on the university Web site.

> SUCCESS Summer Bridge Programs

Central Florida hosts two residential bridge programs in the summer: Seizing Opportunities for Achievement and Retention (SOAR) and the Pegasus Success Program (PSP). Each of these programs provides academic enrichment, support, and community for students from disadvantaged backgrounds or those whose standardized test scores are below regular admissions standards.

> SUCCESS Academic Support Program

The University of Central Florida provides a range of academic support services for first-generation and minority students. Many of these programs fall under the auspices of the Multicultural Academic and Support Services, now supporting a first-generation component. Other university programs include the Freshman Success and Transition Program, as well as the College Achievement Program and Probation Intervention Program, the latter of which serves students who enter University of Central Florida with SAT or ACT scores below the state-required minimums.

> SUCCESS Connecting the University Community

Connecting the University Community is a new initiative designed to engage the campus community, particularly first-year students, in curricular and co-curricular programs. In its four-year history, this initiative has tackled the issues of *Brown v. Board of Education*, "New America" and "Environmental Issues Around the Globe," which focused on shifting demographics. Courses and extra-curricular programs use the themes to engage the community and provide opportunities for students, faculty and staff to gather and discuss the implications of these issues.

University of Central Florida
Undergraduate Admissions
4000 Central Florida Blvd.
Orlando, FL 32816
Ph: (407) 823-3000
admission@mail.ucf.edu
www.ucf.edu

FAST FACTS

STUDENT PROFILE
# of degree-seeking undergraduates	42,910
% male/female	45/55
% African American	9
% American Indian	<1
% Asian	5
% Hispanic	14
% Pell grant recipients	18

First-generation and minority alumni Eric Vasquez, soccer player; Asante Samuel, professional football player; Atari David Bigby, professional football player

ACADEMICS
full-time faculty	1,195
minority faculty	282
student-faculty ratio	30:1
average class size	20-29
% first-year retention rate	86
% graduation rate (6 years)	63

Popular majors Business, Engineering, Psychology, Sciences, Hospitality Management

CAMPUS LIFE
% live on campus (% freshmen)	25 (61)

Multicultural student clubs and organizations African American Student Union, Asian Pacific American Coalition, Asian Student Association, Black Female Development Circle, Caribbean Students Association, Chinese American Student Association, Chinese Student and Scholar Association, Club Kreyol, The Elements Hip Hop Association, Filipino Students Association, French Club, Hispanic American Student Association, International Student Association, Iranian Student Organization, Italian Club, Korean Student Association, Latin Rhythm, Multicultural Student Center, Muslim Student Association, Pulso Caribe, Sangam, Vietnamese American Student Association

Athletics NCAA Division I, Conference USA

ADMISSIONS
# of applicants	28,659
% accepted	48
# of first-year students enrolled	7,352
SAT Critical Reading range	530-630
SAT Math range	550-640
SAT Writing range	510-600
ACT range	23-27
average HS GPA	3.7

Deadlines
regular admission	5/1
rolling	yes
application fee (online)	$30 ($30)
fee waiver available	yes

COST & AID
tuition	in-state $4,526; out-of-state $20,005
room & board	$8,574
total need-based institutional scholarships/grants	$42,997,502
% applying for aid	60
% of students receiving aid	58
% receiving need-based scholarship or grant aid	59
% receiving aid whose need was fully met	19
average aid package	$7,567
average student loan debt upon graduation	$14,601

University of Florida

The University of Florida is a leading research institution and is ranked in the top 20 of U.S. public universities. Prestigious rankings are the result of quality education that promotes excellence and respect for diverse ideas, thoughts and perspectives. The University of Florida is committed to enrolling a community of learners, leaders and thinkers who want to leave their mark on the world. UF is the oldest and largest of Florida's 11 universities.

> ACCESS **Upward Bound**

Upward Bound at UF is a year-round program consisting of an intensive six week Summer Session and the Fall-Spring Academic Year. During the summer, students live on campus, enroll in college prep classes, and participate in educational, cultural, and other youth development activities. The Fall and Spring Sessions offer tutoring, workshops, counseling, and other support services. Upward Bound staff members work with each student to develop and implement an Individualized Educational Plan (IEP) according to the student's needs, potential, interests, and goals.

> ACCESS **UF Alliance**

UF Alliance is a partnership between the University of Florida and several high-poverty low-performing high schools in the State of Florida. The program enhances college access for historically underrepresented urban youth by providing outreach/awareness activities; parental involvement strategies; cultural responsive teaching and learning; professional development of teachers and administrators, and high school reform initiatives.

> ACCESS **UF Shadow Days**

UF's Shadow Day programs invite high-achieving African-American high school seniors to come to UF for a day to 'shadow' a UF student and learn about educational opportunities and student life at the university. Shadow Day lets students experience for themselves what it is like to be a college student at UF. Students have the opportunity to attend UF classes and see all of campus, then UF's historically black Greeks will also provide a special step show.

> ACCESS **African-American, Hispanic-Latino Recruitment Conferences**

These conferences provided the opportunity for African-American and Hispanic-Latino 7th-11th graders to learn more about admission requirements, student life at UF, leadership development opportunities, community resources and mentoring. Students participate in strategic academic workshops based on grade level, financial aid and scholarship workshops and a University of Florida college fair.

> SUCCESS **Florida Opportunity Scholars Program**

The Florida Opportunity Scholars Program is an initiative to ensure first-generation students from economically disadvantaged backgrounds have the resources they need to be academically successful at the University of Florida. The goal of the program is to retain these students and have them graduate at rates equal to or greater than the undergraduate population at large.

"Being a Florida Opportunity Scholar in addition to serving as an FOS Mentor has allowed me to see the complexity and importance of the FOS program. I am honored to be part of a program that gives an opportunity to those individuals who are more than qualified to attend the University of Florida yet struggle to meet the financial obligations of attending the University."

*– Beatriz H., '12
Miami, FL
Family Youth and
Community Sciences and
Political Science*

University of Florida
201 Criser, Box 114000
Gainesville, FL 32611-4000
Ph: (352)392-1365
freshman@ufl.edu
www.admissions.ufl.edu

F A S T   F A C T S

STUDENT PROFILE

# of degree-seeking undergraduates	33,628
% male/female	45/55
% African-American	10
% American Indian or Alaska Native	1
% Asian or Pacific Islander	9
% Hispanic	15
% White	61
% International	1
% Pell grant recipients	22

First-generation and minority alumni William "Willie" George Allen, '62, Law Office of W. George Allen; Hon. Stephan P. Mickle, '65 BA, '66 M. Ed., '70 JD, U.S. District Court Judge; Emmitt Smith, '96, President, SmithCypress and former Dallas Cowboy; Dr. Nils J. Diaz, '64 MS, '69 PhD, former Chairman, Nuclear Regulatory Commission; Dr. Pedro Jose "Joe" Greer, '78, Chair of Department of Humanities, Florida International University, and recipient of the Presidential Medal of Freedom

ACADEMICS

full-time faculty	3,596
full-time minority faculty	847
student-faculty ratio	22:1
average class size	30
% first-year retention rate	90
% graduation rate (6 years)	81

Popular majors Finance, Political Science, Psychology, Engineering

CAMPUS LIFE

% live on campus (% freshmen)	23 (84)

Multicultural student clubs and organizations Asian American Student Union, Black Student Union, Hispanic Student Organization, Islam on Campus, Jewish Student Union

Athletics NCAA Division I, Southeastern Conference (SEC)

ADMISSIONS

# of applicants	25,798
% accepted	42
# of first-year students enrolled	6,253
SAT Critical Reading range	560-670
SAT Math range	580-690
SAT Writing range	560-670
ACT range	26-31
average HS GPA	3.9

Deadlines

regular decision	11/1
application fee (online)	$30 ($30)
fee waiver for applicants with financial need	yes

COST & AID

tuition	in-state: $4,373; out-of-state: $23,744
room & board	$7,500
total need-based institutional scholarships/grants	$48,310,873
% of students apply for need-based aid	53
% receiving need-based scholarship or grant aid	26
% receiving aid whose need was fully met	12
average aid package	$12,792
average student loan debt upon graduation	$15,932

University of South Florida

University of South Florida
4202 East Fowler Avenue, SVC 1036
Tampa, FL 33620
813-974-3350
admission@usf.edu
www.usf.edu/admissions

One of Florida's top three research universities, USF provides a dynamic and diverse learning environment that inspires innovation, creativity and collaboration. Academics are anchored by distinguished faculty and supported by cutting-edge facilities and technology. From biochemistry to ballet, economics to engineering, USF's extensive range of disciplines enables students to discover their passions. In 2009, Diverse Issues in Higher Education ranked USF 26th overall among the nation's leading colleges and universities for awarding bachelor's degrees to Black, Asian American, Hispanic and Native American students. USF students are engaged in their disciplines through internships, research opportunities, study abroad, work and community service experiences. USF offers several summer bridge programs for first generation to college students. These programs provide specialized advising, programs and activities designed to enhance students' transition from high school to college and you are automatically considered for them by applying to USF.

> ACCESS **Access USF**

Held biannually in the fall and in the spring, Access USF is a special event for students that will be the first generation in their family to graduate from college. By attending Access USF students and their families will be introduced to many aspects of USF and the college selection process, including: the admissions process, programs that support student success, the financial aid application process and scholarship opportunities.

"The University of South Florida gave me a tremendous opportunity to expand my horizons and receive an education that will allow me to make a positive impact in our world."
– Monica Z.

> OPPORTUNITY **History of Achievement Award**

The University of South Florida's Scholastic Achievement Scholarship recognizes select bilingual and multilingual students from diverse ethnic backgrounds who have achieved above average academic records in high school while facing significant socioeconomic, educational, cultural or personal challenges. This $6,000 award ($1,500 per year for four years) may be offered in combination with other university scholarships.

> OPPORTUNITY **Freshman Summer Institute**

Student Support Services is a federally funded two-year retention program providing effective academic and personal support for eligible students. These students must demonstrate a need for academic support, be low-income students based on federal guidelines, and/or be a first generation student. Student Support Services provides personal, academic and career counseling. Students participate in college survival seminars, social and cultural enrichment programs and activities designed to broaden career perspectives and promote self-confidence. The Freshman Summer Institute tackles the challenges of the first year with an active concern for students' personal and academic welfare. Counselors, a crucial element of the program, personally advise and monitor student progress throughout the first year.

> SUCCESS **Summer Stampede**

Summer Stampede students become part of a community of first-year students enrolling at USF for the Summer session. This cohort of students attends specially developed workshops emphasizing topics relevant to academic success.

FAST FACTS

STUDENT PROFILE

# of degree-seeking undergraduates	35,951
% male/female	43/57
% African American	11
% American Indian	<1
% Asian	6
% Hispanic	13
% Caucasian	64
% International	33
% Pell grant recipients	32

First-generation and minority alumni Chucky Atkins, professional basketball player; Mark Consuelos, actor; Frank Davis, professional football player; Emilio Gonzalez, director, United States Citizenship and Immigration Services; Kenyatta Jones, professional football player; Kawika Mitchell, professional football player; Anthony Henry, professional football player; Roy Wegerle, professional soccer player

ACADEMICS

full-time faculty	1,585
student-faculty ratio	28:1
average class size	37
% first-year retention rate	86
% graduation rate (6 years)	48

Popular majors Pre-Medical Sciences, Engineering, Pre-Business Administration, Psychology, Biology

CAMPUS LIFE

% live on campus (% freshmen)	14 (64)

Multicultural student clubs and organizations Africana Students Association (ASA), American Minority Inspriring Genuine Overall Success (AMIGOS), Black Student Union (BSU), Caribbean Cultural Exchange (CCE), Club Creole, Cuban American Student Association (CASA), Dominican American Student Association (DASA), Gospel Choir@USF, Latin American Student Association, Mexican American Student Association

Athletics NCAA Division I, Big East Conference

ADMISSIONS

# of applicants	22,138
% accepted	41
# of first-year students enrolled	4,401
SAT Critical Reading range	550-640
SAT Math range	540-630
ACT range	22-28
average HS GPA	3.72

Deadlines

regular decision	4/15
application fee	$30
fee waiver for applicants with financial need	yes

COST & AID

tuition	in-state: $4,580; out-of-state: $15,390
room & board	$8,750
total need-based institutional scholarships/grants	$9,441,910
% of students apply for need-based aid	63
% receiving need-based scholarship or grant aid	45
% receiving aid whose need was fully met	4
average aid package	$8,758
average student loan debt upon graduationon	$19,963

University of Tampa

University of Tampa
401 West Kennedy Blvd.
Tampa, FL, 33606
Ph: (813) 253-3333
admissions@ut.edu
www.ut.edu

The University of Tampa is a mid-sized, private, comprehensive university. Situated on a beautiful 120-acre campus in the heart of Tampa, Fla., the university offers ready access to the Hillsborough River and other leisure areas. The university's student body consists of more than 5,300 students who, in this setting, enjoy a traditional, self-contained campus just steps away from the excitement and opportunity of the vibrant city. In addition, the student body is diverse — 23 percent are minorities, all 50 states are represented and students come from more than 100 countries to study at the University of Tampa. The university offers more than 100 programs and each program challenges students to not only succeed in their coursework, but also beyond the academic context.

> ACCESS Admissions Counselor Outreach

At the University of Tampa, admissions counselors frequently make trips into underserved communities to speak with prospective students at length about the educational and financial aid opportunities offered by the University of Tampa. Outreach efforts are broad and take place collaboratively with a range of stakeholders including Hispanic organizations, Urban Leagues and first-generation outreach organizations. The university brings inner-city youth to campus to excite them about college and their future. Moreover, all admissions counselors at the University of Tampa actively seek out schools in communities with large numbers of first-generation students who aspire to higher education. The university participates in the organization "A Better Chance" and waives the application fee for students with financial need.

> OPPORTUNITY Campus Visit Days

The best way to learn about the University of Tampa is to visit. High school juniors, seniors and other prospective students may meet with an admission counselor, observe classes, tour the campus, or speak with faculty and students. Campus Visit Days allow participants to visit residence halls, attend presentations, learn about campus life, and obtain financial aid information. Participants may choose from more than 20 information sessions ranging from academics to ROTC. The University of Tampa has four Campus Visit Day events for prospective students each year and has regional receptions for admitted students in Chicago, Philadelphia, New Jersey, Long Island, Connecticut, Boston, Ft. Lauderdale, Fla. and Bethesda, Md.

> SUCCESS Gateways Program

The Gateways Program gives entering first-year students the tools to make intelligent decisions about personal matters, academic direction and careers. The program is composed of a two-course sequence for all first-year students. A faculty member teaches both Gateways courses. The faculty member is an adviser, mentor and helps students adjust. The Gateways faculty are especially dedicated educators committed to helping students, offering guidance in making these adjustments and periodically discussing with students individually how they are succeeding. Most importantly, the Gateways Program provides a constant support for students — they have a faculty member who is always willing to offer guidance related to their academic lives.

FAST FACTS

STUDENT PROFILE
# of degree-seeking undergraduates	5,128
% male/female	39/61
% African-American	6
% American Indian or Alaska Native	<1
% Asian or Pacific Islander	2
% Hispanic	10
% White	64
% Pell grant recipients	20

First-generation and minority alumni Bob Martinez, former governor, Florida; Lou Pinella, manager, Chicago Cubs; Freddie Soloman, former professional football player, San Francisco 49ers; Tino Martinez, former professional baseball player, New York Yankees

ACADEMICS
full-time faculty	237
full-time minority faculty	n/a
student-faculty ratio	15:1
average class size	21
% first-year retention rate	76
% graduation rate (6 years)	58

Popular majors Communication, Biology, Management, Criminology, Performing Arts

CAMPUS LIFE
% live on campus (% freshmen)	60 (88)

Multicultural student clubs and organizations African Student Association, Black Student Union, Caribbean Student Association, Diversity Fellowship, Greek American Society, International Student Association, Hispanic Organization for Latin Americans, NAACP, Alpha Phi Alpha Fraternity Inc., Alpha Kappa Alpha, Phi Beta Sigma, Zeta Phi Beta, Delta Sigma Theta, Sigma Lambda Beta, Sigma Lambda Gamma

Athletics NCAA Division II, Sunshine State Athletic Conference

ADMISSIONS
# of applicants	8,408
% accepted	52
# of first-year students enrolled	1,495
SAT Critical Reading range	490-580
SAT Math range	500-590
SAT Writing range	500-580
ACT range	21-25
average HS GPA	3.3

Deadlines
early decision	rolling
application fee (online)	$40 ($40)
fee waiver for applicants with financial need	yes

COST & AID
tuition	$22,482
room & board	$8,296
total need-based institutional scholarships/grants	$35,000,000
% of students apply for need-based aid	62
% of students receive aid	50
% receiving need-based scholarship or grant aid	95
% receiving aid whose need was fully met	22
average aid package	$16,193
average student loan debt upon graduation	$23,807

Emory University

One of Emory University's greatest strengths lies in the diversity of students, faculty, and staff. Collectively they value difference, believing the intellectual and social energy that stems from varied voices and perspectives is one of their best assets. The richness of Emory's diversity extends beyond socio-economic background, race, ethnicity, religion, sexual orientation, gender, ableness, and national origin to include a wide range of interests, intellectual pursuits, beliefs, perspectives, political affiliations, and the like. The multiplicity of organizations, events, and programming here means that you'll be able to explore, take risks, and discover the unique identity only you possess. Whatever your interests, background, or beliefs, at Emory you'll find a diverse group of people to share them with.

> ACCESS Exito Emory

Exito Emory is a program for Latino/Hispanic high school students in the Atlanta area. Students are invited to campus to learn about the college admission process. Participants tour campus and meet with several of Emory's Latino/Hispanic student leaders, faculty, and staff members.

> OPPORTUNITY Essence of Emory

Essence of Emory is an event specifically for Black/African American and Latino/Hispanic students who have been admitted to Emory. This program allows admitted students to experience Emory University firsthand and to meet current students, faculty, and administrators prior to making a decision about enrolling at Emory. Students spend three nights in one of Emory's residence halls, attend classes, eat in the dining hall, explore the beautiful campus, and have the chance to meet with members of various multicultural groups.

> OPPORTUNITY QuestBridge

Emory is a Partner College with the QuestBridge program, which helps low-income high school seniors gain admission and full four-year scholarships to colleges like Emory. Students matched with Emory through the QuestBridge program are awarded with scholarships that cover full tuition, fees, room, and board.

> SUCCESS MORE Mentoring Program

The Multicultural Outreach and Resources at Emory (MORE) Mentoring Program assists first-year students with the social and academic transition to Emory through one-on-one mentoring relationships with upperclassmen. The organization also engages in a number of group activities including the Fall Carnival and other social and academic-related programs.

> SUCCESS Emory Crossroads Retreat

The Emory Crossroads Retreat is held for incoming freshmen of any racial or ethnic background one week prior to their arrival on Emory's campus. Retreat participants continue to praise the program for easing the transition into college, creating lasting friendships, and providing a memorable experience through a ropes course, community building games, and story circles.

> SUCCESS Multicultural Council

The Multicultural Council seeks to foster collaboration amongst and within all undergraduate student organizations on campus. By fostering interaction between diverse groups, the Council hopes that its members collaborate effectively and learn to appreciate people whose race, sexual identity, religion, ethnicity, and interests may be different from his or her own.

> *"I like to call Emory 'The United Nations of universities.' It's great to see so many different people with so much potential. This diversity is what drives me to be more focused and driven in and out of the classroom."*
>
> *– Justin H., '10*
> *College Park, GA*
> *Anthropology, Human Biology*

Emory University
200 Boisfeuillet Jones Center
Atlanta, GA 30322
Ph: (800) 727-6036
admiss@emory.edu
www.emory.edu

FAST FACTS

STUDENT PROFILE
# of degree-seeking undergraduates	6,787
% male/female	44/56
% African-American	10
% American Indian or Alaska Native	<1
% Asian or Pacific Islander	20
% Hispanic	4
% White	52
% International	7
% Pell grant recipients	14

First-generation and minority alumni Glenda Hatchett, Judge Hatchett television courtroom show; Michael Lomax, President and CEO of the United Negro College Fund; Patricia Lottier, co-owner and publisher, The Atlanta Tribune; James B. O'Neal, Attorney and founder, Legal Outreach (Harlem); Leah Ward Sears, former Chief Justice of the Supreme Court of the State of Georgia

ACADEMICS
full-time faculty	1,255
full-time minority faculty	249
student-faculty ratio	7:1
average class size	19
% first-year retention rate	95
% graduation rate (6 years)	82

Popular majors Business/Economics, Psychology, Political Science, Biology, and Neuroscience & Behavioral Biology

CAMPUS LIFE
% live on campus (% fresh.)	66 (99)

Multicultural student clubs and organizations All Mixed Up, Black Student Alliance, Brotherhood of Afrocentric Men, Latino Student Organization, Multicultural Council, Ngambika (organization for women), Racial and Cultural Education Sources, Students in Alliance for Asian American Concerns.
Athletics NCAA Division III, University Athletic Association

ADMISSIONS
# of applicants	17,446
% accepted	27
# of first-year students enrolled	1,299
SAT Critical Reading range	640-740
SAT Math range	670-760
SAT Writing range	650-740
ACT range	30-33
average HS GPA	3.82
Deadlines	
regular decision	1/15
application fee	$50
fee waiver for applicants with financial need	yes

COST & AID
tuition	$37,500
room & board	$10,896
total need-based institutional scholarships/grants	$55,209,328
% of students apply for need-based aid	46
% of students receive aid	86
% receiving need-based scholarship or grant aid	37
% receiving aid whose need was fully met	86
average aid package	$29,627
average student loan debt upon graduation	$23,181

Georgia College & State University

As a public liberal-arts university, Georgia College & State University provides an alternative to a large, one-size-fits-all state school. At Georgia College, students benefit from small classes and a strong liberal arts foundation. In addition to participating in social events on campus, many students take advantage of the GIVE Center, which is the university's clearinghouse for volunteerism. Just beyond the campus, students can enjoy the small, historically significant town of Milledgeville.

> ACCESS Academic Initiative for Males (AIM) Academy

African-American teenagers aged 12 to 14 from central Georgia can benefit from the AIM Academy, a two-week, residential program funded by the university. Students complete a project addressing current social issues and hear from representatives from the Milledgeville 100 Black Men of America, the Macon Alumnae Chapter of Kappa Alpha Psi Fraternity and the Mu Gamma Chapter of Alpha Phi Alpha, who act as role models.

> OPPORTUNITY Joint Enrollment / Early Admissions

Area students who have completed at least 10th grade and who meet certain admissions criteria may apply to the university's joint enrollment program. This program allows students to concurrently enroll in high school and college-level classes. If participants choose to remain at Georgia College after high school graduation, they must re-apply and meet freshmen application criteria. High school students from further distances may elect to participate in a full-time, residential Joint Enrollment/Dual Enrollment program with the permission of their high school.

> SUCCESS Office of Diversity and Multicultural Affairs

The Office of Diversity and Multicultural Affairs oversees programs and resources used to promote diversity on campus and to support multicultural students. Through the office's Minority Advisement Program, for example, minority students are assigned a peer mentor who guides them through freshman year. The office also supports a range of academic and social support services.

> SUCCESS Center for Student Success

An extension of the University Advising Center, the Center for Student Success reinforces the First Year Experience and provides supplemental academic support for struggling students. The center also organizes the advising and registration for incoming freshmen, sustains the First Year Academic Seminars and assists academic advisers.

Georgia College & State University
Campus Box 23
Milledgeville, GA 31061-0490
Ph: (478) 445-2774 / (800) 342-0471
info@gcsu.edu
www.gcsu.edu

F A S T   F A C T S

STUDENT PROFILE

# of degree-seeking undergraduates	5,490
% male/female	n/a
% African-American	6
% American Indian or Alaska Native	<1
% Asian or Pacific Islander	1
% Hispanic	3
% White	n/a
% International	n/a
% Pell grant recipients	16

ACADEMICS

full-time faculty	297
full-time minority faculty	n/a
student-faculty ratio	17:1
average class size	25
% first-year retention rate	80
% graduation rate (6 years)	42

Popular majors Business Administration/Management, Nursing, Psychology, Biology, Mass Communication

CAMPUS LIFE

% live on campus (% freshmen)	39 (99)

Multicultural student clubs and organizations Anime-bu Nibunnoichi, Black Student Alliance, Gay-Straight Alliance, International Club, NAACP, Art as an Agent for Change

Athletics NCAA Division II, Peach Belt Conference

ADMISSIONS

# of applicants	3,906
% accepted	59
# of first-year students enrolled	1,588
SAT Critical Reading range	520-600
SAT Math range	510-600
SAT Writing range	510-590
ACT range	22-25
average HS GPA	3.4

Deadlines

regular admission	rolling
application fee (online)	$40 ($40)
fee waiver for applicants with financial need	yes

COST & AID

tuition	in-state: $6,902; out-of-state: $23,940
room & board	$8,228
total need-based institutional scholarships/grants	n/a
% of students apply for need-based aid	90
% of students receive aid	37
% receiving need-based scholarship or grant aid	41
% receiving aid whose need was fully met	<1
average aid package	$6,585
average student loan debt upon graduation	$14,312

Georgia State University

Georgia State University is one of the premiere public research institutions in the country. Located in vibrant downtown Atlanta, Georgia State has the most diverse student body in the Southeast. Georgia State students come from every state in the nation and over 160 countries. The 2010 Report of the Education Trust ranked Georgia State as top in the nation in both access and success for minority and low income students, crediting Georgia State with the fastest rising graduation rates for minority students nationwide. *Forbes* magazine ranks Georgia State #2 in Georgia and #63 in the nation for overall student satisfaction with their classes, the affordability of education, and student job placement after graduation. GSU offers over 200 different academic programs, with a student-faculty ratio of 19 to 1.

> OPPORTUNITY Hispanic Scholarship Fund Scholar Chapter at Georgia State

The Scholar Chapter is a student group committed to promoting Latino/a student success in support of HSF's mission. The Scholar Chapter provides programming and opportunities for Latino/a students on campus to concentrate on developing the academic, pre-professional, leadership and social skills necessary for graduation and beyond.

> OPPORTUNITY The Goizueta Foundation Scholars Fund Award

Students eligible for this award include those for whom Spanish is a first language or who demonstrate a strong interest in and familiarity with Latino/Hispanic culture through participation in Latino/Hispanic community activities. Scholarships are awarded based on academic merit, service, and financial need.

> OPPORTUNITY The Office of African-American Student Services and Programs (OAASS&P)

OAASS&P's mission is to promote quality services and programs related to the retention, progression and graduation of African-American students at Georgia State by advocating for academic success, degree attainment, cultural awareness, civic awareness and co-curricular involvement.

"Georgia State has offered me an excellent opportunity. I received a full ride scholarship through the Goizueta Fund at GSU, which allowed me to live on campus. With 200+ plus student organizations, I transitioned easily into college life and my network grew instantaneously. I've had amazing advisors and mentors throughout my time here, and I have in turn chosen to mentor Latino high school students and steer them towards the path to college and scholarship."

– Grace M., Jr,
Omaha, AL
Sociology

> SUCCESS Freshman Learning Communities

Freshman Learning Communities provide the opportunity for students to make a smooth transition from high school to university life and culture. Participating incoming freshmen are placed with 24 other students who take 5 classes that center around an academic theme. Freshman Learning Communities enable students to make immediate connections to other students, faculty, campus and Atlanta communities. Past participating students have had higher success rates in GPA, retention and time it takes to graduate.

Georgia State University
PO Box 4009
Atlanta, GA 30302-4009
Ph: (404) 413-2580
admissions@gsu.edu
www.gsu.edu/admissions/apply.html

FAST FACTS

STUDENT PROFILE
# of degree-seeking undergraduates	21,727
% male/female	39/61
% African American	34
% American Indian	1
% Asian	11
% Hispanic	7
% Caucasian	39
% International	2
% Pell grant recipients	40

ACADEMICS
full-time faculty	1,096
full-time minority faculty	253
student-faculty ratio	19:1
average class size	16.9
% first-year retention rate	83
% graduation rate (6 years)	50

Popular majors Biological Sciences, Psychology, Accounting, Marketing, Early Childhood, Finance

CAMPUS LIFE
% live on campus	13

Multicultural student clubs and organizations
African American Student Services and Programs, African Student Association, Arab Society Latin American Student Association (LASA), Latino Leadership Council, Multicultural Greek Council, Black Student Alliance
Athletics NCAA Division I, Colonial Athletic Association

ADMISSIONS
# of applicants	11,913
% accepted	51
# of first-year students enrolled	2,938
SAT Critical Reading range	490-590
SAT Math range	490-590
SAT Writing	n/a
ACT range	21
average HS GPA	3.3

Deadlines
early decision	11/1
regular decision	3/1
application fee	$60
fee waiver for applicants with financial need	yes

COST & AID
tuition	in-state: $6,070; out-of-state: $24,280
room & board	$11,490
total need-based institutional scholarships/grants	$415,344
% of students apply for need-based aid	77
% receiving need-based scholarship or grant aid	335
% receiving aid whose need was fully met	15
average aid package	$10,549
average student loan debt upon graduation	$15,950

Morehouse College

Founded in 1867, Morehouse College is the nation's only private, historically black, four-year liberal arts college for men. The mission of Morehouse College is to develop men with disciplined minds who lead lives of leadership and service. The college recognizes this mission by emphasizing the intellectual and character development of all of its students. Additionally, the college assumes special responsibility for teaching the history and culture of black people. As such, the college seeks students who are willing to carry the torch of excellence and who are willing to pay the price of gaining strength and confidence by confronting adversity, mastering their fears and achieving success by earning it.

> ACCESS Upward Bound Math/Science State Center

The Morehouse College Upward Bound Math/Science State Center provides an intensive six-week summer curriculum to currently enrolled high school sophomores and juniors throughout the state of Georgia. This program assists students to develop critical thinking, scientific, analytical and language-arts skills. Students are given the opportunity to work in various laboratories and receive hands-on computer experience and exposure to a variety of science, math and engineering careers. Conducting research at various lab sites throughout southeast Georgia, students take classes in mathematics, technical writing, two sciences (including a laboratory science) and a foreign language. Applicants to the program must be first-generation and/or low-income students.

> OPPORTUNITY Prospective Student Seminar (PSS)

Morehouse College's Prospective Student Seminar is an event designed for high school seniors to experience life at Morehouse in a unique way. During the three-day special event, prospective parents and students visit the college campus and have the opportunity to participate in panel discussions with departments such as admissions, financial aid, residential life and other student service departments. Other PSS activities include tours of the Atlanta University Center (the campuses surrounding Morehouse College), a tour of a dormitory room, class observation, academic concentration fairs for students and parents, one-on-one interaction with faculty, a historical Atlanta city tour and a visit to Atlanta's newest metropolitan center, Atlantic Station.

> SUCCESS Peer Mentoring

To support students, Morehouse College sponsors a peer mentoring program. Upon arriving at the college, freshmen are assigned to a mentor group leader. The mentor group leader meets weekly with the mentee(s) in an individual and group setting. Upperclassmen may also participate in mentor groups to provide support and input. At the end of each semester, peer mentor group leaders host a social event for the mentor group to celebrate the end of the semester. The freshmen mentor groups are encouraged to complete community service projects together.

> SUCCESS Office of Student Support Services

To increase the college's retention rate and promote the growth and development of an institutional climate supportive of the success of program participants, Morehouse College houses the Office of Student Support Services. Funded by the U.S. Department of Education, the program provides an interconnected series of academic support services, including study skills development, peer tutoring and counseling, both for academic and personal reasons. The office seeks to provide students with academic, cultural and career-oriented activities designed to support academic life at Morehouse College while fostering healthy intellectual, social and moral development during the student's college experience.

Morehouse College
830 Westview Drive, SW
Atlanta, GA 30314
Ph: (404) 681-2800 x2632
admissions@morehouse.edu
www.morehouse.edu

F A S T   F A C T S

STUDENT PROFILE
# of degree-seeking undergraduates	2,796
% male/female	100/0
% African-American	96
% American Indian or Alaska Native	<1
% Asian or Pacific Islander	<1
% Hispanic	<1
% White	<1
% International	2.4
% Pell grant recipients	36.4

First-generation and minority alumni Dr. Martin Luther King, Jr., Nobel Laureate and civil rights leader; Spike Lee, Academy Award nominated and acclaimed filmmaker; Mordecai Wyatt Johnson, first African American president of Howard University; Julian Bond, Executive Director of the NAACP; Calvin O. Butts, III, Pastor of Abyssinian Baptist Church; Michael Lomax, Executive Director of the UNCF; James Nabrit, U.S. Ambassador to the United Nations; Edwin Moses, Olympic champion and professional track and field athlete; Sanford Bishop, United States congressman; Samuel L. Jackson, Academy Award nominated actor

ACADEMICS
full-time faculty	155
average class size	14
% first-year retention rate	85
% graduation rate (6 years)	67

Popular majors Business Administration/Economics, Political Science, Biology, Engineering, Religion/Philosophy, Psychology

CAMPUS LIFE
% live on campus (% freshmen)	n/a

Multicultural student clubs and organizations National Society of Black Engineers, Morehouse College Executive Lecture Series, Black Scholars Association, NAACP, International Student Organization

Athletics NCAA Division II, Southern Intercollegiate Athletic Conference

ADMISSIONS
# of applicants	2,279
% accepted	72
# of first-year students enrolled	904
SAT Critical Reading range	480-560
SAT Math range	450-570
ACT range	18-24
average HS GPA	3.2

Deadlines
regular decision	2/20
application fee (online)	$45 ($45)
fee waiver for applicants with financial need	yes

COST & AID
tuition	$21,376
room & board	$10,946
total need-based institutional scholarships/grants	n/a
% of students apply for need-based aid	95
% of students receive aid	96.7
% receiving need-based scholarship or grant aid	42.1
% receiving aid whose need was fully met	2.2
average aid package	$11,054
average student loan debt upon graduationn	$18,000

Spelman College

Spelman College
350 Spelman Lane
Atlanta, GA 30314
Ph: (800) 982-2411
admiss@spelman.edu
www.spelman.edu

As a historically black college for women that dates back to the late 1800s, Spelman enjoys a world-wide reputation enhanced by its many centers of distinction, including the Women's Research and Resource Center, the first of its kind on a black campus, and the Center for Leadership Development and Civic Engagement. Spelman also benefits from its high-caliber professors, including endowed chairs and a small faculty-to-student ratio.

> ACCESS Early College Summer Program and the College Prep Institute

Qualified high school girls are invited to participate in these programs designed to prepare them for the college experience. Offered are math and English courses for college credit, leadership and personal development seminars and cultural activities, just to name a few.

> OPPORTUNITY Research, Scholarships and Access

Whether aspiring writers or future NASA engineers, Spelman has research and scholarship opportunities to support its students' interests. The college's Bonner, Women in Science and Engineering (WISE), Smith and Flanigan scholarship programs are just a few of the initiatives to support the future leaders of the world who come through Spelman. Interested high school seniors are welcome to attend our Open House program "A Day in Your Life at Spelman College" offered twice in the fall semester. "A Day in Your Life" provides prospective students and their families with a comprehensive look at the Spelman College experience.

> SUCCESS Peer Tutoring Program / Freshman Success Program

Students of all majors can take advantage of Spelman's peer-tutoring program, which provides College Reading and Language Association (C.R.L.A.)-certified peer tutors to help students with study techniques, content-area reading, note-taking and test strategies. Students pursuing science, technology, engineering and mathematics (STEM) majors benefit from the Freshman Success Program, which provides support and academic assistance for freshmen and a small group of sophomores whose studies are in these areas. Program support services include an orientation for incoming STEM majors, workshops in time management and textbook mastery and tutoring sessions for sophomores.

"As a first-generation college student, Spelman College provides opportunities that I never thought I would have a chance to be exposed to. What I admire the most is how Spelman encourages us to become agents of change in our communities. I have been given the opportunity to really make an impact."

– Brittaney B., '11
Atlanta, GA
Sociology, Public Health

> SUCCESS African Diaspora in the World (ADW)

As a two-semester, interdisciplinary course, ADW provides a formal introduction to the background and culture of Spelman students. The course explores such essential issues as identity and values, and it seeks to reinforce those beliefs that are integral to the college's Statement of Purpose, especially in its institutional goals and behavioral expectations. This required, first-year course is designed to develop students' critical reflection skills as they examine contemporary political, economic, and social issues through the lens of the African Diaspora.

FAST FACTS

STUDENT PROFILE
# of degree-seeking undergraduates	2,270
% male/female	0/100
% African American	96
% American Indian or Alaska Native	<1
% Asian or Pacific Islander	<1
% Hispanic	0
% White	<1
% International	3
% Pell grant recipients	35.9

First-generation and minority alumni Marian Wright Edelman, founder, Children's Defense Fund; Marcelite J. Harris, first African-American female general, United States Air Force; Alberta Christine Williams King, mother of Dr. Martin Luther King, Jr.; Dr. Audrey Forbes Manley, former acting U.S. Surgeon General

ACADEMICS
full-time faculty	174
full-time minority faculty	n/a
student-faculty ratio	11:1
average class size	30
% first-year retention rate	89
% graduation rate (6 years)	79

Popular majors Biology, Psychology, Political Science, Economics, English

CAMPUS LIFE
% live on campus (% fresh.)	n/a

Multicultural student clubs and organizations International Student Organization, Caribbean American Student Association (CASA)
Athletics NCAA Division III, Great South Athletic Conference

ADMISSIONS
# of applicants	5,435
% accepted	39
# of first-year students enrolled	550
SAT Critical Reading range	490-570
SAT Math range	470-550
SAT Writing	n/a
ACT range	20-24
average HS GPA	3.61

Deadlines
early decision	11/1
regular decision	2/1
application fee (online)	$35 ($25)
fee waiver for applicants with financial need	yes

COST & AID
tuition	$17,818
room & board	$10,062
total need-based institutional scholarships/grants	n/a
% of students apply for need-based aid	93
% of students receive aid	99
% receiving need-based scholarship or grant aid	79
% receiving aid whose need was fully met	24
average aid package	$12,691
average student loan debt upon graduation	$17,500

University of Georgia

The University of Georgia is America's first state chartered university. The university enrolls more than 33,000 students from 50 states and 127 countries. UGA offers almost 170 majors and 500 student organizations. Athens is consistently rated as one of the best college towns in America. They have previously been ranked "Best Values" by *Money Magazine* and *U.S. News & World Report*.

Through its programs and practices, UGA seeks to foster the understanding of and respect for cultural differences necessary for an enlightened and educated citizenry. It further provides for cultural, ethnic, gender and racial diversity in the faculty, staff and student body. The university is committed to preparing the university community to appreciate the critical importance of a quality environment to an interdependent global society.

> ACCESS Sígueme: Latino Shadow Day at UGA

Sígueme is a one-day event hosted by the UGA student organization Students for Latino/a Empowerment that focuses on bringing Latino high school juniors and seniors from surrounding counties to the UGA campus to shadow a UGA student. Each Sígueme participant, based on their interests, is matched up with a current UGA student. Sígueme participants attend classes, eat at the dinning halls, and take part in a campus tour and admissions workshop.

> ACCESS Padres e Hijos Fin de Semana

The Parent-Student Bilingual UGA Weekend, known as Padres e Hijos, a program of the Fanning Institute, invites 25 highly academically competitive high school seniors and their parents to visit the University of Georgia. The weekend is an English/Spanish bilingual educational forum specially designed to welcome and encourage potential UGA applicants. Current Latino UGA students, parents, faculty, and alumni welcome the visitors and share their experiences. English/Spanish interpreters are available throughout the program.

> OPPORTUNITY UGA Diversified

This is a campus visitation program for high ability African American and Hispanic students and their families that have not gotten a chance to visit campus. The program includes campus tours, a student panel, workshops on housing, financial, and study abroad opportunities. In addition, students are given the chance to enjoy lunch in a campus dining hall as well as participate in a campus resources fair.

> SUCCESS Freshman College Experience

Freshman College Experience is a unique summer program that streamlines a student's introduction to the collegiate environment. Students attend one of several introductory courses that fulfill core curriculum requirements, as well as in courses specifically designed to teach first-year students how to find and utilize the wealth of resources available at UGA. Enrollees are also granted early access to UGA housing. Freshman College participants are assigned rooms in Russell Hall that they will keep not only for the summer program but through the following academic year as well.

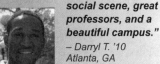

"I like the fact that UGA offers the perfect college experience. UGA has excellent academics, a busy social scene, great professors, and a beautiful campus."
– *Darryl T. '10 Atlanta, GA Environmental Health Science*

> SUCCESS Latinos Investing in the Students of Tomorrow (LISTo)

LISTo is a peer-mentoring program that pairs upper class Latino/a students with first-year Latino/a students to provide a successful transition from high school to college and aid in the navigation of campus resources and leadership opportunities.

University of Georgia
Office of Admissions Terrell Hall
Athens, GA 30602
Ph: (706) 542-8776
undergrad@admissions.uga.edu
www.admissions.uga.edu

F A S T   F A C T S

STUDENT PROFILE
# of degree-seeking undergraduates	25,201
% male/female	58/42
% African-American	8
% American Indian or Alaska Native	1
% Asian or Pacific Islander	8.8
% Hispanic	3
% White	78
% International	3
% Pell grant recipients	9

First-generation and minority alumni Deborah Roberts, ABC news correspondent '82; Hines Ward of the NFL's Pittsburgh Steelers, '98; Natasha Trethewey, Pulitzer Prize-winning poet '89; Henry Cameron "Hadjii" Hand, creator of BET's first scripted series, *Somebodies*, '98

ACADEMICS
full-time faculty	1,751
full-time minority faculty	100
student-faculty ratio	18:1
average class size	33
% first-year retention rate	94
% graduation rate (6 years)	70

Popular majors Psychology, Public and International Affairs, Business, Biology, Pharmacy

CAMPUS LIFE
% live on campus (% freshmen)	n/a

Multicultural student clubs and organizations Pamoja Dance Ensemble, NAACP, Black Affairs Council, Indian Cultural Exchange, Latino Student Association
Athletics NCAA Division I, Southeastern Conference

ADMISSIONS
# of applicants	18,062
% accepted	10,000
# of first-year students enrolled	4,800
SAT Critical Reading range	560-660
SAT Math range	570-670
SAT Writing range	570-660
ACT range	25-29
average HS GPA	3.8

Deadlines
early decision	10/15
regular decision	1/15
application fee	$60
fee waiver for applicants with financial need	yes

COST & AID
tuition in-state: $3,865; out-of-state:	$12,970
room & board	$4,023
total need-based institutional scholarships/grants	n/a
% of students apply for need-based aid	40
% of students receive aid	n/a
% receiving need-based scholarship or grant aid	n/a
% receiving aid whose need was fully met	n/a
average aid package	$9,509
average student loan debt upon graduation	$14,766

Wesleyan College

Wesleyan College
4760 Forsyth Road
Macon, GA 31210
Ph: (478) 757-5206
admission@wesleyancollege.edu
www.wesleyancollege.edu

Founded in 1836 as the world's first college chartered to grant degrees to women, Wesleyan College is recognized as one of the nation's most diverse and affordable four-year liberal arts colleges. Wesleyan, which *The Princeton Review* ranked third for diversity in population, is a small, private women's college with a 36 percent first-generation student population. Undergraduate degrees are offered in 35 majors and 29 minors — including self-designed majors and interdisciplinary programs — plus eight pre-professional programs including seminary, engineering, medicine, pharmacy, veterinary medicine, health sciences, dental and law. Pioneers for women in many fields, Wesleyan College graduates include the first woman to receive a doctor of medicine and the first woman to argue a case before the Georgia Supreme Court.

> ACCESS Center for Women in Science and Technology

Wesleyan's academic centers strengthen existing programs for its students and reach out to the community. The Center for Women in Science and Technology, for example, not only provides resources for Wesleyan students studying mathematics, natural science and technology but also promotes interest in science among young girls. Successful outreach efforts include summer camp experiences for middle school girls and regular classroom visits by Wesleyan science scholars to local elementary schools for help with hands-on experiments. The center also sponsors visits by nationally known scientists. Wesleyan's state-of-the-art science facilities serve an increasing number of Wesleyan students enrolled and majoring in biology, chemistry, psychology and computer science while also addressing the great need throughout the nation for women who are skilled in medicine, scientific research, computer technology and mathematics.

> OPPORTUNITY Low Tuition and Generous Financial Aid

As one of the nation's most affordable selective colleges, Wesleyan offers a strong merit scholarship program as well as a comprehensive financial aid program. In part, this commitment to creating financial access for students and their families has enabled Wesleyan to attract an extremely talented and diverse student body. Tuition at Wesleyan is 48 percent less than the national average of other private colleges. In addition, tuition costs are offset with generous financial gifts from donors. The Princeton Review recently selected Wesleyan as one of America's Best Values in education. A wide variety of merit and need-based scholarships are available for women with outstanding academic records, community or faith-based leadership accomplishments, or special interests in music, art and theatre. Awards range from $1,000 to $16,000 per year, renewable for four years. Wesleyan offers many special scholarship opportunities for Methodist students demonstrating outstanding academic achievement or a commitment to faith and community service.

> SUCCESS Community Service

Wesleyan students are united through a commitment to serve others. Service is part of Wesleyan's curriculum and is integrated into the classroom experience through The Lane Center for Community Engagement and Service, which initiates community leadership development and coordinates projects such as Wesleyan Volunteers for Literacy, Habitat for Humanity, "WOW! Days" for Macon and a community immersion experience for first-year students. Wesleyan organized more than 150 volunteers through its last "WOW! A Day" community-wide service event and completed multiple projects simultaneously at more than a dozen separate work sites throughout the city of Macon. Events like "WOW! A Day" are an integral part of Wesleyan's goal to promote service-based learning among its students. Service can't be limited to the efforts of a single day, but the accomplishments of "WOW!" projects provide an enriching introduction to the power of engagement, inspiring many students to make longer-term commitments.

FAST FACTS

STUDENT PROFILE
# of degree-seeking undergraduates	624
% male/female	0/100
% African-American	33
% American Indian or Alaska Native	<1
% Asian or Pacific Islander	3
% Hispanic	2
% White	46
% Pell grant recipients	44

First-generation and minority alumni The Soong Sisters: Ai-ling (Madame H. H. Kung), Ching-ling (Madame Sun Yat-sen), May-ling (Madame Chiang Kai-shek), first Chinese women to be educated in America (1908)

ACADEMICS
full-time faculty	47
full-time minority faculty	n/a
student-faculty ratio	9:1
average class size	11
% first-year retention rate	68
% graduation rate (6 years)	54

Popular majors Business, Education, Sciences, Fine Arts, Psychology

CAMPUS LIFE
% live on campus (% freshmen)	82 (90)

Multicultural student clubs and organizations A.X.I.S., Black Student Alliance, French Club, GLBAL, Spanish Club

Athletics NCAA Division III, Great South Athletic Conference

ADMISSIONS
# of applicants	536
% accepted	53
# of first-year students enrolled	90
SAT Critical Reading range	500-610
SAT Math range	460-610
SAT Writing	n/a
ACT range	20-28
average HS GPA	35

Deadlines
early decision	11/15
regular decision	rolling
application fee (online)	$30($30)
fee waiver for applicants with financial need	yes

COST & AID
tuition	$17,500
room & board	$8,000
total need-based institutional scholarships/grants	n/a
% of students apply for need-based aid	80
% of students receive aid	100
% receiving need-based scholarship or grant aid	n/a
% receiving aid whose need was fully met	27
average aid package	$11,641
average student loan debt upon graduation	$20,988

Chaminade University

Chaminade University, the only Catholic university in Hawaii, offers its students an education in a collaborative learning environment that prepares them for life, service and successful careers. Guided by its Catholic, Marianist and liberal arts educational traditions, Chaminade encourages the development of moral character, personal competencies, and a commitment to build a just and peaceful society. The University offers both the civic and church communities of the Pacific region its academic and intellectual resources in the pursuit of common aims.

> SUCCESS **Summer Bridge**

Summer Bridge is a mandatory program for students who have been accepted conditionally to Chaminade based on High School GPA and SAT/ACT scores. The program provides conditional students with the opportunity to take pre-college or first year level courses to prepare for their first semester in college. Students will also participate in Charminade activities and familiarize themselves with the campus, staff, and faculty. Summer Bridge must be completed successfully with C's or better in order to enroll in the fall.

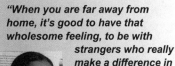

"When you are far away from home, it's good to have that wholesome feeling, to be with strangers who really make a difference in your life."
– Jenise T. '09
Saipan
Biology

> SUCCESS **Academic Achievement Program**

The Academic Achievement Program is designed to assist eligible students in completing their academic goals. The AAP is a TRIO Student Support Services program, which seeks to increase retention and graduation rates for eligible students. They provide a variety of services that help students make the transition to college both academically and socially, including: tutoring, workshops, cultural events, grant aid, a laptop and media loan-out program, academic/personal advising, and preparation for graduate school exams.

> SUCCESS **Multicultural Student Orientation Program**

Chaminade is one of the most diverse in the U.S., and provides a model of multi-cultural interaction and understanding. The greater community of Honolulu provides another dimension of resources for cultural study and awareness. This degree program provides a background for those who would pursue specialized careers in human services, health services, planning, international relations, and education that require a knowledge of cultural diversity.

> SUCCESS **Four Year Plans**

The Academic Advising Office works closely with the registrar, deans, and faculty advisors to create semester schedules that work for every student. They publish four-year plans for every major so all students and advisors have a game plan.

Chaminade University
3140 Waialae Avenue
Honolulu, HI 96816
Ph: (800) 735-3733 / (808) 735-4711
admissions@chaminade.edu
www.chaminade.edu

FAST FACTS

STUDENT PROFILE
# of degree-seeking undergraduates	1,030
% male/Female	35/65
% African American	3
% American Indian	0.5
% Asian American	66
% Hispanic/Latino	7
% Caucasian	21
% International	2
% Other/Unknown	0.5
% Pell grant recipients	n/a

ACADEMICS
full-time faculty	76
full-time minority faculty	n/a
student-faculty ratio	12:1
average class size	16
% first-year retention rate	75
% graduation rate	45

Popular majors Criminal Justice, Forensic Science, Business Administration

CAMPUS LIFE
% live on campus	31

Multicultural student clubs and organizations
Diversity at Its Finest, Pacific Islander Club, Tahitian Club

Athletics NCAA Division II, Pacific West Conference

ADMISSIONS
# of applicants	781
% accepted	94
# of first-year students enrolled	508
SAT Critical Reading range	410-430
SAT Math range	410-430
SAT Writing range	n/a
ACT range	19
average HS GPA	3.14

Deadlines
regular decision	5/1
application fee (online)	$50 ($0)
fee waiver for applicants with financial need	no

COST & AID
tuition	$17,600
room & board	$10,380
total need-based institutional scholarships/grants	$20,000,000
% of students apply for need-based aid	82
% receiving need-based scholarship or grant aid	74
% receiving aid whose need was fully met	14
average aid package	$12,846
average student loan debt upon graduation	$22,263

Benedictine University

Benedictine University is a small, private university in the Catholic and Benedictine tradition. The school prides itself on the individual attention professors give students, and the relationships formed between faculty, staff and students on campus. Benedictine University is dedicated to the education of students from diverse ethnic, racial and religious backgrounds and is nationally recognized for its commitment to diversity. The school's liberal arts and professional education programs are guided by the Roman Catholic tradition and Benedictine heritage and prepare students for life after college as informed, active and responsible citizens and leaders. Benedictine University is proud to welcome students from 44 states and 16 countries who bring a variety of backgrounds to the campus community. Thirty-two percent of the freshmen are minorities with Asians comprising the largest group at 18 percent. Located 25 miles outside of Chicago, the city is easily accessible to students.

> ACCESS St. Ethelreda Partnership

Benedictine University and St. Ethelreda, a parochial grammar school on Chicago's South Side, have a partnership that allows St. Ethelreda students to experience a college atmosphere and improve their math and science skills. Meanwhile, Benedictine education students have the opportunity to mentor the St. Ethelreda students. As part of this partnership, any St. Ethelreda student who graduates from eighth grade with a "B" or better average and maintains that average through high school are given a four-year scholarship to Benedictine if they commit to a major in education. The purpose of this program is to encourage minority students to pursue education as a career.

> OPPORTUNITY The Benedictine Incentive Award

The Benedictine Incentive Award is a scholarship designed to serve underrepresented students on the Benedictine campus. Eligible groups include African-American, Latino and Native American students. Awards of up to $3,000 are given each year and are renewable if the student maintains a GPA of 2.5 or above.

> OPPORTUNITY The Benedictine Need Award

The Benedictine Need Award is a scholarship designed for need-based students. Students demonstrating financial need are eligible. Award amounts vary each year and are renewable if the student continues to demonstrate a financial need and maintains a GPA of 2.5 or above while enrolled full-time.

> SUCCESS Student Success Center

Benedictine University's Student Success Center facilitates students' transition to the university through academic advising and support. Services include individual tutoring, group study sessions, the "Study Zone" learning area, a structured learning assistance program, academic advising and more.

> SUCCESS New Student Advising Center

The New Student Advising Center serves as a source of academic information and support for new students. The academic adviser is a student liaison for information about the university's curriculum, policies, procedures and expectations. This, in turn, provides the student with the tools they need to be academically successful. The goal is to encourage students to foster their own growth and to become proactive in terms of their education.

Benedictine University
5700 College Road
Lisle, IL 60532
Ph: (630) 829-6300
admissions@ben.edu
www.ben.edu

F A S T   F A C T S

STUDENT PROFILE

# of degree-seeking undergraduates	3,110
% male/female	44/56
% African-American	10
% American Indian or Alaska Native	<1
% Asian or Pacific Islander	13
% Hispanic	6
% White	35
% International	1
% Pell grant recipients	23.7

First-generation and minority alumni Dr. Donald Pope-Davis, Vice President and Associate Provost, Notre Dame University; Christopher Mays, Assistant to the Mayor of Detroit, Michigan; Gilberto Barrantes, Corporate Affairs Director, Costa Rica; Ken Carruthers, Benedictine University Athletic Hall of Fame, Vice President of Sales, CorSolutions, Chicago

ACADEMICS

full-time faculty	102
full-time minority faculty	n/a
student-faculty ratio	n/a
average class size	n/a
% first-year retention rate	78
% graduation rate (6 years)	60

Popular majors Management, Health Science, Biology

CAMPUS LIFE

% live on campus (% freshmen)	17 (48)

Multicultural student clubs and organizations African American Student Union, Association of Latin American Students, International Club, Mediterranean Club, Muslim Student Association, South Asian Student Association

Athletics NCAA Division III, Northern Athletic Conference (NAC)

ADMISSIONS

# of applicants	1,566
% accepted	80
# of first-year students enrolled	781
SAT Critical Reading range	n/a
SAT Math range	n/a
SAT Writing	n/a
ACT range	20-26
average HS GPA	3.35

Deadlines

regular decision	rolling
application fee (online)	$25
fee waiver for applicants with financial need	yes

COST & AID

tuition	$22,310
room & board	$6,945
total need-based institutional scholarships/grants	n/a
% of students apply for need-based aid	74
% of students receive aid	65
% receiving need-based scholarship or grant aid	65
% receiving aid whose need was fully met	n/a
average aid package	$14,391
average student loan debt upon graduation	$16,802

Columbia College Chicago

Columbia College Chicago
600 S. Michigan Avenue
Chicago, IL 60605
(312) 369-7130
admissions@colum.edu
www.colum.edu

The largest and most diverse private arts, media, and communication college in the nation, Columbia College Chicago has 120 academic programs and nearly 12,500 students. Columbia is an urban institution located in the heart of Chicago's Education Corridor and its students reflect the economic, racial, cultural, and educational diversity of contemporary America. A Columbia education focuses on a strong liberal arts core and close interaction with a faculty of working artists and professionals. Columbia College allows students to begin work in their chosen fields in their freshman year and offers them extensive support in building and polishing their own portfolios. Columbia students are encouraged to treat the entire city of Chicago as an extended campus and a resource to further their academic and professional goals.

> *"I come from kind of a diverse background growing up, so coming to Columbia was a great way to surround myself with that again. I was shy as a kid and coming here really gave me the chance to open up; I've made so many friends."*
>
> *– Branick G., '11*
> *Chicago, IL*
> *Film: Animation*

> ACCESS Community

The Center for Community Arts Partnership, which has played an integral role at Columbia since 1998, oversees a variety of college-community partnerships in the arts. Two of its initiatives, Project AIM and Community Schools, are committed to building meaningful, sustainable partnerships by uniting the college, public schools, and the local community. It is through these unique relationships that all partners are able to create innovative arts programming that builds stronger schools and neighborhoods, and ultimately, better-educated students. Under the auspices of the Center for Community Arts Partnerships, Columbia College also offers a graduate concentration in Arts in Youth and Community Development.

> OPPORTUNITY High School Summer Institute

Students who have completed at least their sophomore year of high school are eligible to participate in the High School Summer Institute, a five-week program geared toward students with an interest in the visual, media, performing, and communications arts. Participants not only get to work in Columbia's state-of-the-art labs, studios, concert halls, and theaters, but also receive training from the same professionals and scholars who teach at Columbia year round. Students can choose from programs in film & video production, television writing and production, radio, dance, theater, fiction and poetry writing, graphic arts, animation, fashion design, journalism, and others.

> OPPORTUNITY Scholarships

A number of scholarships are offered to Columbia students, including the Open Doors Scholarships for Chicago public school graduates and Opportunity Scholarships, for low-income students who demonstrate academic merit. Columbia also has a Diversity Scholarship program that provides funding for students who the college believes will contribute to diversity within the Columbia community.

> SUCCESS Summer Bridge Program

Applicants to Columbia College whose academic backgrounds have not adequately prepared them for college-level academics may be offered the chance to successfully complete the Summer Bridge Program before they are admitted to the College. During the program students have the opportunity to reinforce their academic skills through coursework, tutoring, counseling, enrichment activities, and access to all college facilities. The Bridge Program is free of charge.

FAST FACTS

STUDENT PROFILE

# of degree-seeking undergraduates	11,592
% male/female	48/52
% African American	16
% American Indian or Alaska Native	1
% Asian or Pacific Islander	3
% Hispanic	10
% White	62
% Pell grant recipients	31

ACADEMICS

full-time faculty	353
full-time minority faculty	n/a
student-faculty ratio	14:1
average class size	17
% first-year retention rate	66
% graduation rate (6 years)	35

Popular majors Film & Video, Art/Design, Photography, Theater

CAMPUS LIFE

% live on campus	22

Multicultural student clubs and organizations
Asian Student Organization, Black Actor's Guild, Black Student Union, Common Ground (GLBTQQIA organization), Hillel, Hispanic Journalists of Columbia, Latino Alliance, Muslim Student Association, American Sign Language Club, Association of Black Journalists

ADMISSIONS

# of applicants	5,581
% accepted	95
# of first-year students enrolled	2,158
SAT Critical Reading range	n/a
SAT Math range	n/a
SAT Writing	n/a
ACT range	18-25
average HS GPA	2.9

Deadlines

priority application	5/15
regular decision	rolling
application fee (online)	$35 ($35)
fee waiver for applicants with financial need	yes

COST & AID

tuition	$19,418
room & board	$12,360
total need-based institutional scholarships/grants	n/a
% of students apply for need-based aid	n/a
% of students receive aid	n/a
% receiving need-based scholarship or grant aid	n/a
% receiving aid whose need was fully met	n/a
average aid package	n/a
average student loan debt upon graduation	n/a

Dominican University

Dominican University
7900 W. Division St.
River Forest, IL 60305
Ph: (800) 828-8475 / (708) 524-6800
domadmis@dom.edu
www.ican.dom.edu

Founded by the Sinsinawa Dominican Sisters in 1901, Dominican University prides itself on being both academically rigorous and committed to social justice and diversity. To this end, the university seeks to embody its motto of *Caritas et Veritas* ("truth and compassion") through its strategic plan, which identifies six specific ways — including supporting underserved students — by which it will ensure diversity on campus. A Dominican education combines study in the liberal arts and professional preparation. Students are encouraged to prepare for their future careers through internships and leadership in campus organizations, as well taking advantage of nearby Chicago, which is easily accessible by public transportation.

> ACCESS Service Learning

Dominican University offers students an opportunity to combine their academic pursuits with the school's mission of social justice by engaging in service learning projects. These community service components are either requirements of a particular course, or can be added onto regular courses for additional credit. Among the predominately educational service options, students have a myriad of opportunities to work with Chicago's burgeoning Latino community.

> OPPORTUNITY The Transitions Program

The Transitions Program is designed for students who may not meet all of the admissions requirements, but due to their zeal for academic success have the potential to successfully complete college. Students begin with a five-week summer program, which includes their freshman seminar and English composition courses, as well as the chance to learn about the academic resources available to them at Dominican. The support continues throughout their time at Dominican with a team of faculty and peer advisors who guide the students and monitor their success.

> SUCCESS Information Access Workshop / Study Skills Seminar

The university offers a workshop in library research and a study skills seminar to its students. While these courses do not count toward graduation requirements, they enable students to receive support in the areas of research, note-taking and educational goal-setting. These courses are particularly suited for students whose previous academic experience may not have fully prepared them for university study, allowing them to quickly acquire requisite skills.

> SUCCESS The Office of Multicultural Affairs

The Office of Multicultural Affairs promotes Dominican University's vision of an inclusive campus community that welcomes a diverse population and honors each individual's heritage and experience. The office provides academic support, student advocacy, financial aid education, cultural events and diversity education programs.

FAST FACTS

STUDENT PROFILE

# of degree-seeking undergraduates	1,807
% male/female	30/70
% African-American	7
% American Indian or Alaska Native	<1
% Asian or Pacific Islander	3
% Hispanic	24
% Pell grant recipients	28

First-generation and minority alumni Calvin Jackson, fashion designer, entrepreneur; Kevin Austin, customer service manager, AT&T; Jonathan de la Cruz, banker; Manny Flores, alderman, City of Chicago

ACADEMICS

full-time faculty	132
full-time minority faculty	n/a
student-faculty ratio	12:1
average class size	17
% first-year retention rate	79
% graduation rate (6 years)	70

Popular majors Business Administration/ Management, Psychology, Health Science

CAMPUS LIFE

% live on campus (% freshmen)	37 (58)

Multicultural student clubs and organizations Asian Student Association, Black Student Union, CIAO (Italian Club), French Club, Indian Student Association, International Club, Organization of Latin American Students

Athletics NCAA Division III, Northern Athletic Conference

ADMISSIONS

# of applicants	1,723
% accepted	71
# of first-year students enrolled	528
SAT Critical Reading range	450-580
SAT Math range	410-560
SAT Writing range	440-580
ACT range	20-25
average HS GPA	3.4

Deadlines

regular admission	rolling
application fee (online)	$25 ($25)
fee waiver for applicants with financial need	yes

COST & AID

tuition	$24,850
room & board	$7,620
total need-based institutional scholarships/grants	n/a
% of students apply for need-based aid	89
% of students receive aid	87
% receiving need-based scholarship or grant aid	99
% receiving aid whose need was fully met	16
average aid package	$17,570
average student loan debt upon graduation	$17,066

Elmhurst College

Founded in 1871 and ranking among the top colleges in the Midwest, Elmhurst College draws from its ties with the United Church of Christ to offer a quality comprehensive education. The college's 38-acre campus rests in Elmhurst, Illinois, ranked No.1 in a *Chicago Magazine* survey of the best places to live. Recognizing that diversity is not defined only by race and ethnicity, the college offers Enrichment Scholarships to qualified students from various traditionally underrepresented groups.

> ACCESS **Summer Mathematics and Science Academy**

The Summer Mathematics and Science Academy is a two-week program for high school students who are considering careers in mathematics, computer science, engineering, biology, chemistry, physics, medicine and nursing. In classes and seminars, students sharpen math skills, explore topics in science and master computer programs. The program is designed specifically for students from groups underrepresented in these professions, however, all high school students are encouraged to apply.

> OPPORTUNITY **The Enrichment Scholarships**

The Enrichment Scholarships are offered to qualified students who are members of traditionally underrepresented groups. Elmhurst College does not limit this designation to racial or ethnic minorities, as scholarships can be given to international students or students who have overcome significant barriers to enroll at Elmhurst. The award is valued at $8,000 and recipients must be enrolled on a full-time, degree-seeking basis. The scholarship is renewable for up to four years, given the recipient maintains full-time enrollment and a cumulative GPA of at least 2.5 or above. Applicants must complete the admission application by May 1 to be considered.

> SUCCESS **B.R.I.D.G.E.S. Newsletter**

Building Respect for Individuality and Diversity in a Globally Evolving Society (B.R.I.D.G.E.S.) is the monthly newsletter of Elmhurst's Office of Intercultural Student Affairs. The publication presents student-written stories from a variety of perspectives on diversity and other news not traditionally found in the mainstream press.

> SUCCESS **Office of Intercultural Education**

The Office of Intercultural Education seeks to provide intercultural students with a welcoming environment and a celebration of ethnic, cultural and racial diversity. The office coordinates programs and services that bring cultural perspectives into the college's academic and social life: Off-Campus Intercultural Retreat, Hispanic Heritage Month, Native American Awareness Month, World AIDS Day, Black History Month, European Heritage Month, Women's History Month, Asian Heritage Month, documentary video series and discussion, discussion series, entertaining and educational cultural events, off-campus diversity conferences, guest speakers and lecturers, peer advising program, career mentoring program and cultural visits to Chicago.

"I plan to go into nursing so I can make a difference. In my clinical rotations, I've already experienced the impact a compassionate nurse can have on a patient. I feel fortunate to be at Elmhurst, where I'm getting the kind of education that will help me reach my goals."
– Glen G.
Bensenville, IL
Nursing

Elmhurst College
190 Prospect Avenue
Elmhurst, IL 60126
Ph: (800) 697-1871 / (630) 617-3400
admit@elmhurst.edu
www.elmhurst.edu

F A S T   F A C T S

STUDENT PROFILE
# of degree-seeking undergraduates	2,400
% male/female	40/60
% African-American	3
% American Indian or Alaska Native	<1
% Asian or Pacific Islander	4
% Hispanic	9
% White	78
% International	1
% Pell grant recipients	22

First-generation and minority alumni Hon. William J. Bauer, judge, Seventh Circuit Court of Appeals; Rev. Dr. Joseph J. Richardson, pastor and community leader; Fred Gretsch, president, Gretsch Musical Instruments; Himeo Tsumori, physician

ACADEMICS
full-time faculty	132
full-time minority faculty	14
student-faculty ratio	13:1
average class size	19
% first-year retention rate	85
% graduation rate (6 years)	71

Popular majors Business, Education, Health Sciences, Nursing

CAMPUS LIFE
% live on campus (% freshmen)	37 (61)

Multicultural student clubs and organizations Black Student Union, H.A.B.L.A.M.O.S., International Student Organization and the Coalition for Multicultural Student Empowerment
Athletics NCAA Division III, College Conference of Illinois & Wisconsin

ADMISSIONS
# of applicants	2,770
% accepted	69
# of first-year students enrolled	580
SAT Critical Reading range	490-630
SAT Math range	490-590
SAT Writing range	490-590
ACT range	22-26
average HS GPA	3.48

Deadlines
regular decision	rolling to 4/15
application fee (online)	$0 ($0)

COST & AID
tuition	$27,270
room & board	$7,864
total need-based institutional scholarships/grants	$30,000,000
% of students apply for need-based aid	97
% of students receive aid	97
% receiving need-based scholarship/grant aid	88
% receiving aid whose need was fully met	62
average aid package	$17,400
average student loan debt upon graduation	$20,675

Illinois Institute of Technology

Since its founding in 1890, Illinois Institute of Technology has dedicated significant resources to enable students from a wide range of financial backgrounds to attend. A private, independent, Ph.D.-granting, co-educational research university, Illinois Institute of Technology offers students a superb education in engineering, business, architecture, the sciences, psychology and the humanities, in an environment geared toward the undergraduate student. The university is committed to providing students a distinctive and relevant experience through hands-on learning, dedicated teachers, small class sizes, and undergraduate research opportunities. Classes are taught by senior faculty, not teaching assistants, who foster a culture of innovation with their own firsthand research experience. The school's location in the world class city of Chicago gives students priceless access to the professional world through internships and employment. The university's own diverse student population mirrors the global work environment faced by all graduates.

> ACCESS Perspectives Charter Schools Partnership

Illinois Institute of Technology and Perspectives Charter Schools have partnered to create a groundbreaking, new math and science academy dedicated to improving students' achievement in these important fields. Supported through a $500,000 grant from the Motorola Foundation in partnership with the Renaissance Schools Fund, Perspectives Charter Schools/IIT Math & Science Academy is a world-class laboratory school that will provide students invaluable tools for personal and academic growth. The school's strong curriculum includes a focus on technology and engineering skills and will be the first Chicago charter school to offer a four-year Chinese language program. Perspectives Charter Schools is working in full partnership with Norman Lederman, chair, and Judith Lederman, director of teacher education, of the Mathematics and Science Education Department at Illinois Institute of Technology IT to develop a comprehensive curriculum and mentorship initiative. The new school will be based within the Benjamin W. Raymond School at 3663 S. Wabash Ave, in close proximity to the university.

> OPPORTUNITY Collens Scholarship

As a continuation of its growing relationship with Chicago Public Schools, Illinois Institute of Technology offers the Collens Scholarship. The scholarship offers eligible high school graduates the opportunity to attend with full financial support for all tuition, books and fees. In fall 2008, 34 students from 19 Chicago high schools entered Illinois Institute of Technology on the Collens Scholarship, to study 13 different majors. This need-based scholarship honors former university President Lew Collens, who served the university from 1990 to 2007, and marks his legacy of commitment to Chicago Public Schools and the city at large.

"When I looked at my award package I was so surprised at how much they were able to award me. It made me feel like my success was IIT's priority. And now that I am here, I know it is."
– Julia G., '12
Chicago, IL
Physics

> SUCCESS Summer Institute

IIT knows the transition to university life and the academic rigors of college are difficult. For over 30 years, Illinois Institute of Technology has sought to develop some of the finest and most comprehensive summer programs to help students make this transition to college. The Summer Institute for First-Year Students is a four-week, non-residential academic and community-building summer program for admitted freshmen that positions students to thrive during their academic careers. Through workshops and group learning activities, students gain subject mastery of mathematics, chemistry and physics; explore intended academic majors through reading, writing and discussion; and develop analytical thinking and communication skills. There are also extra-curricular activities, including field trips and opportunities to build social networks and faculty connections.

Illinois Institute of Technology
Office of Undergraduate Admission
Perlstein Hall 101
10 West 33rd Street
Chicago, IL 60616
Ph: (312) 567-3025
admission@iit.edu
www.admission.iit.edu

FAST FACTS

STUDENT PROFILE
# of degree-seeking undergraduates	2,590
% male/female	72/28
% African American	4
% American Indian or Alaska Native	1
% Asian or Pacific Islander	13
% Hispanic	7
% White	46
% International	17
% Pell grant recipients	25

First-generation and minority alumni Yasuhire Ishimoto, photographer; Susan Soloman, chemist, Nobel Peace Prize, recipient; Jorge Zepeda, Bell Labs engineer, designer, optical communications systems; Walter Cambell, architect, founder, National Organization of Minority Architects; Jimmy Akintonde, architect, entrepreneur and founder, Ujaama Construction

ACADEMICS
full-time faculty	370
full-time minority faculty	57
student-faculty ratio	9:1
average class size	10-19
% first-year retention rate	88
% graduation rate (6 years)	67

Popular majors Architecture, Engineering, the Sciences, Business, Psychology, Humanities

CAMPUS LIFE
% live on campus (% fresh.)	46 (76)

Multicultural student clubs and organizations African Student Organization, Iranian Students Association, Japanese Film and Animation Society, Korean Hope, Korean Student Association, Latino Fuzion, Latinos Involved in Further Education, National Organization of Minority Architecture Students, National Society of Black Engineers (NSBE), Pakistan Student Association, Arquitectos, Thai Student Association, Turkish Student Association, Vietnamese Students Association, Asian Pacific Gays, Lesbians, Allies, & More (GLAM), Black Student Union, Omega Delta, Chinese Student and Scholars Association, Indian Students Association, Indonesian Students Association, International Students Organization
Athletics NAIA Division I, Chicagoland Collegiate Athletic Conference

ADMISSIONS
# of applicants	3,092
% accepted	57
# of first-year students enrolled	530
SAT Critical Reading range	520-640
SAT Math range	610-700
SAT Writing	520-630
ACT range	25-30
average HS GPA	3.84

Deadlines
early action	1/7
regular decision	rolling
application fee (online)	$0 ($0)

COST & AID
tuition	$29,362
room & board	$9,940
total need-based institutional scholarships/grants	$15,615,371
% of students apply for need-based aid	65
% of students receive aid	100
% receiving need-based scholarship or grant aid	99
% receiving aid whose need was fully met	19
average aid package	$24,394
average student loan debt upon graduation	$20,308

Illinois Wesleyan University

Founded in 1850, Illinois Wesleyan University is a four-year, private co-educational university. The university strives to attain the ideals of liberal education by providing students with opportunities to realize individual potential while at the same time, preparing students for life in a global society. Offering diverse curricula in liberal arts, fine arts and professional programs, as well as opportunities for interdisciplinary study and off-campus learning, Illinois Wesleyan allows students to pursue a wide variety of interests and career paths. Personal growth is cherished at Illinois Wesleyan, and the small size and dedication to student-faculty interaction imbues the university with a real sense of community, an atmosphere that is particularly conducive to both personal and intellectual development.

"Illinois Wesleyan was the most supportive academic environment that I encountered in my college search. When I began my college search, my mom and I felt lost and confused. But when I visited Illinois Wesleyan, my admissions counselor went out of her way to make me feel as though no question was too stupid or too small. Her support was also echoed by the students I met during my overnight visit and by my academic advisor."

– Bevin C., '10
Braidwood, IL
Sociology

> ACCESS **College Quest**

College Quest is a summer program assisting promising Chicago public high school students in the college admission process. Successful applicants spend four days and three nights on the Illinois Wesleyan campus, where they attend seminars such as "Finding the Right College Fit," "What Colleges Are Looking For in the Application" and "Understanding the Financial Aid Process." Additionally, participants enjoy entertainment such as bowling and the local Shakespeare Festival, and they have opportunities to interact with university faculty and students on an individual and small group basis.

> OPPORTUNITY **Multicultural Weekend (MCW)**

Multicultural Weekend is an all-expenses-paid opportunity for students to learn more about Illinois Wesleyan and experience campus as a real student. Held in both the fall and spring, attendees stay on campus Thursday evening through Saturday morning and have the opportunity to sit in on classes, meet with professors, participate in clubs and activities and engage in a diversity workshop.

> OPPORTUNITY **¡TU UNIVERSIDAD!**

¡TU UNIVERSIDAD!, held in February, is designed to assist Latino/a students and families who would like to learn more about the University campus community, the surrounding community, receive admissions assistance, attend a Free Application for Federal Student Aid (FAFSA) completion workshop (offered in English and Spanish), and meet current students, faculty and staff. IWU arranges bus transportation.

> SUCCESS **Summer Enrichment Program (SEP)**

With the goal of increasing personal and intellectual development opportunities for minority students, Illinois Wesleyan offers the Summer Enrichment Program. Over the course of 10 weeks, attendees go to class, work on an internship and participate in at least one volunteer project. Designed to promote academic, professional, and personal growth, the Summer Enrichment Program allows students to develop team building and leadership skills. In addition, a scholarship is awarded to all students who successfully complete the program.

> SUCCESS **Giving Undergraduates Instruments to Develop and Excel (GUIDE) Mentoring Program**

Embodying Illinois Wesleyan's commitment to maintaining a close-knit, supportive university community, Illinois Wesleyan's Giving Undergraduates Instruments to Develop and Excel Program provides first-year students with student mentors to assist them through the transition from high school to college. Mentors also provide peer support, help to create a social network that models healthy behaviors and promote academic excellence and co-curricular involvement.

Illinois Wesleyan University
Admissions Office
103 Holmes Hall
1312 Park Street
Bloomington, IL 61701
Ph: (800) 332-2498 / (309) 556-3031
iwuadmit@iwu.edu
www2.iwu.edu

F A S T   F A C T S

STUDENT PROFILE
# of degree-seeking undergraduates	2,064
% male/female	41/59
% African American	6
% American Indian or Alaska Native	<1
% Asian or Pacific Islander	5
% Hispanic	3
% White	76
% International	4
% Pell grant recipients	11

First-generation and minority alumni Alfred O. Coffin, class of 1889, first African-American to receive a Ph.D. in biology in the U.S. and only the second Ph.D. awarded in any field to an African-American; Frankie Faison, actor; Akito Mizuno, CEO, Mizuno; Michael Mason, assistant director, Chief Security Officer, Verizon

ACADEMICS
full-time faculty	161
full-time minority faculty	22
student-faculty ratio	11:1
average class size	17
% first-year retention rate	93
% graduation rate (6 years)	82

Popular majors Business Administration/ Management, Biology, Music, English, Psychology

CAMPUS LIFE
% live on campus (% freshmen)	80 (100)

Multicultural student clubs and organizations Black Student Union, Spanish and Latino Student Association, Southeast Asian Student Association, Multicultural Women's Group, African Student Association, International Student Organization, Hilel, Hindy Student Association, Muslim Student Association, and Sisters Actively Visualizing Vitality Through Intellect

Athletics Division III, College Conference of Illinois and Wisconsin

ADMISSIONS
# of applicants	3,485
% accepted	53
# of first-year students enrolled	524
SAT Critical Reading range	550-690
SAT Math range	590-710
SAT Writing range	n/a
ACT range	26-30
average HS GPA	3.9/4.0

Deadlines
early admission	11/15
regular decision	rolling after 1/15
application fee (online)	$0 ($0)

COST & AID
tuition	$35,286
room & board	$8,306
total need-based institutional scholarships/grants	$17,598,910
% of students apply for need-based aid	62
% of students receive aid	100
% receiving need-based scholarship or grant aid	100
% receiving aid whose need was fully met	53
average aid package	$26,000
average student loan debt upon graduation	$26,555

Lewis University

A Catholic university located outside of Chicago, Lewis University offers many traditional and innovative programs to students. Of particular interest is the university's long-standing aviation program, through which students can study everything from air traffic control to security. Also popular are the nursing and criminal/social justice programs, both of which poise students to enter dynamic careers. Lewis University offers scholarships to ensure attendance for a wide range of applicants.

> ACCESS Si Se Puede / Fulfilling the Dream Conferences

Led by the Office of Admission and campus multicultural groups, the Si Se Puede and Fulfilling the Dream Conferences reach out to Latino and African-American students, respectively. They were designed to encourage high school students from these backgrounds to pursue higher education and to provide them with information about the application process. Attendees can also participate in workshops and discussions around issues of higher education as they affect their own communities.

> OPPORTUNITY Teacher Scholarships

Lewis students who wish to become teachers in high-need communities may be able to secure a scholarship through either the Diversity at the Blackboard or the Teach Quality Enhancement programs.

> OPPORTUNITY Student Orientation and Registration (SOAR)

All incoming students are required to attend one of the SOAR events, which are held in June and July for the following semester. During this two-day, residential program, students register for classes, meet with advisers and become oriented to the university.

> SUCCESS Aviation Conference for Women and Minorities

In conjunction with the Federal Aviation Administration, Lewis University recently hosted its first Aviation Conference for Women and Minorities. At the event, members of these groups learned about career opportunities in the field, including what skills and schooling are necessary, and how one prepares for positions such as pilots, air traffic controllers, mechanics and managers.

> SUCCESS SUCCESS and Bridge Programs

Incoming students whose records do not meet traditional admissions requirements can participate in the university's SUCCESS program, which provides them with ongoing mentoring and support during their first year of college. SUCCESS participants must complete the Bridge Program — a two-week, residential, preparatory program held on campus — in the summer before their freshman year.

Lewis University
Office of Admission
One University Parkway, Unit 297
Romeoville, IL 60446
Ph: (800) 897-9000 / (815) 836-5250
admissions@lewisu.edu
www.lewisu.edu

FAST FACTS

STUDENT PROFILE
# of degree-seeking undergraduates	3,900
% male/female	47/53
% African American	10
% American Indian or Alaska Native	<1
% Asian or Pacific Islander	4
% Hispanic	11
% Pell grant recipients	19

First-generation and minority alumni Chaka Khan, Grammy Award-winning singer

ACADEMICS
full-time faculty	170
full-time minority faculty	n/a
student-faculty ratio	13:1
average class size	18
% first-year retention rate	78
% graduation rate (6 years)	58

Popular majors Business Administration/ Management, Criminal/Social Justice, Nursing, Education, Aviation

CAMPUS LIFE
% live on campus (% freshmen)	38 (60)

Multicultural student clubs and organizations Black Student Union, Expressions Dance Team, International Student Association, Latin American Student Association, Lewis University Gospel Choir, National Pan Hellenic Council, South Asian Student Association

Athletics NCAA Division II, Great Lakes Valley Conference (GLVC), Midwestern Intercollegiate Volleyball Association (MIVA, Division I), Great Lakes Inter Collegiate Athletic Conference (GLIAC)

ADMISSIONS
# of applicants	2,644
% accepted	69
# of first-year students enrolled	655
SAT Critical Reading range	420-530
SAT Math range	430-620
SAT Writing range	n/a
ACT range	19-24
average HS GPA	3.2

Deadlines
regular decision	rolling to 2/15
application fee (online)	$40 ($40)
fee waiver for applicants with financial need	yes

COST & AID
tuition	$21,990
room & board	$8,000
total need-based institutional scholarships/grants	n/a
% of students apply for need-based aid	79
% of students receive aid	65
% receiving need-based scholarship or grant aid	67
% receiving aid whose need was fully met	39
average aid package	$15,044
average student loan debt upon graduation	$19,976

McKendree University

McKendree University's successful history includes graduates that have served as educators, physicians, state and federal legislators, representatives, congressmen and founders of universities and medical schools. Founded by Methodist missionaries in 1828, McKendree continues to serve students at the small, private university in Lebanon, IL, just 20 miles from St. Louis, MO. The university is mission-driven to encourage broader vision, enriched purpose, engagement with community, commitment to responsible citizenship, openness to new ideas and dedication to lifelong learning. Undergraduate experiences are distinguished by great teaching, a diverse and vibrant community and successful outcomes, including support beyond graduation from McKendree's Office of Career Services, which boasts a 97 percent placement rate for graduates. McKendree University is committed to creating programs that promote access, opportunity and success for first-generation, minority and low-income students.

> **ACCESS College Readiness Program**

The College Readiness Program serves local first generation, minority, and low-income eighth graders through their high school years. Participants attend monthly workshops and classes on McKendree's campus in Lebanon, Ill. that are taught by professors and simulate college courses in subjects that include communication, computer science and history. The engaging courses are designed to encourage students to make higher education a priority.

> **OPPORTUNITY Academic Scholarships**

McKendree University offers academic scholarships to applicants with GPAs of at least 3.4 or composite ACT scores of 25 or higher. Students who qualify are invited to attend one of two on-campus scholarship events offering awards ranging from $4,000 to $17,000. Academic scholarships are renewable for up to four years provided GPA requirements are met and recipients complete 15 hours of community service each year.

> **SUCCESS Academic Support Center and Writing Resource Center**

This center provides peer and faculty instruction and advice outside of the classroom in an environment designed with instructional tools and support that accommodate a variety of learning styles. The Academic Support Center also provides students with both reading and study skill courses.

> **SUCCESS The Office of Multicultural Affairs**

Minority leadership development and cultural activities are promoted on the McKendree campus. The director of multicultural affairs sponsors meetings and workshops on the topics of diversity, leadership development and study skills. This office also offers a summer orientation for all minority students attending McKendree in the fall.

"Since I've started my college journey at McKendree, I have been presented with numerous opportunities. I've had the pleasure of going on mission trips and making a difference in places such as New Orleans and Mexico. Not only have I gone on mission trips, but I actively give back in my community. I regularly volunteer and coordinate after-school activities at local elementary schools. Currently, I am preparing for an exciting experience as a first time Resident Assistant and New Student Orientation Group Leader. In addition to the many activities I am involved with, I also work very hard searching for additional scholarships. I recently received the HSBC First Opportunity Partners $5,000 scholarship. I was only one of three people in Illinois to receive this prestigious scholarship. Furthermore, I am in the process of preparing for my study abroad experience in England next fall. McKendree has proven to be a great university that can provide endless opportunities to all students."

– Rosza B., '11
Cahokia, IL
Management

McKendree University
701 College Road
Lebanon, IL 62254
Ph: (618) 537-6831
inquiry@mckendree.edu
www.mckendree.edu

F A S T   F A C T S

STUDENT PROFILE

# of degree-seeking undergraduates	2,222
% male/female	43/57
% African American	16
% American Indian or Alaska Native	0
% Asian or Pacific Islander	1
% Hispanic	3
% White	76
% International	2
% Pell grant recipients	42

ACADEMICS

full-time faculty	95
full-time minority faculty	7
student-faculty ratio	13:1
average class size	15
% first-year retention rate	74
% graduation rate (6 years)	70

Popular majors Business Administration, Athletic Training, Elementary Education, Biology, Psychology

CAMPUS LIFE

% live on campus	82

Multicultural student clubs and organizations International Student Organization, Black Student Organization, Spectrum Alliance, Rotoract

Athletics NAIA, American Midwest Conference

ADMISSIONS

# of applicants	1,347
% accepted	67
# of first-year students enrolled	309
SAT Critical Reading range	430-600
SAT Math range	405-622
SAT Writing range	430-545
ACT range	20-28
average HS GPA	3.5

Deadlines

regular admission	rolling
application fee (online)	$40 ($0)
fee waiver for applicants with financial need	yes

COST & AID

tuition	$22,070
room & board	$7,850
total need-based institutional scholarships/grants	$8,554,907
% of students apply for need-based aid	91
% of students receive aid	79
% receiving need-based scholarship or grant aid	77
% receiving aid whose need was fully met	85
average aid package	$16,998
average student loan debt upon graduation	$16,801

Millikin University

Millikin University is a private, independent, four-year university in Decatur, Ill. with approximately 2,300 students in traditional and non-traditional undergraduate and master's degree programs. The university has four colleges and schools including, the College of Arts and Sciences, The College of Fine Arts, the College of Professional Studies and the Tabor School of Business, and 19 Big Blue NCAA Division III Athletic Teams, varsity and junior varsity sports and intramural teams. Millikin has a long-standing history of academic excellence. When James Millikin founded the university in 1901, his theory-practice approach to education was unique. Today, Millikin takes this idea a step further by introducing "performance learning" — a unique approach to higher education that builds the confidence to succeed after graduation. Because of this approach, it is no surprise that Millikin students have a history of success after graduation. Millikin University is devoted to its diverse student body, with centers for Multicultural Student Affairs and International Education to serve as valuable resources for and advocates of the school's underrepresented populations. Both centers regularly communicate with the Millikin campus community to keep them updated about multicultural events, conferences and other activities.

"As a first-generation college student, Millikin has been such an important stepping stone in my life. It has given me a chance to grow in my personal life and as a leader. For example, when I need help on an assignment, my professor is a phone call away and knows my name."
- Lindsay C., '12

> **OPPORTUNITY Long-Vanderburg Scholarships**

The Long-Vanderburg Scholars Program recognizes high scholastic achievement among underrepresented (African American, Latino/a, Asian and Asian American, and Native American) students. This program honors the first two African-American graduates of Millikin University, Fred Long and Marian Vanderburg. The program provides recipients $2,000 in scholarship monies from Millikin annually. The scholarship is renewable for up to four years so long as the student maintains a 2.75/4.0 cumulative GPA and actively participates in the Long-Vanderburg Scholars Program.

> **OPPORTUNITY Need-based and Merit-based Scholarships**

In addition to its commitment to educate students and parents about ways to gain financial access to a college education, Millikin University is also committed to offering financial assistance to its own admitted student population. Each year, Millikin awards $19 million in need-based and merit-based financial aid. The university also offers endowed scholarships for both first-generation students and students who are members of historically underrepresented groups.

> **SUCCESS EDGE Program**

The Millikin EDGE program is a pre-orientation summer program that allows students to adjust to college courses and campus life in a small, supportive environment. Freshmen selected for the EDGE program complete an intensive course that introduces them to the academic rigor of a college classroom. EDGE students work on college-level reading and writing, critical thinking, class discussion and time management with the assistance of peer mentors and program staff. EDGE students also benefit from intensive advising through their freshmen year.

> **SUCCESS The First Week Program**

This is designed to help students learn their way around Millikin; all first-years have the privilege of participating in the program. First Week is designed to make students' transition to college a smooth one. While the first week at Millikin may be jam packed with activities and things to do, students will learn indispensable information and make bonds with their peers that will last a lifetime. They will also begin their first-year seminar, in order to jump-start the transition to college academics.

Millikin University
Office of Admission
1184 West Main Street
Decatur, IL 62522
Ph: (800) 373-7733 ext. 7 /
     (217) 424-6317
studentservicecenter@millikin.edu
www.millikin.edu

FAST FACTS

STUDENT PROFILE

# of degree-seeking undergraduates	2,300
% male/female	44/56
% African-American	9
% American Indian or Alaska Native	<1
% Asian or Pacific Islander	1.4
% Hispanic	2.7
% White	81.3
% International	1.3
% Pell grant recipients	28.2

First-generation and minority alumni Preston Jackson, professor and department chair, Art Institute of Chicago; Diane Bolden-Taylor, associate professor of music, University of Northern Colorado; Min Wei Looi, publisher, *Chrome Magazine* (Malaysia); Michael Hall, director of group sales, St. Louis Cardinals; Sherman "Skee" Skinner, independent film producer, director, writer; Dr. Fred Spottsville, cardiologist, Nasser, Smith & Pinkerton Cardiology

ACADEMICS

full-time faculty	154
full-time minority faculty	n/a
student-faculty ratio	10.9:1
average class size	23
% first-year retention rate	75.8
% graduation rate (6 years)	64

Popular majors Nursing, Biology, Theatre, Music, Business

CAMPUS LIFE

% live on campus (% freshmen)	65 (87)

Multicultural student clubs and organizations Alpha Phi Alpha Fraternity Inc., Black Men Incorporated, Black Student Union, International Student Organization, Latin American Student Organization, Multicultural Voices of Praise Gospel Choir, Sister Circle, Multicultural Student Council, Delta Sigma Theta Sorority Inc., Sigma Lambda Gamma Sorority Inc., Chinese Student Union, Dynamic Equilibrium

Athletics NCAA Division III, College Conference of Illinois and Wisconsin

ADMISSIONS

# of applicants	2,820
% accepted	61
# of first-year students enrolled	523
SAT Critical Reading range	490-620
SAT Math range	500-630
SAT Writing range	500-620
ACT range	20-24
average HS GPA	3.35

Deadlines

regular decision	5/1
application fee	$0

COST & AID

tuition	$25,750
room & board	$7,866
total need-based institutional scholarships/grants	n/a
% of students apply for need-based aid	89.7
% of students receive aid	99
% receiving need-based scholarship or grant aid	93.1
% receiving aid whose need was fully met	59.1
average aid package	$18,584
average student loan debt upon graduation	$28,388

North Central College

Located in Naperville, Ill. — ranked in 2006 as the second-best U.S. city to live in — North Central College offers students a recognized small town with easy access to Chicago. To enhance the opportunities that its location affords, North Central provides an optional "Chicago Term" for students, during which they may attend classes and participate in an internship downtown. This program operates under the auspices of the Urban and Suburban Studies Program, in which students can also major or minor. North Central further supports hands-on, cultural study through its comprehensive and well-regarded study abroad program, which offers a number of different options for students.

> ACCESS Junior/Senior Scholars Program

As Junior/Senior Scholars Program volunteers, North Central students work with underserved elementary, middle and high school students both throughout the year and through special summer programs. Volunteers can also advocate for better urban education by writing grants, attending education conferences and meeting with educators and legislators.

> OPPORTUNITY Pipeline to Urban Teaching Scholarship

The Pipeline to Urban Teaching is a way for students to gain knowledge, skills and experiences by working in high-need schools. The program consists of integrated experiences, both on campus and in the field, all the while students are enrolled at North Central College. Participants will be involved early and will participate in ongoing experiences with students and teachers in high-need schools (greater than 50 percent free lunch). Education students interested in teaching in high-need schools upon graduation can receive the Pipeline to Urban Teaching Scholarship, which provides scholarship money for every future year of service. Recipients must sign with the Department of Education, and the scholarship defaults into a loan if the recipient does not fulfill this agreement.

> SUCCESS Premier

The Premier program is a four-week residential summer experience that includes supervised study as well as extensive cultural and recreational activities to help students prepare for academic success. Students have the opportunity to engage in math, English, and psychology courses to strengthen their academic and study skills. Exploration with various study skills and specific disciplines is also included. Through the career development component of the program, students discover career options that will broaden their perspective and increase awareness of the endless opportunities available after graduation. Students become familiar with the college support systems and services, including financial aid and the writing center. By the time the school year begins, Premier students are well-acclimated to the campus.

> SUCCESS LINC

This program encourages students to connect with others from the very beginning of their college experience. Students make these connections through the LINC mentoring program that provides interpersonal and academic support by connecting incoming students with current students of color. Multicultural interests are examined and explored with students who have already spent time with the North Central community.

North Central College
PO Box 3063
Naperville, IL 60566-7063
Ph: (800) 411-1861
admissions@noctrl.edu
www.noctrl.edu

F A S T   F A C T S

STUDENT PROFILE

# of degree-seeking undergraduates	2,302
% male/female	47/53
% African-American	3
% American Indian or Alaska Native	<1
% Asian or Pacific Islander	3
% Hispanic	5
% White	79
% International	<1
% Pell grant recipients	25

First-generation and minority alumni John Daniels Jr. '69, first African-American named head of a major Wisconsin law firm; Bertram Lee '61, first minority owner of an NBA franchise, Denver Nuggets; Sandy (Simmons) Matthews '77, vice president, Illinois Action for Children

ACADEMICS

full-time faculty	119
full-time minority faculty	11
student-faculty ratio	16:1
average class size	20
% first-year retention rate	79
% graduation rate (6 years)	63

Popular majors Business/Managerial Operations, Elementary Education and Teaching, Psychology

CAMPUS LIFE

% live on campus (% freshmen)	53 (80)

Multicultural student clubs and organizations Asian Student Konnection (ASK), Black Student Association (BSA), Cardinals Hablando Espanol (¡CHE!), Gay Straight Alliance (GSA), German Club, International Club, Japan Club, Raza Unida, Students of African-American Brotherhood (SAAB)

Athletics NCAA Division III, College Conference of Illinois & Wisconsin

ADMISSIONS

full-time faculty	119
full-time minority faculty	11
student-faculty ratio	16:1
average class size	20
% first-year retention rate	79
% graduation rate (6 years)	63

Deadlines

regular decision	rolling
application fee (online)	$25 ($0)
fee waiver for applicants with financial need	yes

COST & AID

tuition	$26,916
room & board	$8,379
total need-based institutional scholarships/grants	n/a
% of students apply for need-based aid	81
% of students receive aid	70.9
% receiving need-based scholarship or grant aid	98.6
% receiving aid whose need was fully met	23.9
average aid package	$18,739
average student loan debt upon graduation	$26,395

North Park University

Founded in 1891, North Park University is a private, four-year, co-educational university affiliated with the Evangelical Covenant Church. A distinctively Christian university, North Park prepares students for lives of significance and service through liberal arts, professional and theological education. North Park University works to balance freedom and disciplined responsibility. The school focuses on students and attempts to transform the whole person. In this way, the university advances its unique calling as an intentionally urban and purposefully multicultural university dedicated to the glory of God and the good of its students, the academy, the wider church and the world.

> ACCESS **VIVE**

VIVE is a leadership development and college preparation weekend North Park hosts for select students from ethnic or multi-cultural churches around the United States. Students interact with campus personnel, other students and guest speakers. College preparation seminars focus on the college application and selection process.

> OPPORTUNITY **Whole File Review**

North Park University recognizes that many students have successfully faced serious adversity in their lives which may not be reflected in their academic record. As a consequence, North Park carefully considers all elements of a student's record and application. The opportunity for an additional personal interview is offered to select students who show promise of success in college beyond what their record might suggest. An offer of admission may be extended to students based on this personal interview.

> SUCCESS **Centering Our Minds Passionately Around Student Success**

Centering Our Minds Passionately Around Student Success (COMPASS) is a 10-day pre-college program that provides incoming first-year students with the tools necessary to handle the academic and social challenges of college life. COMPASS participants receive tutoring, academic advising and assistance in career planning. Students' progress is monitored by a team that includes an academic services counselor, an academic adviser, additional faculty and the coaches of any athletic teams on which students intend to participate. In this way, COMPASS helps first-year students adjust to community living and prepare for academic excellence.

> SUCCESS **The Office of Multicultural Development**

The Office of Multicultural Development promotes an inclusive environment in which all students thrive, reflecting what North Park sees as God's will for all people. The office helps the campus community explore, embrace and celebrate diversity. Moreover, it works closely with student-led groups to promote justice and equality among the entire student body.

North Park University
3225 West Foster Avenue Box 19
Chicago, IL 60625-4895
Ph: (800) 888-6728 / (773) 244-5500
admission@northpark.edu
www.northpark.edu

F A S T   F A C T S

STUDENT PROFILE
# of degree-seeking undergraduates	2,188
% male/female	41/59
% African-American	8
% American Indian or Alaska Native	1
% Asian or Pacific Islander	7
% Hispanic	12
% White	59
% International	3
% Pell grant recipients	25

First-generation and minority alumni Michael Harper, professional basketball player; Camille Conway, law firm partner; Greg Crawford, marketing executive; Tim Rose, founder and president, institutional investment advisory firm; Cornelius DuBose, education technology

ACADEMICS
full-time faculty	125
full-time minority faculty	20
student-faculty ratio	11:1
average class size	16
% first-year retention rate	75.5
% graduation rate (6 years)	52.9

Popular majors Business, Nursing, Biology, Communication, Psychology

CAMPUS LIFE
% live on campus (% freshmen)	53 (77)

Multicultural student clubs and organizations Black Student Association, Latin American Student Organization, Asian-American Association, Middle Eastern Student Association, Korean and Scandinavian student groups, International Student Association

Athletics NCAA Division III, College Conference of Illinois & Wisconsin

ADMISSIONS
# of applicants	n/a
% accepted	71
# of first-year students enrolled	2,238
SAT Critical Reading range	500-630
SAT Math range	480-600
SAT Writing range	n/a
ACT range	19-25
average HS GPA	n/a

Deadlines
regular decision	rolling
application fee (online)	$40 ($40)
fee waiver for applicants with financial need	yes

COST & AID
tuition	$18,800
room & board	$8,140
total need-based institutional scholarships/grants	n/a
% of students apply for need-based aid	89.8
% of students receive aid	n/a
% receiving need-based scholarship or grant aid	86.5
% receiving aid whose need was fully met	6.9
average aid package	$11,550
average student loan debt upon graduation	$15,814

Roosevelt University

Roosevelt students benefit from central urban and suburban locations, small, interactive classes, and longstanding commitment to diversity and social justice. Campuses in downtown Chicago and Schaumburg, Ill. put students in the heart of two vibrant commercial and cultural districts, which are an integral part of the curriculum and of co-curricular activities. Founded in 1945, Roosevelt was one of the first institutions of higher learning to admit all academically qualified students, regardless of racial, ethnic or religious background, social or economic class, gender or age. Continuing that tradition, Roosevelt is the second most diverse private college/university in the state of Illinois today. Roosevelt University is a national leader in educating socially conscious citizens for active and dedicated lives as leaders in their professions and their communities.

> ACCESS TRIO Programs

Roosevelt University hosts four Federal TRIO programs: Educational Talent Search, Project Prime, Upward Bound, and Veteran's Upward Bound. Educational Talent Search is an academic outreach program designed to help and motivate individuals in completing their middle and high school education, and to pursue further education or training. Project Prime is an academic support program designed to improve the retention and graduation rates of low-income, first generation and disabled students enrolled at Roosevelt's Chicago Campus. Upward Bound is a pre-collegiate experience designed to assist first-generation, minority high school students to develop the skills and motivation necessary to successfully enroll in and graduate from post-secondary educational institutions. Veterans Upward Bound is a pre-college program designed to assist eligible veterans prepare for entry into the college program of their choice by helping them brush up on their academic skills.

> OPPORTUNITY Social Justice High School Scholarship

Roosevelt University offered free tuition to qualified members of Social Justice High School's first two graduating classes. The high school, located in Chicago's Little Village/Lawndale neighborhood, has a high number of low-income Latino and African-American students who otherwise might not have been able to attend college.

> SUCCESS Centers and Institutes

A strong supplement to Roosevelt's degree and certificate programs are twelve centers and institutes that extend the learning, service, and research opportunities available to students and faculty. Among them are the Education Alliance and the Institute for Metropolitan Affairs, which collaborate on school success programs in the greater Chicago area. In addition, the Mansfield Institute for Social Justice and Transformation elevates and fosters social consciousness among students, faculty and members of the community through transformational learning and rich social justice programming in the areas of human rights, social and political action, and the arts. The St. Clair Drake Center for African and African-American Studies uses research, evaluation and policy analysis as tools to examine some of the issues facing the African and African-American communities. The Drake Center partners with organizations that work in targeted geographic locations and is exploring opportunities to collaborate with several agencies, including the Center for New Horizons, The Abraham Lincoln Centre and Jane Addams Hull House, all located in Chicago.

Roosevelt University
430 S. Michigan Ave
Chicago, IL 60605
Ph: (877) APPLY-RU
applyRU@roosevelt.edu
www.roosevelt.edu

FAST FACTS

STUDENT PROFILE

# of degree-seeking undergraduates	4,264
% male/female	33/67
% African American	22
% American Indian or Alaska Native	<1
% Asian or Pacific Islander	21
% Hispanic	5
% White	51
% International	2
% Pell grant recipients	32.3

First-generation and minority alumni Toni Harp, state senator, Connecticut; Anthony Braxton, musician; Sylvia Flanagan, senior editor, *Jet Magazine*; Harold Washington, first African-American mayor of Chicago; Ramsey Lewis, world-famous jazz pianist; Patricia Harris, chief diversity officer, McDonald's Corporation

ACADEMICS

full-time faculty	219
full-time minority faculty	n/a
student-faculty ratio	n/a
average class size	n/a
% first-year retention rate	70
% graduation rate (6 years)	31

Popular majors Psychology, Elementary Education, Accounting, Management, Biology

CAMPUS LIFE

% live on campus (% fresh.)	15 (62)

Multicultural student clubs and organizations Black Student Union, Gamma Theta Chi Multicultural Sorority, International Student Union, RU Latinos, Turkish Intercultural Club

ADMISSIONS

# of applicants	2,861
% accepted	24
# of first-year students enrolled	502
SAT Critical Reading range	505-635
SAT Math range	465-565
SAT Writing	n/a
ACT range	19-24
average HS GPA	3.06

Deadlines

regular decision	rolling
application fee (online)	$25($25)
fee waiver for applicants with financial need	yes

COST & AID

tuition	$21,000
room & board	$11,094
total need-based institutional scholarships/grants	n/a
% of students apply for need-based aid	91.6
% of students receive aid	93.7
% receiving need-based scholarship or grant aid	65.2
% receiving aid whose need was fully met	15.7
average aid package	$13,142
average student loan debt upon graduation	n/a

Southern Illinois University Edwardsville

Southern Illinois University Edwardsville is a premier Metropolitan University offering a rich mix of cultural opportunities and an extensive inventory of academic programs. Seven academic units include Schools of Pharmacy, Dental Medicine, Engineering, Education, Nursing, Business and a College of Arts and Sciences. As one of the best higher education values in the Midwest, SIUE has the lowest in-state tuition rate of all 12 state universities. SIUE students come from 43 states and 49 nations. 24% are first generation college students. Only 25 minutes from downtown St. Louis—with Fortune 500 companies, sports venues, cultural offerings and transportation within minutes of just about anywhere in the Metro Area—the SIUE campus is situated on 2,660 acres of beautiful, forested woodland atop the bluffs overlooking the natural beauty of the Mississippi River's rich bottom land. SIUE wants to make sure all students succeed in their academic programs, graduate and ultimately land a successful career. A variety of programs and initiatives are in place to support the recruitment, retention and academic success of underrepresented students.

> SUCCESS The Summer Bridge Program

The Summer Bridge Program is an on-campus experience that allows freshman students to experience the Southern Illinois University Edwardsville environment prior to the fall term. Through structured and integrated activities, students will be prepared to meet the demands of college and bridge the gap between high school and college. In addition to classes in reading, writing, and math, students will participate in other activities designed to build academic skills and lead to a sense of community.

"Life is full of challenges but with the support system available at SIUE, success is not far out of reach."
– *Jessica Johnson*
Chicago, IL
Secondary Education

> SUCCESS Project F.A.M.E.

Females of African-Descent Modeling Excellence (F.A.M.E.) is a peer-mentoring program designed to link incoming African-American female freshmen with experienced student mentors while guiding them through their first year of university life.

> SUCCESS Project G.A.M.E.

Goal-Oriented African-American Males Excel (G.A.M.E.) is a two-semester program in which African-American males are selected to participate. Incoming freshmen are selected based on high school gpa, ACT score, leadership potential, volunteer experience and potential for success in higher education.

> SUCCESS The Johnetta Haley Scholars Academy

The Johnetta Haley Scholars Academy supports undergraduate students at SIUE who choose to major in Biological Sciences, Computer Sciences, Engineering, Nursing, Physical Sciences and Teacher Education. Other majors may be considered if funds are available.

> SUCCESS The SOAR Program

The SOAR Program (Student Opportunities for Academic Results) is a multicultural support system dedicated to helping students realize their greatest potential. Participation in SOAR is free and includes resources and benefits like tutoring, mentoring, academic advising and cultural events.

Southern Illinois University Edwardsville
P.O. Box 1600
Edwardsville, IL 62026
(618) 650-3705
admissions@siue.edu
www.siue.edu/prospectivestudents

F A S T   F A C T S

STUDENT PROFILE
# of degree-seeking undergraduates	11,144
% male/female	46/54
% African-American	11
% American Indian or Alaska Native	<1
% Asian or Pacific Islander	2
% Hispanic	2
% White	83
% International	2
% Pell grant recipients (2006)	32

First-generation and minority alumni Judge Milton Wharton – St. Clair County Circuit Court Judge, B.S. Business Administration '69; Dr. Ernest Jackson – Only Board Certified African American Forensic Odontologist in the World and Internationally known Certified Crime Scene Investigator, Doctor of Dental Medicine '87; Shelby Steele – Distinguished Alumnus Award – writer for *New York Times*, *Wall Street Journal*, *Harpers Magazine*. Also, an Emmy Winner, MA Sociology, '71; Reggie Thomas – International jazz pianist, instructor, recording artist, musician, teacher, Master of Music '92

ACADEMICS
full-time faculty	622
full-time minority faculty	93
student-faculty ratio	17:1
average class size	23
% first-year retention rate	71
% graduation rate (6 years)	46

Popular majors English, Psychology, Business

CAMPUS LIFE
% live on campus (% fresh.)	30 (69)

Multicultural student clubs and organizations Association of Latin American Students, French Club, International Club, Irish Heritage Society, Italian Club, Muslim Student Association, Organization of African American Students

Athletics NCAA Division I, Ohio Valley Conference

ADMISSIONS
# of applicants	6,952
% accepted	87
# of first-year students enrolled	1,950
SAT Critical Reading range	n/a
SAT Math range	n/a
SAT Writing range	n/a
ACT range	20-25
average HS GPA	n/a

Deadlines
regular decision	n/a
application fee	$30
fee waiver for applicants with financial need	yes

COST & AID
tuition	in-state $6,201; out-of-state $15,503
room & board	$7,461
total need-based institutional scholarships/grants	$1,479,272
% of students apply for need-based aid	86
% receiving need-based scholarship/grant aid	34
% receiving aid whose need was fully met	46
average aid package	$15,749
average student loan debt upon graduation	$20,603

University of Illinois at Urbana-Champaign

University of Illinois
  at Urbana-Champaign
601 East John St.
Champaign, Illinois 61820
Ph: (217) 333-1000
www.uiuc.edu

Since its founding in 1867, the University of Illinois at Urbana-Champaign has earned a reputation as a world-class leader in research, teaching, and public engagement. Distinguished by the breadth of its programs, broad academic excellence, and internationally renowned faculty, Illinois alumni have earned Nobel and Pulitzer Prizes and Olympic medals, have orbited the earth, and lead international corporations. The campus also offers rich experiences beyond the classroom, from performing arts to Big Ten sports. Centrally located between Chicago, Indianapolis and St. Louis, students come from all 50 states and over 100 countries. Also, there are many cultural study centers at the university – which highlight regions including Africa, East Asia and the Pacific, Latin America, the Caribbean, Russia, Eastern Europe, South Asia and the Middle East. In addition to being responsive to issues of cultural diversity, *New Mobility,* a magazine, has continuously ranked the school as the No. 1 "disability-friendly college" in the country.

"I had really high expectations for the University of Illinois, and I am not the slightest bit disappointed. In fact, the environment far exceeds my expectations. I am really excited about the diversity on campus, the school spirit, the endless opportunities for personal and professional growth, and the new people I meet everyday."
– Paula G., '11
Chicago, IL
Marketing and
Management

> ACCESS Biotechnology Education and Outreach Program (BEOP)

Many teachers do not have the knowledge or resources to carry out state-of-the-art science in their classrooms. The Biotechnology Education and Outreach Program is devoted to training teachers and students in biotechnology concepts and hands-on experiments. This program trains teachers in biotechnology concepts and applications and also loans biotechnology equipment and supplies to high school classrooms. To date, this outreach program has trained over 400 high school and community college teachers throughout Illinois, including both rural and urban regions. In particular, BEOP has trained Chicago Public School teachers in the areas of DNA and genomes, genetically modified organisms and DNA fingerprinting.

> OPPORTUNITY Illinois Promise

Economic situations often threaten the affordability of higher education, particularly for students from the lowest income levels. The University of Illinois at Urbana-Champaign, however, is committed to providing access to quality education for high achieving students from all backgrounds. University of Illinois applicants may receive funding through the Illinois Promise program, which provides grants and scholarships to Illinois residents whose families are at or below the federal poverty level. These families do not have to contribute anything toward college expenses. Recipients are expected to work 10 to 12 hours a week, however, in order to contribute to their aid package. To be considered for the Illinois Promise, students must submit the FAFSA by March 15 prior to each academic year.

> SUCCESS Transition Program

Students who demonstrate academic promise but whose academic backgrounds have not adequately prepared them for college success, may be placed in the Transition Program upon admission. Once accepted, students participate in an ongoing academic program, which supplies these students with intensive academic and career counseling, extensive academic and personal support services, plus opportunities to enroll in support-based sections of existing courses.

FAST FACTS

STUDENT PROFILE

# of degree-seeking undergraduates	30,386
% male/female	53/47
% African-American	6
% American Indian or Alaska Native	<1
% Asian or Pacific Islander	14
% Hispanic	7
% White	65
% International	7
% Pell grant recipients	16

First-generation and minority alumni Steve Chen, co-founder, YouTube; Sheila Crump Johnson, co-founder, Black Entertainment Television, America's first black female billionaire; Mannie Jackson, owner, Harlem Globetrotters, chairman, Basketball Hall of Fame; Ang Lee, director

ACADEMICS

full-time faculty	1,979
full-time minority faculty	457
student-faculty ratio	17:1
average class size	25
% first-year retention rate	92
% graduation rate (6 years)	82

Popular majors Business, Biology, Communications, Engineering, Architecture, Psychology

CAMPUS LIFE

% live on campus (% freshmen)	50 (100)

Multicultural student clubs and organizations African American Research and Professional Network, African Cultural Association, Asian American Association, Asian Pacific American Coalition, Baltic Club, Bangladeshi Students Association, Black Chorus at the University of Illinois, Chinese Undergraduate Student Association, Ebony Umoja Black Student Union, Indian Student Association, Japan Intercultural Network, Latino Law Students Association, MIXED, Polish Club Zagloba, PRIDE, Red Roots, Society of Signers, Women of Color and many more
Athletics NCAA Division I, Big Ten Conference

ADMISSIONS

# of applicants	23,146
% accepted	69
# of first-year students enrolled	8,242
SAT Critical Reading range	530-650
SAT Math range	650-750
SAT Writing range	n/a
ACT range	26-31
average HS GPA	n/a

Deadlines

regular admission	1/2
application fee (online)	$40
fee waiver for applicants with financial need	yes

COST & AID

tuition	in-state $12,524; out-of-state $26,666
room & board	$9,284
total need-based institutional scholarships/grants	$76,775,836
% of students apply for need-based aid	58
% of students receive aid	77
% receiving need-based scholarship or grant aid	39
% receiving aid whose need was fully met	28
average aid package	$11,029
average student loan debt upon graduation	$17,930

Western Illinois University

Western Illinois University is a mid-sized, public, co-educational university. Granted recognition by the Pell Institute for the Study of Opportunity as a "Best Practice Institution" for the retention of first-generation and low-income students, the University offers small class sizes and a low faculty-to-student ratio. Western Illinois students receive personal attention from their professors and mentors, and the University is comprised of two campuses that provide a wide range of academic programs, including a strong teacher education program.

> ACCESS Role Models and Success Stories

Western Illinois University's current minority students visit high schools in the region to speak with students about college life and academics.

> ACCESS Pride and Responsibility in My Environment (PRIME)

The University sponsors transportation to various educational programs and activities for this local minority youth program.

> ACCESS Multicultural Recruitment Advisory Board (MRAB)

Western Illinois' Multicultural Recruitment Advisory Board (MRAB), comprised of faculty and students, hosts multicultural group visits and promotes the Western Illinois University experience to prospective minority student

> OPPORTUNITY Western Illinois University Scholarship Program

In 2009, the program distributed more than $2.8 million in scholarship support. Western Illinois scholarships include a number of offerings specifically for entering minority students, including the DuSable scholarship ($1,000 per year, renewable at $500), the Western Opportunity Grant ($1,000), the Western Opportunity Scholarship ($500 to $2,000) and the Student Services Minority Achievement Access/Retention Grant (multiple awards ranging from $500 to $1,000).

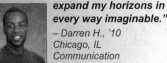

"As president of the WIU Student Government Association and as a member of Beta Phi Pi Fraternity, Inc., I have gained outstanding leadership skills. I love WIU because it has allowed me to expand my horizons in every way imaginable."
– Darren H., '10
Chicago, IL
Communication

> OPPORTUNITY Cost Guarantee

Western's Cost Guarantee is the only program in Illinois that ensures a four-year lock on total costs – tuition, fees, room and board – for undergraduate, transfer and graduate students. Transfer students earning an associate's degree and transferring to WIU the following semester receive the previous year's Cost Guarantee rates. Students from Iowa, Wisconsin and Missouri pay Illinois in-state rates for tuition and fees.

> SUCCESS Diversity and Cultural Awareness

Western provides a wealth of resources that promote diversity and cultural awareness, including Casa Latina Cultural Center, Gwendolyn Brooks Cultural Center and the Women's Center, housed in the new Multicultural Center; Disability Support Services; the Center for International Studies; the University Diversity Council; the University Committee on Sexual Orientation, to name just a few.

Western Illinois University
University Circle
115 Sherman Hall
Macomb, IL 61455-1390
(309) 298-3157
admissions@wiu.edu
www.wiu.edu

FAST FACTS

STUDENT PROFILE
# of degree-seeking undergraduates	10,487
% male/female	54/46
% African-American	9
% American Indian or Alaska Native	<1
% Asian or Pacific Islander	1
% Hispanic	5
% White	77
% International	2
% Pell grant recipients (2006)	30.3

ACADEMICS
full-time faculty	672
full-time minority faculty	105
student-faculty ratio	16:1
average class size	22.6
% first-year retention rate	73.6
% graduation rate (6 years)	59.3

Popular majors Law Enforcement, Biology, Elementary Education, Psychology, Agriculture

CAMPUS LIFE
% live on campus (% fresh.)	36 (95)

Multicultural student clubs and organizations Black Student Association, Latin American Student Organization, NAACP, International Friendship Club, Cultural Expressions Club, Gwendolyn Brooks Cultural Center, Korean Student Association, Tradicion Hispana Dance Troupe, Unity

Athletics NCAA Division I (NCAA Football Championship Subdivision), The Summit League and Missouri Valley Football Conference

ADMISSIONS
# of applicants	8,331
% accepted	64
SAT Critical Reading range	n/a
SAT Math range	n/a
ACT range	19-23
average HS GPA	3.01

Deadlines
regular decision	5/15
fee waiver for applicants with financial need	yes

COST & AID
tuition	in-state $6,779; out-of-state $10,168
room & board	$7,642
total need-based institutional scholarships/grants	$3,600,000
% of students apply for need-based aid	76
% of students receive aid	69
% receiving need-based scholarship/grant aid	68
% receiving aid whose need was fully met	75
average aid package	$11,000
average student loan debt upon graduation	$19,800

Franklin College

Franklin College
101 Branigin Boulevard
Franklin, IN 46131-2623
(317) 738-8062
admissions@franklincollege.edu
www.franklincollege.edu

Franklin College offers students an intimate educational experience — classes contain an average of just 17 students. Students' academic experience is further enhanced by the college's winter term, which is a month-long opportunity for students to take non-traditional classes, participate in internships or travel abroad. Because the Franklin College faculty and staff pay special attention to the needs of underrepresented students, there are a number of resources targeted to these students. Additionally, the Student Association in Support of Multiculturalism (SASSOM) has been a sustained resource for the Franklin College community for more than 20 years.

> ACCESS Center for Leadership Development (CLD) Partnership

Minority youth in Central Indiana can take part in college-preparation sessions offered by the Center for Leadership Development. Franklin College, which is one of CLD's institutional partners, offers two full-tuition scholarships to CLD minority scholars. Franklin College also hosts over 170 CLD students and parents for its annual Success Prep program, designed to encourage high school youth and their parents about the importance of early college planning.

> ACCESS College Summit Partner Campus

Rising seniors from Indianapolis who participate in the College Summit program may have the opportunity to attend a four-day college preparation workshop on the Franklin College campus. College Summit is a national non-profit organization that increases the college enrollment rate of low-income students. By working with high schools and colleges, College Summit recruits talented low-income students and helps with their transition to college while creating a college-going culture in their communities.

> OPPORTUNITY 21st Century Scholars

Indiana students enrolled in 21st Century Scholars, a state-funded program designed to help students from low- and moderate-income families attend college, are awarded full tuition to attend Franklin.

> OPPORTUNITY Ambassadors Scholarship

Students who are underrepresented on the Franklin College campus are also eligible for the Ambassadors Scholarship, with a value that ranges from $1,000 to full tuition and is renewable for four years. Ambassadors Scholarships are stackable with other academic awards received by the student.

> OPPORTUNITY Minority Visit Program

Minority students who have applied and been accepted by January 15 can visit Franklin College during the Minority Visit Program. At this time, students spend two nights living in the Franklin College residence halls with current students and can meet the Director of Multicultural Services and learn about other diversity resources on campus. Franklin makes the travel arrangements for those attending this event.

> SUCCESS Academic Resource Center (ARC)

The Academic Resource Center provides free tutors for all classes taught on campus, as well as writing assistance through the Write Place. The director of the ARC also oversees the Student Success Program, which identifies students' academic weaknesses, provides them with additional support and helps students address transitional issues.

FAST FACTS

STUDENT PROFILE
# of degree-seeking undergraduates	1,047
% male/female	48/52
% African-American	3
% American Indian or Alaska Native	<1
% Asian or Pacific Islander	1
% Hispanic	1
% White	84
% Pell grant recipients	26

First-generation and minority alumni Rafael Sanchez, anchor, WRTV-TV

ACADEMICS
full-time faculty	65
full-time minority faculty	n/a
student-faculty ratio	16:1
average class size	16
% first-year retention rate	71
% graduation rate (6 years)	55

Popular majors Elementary Education and Teaching, Journalism, Sociology, Pre-Medicine, Business

CAMPUS LIFE
% live on campus (% freshmen)	69 (97)

Multicultural student clubs and organizations International Club, Intercultural Book Club, Black Student Union, Student Association for Support of Multiculturalism, Grizzly Pride Alliance, Wave 3
Athletics NCAA Division III, Heartland Collegiate Athletic Conference

ADMISSIONS
# of applicants	1,457
% accepted	66
# of first-year students enrolled	333
SAT Critical Reading range	440-550
SAT Math range	450-560
SAT Writing range	440-540
ACT range	18-23
average HS GPA	3.3

Deadlines
regular decision	rolling
application fee (online)	$30 ($30)
fee waiver for applicants with financial need	yes

COST & AID
tuition	$23,100
room & board	$6,885
total need-based institutional scholarships/grants	n/a
% of students apply for need-based aid	91
% of students receive aid	82
% receiving need-based scholarship or grant aid	100
% receiving aid whose need was fully met	17
average aid package	$16,564
average student loan debt upon graduation	$42,908

Goshen College

Goshen College
1700 South Main Street
Goshen, IN 46526
Ph: (800) 348-7422 / (574) 535-7535
admission@goshen.edu
www.goshen.edu

Founded in 1894 as a ministry of the Mennonite Church, Goshen College continues to work toward a student body comprised of Christ-centered students who are global citizens, passionate learners, compassionate peacemakers and servant leaders. A required study abroad program that has a 40-year tradition embodies the core value of global citizenship. Students spend a semester abroad in countries such as Peru, Nicaragua, China, Germany, Senegal, Jamaica and Cambodia. Students interested in environmental stewardship and sustainable living can take advantage of Goshen's 1,189-acre Merry Lea Environmental Learning Center, which encompasses a natural sanctuary and a sustainable village. The Ministry Inquiry Program and the Camping Inquiry Program provides another hands-on opportunity for learning, placing students in three-month internships in the fields of camping, ministry and service.

> ACCESS 21st Century Scholars

Goshen College provides education workshops, both on campus and in surrounding communities, for students who have been designated as 21st Century Scholars. Students are brought onto the Goshen campus in order to help them gain a stronger understanding of how they can continue their education after completing high school. Faculty and staff from Goshen College also go into the surrounding community to talk with the 21st Century Scholars and their parents to encourage the students to think about attending college.

> OPPORTUNITY Special Visits and Scholarships

Goshen College has sponsored both an Academic Achievers Day as well as special visit days in concurrence with Martin Luther King, Jr. Day. Along with specific visit programs, two scholarships are offered to students of color. The Center for Intercultural Teaching and Learning (CITL) Scholarship is a four-year, full-tuition scholarship for Latino/a students. The Stoltzfus scholarship is for all students of color and is awarded to ten students each year. The $5,000/year scholarship comes with the expectation of campus leadership for the students selected. Center for Intercultural Teaching and Learning scholars participate in a four-year leadership development program. The goal of the program is to prepare students to return to their communities after graduation to continue to work towards educational access for other Latino/a students.

> SUCCESS SALT (Student Academic Leadership Training)

This program is a three-week summer program for students of color. The program is free of charge to the student as long as s/he has already been admitted into Goshen College and enrolls for the fall semester after completing Student Academic Leadership Training. Each student earns three college credits, lives in the residence halls, begins orientation to the college, and begins building and strengthening study skills.

> SUCCESS The Multicultural Affairs Office (MAO)

The Multicultural Affairs Office (MAO) mission is to help foster intercultural understandings and promote a campus-wide environment that encourages interracial and intercultural awareness and learning. The Multicultural Affairs Office oversaw the development of the campus diversity plan. The plan's four guiding goals for advancing interracial and intercultural appreciation are to recruit and retain a diverse student body; to recruit and retain a diverse faculty and staff; to strengthen communication and partnerships with local ethnic communities; and to give increased attention to campus wide and community activities that promote racial harmony and cross cultural relationships.

FAST FACTS

STUDENT PROFILE
# of degree-seeking undergraduates	920
% male/female	41/59
% African-American	3.7
% American Indian or Alaska Native	<1
% Asian or Pacific Islander	1.7
% Hispanic	6.1
% White	81.4
% International	5.7
% Pell grant recipients	19

First-generation and minority alumni Said Sheikh Samatar, African scholar

ACADEMICS
full-time faculty	67
full-time minority faculty	2
student-faculty ratio	11:1
average class size	16.5
% first-year retention rate	84
% graduation rate (6 years)	71.6

Popular majors Business Administration/ Management, Elementary Education and Teaching, Nursing

CAMPUS LIFE
% live on campus	91.3

Multicultural student clubs and organizations American Sign Language Club, AMISH (Association of Mennonites for Ice and Street Hockey), Black Student Union, Frente Mennonita de Liberacion National, Goshen Student Women's Association (GSWA), International Student Club, Latino Student Union

Athletics NAIA, Mid-Central College Conference

ADMISSIONS
# of applicants	525
% accepted	64.7
# of first-year students enrolled	172
Middle 50%:	
SAT Critical Reading range	480-650
SAT Math range	600-650
SAT Writing range	468-620
ACT range	21-28
average HS GPA	3.51

Deadlines
regular admission	12/15
application fee	$25
fee waiver for applicants with financial need	yes

COST & AID
tuition	$23,400
room & board	$7,900
total need-based institutional scholarships/grants	$1,975,052
% of students apply for need-based aid	100
% of students receive aid	99.3
% receiving need-based scholarship or grant aid	68.9
% receiving aid whose need was fully met	33.8
average aid package	$19,470
average student loan debt upon graduation	$18,680

Manchester College

Founded in 1889, Manchester College is an independent, undergraduate, co-educational liberal arts college dedicated to encouraging students to improve themselves and the world they live in. Manchester faculty are committed to preparing students to begin careers and assume leadership roles in society, while at the same time, providing them with the tools to attach meaning to their success. Due to long standing traditions of international study and community service, students are well-versed in the perspectives of other cultures, as well as their own. While the college traces its roots to the Church of Brethren, the institution maintains a commitment to being a community of learning and faith for students of all religious backgrounds.

 ACCESS Wal-Mart College Success Award

Manchester College is the recipient of a $100,000 Wal-Mart College Success Award, a nationwide initiative to increase the number of first-generation college students. Manchester, which boasts a current student body of 25 percent first-generation students, is one of only 20 colleges nationwide to receive the award. With the two-year grant from the Wal-Mart Foundation, Manchester is building on its already successful recruiting and retention programs. An outreach program pairs potential first-generation candidates from area high schools with Manchester mentors. At overnight workshops, program participants learn what to expect from an undergraduate experience and how to prepare and apply for college.

 OPPORTUNITY Multicultural Student Leadership Award (MSLA)

At Manchester College, approximately $11 million in need- and merit-based aid is available for first-generation students. There are several scholarships that may be of interest to first-generation students. One such award is the Multicultural Student Leadership Award (MSLA), which provides recipients up to $3,000 in addition to other financial aid. The award, available to all United States students of color, is based on academic potential, character and leadership, experience and community service.

 SUCCESS Success Center

The Success Center provides a wide range of support services, including academic support, study abroad advising, a writing center, and career advising. A special advisory program for first year students provides academic and navigational support for transitioning from high school into college. Approximately 75 percent of the student body makes use of the Success Center, which is a testament to the efficiency and effectiveness of the services offered.

"I decided to attend Manchester College because they offered me a great financial aid package, but once there, I found so much more! I found a place where I could not only be myself, but discover who I am and who I want to be. I found a home! "

*–Ayana B., '09
Lafayette, IN
Psychology*

 SUCCESS Multicultural Center and Multicultural Clubs

The Office of Multicultural Affairs involves students, staff, faculty, parents, and alumni in campus activities, counseling, special events and projects to promote multiculturalism and encourage a global perspective at Manchester. The mission of the office is to provide an avenue for the campus community to experience diversity and cultivate and foster a respect for other cultures through community building activities. Student organizations such as the Hispanos Unidos and Black Students Union help promote culturally diverse experiences through annual events like forums, film series, and other social activities.

Manchester College
604 E. College Ave.
North Manchester, IN 46962
www.manchester.edu
Ph: (800) 852-3648
admitinfo@manchester.edu
www.manchester.edu

F A S T   F A C T S

STUDENT PROFILE

# of degree-seeking undergraduates	1,187
% male/female	49/51
% African American	3
% American Indian or Alaska Native	1
% Asian or Pacific Islander	1
% Hispanic	3
% White	88
% International	4
% Pell grant recipients	41

First-generation and minority alumni Fred Bullock, educator, professional football player; Samuel Gunnerson, business executive; Michael Jarvis, business executive; Melanie May, educator; James Colins, business executive

ACADEMICS

full-time faculty	71
full-time minority faculty	n/a
student-faculty ratio	15:1
average class size	21
% first-year retention rate	66
% graduation rate (6 years)	55

Popular majors Accounting and Business Management, Biochemistry, Education, Athletic Training

CAMPUS LIFE

% live on campus (% fresh.)	76 (96)

Multicultural student clubs and organizations Asian Awareness Association, Black Student Union, Hispanos Unidos, Manchester College International Association

Athletics NCAA Division III, Heartland Collegiate Athletic Conference

ADMISSIONS

# of applicants	2,389
% accepted	79
# of first-year students enrolled	431
SAT Critical Reading range	440-580
SAT Math range	470-580
SAT Writing	430-540
ACT range	19-25
average HS GPA	3.2

Deadlines

regular decision	rolling
application fee (online)	$25 ($0)
fee waiver for applicants with financial need	yes

COST & AID

tuition	$23,790
room & board	$8,550
% of students receive aid	100
% receiving need-based scholarship or grant aid	n/a
% receiving aid whose need was fully met	31
average aid package	$21,380
average student loan debt upon graduation	$16,333

Saint Joseph's College

Saint Joseph's College
US Highway 231
PO Box 870
Rensselaer, IN 47978
Ph: (219) 866-6000
admissions@saintjoe.edu
www.saintjoe.edu

Saint Joseph's College is a private, Catholic, liberal arts college, founded and sponsored by the Missionaries of the Precious Blood. Saint Joseph's strives to prepare men and women to lead successful professional and personal lives consistent with Gospel values. Located in northwest Indiana, Saint Joseph's students receive a quality education from professors and have many opportunities to sharpen leadership skills on campus. The college features the Core Program, a well-rounded academic foundation which allows students to integrate required courses throughout all four years so that students can begin the study of their majors right away. Students are highly involved in campus life, with 86 percent of full-time students involved in campus clubs and organizations.

> OPPORTUNITY **Puma Opportunity Grant**

The Puma Opportunity Grant is directed toward students who demonstrate a potential for success at Saint Joseph's. The grant may be awarded in the amount of up to $7,000 a year, renewable each year with a 2.8 GPA.

> OPPORTUNITY **Access Grant**

The Access Grant is directed toward students who may not have excelled academically at the high school level but still demonstrate a potential for success at the college level. This grant is awarded in amounts of up to $5,000 annually, renewable each year with a 2.0 GPA.

> SUCCESS **Diversity Coalition**

The Diversity Coalition, a campus multicultural organization, is one of Saint Joseph's College's most popular clubs. Students can attend activities hosted by the Diversity Coalition throughout the year that are inspired by a variety of cultures. In addition to dances, food drives, basketball tournaments, and talent shows, the Diversity Coalition also hosts an annual Martin Luther King Jr. parade and program that incorporates members of the Rensselaer community. The organization makes a point to plan activities to celebrate Black History Month in February and Women's History Month in March.

> SUCCESS **Freshman Academic Support Program (FASP)**

The Freshman Academic Support Program is designed to offer admission to exceptionally motivated students whose high school grades and/or standardized test scores do not meet normal college admissions requirements. The FASP then gives students the tools they need to succeed when they reach campus. Capitalizing on students' motivation to succeed, first-year students accepted into the FASP are required to sign a contract that reflects their willingness to actively participate and take advantage of the services provided by the program. Services include: academic counseling, a study skills class, a basic writing composition class and tutorial assistance.

FAST FACTS

STUDENT PROFILE
# of degree-seeking undergraduates	1,076
% male/female	42.5/57.5
% African-American	7.4
% American Indian or Alaska Native	<1
% Asian or Pacific Islander	<1
% Hispanic	4.2
% White	84.9
% International	<1
% Pell grant recipients	23.3

ACADEMICS
full-time faculty	59
full-time minority faculty	n/a
student-faculty ratio	18:1
average class size	10-19
% first-year retention rate	60
% graduation rate (6 years)	56.1

Popular majors Biology-Chemistry, Business Administration/Management, Criminal Justice, Elementary Education and Teaching, Nursing

CAMPUS LIFE
% live on campus (% freshmen)	67 (93)

Multicultural student clubs and organizations Diversity Coalition
Athletics NCAA Division II, Great Lakes Valley Conference

ADMISSIONS
# of applicants	1,325
% accepted	74.3
# of first-year students enrolled	373
SAT Critical Reading range	420-520
SAT Math range	420-540
SAT Writing range	n/a
ACT range	18-24
average HS GPA	3.0

Deadlines
early decision	10/15
regular decision	rolling
application fee (online)	$25
fee waiver for applicants with financial need	yes

COST & AID
tuition	$24,350
room & board	$7,420
total need-based institutional scholarships/grants	n/a
% of students apply for need-based aid	100
% of students receive aid	82
% receiving need-based scholarship or grant aid	97
% receiving aid whose need was fully met	34.9
average aid package	$22,827
average student loan debt upon graduation	$28,135

Saint Mary's College

For over one-hundred and sixty years, Saint Mary's has remained a private, Catholic, residential, college that educates women in the liberal-arts tradition. As one of the nation's oldest women's colleges, Saint Mary's is an academic community where women develop their talents and prepare to make a difference in the world. Founded by the Sisters of the Holy Cross in 1844, Saint Mary's seeks to provide academic, social and spiritual growth. Located near the city of South Bend and directly across the street from the University of Notre Dame, the Saint Mary's community includes 1,650 students from 43 states and 11 foreign countries.

> ACCESS My First Day in College

The My First Day in College program matches high school freshmen and sophomores from diverse socio-economic backgrounds with enrolled Saint Mary's students. The goal of this program is to allow prospective students to taste collegiate life while providing them with a positive role model throughout their college search process. My First Day in College participants spend the day at Saint Mary's, tour campus, attend classes, and even spend the night with their host students. Workshops are also offered on the admission and financial aid processes.

> ACCESS Encuentro: Encounter Yourself

This is a week-long summer camp for first-generation high school students to develop interpersonal skills, strengthen leadership abilities, and expand intercultural awareness. During the camp, participants gain exposure to college life by sampling courses taught by Saint Mary's professors, explore cultural activities and participate in community-building exercises that foster the development of a positive self-image.

> OPPORTUNITY Holy Cross Grants

Saint Mary's offers Holy Cross grants, ranging up to $5,000/year, to Pell eligible, first-generation students. These grants, offered in addition to other aid traditionally extended, are based solely on financial need. To be eligible, necessary financial aid documents must be completed by March 1.

> OPPORTUNITY Diverse Students' Leadership Conference (DSLC)

Saint Mary's students host the Diverse Students' Leadership Conference each year. During this three-day conference, current and former Saint Mary's students combine energies to organize a campus-wide leadership conference that includes lectures, workshops, film presentations and panel discussions on diversity. Topics from the 2009 conference included: "(En) Lightened Beauty: Media (Mis) Representation of Ethnic Beauty," "Still Needed! Affirmative Action in the Age of a Black President," "Learn about Chinese Culture and Society via YouTube," and "The 'Other' Veil – Muslim Women in the Western Mind." Prospective students are invited to spend the weekend on campus and learn about the challenges and benefits of diversity across a variety of settings – academic, social, spiritual and professional.

> SUCCESS Multicultural Services and Student Programs (MSSP)

MSSP is solid evidence of Saint Mary's commitment to be a community that supports the inclusion of women of all races, ethnicities, and cultures. The MSSP Office advances the understanding of diversity at all levels by providing educational programs and services, as well as being a support network for all students. The office maintains a resource library of novels, scholarship information, art, films and literature on multicultural education. It works with faculty and Academic Affairs to help ensure a student's successful academic and social adjustment to Saint Mary's. MSSP also provides a social and professional gathering place for meetings, small classes, study groups and social events.

Saint Mary's College
Office of Admission
Room 122, LeMans Hall
Notre Dame, IN 46556
Ph: (800) 551-7621 / (574) 284-4587
admission@saintmarys.edu
www.saintmarys.edu

FAST FACTS

STUDENT PROFILE

# of degree-seeking undergraduates	1,664
% male/female	0/100
% African American	2
% American Indian	0
% Asian	2
% Caucasian	88.8
% Hispanic	5
% Pell grant recipients	10

First-generation and minority alumni Eddie Bernie Johnson, Congressional Representative; Donna Christensen, Congressional Delegate; Delia Garcia, President/CEO, Arizona Hispanic Chamber of Commerce

ACADEMICS

full-time faculty	130
student-faculty ratio	10:1
average class size	16
% first-year retention rate	79
% graduation rate (6 years)	76

Popular majors Nursing, Education, Business Administration, Communication, Biology/Pre-Med

CAMPUS LIFE

% live on campus (% freshmen)	84 (99)

Multicultural student clubs and organizations Al Zahra, Student Diversity Board, La Fuerza, Sisters of Nefertiti, Pacific Islander Asian Club
Athletics NCAA Division III, Michigan Intercollegiate Athletic Association

ADMISSIONS

# of applicants	1,357
% accepted	86
SAT Critical Reading range	530-630
SAT Math range	520-610
ACT range	23-27
HS GPA range	3.4-3.9

Deadlines

early decision	11/15
regular decision	2/15
application fee	$30

COST & AID

tuition	$31,020
average room & board	$9,480
% of students receiving aid	91
% receiving need-based scholarship or grant aid	63
% receiving aid whose need was fully met	n/a
average aid package	$18,104*
average student loan debt upon graduation	$18,031**

*Does not include PLUS or private loans.
**Federal student loans.

Saint Mary-of-the-Woods College

Saint Mary-of-the-Woods College
Office of Admission
Guerin Hall
Saint Mary-of-the-Woods, IN 47876
Ph: (812) 535-5106
smwcadms@smwc.edu
www.smwc.edu

Saint Mary-of-the-Woods College, a Catholic college for women sponsored by the Sisters of Providence, is committed to the higher education of women in the tradition of the liberal arts. The college serves a diverse community of learners in undergraduate and graduate programs, while maintaining its historical commitment to women in its campus program. By participating in this community, students develop their abilities to think critically, to communicate responsibly, to engage in lifelong learning and leadership, and to affect positive change in a global society.

.

> OPPORTUNITY Academic Scholarships

Saint Mary-of-the-Woods College offers a selection of academic scholarships driven at access and affordability. All students are automatically considered for academic scholarships when they are reviewed for admissions. The college awarded over $3.3 million in institutional financial aid last year. Renewable merit scholarships include the $20,000 Saint Mother Theodore Guerin Scholarship, the $11,000 Trustee Scholarship, the $9,000 Presidential Scholarship, the $7,000 Dean's Scholarship, and the $6,000 Woods Scholarship. In addition to these merit awards, Saint Mary-of-the-Woods College offers unique scholarship opportunities for underserved students attending select high schools and free room and board for 21st Century Scholars.

> SUCCESS Academic Support Team

Saint Mary-of-the-Woods College Academic Support Team is a one-on-one partnership between designated, experienced faculty members and individual students in need of additional academic support. Such students include those who are on restricted or probationary status, who have low GPAs, or simply want to take advantage of additional help. During regularly scheduled meetings, Academic Support Team members discuss student-related issues such as time management, study habits and questions and concerns related to academic struggle and success. Academic Support Team faculty also acts as liaisons between students, their instructors and other college personnel such as the registrar or counseling staff.

> SUCCESS Succeeding in the College Environment

Offered every fall term at Saint Mary-of-the-Woods College, "Academic Support - ID110: Succeeding in the College Environment" is a course modeled on successful programs taught in several major colleges and universities throughout the nation. This foundational course challenges students to understand and optimize their own personal learning styles, while facilitating the development of more effective study skills, test-taking strategies and communication skills. Its interactive format keeps students engaged, while allowing them to apply what they learn. Most importantly, ID110 enables students to develop skills and strategies that will support and enhance their academic performance across the curriculum.

FAST FACTS

STUDENT PROFILE

# of degree-seeking undergraduates	1,483
% male/female	0/100
% African American	2
% American Indian or Alaska Native	<1
% Asian or Pacific Islander	<1
% Hispanic	1
% White	85
% International	1
% Pell grant recipients	32.8

First-generation and minority alumni Carmen Hansen Rivera, businesswoman

ACADEMICS

full-time faculty	64
full-time minority faculty	n/a
student-faculty ratio	11:1
average class size	n/a
% first-year retention rate	77
% graduation rate (6 years)	42

Popular majors Business Administration, Elementary Education, Psychology, Equine Studies, Pre-Professional Studies

CAMPUS LIFE

% live on campus	70

Multicultural student clubs and organizations International Student Organization, World Wide Woodsies

Athletics United States Collegiate Athletic Association, Intercollegiate Horse Show Association

ADMISSIONS

# of applicants	334
% accepted	69
# of first-year students enrolled	100
SAT Critical Reading range	500-550
SAT Math range	430-530
SAT Writing range	410-550
ACT range	20-26
average HS GPA	3.3

Deadlines

regular decision	8/15
application fee (online)	$30($0)
fee waiver for applicants with financial need	yes

COST & AID

tuition (09-10 academic year)	$22,360
room & board	$8,450
total need-based institutional scholarships/grants	n/a
% of students apply for need-based aid	n/a
% of students receive aid	n/a
% receiving need-based scholarship or grant aid	n/a
% receiving aid whose need was fully met	n/a
average aid package	$17,140
average student loan debt upon graduation	$20,180

Clarke College

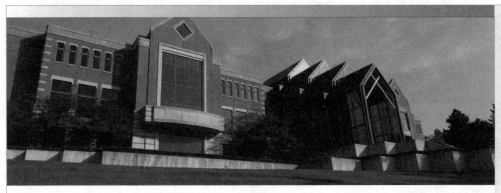

Clarke College
1550 Clarke Drive
Dubuque, IA 52001
Ph: (800) 383-2345
admissions@clarke.edu
www.clarke.edu

A dynamic liberal arts and sciences college in the thriving Mississippi River city of Dubuque, Iowa, Clarke College offers students a personal, values-based education. While the school remains true to its Catholic heritage, it is also "progressive with the times," affording students quality preparation for whichever fields they choose to enter. The college is widely regarded for its health sciences programs and well as its fine arts curriculum.

> ACCESS Campus Ministry Community Service

Reaching beyond the Clarke campus is a regular component of the Clarke experience. Community service opportunities offered through the college's campus ministry office serve organizations in the Dubuque area (such as the Maria House shelter, the Greater Dubuque Boys' & Girls' Club, the Hospice of Dubuque and Big Brother/Big Sister) and beyond (including service trips to New Orleans, Chicago and Ecuador). Each semester, volunteers join Into the Streets, a semi-annual service day that sends hundreds of students into the community.

> ACCESS Student Mentoring

Each year, Clarke students volunteer in the Dubuque Senior High School Mentoring Program, through which they provide students with homework assistance and academic enrichment. Clarke's unique Professional Development School (PDS) method of preparing the teachers of tomorrow puts Clarke education classrooms directly in local schools — providing not only hands-on learning, but also the opportunity to serve area children.

> OPPORTUNITY Catherine Dunn, BVM Endowed Scholarship

Former Clarke College president Catherine Dunn, BVM, Ph.D. served the college for 22 years and upon her retirement supporters of Clarke established the Catherine Dunn, BVM Endowed Scholarship. In line with Dunn's wishes, the scholarship was designed to be awarded to minority students, with an emphasis on those of Hispanic descent, who demonstrate academic ability, good moral character and financial need.

> SUCCESS Smart Start Program

Sometimes students need a jump start as they begin their college experience. That's why Clarke started the "Smart Start" program — to give participating students a jump-start into college life and make the transition easier. This immersion program brings selected students to campus to begin the process of building relationships and becoming familiar with campus resources just prior to Welcome Weekend. Students in the Smart Start program begin college life more engaged and better prepared for the challenges ahead.

> SUCCESS Academic Resource Centers

Clarke offers a variety of academic support resources that are free to all students through the Margaret Mann Academic Resource Centers, which include the Learning Center, the Writing Center and the Technology Center. There, students receive help acquiring a number of skills, such as test-taking, time management and effective studying.

FAST FACTS

STUDENT PROFILE
# of degree-seeking undergraduates	956
% male/female	32/68
% African-American	1
% American Indian or Alaska Native	<1
% Asian or Pacific Islander	<1
% Hispanic	<1
% White	57
% International	2
% Pell grant recipients	78.4

ACADEMICS
full-time faculty	104
full-time minority faculty	n/a
student-faculty ratio	n/a
average class size	n/a
% first-year retention rate	68
% graduation rate (6 years)	55.3

Popular majors Business Administration/ Management, Nursing, Education

CAMPUS LIFE
% live on campus (% freshmen)	85 (90)

Multicultural student clubs and organizations UNITY, Human Rights Action Group

Athletics NAIA, Midwest Collegiate Conference

ADMISSIONS
# of applicants	4,008
% accepted	36
# of first-year students enrolled	634
SAT Critical Reading range	440-530
SAT Math range	420-610
SAT Writing range	410-490
ACT range	21-26
average HS GPA	3.4

Deadlines
regular admission	rolling
application fee (online)	$20
fee waiver for applicants with financial need	yes

COST & AID
tuition	$23,520
room & board	$6,840
total need-based institutional scholarships/grants	n/a
% of students apply for need-based aid	96
% of students receive aid	100
% receiving need-based scholarship or grant aid	98
% receiving aid whose need was fully met	27
average aid package	$28,649
average student loan debt upon graduation	$18,581

Grinnell College

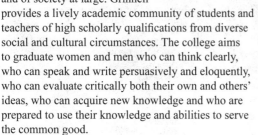

Founded in 1846, Grinnell College is a private, co-educational, liberal-arts college that seeks to educate its students in the liberal arts through free inquiry and the open exchange of ideas. As a teaching and learning community, the college holds that knowledge is a good to be pursued both for its own sake and for the intellectual, moral and physical well-being of individuals and of society at large. Grinnell provides a lively academic community of students and teachers of high scholarly qualifications from diverse social and cultural circumstances. The college aims to graduate women and men who can think clearly, who can speak and write persuasively and eloquently, who can evaluate critically both their own and others' ideas, who can acquire new knowledge and who are prepared to use their knowledge and abilities to serve the common good.

"Growing up in Los Angeles, Grinnell, Iowa was not exactly where I envisioned myself spending my undergraduate years. However, the same is probably true for my best friends, who come from Connecticut, Texas, Ohio, Oregon, and even South Africa. But that's exactly the magic of the best kept secret in the liberal arts. It would take hours to explain why Grinnell is so special and important, but I think bringing students from around the world to an Iowan town of 9,000, and getting us to love it, says enough."
– Zac E., '09
Los Angeles, CA
Psychology

 ACCESS The Galaxy Inc.

In partnership with the Galaxy Inc., a non-profit community youth resource center, Grinnell College organizes fun activities and educational programming for local Iowa youth. With an emphasis on "at risk" and "disadvantaged youth" participation, Galaxy provides fifth through 12th grade students with a safe, innovative space where they have the opportunity to engage in a variety of educational and recreational activities, build positive relationships and take on community initiatives. Grinnell College students provide Galaxy participants with after-school tutoring and homework help; volunteer as chaperones for dances and open evenings; hang out with kids during open afternoon hours; and help with creative programming for the youth center.

> **OPPORTUNITY Fly-In Programs**

Every year, the Grinnell College Office of Admission sponsors several diversity fly-in programs. The goal of these programs is to bring students to campus for an in-depth visit to fully familiarize each of them with Grinnell. Participants receive a formal invitation to visit Grinnell and a stipend that covers transportation, food and lodging for a weekend on campus.

> **OPPORTUNITY Restructured Financial Aid Program**

Committed to need-blind admission and accessibility for academically qualified students, Grinnell College offers significant financial aid to needy students. Beginning with the class of 2012, Grinnell students will potentially graduate from Grinnell with no more than $8,000 in debt, as need-based loans are capped at $2,000 per year. In addition, students' required financial contribution may be eliminated for one summer if they engage in a socially worthwhile or educationally relevant activity.

> **SUCCESS Multicultural Student Orientation Program**

The Grinnell College Multicultural Student Orientation Program is designed to assist new students in making the transition to the college. Held prior to New Student Orientation, this two-day program provides an introduction to resources on campus, in town, and in the surrounding communities. Participants become acquainted with students of color, faculty and staff, and establish useful networking relationships. In addition, participants are automatically assigned to a peer mentor who will help multicultural freshmen transition to a small liberal arts college and rural community throughout the year.

Grinnell College
1103 Park St.
Grinnell, IA 50112
Ph: (641) 269-3600
askgrin@grinnell.edu
www.grinnell.edu

F A S T   F A C T S

STUDENT PROFILE

# of degree-seeking undergraduates	1,639
% male/female	46/54
% African American	5
% American Indian or Alaska Native	<1
% Asian or Pacific Islander	8
% Hispanic	6
% White	62
% International	11
% Pell grant recipients	12.7

First-generation and minority alumni Herbie Hancock, musician; John Garang, vice president, Sudan; George Moose, Assistant Secretary of State for African Affairs, ambassador to Benin and Senegal; Sen Katayama, co-founder, Japan Communist Party; K.C. Wu, governor of Taiwan Province, Mayor of Shanghai

ACADEMICS

full-time faculty	158
full-time minority faculty	27
student-faculty ratio	9:1
average class size	10
% first-year retention rate	94
% graduation rate (6 years)	86

Popular majors Biology, History, English, Political Science, Economics

CAMPUS LIFE

% live on campus	87 (100)

Multicultural student clubs and organizations Asian Students in Alliance, Grinnell Multicultural Alliance, MidEastern-American Solidarity Group, African Student Union, Native American Student Alliance, South Asian Students in Alliance, Asian American Coalition, Concerned Black Students, International Student Organization, Student Organization of Latinas/Latino

Athletics NCAA Division III, Midwest Conference

ADMISSIONS

# of applicants	3,217
% accepted	43
# of first-year students enrolled	464
SAT Critical Reading range	620-740
SAT Math range	620-710
SAT Writing range	n/a
ACT range	28-32
average HS GPA	n/a

Deadlines

early decision	11/15
regular decision	1/2
application fee (online)	$30 ($0)
fee waiver for applicants with financial need	yes

COST & AID

tuition	$34,932
room & board	$8,272
total need-based institutional scholarships/grants	$23,227,157
% of students apply for need-based aid	68
% of students receive aid	100
% receiving need-based scholarship or grant aid	99
% receiving aid whose need was fully met	100
average aid package	$30,751
average student loan debt upon graduation	$19,526

Mount Mercy College

Small campus. Big results. Mount Mercy's intimate campus and small size make it a great choice. Students easily get involved in campus activities and gain valuable leadership experience. Every entering freshman receives an institutional grant or scholarship. With a wide range of majors, athletic and intramural opportunities, clubs and organizations, and residential options, students find their unique paths and achieve big results. Mount Mercy offers resources through the Classroom Connection Program, Mentoring Program, and Student Alumni Career Ambassadors (SACA) that connect students with alumni who work in fields of potential interest. In the spirit of the Sisters of Mercy, founders of Mount Mercy, the campus community nurtures and promotes reflective judgment, strategic communication, service to the common good and the development of a purposeful life.

> ACCESS **Students in Free Enterprise (SIFE)**

Mount Mercy's nationally recognized Students in Free Enterprise (SIFE) team offers a multitude of learning experiences for elementary and high school students in the area to learn success skills, entrepreneurship, financial literacy and business ethics. Last year, SIFE team members volunteered more than 1,566 hours and taught more than 3,339 people about free enterprise principles in the global market. SIFE students condense these experiences into a cumulative presentation showcasing their community partnership successes, and compete against students from more than 800 college campuses nationwide. The team won its 13th consecutive SIFE regional championship in 2010.

> ACCESS **Elementary School Partnership / High School Art Day**

Education, nursing, social work and fine arts students can take advantage of Mount Mercy's partnership with local elementary schools to share their time and talents with students. Activities include theatre lessons that encourage students to find their voice on stage and express themselves artistically. Regional high school students are also recognized at Mount Mercy during High School Art Day, where they can participate in art reviews and have their art showcased in the newly enhanced Janalyn Hanson White Gallery.

> ACCESS **College for a Day**

Mount Mercy partners with two local elementary schools to facilitate "college for a day," in which elementary school students attend classes in biology, business, art, criminal justice, theater and nursing. The experience culminates in campus tours led by Mount Mercy Student Ambassadors and lunch in the renovated dining center with Mount Mercy students and faculty.

> OPPORTUNITY **Iowa Private College Week**

Mount Mercy participates in the annual Iowa Private College Week, an initiative that allows students to explore all of Iowa's private colleges. Participation in this event is of particular importance to Mount Mercy, as over 70 percent of Mount Mercy's students are first-generation students who come from small rural communities. By visiting three or more colleges that week, students may be eligible to receive free books.

> SUCCESS **Faculty Mentoring**

Mount Mercy ensures that all first-year students are placed in small classes so that they may benefit from more individual support from faculty and learn valuable study skills and time management. Mount Mercy faculty also monitor the academic progress of new freshmen in order to identify potentially problematic areas. Portal courses in Mount Mercy's core curriculum also focus on successful college transitions while exploring key Mercy themes of service, volunteerism and hospitality.

"My scholarship has opened so many doors for me. Without receiving this help there is a good chance that I could not have attended college. I feel so fortunate to have been able to enroll at Mount Mercy."

– Bryce S., '10
Prescott , IA
Outdoor Conservation

Mount Mercy College
1330 Elmhurst Drive NE
Cedar Rapids, IA 52402
Ph: (319) 368-6460
admission@mtmercy.edu
www.mtmercy.edu

F A S T   F A C T S

STUDENT PROFILE
# of undergraduate enrollment	1,498
% male/female	30/70
% African American	1.6
% American Indian	<1
% Asian	1.5
% Caucasian	84.1
% Hispanic	2.7
% Pell grant recipients	22

First-generation and minority alumni Nancy Penner '81, attorney, Shuttleworth & Ingersoll Law Firm; Sherrie Fletcher '79, archivist, Ronald Reagan Presidential Library; Tammy Koolbeck '86, vice president of Venue Services, VenuWorks; Jean-Paul Calabio '07, SAP & application security, Rockwell Collins; Rachel Collins '01, guidance counselor, Cedar Rapids (Iowa) Kennedy High School

ACADEMICS
full-time faculty	81
student-faculty ratio	13:1
average class size	15
% first-year retention rate	83.7
% graduation rate (6 years)	64.6

Popular majors Management, Criminal Justice, Education, Nursing, Social Work, Biology, Outdoor Conservation

CAMPUS LIFE
% live on campus	37

Multicultural student clubs and organizations International Club, Mount Mercy Women's Organization, College Pastoral Council, Stangs Christian Fellowship
Athletics NAIA, Midwest Collegiate Conference

ADMISSIONS
# of applicants	366
% accepted	78
SAT range	940-1160
ACT range	20-29
average HS GPA	3.42
Deadlines	
regular admission	rolling

COST & AID
tuition	$23,260
room & board	$7,260
% of students receiving aid	97
% receiving need-based scholarship or grant aid	78
% receiving aid whose need was fully met	37

University of Iowa

Students attending the University of Iowa can have it all: the benefits of a large research institution and the intimacy of a small, yet vibrant city. Home to the world-renowned Writer's Workshop, International Writing Program and the Playwright's Workshop, writing and literature enthusiasts will feel comfortable here. The university has won international recognition for its wealth of achievements in the arts, sciences and humanities. The first public university in the country to admit women and men on an equal basis, the University of Iowa is already a groundbreaker in equal opportunity and diversity. The University of Iowa is a comprehensive public university with a long-standing commitment to teaching, research and service.

> ACCESS Iowa First Nations Summer Program

The Iowa First Nations Summer Program is a unique research, social, recreational and educational opportunity for Native American students entering eighth or ninth grade who have some science or laboratory background. Students attend chemistry and biotechnology classes and, after completing their research, make a visual presentation and write a mini-journal article on their topic.

> ACCESS Iowa Talent Project

Minority and economically disadvantaged students with considerable talent from the Des Moines and Cedar Rapids school districts may take part in the free three-week summer residential program focused on improving critical reading and writing skills.

> OPPORTUNITY Advantage Iowa Awards

These awards are for low-income or first-generation students that meet certain admissions criteria or who participate in a federally funded Upward Bound program. Awards range from $2,000 to full tuition; FAFSA must be on file by March 1.

> OPPORTUNITY Diversity-Focused Scholarships

Students are automatically considered for a number of diversity scholarships. The Tom Brokaw Scholarship Fund supports first-year Native American students who demonstrate need and meet merit requirements, the Madeline P. Peterson Scholarship is awarded to a first-year woman student of American Indian descent and African-American students intending to major in the physical sciences are given preference for the Ezra L. Totton Scholarship, and many more.

> SUCCESS Iowa Edge Program

Iowa Edge is an early leadership, communication and skill-building program for 72 minority and first-generation students. Participants meet peers and campus leaders, tour the campus and take advantage of leadership and communication skill-building activities.

> SUCCESS Center for Diversity and Enrichment / Iowa Biosciences Advantage

The Center coordinates supplemental instruction and programming in conjunction with its TRIO services: Friday After Class is an opportunity for students to talk informally with diverse faculty, and the Life Science Summer Program gives students hands-on lab training in developmental biology. Academically talented minority students also benefit from the Iowa Biosciences Advantage, which provides first-rate training in biomedical, behavioral, and biophysical sciences to facilitate entry into doctoral programs.

"Iowa is really welcoming and it's easy to find a place to fit in. It's a large campus, so you're always able to find people with similar interests and backgrounds. And there are so many resources available to help you succeed. At the Center for Diversity & Enrichment, for example, multicultural coordinators can answer any questions you have. They want you to come here, and they want you to do well.""
– Jostten S., '12
Fort Dodge, IA
Business

The University of Iowa
107 Calvin Hall
Iowa City, IA 52242-1396
Ph: (800) 553-4692 / (319) 335-3847
admissions@uiowa.edu
www.uiowa.edu

FAST FACTS

STUDENT PROFILE
# of degree-seeking undergraduates	19,899
% male/female	48/52
% African-American	2
% American Indian or Alaska Native	1
% Asian or Pacific Islander	4
% Hispanic	3
% White	85
% International	4
% Pell grant recipients	16

First-generation and minority alumni Rita Dove, former Poet Laureate and Pulitzer Prize winner; B.J. Armstrong, professional basketball player, Chicago Bulls; Cornelius (Perk) Thornton, Retired Vice President, Investment Research, Goldman, Sachs & Co.; Tiffani Orange, diversity and inclusion manager for the Americas, Ford Motor Company; Herbert Nipson — Award-winning journalist who spent nearly forty years of his professional career at *Ebony* magazine.

ACADEMICS
full-time faculty	1,588
full-time minority faculty	264
student-faculty ratio	15:1
average class size	25
% first-year retention rate	83
% graduation rate (6 years)	66

Popular majors Business; Health Sciences; Education; Communications/English; Psychology

CAMPUS LIFE
% live on campus (% freshmen)	27 (94)

Multicultural student clubs and organizations African Student Association, American Indian Student Association, Asian American Coalition, Black Student Union, Chinese Dance Club, Chinese Students and Scholars Association, International Crossroads Community, Japanese Cultural Association, Korean Student & Scholars Association, Malaysian Student Society, Romanian Cultural Organization, Multicultural Business Student Association, National Society of Black Engineers
Athletics NCAA Division I, Big Ten Conference

ADMISSIONS
# of applicants	15,060
% accepted	83
# of first-year students enrolled	4,063
SAT Critical Reading range	500-640
SAT Math range	560-690
SAT Writing range	n/a
ACT range	28-28
average HS GPA	3.57

Deadlines
regular application	4/1
application fee (online)	$40 ($40)
fee waiver for applicants with financial need	yes

COST & AID
tuition in-state: $5,782; out-of-state: $21,156	
room & board	$8,004
total need-based institutional scholarships/grants	$22.572,128
% of students apply for need-based aid	72
% of students receive aid	71
% receiving need-based scholarship or grant aid	30
% receiving aid whose need was fully met	44
average aid package	$7,900
average student loan debt upon graduation	$22,856

University of Northern Iowa

The University of Northern Iowa prides itself on putting "Students First" and has a reputation for providing exceptional undergraduate education. Building on its historic excellence in teacher education, the university has developed outstanding programs in business, natural sciences, humanities and fine arts, and social and behavioral sciences. The university's size — just more than 13,000 students — allows it to offer faculty, facilities, and academic choices of a large university, while retaining a friendly, small-college atmosphere on a compact, park-like campus. With more than 40 major buildings on 940 acres, the campus can still be crossed in an easy 15-minute walk.

> ACCESS **Multicultural Super Saturday**

Multicultural Super Saturday is a comprehensive program designed for high school freshmen, sophomore, juniors, seniors and their guests. During this visit, prospective students and their parents will learns about admissions, the financial aid/scholars process, campus housing, preparing for college and academic programs. Multicultural Super Saturday also provides the opportunity to meet with UNI students, staff and faculty, tour the campus, and have lunch in one of the dining centers.

"It gives me confidence to know I'm in an environment in which my professors want to see me succeed, not fail. I was surprised most by their willingness to help me with whatever I needed, even outside of the classroom. Having that kind of support system makes it easy to be successful at UNI."

*– Andrea C., '11
Marshalltown, IA
Elementary Education/Early Childhood Education*

> OPPORTUNITY **Financial Aid Office**

Paying for college can seem like a daunting task, leaving many students and their families unsure of what to ask or where to start. The UNI Financial Aid Office prides itself on assisting families in understanding the aid process and ensuring that they can make the University of Northern Iowa accessible and affordable. Notable grants and scholarships include Iowa Minority Academic Grants for Economic Success (IMAGES), Tuition Guarantee Program for Iowans, and Tuition Guarantee Program for Multicultural Community College Iowans, Multicultural Scholar Awards, Out of State Scholar Awards, and Distinguished Scholar Awards for Iowans.

> SUCCESS **Jump Start Orientation Program**

For over a decade, The UNI Jump Start Orientation Program has provided new students from ethnically, culturally, and socioeconomically diverse backgrounds with a "jump start" on their first year at the University. Jump Start is a special orientation program that provides students with an opportunity to make a smooth transition to the University. Students move to campus one week early to learn about campus resources, network with multicultural faculty and staff, and meet with other multicultural students on campus. Additional activities include sessions on academic success, library resources, computer lab training, on-campus job fair, and money management. Many participants are enrolled in Strategies for Academic Success, a course designed to develop effective study techniques and other skills necessary for courses at the collegiate level.

> SUCCESS **Gaining Panther Success (GPS) Mentor Program**

This program is designed to support and encourage new students from diverse backgrounds in their academic and personal growth during their first year at UNI. The GPS program provides an excellent opportunity for students to enhance their academic and personal success in a university environment. Mentors are students who have successfully transitioned into university life at UNI. They serve as guides who meet with their new mentees in individual and group meetings. Mentees receive one-on-one encouragement, information on academic and community resources, and many opportunities to attend on- and off-campus activities with their mentors.

University of Northern Iowa
1227 West 27th Street
Cedar Falls, IA 50614
Ph: (319) 273-2281
admissions@uni.edu
www.uni.edu

F A S T   F A C T S

STUDENT PROFILE

# of degree-seeking undergraduates	11,086
% male/female	43/57
% African-American	2.7
% American Indian or Alaska Native	<1
% Asian or Pacific Islander	1.1
% Hispanic	1.8
% White	88.3
% International	2.4
% Pell grant recipients	23.8

First-generation and minority alumni Inta Eppright, Assistant Principal, Nashville TN Public Schools; Clarence Lobdell, Auditor, Office of Inspector General, U.S. Government, Washington DC; Stephanie Mohorne, Assistant Principal, Waterloo (IA) Public Schools

ACADEMICS

full-time faculty	639
full-time minority faculty	n/a
student-faculty ratio	16:1
average class size	n/a
% first-year retention rate	84
% graduation rate (6 years)	63

Popular majors Elementary Education, Biology, Accounting, Management, Communications

CAMPUS LIFE

% live on campus (% fresh.)	40 (90)

Multicultural student clubs and organizations Asian Alliance, Black Greek Alliance, Black Male Leaders Union, Black Student Union, EXCEL, Ethnic Student Promoters, George Walker Society of Music, Hispanic/Latino Student Union, Minority Graduate Student Association, Multicultural Student Advisory Board, Multicultural Teaching Alliance
Athletics NCAA Division I, Missouri Valley Conference

ADMISSIONS

# of applicants	4,584
% accepted	84
# of first-year students enrolled	2,522
SAT Critical Reading range	461-581
SAT Math range	441-591
SAT Writing range	n/a
ACT range	21-26
average HS GPA	3.39

Deadlines

regular decision	8/15
application fee	$40
fee waiver for applicants with financial need	no

COST & AID

tuition	in-state: $7,008; out-of-state: $15,348
room & board	$6,960
total need-based institutional scholarships/grants	n/a
% of students apply for need-based aid	85.2
% of students receive aid	97.8
% receiving need-based scholarship or grant aid	45.4
% receiving aid whose need was fully met	28.2
average aid package	$7,867
average student loan debt upon graduation	$24,176

Wartburg College

Wartburg College, affiliated with the Lutheran Church (ELCA), is recognized for outstanding liberal arts and pre-professional programs, competitive athletic teams, stellar music ensembles and active, involved students. Wartburg College has been nationally classified by the Carnegie Foundation for the Advancement of Teaching as one of 62 colleges that foster community engagement in the curriculum and through community outreach and partnerships. The college's high placement rates in jobs, graduate and professional schools includes an 89 percent medical school placement rate and 100 percent placement in other medical programs. Wartburg is included on a list of best Midwestern colleges and among top 200 colleges for science. The college administers more than $37 million in financial aid, providing access to students from a wide variety of socioeconomic backgrounds. The college is named after the Wartburg Castle in Eisenach, Germany.

> OPPORTUNITY The Center for Community Engagement Fellows

The Wartburg Center for Community Engagement offers a unique opportunity for students to serve the community and earn a $1,000 educational voucher as CCE Fellows. Fellows enroll as part-time AmeriCorps members and complete 300 hours of service over the course of the academic year. Service can involve internships with nonprofit organizations, completing a leadership class, participating in a service trip or service-learning project, tutoring and other volunteer opportunities. The $1,000 voucher can be used toward tuition, loans or graduate school.

> OPPORTUNITY Scholarships for Underrepresented Students

The McElroy Minority Scholarship and Slife Minority Scholarship provide full-tuition scholarships for first-year underrepresented students. GPA and letters of recommendation are considered and reviewed. Preference is given to students from the Waterloo or Cedar Falls, Iowa area and scholarships are renewable based on academic performance. The "Be Orange Scholarship" is awarded to incoming first-generation students. Applicants are recommended by the Admissions Office and approved by the Financial Aid Office.

> OPPORTUNITY Diversity Grant

This grant is awarded to underrepresented students with academic potential. The grant amount, up to $2,500 annually, is determined by financial need. A FAFSA must be completed for consideration.

> SUCCESS The Pathways Center

The Pathways Center provides comprehensive support to students from orientation to preparing for life after college. Pathways' First Year Experience program helps students make a successful transition to college.

> *"Wartburg College has provided me with an incredible support system of faculty, staff, and coaches. Thanks to faculty advisers, academic support services, and financial assistance from the college, I will join my brother in becoming the first generation of our family to graduate from college. Along the way, I have made great friends from across the country and around the world, earned a national individual championship in wrestling, and participated in college service trips as a way to help others."*
>
> *– Romeo D., '09*
> *Cameroon*
> *Religion*

FAST FACTS

STUDENT PROFILE

# of degree-seeking undergraduates	1,800
% male/female	48/52
African American	4.8
% American Indian or Alaska Native	0.2
% Asian or Pacific Islander	1.5
% Hispanic	1.5
% White	82.2
% International	5
% Pell grant recipients	26

First-generation and minority alumni
Walter Reed, Jr., director, Iowa Department of Human Rights

ACADEMICS

full-time faculty	109
full-time minority faculty	5
student faculty ratio	12:1
average class size	22
% first-year retention rate	82
% graduation rate (6 years)	64

Popular majors Business Administration, Biology, Communication Arts, Elementary Education, Music Education

CAMPUS LIFE

% live on campus (% fresh.)	81 (98)

Multicultural student clubs and organizations
Mosaico, Black Student Union, International Club
Athletics NCAA Division III, IIAC

ADMISSIONS

# of applicants	2,451
% accepted	70.7
# of first year students enrolled	480
SAT Critical Reading range	420-600
SAT Math range	510-600
SAT Writing range	470-610
ACT range	21 - 27
Average HS GPA	3.5

Deadlines

early action	12/1
regular decision	rolling
application fee	$0
fee waiver for applicants with financial need	n/a

COST & AID

tuition (09/10 Academic year)	$26,650
room & board (09/10 Academic year)	$7,615
Total need-based institutional scholarships and grants	$21,509,387
% of students apply for need-based aid	88
% of students receive aid	98
% receiving need-based scholarship or grant aid	76
% receiving aid whose need was fully met	32
average aid package	$31,063
average student loan dept upon graduation	$20,435

Southwestern College

Southwestern College
100 College Street
Winfield, KS 67156-2499
Ph: (620) 229-6236
scadmit@sckans.edu
www.sckans.edu

Southwestern College is a private, comprehensive, four-year college affiliated with the United Methodist Church. Southwestern is dedicated to its small student body and supports its students' success with a large variety of services and merit scholarships, even providing each student with a laptop upon enrollment. Southwestern's cutting-edge, computer-based curriculum makes for a unique and rewarding academic experience. The college recruits heavily in local Wichita, Kansas City, Oklahoma City and Tulsa areas, and targets urban high schools with significant populations of minority and first-generation students.

> ACCESS **Stucky Middle School Partnership**

Southwestern College's partnership with Stucky Middle School, a local, diverse public school in Wichita, encourages middle school students to attend college, especially Southwestern. The partnership includes a mentoring program between Southwestern and Stucky students throughout the academic year and field trips to the Southwestern campus for athletic events, concerts and other programs. Southwestern hosts a select group of Stucky students over the summer for a three-day Academic Camp devoted to college admission and coursework preparation. The college guarantees a $25,000 scholarship to any Stucky graduate admitted to Southwestern. Similar partnerships exist between Southwestern and other Wichita public schools through school-based organizations.

> OPPORTUNITY **Explore More**

Special sessions during "Explore More" campus visit days allow first-generation and minority students to examine issues of particular interest, including finance, campus activities and support for these groups. "Explore More" days are scheduled three times during each school year.

> SUCCESS **Laptop Learning**

Southwestern College issues Dell laptop computers to all incoming students on its main campus, ensuring easy access to its wireless network and Blackboard academic software anywhere on campus. Connecting to faculty, staff and fellow students is seamless and convenient, and every two years the computers are switched out for brand new hardware and software. Graduates pay a minimal transfer fee to keep the computer when they receive their degrees.

> SUCCESS **Student Success Center**

Southwestern College's Student Success Center runs all student services programs that encourage student retention and success. This includes academic advising, tutoring, study skills assistance and mentoring. Students are individually identified for Success Center services by the College Student Inventory, through which new students self-evaluate their challenges in preparation for college. Students are also referred to the Success Center by advisers, Student Life staff and faculty members. Services are available to all students, but the majority of programs are aimed at minority, low-income and first-generation students.

FAST FACTS

STUDENT PROFILE

# of degree-seeking undergraduates	1,623
% male/female	48.9/51.1
% African-American	9
% American Indian or Alaska Native	1
% Asian or Pacific Islander	2
% Hispanic	5
% White	68
% Pell grant recipients	27

First-generation and minority alumni Elizabeth Baumgart '60, educator, developed criteria for and was principal of magnet school that became model for more than 100 Los Angeles magnet schools; Arlyn Hackett '67, professional consultant, Annie's Gourmet Kitchens; C. Darnell Jones '72, president judge, Court of Common Pleas of Philadelphia County, member since 1987; Hector Rios '90, Wichita optometrist; Christy Grealis '98, event manager, Country Music Association

ACADEMICS

full-time faculty	49
full-time minority faculty	n/a
student-faculty ratio	13:1
average class size	15
% first-year retention rate	69
% graduation rate (6 years)	49

Popular majors Business Administration, Liberal Studies, Nursing

CAMPUS LIFE

% live on campus (% freshmen)	76 (99)

Multicultural student clubs and organizations Black Student Union, Dixon Fellows, Phi 54 Phi, Phi Delta Theta

Athletics NAIA, Kansas Collegiate Athletic Conference

ADMISSIONS

# of applicants	328
% accepted	90
# of first-year students enrolled	159
SAT Critical Reading range	420-510
SAT Math range	430-530
SAT Writing range	400-480
ACT range	19-25
average HS GPA	3.4

Deadlines

regular decision	rolling
application fee (online)	$20 ($20)
fee waiver for applicants with financial need	yes

COST & AID

tuition	$19,680
room & board	$5,750
total need-based institutional scholarships/grants	n/a
% of students apply for need-based aid	85
% of students receive aid	75
% receiving need-based scholarship or grant aid	100
% receiving aid whose need was fully met	33
average aid package	$22,382
average student loan debt upon graduation	$25,697

Berea College

Berea College offers a high quality liberal arts education to students of all races, who have great promise but limited economic resources. Every admitted student receives a four-year tuition scholarship and the opportunity to work on campus to assist with costs of room and board and to learn valuable skills. Additionally, Berea provides a laptop computer for all new students. Founded in 1855 as the first interracial and co-educational college in the South, Berea promotes understanding and kinship among all people, service to communities in Appalachia and beyond, and sustainable living practices which set an example of new ways to conserve our limited natural resources. The college's motto lays a firm foundation for this one-of-a-kind institution: "God has made of one blood all peoples of the earth."

> ACCESS Women's Equality in Education Act (WEEA) Project

The Berea College Women's Equality in Education Act (WEEA) Project provides direct services to 50 Kentucky high school women interested in obtaining college degrees in math and science. Services include hands-on science academic opportunities, science professional development for high school educators, job shadowing and internship experiences, and providing STEM career planning information to students and parents. Berea College students work throughout the year and summer with the project through mentoring and tutoring the WEAA students.

> ACCESS Upward Bound

Upward Bound helps young people in grades nine through twelve prepare for higher education. The program provides tutoring, instruction, counseling, career orientation, and an opportunity to experience educational development and personal growth in a college setting while still in high school. Berea College serves 85 participants in selected schools in south central Kentucky.

> *"I never knew that I could do as well in college as I have. The professors at Berea are so helpful. I could not have done it alone. Now I will walk away with a prestigious education that will always benefit me."*
>
> *– Katie L., '08*
> *Dalton, GA*
> *Nursing*

> SUCCESS Four-Year Tuition Scholarship

Berea provides all students a four-year tuition scholarship, which covers remaining tuition costs after all federal, state, institutional, and private grants have been awarded. The cost of education does not include room, board, fees, books, and supplies, but additional financial aid is available to support these costs. The average freshman pays on average only $1,500 for these costs during the first year of enrollment, but many pay nothing if their family cannot afford to contribute.

> SUCCESS Work-Learning Program

Another distinctive feature of Berea College is its work-learning program. Berea requires all students to work 10-15 hours per week while carrying a full academic course load. The program provides students with valuable work experience such as teamwork, leadership, and supervising others. Students may work in any one of 130 departments — jobs range from working in food service at Berea's historic Boone Tavern to serving as a teaching assistant for an academic major to helping the local Boys & Girls Club of Madison County.

> SUCCESS The Center for Excellence in Learning Through Service (CELTS)

CELTS was created in 2000 to house all of the student-led service programs and community outreach offices and to lead an initiative to integrate service into the academic curriculum. Berea College was named to the 2007 President's Higher Education Community Service Honor Roll with Distinction. This award, given annually to only a few institutions, is the highest federal recognition a college can receive in regards to innovative and effective volunteering, service-learning and civic engagement.

Berea College
CPO 2220
Berea, KY 40404
Ph: (859) 985-3500
askadmissions@berea.edu
www.berea.edu

FAST FACTS

STUDENT PROFILE

# of degree-seeking undergraduates	1,548
% male/female	41/59
% African American	18
% American Indian or Alaska Native	1
% Asian or Pacific Islander	2
% Hispanic	3
% White	68
% International	7
% Pell grant recipients	86

First-generation and minority alumni Carter G. Woodson, father of black history; John Fenn, Nobel Prize winner; Juanita M. Kreps, former U.S. Secretary of Commerce; Tharon Musser, Tony Award winner; Jack Roush, automotive engineer and designer, owner of Roush Racing

ACADEMICS

full-time faculty	130
full-time minority faculty	22
student-faculty ratio	10:1
average class size	15
% first-year retention rate	81.8
% graduation rate (6 years)	64.9

Popular majors Biology, Business Administration, Child/Family Studies, Psychology, Technology/Industrial Arts

CAMPUS LIFE

% live on campus (% fresh.)	3 (13)

Multicultural student clubs and organizations African Student Association, Asian Student Union, Black Music Ensemble, Berea Middle Eastern Dance, Buddhist Student Association, Hispanic Student Association, Center for International Education

Athletics NAIA, Kentucky Intercollegiate Athletic Conference

ADMISSIONS

# of applicants	2,745
% accepted	19
# of first-year students enrolled	392
SAT Critical Reading range	500-620
SAT Math range	465-585
SAT Writing	510-590
ACT range	21-26
average HS GPA	3.37

Deadlines

regular decision	rolling to 4/30
application fee (online)	$0 ($0)
fee waiver for applicants with financial need	n/a

COST & AID

tuition	$0
room & board	$5,496
total need-based institutional scholarships/grants	$3,592,320
% of students apply for need-based aid	100
% of students receive aid	100
% receiving need-based scholarship or grant aid	100
% receiving aid whose need was fully met	100
average aid package	$33,573
average student loan debt upon graduation	$7,849

Centre College

Centre College, a private, Presbyterian, liberal arts college founded in 1819, is known for its outstanding professors, beautiful 115-acre Greek Revival campus and remarkable alumni. By attracting and nurturing highly motivated students, the college has produced two-thirds of Kentucky's Rhodes Scholars (postgraduate study at Oxford University) in the past 50 years and more than 34 Fulbright recipients (postgraduate study and work around the world). The Centre Commitment guarantees every student an internship, study abroad and graduation within four years or the college provides up to one additional year of tuition-free study. The college's alumni include U.S. vice presidents, Supreme Court justices and the founder of Hard Rock Café.

> ACCESS **Centro Latino and Spanish Program**

Centre's Spanish Program established and continues to work with Centro Latino, which serves the area Latino community with translation help and through social and educational programs. Spanish students also provide tutoring, after-school programs and reading camps for the Latino community.

> ACCESS **Whitney M. Young Scholars**

Whitney M. Young Scholars spend two weeks on campus each summer through a Louisville-based program that identifies talented, low-income, predominantly African-American students in seventh grade and works with them through high school to prepare for college.

> OPPORTUNITY **Posse Foundation**

Centre participates in the Posse Foundation, a program that brings talented inner-city youth to campus to pursue their academics and to help promote cross-cultural communication. Posse students are nominated by their high school to the program and share a collaborative support system with a special mentor to adjust to campus and college life. Centre's Posse Scholars hail from Boston.

> OPPORTUNITY **New Horizons Scholarship**

This Centre scholarship program recognizes talented students who are likely to provide campus diversity leadership. As many as 40 students from each class are awarded a scholarship ($16,000 in 2007-08) and guaranteed priority consideration for need-based grants.

> OPPORTUNITY **Bonner Scholarship**

This Centre scholarship provides access to higher education for students from underrepresented populations who demonstrate financial need and an ability to have a strong positive impact on campus and the surrounding community through their service work.

> SUCCESS **Pre-Freshman Research Program**

The Pre-Freshman Research Program enables students who will be attending Centre to conduct science research during the summer before beginning their freshman year at Centre. The program is open to African-American, Hispanic, Native American and Asian and Pacific Islanders who will enroll at Centre in the fall.

> SUCCESS **Academic Affairs Diversity Office**

Centre College strives for a campus community that reflects global society's racial and ethnic diversity. The Academic Affairs Diversity Office recruits and retains diverse faculty, staff and students and also promotes campus diversity by working with the Diversity Student Union, Admission Office, Student Life Office and Human Resources. Activities for the Annual Martin Luther King Celebration and other community relations are also planned through the office.

Centre College
600 W. Walnut St.
Danville, KY 40422-1394
Ph: (859) 238-5350
admissions@centre.edu
www.centre.edu

F A S T   F A C T S

STUDENT PROFILE
# of degree-seeking undergraduates	1,214
% male/female	45/55
% African-American	4
% American Indian or Alaska Native	<1
% Asian or Pacific Islander	3
% Hispanic	2
% White	88
% International	2
% Pell grant recipients	15.6

First-generation and minority alumni John Henrey Rogers, U.S. Representative; Issac Tigrett, founder of Hard Rock Café.

ACADEMICS
full-time faculty	103
full-time minority faculty	11
student-faculty ratio	11:1
average class size	18
% first-year retention rate	91
% graduation rate (6 years)	81

Popular majors Economics, English Language and Literature, History, Biology, Anthropology/Sociology

CAMPUS LIFE
% live on campus (% freshmen)	98 (99)

Multicultural student clubs and organizations Diversity Student Union, International Student Association, Hispanic Society, Muslim Student Association, Japanese Club, NAACP

Athletics NCAA Division III, Southern Collegiate Athletic Conference

ADMISSIONS
# of applicants	2,176
% accepted	63
# of first-year students enrolled	333
SAT Critical Reading range	600-699
SAT Math range	600-699
SAT Writing range	500-599
ACT range	24-29
average HS GPA	3.58

Deadlines
early decision	12/1
regular admission	2/1
application fee (online)	$40
fee waiver for applicants with financial need	yes

COST & AID
tuition	$26,400
room & board	$8,500
total need-based institutional scholarships/grants	$15,610,982
% of students apply for need-based aid	71
% of students receive aid	83
% receiving need-based scholarship or grant aid	59
% receiving aid whose need was fully met	25
average aid package	$25,091
average student loan debt upon graduation	$17,190

Thomas More College

Thomas More College
333 Thomas More Parkway
Crestview Hills, KY 41017-3495
Ph: (859) 344-3332
admissions@thomasmore.edu
www.thomasmore.edu

Founded in 1921 as a teaching college by the Benedictine Sisters at Villa Madonna College, Thomas More College is a small, Catholic liberal arts school located 10 miles outside Cincinnati. The school is well-respected for its focus on individual student development, achievement and life-long learning. From the beginning, Thomas More has emphasized critical thinking and responsibility. All students are encouraged to become involved in the direction of their future through independent study, building relationships with advisors and taking courses that support self-advocacy. The school's core curriculum was designed by the faculty to ensure a solid liberal arts education for their students.

> OPPORTUNITY College Access Program (CAP)

Thomas More's College Access Program is a six-week summer program that offers students with scores and grades below admissions requirements an opportunity for entrance to the school. Students must go through the standard application procedure for consideration. If a student does not gain unconditional acceptance, CAP is a viable alternative. The summer session consists of a remedial class in English, math and a study skills course. Students receiving a 3.5 GPA from the summer courses gain unconditional acceptance into Thomas More for the fall. Students whose grade point average is lower must undergo an admissions committee review to determine their status.

> OPPORTUNITY Diversity Award

Thomas More College offers a Diversity Award of $2,500 given annually to students from traditionally underrepresented African American, Hispanic, Asian American and American Indian student groups. The award is also available to students with physical disabilities. Students need only to apply for admission to the college to be considered.

> SUCCESS Office of Multicultural Affairs

The Office of Multicultural Affairs works to ensure that the campus population respects and appreciates diversity issues. They provide support and programs to foster a campus community that values diversity. The office also works to encourage academic achievement and personal growth within its diverse student population by promoting diversity-related programs and a neutral ground for students to express their concerns. The director of this office serves as the adviser to the African American Student Association, which sponsors several educational and social events for the entire campus throughout the year. The group also serves as mentors to new African American students.

FAST FACTS

STUDENT PROFILE
# of degree-seeking undergraduates	1,303
% male/female	47/53
% African-American	5
% American Indian or Alaska Native	<1
% Asian or Pacific Islander	<1
% Hispanic	<1
% White	75
% Pell grant recipients	27

First-generation and minority alumni Carol Burns '70, vice president, Education Junior Achievement; Joe Kohrs '82, president, Kohrs, Lonneman, Heil Engineers

ACADEMICS
full-time faculty	71
full-time minority faculty	n/a
student-faculty ratio	16:1
average class size	17
% first-year retention rate	74
% graduation rate (6 years)	42

Popular majors Business Administration, Biology, Nursing, Education

CAMPUS LIFE
% live on campus (fresh.)	23 (56)

Multicultural student clubs and organizations African American Student Association
Athletics NCAA Division III, President's Athletic Conference

ADMISSIONS
# of applicants	1,055
% accepted	80
# of first-year students enrolled	274
SAT Critical Reading range	440-570
SAT Math range	460-570
SAT Writing range	n/a
ACT range	19-25
average HS GPA	3.3

Deadlines
early decision	8/15
application fee (online)	$25 ($25)
fee waiver for applicants with financial need	yes

COST & AID
tuition	$23,220
room & board	$6,560
total need-based institutional scholarships/grants	n/a
% of students apply for need-based aid	80
% of students receive aid	99
% receiving need-based scholarship or grant aid	92
% receiving aid whose need was fully met	27
average aid package	$10,797
average student loan debt upon graduation	$25,265

Transylvania University

Transylvania University
300 North Broadway
Lexington, KY 40508
800-872-6798
admissions@transy.edu
www.transy.edu

Founded in 1780, Transylvania is the sixteenth oldest college in the United States. Consistently ranked as one of the nation's top liberal arts colleges, it is one of only a few schools in that group located in the heart of city. Transylvania's location in vibrant Lexington, Kentucky, a city of 270,000 people, provides studens with professional, cultural, and social opportunities only available in such an environment. Over one-third of Transylvania's students are the first in their families to attend a four-year college, and they thrive in Transylvania's challenging yet supporting environment. Transylvania's faculty is among the strongest in the nation. Professors know their students well, they push students in their areas of strength, and they support students in their areas of weakness.

> ACCESS **Community Outreach**

Transylvania students serve local children through a number of service opportunities, including Ready, Set, Study (a partnership between Transylvania University, the Carnegie Center for Literacy and Learning, and Breckinridge Elementary School), TUTORS (Transylvania University Teaching and Outreach to Refugee Children), and special tutoring programs through organizations like 3M Tutors and the Optimists Club. The Transylvania community holds an annual holiday party, Crimson Christmas, for children who participate in the local Big Brother/Big Sister Program. Transylvania partners with a variety of other organizations each year to prepare and distribute backpacks with school supplies. Transylvania also offers summer sports and academic camps for students from kindergarten through high school

"What sets Transy apart is its very friendly environment. Other schools I visited seemed fake - like they were giving me the same set speech they give every prospective student who walks in the door. But here, I'm not just another name. I feel like people really want me to be here. And my financial aid package, scholarships, and campus work-study make it possible for me and my family."

– Quanta T., '12
Lexington, KY
Cultural and Ethical Studies

> OPPORTUNITY **Scholarships**

Transylvania offers a wide range of academic scholarships and need-based awards that help bridge the cost of a Transylvania education with what students and their families can afford. Of all students, 98 percent - and 100 percent of all freshmen - receive scholarships and/or financial aid. Transylvania is well known for meeting student need, especially those with the highest level of need.

> SUCCESS **Diversity Action Council (DAC)**

The Diversity Action Council is a student leadership organization created to promote a campus environment that respects and celebrates diversity in all dimensions. DAC works directly with the Office of Multicultural Affairs to plan diversity programs for the Transylvania community. DAC maintains a consistent working relationship with the Office of Community Service and Civic Engagement, the Office of Admissions, and the Student Activities Board while also operating as an umbrella organization for other student organizations like the Black Student Alliance and TUnity.

FAST FACTS

STUDENT PROFILE

# of degree-seeking undergraduates	1,092
% male/female	41/59
% African-American	4
% American Indian or Alaska Native	<1
% Asian or Pacific Islander	2
% Hispanic	1
% White	82
% International	<1
% Pell grant recipients	20

First-generation and minority alumni
Everett Bass '72, Vice President, Waste Management Inc.; Erwin Roberts '94, Attorney and Former secretary of the Kentucky Personnel Cabinet; Latarika Young '03, Software Engineer, Lexmark International; C. Shawn McGuffey '98, Assistant Professor of Sociology, Boston College

ACADEMICS

full-time faculty	90
full-time minority faculty	5
student-faculty ratio	12:1
average class size	17
% first-year retention rate	86
% graduation rate (6 years)	75

Popular majors Business, Biology, Psychology, Political Science, Spanish

CAMPUS LIFE

% live on campus (% freshmen)	80 (98)

Multicultural student clubs and organizations
Diversity Action Council, Black Student Alliance, TUnity, TERRA, International House, TUTORS (Teaching and Outreach for Refugee Children)
Athletics NCAA Division III, Heartland Collegiate Athletic Conference

ADMISSIONS

# of applicants	1,423
% accepted	79
# of first-year students enrolled	283
SAT Critical Reading range	530-650
SAT Math range	510-630
SAT Writing	n/a
ACT range	23-29
average HS GPA	3.73

Deadlines

early decision	12/1
regular decision	2/1
application fee (online)	$30 ($0)
fee waiver for applicants with financial need	yes

COST & AID

tuition	$25,650
room & board	$8,090
total need-based institutional scholarships/grants	n/a
% of students apply for need-based aid	75
% receiving need-based scholarship or grant aid	100
% receiving aid whose need was fully met	21
average aid package	$21,670
average student loan debt upon graduation	$17,595

Dillard University

Dillard University
2601 Gentilly Boulevard
New Orleans, LA 70122
Ph: (504) 283-8822
admissions@dillard.edu
www.dillard.edu

Set on a beautiful 55-acre campus in historic New Orleans, Louisiana, Dillard University offers a high-quality, comprehensive—and affordable—education in an intimate and supportive environment that helps students reach their full potential. The faculty at Dillard not only teach, but are true mentors. Dillard's internships, rate of placements in the workplace and admissions to graduate schools are among the highest in the nation. Dillard is preparing them for world-class graduate and professional schools, and successful careers in law, medicine, science and research, education, business, and the arts and entertainment. Dillard students are being prepared for leadership roles and for giving back to their communities, their states, their nation and the world.

"Dillard University allows me to be in a loving environment while receiving a quality education. Dillard is truly preparing me for graduate level programs and a very rewarding, successful life."
– Terrance M., '12 Houston ,TX Biology

> ACCESS Eighth Grade Initiative

The Dillard University Eighth Grade Initiative program is a cutting edge, pre-collegiate program that is designed to encourage New Orleans students from diverse backgrounds to successfully negotiate high school and to attend college. A cohort of 100 students is enrolled into the Dillard University's Eighth Grade Initiative program each year. These students remain in the Eighth Grade Initiative program until their matriculation into Dillard University. Dillard University also participates in a number of federally funded TRiO programs, including Student Support Services, Educational Talent Search, and Upward Bound.

> OPPORTUNITY UNCF Gates Millennium Scholars Program

Dillard University promotes the UNCF Gates Millennium Scholars Program, a scholarship sponsored by Bill Gates, as the university is a member institution with UNCF. The scholarship criteria is as follows: Students submit a nominee form (i.e. student application, nominator form, recommender form); student must be of African American, American Indian, Asian, Pacific Islander, or Hispanic American descent; be a US citizen; have a 3.3 GPA on a 4.0 scale; be a first year student attending an accredited institution; have demonstrated leadership abilities; and meet federal Pell Grant criteria.

> OPPORTUNITY Emerging Scholars Program

Students whose GPA or standardized test scores fall below traditional admissions requirements may nevertheless qualify for the Emerging Scholars program, which provides sliding scores for students hailing from the metropolitan New Orleans area. Emerging Scholars receive academic, cultural and social enrichment during the summer after their senior year and, if they complete it successfully, matriculate in the fall semester.

> SUCCESS Student Orientation, Advisement and Registration (S.O.A.R.)

All students are required to participate in an orientation program, during which they learn about the university resources available to them. Academic advising and class registration are major elements of the program, which is offered in a number of sessions.

FAST FACTS

STUDENT PROFILE

# of degree-seeking undergraduates	781
% male/female	29/71
% African-American	71
% American Indian or Alaska Native	0
% Asian or Pacific Islander	<1
% Hispanic	<1
% White	<1
% International	n/a
% Pell grant recipients	73

First-generation and minority alumni Lisa Frazier-Page, writer, The Washington Post; Ellis Marsalis, jazz musician; Garrett Morris, comedian, actor; Ruth J. Simmons, first African-American president of an Ivy League School (Brown University)

ACADEMICS

full-time faculty	104
full-time minority faculty	94
student-faculty ratio	7:1
average class size	13
% first-year retention rate	69
% graduation rate (6 years)	37

Popular majors Biology, Nursing, Mass Communication, Business Management, Sociology

CAMPUS LIFE

% live on campus (% freshmen)	47 (100)

Multicultural student clubs and organizations International Language Club, Melton Foundation, Vision Quest

Athletics NAIA, Gulf Coast Athletic Conference

ADMISSIONS

# of applicants	1,974
% accepted	35
# of first-year students enrolled	173
SAT Critical Reading range	310-560
SAT Math range	400-560
SAT Writing range	310-440
ACT range	16-20
average HS GPA	2.8

Deadlines

regular admission	rolling
application fee (online)	$30
fee waiver for applicants with financial need	yes

COST & AID

tuition	$13,000
room & board	$8,285
total need-based institutional scholarships/grants	$5,844,681
% of students apply for need-based aid	92
% of students receive aid	92
% receiving need-based scholarship or grant aid	52
% receiving aid whose need was fully met	73
average aid package	$15,421
average student loan debt upon graduation	$26,000

Loyola University New Orleans

Loyola University New Orleans is a private, co-educational Catholic university located in the heart of the city. Loyola offers students a wide variety of academic programs, ranging from arts and sciences to business to music, all taught in the Jesuit tradition of educating the whole person. While students are challenged to seek personal excellence, they are also guided in their efforts, helped by Loyola's "person-centered" learning community. Consistent with its Jesuit and Catholic heritage, Loyola strives to develop students into a new generation of leaders who possess a love for truth, the critical intelligence to pursue it and the courage to articulate it.

> ACCESS **Upward Bound**

Committed to providing students with a quality education, Loyola reaffirms its social responsibility by hosting an Upward Bound program open to local underserved high school students. Upward Bound consists of a six-week summer course that provides intense instruction and college credit, and a Saturday and after-school course that provides instructional and tutorial assistance to increase developmental skills in language arts, mathematics, science and foreign language. Additionally, Upward Bound students receive academic and career advisement, postsecondary orientation and preparation and participate in a variety of motivational and cultural enrichment activities.

> OPPORTUNITY **Jazz Brunch and President's Open House**

Each fall Loyola hosts a Jazz Brunch open house for prospective students; and each spring an open house for all admitted students. The latter, the President's Open House, offers families an opportunity to gain further insight into the Loyola collegiate experience. Students and guests take part in several events held throughout the day, including a talk with the president, a meeting with the academic deans and special interest sessions.

> SUCCESS **Summer Bridge**

In keeping with its philosophy of "person-centered" education, Loyola serves the needs of students going through the college admissions process who might need a "jump start" through the Summer Bridge program. In Summer Bridge, traditionally underserved high school seniors are conditionally admitted to Loyola with the understanding that they must attend college preparatory classes. Loyola's Summer Bridge program provides a study skills class, the opportunity to earn six college credits over the summer. With this kind of intense, individualized guidance, Summer Bridge students enter Loyola academically prepared and confident.

"I was an intern at Entergy, a utility company that serves Louisiana, Texas, Mississippi, and Arkansas. Entergy is one of the largest companies in Louisiana and employees more than 14,000 people in various fields such as engineering, management, finance, and my field, accounting. Thanks go to Loyola and the College of Business for helping me to discover such a great opportunity in the city of New Orleans."

– Ryan J., '08
Missouri
Accounting

> SUCCESS **Mathematics Center**

The Loyola Mathematics Center offers one-on-one tutoring for students from developmental math through calculus, differential equations, linear algebra and discrete math. In an effort to support low-income students, the Mathematics Center also offers a wide variety of mathematics tools. Interactive computer software as well as video tapes are available to those who prefer these methods of assistance.

Loyola University
6363 St. Charles Avenue
Campus Box 18
New Orleans, LA 70118
Ph: (800) 4-LOYOLA / (504) 865-3240
admit@loyno.edu
www.loyno.edu

FAST FACTS

STUDENT PROFILE
# of degree-seeking undergraduates	2,600
% male/female	47/53
% African American	18
% American Indian or Alaska Native	>1
% Asian or Pacific Islander	5
% Hispanic	15
% Pell grant recipients	19

First-generation and minority alumni Ellis Marsalis, jazz pianist, recording artist; Manuel A. Esquivel, former Prime Minister, Belize; Cassandra McWilliams Chandler, assistant director of the Office of Public Affairs, national spokesperson, FBI; Dr. Rose-Marie Toussaint, liver transplant surgeon, author; Michael Smith, ESPN

ACADEMICS
full-time faculty	255
full-time minority faculty	34
student-faculty ratio	11:1
average class size	19
% first-year retention rate	73
% graduation rate (6 years)	68

Popular majors Communications, Biology, Psychology, Music Industry Studies, International Business, English Writing

CAMPUS LIFE
% live on campus (% freshmen)	37 (73)

Multicultural student clubs and organizations Black Student Union, International Student Association (ISA), Loyola Asian Student Organization (LASO), Bridging the Gap

Athletics NAIA, Gulf Coast Athletic Conference

ADMISSIONS
# of applicants	3,651
% accepted	63
# of first-year students enrolled	709
SAT Critical Reading range	560-660
SAT Math range	520-630
SAT Writing range	n/a
ACT range	23-28
average HS GPA	3.7

Deadlines
priority application	12/1
regular decision	rolling
application fee (online)	$20 ($20)
fee waiver for applicants with financial need	yes

COST & AID
tuition	$28,770
room & board	$9,826
total need-based institutional scholarships/grants	$26,335,479
% of students apply for need-based aid	73
% of students receive aid	57
% receiving need-based scholarship or grant aid	57
% receiving aid whose need was fully met	16
average aid package	$23,322
average student loan debt upon graduation	$21,401

Bowdoin College

Located on a 205-acre campus in coastal Brunswick, Maine, Bowdoin College has provided students with a nonsectarian liberal arts education since 1794. The college prides itself in the recruitment of first-generation and minority students, who make up approximately 40 percent of the student body. For all students, Bowdoin has a 92 percent graduation rate over six years and a 96 percent first-year retention rate. Offering more than 40 academic majors and award-winning educational facilities, Bowdoin offers an education and a residential experience focused on instilling principled leadership, lifelong learning, and service to the common good.

> ACCESS Upward Bound

At Bowdoin College, Upward Bound serves first-generation, low-income students from 16 high schools in rural Maine. The program has two components — the summer program and the academic year program. Students apply to the summer program during the second semester of their sophomore year in high school. The students visit the Bowdoin College campus for two six-week summer sessions — one before the junior year and another before the senior year of high school. During the regular academic year, Upward Bound counselors visit students each month to provide academic counseling. A few Upward Bound students are accepted into the Bridge Program for the summer after high school graduation. Students earn college credit in Composition and Art History while working and living in a Bowdoin College residence.

"I am from Florida, so people always ask why I would even think of going to school in Maine. The answer is as simple as this: I fell in love with Bowdoin during my Invitational trip. With friendly students, welcoming professors, helpful staff, and gorgeous fall foliage (not to mention the delicious food), how could anyone not?"

– Carina S., '10
Coral Springs, FL
Visual Arts

> OPPORTUNITY QuestBridge

Bowdoin is a partner with QuestBridge, a non-profit program that links low-income students with educational and scholarship opportunities at 26 top colleges and universities throughout the U.S. Through the QuestBridge National College Match Program, Bowdoin has enrolled low-income students from many parts of the U.S. In many cases, these are students who became interested in Bowdoin through partnership with QuestBridge.

> OPPORTUNITY The Bowdoin Invitational and Experience

The Bowdoin Invitational and Experience programs are all–expense paid college visit programs for talented students from around the country who can contribute the college's diversity. Bowdoin knows that the most influential factor in a student's decision to attend Bowdoin is a campus visit. The programs are crucial for students who are unable to afford the trip to Maine.

> SUCCESS Baldwin Program for Academic Development

The Baldwin Program offers counseling in academic skills and training in time- and stress-management techniques. The program also offers peer tutoring, study skills development, study groups for particular classes and assistance for students with different learning styles.

Bowdoin College
5000 College Station
Brunswick, ME 04011-8441
Ph: (207) 725-3100
admissions@bowdoin.edu
www.bowdoin.edu

F A S T   F A C T S

STUDENT PROFILE

# of degree-seeking undergraduates	1,777
% male/female	49/51
% African American	7
% American Indian or Alaska Native	1
% Asian or Pacific Islander	11
% Hispanic	10
% White	66
% International	4
% Pell grant recipients	12

First-generation and minority alumni John Brown Russwurm, Bowdoin's first (and the nation's third) African-American graduate, teacher, writer, editor, "The Freedom's Journal," governor of Liberia; Kenneth I. Chenault, chairman and CEO, American Express; Geoffrey Canada, author, educator, president and CEO, Harlem Children's Zone

ACADEMICS

full-time faculty	177
full-time minority faculty	32
student-faculty ratio	9:1
average class size	13
% first-year retention rate	96
% graduation rate (6 years)	92

Popular majors Economics, History, Government, Biology, English

CAMPUS LIFE

% live on campus (% fresh.)	94 (100)

Multicultural student clubs and organizations African American Center, International Students Association, Latin American Students Association, Korean American Students Association, Asian Students Association, Southeast Asian Students Association, Caribbean Students Association
Athletics NCAA Division III, New England Small Colleges Athletic Conference

ADMISSIONS

# of applicants	5,940
% accepted	19
# of first-year students enrolled	494
SAT Critical Reading range	660-750
SAT Math range	660-750
SAT Writing range	660-750
ACT range	30-33

Note: Submission of standardized test is optional for admission to Bowdoin

average HS GPA	n/a

Deadlines

early decision I	11/15
early decision II	1/1
regular decision	1/1
application fee (online)	$60 ($60)
fee waiver for applicants with financial need	yes

COST & AID

tuition	$39,605
room & board	$10,880
total need-based institutional scholarships/grants	$21,472,864
% of students apply for need-based aid	51
% of students receive aid	42
% receiving need-based scholarship or grant aid	42
% receiving aid whose need was fully met	100
% of students with loans in aid packages	0
average aid package	$33,139
average student loan debt upon graduation	$18,135

Colby College

Colby College
4800 Mayflower Hill
Waterville, ME 04901
Ph: (800) 723-3032
admissions@colby.edu
www.colby.edu

Colby College, one of the country's oldest independent liberal arts colleges, is a small, private college located in Waterville, Maine. Colby is a national leader in research and project-based undergraduate learning and has won awards for campus internationalization and environmental studies and stewardship. Colby's focus on diversity and internationalization is renown; 70 percent of Colby students study abroad and 66 countries are represented on campus. Colby's Oak Institute for the Study of International Human Rights supports international Oak Scholars, promotes interaction among international and American students on campus and brings a human rights practitioner to Colby for one semester every year.

> OPPORTUNITY **Ralph J. Bunche Scholars Program**

The Ralph J. Bunche Scholars Program supports students of color who demonstrate leadership potential and academic strength. Each year 10 to 15 students enroll at Colby College as Bunche Scholars. Bunche Scholar weekend symposia are held each spring on the Colby campus. Additionally, as Bunche Scholars pursue internship opportunities, a stipend of $3,000 will be provided for one summer internship during the student's Colby career.

> OPPORTUNITY **Posse Foundation**

Colby participates in the Posse Foundation, a program that brings talented inner-city youth to campus to pursue their academics and to help promote cross-cultural communication. Posse students are nominated by their high school to the program and share a collaborative support system with a special mentor to adjust to campus and college life. Colby's Posse Scholars hail from New York City.

> OPPORTUNITY **Experience Colby and Colby Live**

Experience Colby (fall) and Colby Live (early spring) are all-expense paid college visit programs for U.S. citizens and permanent residents with African, Latino/a, Asian, and Native heritage. Colby continues to have a deep commitment to increasing campus diversity, with the ultimate goal of developing a truly multicultural community. We understand that the campus visit is an important part of any student's decision-making process, and Colby has committed resources necessary to make such visits possible.

> SUCCESS **Advising Dean Program**

The Advising Dean program supports and enhances Colby's commitment to first rate individual advising of students. Designed to complement Colby's academic advising, the Advising Dean program ensures that all students have a point of contact for advice and counsel. The Advising Deans are knowledgeable about issues and problems that arise for student and are a good source of information about College resources and policies.

> SUCCESS **Colby Achievement Program in the Sciences (CAPS)**

Colby Achievement Program in the Sciences is a six-week summer program designed to provide participating pre-first year students with the tools and experience to excel in their chosen science major, and to encourage career development at an early stage of their Colby education. This program, funded in large part by a grant from the Howard Hughes Medical Institute accepts ten students per summer.

FAST FACTS

STUDENT PROFILE

degree-seeking undergraduates	1,838
% male/female	46/54
% African-American	3
% American Indian or Alaska Native	<1
% Asian or Pacific Islander	8
% Hispanic	3
% White	57
% International	11
% Pell grant recipients	8

First-generation and minority alumni Ms. Hannah Beech '95 Journalist for *TIME*; Dr. Norman Fernandez Navarro '88 Obstetrician and Gynecologist; Rev. Richard L. Freeman '82 Pastor of Ocean View Baptist Church; Dr. Lynn McKinley-Grant '69, Specialized Dermatologist; Dr. Don Roland Heacock '49, Doctor of Child Psychiatry

ACADEMICS

full-time faculty	164
full-time minority faculty	17
student-faculty ratio	10:1
average class size	16
% first-year retention rate	96
% graduation rate (6 years)	90

Popular majors Biology, English, Government

CAMPUS LIFE

% live on campus (% fresh.)	94 (100)

Multicultural student clubs and organizations Anime Club, Asian-American Student Association, Asian Cultural Society, Bulgarian Club, Colby Taiko, Desi/South Asian Club, Filipino Club, Four Winds (Native American group), International Club, Irish Club, Project Ally, Society Organized Against Racism, Student Organization for Black and Hispanic Unity, The Bridge, Women's Group
Athetics NCAA Division III, New England Small College Athletic Conference

ADMISSIONS

# of applicants	4,520
% accepted	34
# of first-year students enrolled	480
SAT Critical Reading range	630-720
SAT Math range	640-720
SAT Writing range	n/a
ACT range	28-31
average HS GPA	n/a

Deadlines

early decision I	11/15
early decision II	1/1
regular decision	1/1
online application fee	$0
fee waiver for applicants with financial need	yes

COST & AID

tuition (including room & board)	$50,320
total need-based institutional scholarships/grants	$24,784,000
% of students apply for need-based aid	66
% of students receive aid	65
% receiving need-based scholarship or grant aid	40
% receiving aid whose need was fully met	100
average aid package	$35,810
average student loan debt upon graduation	$17,000

University of Maine at Farmington

University of Maine at Farmington
246 Main St.
Farmington, ME 04938
Ph: (207) 778-7050
umfadmit@maine.edu
www.farmington.edu

The University of Maine at Farmington is a selective, public, liberal-arts college, offering quality programs in teacher education, human services and arts and sciences. Enrollment is limited to just 2,000 students. Farmington is also one of just 20 colleges and universities across the nation featured in *Student Success in College: Creating Conditions That Matte*r, a book that identifies schools that serve as models of educational effectiveness. The university features developed individualized course "tracks" in each pre-professional area — specific courses identified as ideal for meeting the entrance requirements of medical schools, law schools and MBA programs. From Ivy League universities to prestigious research institutions, Farmington students are regularly accepted to some of the finest medical schools, law schools, MBA programs and graduate schools in the nation.

> ACCESS GEAR UP

Farmington participates in the national GEAR UP program, which provides grants to states and organizations to provide services to high-poverty middle and high school students. In 2005, Farmington received a six-year, $2 million GEAR UP grant from the U.S. Department of Education.

> OPPORTUNITY Diversity Scholarships / Native American Waiver and Scholarship Program

Diversity Scholarships are available each year for outstanding new first-year students whose attendance at Farmington would help create a more diverse population. Preference is given to students who have demonstrated academic achievement, who have contributed to their schools and communities, and who can contribute to diversity on campus. Farmington also offers a Native American Waiver and Scholarship Program, which covers tuition, mandatory fees and room and board charges. This program is for Native North Americans who have resided in Maine for at least one year.

> OPPORTUNITY New England Regional Student Program

Students admitted from other New England states into a Farmington program major that is not offered by the public institutions in their home state may be eligible for reduced tuition.

> SUCCESS Summer Experience

A week-long program where high schools students live on campus, Summer Experience is a college "test run" of sorts. Participants are enrolled in a one-credit course that gives them great insight into the liberal arts and the Farmington faculty. It is also a great opportunity for students to meet some of their classmates and get acquainted before move-in day. Summer Experience is an optional program but has proven year after year to be a great academic and social introduction to Farmington.

> SUCCESS Summer Orientation

A four-day orientation begins students' Farmington career. On move-in day, there is an abundance of Orientation Events Staff ready to help students move in and get acquainted with their new residential community. Throughout those four days, students also participate in a number of off-campus trips, from whitewater rafting to trail riding and everything in between. The four days are designed for new students to get comfortable in their new surroundings before the upperclassmen return.

F A S T   F A C T S

STUDENT PROFILE

undergraduate enrollment	2,265
% male/female	34/66
% African American	1
% American Indian	1
% Asian	1
% Caucasian	97
% Hispanic	<1
% Pell grant recipients	39

ACADEMICS

full-time faculty	130
student-faculty ratio	15:1
average class size	19
% first-year retention rate	73
% graduation rate (6 years)	59

Popular majors Elementary Education, Psychology

CAMPUS LIFE

% live on campus (% freshmen)	52 (95)

Multicultural student clubs and organizations
Otaku Club, Voices of Women on Campus
Athletics NAIA/NCAA Division III, Sunrise Conference

ADMISSIONS

# of applicants	1.902
% accepted	68
SAT Critical Reading range	460-580
SAT Math range	440-560
ACT range	n/a
average HS GPA	3.0

Deadlines

early action	11/15
regular admission	rolling
application fee (online)	$40 ($40)
waiver for applicants with financial need	n/a

COST & AID

tuition in-state: $9,020; out-of-state:	$17,756
room & board	$7,854
total need-based institutional scholarships/grants	n/a
% of students apply for need-based aid	n/a
% of students receive aid	84
% receiving need-based scholarship or grant aid	n/a
% receiving aid whose need was fully met	13.4
average aid package	$8,719
average student loan debt upon graduation	$19,490

University of New England

University of New England
Hills Beach Road
Biddeford, ME 04005
Ph: (800) 477-4863 / (207) 283-0170
admissions@une.edu
www.une.edu

With the university campus sitting right on the ocean, students have ready access to field experience in majors like aquaculture and aquarium science and marine biology at the University of New England. The university also offers a range of opportunities for students interested in pursuing degrees — and careers — in other fields. For example, students interested in health professions, such as dental hygiene and nursing, have their own College of Health Sciences and College of Pharmacy on the Westbrook College campus in Portland. There is also the College of Osteopathic Medicine on the university campus in Biddeford, and the College of Arts and Sciences offers a host of programs in the liberal arts, including sociology, psychology, mathematics, English, education, history and political science, as well as a number of programs in the biological sciences.

> **ACCESS College Exploratory Program**

Through the College Exploratory Program qualified high school juniors and seniors are offered tuition-free enrollment in a number of classes taught at the University of New England.

> **OPPORTUNITY Scholarships**

The University of New England offers a number of scholarships to incoming students, including the U-Lead Scholarship, which goes to students who demonstrate the potential for involvement in the campus community, and the Diversity Scholarship, which goes to students who demonstrate the ability to contribute to campus diversity. The university also offers academic scholarships that range up to $13,000, and an Honors Program which carries with it enough scholarship funding to cover 75 percent of tuition costs. A number of other school, state and federal scholarships and grants are also available.

> **SUCCESS MELMAC Retention Programs**

The University of New England recently received a substantial grant from the MELMAC Education Foundation to help promote first-year student retention. The money supports individualized advising and the integration of basic academic skills into core classes, among other initiatives.

> **SUCCESS Academic Support**

Incoming students who do not meet the minimum requirements in math and language arts — as indicated by their placement tests, SAT scores and transcripts — are automatically placed into an appropriate developmental courses in these areas. The entire student body, undergraduate and graduate, may utilize the academic support available through the Learning Assistance Center which is staffed by learning specialists, professional tutors, peer tutors and specialists in math and English.

FAST FACTS

STUDENT PROFILE
# of degree-seeking undergraduates	2,140
% male/female	26/74
% African-American	1
% American Indian or Alaska Native	<1
% Asian or Pacific Islander	2
% Hispanic	1
% White	89
% Pell grant recipients	22

ACADEMICS
full-time faculty	180
full-time minority faculty	10
student-faculty ratio	15:1
average class size	20
% first-year retention rate	77
% graduation rate (6 years)	39

Popular majors Athletic Training, Marine Biology, Political Science, Psychology, Exercise Science, Medical Biology, Environmental Studies, Nursing, History, English, Business, Education

CAMPUS LIFE
% live on campus (% freshmen)	49 (90)

Multicultural student clubs and organizations Multicultural Services, Alliance for Sexual Diversity, Campus Diversity Club, Latin American Student Association, Student National Medical Association, The ULead Student Leadership Program, Orientation Leader Program
Athletics NCAA Division III, Commonwealth Coast Conference

ADMISSIONS
# of applicants	3,149
% accepted	78
# of first-year students enrolled	2,449
SAT Critical Reading range	480-570
SAT Math range	470-590
SAT Writing range	n/a
ACT range	n/a
average HS GPA	n/a

Deadlines
regular decision application	2/15
application fee (online)	$40 ($40)
fee waiver for applicants with financial need	yes

COST & AID
tuition	$27,920
room & board	$10,870
total need-based institutional scholarships/grants	n/a
% of students apply for need-based aid	89
% of students receive aid	83
% receiving need-based scholarship or grant aid	99
% receiving aid whose need was fully met	19
average aid package	$23,956
average student loan debt upon graduation	$44,325

Bowie State University

Bowie State University
14000 Jericho Park Road
Bowie, MD 20715-9465
Ph: (301) 860-4000
ugradadmissions@bowiestate.edu
www.bowiestate.edu

Founded in 1865 and located in vibrant, affluent Prince George's County, Bowie State University is Maryland's oldest historically black institution and has recently been designated as a "growth" institution by the University System of Maryland. A comprehensive university, Bowie State won a $27 million award covering an eleven-year period from the National Aeronautics and Space Administration/National Science Foundation in 1995, making it a Model Institution for Excellence in science, engineering and mathematics — one of six in the nation. Bowie State continues to make strides and is one of the nation's top five producers of African Americans earning master's degrees in technology, science and mathematics.

"TRIO has been an integral part of my success at Bowie State University. TRIO provided me with tutoring (Math & English), access to a computer lab, and a job. More importantly, TRIO has been a family that provided the love, support, and encouragement I needed to graduate successfully in four years."

– Anthony S., '09
Waldorf, MD
Business Administration

FAST FACTS

STUDENT PROFILE
# of degree-seeking undergraduates	4,362
% male/female	35/65
% African American	88.4
% American Indian or Alaska Native	<1
% Asian or Pacific Islander	1.8
% White	4.2
% International	1.3
% Pell grant recipients	36.4

First-generation and minority alumni Joanne Benson, Maryland State Assembly delegate; William Missouri, Maryland Circuit Court judge; Toni Braxton, R&B singer

ACADEMICS
full-time faculty	219
full-time minority faculty	n/a
student-faculty ratio	18:1
average class size	18
% first-year retention rate	74
% graduation rate (6 years)	46

Popular majors Education, Computer Science, Business, Nursing, Communication, Psychology

CAMPUS LIFE
% live on campus (% freshmen)	26 (33)

Multicultural student clubs and organizations African Student Association, Caribbean Students Association, Eyes Wide Shut, Friends of Africa Association, International Student Association, Latino/Hispanic Student Association, Muslim Student Association

Athletics NCAA Division II, Central Intercollegiate Athletic Conference

ADMISSIONS
# of applicants	4,928
% accepted	53
# of first-year students enrolled	714
SAT Critical Reading range	447
SAT Math range	434
SAT Writing range	n/a
ACT range	n/a
average HS GPA	2.77

Deadlines
regular decision	4/1 (rolling after 4/1)
application fee (online)	$40 (40)
fee waiver for applicants with financial need	no

COST & AID
tuition	in-state $4,286; out-of-state $13,976
room & board	$7,535
total need-based institutional scholarships/grants	$3,590,188
% of students apply for need-based aid	65
% of students receive aid	75
% receiving need-based scholarship or grant aid	48
% receiving aid whose need was fully met	27
average aid package	$8,016
average student loan debt upon graduation	$13,730

> OPPORTUNITY Financial Aid Survival Guide

In addition to the Bowie State Institutional Scholarship, the Office of Financial Aid publishes an online financial aid guide that explains the basics of applying for financial aid and enumerates additional sources of financial aid for students. The guide also provides links to information about scholarships, many of which are geared toward minority students.

> SUCCESS Summer Bridge Program

Applicants who do not meet admissions requirements at Bowie State University but show significant potential for success are given the opportunity to enroll in a five week summer residential program focused on core studies in reading, mathematics, English, and science. Students must be referred to this program by the Admissions Office. Those students who successfully perform in all core areas of studies are offered an opportunity to enroll in the fall.

> SUCCESS Academic Advisement Center/ Career, Cooperative Education and International Services

Seeking to promote academic performance and retention, the university houses the Academic Advisement Center to provide enhanced academic advisement to new freshmen and undecided majors, and to support students with low grades by helping them address outside factors, such as employment or familial concerns, that may be hindering them. Students can likewise access Career, Co-op and International Services, which provide career planning, job search assistance and programs to assist students and alumni in making meaningful career, educational and life choices.

> SUCCESS NASAP Student Leadership Institute

The annual NASAP Student Leadership Institute provides Bowie State students with an opportunity to learn the techniques of African-centered leadership through Nguzo Saba principles. The Student Leadership Institute offers courses in conflict resolution, effective communication and ethical decision-making. The program culminates in a community service project.

> SUCCESS Counseling Services

A component of the University Wellness Center, the center provides personal, social, career and academic counseling. To assist in the retention of freshmen and sophomore students, the center conducts freshmen and sophomore interviews to assess their psychosocial needs and provide intervention.

Loyola University Maryland

Because of its Jesuit affiliation, Loyola University Maryland takes its commitment to ethics and values seriously. It takes its academic program equally seriously, offering students a comprehensive liberal arts core designed to help them explore different fields while achieving a broad-based educational foundation. At the same time, the school presents several opportunities for advanced studies, including an honors program and multiple fellowships. Diversity is also a central concern for the college, which takes an active interest in focusing on issues relevant to ALANA (African-American, Latino, Asian, Native American) students.

> ACCESS St. Mary of the Assumption School Partnership

Loyola University Maryland enjoys a strong relationship with a local primary school, St. Mary's of the Assumption, whose students are from minority backgrounds. Because of this relationship, St. Mary's students benefit from homework help, field trips, and speech and hearing screenings, all offered by Loyola's students and institutions.

> OPPORTUNITY Claver Scholarships and Grants

ALANA students are eligible to receive the Claver Scholarships and Grants. The Claver Scholarships are valued from $7,500 to full tuition and are based on academic achievement and school and community involvement, while Claver Grants are based on financial need. Candidates, who must self-identify as ALANA students, must apply for these scholarships and grants.

> SUCCESS Upperclassman Mentors

Loyola University Maryland has a department of ALANA Student Services, which helps meet the needs of underrepresented students. Among its programs, the school offers the pre-orientation Multicultural Awareness Program (MAP), which helps first-year ALANA students adjust to campus life, and the ALANA Mentoring Program (AMP), which pairs first-year students with upperclassmen mentors.

Loyola University Maryland
4501 N. Charles Street
Baltimore, MD 21210
Ph: (800) 221-9107 / (410) 617-2000
admission@loyola.edu
www.loyola.edu

FAST FACTS

STUDENT PROFILE
# of degree-seeking undergraduates	3,716
% male/female	41/59
% African-American	4
% American Indian or Alaska Native	<1
% Asian or Pacific Islander	3
% Hispanic	4
% Pell grant recipients	8

First-generation and minority alumni Robert Kelly '94, VP for Student Development, Seattle University; Jose Vargas '99, Loyola's first Rhodes Scholar, attended Harvard Medical School; Haydee Rodriguez, director, PBS Diversity Initiative, former executive director, Maryland Governor's Commission on Hispanic Affairs; Anjan Shah, MBA '07, director of sales and marketing, IKEA

ACADEMICS
full-time faculty	334
full-time minority faculty	32
student-faculty ratio	12:1
average class size	17
% first-year retention rate	91
% graduation rate (6 years)	86

Popular majors Communication, Business, Psychology, Biology

CAMPUS LIFE
% live on campus (% freshmen)	79 (98)

Multicultural student clubs and organizations ALANA Services, South Asian Student Association, African Student Union, Asian Students Organization, Hispanic Student Association, Black Student Association, Caribbean Students Association, Filipino Organization, Association of Latin American and Spanish Students

Athletics NCAA Division I, Big East Conference, Eastern College Athletic Conference, Metro Atlantic Athletic Conference

ADMISSIONS
# of applicants	7,623
% accepted	69
# of first-year students enrolled	1,068
SAT Critical Reading range	540-630
SAT Math range	560-650
SAT Writing	550-650
ACT range	23-28
average HS GPA	3.5

Deadlines
regular decision	1/15
application fee (online)	$50 ($50)
fee waiver for applicants with financial need	yes

COST & AID
tuition	$36,510
room & board	$10,200
total need-based institutional scholarships/grants	$33,413,293
% of students apply for need-based aid	58
% of students receive aid	82
% receiving need-based scholarship or grant aid	86
% receiving aid whose need was fully met	97
average aid package	$25,360
average student loan debt upon graduation	$26,340

Salisbury University

A member of the University System of Maryland, Salisbury University is a four-year, comprehensive institution offering 55 distinct graduate and undergraduate programs. The Salisbury curriculum emphasizes undergraduate research, study abroad, professional internships and community engagement. In guidebooks and surveys by *US News & World Report*, the *Princeton Review*, *Newsweek-Kaplan*, *Kiplinger's Personal Finance* and others, the university consistently ranks in the top 10 percent of public and private institutions nationwide. Located on Maryland's beautiful and historic Eastern Shore, all four of Salisbury's academic schools are endowed, a rarity among public institutions. Exceptional students, a highly regarded faculty and dynamic administration have made Salisbury a Maryland university of national distinction.

> OPPORTUNITY SAT Optional

As part of a five-year pilot study, Salisbury is the first in the University System of Maryland to make submission of SAT and ACT scores optional for applicants with a high school GPA of 3.5 or higher. The new policy is expected to attract an even more diverse pool of highly motivated, civic-minded students with distinct talents in academics, the arts, leadership and other fields of achievement.

> SUCCESS MOSAIC (Maximizing Opportunities for Students to Achieve an Inclusive Campus)

Through Salisbury's New Student Experience Program, freshmen may enroll in this week-long course designed to foster inclusion in the campus environment, as well as an understanding and appreciation for those who differ culturally, ethnically and racially. A peer-education program, MOSAIC involves cultural events, volunteer work and small group discussions about cultural identities, stereotypes and leadership skills.

> SUCCESS Cultural Events

Salisbury offers a variety of cultural events, such as this year's African-American Cultural Celebration featuring the Preservation Hall Jazz Band, the Harlem Renaissance Orchestra, the American Spiritual Ensemble and the Alvin Ailey II Dance Company, among others. Each spring, the university also hosts a Multicultural Festival with musical performances, speakers and awards ceremonies that feature both nationally acclaimed artists and those hailing from campus.

> SUCCESS Diversity Awards

Every year, Salisbury recognizes faculty, staff and students with Diversity Awards given to honor those who promote the educational benefits of diversity within the campus community.

> SUCCESS Diversity Initiatives

From faculty and peer mentoring programs to annual Hispanic Heritage Month and African-American History Month activities, Salisbury's Office of Multicultural Student Services helps students adapt to and survive in the campus environment. In addition, the university's Office of Diversity hosts workshops recognizing the educational benefits of a diverse community. Students of different faiths and backgrounds often use the Guerrieri University Center Spirituality Room for meetings, mediation and prayer. In addition, a longtime collaborative agreement also allows students to take advantage of programs, facilities and resources at the University of Maryland Eastern Shore, a historically black institution.

Salisbury University
1101 Camden Ave.
Salisbury, MD 21801
Ph: (410) 543-6161
admissions@salisbury.edu
www.salisbury.edu

FAST FACTS

STUDENT PROFILE
# of degree-seeking undergraduates	6,342
% male/female	44.8/55.2
% African-American	10.3
% American Indian or Alaska Native	<1
% Asian or Pacific Islander	2.6
% Hispanic	2.6
% White	80.3
% International	<1
% Pell grant recipients	15.2

First-generation and minority alumni
Byron Westbrook, football player; Talmadge Branch, Maryland delegate; Andre Foreman, basketball player

ACADEMICS
full-time faculty	379
full-time minority faculty	n/a
student-faculty ratio	16:1
average class size	20-29
% first-year retention rate	82.8
% graduation rate (6 years)	68

Popular majors Business Administration, Communication Arts, Biology, Education

CAMPUS LIFE
% live on campus (% fresh)	40 (83)

Multicultural student clubs and organizations
African Student Association, Asian and Pacific Islander Club, BT GLASS (Bisexual, Transgender, Gay, Lesbian and Straight Supporters), Casser Le Moule, German Club, Jewish Student Association, Muslim Student Association, NAACP, Salisbury Activists for Gender Equality, Spanish Club, Step Squad, Untouchables Dance Company

Athletics NCAA Division III, Capital Athletic Conference, Eastern College Athletic Conference

ADMISSIONS
# of applicants	7,275
% accepted	53
# of first-year students enrolled	1,929
SAT Critical Reading range	520-600
SAT Math range	520-610
SAT Writing	510-590
ACT range	22-25
average HS GPA	3.53

Deadlines
regular decision	1/15
application fee	$45
fee waiver for applicants with financial need	no

COST & AID
tuition	$6,412
room & board	$4,310
total need-based institutional scholarships/grants	n/a
% of students apply for need-based aid	76.5
% of students receive aid	95
% receiving need-based scholarship or grant aid	83.7
% receiving aid whose need was fully met	61
average aid package	$7,414
average student loan debt upon graduation	$15,939

St. Mary's College of Maryland

St. Mary's College of Maryland has a unique status in public higher education as Maryland's public honors college. This co-educational state college is committed to the ideals of affordability, accessibility and diversity while providing an outstanding faculty, high academic standards, a challenging curriculum, small classes, a sense of community, and a spirit of intellectual inquiry. By combining the virtues of public and private education, St. Mary's provides a valuable opportunity for students and their families. The College is set in the heart of the Chesapeake Bay region, 70 miles southeast of Washington, D.C. and 95 miles south of Baltimore.

> ACCESS **Student Ambassadors**

The Student Ambassador Program connects high school students with their counterparts at St. Mary's College. This program gives high school students a more familiar contact than an Admissions staff member. St. Mary's sends an alumnus or alumna back to their high schools several times a year to touch base with students who may be interested in St. Mary's. Once the prospective student and St. Mary's student have met, they are encouraged to keep in touch to assist with any questions or concerns the students might have.

"St. Mary's offers numerous opportunities for a smooth transition into college, such as The De Sousa-Brent Scholars Program. It's a great outlet for students to take full advantage of the college lifestyle; learning early about time management, workloads, and other first-year issues."
– Octavia D., '12
Baltimore, MD
English

> OPPORTUNITY **CollegeBound Foundation (CBF)**

The CollegeBound Foundation recognizes the hard work and dedication of the talented youth of Baltimore, many of whom face significant financial and personal challenges in their lives. The partnership between CBF and St. Mary's helps meet a common mission of encouraging and enabling Baltimore's underserved youth to go to college by motivating other youth to consider higher education. Since 2002, St. Mary's has helped Baltimore city students achieve their dream of going to college by matching dollar-for-dollar any CBF grant to an accepted student.

> SUCCESS **Office of Student Development**

The multicultural programs, under the Office of Student Development, serve as an advocate for students of color and provide them with support in academic, social and personal areas as they pursue their college education. The program's aim is to reach students, faculty and staff to educate the campus community about diversity and to foster awareness of and appreciation for difference. The coordinator of multicultural programs works closely with other departments and organizations on campus to meet the needs of diverse students.

> SUCCESS **Multicultural Achievement Peer Program (MAPP)**

The Multicultural Achievement Peer Program is a retention program designed to maximize the opportunity for multicultural students to be successful at St. Mary's. The program assists multicultural students acclimate to college beyond orientation. First-year students are assigned a MAPP mentor who is responsible for guiding the students through their first year. Mentors help students around campus and discover its many resources. Mentors will also serve as liaison between Student Development and other departments at the college. Mentors are selected based on their knowledge of campus resources, proven academic proficiency, class standing, academic major and involvement in campus activities. Previous participants in the program have concurrently held major positions or moved on to hold major positions in a variety of campus organizations.

St. Mary's College of Maryland
18952 E. Fisher Road
St. Mary's City, MD 20686-3001
Ph: (240) 895-2000
admissions@smcm.edu
www.smcm.edu

F A S T   F A C T S

STUDENT PROFILE
# of degree-seeking undergraduates	1,978
% male/female	43/57
% African-American	8
% American Indian or Alaska Native	1
% Asian or Pacific Islander	4
% Hispanic	4
% White	77
% International	1
% Pell grant recipients	11

First-generation and minority alumni W. Michael Kelley, author; Kevin Crutchfield, neurologist; Hon. Judith Guthrie, judge, Federal District Court

ACADEMICS
full-time faculty	142
full-time minority faculty	22
student-faculty ratio	12:1
average class size	16
% first-year retention rate	91
% graduation rate (6 years)	79

Popular majors Economics, Biology, Political Science, Psychology, English

CAMPUS LIFE
% live on campus (%fresh.)	85 (96)

Multicultural student clubs and organizations Black Student Union, Raíces Hispanas, International Student Organization, Asian Studies, Sister to Sister
Athletics NCAA Division III, ICSA (sailing)

ADMISSIONS
# of applicants	2,411
% accepted	57
# of first-year students enrolled	488
SAT Critical Reading range	580-670
SAT Math range	550-650
SAT Writing range	560-670
ACT range	24-29
average HS GPA	3.78

Deadlines
early decision	11/1, 12/1
regular decision	1/1
application fee	$50
fee waiver for students with financial need	yes

COST & AID
tuition& fees in-state $13,630; out-of-state $25,023	
room & board	$10,250
total need-based institutional scholarships/ grants	$3,508,000
% of students apply for need-based aid	68
% of students receive aid	100
% receiving need-based scholarship/grant aid	33
% receiving aid whose need was fully met	n/a
average aid package	$8,500
average student loan debt upon graduation	$21,000

Amherst College

Amherst College has an educational tradition that stretches back to its founding in 1821. Since that time, the college has become one of the nation's premier liberal arts schools. Amherst's 1,697 talented and energetic students — 35 percent of whom are students of color — benefit from the personal attention afforded by an 8:1 student-to-professor ratio. Amherst, Mass., a town of 35,000 people in the western part of the state, is home to the college's scenic 1,000-acre campus. In this setting, Amherst "educates men and women of exceptional potential from all backgrounds so that they may seek, value and advance knowledge, engage the world around them and lead principled lives of consequence." Beginning in the 2008-2009 academic year, the loan component of all financial aid awards was replaced with scholarship aid.

> ACCESS **Tele-mentoring Program**

Amherst College offers a tele-mentoring program in which Amherst students use e-mail and the telephone to help high school students locate and gain acceptance to colleges and universities. The Tele-mentoring Program allows nearly 30 Amherst students from socio-economic disadvantaged backgrounds to serve as mentors to talented high school students from underserved schools across the nation.

> ACCESS **ABC Tutoring and Mentoring Program**

The A Better Chance (ABC) tutoring and mentoring program involves Amherst College students willing to make a difference in the lives of the young male members of the Amherst chapter. Amherst students assist participants with homework and general activities in preparation for college level work. The goals of ABC are to offer support and aid in any subjects being taken by the participants, to promote diversity by providing the opportunity for Amherst students to form meaningful relationships with students of different backgrounds, and vice versa.

> OPPORTUNITY **Access to Amherst**

Amherst hosts two Diversity Open House Weekends each fall in which the college funds travel for multicultural and first-generation students. Students attend classes, cultural events and admission workshops during their three-day stay. Twelve diversity interns work for the Admission Office and help organize and coordinate the Open House weekends. The diversity interns also serve as liaisons and mentors to students with diversity questions or concerns during the event.

"I never expected to attend a prestigious liberal arts college, but now Amherst is my home. I wondered about class differences, but I found that everyone was on a level field. You don't have to have money to do anything that is school-sponsored— everything is paid for by Amherst."

– Yasmin N., '10 Houston, TX Psychology

> SUCCESS **Diversity Open House Weekends**

Matriculated students from disadvantaged backgrounds who are interested in the sciences are eligible for the Summer Science Program, while those interested in the humanities and social sciences are eligible for the Summer Humanities and Social Science Program. The two three-week courses occur before first-year orientation. Approximately 20 members of the incoming class participate in each program and gain assistance transitioning between high school and college. Participants in the science program gain further assistance in learning various approaches to math and science while those in the humanities and social science program develop writing and study skills as well as other skills aimed at achieving success.

Amherst College
220 South Pleasant Street
Amherst, MA 01002
Ph: (413) 542-2328
admission@amherst.edu
www.amherst.edu

F A S T   F A C T S

STUDENT PROFILE
# of degree-seeking undergraduates	1,697
% male/female	50/50
% African American	12
% American Indian or Alaska Native	<1
% Asian or Pacific Islander	10
% Hispanic	10
% White	34
% International	8
% Pell grant recipients	20

First-generation and minority alumni Jide Zeitlin, Ambassador to the United Nations, Representative for U.N. Management and Reform

ACADEMICS
full-time faculty	203
full-time minority faculty	38
student-faculty ratio	8:1
average class size	17
% first-year retention rate	96
% graduation rate (6 years)	96

Popular majors English, Political Science, Economics, Psychology, Biology

CAMPUS LIFE
% live on campus (% fresh.)	98 (100)

Multicultural student clubs and organizations Black Student Union, Black Men's Group, Black Women's Group, Drew House, Black Studies Department, La Causa, Chicano Caucus, La Casa, Asian Students Association, Korean Students Association, South Asian Students Association, China Awareness Organization, Asian Culture House, Amherst College Diversity Coalition, Pride Alliance, International Students Association, Marsh Art House, NOOR, African and Caribbean Students Union

Athletics NCAA Division III, New England Small College Athletic Conference

ADMISSIONS
# of applicants	7,745
% accepted	15
# of first-year students enrolled	438
SAT Critical Reading range	660-760
SAT Math range	650-750
SAT Writing range	660-700
ACT range	30-35
average HS GPA	n/a

Deadlines
early decision	11/15
regular decision	1/1
application fee (online)	$60 ($60)
fee waiver for applicants with financial need	yes

COST & AID
tuition	$38,250
room & board	$10,150
total need-based institutional scholarships/grants	$30,132,063
% of students apply for need-based aid	59
% of students receive aid	100
% receiving need-based scholarship or grant aid	54
% receiving aid whose need was fully met	100
average aid package	$37,564
average student loan debt upon graduation	$12,603

Assumption College

Founded in 1904, Assumption College is a four-year, private, co-educational, liberal-arts college affiliated with the Catholic Church. Assumption strives to form graduates known for critical intelligence, thoughtful citizenship and compassionate service. The school pursues these ambitious goals through a curriculum grounded in the liberal arts and extending to the domain of professional studies. Enlivened by the Catholic affirmation of the harmony of faith and reason, Assumption aims, by the pursuit of the truth, to transform the minds and hearts of students. Assumption College favors diversity and ecumenically welcomes all who share its goals.

> ACCESS Assumption College Early Awareness Program

The Assumption College Early Awareness Program works with middle schools students in the Greater Worcester area to expose younger students to the college experience and make them aware that many other colleges exist. The program includes group presentations, "hands-on" activities and long-term projects for students that provide an important motivational experience for students to pursue a college education.

> ACCESS Minority Achievers Program

Assumption is a founding sponsor of the local YMCA's Minority Achievers Program, which attracts high school age students for four years of after-school, curricular and co-curricular activities. Students who complete the program are elible for a full tuition Assumption Scholarship.

> OPPORTUNITY Discover Assumption

Discover Assumption provides an opportunity for prospective students from underrepresented backgrounds to experience the campus and what it has to offer, as well as provide a venue to address the many possibilities and concerns that students and families may have related to students from diverse backgrounds. These events are a great introduction to the Assumption College community.

"At Assumption, I'm not just another number—people here treat me like family. One of my professors invited me to Easter dinner at her house because she knew I was staying on campus. My decision to come to Assumption was a great choice."

– Cerilenne M., '11 Guaynabo, Puerto Rico Accounting

> SUCCESS Office of Multicultural Affairs

Assumption College's Office of Multicultural Affairs (OMA) is committed to the enhancement of a campus that fosters the achievement of all students who are eager to increase their understanding of diversity in a global society. The OMA office is responsible for providing campus-wide programming including advising student organizations and clubs, facilitating faculty and staff partnerships, promoting multicultural awareness and education opportunities in the community.

> SUCCESS ALANA Network

OMA staff advises the ALANA Network, a student organization that serves to foster self-government among its members and to promote student and community activities in the best interest of the ALANA (African-, Latino/Hispanic-, Asian-, and Native-American) population at Assumption College, as it relates to the entire community. ALANA also strives to develop an active interest in community affairs leading to the advancement of the members and the community by working with Residential Life, Reach Out Center volunteer office, Campus Activities Board, Student Government Association and others.

Assumption College
500 Salisbury Street
Worcester, MA 01609
Ph: (508) 767-7285
admiss@assumption.edu
www.assumption.edu

FAST FACTS

STUDENT PROFILE

# of degree-seeking undergraduates	2,157
% male/female	42/58
% African-American	2
% American Indian or Alaska Native	<1
% Asian or Pacific Islander	2
% Hispanic	3
% White	76
% Pell grant recipients	11.3

First-generation and minority alumni Honorable Jay Garcia-Gregory '66; Roselly Ramseyer-Torres '85 – former global head of equity products for Dresdner Kleinwort Benson, Dresdner Bank; Catalina Miranda '76, Metro Opera NY; Christopher Adams '80, CEO Walleye Technologies, Inc.; Cecil Ellis '84, VP Human Resources for CUNA Group

ACADEMICS

full-time faculty	152
full-time minority faculty	9
student-faculty ratio	12:1
average class size	20
% first-year retention rate	66
% graduation rate (6 years)	81

Popular majors Business Studies, English, Natural Sciences, Psychology

CAMPUS LIFE

% live on campus	90 (95)

Multicultural student clubs and organizations ALANA Network, Reach Out Center, Step Team
Athletics NCAA Division II, Northeast-10 Athletic Conference

ADMISSIONS

# of applicants	3,719
% accepted	79
# of first-year students enrolled	512
SAT Critical Reading range	480-590
SAT Math range	490-590
SAT Writing range	n/a
ACT range	20-25
average HS GPA	3.4

Deadlines

regular decision	2/15
application fee (online)	$50 ($50)
fee waiver for applicants with financial need	yes

COST & AID

tuition	$29,806
room & board	$10,070
total need-based institutional scholarships/grants	$21,271,009
% of students apply for need-based aid	84
% of students receive aid	85
% receiving need-based scholarship or grant aid	99
% receiving aid whose need was fully met	23
average aid package	$18,341
average student loan debt upon graduation	$26,691

Babson College

Babson College
231 Forest Street
Babson Park, MA 02457-0310
Ph: (781) 239-5522
ugradadmission@babson.edu
www.babson.edu/ugrad

For students who want to study business in a comprehensive, dynamic environment, Babson College may just be a dream come true. Not content to have students learn by passively sitting in their classrooms, Babson demands that students work hands-on right away; in fact, the school gives all first-year students (grouped in teams) $3,000 start-up loans to create, run and liquidate a business in their first year alone. Babson students also benefit from other professional development opportunities, such as receiving leadership coaching and participating in a management consulting program, through which they can work with real-world firms like Boston Scientific and Stacy's Pita Chips.

"I chose Babson because no other school provided such an innovative business education that placed entrepreneurial thinking and liberal arts at its core. The scholarship program provides students like myself, who have the academic skills to succeed at Babson, with an opportunity that would be unavailable to them."

– Kelvin W., '13
Dallas, TX
Finance & Law

> ACCESS **High School Presentations**

Since the spring of 2007, Babson students have been presenting their student-designed businesses to inner-city high school students. These presentations expose at-risk populations to the various unique opportunities in higher education, as well as facilitate the notion of social responsibility for current students.

> ACCESS **NFTE Conference**

Babson College currently hosts the northeast regional conference of the Network for Teaching Entrepreneurship (NFTE). This organization, which provides both training to students and teachers, helps young people from low-income communities build skills and unlock their entrepreneurial creativity. Thanks to the generosity of the Shelby/Cullom Davis Foundation, there is an endowed scholarship to ensure that there is always one NFTE alumnus at Babson as an undergraduate student.

> OPPORTUNITY **Experience Diversity / Diversity Overnight Program**

Held in conjunction with the college's annual Basically Babson Day for admitted under-represented minority students, Babson's Experience Diversity campus visit program allows admitted seniors to learn about the Babson experience and the resources available to alumni of color, as students are also given the opportunity to interact with alumni. Travel scholarships are available for the program.

> OPPORTUNITY **Posse Foundation**

Babson College participates in the Posse Foundation, a program that brings talented inner-city youth to campus to pursue their academics and to help promote cross-cultural communication. Posse students are nominated by their high school to the program and share a collaborative support system with a special mentor to adjust to campus and college life.

> SUCCESS **Diversity Leadership Award Support**

The Diversity Leadership Awards are a set of four-year, half- or full-tuition merit scholarships awarded to students deemed to have the greatest potential for leadership in creating a richly diverse Babson community. Scholars receive student and faculty mentoring, are provided unique leadership development opportunities, and are able to participate in special academic, social and cultural activities and events.

FAST FACTS

STUDENT PROFILE
# of degree-seeking undergraduates	1,898
% male/female	57/43
% African American	5
% American Indian or Alaska Native	1
% Asian or Pacific Islander	13
% Hispanic	8
% White	40
% International	23
% Pell grant recipients	13.9

First-generation and minority alumni
Gustavo Cisneros, businessman; Rudy Crew, superintendent, Miami-Dade County Public Schools; Mir Ibrahim Rahman, television CEO; Alberto Perlman, entrepreneur

ACADEMICS
full-time faculty	159
full-time minority faculty	25
student-faculty ratio	14:1
average class size	29
% first-year retention rate	97
% graduation rate (6 years)	88

Popular majors Accounting, Entrepreneurship, Finance, Global Business Management, Marketing

CAMPUS LIFE
% live on campus (% fresh.)	84 (93)

Multicultural student clubs and organizations
AMAN, Armenian Students Association, Association of Latino Professionals in Finance and Accounting, Babson African Student Organization, Babson Asian Pacific Student Association, Babson Brazilian Association, Babson Global Outreach through Entrepreneurship, Babson Korean Student Association, Babson Thai Student Association, HOLA, Japanese International Circle, ONE Tower, Open, STAND, The Global Society

Athletics NCAA Division III, ECAC East Ice Hockey League, New England Women's and Men's Athletic Conference, Pilgrim League

ADMISSIONS
# of applicants	4,146
% accepted	37
# of first-year students enrolled	470
SAT Critical Reading range	580-670
SAT Math range	630-730
SAT Writing range	600-690
ACT range	25-29
average HS GPA	3.4

Deadlines
early action	11/1
early decision	11/1
regular decision	1/15
application fee (online)	$65 ($65)
fee waiver for applicants with financial need	yes

COST & AID
tuition	$39,040
room & board	$12,876
total need-based institutional scholarships/grants	$17,400,000
% of students apply for need-based aid	56
% of students receive aid	51
% receiving need-based scholarship or grant aid	41
% receiving aid whose need was fully met	24
average aid package	$30,677
average student loan debt upon graduation	$28,164

Bard College at Simon's Rock

DANIEL ARTS CENTER

Bard College at Simon's Rock is the only four-year college of the liberal arts and sciences specifically designed to provide bright, highly motivated students with the opportunity to begin college in a residential setting after 10th or 11th grade. The school's small size — approximately 400 students — allows faculty and staff to give students a great deal of individual attention both in and out of the classroom. A faculty-to-student ratio of 10:1, an average class size of 10, an intensive advising program and an active residence life team assist young students in their transition to college. All first-year students attend a week-long orientation that combines writing and thinking workshops with other programs designed to introduce students to campus life. There is a strong institutional commitment to diversity and the W.E.B. Du Bois Scholarship supports academically talented students from underrepresented backgrounds.

> ACCESS Young Writers Workshop (YWW)

The Young Writers Workshop at Simon's Rock selects 70 to 80 highly motivated high school students to participate in an on-campus writing workshop each summer. Participants strengthen writing, language and thinking skills while living in a college environment. Small workshop groups and intellectual autonomy prepare students for college academics. All YWW faculty are experienced teachers and writers from around the country with an interest in the needs and abilities of young writers. Some financial aid is available for students with demonstrated need, and students of color are eligible to apply for the Dorothy West Scholarship, which covers the full cost of tuition and room and board for the YWW at Simon's Rock.

> OPPORTUNITY W.E.B. Du Bois Scholarships

Simon's Rock's W.E.B. Du Bois Scholarships meet a significant portion of financial need for eligible students from underrepresented backgrounds who enroll following 10th or 11th grade. Students must have a record of academic achievement and motivation. Du Bois Scholarships are renewable for four years with a cumulative grade point average of 2.7 and good social standing.

> OPPORTUNITY Acceleration to Excellence Program

The Acceleration to Excellence Program awards merit scholarships that cover up to the full cost of tuition for outstanding students who enter Simon's Rock following 10th or 11th grade. Simon's Rock faculty members select recipients of this award based on academic excellence, extracurricular distinction, personal motivation and character. The most highly qualified applicants are invited to attend the Acceleration to Excellence Finalist Day, where they are introduced to the college's academic and social programs, interview with faculty and have the opportunity to receive one of the college's most substantial merit awards.

"Sure we have a great time, but when it comes to education, I think we value it more than anything else in our lives...I'm always very, very astonished at just how much the class and the academics become part of us, and actually we build a lot of relationships and friendships amongst ourselves with that kind of bond."

– R. A., '09
Bronx, NY
Biology, Cross-Cultural Relations

> SUCCESS Diversity Studies

The college's faculty offer classes and develop academic concentrations in fields that directly address issues of diversity: African American studies, Asian studies, cross-cultural relations, gender studies and Spanish and Latin American studies. Academic and personal support services are coordinated through the Win Student Resource Commons, which explores and celebrates diversity and nurtures mind, body and spirit.

Bard College at Simon's Rock
Office of Admission
84 Alford Road
Great Barrington, MA 01230-1990
Ph: (413) 538-7312
admit@simons-rock.edu
www.simons-rock.edu

FAST FACTS

STUDENT PROFILE

# of degree-seeking undergraduates	427
% male/female	40/60
% African American	7
% American Indian or Alaska Native	<1
% Asian or Pacific Islander	4
% Hispanic	5
% White	49
% International	5
% Pell grant recipients	19.3

First-generation and minority alumni John McWhorter, linguist; Veronica Chambers, writer

ACADEMICS

full-time faculty	48
full-time minority faculty	6
student-faculty ratio	10:1
average class size	10
% first-year retention rate	75
% graduation rate (6 years)	73.1

Popular majors Literary Studies, Politics/Law/Society, Psychology, Creative Writing, Engineering (in conjunction with Columbia University)

CAMPUS LIFE

% live on campus (% fresh.)	89 (96)

Multicultural student clubs and organizations Black Student Union, Multicultural Student Organization, International Students Club, Latino Student Organization

Athletics Recreational Athletic Program; basketball, climbing, fencing, racquetball, squash, swimming, soccer, tennis, volleyball, yoga

ADMISSIONS

# of applicants	333
% accepted	80
# of first-year students enrolled	181
SAT Critical Reading range	640-720
SAT Math range	560-710
SAT Writing range	570-700
ACT range	26-29
average HS GPA	n/a

Deadlines

regular decision	rolling
application fee	$50
fee waiver for applicants with financial need	yes

COST & AID

tuition	$37,860
room & board	$10,600
total need-based institutional scholarships/grants	$3,313,882
% of students apply for need-based aid	60
% of students receive aid	98
% receiving need-based scholarship or grant aid	77
% receiving aid whose need was fully met	43
average aid package	$25,359
average student loan debt upon graduation	$20,000

Bay Path College

Founded in 1897, Bay Path College is a private college with an enrollment of more than 2,000 students at its Longmeadow campus and satellite campuses in Sturbridge/Charlton (MA) and Burlington (MA). The College offers undergraduate degrees for women; graduate degrees for men and women; and Bay Path Online, the College's distance-learning center, offering graduate degrees and certificates. Bay Path is committed to women's undergraduate education that emphasizes leadership, communication, and technology, enabling women to make a difference once they graduate. A dedicated faculty enriches and supports the social and intellectual development of all students with a career-focused curriculum, which prepares students to become leaders in their fields. At Bay Path, 64 percent of undergraduates are first-generation students. The College values and promotes diversity, while fostering an environment for learning both inside and outside the classroom. The financial aid staff works with students to ensure financial barriers do not stand in their way of a college education.

"From the moment I arrived on campus, Bay Path has opened the door to endless opportunities for me. By providing me with a top-rate education, Bay Path is encouraging me to make a difference in the lives of others. Bay Path is serving me well by broadening my horizons and supporting me in my future endeavors as a scientist."

– Brittany T., '13
Springfield, MA
Biology
First-generation Student

> ACCESS   Pathways to College

Pathways to College is a set of programs to help underserved, young women in middle and high schools strengthen their academic skills in preparation for college and develop the confidence they need to succeed. "It's MY Business!" engages young women in entrepreneurship as a way to envision the many possibilities for their future. "Science Matters!" is a unique hands-on science discovery summer program, introducing the intricacies of science to young women and encouraging them to continue study in this field.

> OPPORTUNITY   National Science Foundation Grant

Bay Path was awarded a grant of over $500,000 from the National Science Foundation to support scholarships and activities designed to attract women and minority students in the scientific fields, including biology, biotechnology, and forensic science. The grant provides students with scholarships of up to $10,000 per year for four years, giving academically talented, but financially challenged students the opportunity to pursue a career in science.

> OPPORTUNITY   Scholarships

Bay Path offers scholarships for the support of low-income students, students from rural New England towns, students of color, and first-generation students to ensure college remains accessible and affordable to young women regardless of their level of financial need. In addition, students can qualify for merit scholarships worth up to $13,000 a year. The average total aid package for students with financial need in the Class of 2013 was $24,000. Bay Path also offers a three-part Education Stimulus Plan, which includes $10,000 grants toward the College's graduate programs, helping students and their families get the best value in higher education.

> SUCCESS   Walmart College Success Award

Bay Path was selected by the Council of Independent Colleges to receive a $100,000 Walmart College Success Award. The award expands Bay Path's successful work in enrolling, retaining and graduating first-generation college students. Nearly two-thirds of students at Bay Path are first in their families to attend college. Bay Path is committed to increasing resources to support the academic achievement of it students, as well as encouraging personal growth and engagement in their college experiences. Bay Path offers a first-year leadership course, discussion groups focusing on academic skills, peer tutoring, a mentorship program, increased funding for study abroad, and expanded community service opportunities.

Bay Path College
588 Longmeadow Street
Longmeadow MA 01106
Ph: (413) 565-1331
admiss@baypath.edu
www.baypath.edu

FAST FACTS

STUDENT PROFILE

# of degree-seeking undergraduates	1,481
% male/female	0/100
% African American	11
% American Indian or Alaska Native	<1
% Asian or Pacific Islander	6
% Hispanic	8
% White	77
% International	3
% Pell grant recipients	39.2

First-generation and minority alumni Jan Melnik '76, published author and president, Absolute Advantage; JoAnna Rhinehart '78, actress and producer; Ashley Uhey Carter '06, forensic scientist, Oregon State Police Crime Lab; Jennifer Fay '06, Campbell University School of Law; Sara Klimoski '08, Ross University School of Medicine

ACADEMICS

full-time faculty	44
student-faculty ratio	15:1
average class size	17
% first-year retention rate	73
% graduation rate (6 years)	52

Popular majors Forensic Science, Business, Education, Psychology, Occupational Therapy

CAMPUS LIFE

% live on campus (% freshmen)	64 (82)

Multicultural student clubs and organizations All Women Excel, Black Student Association, Essence Step Team, Hispanic American Leadership Organization, Native Cultures Club, and Women of Culture

Athletics NCAA Division III, New England Collegiate Conference (NECC)

ADMISSIONS

# of applicants	635
% accepted	83
SAT Critical Reading range	530-540
SAT Math range	520-530
ACT range	17-21
average HS GPA	3.15

Deadlines

early action	12/15
regular decision	rolling
application fee (online)	$25 ($0)
fee waiver for applicants with financial need	yes

COST & AID

tuition	$24,530
room & board	$10,035
total need-based institutional scholarships/grants	n/a
% of students apply for need-based aid	100
% of students receive aid	100
% receiving need-based scholarship or grant aid	100
% receiving aid whose need was fully met	12
average aid package	$22,024
average student loan debt upon graduation	$18,200

Bentley University

Founded in 1917 as a school of accounting and finance, Bentley University is a private, coeducational university committed to ensuring social and cultural diversity in every dimension of institutional life. Bentley distinguishes itself from other institutions in its commitment to provide liberally educated business students, with hands on, technologically-rich learning. At the intersection of the University's curriculum and research is a commitment to Business and Information Technology, Ethics and Social Responsibility, and Global Commerce and Culture.

> ## OPPORTUNITY **Summer Transition Education Program (STEP)**

The Summer Transition Education Program provides annual college admission support to 25 high-potential high school students, traditionally from urban areas, who do not meet all standard admission requirements. Program support includes mentoring and monitoring academic progress and academic advising and counseling. Realizing the importance of support at home, the STEP staff collaborates with students' families and guardians. Students also attend a six-week summer residential program, upon the completion of which they receive two Bentley course credits.

> ## SUCCESS **ALANA Experience**

The ALANA Experience is a four-day program for all incoming Asian/Asian American, Latino/a, African American, Native American and Multiracial students. The program gives students the opportunity to network through a series of workshops, information sessions, and social events. Staff and upperclassmen help guide students in gathering the tools needed for success at Bentley University.

> ## SUCCESS **The Multicultural Center**

The Multicultural Center serves as a "home" for many ALANA students at Bentley University. The center serves to further the retention and success of the ALANA students through academic mentoring, guidance, leadership development, advocacy and personal support services. There is a committed staff that helps students with personal, academic, and career counseling. Additionally, the Multicultural Center serves as the campus-wide resource for promotion, exploration and celebration of the University's diversity mission. It organizes a full calendar of events in collaboration with all cultural organizations.

"Bentley supports me on all levels: academic, professional and social. My professors are interested in learning about me as a person, not just a student. Professionally, Career Services has helped me land an internship with McDonalds. Socially, I met new friends through the ALANA Experience, a four-day orientation program through the Multicultural Center."
– Nomble C., '11
Downingtown, PA

> ## SUCCESS **The ALANA Student Advancement Program (ASAP)**

ASAP pairs first-year ALANA students with upperclassmen to assist them in acclimating to campus life at Bentley. ASAP Mentors play an integral role in helping first-year students gain an understanding and appreciation for the Bentley culture, introducing them to co-curricular activities and supporting them in their academic and personal growth.

Bentley University
Office of Admission
175 Forest St.
Waltham, MA 02452-4705
Ph: (800) 523-2354
ugadmission@bentley.edu
www.bentley.edu

F A S T   F A C T S

STUDENT PROFILE

# of degree-seeking undergraduates	4,235
% male/female	60/40
% African American	3
% American Indian	<1
% Asian or Pacific Islander	7
% White	62
% Hispanic	5
% International	9
% Pell grant recipients	13.9

ACADEMICS

full-time faculty	279
full-time minority faculty	37
student-faculty ratio	12:1
average class size	24
% first-year retention rate	93
% graduation rate (6 years)	88

Popular majors Finance, Accounting, Marketing, Management, International Studies

CAMPUS LIFE

% live on campus (% fresh.)	83 (98)

Multicultural student clubs and organizations Asian Students' Association, Association of Latino Professions in Finance and Accounting, Bentley Asian Students' Christian Fellowship, Association of Chinese Students, Black United Body, International Students' Association, La Cultura Latina, National Association of Asian American Professionals, National Association of Black Accountants, National Black MBA Association, Portuguese Across Continents, PULSE Newspaper, South Asian Student Association, Vietnamese Students Association

Athletics NCAA Division II, Northeast-10 Athletic Conference, Atlantic Hockey League, Division I

ADMISSIONS

# of applicants	6,675
% accepted	43
SAT Critical Reading range	540-630
SAT Math range	600-680
ACT Range	25-28
average HS GPA	3.4/4.0 A-/B+

Deadlines

early decision	11/1
early action	11/15
regular decision	1/15
application fee (online)	$50 ($50)
fee waiver for applicants with financial need	yes

COST & AID

tuition	$34,360
room & board	$11,740
total need-based institutional scholarships/grants	$29,538,458
% of students apply for need-based aid	70
% students receive aid	100
% receiving need based scholarship or grant aid	84
% receiving aid whose need was fully met	92
average aid package	$29,415
average student loan debt upon graduation	$33,073

Boston University

Boston University is the alma mater of Dr. Martin Luther King, Jr., and Dr. Solomon Carter Fuller, the first African American psychiatrist in the United States. BU has been committed to diversity since its charter in 1868, when it promised to admit students of both sexes and every race and religion. It was the first university in the nation to award a Ph.D. to a woman and to award a medical degree to an American Indian student. Boston University is one of the foremost private teaching and research institutions in the world, with two main campuses in downtown Boston and affiliate programs located around the globe. The University prepares students for success with an education that combines the liberal arts with practical skills and experience offered through the University's professional programs.

> ACCESS **COACH (College Opportunity and Career Help)**

This Boston University program supports Boston public school juniors and seniors as they form post-secondary plans. Boston University student coaches work in high school classrooms, providing information on college applications, college access, and financial aid. The coaches help motivate students to make good decisions about their futures.

> ACCESS **Summer Pathways**

Summer Pathways is a one-week residential summer program for female high school students who demonstrate promise in the fields of science and engineering. The Summer Pathways program is free of charge and seeks students from Boston public schools who would not otherwise have the opportunity to attend a summer enrichment program. Summer Pathways students learn about the wide range of academic and career opportunities in science and engineering and are connected to women working in these fields.

"When looking at BU, I thought it was important to find my home away from home. I found just that during my freshman year living in the Spanish House. I met students from Latin America, Latinos from across the U.S., and others who were interested in Latino culture and Spanish language."
– Melissa B., '10
Lagrangeville, NY
Education

> OPPORTUNITY **Martin Luther King, Jr. Scholarship**

Awarded in honor of Boston University's most prominent alumnus, the Dr. Martin Luther King, Jr. Scholarship provides renewable four-year, full-tuition awards to academically gifted students who have leadership abilities and a strong commitment to social justice and community involvement.

> OPPORTUNITY **National Hispanic Recognition Program**

The National Hispanic Recognition Program offers academic recognition to Hispanic students who have received high achieving scores on the PSAT/NMSQT, taken during their junior year in high school, and who have a 3.0 GPA or higher. The program sends a list of recognized students to subscribing colleges. Boston University awards a four-year, half-tuition scholarship to National Hispanic Recognition Program finalists with exceptional high school academic records.

> OPPORTUNITY **The Howard Thurman Center for Race, Culture and Ethnicity**

The Howard Thurman Center for Race, Culture and Ethnicity supports the academic success and personal development of all Boston University students. The Thurman Center offers programs and resources that encourage minority students to develop a sense of community on campus. The Thurman Center provides an orientation to minority freshmen at the beginning of the year to introduce them to the resources and cultural organizations on campus. Students also work with upperclassmen who serve as mentors through the cultural mentorship program.

Boston University Admissions
121 Bay State Road
Boston, MA 02215
Ph: (617) 353-2300
admissions@bu.edu
www.bu.edu

FAST FACTS

STUDENT PROFILE
# of degree-seeking undergraduates	16,295
% male/female	40/60
% African-American	3
% American Indian or Alaska Native	<1
% Asian or Pacific Islander	14
% Hispanic	7
% White	50
% International	9
% Pell grant recipients	14.5

First-generation and minority alums Dr. Martin Luther King, Jr., civil rights activist; Alfre Woodard, actress; Karen Holmes Ward, producer/host, ABC; Dr. Elizabeth Alexander, poet who composed and read her poem at President Obama's inauguration; Senator Edward Brooke, the first African American to be elected by popular vote to the US Senate

ACADEMICS
full-time faculty	1,549
full-time minority faculty	189
student-faculty ratio	13:1
average class size	27
% first-year retention rate	90
% graduation rate (6 years)	82

Popular majors Business Administration/Management, Communications and Media Studies, International Relations, Pre-Medical Studies, Psychology

CAMPUS LIFE
% live on campus (% fresh.)	67 (99)

Multicultural student clubs and organizations African Students Organization, Alianza Latina, Asian Student Union, Associacion de Estudiantes, Bangladeshi Student Association, Bhangra, Brazilian Association, BU por Columbia, Chinese Student and Scholar Association, Filipino Student Association, Hong Kong Student Association, India Club, Indonesian Society, Italian Students Association, Japanese Student Association, Kalaniot, Korean Student Association, Lebanese Club, Mexican Student Association, Organization of Pakistani Students, Palestinian-Israeli Peace Alliance, Persian Student Cultural Club, Singapore Society, Taiwanese Student Association, Indian Students Association, Thai Student Association, UMOJA (Black Student Union), Vietnamese Student Association

Athletics NCAA Division I, American East Conference, Colonial Athletic Association, Hockey East Association

ADMISSIONS
# of applicants	37,795
% accepted	58
# of first-year students enrolled	4,130
SAT Critical Reading range	570-660
SAT Math range	600-690
SAT Writing range	590-680
ACT range	26-30
average HS GPA	3.5

Deadlines
early decision	11/1
regular decision	1/1
application fee (online)	$75 ($75)
fee waiver for applicants with financial need	yes

COST & AID
tuition	$37,910
room & board	$11,848
total need-based institutional scholarships/grants	$145,834,044
% of students apply for need-based aid	48
% of students receive aid	100
% receiving need-based scholarship or grant aid	95
% receiving aid whose need was fully met	51
average aid package	$34,896
average student loan debt upon graduation	$30,998

Emmanuel College

Emmanuel College promises to deliver students an education that will "sharpen minds, unleash potential, free spirit and expand horizons." It's a hefty promise, but one that the college lives up to by offering students small classes and a dedicated faculty. As an investment in this promise and in its students, Emmanuel is in the process of building a green, state-of-the-art Academic Science Center. The center, opening in 2009, will offer numerous classroom and meeting spaces. In further support of its mission, Emmanuel also houses the Center for Mission and Spirituality, a clearinghouse for lectures and programs.

> OPPORTUNITY Road to Intellectual Success at Emmanuel (R.I.S.E.)

The Road to Intellectual Success at Emmanuel program is designed for highly motivated and academically talented students from diverse backgrounds. Students are accepted conditionally, having to participate in a mandatory summer program, taking classes for college credit prior to their first year at Emmanuel. Upon successful completion of R.I.S.E., students enroll at the college and are provided with additional academic and social support mechanisms throughout their four-year academic journey.

> OPPORTUNITY Multicultural Telethon Series / Emmanuel's Multicultural Experience Weekend

Current Emmanuel students from underrepresented groups take pride in helping with the recruitment process through the Multicultural Telethon Series. During the admissions application cycle, current students of color call prospective students of similar backgrounds to convince them to attend Emmanuel College. Once prospective students are accepted, students are invited to attend Emmanuel's Multicultural Experience Weekend, which brings students of color to campus for a chance to meet current students, attend classes and participate in events led by multicultural groups such as the Black Student Union.

> OPPORTUNITY City of Boston and Femi Esan Memorial Scholarships

First-year or transfer students from Boston are eligible for a renewable, $4,500 City of Boston scholarship. One junior at Emmanuel College can also receive the Femi Esan Memorial Scholarship. This award, created five years ago after an Emmanuel College student was murdered while trying to stop a fight, honors a student who is committed to peace and social activism.

> SUCCESS International Hospitality Night (IHN)

International Hospitality Night is a multicultural celebration that allows students to share their respective cultures with the campus community. Students present informational display boards in the Jean Yawkey Center on their native countries, and for more than 18 years, IHN has allowed the campus to learn about the customs and cuisine of a variety of cultures of the international student body population. In the past, performances have included a Vietnamese folk dance, traditional belly dancing and a martial arts demonstration.

> SUCCESS Through the Wire

Through the Wire is a diversity lecture series that serves to stimulate intellectual discourse on campus, with an emphasis on issues of race, racism and socioeconomic status. The series provides a mix of dynamic speakers with the ability to engage and challenge all Emmanuel students to affirm identity, challenge stereotypes and become active learners of their cultures and history. Past speakers have included minister Dorian Cast, activist Leon Williams, genocide survivor Luong Ung and most recently, Tim Wise, one of the most prominent anti-racist writers and activists in the country.

Emmanuel College
Admissions Office
400 The Fenway
Boston, MA 02115
Ph: (617) 735-9715
enroll@emmanuel.edu
www.emmanuel.edu

FAST FACTS

STUDENT PROFILE

# of degree-seeking undergraduates	1,665
% male/female	26/74
% African-American	5
% American Indian or Alaska Native	<1
% Asian or Pacific Islander	3
% Hispanic	5
% Pell grant recipients	17

First-generation and minority alumni Dr. Sheilah Shaw Horton, interim vice president for student affairs, Boston College; Elizabeth Hayes Patterson, Esq., deputy director, Association of American Law Schools

ACADEMICS

full-time faculty	92
full-time minority faculty	n/a
student-faculty ratio	15:1
average class size	17
% first-year retention rate	76
% graduation rate (6 years)	62

Popular majors Biology, Chemistry, Business Management, English, Communications, Psychology, Political Science

CAMPUS LIFE

% live on campus (% freshmen)	72 (98)

Multicultural student clubs and organizations Black Student Union, Helping Unite Emmanuel Latinos to Lead and Achieve Success, Cape Verdean Student Association, Asian Student Association, ACCENT, Uprising Magazine, The Untouchables, Broken Silence
Athletics NCAA Division III, Eastern College Athletic Conference

ADMISSIONS

# of applicants	4,931
% accepted	56
# of first-year students enrolled	582
SAT Critical Reading range	490-590
SAT Math range	480-580
SAT Writing range	n/a
ACT range	20-24
average HS GPA	3.5

Deadlines

early decision	11/1
regular decision	3/1
application fee (online)	$40 ($40)
fee waiver for applicants with financial need	yes

COST & AID

tuition	$29,490
room & board	$11,950
total need-based institutional scholarships/grants	n/a
% of students apply for need-based aid	89
% of students receive aid	75
% receiving need-based scholarship or grant aid	97
% receiving aid whose need was fully met	41
average aid package	$21,263
average student loan debt upon graduation	$24,375

Harvard University

Harvard University is a private, co-educational, non-denominational liberal arts college located in Cambridge, Massachusetts. Founded in 1636, Harvard is the oldest institution of higher learning in the United States, as well as the first corporation in the Americas. The College strives to open the minds of students to knowledge and to enable them to take advantage of their educational opportunities, and the support it provides is a foundation upon which self-reliance and life-long learning habits are built. Through the scholarship it fosters, Harvard seeks to promote understanding and a desire to serve society.

> ACCESS Crimson Summer Academy

The Crimson Summer Academy offers select high school freshmen from Boston and Cambridge the opportunity to experience college life. After a period of orientation, participants live on Harvard's campus from Sunday evenings through Friday afternoons. Over the course of three consecutive summers, Crimson Scholars engage in classes, projects, field trips and recreational activities as they prepare for success in college and beyond. Each student receives full financial support, and upon completion of the three-year program is awarded a $3,000 scholarship for use at the college or university of their choice.

> ACCESS Campus Visits

Throughout the year, Harvard seeks to identify organizations and schools that work with low-income, high-achieving student populations and invites those groups to visit campus. Student coordinators and admissions officers provide a customized information session stressing the importance of higher education and the availability of financial aid, give a tour of the campus, and provide an "insider's look" into the Harvard experience in a small group setting.

> ACCESS Harvard Student Ambassadors

In order to reach students who might not be able to travel to campus prior to applying, current undergraduates from modest backgrounds are hired to return to their hometowns and visit local middle schools as well as high schools, where they discuss Harvard and higher education in general.

> OPPORTUNITY The Harvard Financial Aid Initiative (HFAI)

The Financial Aid Initiative has reduced the amount families with incomes below $180,000 are expected to contribute to college costs, and parents of families with incomes below $60,000 are not expected to contribute at all. Harvard no longer considers home equity as a resource in determination of family contribution, and need-based scholarships have replaced student loans. The Initiative has reduced the cost to middle income families by one-third to one-half, making the price of education for Harvard students with financial aid comparable to the cost of in-state tuition and fees at leading public universities. The Initiative benefits all accepted students who qualify.

> SUCCESS Harvard Financial Aid Initiative Newsletter and Initiatives

Students are provided with a monthly electronic newsletter highlighting events and opportunities on campus of special interest to students from modest backgrounds. Each newsletter includes information on research funding, travel grants, internships and other opportunities, along with general information about understanding financial aid or ways to take advantage of the many free social and cultural campus events. Each student receives a copy of "Shoestring Strategies for Life @ Harvard," a guide to living on a budget while taking advantage of the Harvard and Cambridge community opportunities. The Financial Aid Office administers the Student Events Fund for currently enrolled undergraduates from low-income backgrounds, enabling students to receive tickets to campus events free of charge. Students receiving financial aid may also be eligible for additional funds for personal and unexpected expenses.

Harvard University
Office of Admissions and Financial Aid
86 Brattle Street
Cambridge, MA 02138
Ph: (617) 495-1551
college@fas.harvard.edu
www.admissions.college.harvard.edu

F A S T F A C T S

STUDENT PROFILE

# of degree-seeking undergraduates	6,678
% male/female	50/50
% African American	8
% American Indian or Alaska Native	1
% Asian or Pacific Islander	16
% Hispanic	7
% White	45
% International	10
% Pell grant recipients	12.5

First-generation and minority alumni W. E. B. Du Bois, civil rights activist; Yo Yo Ma, cellist; Fan Noli, writer, former regent, prime minister, Albania; Alan Keyes, political figure; Jose Angel Navarro, former Texas legislator; Clifton Dawson, professional football player

ACADEMICS

full-time faculty	1,712
full-time minority faculty	298
student-faculty ratio	6.8:1
average class size	10-19
% first-year retention rate	97
% graduation rate (6 years)	97

Popular majors Economics, Political Science and Government, Psychology

CAMPUS LIFE

% live on campus (% fresh.)	99 (100)

Multicultural student clubs and organizations The Harvard Foundation for Intercultural and Race Relations, Asian-American Association, Black Student Association, Society of Black Scientists and Engineers, Fuerza Latina, RAZA, Native Americans at Harvard College, Woodbridge International Student Association

Athletics NCAA Division I, Collegiate Water Polo Association, Eastern College Athletic Conference (football I-AA), Eastern Intercollegiate Volleyball Association, Eastern Intercollegiate Wrestling Association, Ivy League (football I-AA)

ADMISSIONS

# of applicants	29,000
% accepted	7
# of first-year students enrolled	1,666
SAT Critical Reading range	700-800
SAT Math range	700-790
SAT Writing range	690-790
ACT range	31-35
average HS GPA	n/a

Deadlines

regular decision	1/1
application fee (online)	$65 ($65)
fee waiver for applicants with financial need	yes

COST & AID

tuition	$33,696
room & board	$11,856
total need-based institutional scholarships/grants	$100,143,628
% of students apply for need-based aid	57
% of students receive aid	100
% receiving need-based scholarship or grant aid	84
% receiving aid whose need was fully met	100
average aid package	$35,831
average student loan debt upon graduation	$9,290

Lesley University

Lesley University
29 Everett Street
Cambridge, MA 02138
Ph: (800) 999-1959 / (617) 349-8800
lcadmissions@lesley.edu
www.lesley.edu/lc/cso

Located in Cambridge, Mass., just steps from Harvard Square and minutes from Boston, Lesley students are committed to making a difference in the lives of others. Field-based internships begin freshman year for every program and include 450 to 600 hours of professional career exposure. Classes of 16-20 students, faculty committed to teaching undergraduates, and the option to self-design your own academic program ensures that Lesley students are never just a number. Students interested in Lesley's Dual Degree Programs have the opportunity to pursue both a Bachelor's and Master's degree within an accelerated timeframe, and those interested in the visual arts can access the curriculum of the Art Institute of Boston.

> ACCESS Admissions Office Events

The Lesley College Admissions Office works with the coordinators of various TRIO, AVID, Kids 2 College, The Bottom Line, Stepping Stone, summer enrichment camps sponsored by the Mayor's Office, and other pre-college programs to host tours, information sessions, class visits, and interviews on campus.

> OPPORTUNITY Need-Based Scholarships

"Being at Lesley is great! I'm part of an awesome community where people really care about each other and help each other out. And, by doing my teaching practicum at Brookline High School, I learned what it's really like to be a classroom teacher and how to help students succeed."

*– Nairobi M., '11
Roxbury, MA
Education*

Lesley offers a guaranteed scholarship program based on prior academic performance. Merit Scholarships range from $8,000 to full tuition and are awarded annually over a student's four years of study.

Additionally, in support of local communities, any student graduating from a public or charter high school in the cities of Boston, Brockton, Cambridge, Chelsea, Lawrence, Lowell, Lynn, or Somerville is automatically eligible for an $8,000 annual Urban Scholarship, assuming s/he starts at Lesley College the semester following their high school graduation. Graduates with an Associates Degree from any two-year community college in the United States are automatically eligible for an $8,000 annual Lesley University Community College Scholarship. Phi Theta Kappa Honor Society students who have graduated from a two-year institution are automatically eligible for a $13,000 annual scholarship.

> OPPORTUNITY Summer Orientation, Advisor and Tutorial Programs

With a grant from the Council of Independent Colleges and the Wal-Mart Foundation, Lesley University has created a network of current Lesley College, Art Institute of Boston, and Adult Learning students who are the first in their families to attend college. First 2 Lesley Fellows meet to discuss issues affecting first-generation students, participate in leadership training, and act as mentors to current middle school, high school, and community college students who are considering post-secondary education. Fellows are also committed to serving as mentors to other first generation students within Lesley University.

> SUCCESS Advisor and Tutorial Programs

Through the University's Advising Center, first-year students are assigned a professional advisor who will work with them through sophomore year. Freshman Transition Seminars serve to connect new students with faculty and help prepare them for their first internship/experiential learning course second semester. Tutorial assistance and help with writing or editing papers and support for learning disabilities or English as a second language may be found in the Center for Academic Achievement.

FAST FACTS

STUDENT PROFILE
# of degree-seeking undergraduates	1,377
% male/ female	25/75
% African-American	5
% American Indian or Alaska Native	1
% Asian or Pacific Islander	3
% Hispanic	4
% White	73
% International	4
% Pell grant recipients	34

First-generation and minority alumni Lynette Correa, Founder/CEO of Career Coaching 4 Kidz, Named Top 100 Most Influential Individual in Massachusetts by *El Planeta*; Natalia Santiago, Recipient of Lesley College's Presidential Full Tuition Scholarship, English teacher; Reena Patel, Recipient of the Rotary Foundation Academic Year Ambassadorial Scholarship, studying and working with children, Mumbai; Virginia Chau, former President of LU Student Government, preparing for law school; Thomas Morgan, former President of LU Student Government, summer internship in Ghana, attending graduate school for counseling.

ACADEMICS
full-time faculty	73
full-time minority faculty	11
student-faculty ratio	10:1
average class size	16-20
% first-year retention rate	75
% graduation rate (6 yr)	62

Popular majors Counseling Psychology, Education (Early Childhood, Elementary & Secondary) Management, Creative Writing, Art Therapy

CAMPUS LIFE
% live on campus (% freshmen)	54 (85)

Multicultural student clubs and organizations ALANA Student Organization, International Student Association, Lesley UNITY Chorus

Athletics NCAA Division III, New England Collegiate Conference

ADMISSIONS
# of applicants	2,611
% accepted	67
# of first-year students enrolled	384
SAT Critical Reading range	470-600
SAT Math range	450-580
SAT Writing range	470-600
ACT range	20-26
average HS GPA	2.9

Deadlines
early action	12/1
regular decision	rolling
application fee (online)	$50($0)
fee waiver for applicant with financial need	yes

COST & AID
tuition	$29,150
room & board	$12,800
total need-based institutional scholarships/ grants	$9,700,000
% of students apply for need-based aid	90
% of students receive aid	80
% receiving need-based scholarship/ grant aid	70
% receiving aid whose need was fully met	15
average aid package	$16,977
average student loan debt upon graduation	$18,000

Massachusetts College of Liberal Arts

At a cost that is much lower than that of private New England institutions, Massachusetts College of Liberal Arts is an attractive option for Massachusetts residents. With residents from Southern Vermont, Maine, Rhode Island and New York also qualifying for select tuition reductions, and 80 percent of students receiving some kind of financial aid and/or scholarships, it is no wonder the college ranked in *Newsweek*'s "Most for Your Money" category. Students at MCLA can take advantage of the beautiful Berkshire surroundings, which include Mt. Greylock (the highest peak in the state), access to three major ski resorts, as well as a vibrant arts community with world-renowned museums such as MASS MoCA and the Clark Art Institute. A comprehensive liberal arts and pre-professional program features small class sizes, providing programs in arts management, computer science, English/communications, business administration, physics, education and many more.

> ## ACCESS **Berkshire Compact for Education**

Massachusetts College of Liberal Arts is the lead partner in the Berkshire Compact for Education. Established in February 2005, the compact is assessing the higher education and lifelong learning needs of Berkshire County residents and employers, and identifying new opportunities and strategies to better meet those needs.

> ## ACCESS **Massachusetts Campus Compact College Access Corps**

MCLA recently was selected as a host site for the Massachusetts Campus Compact College Access Corps, a collaborative program between Tufts University and the Massachusetts Campus Compact. For its part in this collaboration, MCLA will work closely with local Drury High School to support qualified students' path toward higher education. The program also will build on current projects underway at the college, including Pathways to College Success, The Write Stuff, Friends of Foster Families and other community-centered collaborations.

> ## OPPORTUNITY **Scholarships**

MCLA offers and distributes more than $13 million each year in need-based and scholarship aid. This includes donor-funded scholarships to underrepresented students. The aid includes the Margaret A. Hart Scholarship, in honor of the first student of color to graduate from the college, and the Mitchell L. West Opportunity Scholarship, in honor of a college administrator who supported multicultural services.

> ## OPPORTUNITY **Multicultural Overnights**

MCLA provides students from urban cities like New York, Boston and Springfield with an opportunity to visit the campus. Students spend a night in the residence halls, attend classes, meet faculty and tour the MCLA campus. Nearly 80 percent of these students ultimately enroll at MCLA.

> ## SUCCESS **Learning Services Center (LSC) & Summer Enrichment Program (IEP)**

The Learning Services Center administers several key support services on campus, including the Individual Enrichment Program (IEP), which provides an intensive, four-week residential program to select students prior to the fall of their freshman year. Other center services include the Tutor Exchange Network and writing assistance offered through the Writing and Research Center.

> ## SUCCESS **Students Working to Assist Transitions (SWAT)**

Based on their majors and co-curricular interests, all first-year students are assigned a peer adviser through SWAT, a campus peer-advising group staffed by upperclassmen. SWAT support includes peer tutoring, workshop, and seminars designed to foster student development and enhance the relationship between advisers and advisees.

"Hosting fellow students for Multicultural Overnights gives me the opportunity to inspire them to not only attend college, like MCLA, but also to help create a more diverse campus community."

– Hawa U. '12 Chelsea, MA Interdisciplinary Studies with concentration in business and history, minor in political science

---

Massachusetts College of Liberal Arts
375 Church Street
North Adams, MA 01247-4100
Ph: (413) 662-5410
admissions@mcla.edu
www.mcla.edu

F A S T   F A C T S

STUDENT PROFILE

# of degree-seeking undergraduates	1,675
% male/female	40/60
% African-American	6
% American Indian or Alaska Native	<1
% Asian or Pacific Islander	<1
% Hispanic	5
% White	83
% Pell grant recipients	30.6

First-generation and minority alumni Dr. Mary K. Grant '83, president, Massachusetts College of Liberal Arts; John Barrett III '69, former mayor, North Adams, Mass., longest-serving mayor in the state; Daniel E. Bosley '76, Massachusetts state representative; Thomas Calter '80, Massachusetts state representative; Henry Reynolds '58, former deputy director, U.S. Agency for the International Development Mission; Bob Underhill '75, executive vice president/COO, Channing Bete Company Inc.; Kevin Barbary '85, principal, Office Resources; Cynthia Borek Normandin '76, owner, Braun's Express; Paul Serino '81, president, Serino's Italian Food, Inc.; Christine Keville '85, owner, Keville Enterprises; Oscar Lanza-Galindo '01, program associate for student leadership, Amherst College; Theresa O'Bryant, '86, Associate Dean of Students, MCLA; Carla Daugherty Holness, '95, account executive, Sun Trust Bank

ACADEMICS

full-time faculty	19
full-time minority faculty	n/a
student-faculty ratio	14:1
average class size	19
% first-year retention rate	75
% graduation rate (6 years)	50

Popular majors English, Business, Education, Psychology, Sociology, Fine and Performing Arts

CAMPUS LIFE

% live on campus (% freshmen)	68 (91)

Multicultural student clubs and organizations Aikido Club, African American Studies Club, Anime Club, Asian Club, B-GLAD Bi-sexuals, Gays & Lesbians Making A Difference, Christian Fellowship, Jewish Student Union, Latin American Society, Multicultural Student Society

Athletics NCAA Division III, Massachusetts State College Athletic Conference & Eastern Conference Athletic Conference

ADMISSIONS

# of applicants	1,690
% accepted	65
# of first-year students enrolled	351
SAT Critical Reading range	470-590
SAT Math range	440-560
SAT Writing range	n/a
ACT range	20-24
average HS GPA	3.1

Deadlines

regular decision	rolling
application fee (online)	$35 ($35)
fee waiver for applicants with financial need	yes

COST & AID

tuition	in-state: $7,015; out-of-state: $15,960
room & board	$7,868
total need-based institutional scholarships/grants	$2,000,000
% of students apply for need-based aid	87
% of students receive aid	64
average student loan debt upon graduation	$19,090

Massachusetts Institute of Technology

Massachusetts Institute of Technology is widely known for both its quality of education and the exceptional alumni that it produces. The benefit of MIT, however, is not limited to those destined for careers in science. Moreover, MIT is truly accessible to qualified students from all backgrounds; and as a closer look reveals, MIT does a great deal to create an environment that is conducive to learning and growth. The Admissions Office makes its desire for student diversity transparent: women, minority and LGBT students — as well as those with unique talents and passions to bring to the table — are all especially welcomed. Despite the rigor of its academic curriculum, MIT also does not allow students to fail — freshmen cannot receive failing grades; failed courses are simply dropped from their records. Academic collaboration is also valued, and students are given the entire month of January to experience the Independent Activities Period.

> ACCESS   Educational Outreach Programs

Massachusetts Institute of Technology supports several major engineering outreach programs. Two such programs are Minority Introduction to Engineering and Science (MITES) and Saturday Engineering, Enrichment, and Discovery (SEED) Academy. Both of these programs target communities underrepresented in science and engineering. MITES is a rigorous six-week residential, academic enrichment summer program for promising high school juniors who are interested in studying and exploring careers in science, engineering and entrepreneurship. SEED addresses the needs of area high schoolers by helping them to increase their academic performance in math and science and builds problem solving skills for students who want to excel in technologically focused fields. There is no cost to participate in either MITES or SEED, and more information on both programs can be found on the MIT Web site.

> OPPORTUNITY   Need-Blind Admissions / Need-Based, Full-Need Financial Aid

One of only a few U.S. institutions with a completely need-blind admissions process and a purely need-based financial aid award system, the Massachusetts Institute of Technology makes its sterling education affordable to all U.S. citizens, permanent residents and citizens from other countries. Affirmative action also brings students from ALANA (African-American, Latino, Asian, Native American) and low-income backgrounds to campus, creating an incoming freshman class that includes 16 percent first-generation and 63 percent ALANA students.

> SUCCESS   Office of Minority Education (OME)

Students can benefit from a number of student support services offered by the Office of Minority Education. Of particular interest is Project Interphase, a rigorous, seven-week, residential, academic bridge program for incoming ALANA students. Interphasers have access to award-winning teachers, one-on-one tutors and intensive courses in calculus, physics and writing. During their time on campus, participants gain experience in self-reliance and time management, make new friends and become better oriented to MIT's campus. Seminar XL is another OME-sponsored program where freshmen meet weekly to learn innovative and effective small-group learning concepts. Students taking part in Seminar XL meet in small groups for up to six hours each week with a graduate student facilitator who helps develop their problem-solving abilities, analytical reasoning skills and test-taking strategies. OME also provides funding for significant research experiences for undergraduates, as well as summertime internships that help introduce freshmen to the engineering process.

Massachusetts Institute of Technology
77 Massachusetts Avenue
Cambridge, MA 02139-4307
Ph: (617) 253-3400
admissions@mit.edu
www.mit.edu

F A S T   F A C T S

STUDENT PROFILE

# of degree-seeking undergraduates	4,153
% male/female	55.9/44.1
% African-American	8
% American Indian or Alaska Native	1
% Asian or Pacific Islander	25.4
% Hispanic	12.4
% White	36.5
% International	9.4
% Pell grant recipients	15.2

First-generation and minority alumni Kofi Annan, former UN Secretary General; Alex Padilla, California state senator; Luis Ferre, former governor, Puerto Rico; Virgilio Barco, former president, Columbia; Jullalan Weber, actor/dancer; Shirley Ann Jackson, president, RPI

ACADEMICS

full-time faculty	1,365
full-time minority faculty	390
student-faculty ratio	6:1
average class size	10-19
% first-year retention rate	98
% graduation rate (6 years)	94.0

Popular majors Electrical Engineering/Computer Science, Biology, Management, Mechanical Engineering, Biological Engineering

CAMPUS LIFE

% live on campus (% freshmen)	93 (100)

Multicultural student clubs and organizations African Student Association, American Indian Science & Engineering Society, Arab Student Organization, Armenian Student Association, Association of Puerto Rican Students, Black Students' Union, Black Christian Fellowship, Black Theater Guild, Black Women's Alliance, Caribbean Club, Chocolate City, Haitian Alliance, La Union Chicano por Aztlan, Mujeres Latinas, Mexican Student Association, National Society of Black Engineers, Native American Student Association, Society of Mexican American Engineers & Scientists, Hispanic Professional Engineers, Mes Latino, Spanish House, Vietnamese Students' Association

Athletics NCAA Division III, New England Women's and Men's Athletic Conference

ADMISSIONS

# of applicants	13,396
% accepted	12
# of first-year students enrolled	1,051
SAT Critical Reading range	660-760
SAT Math range	720-800
SAT Writing range	660-750
ACT range	31-34
average HS GPA	n/a

Deadlines

regular decision	1/1
application fee (online)	$75
fee waiver for applicants with financial need	yes

COST & AID

tuition	$37,782
room & board	$11,360
total need-based institutional scholarships/grants	n/a
% of students apply for need-based aid	78.2
% of students receive aid	100
% receiving need-based scholarship or grant aid	97.3
% receiving aid whose need was fully met	100
average aid package	$32,129
average student loan debt upon graduation	$14,148

Mount Holyoke College

Mount Holyoke College
Newhall Center, 50 College Street
South Hadley, MA 01075
Ph: (413) 538-2023
admission@mtholyoke.edu
www.mtholyoke.edu

A highly selective women's liberal arts college, Mount Holyoke College has a global reputation for educating women who change the world. With 49 departmental and interdepartmental majors, including an option for students to design their own concentration of study, the college offers plenty of academic opportunity to its 2,100 talented, dynamic students. Mount Holyoke College is also a member of the Five College Consortium, a program which links its students to a collegiate community of some 30,000 students and a variety of academic opportunities at nearby Amherst, Hampshire, and Smith Colleges and the University of Massachusetts at Amherst.

"After coming to 'Experience Diversity' at Mount Holyoke College, I knew that MHC was the place for me. I met an intelligent, ambitious and fascinating group of women who welcomed me with open arms. Four years later, the feeling has not gone away, I am still supported by my peers, my professors and even by our strong network of alumnae."

– Dawnell P., '10
Valley Stream, NY
Psychology, Education

> ACCESS Kids To College

Mount Holyoke's Admission Office takes part in the Kids2College program, which invites Springfield-area sixth graders from urban schools to participate in a college-awareness program. The program consists of several sessions that introduce students to issues like career options and planning for post-secondary education. The Kids2College program culminates in a day-long campus visit for students and their teachers, which provides the experiential component of the program and allows students to learn about available academic and social opportunities.

> ACCESS Focus on Diversity and Experience Diversity

Yearly, Mount Holyoke College sponsors Focus on Diversity and Experience Diversity — two programs that allow students who are particularly interested in and committed to issues on diversity — to visit Mount Holyoke, experience the college's tight-knit and dynamic student body, and dialogue about these issues. Focus on Diversity occurs in the fall for prospective students, while the Experience Diversity program takes place in the spring for accepted students and their families. Both programs have fly-in and bus-in travel arrangements for students.

> OPPORTUNITY Science Scholars Program

The Science Scholars program is an academic honors program that provides advanced research experiences and early career development opportunities for highly talented science and math students from diverse backgrounds who enroll at Mount Holyoke College. The program takes place in the summer before first year and consists of a four-week scientific research experience, which is guided and supported by current student mentors and science faculty. Science Scholars receive transportation to and from Mount Holyoke, on-campus housing, meals, and a stipend.

> SUCCESS Passages and ALANA Student Advising Pre-Orientation Program

Promoting InterCultural Dialogue and Creating Inclusion is an optional three-day program for incoming first year students just before Orientation. Designed to further promote an inclusive campus community, this program invites all students to partake in dialogues that will meet following three distinct goals: (1) deepening self-understanding of individual identity issues and cross cultural awareness; (2) increasing sensitivity to the complexity of other racial/ethnic groups as well as your own; and (3) developing a strong set of communication and leadership skills.

FAST FACTS

STUDENT PROFILE
# of degree-seeking undergraduates	2,173
% male/female	0/100
% African American	5
% American Indian or Alaska Native	<1
% Asian or Pacific Islander	12
% Hispanic	5
% White	49
% International	17
% Pell grant recipients	21.4

First generation and minority alumni Naomi Barry-Perez, civil rights lawyer, U.S. Department of Labor; Elaine Chao, U.S. secretary of labor; Suzan-Lori Parks, Pulitzer Prize-winning playwright; Gloria Johnson-Powell M.D., psychiatrist/author; Mona K. Sutphen, White House Deputy Chief of Staff

ACADEMICS
full-time faculty	208
full-time minority faculty	57
student-faculty ratio	10:1
average class size	20
% first-year retention rate	92
% graduation rate (6 years)	81

Popular majors Biology, English, International Relations, Psychology, Economics

CAMPUS LIFE
% live on campus (% fresh.)	94 (100)

Multicultural student clubs and organizations Arab/American and International Women's Association, Asian American Sisters in Action, Asian Students Association, Association of Pan-African Unity, South Asian Club, Bulgarian Club, Chinese Cultural Association, Hawai'i Club, Korean American Sisters Association, La Unidad, Liga Filipina, Community of Portuguese Speaking Countries, Movimiento Estudiantial Chicano de Aztlan, African and Caribbean Student Association, Native Spirit, Romanian Student Association, Vietnamese Students Association, Zim Club (Zimbabweans)

Athletics NCAA Division III, NEWMAC Conference

ADMISSIONS
# of applicants	3,127
% accepted	53
# of first-year students enrolled	527
SAT Critical Reading range	620-720
SAT Math range	590-700
SAT Writing range	625-700
ACT range	27-31
average HS GPA	3.65

Deadlines
early decision	11/15
regular decision	1/15
application fee (online)	$60($0)
fee waiver for applicants with financial need	yes

COST & AID
tuition	$38,940
room & board	$11,450
total need-based institutional scholarships/grants	$34,083,549
% of students apply for need-based aid	70
% of students receive aid	100
% receiving need-based scholarship or grant aid	95
% receiving aid whose need was fully met	100
average aid package	$31,459
average student loan debt upon graduation	$23,841

Northeastern University

Northeastern University is a leader in integrating rigorous classroom studies with experiential learning opportunities, anchored by the nation's largest, most innovative cooperative education (co-op) program. In addition to the signature co-op program, in which students alternate between classroom learning and work experience, Northeastern offers students several other experiential learning opportunities, including student research, service learning and global learning experiences. All of this takes place on a vibrant, 73-acre campus located in the heart of Boston, which offers modern academic, residential and recreational facilities.

> ACCESS Diversity Initiatives

Northeastern is a community that is comprised of students, faculty and staff from a diversity of backgrounds and experiences. The university values the contributions of all its members and works to support its underrepresented populations through a network of active cultural centers and mentoring programs. In recruiting students, Northeastern outreaches to a wide variety of geographically distant locations nationally and internationally and works closely with a host of support programs such as Upward Bound, Gear UP and Kids to College.

> OPPORTUNITY Linking Education and Diversity Mentoring Program (LEAD)

Continuing a century-old commitment to educational access, the Torch Scholars Program is a bold and innovative scholarship initiative awarded to individuals who have overcome exceptional odds and who demonstrate the potential to excel academically. Torch Scholars receive full tuition, fees, and room and board, as well as significant personal and academic support throughout their undergraduate careers.

> OPPORTUNITY $118 Million in Financial Aid

Northeastern is committed to making college accessible and affordable for all students interested in pursuing their passions. The university offers more than $118 million in grant and scholarship assistance, participates in all federal aid programs and offers an array of alternative financing and payment plans. In addition, Northeastern offers a number of scholarships that are awarded to students who are well-prepared for success in college and demonstrate strong leadership and community values.

> SUCCESS Diverse University Community

Reflecting the city of Boston and the world beyond, Northeastern is a rich blend of cultures, languages, religions and traditions. The university supports and celebrates these characteristics through many centers, institutes and programs including the John D. O'Bryant African-American Institute, Asian American Center, Latino/a Student Cultural Center, GLBT Community, Hillel Jewish Community, Catholic Center, Spiritual Life Center and International Student and Scholar Institute.

> SUCCESS Legacy Mentoring/Retention Program

The Legacy Mentoring Program provides a sense of belonging, retention and academic success for the black and Latino/a community. This active program includes events such as Black and Latino New Student Orientation, a study abroad forum, financial aid and professional development workshops, community service projects and many social outings.

"Torch is a program that encompasses all the hopes and dreams for students who are willing to work hard to achieve their goals. Without Torch, I don't know where I would be. Torch is my life, and it's a program I strive to progress and support now and in the future."

– Kathy M., '13
Boston, MA
Business/Management

Northeastern University
Office of Undergraduate Admissions
150 Richards Hall
360 Huntington Avenue
Boston, MA 02115
Ph: (617) 373-2200
admissions@neu.edu
www.northeastern.edu

F A S T F A C T S

STUDENT PROFILE

# of degree-seeking undergraduates	15,669
% male/female	49/50
% African American	6
% American Indian or Alaska Native	<1
% Asian or Pacific Islander	12
% Hispanic	7
% White	57
% International	8
% Pell grant recipients	10

First-generation and minority alumni Aisha Kahlil, singer, actor, dancer; Reggie Lewis, professional basketball player, Boston Celtics; José Juan Barea, professional basketball player, Dallas Mavericks

ACADEMICS

full-time faculty	984
full-time minority faculty	165
student-faculty ratio	15:1
% first-year retention rate	93
% graduation rate (6 years)	70

Popular majors Business/International Business, Engineering, Health Services/Allied Health

CAMPUS LIFE

% live on campus (% fresh.)	47 (96)

Multicultural student clubs and organizations African Student Organization, Arab Student Association, Armenian Student Association, Asian Student Association, Barkada, Black Student Association, Cape Verdean Student Association, Caribbean Students' Association, Cultural & Language Learning Society of NU, Haitian Student Unity, Hip Hop Culture Club, International Students Association, Italian Culture Society, Korean American Students Association, Latin American Students Organization (LASO), Students for Israel at Northeastern, UTSAV (South Asian Student Organization), Vietnamese Student Association

Athletics NCAA Division I, Colonial Athletic Association

ADMISSIONS

# of applicants	37,650
% accepted	49
# of first-year students enrolled	2,833
SAT Critical Reading range	590-680
SAT Math range	630-710
SAT Writing range	600-690
ACT range	28-31
average HS GPA	3.6-4.1

Deadlines

early action	11/1
regular decision	1/15
application fee (online)	$70 ($70)
fee waiver for applicants with financial need	yes

COST & AID

tuition	$34,950
room & board	$11,910
total need-based institutional scholarships/grants	$84,772,946
% of students apply for need-based aid	65
% of students receive aid	81
% receiving need-based scholarship or grant aid	94
% receiving aid whose need was fully met	16
average aid package	$17,877
average student loan debt upon graduation	n/a

Pine Manor College

Pine Manor College is a four-year, liberal-arts college dedicated to preparing women for inclusive leadership, social responsibility and academic success. For five of the last six years, Pine Manor has been ranked No. 1 for campus diversity by *US News & World Report*. The school distinguishes itself in its Inclusive Leadership and Social Responsibility (ILSR) program with a focus on community-based leadership, and its outcomes-based Portfolio Learning Program, which assists young women in creating and achieving academic goals. With such a small student body students receive individual attention from professors and a strong feeling of community and solidarity on campus. Student groups such as ALANA (African American, Latina, Asian, Native American and All) celebrate diversity in the student body. The school is located five miles from downtown Boston, accessible by subway.

"The mentoring class brought me out of my shell. I could not remain reserved and quiet, as I usually am. I had to be proactive, able to engage everyone within the team to participate and bring forth change. I never in a million years thought that I would have the opportunity to do any kind of mentoring. I was to busy looking for one myself, that I forgot that I could impart some advice to another human-being. "

– Jeanette D., '08
Boston, MA
Business Administration

Pine Manor College
400 Heath Street
Chestnut Hill, MA 02467
Ph: (800) 762-1357
admissions@pmc.edu
www.pmc.edu

FAST FACTS

STUDENT PROFILE

# of degree-seeking undergraduates	486
% male/female	0/100
% African-American	46
% American Indian or Alaska Native	<1
% Asian or Pacific Islander	6
% Hispanic	13
% White	17.7
% International	7
% Pell grant recipients	66

First-generation and minority alumni Merle Wolin, journalist; Gloria Harrison-Hall, radio and television producer

ACADEMICS

full-time faculty	66
full-time minority faculty	n/a
student-faculty ratio	10:1
average class size	< 20
% first-year retention rate	65
% graduation rate (6 years)	40

Popular majors Business Administration/ Management, Communications and Media Studies, Psychology

CAMPUS LIFE

% live on campus (% freshmen)	70 (69)

Multicultural student clubs and organizations ALANA, Alianza Latina, Asian Student Club, BGLAD, Diversity Committee, Haitian-American Women's Alliance, International Student Organization (ISC), Ladies of Various Ebony Shades (LOVES)

Athletics NCAA Division III, Great Northeast Athletic Conference

ADMISSIONS

# of applicants	556
% accepted	64
# of first-year students enrolled	142
SAT Critical Reading range	370-480
SAT Math range	350-460
SAT Writing range	n/a
ACT range	18
average HS GPA	n/a

Deadlines

regular admission	rolling
application fee	$25
fee waiver for applicants with financial need	yes

COST & AID

tuition	$20,189
room & board	$11,670
total need-based institutional scholarships/grants	n/a
% of students apply for need-based aid	95
% of students receive aid	92.4
% receiving need-based scholarship or grant aid	n/a
% receiving aid whose need was fully met	4.9
average aid package	$15,545
average student loan debt upon graduation	$32,875

> **ACCESS** **Center for Inclusive Leadership and Social Responsibility (ILSR)**

Pine Manor's Center for Inclusive Leadership and Social Responsibility builds leadership skills in high school girls from around the country. The center provides free, two-hour Leadership Workshops in local high schools, hosts an annual Summer Summit on Leadership for high school girls from around the country and supports the Susan and Jack Rudin Conference, a two-day leadership conference on campus. The aim of ILSR is to encourage leadership in girls and to prepare them for success in college. Workshops titled College 101 emphasize self-esteem, getting into college, goal setting, balancing work and family, managing relationships and working as a team. The center annually presents the Pine Manor College Award for Inclusive Leadership and Social Responsibility to women who make a positive difference in the lives of others through compassion, collaboration and inclusiveness.

> **OPPORTUNITY** **Pine Manor College Scholarships**

Pine Manor College is committed to making their highly personalized, relationship-based education available and affordable to women regardless of their financial means. In addition to reducing tuition by one-third, making the college one of the least expensive private colleges in New England, Pine Manor also offers nearly $4 million in need-based scholarships to deserving students.

> **SUCCESS** **Multicultural, International and Spiritual Affairs Office (MISA)**

The MISA Office provides programs to encourage the awareness of diverse cultures and spirituality for all women on campus. The MISA Office also offers ongoing guidance and support for students of color and international students on the Pine Manor campus, and MISA staff make sure that students maintain their legal status while pursuing an undergraduate degree.

Regis College

Regis College, a leading co-educational Catholic liberal arts college, offers innovative academic programs allowing students to take integrated and interdisciplinary courses, to interact with faculty and students within different majors, and to participate in workshops, lectures, and co-curricular programs. Regis College develops each student's individual success and encourages students to take leadership roles in their own education. Regis College is located just 12 miles west of Boston, on a secure and beautiful 132-acre campus. The college's suburban campus and location provides the ideal setting for learning, making friends, and experiencing college life. The college provides access to the public transportation system, allowing students the opportunity to explore a variety of cultural, educational, and professional opportunities throughout the metropolitan Boston area.

"Regis is the kind of school where professors hand out their cell phone numbers at the end of the first class and encourage you to call or text them with any questions. The open door policy at Regis makes the transition to college life as smooth as possible."
– Michael V., '12
Daegu, South Korea
Political Science/English

> ACCESS **The College Awareness Program**

The College Awareness Program is an outreach program sponsored by Regis College to give Latino youth in Boston Public Schools preparation and support as they transition from high school to college. Students spend a month-long residency on the Regis campus taking academic classes and building leadership and social skills. Regis College staff, faculty, current Latino Regis students and members of the Boston Latino community speak to program participants about college life and encourage students to pursue higher education.

> ACCESS **Family College Partnership Program (FCP)**

Success in earning a college degree is not only the result of intelligence and effort; it is a product of the support systems that assist students in their journey to graduation. Parents and family members play a key role in this process. The Regis Family College Partnership Program provides parents and guardians with information they can use to help direct their daughter or son to the many resources of Regis.

> OPPORTUNITY **Merit Scholarships**

Regis College offers a variety of merit scholarships to entering full-time, first-year and transfer students. Students are notified of scholarship eligibility by the Office of Admission at the time of their acceptance. Merit scholarships are renewable for four years, provided the student maintains the minimum requirements, and range from $6,000 to $12,000 per year.

> SUCCESS **Experiential Learning and Career Center**

Preparing for a career is a long-term process that should begin well before a student graduates from college. The Experiential Learning & Career Center (ELCC) at Regis College is designed to help students every step of the way. The ELCC assists Regis College students and graduates in identifying, planning, and achieving their academic and career goals by providing a range of services and programs, including career counseling/assessment, conducting a job search, and advising on graduate school.

Regis College
235 Wellesley Street
Weston, MA 02493-1571
Ph: (781) 768-7100
admission@regiscollege.edu
www.regiscollege.edu

F A S T   F A C T S

STUDENT PROFILE
# of degree-seeking undergraduates	991
% male/female	1/99
% African American	20
% American Indian or Alaska Native	<1
% Asian or Pacific Islander	6
% Hispanic	11
% Pell grant recipients	28

ACADEMICS
full-time faculty	55
full-time minority faculty	n/a
student-faculty ratio	14:1
average class size	14
% first-year retention rate	77
% graduation rate (6 years)	60

Popular majors Nursing, Communication, Education, Management and Leadership, Health and Fitness

CAMPUS LIFE
% live on campus (% fresh.)	50 (77)

Multicultural student clubs and organizations AAA (Asian-American Association), AHANA (African-American, Hispanic, Asian and Native American Organization), CVSA (Cape Verdean Student Association), HASO (Hatian-American Student Organization), LASO (Latin-American Student Organization), STAND (Students Taking Action Now in Darfur), START (Students Teaching Acceptance and Respect Together)

Athletics NCAA Division III, Commonwealth Coast Conference

ADMISSIONS
# of applicants	1,549
% accepted	75
# of first-year students enrolled	250
SAT Critical Reading range	390-490
SAT Math range	400-500
SAT Writing range	400-510
ACT range	16-21
average HS GPA	2.8
Deadlines	
regular decision	rolling
application fee (online)	$50 ($50)
fee waiver for applicants with financial need	yes

COST & AID
tuition	$28,900
room & board	$12,190
total need-based institutional scholarships/grants	n/a
% of students apply for need-based aid	78
% of students receive aid	72
% receiving need-based scholarship or grant aid	93
% receiving aid whose need was fully met	15
average aid package	$22,111
average student loan debt upon graduation	$24,178

Smith College

Smith College
Office of Admission
7 College Lane
Northampton, MA 01063
Ph: (800) 383-3232
admission@smith.edu
www.smith.edu

As the nation's largest undergraduate women's college, Smith is distinguished by a diverse student body, a culturally vibrant surrounding area, and participation in the Five College Consortium. Smith offers unique educational resources and outstanding facilities rivaling those in many universities with special programs including an engineering major, funded summer internships, and research with faculty. Smith educates women of promise to lead lives of distinction.

> ACCESS Urban Education Initiative

The Urban Education Initiative is a service-learning program that brings Smith students to elementary, middle and high schools in New York City, Chicago and nearby Springfield, Mass. Urban Education Fellows spend three weeks in January at one of the partner schools providing one-on-one tutoring and classroom assistance.

> ACCESS Smith Summer Science and Engineering Program

High school students from around the globe participate in a month-long summer program in science and engineering. Funding is available for low-income students.

> ACCESS Women of Distinction

The Women of Distinction program for high school seniors highlights the opportunities at Smith for African American, Asian American, Latina and Native American students. Participants in the three-day program live in campus houses, experience academic life, and attend panels and workshops on student life and the college admission process. There is a required application and students are chosen on the basis of academic and personal qualities. All expenses are covered by Smith.

> OPPORTUNITY Springfield and Holyoke Partnership

Through this partnership, four graduates from the Springfield and Holyoke, Mass. public schools are selected to receive a full-tuition scholarship for each of their four undergraduate years at Smith. Students are selected based on their academic record and leadership potential.

> SUCCESS Student Support Groups

There are a number of groups for low-income students and students of color: Low-Income Students of Smith, the Minority Association of Pre-Health Students, the Union of Underrepresented Students in the Sciences and AEMES (Achieving Excellence in Mathematics, Engineering and Sciences).

> SUCCESS Bridge Pre-Orientation Program

Through a variety of interactive student-led seminars and group activities, participants are encouraged to share their perspectives and hear the voices of their peers to better understand and appreciate their similarities and differences. The goal of the program is an examination of cultural diversity in all its forms.

"It's empowering to look around a lecture of 40 and realize the women surrounding you aren't built to think a certain way, but that we each have something unique to contribute. Smithies aren't just top students but amazing leaders, athletes, researchers and artists. They don't just graduate with degrees in a given topic, but leave Smith with a supreme sense of personal development, confidence and accomplishment, ready to change the world."

– Chloe W., '11
White Plains, NY
Psychology

FAST FACTS

STUDENT PROFILE

# of degree-seeking undergraduates	2,614
% male/female	0/100
% African-American	7
% American Indian or Alaska Native	1
% Asian or Pacific Islander	13
% Hispanic	7
% White	41
% International	8
% Pell grant recipients	28

First-generation and minority alums Yolanda King, civil rights activist, daughter of Dr. Martin Luther King, Jr.; Maria Lopez, judge; Evelyn Boyd Granville, mathematician; Sian DeVega, model, actress; Ng'endo Mwangi, first woman physician in Kenya; Sharmeen Obaid-Chinoy, award-winning documentary filmmaker; Thelma Golden, deputy director of Studio Museum in Harlem; Martha Southgate, writer

ACADEMICS

full-time faculty	278
full-time minority faculty	48
student-faculty ratio	9:1
average class size	19
% first-year retention rate	91
% graduation rate (6 years)	88

Popular majors Psychology, Government, English Language/Literature, Biology, Economics and Art

CAMPUS LIFE

% live on campus (% fresh.)	90 (100)

Multicultural student clubs and organizations Asian Students Alliance, Black Students Alliance, Ekta, International Students Organization, Indigenous Smith Students and Allies, Korean American Students, Multiethnic Interracial Smith College, Nosostras, Smith African and Caribbean Students Association

Athletics NCAA Division III, Eastern College Athletic Conference

ADMISSIONS

# of applicants	4,011
% accepted	47
# of first-year students enrolled	665
SAT Critical Reading range	610-710
SAT Math range	580-690
SAT Writing range	610-710
ACT range	25-31
average HS GPA	3.89

Deadlines

early decision I	11/15
early decision II	1/2
regular decision	1/15
application fee (online)	$60 ($0)
fee waiver for applicants with financial need	yes

COST & AID

tuition	$38,640
room & board	$13,000
total need-based institutional scholarships/ grants	$43,935,108
% of students apply for need-based aid	74
% of students receive aid	86
% receiving need-based scholarship/grant aid	60
% receiving aid whose need was fully met	100
average aid package	$34,526
average student loan debt upon graduation	$21,573

Stonehill College

Boston is within easy reach of Stonehill College, a selective Catholic college located in Easton, Massachusetts. Students who study at Stonehill emerge with a comprehensive education that honors leadership, personal growth and discovery. To this end, students are required to participate in the Cornerstone Program of General Education to prepare for a life of learning and responsible citizenship by leading them to examine critically the self, society, culture and the natural world. Stonehill offers 42 major programs, the opportunity to double major and 42 minor programs.

> *"Stonehill has proven to me to be a place offering many resources. These resources have helped me to build a solid foundation. Now I am confident that I will attain my professional goals."*
> – Alexandre S., '11
> Natick, MA
> Psychology

> ACCESS **Project SEED**

Project SEED provides a number of academically talented, economically disadvantaged high school students the opportunity to conduct meaningful summer research with Stonehill chemistry professors and advanced level college students.

> OPPORTUNITY **Minority, Low-Income and First-Generation Scholarships**

Stonehill College offers several Minority, Low-Income, and First-Generation Scholarships to those who meet certain other criteria. Among the aforementioned scholarships are: the Ely Scholarship, specifically earmarked for minority males whose families are facing undue economic hardship; the William Randolph Hearst Foundation Scholars Program Scholarship, open to all minority students from low-income backgrounds; the Ron Burton Scholarship, available only to alumni from the Ron Burton Training Village summer program for disadvantaged boys; the John and Margarete McNeice Scholars Program award, open to minority students from low-income backgrounds; and, The Yawkey Scholarship, available to eligible students residing in New England or Georgetown County, South Carolina who are financially needy, academically qualified and have a life circumstance that have made study and achievement challenging.

> SUCCESS **The Path Program**

Run by the Office of Academic Services, The Path Program is an intensive transition program designed to develop needed academic skills for first-year students. In addition to skill development in areas such as note-taking, research and text book reading, students learn about the nuts and bolts of college life such as reading a course syllabus, calculating a GPA and exploring a major area of study. This program eases the transition on campus and puts students in touch with a diverse group of upper-class students, staff and resources on campus.

> SUCCESS **The Summer Bridge Program**

This pre-orientation program is designed for high school seniors who are accepted and plan to enroll in the science program at Stonehill. The Summer Bridge Program affords the pre-college student who may not have the most rigorous science preparation in high school the opportunity to work alongside Stonehill science faculty to gain lab experience, knowledge and added skills prior to the start of Fall classes. This program is designed to aid in the college transition process especially within a competitive science program.

Stonehill College
320 Washington Street
Easton, MA 02357
Ph: (508) 565-1373
admissions@stonehill.edu
www.stonehill.edu

FAST FACTS

STUDENT PROFILE
# of degree-seeking undergraduates	2,448
% male/female	40/60
% African-American	3
% American Indian or Alaska Native	0
% Asian or Pacific Islander	1
% Hispanic	4
% White	92
% International	0
% Pell grant recipients	10.9

First-generation and minority alumni Ed Cooley '94, Division I head coach, men's basketball, Fairfield University; Lois Commodore '00, Christian recording artist, founder of Soldiers of Destiny Foundation; Andrea Vandross '02, medical school, University of Chicago; Christopher Tirrell '09, law school, Stanford University

ACADEMICS
full-time faculty	152
full-time minority faculty	13
student-faculty ratio	13:1
average class size	20
% first-year retention rate	89
% graduation rate (6 years)	82

Popular majors Psychology, English, Political Science, Biology, Accounting

CAMPUS LIFE
% live on campus (% fresh.)	88 (97)

Multicultural student clubs and organizations Diversity Committee of Student Government, International Club, PRIDE, Diversity on Campus (D.O.C.), Asian American Society, La Unidad/Spanish Club, ALANA Brothers and Sisters Leadership Program, Stonehill College chapter of Jane Doe, Raising Awareness of our Cultural Experiences (R.A.C.E.), Stonehill Alumni of Color Group

Athletics NCAA Division II, Northeast-10 Conference

ADMISSIONS
# of applicants	5,871
% accepted	56
# of first-year students enrolled	683
SAT Critical Reading range	550-630
SAT Math range	570-650
SAT Writing range	n/a
ACT range	24-28
average HS GPA	3.49

Deadlines
early decision	11/1
regular decision	1/15
application fee (online)	$60 ($60)

COST & AID
tuition	$31,210
room & board	$12,240
total need-based institutional scholarships/grants	$20,817,223
% of students apply for need-based aid	81
% receiving need-based scholarship or grant aid	64
% of students recieve aid	84
average aid package	$20,972
average student loan debt upon graduation	$29,163

Suffolk University

Founded in 1906, Suffolk University is a private, co-educational, non-denominational, comprehensive, urban university that takes pride in being a personal, student-centered school where faculty and administrators know students by name. Providing quality education at a reasonable cost for students of all ages and backgrounds with strong emphasis on diversity, the university is committed to educational access and opportunity for all students. Suffolk University seeks to prepare students to become life-long learners, as well as professionals who lead and serve the communities in which they live and work.

> ACCESS Connections to College

Connections to College is a partnership between Bird Street Community Center and Suffolk University, providing non-traditional college-bound Boston High School students with the tools they need to pursue higher education. During the program, participants take college-level courses instructed by university professors for six weeks during the summer and participate in an internship at Suffolk University, Massachusetts State House or City Hall. Participants take courses weekday mornings and perform their internship in the afternoon. The courses provide students with the academic knowledge necessary to be productive in their summer internship positions and other work that their supervisors believe will make for a meaningful learning experience.

> *"As an international student, I have developed a passion for traveling. Being a Suffolk student has given me the opportunity to explore my passion for travel by studying abroad while completing my degree in international relations."*
> – Padmini S., '11
> San Fernando, Trinidad and Tobago

> OPPORTUNITY The Miller Scholarship Program

This program offers full tuition scholarships to academically qualified graduates of Boston Public High Schools who reside in Boston and demonstrate financial need. During freshman year Miller Scholars participate in weekly enrichment seminars offered by the staff of the Learning Center, to cover time management and study skills. Additionally, numerous cultural excursions (to museums, plays, etc.) are available to Miller Scholars during the first year of enrollment. Miller Scholars are required to participate in a minimum of 15 hours of community service during the spring semester of freshman year. Awards are renewable provided the recipient maintains a 2.8 GPA, is a full-time student, and continues to demonstrate financial need.

> SUCCESS Math & Computer Science Support Center

Suffolk University's Math & Computer Science Support Center offers students high-quality tutorials for both math and computer science courses. These support services are designed to help students to succeed in reaching their full potential and to overcome particular difficulties. The center offers a variety of services designed to strengthen students' foundations in math and computer science, while expanding their knowledge in specific subject areas. Services offered include math placement exams, special review sessions, math survival guides, math drop-in help, math one-on-one, as well as computer science drop-in help, programming and workshops.

> SUCCESS Ronald E. McNair Post-Baccalaureate Achievement Program

With a goal of increasing the number of students from underrepresented segments of society who successfully pursue Ph.D. programs, The McNair Scholars program at Suffolk University encourages graduate studies by providing opportunities for undergraduates to define their goals, engage in research and develop the skills and faculty-mentor relationships critical to success at the doctoral level. The university also tracks the progress of these students as they complete their advanced degrees.

Suffolk University
8 Ashburton Place
Boston, MA 02108
Ph: (617) 573-8460
admission@suffolk.edu
www.suffolk.edu

FAST FACTS

STUDENT PROFILE
# of degree-seeking undergraduates	5,639
% male/female	43/57
% African American	3
% American Indian or Alaska Native	0
% Asian or Pacific Islander	6
% Hispanic	6
% White	59
% International	10
% Pell grant recipients	20.5

ACADEMICS
full-time faculty	342
full-time minority faculty	39
student-faculty ratio	13:1
average class size	20
% first-year retention rate	72
% graduation rate (6 years)	55

Popular majors Communications, Sociology

CAMPUS LIFE
% live on campus (% freshmen)	23 (69)

Multicultural student clubs and organizations
African Student Association, Black Student Union, Caribbean Student Network, Asian American Association, Vietnamese Student Association, Suffolk University Hispanic Association, International Student Association, Cape Verdean Student Association, Greek Student Association, Japanese Student Association, South Asian Student Association

Athletics NCAA Division III, Great Northeast Athletic Conference, ECAC Northeast Ice Hockey League

ADMISSIONS
# of applicants	8,045
% accepted	80
SAT Critical Reading range	460-560
SAT Math range	450-570
ACT range	20-24
average HS GPA	3.03

Deadlines
early decision	12/20
regular decision	3/1
application fee (online)	$50 ($50)
fee waiver for applicants with financial need	yes

COST & AID
tuition	$27,000
room & board	$14,544
total need-based institutional scholarships/grants	$21,149,422
% of students apply for need-based aid	66
% of students receive aid	95
% receiving need-based scholarship or grant aid	84
% receiving aid whose need was fully met	60
average aid package	$15,232
average student loan debt upon graduation	n/a

Tufts University

Located 5 miles outside of Boston, Tufts is a highly selective university which draws a diverse student body from all over the world. The University has students from all 50 states and over 65 countries, and approximately 28 percent of undergraduates are students of color and 10 percent are first-generation students. Dedicated to preparing leaders who will address the intellectual and social challenges of the new century, Tufts values globalism, active citizenship and environmentalism in over 60 academic programs in the School of Arts & Sciences and the School of Engineering.

Tufts University
Bendetson Hall
Medford, MA 02155
Ph: (617) 627-3170
admissions.inquiry@ase.tufts.edu
www.tufts.edu

> ACCESS **Early Awareness Initiative**

Tufts' Office of Undergraduate Admissions runs an Early Awareness Initiative, which brings Boston middle school students (with a focus on those from under-served areas) to campus weekly to expose them to college life. Current undergraduates and admissions officers explain how participants can begin preparing for the college application process, placing emphasis on the steps middle and early high school students should take to access higher education.

> *"It's undeniable that Tufts works very hard to extend a hand of friendship to all students. No where else in my tours of colleges and universities did I find a prospective student program like Tufts' Voices of Tufts program, which reached out to high school seniors like me."*
>
> *– Mary Jo P., '11 Springfield, MA International Relations, Chinese*

> ACCESS **College Advising**

Current Tufts students volunteer with the Let's Get Ready program to help juniors at Somerville High School prepare for the SATs and admissions process. Recent graduates serve in the College Advising Corps, a collaboration between Massachusetts Campus Compact and Tufts. Selected graduates work in high schools across Massachusetts, serving as college advisers for one to two years.

> OPPORTUNITY **Loan Replacement Policy/Financial Aid**

Beginning with the class of 2011, Tufts will replace loans with scholarship grants for all undergraduates whose annual family income is below $40,000. The ability to provide need-blind financial aid is the top priority of the University's fundraising campaign and it is committed to meeting all demonstrated need of admitted students.

> OPPORTUNITY **Voices of Tufts**

The Office of Undergraduate Admissions invites traditionally underrepresented students to visit the Tufts campus for a two-day fly-in program each fall that provides a multicultural prospective on attending the university. Bus transportation is provided from New York City and students traveling from elsewhere can apply for a travel grant.

> SUCCESS **Health Careers Fellows Program (HCFP)**

The Health Careers Fellows Program seeks to support minority and disadvantaged students interested in the health professions. HCFP ensures that each student maximizes his or her academic career by providing academic tutoring, counseling and advising. Fellows have the opportunity to attend review sessions, participate in seminar series on health-related topics, and visit off-campus sites. They receive individualized support from the Program Director and Associate Director of Health Professions Advising while they are students at Tufts and go on to graduate study in health-related careers.

> SUCCESS **Computer Science, Engineering and Mathematics Scholars**

Through weekly, individualized advising and scholarship funding, Tufts seeks to promote the academic advancement and degree achievement of talented undergraduate students from low-income backgrounds seeking degrees in math, computer science and engineering. Particular emphasis is placed on minority and female students.

FAST FACTS

STUDENT PROFILE

# of degree-seeking undergraduates	5,044
% male/female	49/51
% African American	8
% American Indian or Alaska Native	<1
% Asian or Pacific Islander	12
% Hispanic	8
% White	57
% International	12
% Pell grant recipients	13

First-generation and minority alumni Cathy Bao Bean, author, advocate; Bill Richardson, Governor, New Mexico, former presidential candidate; Bill Thompson, comptroller, City of New York; Tracy Chapman, singer/songwriter

ACADEMICS

full-time faculty	640
full-time minority faculty	n/a
student/faculty ratio	8:1
average class size	20
% first year retention rate	96
% graduation rate (6 years)	92

Popular majors International Relations, Biology, English, Economics, Psychology

CAMPUS LIFE

% live on campus (% fresh.)	65.9 (99.9)

Multicultural student clubs and organizations African Student Organization, Arab Student Association, Asian Community at Tufts, Association of Latin American Students, Black Men's Group, Chinese Student Association, Gen-1 (First Generation College Student Organization), Multiracial Organization of Students at Tufts, Tufts Association of South Asians, Vietnamese Student Club

Athletics NCAA Division III, New England Small College Athletic Conference (NESCAC)

ADMISSIONS

# of applicants	15,642
% accepted	25
# of first-year students enrolled	1300
SAT Critical Reading range	670-750
SAT Math range	670-750
SAT Writing range	670-760
ACT range	30-33
average HS GPA	n/a

Deadlines

early decision	11/2
regular decision	1/4
application fee (online)	$70 ($70)
fee waiver for applicants	yes

COST & AID

tuition	$37,952
room and board	$10,518
total need-based institutional scholarships and grants	$52,000,000
% students apply for need-based aid	48
% receiving need-based scholarship or grant aid	40
% receiving aid whose need fully met	100
average aid package	$30,000
average student loan debt upon graduation	$15,000

Wellesley College

Wellesley College
Admission Office
106 Central Street
Wellesley, MA 02481
Ph: (781) 283-2270
admission@wellesley.edu
www.wellesley.edu/admission

Located a dozen miles from Boston, Wellesley College offers bright, motivated women a comprehensive, liberal arts education in a small college environment. Due to its need-blind admission policy for U.S. citizens and permanent residents, generous financial aid, and support of students throughout their undergraduate education, Wellesley is considered one of the most socio-economically diverse colleges or universities in the nation. Wellesley considers students for admission solely on their talents and personal qualities, not on their financial resources, and is committed to meeting 100 percent of each admitted student's demonstrated financial need. Women interested in science and technology particularly benefit from attending the College, which provides opportunities for research with faculty, and offers cross-registration with the Massachusetts Institute of Technology and Olin College of Engineering.

"I knew nothing about Wellesley, and it was a world away from my LA roots, but my counselor's blunt advice, 'If you really want to do good for your community like you claim you do, then you should really consider Wellesley,' sealed the deal. I'm really glad I left my comfort zone."

*– Krizia V., '10
Bell, CA
Political Science*

> ACCESS Kids2College

Boston-area sixth graders from urban schools can benefit from Kids2College, an initiative of the Wellesley College Admission Office. This college-awareness program introduces students to career options and planning for post-secondary education by providing them with a series of hands-on sessions. Kids2College culminates in a day-long campus visit for students and their parents or guardians. Wellesley has partnerships with secondary schools in nearby Framingham, a city with a diverse student population.

> OPPORTUNITY Campus Visit Financial Assistance

Wellesley's outreach includes recruitment efforts directed at students from a wide range of socioeconomic experiences in all areas of the country, including making connections with those from high schools with more limited resources and with students who may be the first in their families to attend college. Wellesley brings talented high school students from lower socioeconomic backgrounds — those who are thinking of applying and those who have been admitted — to campus at the college's expense.

> OPPORTUNITY QuestBridge National College Match Program

The QuestBridge National College Match program provides students who have achieved academic excellence in the face of economic hardship with a free QuestBridge application that enables these students to highlight their academic achievements in light of their low-income background and links them with financial aid and scholarship opportunities.

> SUCCESS Supplemental Instruction Program

Wellesley's Pforzheimer Learning and Teaching Center provides academic support and advising, including peer tutoring to underrepresented students. Wellesley is also piloting a version of the nationally recognized Supplemental Instruction program, which provides additional peer-led learning opportunities in high-risk courses. In its first year, Wellesley introduced the Supplemental Instruction Program to entry-level courses in biology and chemistry, and it now offers an advanced chemistry course. A cultural advising network also provides a range of support services for students from diverse backgrounds.

FAST FACTS

STUDENT PROFILE
# of degree-seeking undergraduates	2,177
% male/ female	0/100
% African-American	6
% American Indian or Alaskan Native	1
% Asian or Pacific Islander	25
% Hispanic	7
% White	41
% International	10
% Pell grant recipients	16

First-generation and minority alumni Michelle Ye, former Miss Chinese International; Regina Montoya, Latina business leader, advocate; Nayantara Sahgal, writer; Michelle Caruso-Cabrera, host, anchor, CNBC; Amalya L. Kearse, judge, U.S. Court of Appeals

ACADEMICS
full-time faculty	259
full-time minority faculty	63
student-faculty ratio	8:1
average class size	18
% first-year retention rate	94
% graduation rate (6 yrs)	90

Popular majors Economics, Political Science, English, Psychology, Biological Sciences

CAMPUS LIFE
% live on campus (% freshmen)	98 (100)

Multicultural student clubs and organizations African Students' Association, Asian Student Union, Chinese Students Association, Club Filipina, Ethos, Korean Students Association, Mezcla, Native American Student Organization, Slater International Association, Spectrum, Taiwanese Cultural Organization, United World Colleges, Association for South Asian Cultures

Athletics NCAA Division III, NEWMAC

ADMISSIONS
# of applicants	4,156
% accepted	35
# of first-year students enrolled	589
SAT Critical Reading range	640-740
SAT Math range	640-730
SAT Writing range	650-740
ACT range	29-32
average HS GPA	n/a
% in top 20% of class, if ranked	94

Deadlines
early decision	11/1
regular decision	1/15
application fee (online)	$50($0)
fee waiver for applicants with financial need	yes

COST & AID
tuition	$39,420
room & board	$12,284
total need-based institutional scholarships/ grants	$44,592,163
% of students apply for need-based aid	71
% of students receive aid	56
% receiving need-based scholarship/ grant aid	97
% receiving aid whose need was fully met	100
average aid package	$35,951
average student loan debt upon graduation	$13,324

Westfield State College

Westfield State College
333 Western Avenue
Westfield, MA 01086
Ph: (413) 572-5218
admissions@wsc.ma.edu
www.wsc.ma.edu

Founded in 1838 by Horace Mann, Westfield State is an education leader committed to providing every generation of students with a learning experience built on its founding principle as the first co-educational college in America to offer an education without barrier to race, creed or economic status. This spirit of innovative thinking and social responsibility is forged in a curriculum of liberal arts and professional studies that creates a vital community of engaged learners who become confident, capable individuals prepared for leadership and service to society.

> ACCESS Urban Education Program (UEP)

Recognized across campus for its development of pre-college first-generation, low-income, and ethnically diverse student scholars, UEP is an academic support progam designed to increase the enrollment, retention, and graduation rates of these students. By way of comprehensive summer and academic year programming and services, the Urban Education Program has created and maintained a dynamic program environment that promotes intellectual, social, and emotional development, both collaboratively and individually. The Urban Education Program is comprised of five identifiable components: recruitment and participant selection, summer bridge program, academic year programming, leadership development, and career/graduate school preparation.

> OPPORTUNITY Discover Westfield State College Day

The annual Discover Westfield State College Day is geared toward first-generation college students and students of color. Westfield provides transportation from the high schools to campus so that prospective students can meet with WSC faculty, staff, and students. The participants receive a student-guided tour of the campus and hear presentations from the Admission, Financial Aid, and Urban Education offices. Prospective students also receive an admission application with an application fee waiver.

"Through the Urban Education Program, I established a support group which only grows as I continue my education at Westfield State. I often hear minorities complain about the things they can not do, however Westfield State College along with the Urban Education program showed me all of the things I can do and how to attain each goal."

*– Kiara D., '11
Springfield, MA
Communications*

> SUCCESS TRiO Student Support Services

TRiO Student Support Services is a comprehensive federally funded TRiO Program serving matriculated students who are low performing academically and are either first-generation, low-income, or disabled (learning, physical, psychological/emotional). This program is designed to improve academic performance, retention to graduation, and assist with graduate and professional school preparation. Services such as professional tutoring, academic advisement, peer mentoring, cultural enrichment, assistance with obtaining financial aid, to name a few, are available to program students for as long as they are enrolled at the college.

FAST FACTS

STUDENT PROFILE

# of degree-seeking undergraduates	4,562
% male/female	47/53
% African American	4
% American Indian or Alaska Native	<1
% Asian or Pacific Islander	2
% Hispanic	4
% White	83
% International	<1
% Pell grant recipients	23

First-generation and minority alumni Dr. Yolanda Johnson '87, Principal, Atlanta School System, GA; George Gilmer '92, Senior Vice President, Bank of New York Mellon; Eduardo C. Robreno '67, Federal Court Judge, PA; Lance Campbell '91, Urban City Planner, Boston; Tyrone Abrahamian '95, Probation Officer Supervisor, CT

ACADEMICS

full-time faculty	212
full-time minority faculty	29
student/faculty ratio	17:1
average class size	23
% first year retention rate	79
% graduation rate (6 years)	58

Popular majors Business Management, Communication, Criminal Justice, Education, Psychology

CAMPUS LIFE

% live on campus (% fresh.)	60 (90)

Multicultural student clubs and organizations Asian Appreciation Club, Latino Association for Empowerment

Athletics NCAA Division II, Massachusetts State College Athletic Conference

ADMISSIONS

# of applicants	5,806
% accepted	53
# of first-year students enrolled	1,193
SAT Critical Reading average	520
SAT Math average	530
SAT Writing range	n/a
ACT range	n/a
average HS GPA	3.12

Deadlines

regular decision	3/1
application fee (online)	$50 ($50)
fee waiver for applicants	yes

COST & AID

tuition	in-state $6,515; out-of-state $12,595
room and board	$8,065
total need-based institutional scholarships and grants	$1,313,506
% students apply for need-based aid	76
% receiving need-based scholarship or grant aid	31
% receiving aid whose need fully met	2
average aid package	$7,262
average student loan debt upon graduation	$12,942

Wheaton College

Wheaton College is a classic, selective, private, coeducational liberal arts college. The College boasts nearly 1600 students hailing from 42 states and almost 38 countries. Wheaton's 400 acre campus is ideally located in suburban Norton, Massachusetts, 35 miles south of Boston and 20 miles north of Providence, Rhode Island. Among its many academic opportunities include internships in every professional field, community service, and study abroad. More than 127 Wheaton students have won national academic awards since 2001, including 3 Rhodes Scholars.

> ACCESS Davis United World Scholars Program

The program provides grants to Wheaton for scholars from both the United States and from overseas who have proven themselves by completing their last two years of high school at a group of international schools called United World Colleges. These UWC schools are located in the United States, Bosnia, Canada, Costa Rica, Hong Kong, India, Italy, Norway, Singapore, Swaziland, the United Kingdom, and Venezuela. By supporting scholars who are energized by building understanding in active, personal ways, the Davis UWC Scholars Program exemplifies how diversity can contribute to a much richer education and to a more internationally oriented undergraduate experience for everyone on campus.

> OPPORTUNITY Posse Foundation

Wheaton College and The Posse Foundation, Inc., identify public high school students with extraordinary academic and leadership potential who may be overlooked by traditional college selection processes. Posse extends to these students the opportunity to pursue personal and academic excellence by placing them in supportive, multicultural teams. Posse Scholars receive four-year, full-tuition leadership scholarships.

> OPPORTUNITY Diversity Overnight Program

Every year Wheaton invites a group of diverse and talented high school seniors to come together for an overnight visit and experience the Wheaton community. This program is designed to explore academic, extracurricular opportunities, and other important aspects of college life. Students chosen to participate are provided with housing and meals as guests of Wheaton.

> OPPORTUNITY HERO Program

The Higher Education Readiness Opportunity (HERO) program partners with Brockton high school students who will be the first from their families to attend college. Students pair up with Wheaton mentors. Through the program, students get a better sense of college life and develop the abilities and confidence to acquire—and excel during—a college education.

"I came to Wheaton College through the Bottom Line College Counseling Program. I am the first of my immediate family to attend a four-year college. My mother is originally from El Salvador and came to the U.S. to give my brother and I a better life. The program gave me the resources I needed to be successful."

– Vanessa H., '11
Hyde Park, MA
Psychobiology

> SUCCESS The Marshall Center for Intercultural Learning

Wheaton College recognizes that individuals have complex identities formed by biology, society, history and choice. These varied facets shape who we are, form our uniqueness, and contribute to the rich educational community that is Wheaton College. The Marshall Center exists to affirm these unique identities, to build a community that draws from them and to cultivate leaders who will introduce to the world the value of human diversity.

Wheaton College
26 East Main Street
Norton, MA 02766
admission@wheatoncollege.edu
www.wheatoncollege.edu

FAST FACTS

STUDENT PROFILE

# of degree-seeking undergraduates	1,632
% male/female	38/62
% African-American	5
% American Indian or Alaska Native	0
% Asian or Pacific Islander	2
% Hispanic	4
% White	76
% Pell grant recipients	n/a

First-generation and minority alumni Patricia A. King '63, Professor of Law, Medicine, Ethics and Public Policy at Georgetown University; Ruth Ann Stewart '63, Professor of Public Policy, New York University; Derron JR Wallace '07, Posse Scholar and Marshall, Watson, and Fulbright Scholar, Indira Henard '03, President Obama Administration

ACADEMICS

full-time faculty	139
full-time minority faculty	26
student-faculty ratio	11:1
average class size	30
% first-year retention rate	88
% graduation rate (6 years)	75

Popular majors Psychology, History, English, Economics, Biology, Political science

CAMPUS LIFE

% live on campus (% fresh)	93 (99)

Multicultural student clubs and organizations Black Students Association, International Students Association, South Asian Students Association, Asian Student Association, Latino Students Association, Middle Eastern Students Association, Multi-Ethnic

Athletics NCAA Division III, NEWMAC

ADMISSIONS

# of applicants	3,304
% accepted	59
# of first-year students enrolled	424
SAT Critical Reading range	570-680
SAT Math range	560-670
SAT Writing range	n/a
ACT range	27-30
average HS GPA	3.5

Deadlines

early decision	11/1, 1/15
regular decision	1/15
application fee (online)	$55 ($55)
fee waiver for applicants with financial need	yes

COST & AID

tuition	$40,790
room & board	$10,180
total need-based institutional scholarships/grants	$20,988,963
% of students apply for need-based aid	62
% of students receive aid	56
% receiving need-based scholarship or grant aid	53
% receiving aid whose need was fully met	57
average aid package	$31,770
average student loan debt upon graduation	$25,540

Williams College

Williams College
33 Stetson Court
Williamstown, MA 01267
Ph: (413) 597-2211
admission@williams.edu
www.williams.edu

Williams offers the best in a college education. With a committed and accomplished faculty, more than 30 majors, exciting events and student groups and a breathtaking campus, Williams College is a highly ranked liberal arts school regarded as one of the finest in the country. When visiting in 1844, Henry David Thoreau remarked, "It would be no small advantage if every college were thus located at the base of a mountain." Williams, resting in the Berkshires in northwestern Massachusetts, at the foot of Mount Greylock, is a small college with a far-reaching name. Respected and revered by academia, this co-educational school, founded in 1793, has produced 37 Rhodes Scholars, more than any other liberal arts college in the country.

"Williams offers everything a student needs to succeed. From some of the smallest class sizes, to one-on-one tutoring in most classes. Earlier on this semester my professor even pulled an all-nighter with us, helping us study for an exam. Moreover, within my first week at Williams all my professors knew my name. It was amazing to know that they cared about me."

– Maxwell R., '13
New York, NY
Undecided

> ACCESS **Counselor Visitation Program**

Every summer Williams teams up with Middlebury College to bring twenty-five counselors to the two campuses. Counselors spend three days on each campus, exploring the academic, cultural, and social offerings available to students. Time is spent networking with one another and discussing college admission processes with admission counselors, seeking ways to collaborate on improving college access. To inquire about the program, or to nominate yourself or your counselor for the trip, please contact the Office of Admission at 413.597.2214 and ask for the Director of Diversity Recruitment.

> OPPORTUNITY **Windows on Williams (WoW): Student Fly-In Program**

Williams offers low-income and first-generation prospective students a three-day, all expenses paid trip to the college. Participants are able to sit in on classes, meet professors and current students, and try Williams on for size. Applications for this program are available at the beginning of each summer.

> SUCCESS **Summer Science / Summer Humanities and Social Sciences**

About 150 students participate in Summer Science and Summer Humanities and Social Sciences at Williams, special orientation programs during the month of July. Priority for admission is given to first-generation students. Participants take four courses and engage in research, allowing for an academically enriching experience that familiarizes students with campus life before the fall semester.

> SUCCESS **BRIDGES**

BRIDGES is a mid-orientation diversity program to introduce new students to alumni, faculty, and staff that will guide them toward all available resources. Through enlightening workshops and discussions, examining the Berkshire's heritage, interfacing with key college administrators, community dinners, visits to nearby towns and one-on-ones with talented college seniors, meaningful connections are inevitable.

> SUCCESS **Williams Community Building Program**

The Multicultural Center at Williams College provides students with a social and academic center on campus. A diverse community is supported through cultural programs, clubs and events. Through speakers, student group meetings, and other activities, over 200 multicultural events are sponsored at Williams.

FAST FACTS

STUDENT PROFILE

# of degree-seeking undergraduates	1,997
% male/female	50/50
% African American	10
% American Indian or Alaska Native	<1
% Asian or Pacific Islander	11
% Hispanic	9
% White	61
% International	7
% Pell grant recipients	13.3

First-generation and minority alumni Mayda del Valle '00, youngest-ever winner, National Poetry Slam Contest, voted one of 37 young innovators by Smithsonian magazine in 2007; Aaron Jenkins, former legislative aide for U.S. Senator John Kerry, now a director of educational access in Washington DC.

ACADEMICS

full-time faculty	267
full-time minority faculty	50
student-faculty ratio	7:1
average class size	15
% first-year retention rate	97
% graduation rate (6 years)	96

Popular majors Art/Art Studies, Economics, Political Science, Psychology, Research Sciences

CAMPUS LIFE

% live on campus (% fresh.)	96 (100)

Multicultural student clubs and organizations Asian American Students in Action, South Asian Student Organization, Chinese American Student Organization, Koreans of Williams, Students of Mixed Heritage, VISTA (Latino/a Student Organization), Williams Black Student Union, Minority Coalition

Athletics NCAA Division III, New England Small College Athletic Conference

ADMISSIONS

# of applicants	6,633
% accepted	18
# of first-year students enrolled	550
SAT Critical Reading range	660-760
SAT Math range	660-760
SAT Writing range	n/a
ACT range	29-33
average HS GPA	n/a

Deadlines

early decision	11/10
regular decision	1/1
application fee (online)	$60 ($60)
fee waiver for applicants with financial need	yes

COST & AID

tuition	$41,190
room & board	$10,906
total need-based institutional scholarships/grants	$32,372,041
% of students apply for need-based aid	57
% of students receive aid	100
% receiving need-based scholarship or grant aid	100
% receiving aid whose need was fully met	100
average aid package	$37,857
average student loan debt upon graduation	$9,214

Kalamazoo College

Kalamazoo College Office of Admission
1200 Academy Street
Kalamazoo, MI 49006
Ph: (800) 253-3602 / (269) 337-7166
admission@kzoo.edu
www.kzoo.edu

Kalamazoo College is a small, private, selective, four-year liberal arts college located in southwest Michigan. Kalamazoo prides itself on being internationally oriented — the college seeks talented students from diverse backgrounds and students are introduced to global perspectives and intercultural awareness in all programs of study. The college's commitment to on-campus diversity includes several minority and first-generation endowed scholarships and travel subsidies for potential low-income students and their families to visit the school. Kalamazoo's dedication to students' individual needs and success is evident through the unique First Year Experience program, renowned as one of the nation's leading first-year programs.

> ACCESS College Advising

Kalamazoo College sponsors a college advising program for local Hispanic ESL students in Kalamazoo's public middle and high schools. The College Advising Program encourages ESL students to explore the possibilities of higher education and assists them with the college application process. The program is run by staff members from the college's enrollment division.

> ACCESS Sisters in Science

Kalamazoo's female science majors partner with local middle school girls to encourage science learning and exploration through the Sisters in Science program. Sisters in Science also encourages high school girls to pursue science degrees through higher education.

> OPPORTUNITY John T. Williamson Scholarship

The John T. Williamson Scholarship is awarded to competitive applicants of Kalamazoo College who are African American or Hispanic.

> OPPORTUNITY William Randolph Hearst Endowed Scholarship

Kalamazoo's Hearst Foundation Scholarship was established by the Hearst Foundation to award scholarships annually to two first-generation students at the college.

> SUCCESS First Year Experience

The award-winning First Year Experience program at Kalamazoo intertwines hands-on activity, experiential learning and mentorship within the context of rigorous undergraduate academics. First Year Experience fosters academic success, intercultural understanding and balance through First Year Seminars, First Year Forums, Academic Advising and Peer Leaders. Peer Leaders are carefully selected student-mentors that are trained to share knowledge and experiences with first-year students at the college. First Year Forums are special programs in the form of dramatic presentations, interactive learning sessions and structured conversations that focus on the goals of the First Year Experience program. They help first-year students successfully continue academic and personal growth at Kalamazoo.

FAST FACTS

STUDENT PROFILE
# of degree-seeking undergraduates	1,387
% male/female	43/57
% African-American	4
% American Indian or Alaska Native	<1
% Asian or Pacific Islander	6
% Hispanic	3
% Pell grant recipients	13

ACADEMICS
full-time faculty	92
full-time minority faculty	17
student-faculty ratio	13:1
average class size	n/a
% first-year retention rate	92
% graduation rate (6 years)	76

Popular majors Economics/Business, Psychology, Biology

CAMPUS LIFE
% live on campus (% freshmen)	78 (100)

Multicultural student clubs and organizations
Asian-American Student Organization, Black Student Organization, Cultural Awareness Troupe, International Student Organization, Jewish Student Organization, Latino Student Organization, Hindu Student Organization, Buddhist Group, Muslim Student Association

Athletics NCAA Division III, Michigan Intercollegiate Athletic Association

ADMISSIONS
# of applicants	2,059
% accepted	70
# of first-year students enrolled	364
SAT Critical Reading range	600-710
SAT Math range	590-670
SAT Writing range	580-680
ACT range	26-30
average HS GPA	3.6

Deadlines
early decision	11/20
regular decision	2/1
application fee (online)	$40 ($40)
fee waiver for applicants with financial need	yes

COST & AID
tuition	$32,643
room & board	$7,776
total need-based institutional scholarships/grants	$12,326,110
% of students apply for need-based aid	64
% of students receive aid	100
% receiving need-based scholarship or grant aid	95
% receiving aid whose need was fully met	53.7
average aid package	$24,710
average student loan debt upon graduation	n/a

Michigan State University

Students at Michigan State have a plethora of educational, social and recreational opportunities to choose from — after all, Michigan State is an internationally recognized research institution. The university's academic offerings are particularly extensive and will especially benefit those interested in studying agriculture, agribusiness or any of the many subsets of environmental studies. Michigan State further supports those interested in the farming aspect of these fields, offering certificate programs in both beef and dairy production/management.

> ACCESS High School Summer Programs

Michigan State offers a number of summer programs for high school students interested in furthering their education. For example, the Broad Summer High School Scholars Program in the College of Education targets students entering 11th and 12th grades from Detroit Public Schools, providing them a four-week residential program on the university campus. Other programs, such as the Summer Business Institute and the Multicultural Apprenticeship Program (MAP), offer a more targeted experience, providing students with coursework in the business and math and science areas, respectively.

> ACCESS GEAR UP / College Day Programs and Talent Search

These programs utilize a variety of strategies to educate low-income and first-generation students about the challenges and rewards of a higher education. The program begins with outreach efforts involving program representatives fostering a connection with middle school students, who then participate in campus visits. Students and parents may also take part in the social and academic workshops that are held on campus throughout the year, while other students participate in the Summer Residency Program.

> OPPORTUNITY The Michigan-Louis Stokes Alliance for Minority Participation (MI-LSAMP)

MI-LSAMP is a comprehensive initiative designed to substantially increase the quantity and quality of minority students pursuing baccalaureate degrees and careers in science, technology, engineering and mathematics. This five-year, $5 million initiative is underwritten by the National Science Foundation and four institutions: The University of Michigan (lead institution), Michigan State University, Wayne State University and Western Michigan University.

> OPPORTUNITY College Assistance Migrant Program (CAMP)

CAMP is an educational program designed to assist migrant and/or seasonal farm-worker students in their first-year transition to the university. The program is a collaboration of campus faculty, student services and community-based agencies meant to improve educational opportunities. Services include assistance in the admission and financial aid processes, help securing on-campus housing, assistance in developing a support system for academic success, tutorial assistance and limited supplemental financial assistance.

> SUCCESS Office of Supportive Services (OSS) / College Achievement Admissions Program (CAAP)

Under the auspices of the Office of Supportive Services, Michigan State offers CAAP, which allows low-income and first generation students and students with disabilities who have the potential, but not the prerequisite background, to gain admittance to Michigan State. As a condition of their acceptance, CAAP students must enroll in particular seminars and tutorials, as well as meet with an OSS academic specialist. The OSS also provides academic advising, social counseling, personal planning, career guidance and skill enrichment seminars.

> SUCCESS Office of Cultural and Academic Transitions (OCAT)

OCAT is designed to connect diverse peoples, programs and ideas to enhance student success. The office helps students to better understand themselves and others through cultural and social activities. OCAT strives to bring together individuals as well as groups of students from diverse racial, ethnic, international and domestic backgrounds for meaningful interaction. The Transition and Cultural Aide Program fosters a connection for students living in residence halls.

Michigan State University
250 Administration Building
East Lansing, MI 48824
Ph: (517) 355-8332
admis@msu.edu
www.msu.edu

F A S T   F A C T S

STUDENT PROFILE
# of degree-seeking undergraduates	36,337
% male/female	46/54
% African-American	8.3
% American Indian or Alaska Native	< 1
% Asian or Pacific Islander	5.1
% Hispanic	2.9
% White	75.7
% International	6
% Pell grant recipients	19.2

First-generation and minority alumni Dr. Akhtar Hameed Khan, social scientist; George Ryoichi Ariyoshi, former governor, Hawaii; Adnan Badran, former prime minister, Jordan; Dee Dee Bridgewater, jazz singer; Areeya Chumsai, Miss Thailand

ACADEMICS
full-time faculty	2,616
full-time minority faculty	22
student-faculty ratio	16:1
average class size	20-29
% first-year retention rate	91
% graduation rate (6 years)	74.0

Popular majors Business Administration/ Management, Communications Studies/Speech Communication and Rhetoric

CAMPUS LIFE
% live on campus (% freshmen)	42 (95)

Multicultural student clubs and organizations African Students Union, American Indian Science and Engineering Society (AISES), Association of Vietnamese Scholars and Students, Baha'i Association, Brazilian Community Association, Brothers of the Struggle, Caribbean Student Association, Chaldean American Student Association, Chicanos/Latinos in Health Education, Chinese Students and Scholars Association, Coalition of Indian Undergraduate Students, Delta Xi Phi Multicultural Sorority, Hausa Cultural Society, and many more

Athletics NCAA Division I, Big Ten Conference

ADMISSIONS
# of applicants	25,589
% accepted	70
# of first-year students enrolled	9,417
SAT Critical Reading range	480-620
SAT Math range	540-660
SAT Writing range	480-610
ACT range	23-27
average HS GPA	3.61

Deadlines
regular admission	rolling
application fee (online)	$35
fee waiver for applicants with financial need	yes

COST & AID
tuition	in-state: $11,434; out-of-state: $27,832
room & board	$8,044
total need-based institutional scholarships/grants	n/a
% of students apply for need-based aid	71.2
% of students receive aid	99.2
% receiving need-based scholarship or grant aid	52.7
% receiving aid whose need was fully met	28.5
average aid package	$10,789
average student loan debt upon graduation	$17,347

Augsburg College

Augsburg College
Office of Undergraduate Admission
2211 Riverside Avenue
Minneapolis, MN 55454
Ph: (800) 788-5678 / (612) 330-1001
admissions@augsburg.edu
www.augsburg.edu

Augsburg College is a private, co-educational, liberal arts college affiliated with the Lutheran church. Nurturing future leaders in service to the world, Augsburg provides high-quality education opportunities that are shaped by the faith and values of the Christian church. Founded in 1869, Augsburg College is committed to preparing students for service in community and church and providing a core liberal arts education with a practical dimension in order to send out productive, creative and successful citizens.

"Augsburg is where you leave the nest, step off the branch, and attempt to soar. If you happen to fall, there are so many people here to catch you and encourage to keep going. Never give up until you succeed!"
– Sama S. '08
Osseo, MN
Business

> ACCESS College Goal Sunday

To help low-income students in the college application process, Augsburg College sponsors a College Goal Sunday site. College Goal Sunday is a national one-day event that provides free information and assistance to families who are filling out the Free Application for Federal Student Aid (FAFSA).

> ACCESS Girls in Engineering, Math and Science Summer Program

To give young urban women a greater understanding of complex problem solving while learning and using technology, science and mathematics, Augsburg College sponsors the Girls in Engineering, Math and Science Summer (GEMS) Program. Each summer, the program brings together 120 middle school girls from the Minneapolis Public Schools to learn about monarch butterfly research, to develop robots and program them to do various tasks using Lego-Logo and to create and developing e-musik.

> OPPORTUNITY Scholastic Connections Scholarship

Augsburg College's Scholastic Connections Scholarship is a unique scholarship program designed to assist high-achieving multicultural students reach their goal of succeeding as students at Augsburg. The program uses proceeds from a $500,000 endowment to pair multicultural students and alumni in mentoring relationships. Scholastic Connections recipients receive $5,000 scholarships.

> OPPORTUNITY Augsburg College Achievement Program (ACAP)

With a goal of helping underserved students afford their college education, Augsburg sponsors the Augsburg College Achievement Program. The program recognizes students who have participated in college-readiness programs such as TRIO, MMEP, Admission Possible and AVID by providing additional financial support. ACAP recipients receive a $4,500 grant per year for four years.

> SUCCESS TRIO/Student Support Services

TRIO/Student Support Services is a government-funded, Augsburg College-sponsored program whose objective is to help students overcome class, social and cultural barriers to complete their college education. With a goal of increasing the retention and graduation rates of low-income and first-generation Augsburg students, TRIO/Student Support Services students may receive assistance in individual academic work plans, study skills development, computer skills assistance, financial aid workshops, budget-management skills, career exploration, cultural enrichment and stress management.

FAST FACTS

STUDENT PROFILE

# of degree-seeking undergraduates	3,049
% male/female	50/50
% African-American	6
% American Indian or Alaska Native	2
% Asian or Pacific Islander	5
% Hispanic	3
% Pell grant recipients	22

First-generation and minority alumni Devean George, professional basketball player

ACADEMICS

full-time faculty	188
full-time minority faculty	n/a
student-faculty ratio	15:1
average class size	15
% first-year retention rate	80
% graduation rate (6 years)	58

Popular majors Business Administration, Elementary Education, Biology, Psychology, English

CAMPUS LIFE

% live on campus (% fresh.)	55 (90)

Multicultural student clubs and organizations Augsburg Asian Student Association, Muslim Student Association, Pan Afrikan Student Association, Augsburg Indigenous Student Association, Allies

Athletics NCAA Division III, Minnesota Intercollegiate Athletic Conference

ADMISSIONS

# of applicants	1,924
% accepted	56
# of first-year students enrolled	644
SAT Critical Reading range	510-640
SAT Math range	500-640
SAT Writing range	480-600
ACT range	20-25
average HS GPA	3.27

Deadlines

regular decision	rolling
application fee (online)	$25 ($25)
fee waiver for applicants with financial need	yes

COST & AID

tuition	$27,628
room & board	$7,514
total need-based institutional scholarships/grants	n/a
% of students apply for need-based aid	91
% of students receive aid	77
% receiving need-based scholarship or grant aid	88
% receiving aid whose need was fully met	15
average aid package	$17,449
average student loan debt upon graduation	$25,155

Carleton College

Carleton College
One North College Street
Northfield, MN 55057
Ph: (507) 222-4190
admissions@carleton.edu
www.carleton.edu

Founded in 1866, Carleton College is a small, co-educational, non-denominational, private liberal arts college. Best known for its academic excellence and warm, welcoming campus community, Carleton College is committed to challenging students to learn broadly and think deeply. Instead of training for one narrow career path, Carleton students develop the knowledge and skills to succeed in any walk of life. A community that fosters diversity of thought and an open exchange of ideas can only emerge from the participation of individuals with different backgrounds and worldviews. Toward this end, Carleton embraces diversity, educating talented and diverse students and acknowledging a strong commitment to underrepresented groups.

> ACCESS **Northfield Reads and Counts**

Northfield Reads and Counts is part of Carleton College's Community Work Study. This program offers Carleton College students the opportunity to earn work-study awards off-campus performing jobs in the community's interest. Northfield Reads and Counts is a local implementation of two national educational initiatives (America Reads and America Counts) that involves community members in helping children — from kindergarten through high school — develop critical reading and mathematics skills. For two decades, Carleton has had a federally sponsored TRIO-Student Support Services program that provides assistance to both first-generation and low-income enrolled students. This student support service program serves up to 100 students and complements the support efforts of Carleton's Office of Intercultural Life.

> OPPORTUNITY **Carleton Access Scholarship**

The Carleton Access Scholarship program is a Carleton College program of assistance targeted towards needy students. The Access Scholarship is awarded to reduce the loan debt that often becomes a financial obstacle in a student's pursuit of learning or career path. Students from families with an income level less than $40,000 are eligible for a renewable $4,000 Access Scholarship, while students from families with an income level less than $60,000 are eligible for $3,000 and students from families with an income level less than $75,000 receive $2,000. Students receiving a $4,000 Access Scholarship will likely have their total indebtedness reduced by about 70 percent when they graduate, $3,000 scholarship recipients can expect a reduction of 50 percent and $2,000 Access Scholarship recipients see a reduction of 33 percent.

> OPPORTUNITY **Posse Foundation**

Carleton College participates in the Posse Foundation, a program that brings talented inner-city youth to campus to pursue their academics and to help promote cross-cultural communication. Posse students are nominated by their high school to the program and share a collaborative support system with a special mentor to adjust to campus and college life. Carleton's Posse Scholars hail from Chicago.

> SUCCESS **Intercultural Peer Leader (IPL) Program**

Carleton College's Intercultural Peer Leader Program offers a variety of services to address the academic, cultural and professional development of students of color at Carleton. Intercultural Peer Leaders are sophomores, juniors and seniors who have done well academically, are active in the Carleton community and are enthusiastic about meeting and assisting new students, sharing with them their knowledge and experience. IPLs also plan programs and activities for the community as a whole. Intercultural Peer Leaders offer first-year students a personal perspective on the experience of living, growing and succeeding in a community that encourages diversity and individual differences and have often served as friends and mentors.

FAST FACTS

STUDENT PROFILE
# of degree-seeking undergraduates	1,975
% male/female	48/52
% African-American	5
% American Indian or Alaska Native	<1
% Asian or Pacific Islander	10
% Hispanic	5
% White	73
% International	6
% Pell grant recipients	11

First-generation and minority alumni Walter Alvarez, geologist; Masanori Mark Christianson, musician/art director

ACADEMICS
full-time faculty	215
full-time minority faculty	46
student-faculty ratio	9:1
average class size	18
% first-year retention rate	95
% graduation rate (6 years)	93

Popular majors Biology, English, Political Science

CAMPUS LIFE
% live on campus (% fresh.)	90 (100)

Multicultural student clubs and organizations
Carleton African Students Association, Coalition of Women of Color, Latin American Students Organization, Phase 2, Men of Color, Middle Eastern Society and Politics, Minority Students Prehealth Coalition, Pangea, American Native Peoples Organization, A.S.I.A, Coalition of Hmong Students, D.E.S.I., Korean Students in America, Vietnamese Student Association, Black Students Alliance, Club Caribe
Athletics NCAA Division III, Minnesota Intercollegiate Athletic Conference

ADMISSIONS
# of applicants	4,956
% accepted	27
# of first-year students enrolled	490
SAT Critical Reading range	660-750
SAT Math range	650-740
SAT Writing range	650-750
ACT range	29-33
average HS GPA	3.29

Deadlines
early decision application	11/15
regular admission	1/15
application fee (online)	$30 ($30)
fee waiver for applicants with financial need	yes

COST & AID
tuition	$34,272
room & board	$9,796
total need-based institutional scholarships/grants	$26,349,565
% of students apply for need-based aid	87
% of students receive aid	63
% receiving need-based scholarship or grant aid	55
% receiving aid whose need was fully met	63
average aid package	$32,132
average student loan debt upon graduation	$20,083

College of Saint Benedict and Saint John's University

The College of Saint Benedict (CSB) for women and Saint John's University (SJU) for men are two nationally-leading liberal arts colleges whose partnership offers students the educational options of a large university and the individual attention of a premier small college. Ranked among the top undergraduate colleges for the number of students who study abroad, the two colleges enroll nearly 250 international students, and offer more than 200 courses with a global focus. Students from both colleges attend classes and activities together and have access to the libraries and athletic facilities on both campuses. With 15 miles of hiking trails, a private beach, and a walking path between campuses, the College of Saint Benedict and Saint John's University are near the St. Cloud metropolitan area in central Minnesota, an hour from Minneapolis and St. Paul.

> ACCESS Upward Bound

Local high school students who come from low-income families in which neither parent holds a bachelor's degree can benefit from the College of Saint Benedict and Saint John's University's Upward Bound, a pre-college program that provides a group of students with the right tools to pursue their goal of earning a college degree. Students benefit from weekly tutoring, field trips, workshops, and a six-week summer enrichment program at the College of Saint Benedict and Saint John's University.

> *"I have developed the confidence, energy, and love that I-LEAD promotes every time I talk to a staff member, lead a seminar or ask for help with questions. I will remember I-LEAD for the amount of time and knowledge that has helped me and other students succeed in college."*
>
> *– Virigina O., '10*
> *St. Paul, MN*
> *English, Secondary Education*

> ACCESS Fast Forward Youth Program

College of Saint Benedict and Saint John's University College Mentors and staff help underrepresented high school students to prepare for college. Participants practice the ACT, visit colleges, fill out applications, navigate the financial aid process, and successfully complete high school course work.

> OPPORTUNITY Diversity Leadership Scholarships

A four-year renewable scholarship for up to $5,000 for students who have demonstrated leadership and service in the area of cultural and ethnic diversity.

> OPPORTUNITY Twin Cities Bus Trips

Designed for prospective students from Minnesota's Twin Cities high schools, the program arranges complimentary bus trips to the two colleges to attend special events and learn more about the campuses.

> OPPORTUNITY National Fly-Ins

The College of Saint Benedict and Saint John's University pay up to half of the travel costs for prospective students outside of Minnesota and arranges a three-day campus experience for them along with their fellow prospective students.

> SUCCESS Intercultural Leadership, Education and Development (I-LEAD) Fellowship Program

First-generation college students receive financial and educational support to build on the leadership skills they already demonstrate. These college student leaders attend national and international leadership conferences and promote ideals of equality, diversity and civic leadership.

> SUCCESS Retreat on Race and Ethnicity (RORE)

This three day retreat sponsored by the Intercultural Center creates a safe atmosphere for intercultural dialogue. Participants engage in discussion and activities that highlight the realities of racism, privilege and bigotry.

College of Saint Benedict and Saint John's University
PO Box 7155
Collegeville, MN 56321
Ph: (320) 363-2196
admissions@csbsju.edu
www.csbsju.edu

F A S T   F A C T S

STUDENT PROFILE
# of degree-seeking undergraduates	4,048
% male/female	52/48
% African-American	1
% American Indian or Alaska Native	<1
% Asian or Pacific Islander	3
% Hispanic	2
% White	88
% International	6
% Pell grant recipients	17

ACADEMICS
full-time faculty	300
full-time minority faculty	25
student-faculty ratio	12:1
average class size	20
% first-year retention rate	90
% graduation rate (6 years)	84

Popular majors Business Management, Communication, Biology, Nursing, Psychology

CAMPUS LIFE
% live on campus	up to 95

Multicultural student clubs and organizations
Asia Club, Cultural Fusion, Archipeligo Association, Kaliente (Latino/a Student Club), International Affairs Club

Athletics NCAA Division III, Minnesota Intercollegiate Athletic Conference (MIAC)

ADMISSIONS
# of applicants	2,894
% accepted	80
# of first-year students enrolled	980
SAT Critical Reading range	493-655
SAT Math range	529-658
SAT Writing range	n/a
ACT range	23-28
average HS GPA	3.67

Deadlines
regular decision	rolling
application fee (online)	$0 ($0)

COST & AID
tuition	$29,388
room & board	$8,036
total need-based institutional scholarships/ grants	$31,600,000
% of students apply for need-based aid	71
% receiving need-based scholarship or grant aid	61
% receiving aid whose need was fully met	42
average aid package	$22,820
average student loan debt upon graduation	85

Millsaps College

Founded in 1890, Millsaps College is dedicated to undergraduate teaching and is praised by the *Fiske Guide to Colleges* for "its focus on scholarly inquiry, spiritual growth, and community service." Located in Jackson, Mississippi, Millsaps is home to 1,200 students and offers undergraduate degrees in 34 subjects. Once on campus, students join a close-knit community with opportunities to become involved in more than 85 clubs, intramural sports, campus ministries, student government, and student publications. Athletes successfully compete in 18 men's and women's NCAA Division III sports. Millsaps College is one of only 40 colleges from across the country included in *Colleges That Change Lives* and is included in the 2008 edition of the Princeton Review's *America's Best Value Colleges*. Through Millsaps' aggressive scholarships program, more than 90 percent of students receive some financial aid.

> ACCESS 1 Campus, 1 Community Program

The Millsaps College 1 Campus, 1 Community program enhances higher education opportunities for first-generation and underserved K-12 students in the Jackson community. Working in partnership with local public schools and nearby North Midtown, the college hosts youth for a range of events including sports camps, arts and enrichment events, and an annual block party attended by many Millsaps faculty, staff, alumni and their children, as well as North Midtown children and families. The block party includes music, food, health screenings, face painting and other games and activities, allowing students to familiarize themselves with the Millsaps campus and environment. In addition, Millsaps students work in local public schools, which are 96 percent African American and majority low income, through diverse service-learning projects in conjunction with Millsaps academic courses and through a broad array of volunteer activities such as judging book fair projects, serving as literacy mentors, staffing after-school programs, and raising money for school uniforms and supplies.

"The Multicultural Association Diversity Club is an organization that encourages and promotes multiculturalism and cultural awareness throughout Millsaps College and the Jackson community through group discussions, films, cultural displays, and special programs. The members put a lot of effort in emphasizes the importance of friendship, unity, and respect –especially needed in modern times."

– Wrijoya R., '12
Columbus, MS

> OPPORTUNITY Open Door Days

Millsaps College's Open Door Days visit program provides a full day at Millsaps for prospective high school students, transfer students, and their families. Offered throughout the year, the program encourages students to explore the college's academic programs and learn about the wide range of student services and campus activities offered. Participants are invited to attend classes, tour campus, speak with faculty, enjoy lunch in the cafeteria and hear more about the scholarship and financial aid application process.

> SUCCESS Millsaps College Advising and Mentoring Program (M-CAMP)

Each student is assigned a faculty adviser as part of the Millsaps College Advising and Mentoring Program. First-year students meet several times per semester with their M-CAMP adviser, who also serves as one of their first-semester classroom teachers. Students are advised individually and also in groups of five to seven peers. The M-CAMP curriculum invites students to embrace their own socio-cultural heritage as an important and valued source of identity formation and vocational wisdom.

Millsaps College
Office of Admissions
1701 North State Street
Jackson, MS 39210
Ph: (601) 974-1050
admissions@millsaps.edu
www.millsaps.edu

FAST FACTS

STUDENT PROFILE

# of degree-seeking undergraduates	999
% male/female	49/51
% African American	11
% American Indian or Alaska Native	<1
% Asian or Pacific Islander	4
% Hispanic	2
% White	80
% International	1
% Pell grant recipients	22.6

First-generation and minority alumni Randall Pinkston, news correspondent; Cassandra Wilson, jazz singer; Manisha Sethi, pediatrician; Casey Parks, journalist; James Graves, justice, Mississippi Supreme Court

ACADEMICS

full-time faculty	97
full-time minority faculty	10
student-faculty ratio	10:1
average class size	15
% first-year retention rate	79
% graduation rate (6 years)	68

Popular majors Business Administration, Psychology, English

CAMPUS LIFE

Multicultural student clubs and organizations
Black Student Association, Future Black Law Students Association, International Students Association, Millsaps International Buddy System, Millsaps Multicultural Association, Mississippi Masala, Multicultural Association Diversity Group, Multicultural Culinary Club

Athletics NCAA Division III, Southern Collegiate Athletic Conference

ADMISSIONS

# of applicants	1,266
% accepted	77
# of first-year students enrolled	271
SAT Critical Reading range	538-673
SAT Math range	538-650
ACT range	23-29
average HS GPA	3.46

Deadlines

early action	1/8
regular decision	rolling
application fee (online)	$0 ($0)

COST & AID

tuition	$24,608
room & board	$9,252
total need-based institutional scholarships/grants	$7,994,145
% of students apply for need-based aid	68
% of students receive aid	100
% receiving need-based scholarship or grant aid	99
% receiving aid whose need was fully met	35
average aid package	$22,707
average student loan debt upon graduation	$17,175

Mississippi State University

Mississippi State University is a public, land-grant, co-educational university that provides access and opportunity to students from all sectors of Mississippi's diverse population. The university offers excellent and extensive programs in teaching, research and outreach that improve the lives and opportunities of the citizens of the state, region and world. Mississippi State maintains its tradition as the "People's University" by offering integrated programs in learning, research, and service; traditional scholarship; statewide extension and outreach; and engagement with business, industry, government, communities and organizations. *Forbes* has ranked Mississippi State among the top 20 of its top 100 best college buys in America, and *Kiplinger's Personal Finance* ranked Mississippi State among the "100 Best Values in Public Colleges."

> OPPORTUNITY **Mississippi State Promise Program**

In fulfilling Mississippi State's traditional role as the "People's University" and in keeping with the needs of Mississippi, the Mississippi State Promise Program combines access and excellence. The Promise Program helps support low-income students (either entering freshmen or community college transfer students) in their matriculation at Mississippi State University. Tuition and fees are paid with grants, scholarships and waivers. In addition, the program provides on-campus work opportunities to help offset other non-tuition costs.

> OPPORTUNITY **Minority Student Achievement Day/Fall Showcase Day**

The Minority Student Achievement Day provides an opportunity to visit the Mississippi State University campus for minority scholars and their parents. Invitations to the annual event are sent to high school seniors who have scored well on the ACT and SAT or who have been nominated by school counselors. Activities include campus tours, a general assembly and opportunities to visit with academic advisers.

> SUCCESS **Summer Bridge Program**

Mississippi State University uses the Summer Bridge Program to help incoming freshmen students adjust to university life. Incoming freshmen will be selected to participate from the following areas of study: Science, Including Agricultural Sciences, Biological Sciences, Chemistry, and Physics; Mathematics; Engineering, Including Computer Sciences; and Technology.

> SUCCESS **IMAGE**

Mississippi State University is home to the Increasing Minority Access to Graduate Education (IMAGE) Program. Bringing together all levels of students through financial support and mentoring, IMAGE provides partial scholarships for eligible minority students in the SME (science, mathematics, and engineering) curricula. Each participant is assigned to an upperclassman mentor before they attend the freshman orientation.

> SUCCESS **The Holmes Cultural Diversity Center**

The Holes Cultural Diversity Center enhances the college experience of culturally diverse students at Mississippi State University. The Center encourages the development of a climate within which all cultures are appreciated as valued members of the campus community. Specific endeavors include cultural diversity workshops, seminars, classroom lectures, problem-solving assistance, scholarship resources and employment opportunities. The Holmes Center is essential in recruiting and retaining multicultural students and in creating a college experience that is productive and successful for all.

"As a first-generation student from a low-income area, Mississippi State University has granted me so many opportunities. Not only was I able to obtain a degree in Political Science, I was a member of several student led organizations such as, Stennis Montgomery Association, Pre-Law Society, IMAGE, and Alpha Kappa Alpha. MSU has given so much to me that I am now giving back to it as a student recruiter informing students of my undergraduate experiences that I believe can impact the lives of others.

– Chara S. '08
Macon, MS
Political Science

Mississippi State University
Office of Admissions and Scholarships
P.O. Box 6334
25 Old Main, 101 Montgomery Hall
Mississippi State, MS 39762-6334
Ph: (662) 325-2224
admit@msstate.edu
www.admissions.msstate.edu

F A S T   F A C T S

STUDENT PROFILE
# of degree-seeking undergraduates	14,602
% male/female	52/48
% African-American	19
% American Indian or Alaska Native	<1
% Asian or Pacific Islander	1
% Hispanic	1
% White	70
% International	2
% Pell grant recipients	31

First-generation and minority alumni Rafael Palmeiro, professional baseball player; Eric Dampier, professional basketball player; Lawrence Roberts, professional basketball player; Jerome Keys, professional football player

ACADEMICS
full-time faculty	844
full-time minority faculty	114
student-faculty ratio	18:1
average class size	n/a
% first-year retention rate	82
% graduation rate (6 years)	60

Popular majors Biological Science, Communications, Marketing, Education, Engineering

CAMPUS LIFE
% live on campus (% freshmen)	n/a

Multicultural student clubs and organizations African Students Association, Japanese Club, Korean Student Association, NAACP, Native American Association, Pakistani Student Association, Sri Lankan Association, Taiwan Student Association, Thai Students and Scholars Association, Vietnamese Students Association, Association of Chinese Students and Scholars, Black Student Alliance, Chinese Student Association, Graduate Minority Council, Hispanic Student Association, Indian Student Association, Minorities in Agriculture, Natural Resources and Related Sciences

Athletics NCAA Division I, Southeastern Conference

ADMISSIONS
# of applicants	7,839
% accepted	65
# of first-year students enrolled	1,238
SAT Critical Reading range	470-610
SAT Math range	490-640
SAT Writing range	n/a
ACT range	20-27
average HS GPA	3.17

Deadlines
regular decision	rolling
application fee	$35
fee waiver for applicants with financial need	yes

COST & AID
tuition in-state: $5,151; out-of-state: $13,021	
room & board	$7,520
total need-based institutional scholarships/grants	$35,994,809
% of students apply for need-based aid	65
% receiving need-based scholarship or grant aid	49
% receiving aid whose need was fully met	25
average aid package	$4,475
average student loan debt upon graduation	$23,413

Lincoln University

Lincoln University is a historically black, public, comprehensive institution, founded in 1866 by the soldiers of the 62nd and 65th United States Colored Infantries at the close of the Civil War, and enrolls over 3,200 students from 36 states and over 30 countries. Set upon nearly 160 acres in the state capital of Missouri, Jefferson City, it offers services to a diverse body of traditional and non-traditional students with a broad range of academic preparation and skills. Lincoln offers seven undergraduate degrees in more than 50 areas of study and graduate programs in selected disciplines that prepare students for citizenship and leadership in the global community. Alumni can be found in all corners of the globe, serving communities, regions and nations of the world.

> OPPORTUNITY **Open Houses**

The Office of Admissions and Recruitment hosts Open House events for prospective students, one held in the fall and another in spring. These events allow future Lincolnites to get an up-close look at campus, as well as to meet and interact with administrators, faculty, staff, students and alumni. Each event allows the student to become an instant Blue Tiger – on-site admissions is offered to those students who come with a completed application, ACT or SAT test scores and their official high school transcript.

"The faculty and staff at Lincoln are great. I have had the privilege of getting to know many of them and each one wants to see students succeed. Each professor that I have encountered at Lincoln has a strong grasp on their specific field and a diverse background in many others."

– Alexander E., '11
Chicago, IL
Wellness

> SUCCESS **Lincoln Educational Access Program (LEAP)**

LEAP is designed to strengthen the first-year experience at Lincoln University of Missouri by providing students with tools necessary to persist and succeed in college. This is a rigorous program, and is designed to assist students both academically and socially by providing access to one-on-one tutoring, academic advising and peer leaders.

> SUCCESS **Learning Communities**

Learning Communities provide students with an opportunity to enroll in three common courses with peers who share similar interests. This group setting allows students the opportunity to get to know their professors and classmates better, attend out-of-class programs, learn about resources at Lincoln University and get involved with the campus community. Each Learning Community has a Peer Leader to guide the students throughout these courses.

> SUCCESS **Center for Academic Enrichment (CAE)**

The Center for Academic Enrichment provides tutorial assistance in writing and mathematics and coordinates the Supplemental Instruction (SI) program, which gives students in difficult courses an opportunity to study with a group of students from the same class. Students who participate in these study sessions generally earn higher course grades.

> SUCCESS **Student Support Services (SSS)**

Student Support Services provide tools and programs to help students to stay in college until they earn a degree. Tutoring, counseling, and remedial instruction are among services offered to first-generation, low-income students. Weekly workshops are held to aid students in adjusting to campus life, with the purpose of cultivating study and life skills, as well as self-sufficiency.

Lincoln University
Office of Admission and Recruitment
820 Chestnut St., B7 Young Hall
Jefferson City, MO 65101
Ph: (573) 681-5599
enroll@lincolnu.edu
www.lincolnu.edu

F A S T   F A C T S

STUDENT PROFILE
# of degree-seeking undergraduates	3,116
% male/female	40/60
% African-American	38
% American Indian or Alaska Native	1
% Asian or Pacific Islander	1
% Hispanic	2
% White	54
% International	4
% Pell grant recipients	57

First-generation and minority alumni Wendell Oliver Pruitt, Tuskegee Airman, recipient of Congressional Gold Medal for service to his country, George Howard, Jr., first African-American to serve as a judge on the Arkansas Court of Appeals, the Arkansas Supreme Court and the Federal District Court in Arkansas; Lemar Parrish, Eight-Time NFL Pro Bowler; Dr. Edward A. Rankin, first African-American president of the American Academy of Orthopaedic Surgeons; Dr. James Frank, first African-American to serve as President of the NCAA, former President of Lincoln University

ACADEMICS
full-time faculty	120
full-time minority faculty	38
student-faculty ratio	15:1
average class size	10-19
% first-year retention rate	52
% graduation rate (6 years)	26

Popular majors Nursing Science, Criminal Justice, Business Administration, Elementary Education, Psychology

CAMPUS LIFE
% live on campus (% fresh.)	31(59)

Multicultural student clubs and organizations Community Connection of Lincoln University, International Student Association, Orientation Leader Board, Lincoln University NAACP, Impact Movement
Athletics NCAA Division II, Mid-America Intercollegiate Athletic Association (MIAA)

ADMISSIONS
# of applicants	2,485
% accepted	95
# of first-year students enrolled	745
SAT Critical Reading range	380-430
SAT Math range	390-460
SAT Writing range	n/a
ACT range	14-23
average HS GPA	2.62

Deadlines
regular decision	rolling to 7/15
application fee (online)	$20 ($20)
fee waiver for applicants with financial need	no

COST & AID
tuition	in-state $5,505; out-of-state $10,065
room & board	$4,590
total need-based institutional scholarships/grants	$1,266,674
% of students apply for need-based aid	66
% of students receive aid	100
% receiving need-based scholarship or grant aid	71
% receiving aid whose need was fully met	15
average aid package	$8,652
average student loan debt upon graduation	$21,255

Park University

Park University prides itself on a tradition of keeping a private education affordable and within reach of a wide range of students. What distinguishes a private education? Start with access to world-class faculty and learning environments. Small class sizes, new classroom technology, and routine faculty contact support academic excellence. Park combines the best of a liberal arts approach with an emphasis on clear professional paths. Students develop the habits they'll need to think critically, communicate effectively and engage others. Students are surrounded with experienced teachers, mentors and advisors. Students will graduate with more than just a degree. They will go forward with new knowledge and confidence, an abiding sense of purpose and the highest ethical standards. Park's well-balanced liberal arts curriculum trains students to see patterns across disciplines; to combine courses in unexpected ways; and to connect what is learned in the classroom with what is experienced in the world.

"I would like to extend my heartfelt thanks to Park University because I will be the first out of four children to be a college graduate, and the first in my family to be able to say to my children that education is key. I have been given an opportunity to excel within the classes that are dedicated to students; I have by the grace of God been given a feel for a family oriented atmosphere. I have been given the chance to be a proud student of Park University."

– Tiffany R., '11
Kansas City, MO
Business Management

> ACCESS **Parkville Campus Visit Days**

The Office of Admissions hosts Campus Visit days throughout the school year. Prospective students can learn about admissions, financial aid, scholarships, campus housing and academic programs from Park faculty, along with taking a tour of campus and meeting current Park University students.

> OPPORTUNITY **Financial Aid**

Staff members within the Office of Student Financial Services work with students to make meeting financial requirements of a college education as simple and affordable as possible. A mix of scholarships, grants and work-study, as well as student and parent loans, are available.

> SUCCESS **Academic Support Center**

The Academic Support Center offers many services to help students with their academic progress. All services are free of charge to Park University students. The mission of the Academic Support Center is to encourage and help students achieve academic excellence during their studies at Park by helping them learn to think critically, communicate effectively and become independent learners in order that they may engage in lifelong learning and better serve a global community. Park has professional and student tutors to help with math, science, foreign language and other subjects. The Academic Support Center offers writing, test preparation, accommodations for students with special needs, computer lab and computer assistance.

> SUCCESS **StepUP**

StepUP is a program operated through the Academic Support Center. The goal of StepUP is to provide the support and services for students to persist, excel and graduate. StepUP provides a social and support network for students who are willing to work consistently toward their academic goals. StepUP students work with a professional mentor who assists them in setting goals, developing talents and making connections with people and services to help them be successful in their quest for a college degree. StepUP is provided at no charge, but space is limited.

Park University
8700 NW River Park Drive
Parkville, MO 64152
Ph: (816) 584-6214
admissions@park.edu
www.park.edu

F A S T   F A C T S

STUDENT PROFILE
# of degree-seeking undergraduates	11,865
% male/female	49/51
% African American	20
% American Indian or Alaska Native	1
% Asian or Pacific Islander	2
% Hispanic	16
% White	57
% International	0.5
% Pell grant recipients	12

First-generation and minority alumni Bob Kendrick, Vice President of Marketing, Negro Leagues Baseball Museum; Anita Flavors Thompson, City Manager, Tallahassee, Fla.; Mary Lou Jaramillo MPA, President/CEO, El Centro, Inc.; Omar Maden, founder and CEO, Maden Technologies, Inc.; Manuchair Ebadi, Ph.D., leader in Parkinson's research; Louis Quijas, MPA, Assistant Director of Office of Law Enforcement Coordination, Federal Bureau of Investigation

ACADEMICS
full-time faculty	152
full-time minority faculty	n/a
student-faculty ratio	12:1
average class size	12
% first-year retention rate	67
% graduation rate (6 years)	39

Popular majors Management, Criminal Justice, Social Psychology, Management/Computer Information Systems, Management/Human Resources

CAMPUS LIFE
% of fresh. live on campus	35

Multicultural student clubs and organizations Milele Kenyan Club, People to People International, World Student Union, Black Student Union; Muslim Student Organization; Model Organization of American States

Athletics NAIA, American Midwest Conference

ADMISSIONS
# of applicants	626
% accepted	76
# of first-year students enrolled	206
SAT Critical Reading range	n/a
SAT Math range	n/a
SAT Writing range	n/a
ACT range	18-28
average HS GPA	3.4
Deadlines	
regular decision	8/1
application fee (online)	$25 ($25)
fee waiver for applicants with financial need	yes

COST & AID
tuition	$298 per credit hour
room & board	$5,850
total need-based institutional scholarships/grants	$17,156
% of students apply for need-based aid	28
% of students receive aid	31
% receiving need-based scholarship or grant aid	12
% receiving aid whose need was fully met	47.75
average aid package	$6,540
average student loan debt upon graduation	$16,996

Truman State University

Truman State University
100 E Normal Ave
Kirksville, MO 63501
Ph: (660) 785-4114
admissions@truman.edu
www.truman.edu

Truman State University is Missouri's premier liberal arts and sciences university and the only highly selective public institution in the state. Truman has established an impeccable reputation in the Midwest and throughout the nation for the high-quality undergraduate programs offered. In fact, for the thirteenth consecutive year, *U.S. News & World Report* has ranked Truman State University as the number one master's level public institution in the Midwest. It is in the University's mission to provide an affordable education and to maintain a student-centered living and learning environment that will attract, nurture, and challenge diverse, outstanding students.

> ACCESS **Upward Bound**

Truman was among the first five institutions in the country to sponsor Upward Bound, a program that assists high school students in building skills and motivation necessary for college success. Upward Bound provides students with academic skill development, tutoring, and college career assistance.

> OPPORTUNITY **Truman Week**

During Truman Week, an orientation period for new students, underrepresented students participate in Directions, a special orientation program designed to help them become acclimated to campus.

"I was attracted to Truman by the potential for individual attention. Many of the other universities I considered had huge class sizes that would not provide the opportunity to get to know and build relationships with professors. Truman definitely has given me the chance to do so."

*– Hazar K., '12
Jefferson City, MO
Biology*

> SUCCESS **Peer Mentor Program**

The Peer Mentor Program is a program that pairs underrepresented students with upperclassmen mentors. These mentors advise students on picking classes, joining organizations, and becoming ingrained in the campus community.

> SUCCESS **Student Success Center**

The Student Success Center is a multi-faceted academic support program that provides a range of services to enhance both a student's individual learning and in-class performance. The center provides tutoring services, collaborative group study for specific courses, peer mentoring, and learning and study skills workshops.

> SUCCESS **SEE Scholars Program**

The SEE Scholars Program is a two-week summer program for incoming, underrepresented college freshman that takes place on the campus of Truman State University. Through SEE Scholars, students are introduced to college life, resources, and support systems in ways that will help them succeed at the university level.

> SUCCESS **McNair Program**

The McNair program was designed to provide disadvantaged college students with effective preparation for doctoral studies. McNair Scholars are matched with faculty mentors who supervise research and assist students in achieving their individual post-baccalaureate educational goals. Students participate in pre-research internships during their sophomore year and summer research internships during their junior year. During their senior year, the focus is on graduate school placement.

F A S T   F A C T S

STUDENT PROFILE

# of degree-seeking undergraduates	5,359
% male/female	42/58
% African-American	4
% American Indian or Alaska Native	<1
% Asian or Pacific Islander	2
% Hispanic	2
% White	75
% International	5
% Pell grant recipients	14

First-generation and minority alumni Lenvil Elliot, professional football player; Ken Norton, professional boxer; Byron (Bol) Crawford, Hip Hop critic and blogger; Scott Piper, professional opera singer; Dr. Kia (Hartfield) Johnson, Assistant Professor of Communication Sciences and Disorders and the Director of the Developmental Stuttering Research Laboratory at James Madison University

ACADEMICS

full-time faculty	345
full-time minority faculty	39
student-faculty ratio	16:1
average class size	26
% first-year retention rate	84
% graduation rate (6 years)	71

Popular majors Business, Biology, English, Psychology

CAMPUS LIFE

% live on campus (% freshmen)	48 (99)

Multicultural student clubs and organizations African Students Organization, Association of Black Collegians, Coalition of African American Women, Hispanic American Leadership Organization (HALO), International Club, GlobeMed, Hablantes Unidos/United Speakers, Namaste Nepal, Sigma Lambda Beta (formerly Hermanos Unidos), Society for Sino-American Studies

Athletics NCAA Division II, Mid-America Intercollegiate Athletic Association

ADMISSIONS

# of applicants	4,608
% accepted	72
# of first-year students enrolled	1,342
SAT Critical Reading range	540-660
SAT Math range	560-660
SAT Writing range	n/a
ACT range	25-30
average HS GPA	3.74

Deadlines

early decision	12/15
regular decision	rolling
application fee (online)	$0 ($0)
fee waiver for applicants with financial need	yes

COST & AID

tuition	in-state: $6,458; out-of-state: $11,309
room & board	$6,854
total need-based institutional scholarships/grants	n/a
% of students apply for need-based aid	64
% receiving need-based scholarship or grant aid	74
% receiving aid whose need was fully met	82
average aid package	$8,425
average student loan debt upon graduation	$21,858

University of Missouri

University of Missouri
230 Jesse Hall
Columbia, MO 65211
Ph: (573) 882-7786
MU4U@missouri.edu
www.missouri.edu

Located in Columbia, Missouri, Mizzou is an exceptional place, a university where students will find more majors, more talented and dedicated teachers and more top-notch facilities — all of which add up to more opportunities to explore, grow and succeed. The University of Missouri works with students to develop a personalized academic plan for the first semester. Students may join a Freshman Interest Group (FIG), a Learning Community, or consider joining a student organization. At the start of the semester, students participate in Fall and Spring Welcome activities to get better connected with the campus and their department. Mizzou wants students to have a successful start to their college career. The Learning Center, Academic Advising, Academic Retention Services and other programs are available to help develop learning strategies to enhance success. Positive freshman retention rates indicate Mizzou students are well served by these programs by helping them define, clarify and achieve their academic, personal and professional goals throughout their program of study.

> ACCESS MU Engineering Scholars Camp

MU offers a wide variety of academic enrichment and leadership summer opportunities that provide exposure and engagement to college for 6th-12th grade students. MU Engineering Scholars Camp provides an opportunity to learn what engineers really do and the tools they use, introducing students to engineering's various disciplines through hands-on activities and team design competitions.

> ACCESS High School Mini Medical School

This is a one-week experience designed to give students a preview of medical school. The program includes: participation in a medical school style curriculum; hospital tours; hands-on experience in anatomy, microbiology, and clinical skills; meaningful interactions with current medical students, faculty, and staff of the School of Medicine and seminars on college and medical school entrance and medical school life.

> OPPORTUNITY Mizzou Days and Black and Gold Days

Throughout the year Mizzou Days and Black and Gold Days are designed to help prospective students and their families learn everything they'd ever want to know about Mizzou, from the award-winning residential dining halls to a campus rich in tradition. Students visit with admissions staff, explore the campus during a student led tour, interact with faculty in the academic areas that they have the most interest in and visit student facilities.

> SUCCESS Academic Retention Services (ARS)

Academic Retention Services provides services designed to support the academic/intellectual, social, personal and cultural development of students. From the time of admittance to Mizzou and up until graduation, students are offered a wide array of programs and services to enhance their overall campus experience. ARS is committed to the development of students by creating opportunities that foster campus involvement, leadership development and academic excellence. ARS also serves as a resource office to parents, students, faculty and staff by providing culturally related information.

> SUCCESS Exposure to Research for Science Students (EXPRESS)

The EXPRESS program is specially designed for freshmen and sophomores to receive an opportunity to work in a faculty research lab as underclassmen. Students acquire a faculty mentor, learn valuable laboratory skills, become involved in cutting-edge research, and participate in a variety of supplemental activities.

FAST FACTS

STUDENT PROFILE

# of degree-seeking undergraduates	23,529
% male/female	48/52
% African-American	7
% American Indian or Alaska Native	1
% Asian or Pacific Islander	2
% Hispanic	2
% White	83
% International	2
% Pell grant recipients	16

ACADEMICS

full-time faculty	1,266
full-time minority faculty	227
student-faculty ratio	19:1
average class size	n/a
% first-year retention rate	85
% graduation rate (6 years)	68

Popular majors Business, Journalism and Communication, Health professions

CAMPUS LIFE

% live on campus (% freshmen)	30 (86)

Multicultural student clubs and organizations Legion of Black Collegians, Hispanic American Leadership Organization (HALO), From the Four Directions (Native American Student Group) Asian American Association, National Society of Black Engineers (NSBE), Hispanic Professional Engineers (SHPE), Minorities in Agriculture, Natural Resources and Related Sciences, Minority Association of Pre-Health professionals, National Society of Minorities in Hospitality, 9 National Pan-Hellenic Greek Organizations

Athletics NCAA Division I, Big 12 Conference

ADMISSIONS

# of applicants	16,436
% accepted	83
# of first-year students enrolled	5,593
SAT Critical Reading range	530-650
SAT Math range	530-650
SAT Writing range	n/a
ACT range	23-28
average HS GPA	n/a

Deadlines

regular decision	5/1
application fee (online)	$45 ($45)
fee waiver for applicants with financial need	yes

COST & AID

tuition	in-state: $7,368; out-of-state: $18,459
room & board	$8,150
total need-based institutional scholarships/grants	$22,671,170
% of students apply for need-based aid	64
% receiving need-based scholarship or grant aid	37
% receiving aid whose need was fully met	15
average aid package	$12,757
average student loan debt upon graduation	$20,814

Westminster College

Westminster College
501 Westminster Avenue
Fulton, MO 65251-1299
Ph: (573) 592-5251
admissions@westminster-mo.edu
www.westminster-mo.edu

Located in the heart of Missouri, Westminster College is a distinctive, liberal arts and sciences college with a global community. With an 11 percent international student population, Westminster's students benefit from a great range of diversity on campus. Westminster integrates academics with experience by providing students with dynamic, hands-on, real-world experiences and seeks to be students' "gateway to the world." With an enrollment of just under 1,000 students, the college community is intimate enough for each student to have an individualized learning experience and for faculty and staff to know their students well. Community service is a way of life at Westminster. Recently, the college's international organizations have focused their efforts on promoting the use of sustainable products from other countries.

> ## ACCESS **Summer Youth Leadership and Development Camps**

The Center for Leadership and Service hosts summer youth leadership and development camps to cultivate the skills in community youth that will lead them to success in high school and college.

> ## OPPORTUNITY **Triple S Visionary Scholarship**

The Triple S Visionary Scholarship is awarded to a student based on high school academic and extra-curricular activities, community service, citizenship and financial need. Triple S stands for *success*, *significance* and *service*, and the award is amounted for full cost of tuition. Priority consideration is given to first-generation college students and members of underrepresented minority groups. Candidates must submit a one-page essay on why they would be good candidates for this award.

> ## SUCCESS **Cultural Diversity Education Office**

Under the auspices of the Center for Leadership and Service, the Cultural Diversity Education Office supports the college community in understanding the interconnectedness of peoples and cultures. The office offers international students various programs, such as "friendship family" and Christmas International House. A "friendship family" shares with an international student information about American culture. Students are able to eat American food and learn customs of American life. Through interaction with the "friendship family," international students have a chance to improve their English and share their own cultures. The Christmas International House is open to international students to provide a "home away from home" during the holiday season.

> ## SUCCESS **Reading and Study Skills Program (RSSP)**

This program gives special attention during the first semester in college to incoming freshmen whose preparation for college is, in certain respects, inadequate. Offered through the college's Campus Learning Center, the program consists of special courses, a reduced course load, advising and, when appropriate, counseling. Students are selected for RSSP on the basis of their high school records and SAT or ACT scores. Some students are admitted to Westminster only if they agree to participate in the program. A few students who are not required to participate may be invited to enter the program on a space-available basis.

FAST FACTS

STUDENT PROFILE
# of degree-seeking undergraduates	1,000
% male/female	53/47
% African-American	5
% American Indian or Alaska Native	2
% Asian or Pacific Islander	1
% Hispanic	2
% White	73
% Pell grant recipients	21

ACADEMICS
full-time faculty	59
full-time minority faculty	5
student-faculty ratio	15:1
average class size	18
% first-year retention rate	84
% graduation rate (6 years)	61

Popular majors Psychology, General Studies, Human Services, Political Science and Government, Child Development

CAMPUS LIFE
% live on campus (% freshmen)	85 (97)

Multicultural student clubs and organizations African Caribbean Club, Black Student Union, Brown Pride, Calling All Colors, Filipino American Student Association, Hui 'O Hawaii, International Movie and Tea Club, International Taste Testers, Japanese Conversation Group, Latin Student Union, La Mesa Espanola, mEChA (Movimiento Estudiantil Chicano/a de Aztlan), Mixed Identity Student Organization (MISO), MOSAIC, Native American Mentoring Program (NAMP), Native American Student Union, Ritmo Latino, South Asian Student Association, Taiwanese Student Association, Vietnamese Student Association, Western Sister Cities Association

Athletics NCAA Division II, Great Northwest Athletic Conference

ADMISSIONS
# of applicants	966
% accepted	77
# of first-year students enrolled	244
SAT Critical Reading range	430-620
SAT Math range	450-600
SAT Writing range	430-550
ACT range	22-28
average HS GPA	3.5

Deadlines
regular decision	rolling
application fee (online)	$0 ($0)

COST & AID
tuition	$18,700
room & board	$7,120
total need-based institutional scholarships/grants	$11,546,308
% of students apply for need-based aid	67
% of students receive aid	54
% receiving need-based scholarship or grant aid	100
% receiving aid whose need was fully met	71
average aid package	$16,188
average student loan debt upon graduation	$19,845

The University of Montana

The University of Montana offers students academic excellence in addition to outstanding outdoor recreational opportunities and quality of life. Students receive a high-quality, well-rounded education through the university's five colleges — arts and sciences, education and human sciences, forestry and conservation, health professions and biomedical sciences, and technology — and four professional schools — journalism, law, business and fine arts. The University of Montana was founded in 1893 in the pioneer town of Missoula, fewer than 90 years after Lewis and Clark and their Corps of Discovery explored the area. Today, the university dedicates a considerable amount of time, energy and resources to working with first-generation, minority and low-income students. Located in the midst of western Montana's stunning natural landscape, The University of Montana's campus has been deemed the most scenic in America by *Rolling Stone*.

> ACCESS **Minority Admissions Counselor**

The University of Montana Minority Admissions Counselor travels around Montana, the U.S. and Canada speaking with groups about the possibility of college and about The University of Montana. The Minority Admissions Counselor also plans tours, admissions visits, mock orientations, student panels, program presentations, scavenger hunts and hands-on learning experiences for TRIO whose programs also include Upward Bound, Talent Search and GEAR UP.

> OPPORTUNITY **Tribal Colleges**

The state of Montana is home to seven Tribal Colleges, one on each of the seven reservations. In Dual Admissions Agreements with all of the Tribal Colleges, The University of Montana offers dual enrollment to students enrolled in Tribal Colleges, allowing students to get the benefits of being a UM student, complete with advising, an early registration period and an application fee waiver. Approximately 25 percent of The University of Montana's Native American students are transfer students from Tribal Colleges. Many of the Tribal Colleges bring students, faculty and staff to the university to learn about specific programs, to interact with students, to participate in specific campus activities, or to become more acquainted with the campus in general. Transfer Transition provides Tribal College transfer students with an enhanced orientation where students come on campus for one day and register for courses.

"I chose The University of Montana because there were a lot of American Indian Students going there and a lot of support for them. At first it was really awkward because I didn't know anyone but right away I got involved in a lot of activities and clubs on campus. Now I love it!"

– Meryl B., '08
Bishop Paiute
Reservation (CA)

> OPPORTUNITY **Native American Scholarships**

The University of Montana's Native American Studies Department provides Native American students with over $130,000 in scholarships each year. The Davidson Honors College awards $1,500 per year to an American Indian student who has been admitted into the Honors College.

> SUCCESS **The University of Montana Diversity Committee**

The Diversity Committee is formed by students who create working partnerships with other student groups, staff and faculty to create learning and leadership opportunities, explore common interests, identify common problems and possible solutions, engage students in social activities and overall, improve campus life.

The University of Montana
Enrollment Services
Lommasson Center
32 Campus Drive
Missoula, MT 59812
Ph: (800) 462-8636 / (406) 243-6266
admiss@umontana.edu
www.umt.edu

F A S T   F A C T S

STUDENT PROFILE
# of degree-seeking undergraduates	13,072
% male/female	47/53
% African American	1
% American Indian	4
% Asian	1
% Caucasian	82
% Hispanic	2
% Pell grant recipients	37

First-generation and minority alumni Mike Mansfield; Joe McDonald; Bonnie HeavyRunner; Henrietta Mann Morton; Judy Blunt; Dorothy M. Johnson; George M. Dennison; Gary Niles Kimble; Kenneth Ryan

ACADEMICS
full-time faculty	557
student-faculty ratio	19:1
average class size	29
% first-year retention rate	72
% graduation rate (6 years)	42

Popular majors Business Administration, English, Education, Natural Resources/Conservation

CAMPUS LIFE
% live on campus (% freshmen)	18 (99)

Multicultural student clubs and organizations American Indians in Science and Engineering, American Indian Business Leaders, Coalition on Bias and Discrimination, Indian Hall of Fame, Kyi-Yo Native American Student Association, Le Gente Unida, Native American Journalist Association Student Chapter, Native American Law Student Association, ROSNA/PACE, Traditional American Indian Games Association, WA YA WA American Indian Education Association

ADMISSIONS
# of applicants	7,849
% accepted	78
SAT Critical Reading range	n/a
SAT Math range	n/a
ACT range	22+
average HS GPA	3.3

Deadlines
regular admission	rolling

COST & AID
tuition in-state: $5,329.80; out-of-state: $17,763	
room & board	$6,026
% of students receive aid	67
% receiving need-based scholarship or grant aid	53
% receiving aid whose need was fully met	13
average aid package	$6,149
average student loan debt upon graduation	$21,000

Dartmouth College

A member of the Ivy League, Dartmouth is distinctive for being a vibrant and yet highly-accessible and student-centered residential liberal arts college with world-class resources and research opportunities. Aspiring to provide the best undergraduate education in the country, Dartmouth enables students to individualize their experience through its unique academic calendar (the D-Plan) and extensive study abroad programs. Its intellectual and social community is built on the diverse backgrounds, perspectives and interests of its student body and faculty. Dartmouth is committed to the success of all of its students, particularly its high percentage of historically underrepresented and first generation students through its Office of Pluralism and Leadership, First Generation Student Network, students of color advising groups and community-building cultural programming such as the Martin Luther King, Jr. Celebration, annual PRIDE celebration, Dartmouth Asian Organization culture nights, and the largest Pow-Wow in New England.

"The thing that drew me to Dartmouth is the thing that still continues to amaze me on a daily basis – the people. When I first visited Dartmouth, I was shocked by the zeal that the students had for their school. The feeling of Dartmouth pride was palpable. When I finally became a Dartmouth student, I began to understand that feeling for myself. I feel blessed to be surrounded by some of the most intelligent and passionate people I have ever met in my life."
– Andrew R., '10 Chicago, IL English, Education

 ACCESS Dartmouth Bound

Every year Dartmouth's Admissions Office invites a small, promising group of college-bound rising seniors for an extended campus visit through the Dartmouth Bound programs. Participants are provided with roundtrip airfare and overnight accommodations in residence halls, and are given the opportunity to visit lasses and interact freely with Dartmouth faculty, administrators and students. Participating students are selected on the basis of their academic achievement, personal character, and potential for college success.

 OPPORTUNITY Need Blind Admissions

Dartmouth practices need-blind admissions for all applicants, which means students' financial need has no bearing on their admission to Dartmouth. Furthermore, Dartmouth guarantees to meet 100 percent of the demonstrated financial need for all admitted students, including free tuition for students who come from families with total annual incomes below $75,000 with typical assets. Student financial aid packages provide a combination of scholarships and grants, with small loans and employment eligibility.

 SUCCESS Office of Pluralism and Leadership (OPAL)

Dartmouth's Office of Pluralism and Leadership is a critical resource in the College's effort to support historically underrepresented populations and to encourage the building of cultural bridges within the Dartmouth community. In addition to facilitating programs and advising networks designed to support students' academic success, the program also provides opportunities for leadership development, cultural enrichment, and community engagement. Through its collaboration with students and over 50 campus offices, OPAL works to enhance Dartmouth's institutional commitment to diversity.

 SUCCESS Affinity Programs

Dartmouth's affinity programs provide residential learning opportunities for students based on either a self-defined academic or special interest focus. Through Dartmouth's affinity programs, undergraduates have the opportunity to live with other students who share a common interest or background. These programs include the Chinese Language House, the Inter-faith Living and Learning Center (IFLLC), La Casa, the Latin American, Latino & Caribbean Studies House (LALACS), the Cutter-Shabazz African American Center for Intellectual Inquiry, and the Native American House.

Dartmouth College
6016 McNutt Hall
Hanover, NH 03755
Ph: (603) 646-2875
admissions.office@dartmouth.edu
www.dartmouth.edu

FAST FACTS

STUDENT PROFILE

# of degree-seeking undergraduates	4,196
% male/female	49/51
% African American	8
% American Indian or Alaska Native	4
% Asian or Pacific Islander	14
% Hispanic	7
% White	53
% International	7
% Unknown	6
% Pell grant recipients	14.5

First-generation and minority alumni Aisha Tyler, actress, "Friends" and "CSI", former host of "Talk Soup"; Shonda Rhimes, creator, head writer, and executive producer of "Grey's Anatomy"; Keith Boykin, editor of "The Daily Voice", CNBC contributor, co-host of BET's "My Two Cents"; Leah Daughtry, CEO of 2008 Democratic National Convention, Howard Dean's chief of staff; Louise Erdrich, Native American author, 2009 finalist for the Pulitzer Prize in Fiction; Jose W. Fernandez, Assistant Secretary of State

ACADEMICS

full-time faculty	533
full-time minority faculty	88
student-faculty ratio	8:1
average class size	10-19
% first-year retention rate	98
% graduation rate (6 years)	94

Popular majors Economics, Government, Psychological & Brain Sciences, Biology, History, English

CAMPUS LIFE

% live on campus (% fresh.)	85 (100)

Multicultural student clubs and organizations AfriCaSO, Afro-American Society, Dartmouth Asian Organization, Dartmouth Chinese Culture Society, Dartmouth Japan Society, Dartmouth Taiwanese Association, Hokupa'a, International Students Association, Korean American Students Association, La Alianza Latina, M.E.Ch.A. (Movimiento Estudiantil Chicano/a de Aztlan), Milan, MOSAIC, Native Americans at Dartmouth, Vietnamese Student Association.

Athletics NCAA Division I, Eastern College Athletic Conference, Ivy League

ADMISSIONS

# of applicants	18,132
% accepted	12.6
# of first-year students enrolled	1,094
SAT Critical Reading range	670-770
SAT Math range	680-780
SAT Writing range	680-780
ACT range	30-34

Deadlines

early decision	11/1
regular decision	1/1
application fee (online)	$70 ($70)
fee waiver for applicants with financial need	yes

COST & AID

tuition	$39,978
room & board	$11,838
total need-based institutional scholarships/grants	$63,163,730
% of students apply for need-based aid	64.9
% of students receive aid	53.4
% receiving need-based scholarship or grant aid	46.2
% receiving aid whose need was fully met	100
average aid package	$33,232
average student loan debt upon graduation	$15,738

Southern New Hampshire University

With a diverse environment that includes many ages, races and cultures, Southern New Hampshire University is considered the most internationally diverse campus in northern New England. Its multicultural community promotes mutual respect and understanding of others as an integral part of its globally oriented educational purpose. Undergraduate degree programs in business, culinary arts, education, hospitality and liberal arts bring together a culture that inspires every person, every day, to learn more, try harder and exceed expectations, and the school is dedicated to helping students realize their potential.

> ACCESS **SNHU Partnership Program**

The SNHU Partnership Program provides step-by-step support to high school students with great potential to make their dreams come true and to succeed in college. For students who might otherwise think they "can't" go to college, the three-year program beings during the sophomore year and includes academics, tutoring, mentoring, and community service, as well as assistance with applications for admission and financial aid and deadline reminders. Upon successful completion of the program, Southern New Hampshire University will provide financial aid counseling and academic counseling. For graduates applying to Southern New Hampshire University, financial aid opportunities and scholarships will be available, allowing a student, regardless of ability to pay, access to a college education.

> *"SNHU was the one that opened the doors for me and made three years of my life a marvelous, wonderful, experience."*
>
> *– Maria Antonieta M., '08*
> *Ecuador*
> *Finance*

> ACCESS **Destination College**

Destination College is an annual event in March SNHU hosts with the New Hampshire Higher Education Assistance Foundation in an effort to provide information for parents and students about planning and paying for college. The event also features seminars for first-generation college students. Over 1,000 students and families attended this year's Destination College.

> SUCCESS **JumpStart**

Studies show that when students are given an early, formal introduction to higher education, they are more likely to experience satisfaction and to graduate. The Learning Center at SNHU is offering a pre-college program called "JumpStart", to provide this introduction. JumpStart is an early entrance/summer bridge experience for first-year students designed to help them make a satisfactory transition to the SNHU experience and enhance their chances for academic success. JumpStart is offered to all incoming first-year students; however, enrollment is limited to the first 50 eligible applicants. As a residential program, all participants live on campus during the week.

> SUCCESS **101 Scholarship for Success**

All students take SNHU 101 Scholarship for Success, which focuses on academic, personal and social development. LSS 100 Learning Strategies Seminar is for students seeking to develop better study and organizational skills. The course serves as an introduction to college and college-level work, and it prepares students for academic, personal, and social success through the structured practice of critical thinking and decision-making. Students will engage in collaborative efforts that generate, integrate, and apply knowledge.

Southern New Hampshire University
2500 N. River Road
Manchester, NH 03106
Ph: (800) 642-4968 / (603) 645-9611
admission@snhu.edu
www.snhu.edu

F A S T   F A C T S

STUDENT PROFILE
# of degree-seeking undergraduates	3,493
% male/female	41.2/58.8
% African-American	<1
% American Indian or Alaska Native	<1
% Asian or Pacific Islander	<1
% Hispanic	1.4
% White	53.4
% International	4.4
% Pell grant recipients	22.3

ACADEMICS
full-time faculty	132
student-faculty ratio	n/a
average class size	20
% first-year retention rate	74
% graduation rate (6 years)	50.1

Popular majors Business Administration, Culinary Arts, Psychology, Education, Hospitality Management

CAMPUS LIFE
% live on campus (% fresh.)	78 (85)

Multicultural student clubs and organizations International Students Association, Outreach Association, Student Ambassadors
Athletics NCAA Division II, Northeast 10 Conference

ADMISSIONS
# of applicants	3,738
% accepted	69.1
# of first-year students enrolled	720
SAT Critical Reading range	440-520
SAT Math range	440-540
SAT Writing range	430-530
ACT range	18-21
average HS GPA	2.94

Deadlines
early decision	12/15
regular decision	3/15
application fee (online)	$40 ($40)
fee waiver for applicants with financial need	yes

COST & AID
tuition	$26,442
room & board	$10,176
total need-based institutional scholarships/grants	n/a
% of students apply for need-based aid	85.3
% of students receive aid	90
% receiving need-based scholarship or grant aid	95.4
% receiving aid whose need was fully met	11.4
average aid package	$16,704
average student loan debt upon graduation	$21,138

Fairleigh Dickinson University

Fairleigh Dickinson University
285 Madison Avenue
Madison, NJ 07940
Ph: (800) 338-8803
admissions@fdu.edu
www.fdu.edu

Fairleigh Dickinson University, a leader in global education and New Jersey's largest private university, provides professional and career preparation with a global focus on two distinctive campuses in northern New Jersey near New York City. FDU offers more than 100 undergraduate and graduate degrees, 100 student organizations and clubs, and more than three dozen men's and women's Division I and III athletic teams. Students come from 35 states and more than 96 countries, representing a myriad of backgrounds, personalities and cultures. *U.S. News & World Report* ranks FDU among the top 20 schools for "Most International Students" and "Campus Diversity" among comprehensive universities offering master's degrees in the northern United States. The school offers resources of a large university — from great professors to diverse research and computer facilities — but is small enough to ensure students receive the personal attention and support essential to academic success.

> ACCESS Latino Promise

FDU's multi-faceted Latino Promise program provides inspiration and access for Latino students along with encouragement and support aimed at academic success. The program is designed to educate prospective Latino students and their families to the possibilities of a college education. The program also provides pre-college support to guide them through the admission process and provide information on recruitment, financial aid, reduced fee SATs and other important facts. FDU's Latino Promise provides students with generous scholarships and financial support.

> OPPORTUNITY The Educational Opportunity Fund (EOF)

This program was created in 1969 to ensure access and opportunity to higher education for students who are economically and/or educationally disadvantaged. Through this University- and state-sponsored program, EOF assists low-income New Jersey residents by providing financial aid to cover college costs such as books, fees, room and board, as well as a comprehensive network of support ranging from individual and group academic, career and financial aid counseling to tutoring services. A key feature of the EOF program is its Pre-Freshman Summer Program, which helps incoming freshmen — particularly educationally disadvantaged and first-generation college students — transition successfully from high school to college. Students get a head start on college by meeting other students, becoming acquainted with academic advisors, and learning about campus resources and support services.

"I am grateful for the cultural and academic opportunities provided by FDU and the EOF program. Thanks to the guidance and support of the EOF program and the professional development courses offered by the hospitality program, I've gained the tools I need for my professional career in hospitality."
– Natalie G. Elizabeth, N.J.

> SUCCESS Freshman Intensive Studies and Enhanced Freshman Experience

FDU's Freshman Intensive Studies program at the Madison Campus and the Enhanced Freshman Experience program at the Metropolitan Campus each provide a highly structured curriculum and extra support services for first-year students. Through both programs, the directors, faculty and staff work with freshmen to strengthen their academics, ensure retention and eliminate obstacles to their academic success.

FAST FACTS

STUDENT PROFILE

# of degree-seeking undergraduates	2,410
% male/female	47/53
% African American	8
% American Indian or Alaska Native	<1
% Asian or Pacific Islander	3
% Hispanic	7
% White	68
% International	<1
% Pell grant recipients	n/a

First generation and minority alumni Adenah Bayoh, '01, entrepreneur, real estate investor and restaurateur (IHOP franchise); Brenda Blackmon,'01, co-anchor of My9 News, WWOR TV; Angela Gittens, '67, Director General, Airports Council International; Hector I. Erezuma,'76, vice President-Taxation, Colgate-Palmolive Co.; George Martin, '87, (Retired) Defensive Lineman and Co-Captain, New York Giants, National Football League

ACADEMICS

full-time faculty	306
full-time minority faculty	52
student-faculty ratio	n/a
% first-year retention rate	n/a
% graduation rate (6 years)	n/a

Popular majors College at Florham: Business, Psychology, Biology, Communication Studies, Education; Metropolitan Campus: Nursing, Business, Psychology, Criminal Justice. Education

CAMPUS LIFE

% live on campus (% freshmen)	60 (84)

Multicultural student clubs and organizations College at Florham: Association of Black Collegians, Latino American Student Organization; Metropolitan Campus: African American Heritage Society, Asian Club, BARKADA-Filipino Club, Black Men's Alliance, Chinese Students Friendship Association, Haitian Cultural Association, Indian Cultural Experience, International Students Organization, Latin Exchange Organization, Muslin Educational and Cultural Association, Nubian Ladies Making Vital Progress, Organization of Latin Americans

Athletics NAIA, Athletic Conference American Mideast

ADMISSIONS

# of applicants	3,496
% accepted	62
# of first-year students enrolled	606
SAT Critical Reading range	460-550
SAT Math range	460-570
SAT Writing range	460-560
ACT range	n/a
average HS GPA	3.1

Deadlines

regular decision	rolling to 3/1
application fee (online)	$40 ($0)
fee waiver for applicants with financial need	yes

COST & AID

tuition	$30,392
room & board	$11,058
% of students apply for need-based aid	78
% of students receive aid	67
% receiving need-based scholarship or grant aid	56
% receiving aid whose need was fully met	n/a
average aid package	$17,400
average student loan debt upon graduation	n/a

Felician College

Felician College is a co-educational institute of higher learning with 1,300 traditional undergraduate students. It is a Catholic college in the Franciscan tradition, committed to putting STUDENTS FIRST. Felician offers 55 academic and professional programs in the liberal arts tradition to help prepare today's college student to assume their roles as members of an increasingly global community. Felician College has been named one of the top (#5) Best Colleges for racial diversity for Baccalaureate Colleges in the North by the *U.S. News & World Report* ranking. You will find that Felician is small and personable, and students state positively that Felician is a place where students can sit and talk with professors and feel their individual talents are nurtured.

> ACCESS **Jumpstart**

Jumpstart runs for 5 weeks and is designed to help students strengthen their skills in math and English. At the end of the program, Jumpstart students take a placement exam in order to test out of one or more of the developmental courses in which they were originally placed, allowing them to take college-level courses sooner.

> ACCESS **The Educational Opportunity Fund Program (EOF)**

The Educational Opportunity Fund (EOF) program, is designed to provide an opportunity for higher education for New Jersey residents, who are found to be economically and academically disadvantaged. EOF offers great advantages such as: an extra grant towards tuition, additional tutoring for classes, a summer program to prepare students for the first college level English and math courses and an opportunity to get to know future classmates before the semester begins.

> OPPORTUNITY **Scholarships**

Felician College aims to make college more affordable by keeping the cost low and offering generous scholarships. Scholarships are designed to reward students for academic achievement and help pay for college. Please visit www.felician.edu to view merit based scholarships.

> SUCCESS **Freshman Year Experience (FYE)**

This program entails a one-credit course which meets weekly in both the fall and spring semesters of your freshman year. It is taught by a Felician faculty member, usually from the participating student's academic discipline and, in most cases, this faculty member will also serve as their academic advisor during their first year.

> SUCCESS **Academic Support Services**

The Academic Support Services at Felician are in a collaborative and cooperative learning environment where students from all disciplines can discover the tools, strategies and resources necessary to become life-long learners. The Center for Learning is staffed by professors, professional tutors, and peer tutors who provide free consultations to students in areas such as English, math, science, and other selected academic disciplines.

"Initially, I was not sure if I was college material. But, I met Dinela Huertas, EOF Associate Director during my college search process; she believed in me and thought I had what it took to be a college student. Now, I have close to a 3.0 GPA and I am on the road to complete my degree in Education."

– Daniel R.
Newark, NJ
Education

Felician College
262 South Main Street
Lodi, NJ 07644
Ph: (201) 559-6131
admissions@felician.edu
www.felician.edu

F A S T   F A C T S

STUDENT PROFILE

# of degree-seeking undergraduates	1,300
% male/female	23/77
% African-American	12
% American Indian or Alaska Native	<1
% Asian or Pacific Islander	10
% Hispanic	17
% White	40
% International	<1
% Pell grant recipients	49

ACADEMICS

full-time faculty	112
full-time minority faculty	9
student-faculty ratio	12:1
average class size	15
% first-year retention rate	60
% graduation rate (6 years)	n/a

Popular majors Business, Education, Nursing and Criminal Justice

CAMPUS LIFE

% live on campus	25

Multicultural student clubs and organizations International Cultural Club, United Latino Club, and many other professional organizations

Athletics NCAA Division II, CACC

ADMISSIONS

# of applicants	2,018
% accepted	81
# of first-year students enrolled	326
SAT Critical Reading range	400-500
SAT Math range	400-500
SAT Writing range	n/a
ACT range	n/a
average HS GPA	2.7

Deadlines

regular decision	rolling
application fee (online)	$30 ($30)
fee waiver for applicants with financial need	yes

COST & AID

tuition	$23,650
room & board	$9,700
total need-based institutional scholarships/grants	n/a
% of students apply for need-based aid	86
% receiving need-based scholarship or grant aid	73
% receiving aid whose need was fully met	77
average aid package	$22,476
average student loan debt upon graduation	$15,000

Montclair State University

Montclair State offers the advantages of a large university – a comprehensive undergraduate curriculum with a global focus, a broad variety of superior graduate programs through the doctoral level, and a diverse faculty and student body – combined with a small college's attention to students. For over 100 years, ambitious people from all walks of life have come to Montclair State to fulfill their potential and reach for their dreams. In February 2010, Montclair State University was named a "Top Gainer" and a "Top Gap Closer," and listed among the top 25 public four-year colleges and universities in the nation for its improvements in minority graduation rates by The Education Trust, a Washington DC-based, non-profit advocacy group. Among the Carnegie classification's 186 public master's institutions included in the study, Montclair State was the only New Jersey institution to be listed in the top 25.

> ACCESS Upward Bound Program

The Upward Bound Program at Montclair State University assists low-income and first generation students with academic support services to increase their opportunity to graduate from high school. The main thrust of the project is to increase the skills and motivation needed to successfully complete an undergraduate course of studies. Participants are recruited from the federally approved target areas of Newark, Passaic, and Paterson.

> OPPORTUNITY Educational Opportunity Fund Program

The Educational Opportunity Fund (EOF) Program provides special admission, financial aid, and academic support services for highly motivated low-income students who do not meet Montclair State University's regular admission criteria. Students admitted to the program must be members of economically disadvantaged families, have a background of academic under-preparedness, but demonstrate potential to be successful in college. Eligible students who are admitted to the program receive a maximum amount of financial aid based on their individual need. Also students are provided with a broad range of academic support services including counseling, tutoring, leadership development, and workshops. Counselors interact with students in individual and small group settings, which cover academics, course advising, careers, personal and financial aid issues. For more information, visit: http://www.montclair.edu/eop/

"Montclair State University and the EOF Program means having a family where you are given a chance to express yourself, to communicate with your counselor, to set goals for yourself, and knowing that there are people who believe in you. It's a community where your opinion and education matters."

*– Dianne F.
Newark, NJ
Psychology*

> OPPORTUNITY The Health Careers Program

The Health Careers Program (HCP), funded jointly by Montclair State University and the New Jersey Educational Opportunity Fund, is an undergraduate program that provides highly motivated and academically capable students from financially and educationally disadvantaged backgrounds an opportunity for admission to health professions schools and careers in the sciences.

FAST FACTS

STUDENT PROFILE
# of degree-seeking undergraduates	14,139
% male/female	39/61
% African-American	9
% American Indian or Alaska Native	<1
% Asian or Pacific Islander	6
% Hispanic	20
% White	52
% International	5
% Pell grant recipients	27

First-generation and minority alumni Alread Bundy, Producer and Public Relations Specialist, Bundy Productions, BA 1975, MA 1980; Christopher C. Catching, ED.D Dean/Director, Multicultural Engagement, Rutgers, The State University of New Jersey, Office of Undergraduate Education, New Brunswick, NJ, 1999; Dr. Antoinete "Toni" Clay, Assistant Vice President, Instructional Student Support Services, Montclair State University BA in Psychology, 1980; Lynette N. Harris, Director of Judicial Affairs, The College of New Jersey, Bachelor of Arts in Sociology (1990) and a Masters of Arts in Counseling in Higher Education (1995)

ACADEMICS
full-time faculty	553
full-time minority faculty	137
student-faculty ratio	17:1
average class size	23
% first-year retention rate	81
% graduation rate (6 years)	62

Popular majors Business Administration, Family & Child Services, Psychology, English, Biology

CAMPUS LIFE
% live on campus (% fresh.)	26 (51)

Multicultural student clubs and organizations Active Students Serving in Society Together (ASSIST), Caribbean Student Organization (CaribSO), Haitian Student Association (HSA) Helping Each Other and Redefining Tomorrow (HEART), International Student Organization (ISO), Latin American Student Organization (LASO), Minority Association of Pre-Health Students (MAPS), Multicultural Inclusive Teacher Candidates Organization (MINTCO), National Association for the Advancement of Colored People (NAACP), Native African Student Organization (NASO), Organization of Students for African Unity (OSAU)
Athletics NCAA Division III, New Jersey Athletic Conference

ADMISSIONS
# of applicants	13,469
% accepted	47
# of first-year students enrolled	2,117
SAT Critical Reading range	440-540
SAT Math range	460-550
SAT Writing range	450-550
ACT range	n/a
average HS GPA	3.13

Deadlines
regular decision	3/1
application fee (online)	$60 ($60)
fee waiver for applicants with financial need	yes

COST & AID
tuition	in-state $9,771; out-of-state $17,783
room & board	$10,208
total need-based institutional scholarships/grants	$200,000
% of students apply for need-based aid	71
% receiving need-based scholarship or grant aid	32
% receiving aid whose need was fully met	15
average aid package	$9,217
average student loan debt upon graduation	$18,307

Montclair State University
1 Normal Avenue
Montclair, NJ 07043
Ph: (973) 655-4444
undergraduate.admission@montclair.edu
www.montclair.edu

Princeton University

Princeton University is a private, four-year, research university located in Princeton, NJ. The University's commitment to undergraduate education is distinctive among leading research universities. Princeton is recognized globally for its academic excellence; the University embraces open-mindedness, critical thinking, and the core principles of responsibility, integrity, and courage in its students. Although admission to Princeton is highly selective, the institution is committed to building a diverse campus community to ensure that students explore their interests, discover new academic and extracurricular pursuits, and learn from each other. More than ever, through initiatives such as its generous financial aid program, Princeton is making its distinctive education accessible to students from a broad range of cultural, ethnic, and economic backgrounds. Princeton's no-loan financial aid program assists all qualified applicants with generous need-based grants, making the University affordable to low- and middle-income families. More than half of Princeton's student body receives aid each year. The University supports minority students on campus through college preparatory programs, one-on-one mentoring, tutoring, and other programs and resources.

> *"I chose Princeton for many reasons: its generous no-loan financial aid package, commitment to diversity, and unparalleled focus on undergraduate education. I've found that Princeton provides endless opportunities to explore your interests and discover new ones."*
> – Ana G., '11
> Daly City, CA
> Woodrow Wilson School of Public and International Affairs

> ACCESS Princeton University Preparatory Program

The Princeton University Preparatory Program (PUPP) is a rigorous academic and cultural enrichment program that supports high-achieving, low-income high school students from local districts. The program helps students from ninth grade through high school graduation to build the academic skills, confidence, and leadership abilities necessary to both gain access to — and guarantee success in — higher education. Each summer, participants attend an intensive program on the Princeton campus. Participants are also provided year-round academic and cultural enrichment opportunities. Program staff members assist students and their families with the college application process and encourage students through every step, from SAT tutoring to extracurricular involvement.

> OPPORTUNITY Need-Based Financial Aid

Princeton University has one of the strongest need-based financial aid programs in the country, reflecting our core value of equality of opportunity and our desire to attract the most talented students. Princeton does not require student loans in its aid package, only grant aid that students do not have to repay, and part-time campus jobs to meet the full demonstrated need for all students offered admission. The average financial aid grant covers more than 100 percent of tuition. Grants for lower-income students also typically cover room and board costs.

> SUCCESS Black Student Union Leadership and Mentoring Program

Through the Black Student Union Leadership and Mentoring Program, Princeton upperclassmen offer one-on-one mentoring for incoming students. The program provides a support network that encourages academic and social exploration and success.

Princeton University
Undergraduate Admissions Office
P.O. Box 430
Princeton, NJ 08542
Ph: (609) 258-3060
uaoffice@princeton.edu
www.princeton.edu

FAST FACTS

STUDENT PROFILE

# of degree-seeking undergraduates	4,798
% male/female	53/47
% African American	8
% American Indian	1
% Asian	14
% Caucasian	52
% Hispanic	8
% Pell grant recipients	8.6

First-generation and minority alumni Sonia Sotomayor, Supreme Court Justice; Mohsin Hamid, novelist; Stanley Jordan, jazz guitarist; Michelle Obama, lawyer, first lady; Angela Ramirez, executive director, Congressional Hispanic Caucus; Anthony Romero, executive director, ACLU; John Thompson III, men's basketball coach, Georgetown University

ACADEMICS

full-time faculty	825
student-faculty ratio	8:1
% first-year retention rate	98
% graduation rate (6 years)	96

Popular majors History, Economics, Politics, Public and International Affairs, Molecular Biology

CAMPUS LIFE

% live on campus (% freshmen)	98 (100)

Multicultural student clubs and organizations Acción Latina, AKWAABA: African Students Association, Arab Society of Princeton, Asian American Students Association, Asian Pacific American Heritage Council, Black History Month Planning Committee, Black Student Union, Bulgarian Undergraduate Society, Chicano Caucus, Chinese Students Association, Cuban American Undergraduate Student Association, Hillel (Center for Jewish Life), Hong Kong Students Association, International Students Association of Princeton, Japanese Student Association, Korean American Students Association, Latin American Studies Student Organization, Latino Heritage Month Committee, Minority Business Association, National Society of Black Engineers, Native Americans at Princeton, Pehchaan (Pakistanis at Princeton), Persian Society of Princeton, Princeton Association of Black Women, Princeton Caribbean Connection, Singapore Society, South Asian Students Association, Taiwanese American Students Association, Ukrainian Alliance

Athletics NCAA Division I, Ivy League

ADMISSIONS

# of applicants	18,942
% accepted	9.7
SAT Critical Reading range	690-790
SAT Math range	700-790
ACT range	30-34

Deadlines

priority application	12/15
regular admission	1/1

COST & AID

tuition	$34,290
room & board	$11,405
% of students receiving aid	54
% receiving need-based scholarship or grant aid	55
% receiving aid whose need was fully met	100
average aid package	$35,000
average student loan debt upon graduation	$2,700

Rider University

Rider University is a mid-size, private, liberal arts college in New Jersey, within driving distance of New York City and Philadelphia. Rider is well known for its commitment to students — it provides a supportive, community-based learning environment with small classes, personal attention and individualized student services. Rider encourages leadership skills in its student body through a strong system of student government and honors programs. Generous financial aid packages and merit scholarships make the college affordable, and the school reaches out to minority and first-generation college students, particularly those who are residents of New Jersey.

> OPPORTUNITY Educational Opportunity Program (EOP)

The Educational Opportunity Program is a state-sponsored program that makes higher education accessible to low-income New Jersey residents. Along with financial aid assistance, EOP also provides academic support to its participants. Students admitted to the program are given individualized academic programs and tutoring so that they achieve academic success and graduate from college. There is also a five-week residential pre-orientation summer program to familiarize students with college life, where students take courses and participate in leadership workshops on the Rider University campus.

> OPPORTUNITY Rider Advantage Scholarship

The Rider Advantage Scholarship rewards outstanding academic performance and student leadership. Eligible students receive a grant to match the tuition increase between freshman and sophomore year. The grant may be renewed to minimize future tuition increases, thereby increasing students' merit financial aid packages and rewarding those students who may not have received a merit award upon initial enrollment at Rider.

> SUCCESS Rider Achievement Program (RAP)

The Rider Achievement Program is a structured learning program for first-year students who demonstrate the potential to succeed at Rider, but whose high school academic record does not meet regular admission criteria. It includes a Summer Bridge Program, peer assistance, a freshman seminar, specialized advising, linked courses, tutoring, workshops and events for participants. The Summer Bridge Program is a mandatory orientation program for all RAP students, where academic work is mixed with community building activities to ease the transition into the university environment.

Rider University
Lawrenceville Campus
2083 Lawrenceville Rd
Lawrenceville, NJ 08648
Ph: (800) 257-9026
admissions@rider.edu
www.rider.edu

FAST FACTS

STUDENT PROFILE

# of degree-seeking undergraduates	3,896
% male/female	40.6/59.4
% African-American	7.7
% American Indian or Alaska Native	<1
% Asian or Pacific Islander	4
% Hispanic	4.8
% White	74.8
% International	2.9
% Pell grant recipients	19.5

First-generation and minority alumni James Bass, superior judge, Eastern Judicial Circuit Court of Georgia; Wanda Jones Rogers, assistant commissioner of finance, U.S. Department of Treasury

ACADEMICS

full-time faculty	244
full-time minority faculty	n/a
student-faculty ratio	13:1
average class size	n/a
% first-year retention rate	80
% graduation rate (6 years)	58.3

Popular majors Elementary Education, Psychology, Accounting, Communications

CAMPUS LIFE

% live on campus (% freshmen)	54 (89)

Multicultural student clubs and organizations Asian Students at Rider, Black Student Union, Latin American Student Organization, Organization of Caribbean-Affiliated Students, International Student Club

Athletics NCAA Division I, Metro Atlantic Athletic Conference (MAAC), Eastern College Athletic Conference (ECAC)

ADMISSIONS

# of applicants	5,000
% accepted	79
# of first-year students enrolled	926
average SAT Critical Reading score	529
average SAT Math score	540
average SAT Writing score	532
ACT range	18-24
average HS GPA	3.34

Deadlines

early decision	11/15
regular decision	1/15
application fee (online)	$50 ($50)
fee waiver for applicants with financial need	yes

COST & AID

tuition	$28,470
room & board	$6,740
total need-based institutional scholarships/grants	n/a
% of students apply for need-based aid	85.7
% of students receive aid	100
% receiving need-based scholarship or grant aid	98.7
% receiving aid whose need was fully met	19.2
average aid package	$20,878
average student loan debt upon graduation	$33,156

Rutgers University

One of the original colonial colleges in the U.S., Rutgers is ranked among the nation's top five universities for commitment to diversity by *DiversityInc.* magazine. New Jersey is one of the most diverse states in the nation, and Rutgers follows suit with students from every U.S. state and more than 140 countries. *U.S. News and World Report* has named Rutgers-Newark the most diverse national university for 12 straight years. With three regional campuses in Camden, New Brunswick, and Newark, Rutgers is a major state university, offering all of the advantages of a public institution: reasonable tuition, big-time athletics, and some of the best research and academic resources, as well as a contemporary liberal arts education in a traditional northeastern college setting.

> ACCESS Upward Bound

Local high school students who come from low-income families in which neither parent holds a bachelor's degree can benefit from Rutgers' Upward Bound, a pre-college program that provides students with the right tools to pursue their goal of earning a college degree. Students benefit from weekly tutoring, field trips, workshops, and a six-week summer enrichment program on campus.

"With the extensive program support available to help me, I never felt alone or lost at Rutgers. I found the strength and courage that I needed to excel."
– Jackasha-Janaee W., '10
*Plainfield, NJ
History, Women & Gender Studies*

> OPPORTUNITY Rutgers Educational Opportunity Fund

The Rutgers Educational Opportunity Fund (EOF) program provides access to higher education for highly motivated New Jersey residents whose economic and educational circumstances have placed them at a disadvantage. The EOF program's comprehensive services and highly dedicated staff guide students in all areas of university life: academic, financial, personal, career and social. The program includes a Summer Institute to help ease the transition from high school to the university and sharpen students' math, writing, and other skills.

> SUCCESS The Office for Diversity and Academic Success in the Sciences (ODASIS)

The Office for Diversity and Academic Success in the Sciences (ODASIS) has a threefold mission to increase the numbers of Hispanic, African-American, Native American, and New Jersey Educational Opportunity Fund students majoring in the sciences. ODASIS does this by providing a supportive environment, improving retention rates, enhancing students' levels of academic achievement, and increasing students' entry rates into graduate or professional schools, or in their chosen fields in the workforce.

> SUCCESS Student Support Services

Student Support Services (SSS) is a federally funded program maintained by Rutgers to increase retention and graduate rates by helping first-generation and low-income students make the transition from one level of higher education to the next. Student Support Services (SSS) include one-on-one tutoring, mentoring, career and academic counseling, and assistance in pursuing higher level education. SSS participants who are receiving Federal Pell Grants are also eligible to receive grant aid.

> SUCCESS The TRIO Ronald E. McNair Post-Baccalaureate Achievement Program

The Rutgers Ronald E. McNair Program assists students from underrepresented backgrounds with strong academic potential and prepares them to pursue doctoral programs through involvement in research and other scholarly activities. Rutgers works closely with students, providing them with academic and financial support as they complete their undergraduate requirements. Participating students are encouraged to enroll in graduate programs, and their progress is tracked through the successful completion of advanced degrees.

Rutgers University
Office of Undergraduate Admissions
65 Davidson Road - Room 202
Piscataway, NJ 08854-8097
Ph: (732) 445-INFO (4636)
admissions@ugadm.rutgers.edu
www.admissions.rutgers.edu

FAST FACTS

STUDENT PROFILE
# of degree-seeking undergraduates	38,902
% male/ female	50/50
% African-American	11
% American Indian or Alaska Native	<1
% Asian or Pacific Islander	23
% Hispanic	11
% White	49
% International	2

First-generation and minority alums Avery F. Brooks, Actor and Educator, Livingston College 1973, Mason Gross School of the Arts 1976; James Dickson Carr, Attorney and First African-American Graduate of Rutgers, Rutgers College 1892; Clement A. Price, Historian and Professor, Graduate School – New Brunswick 1975; Paul Robeson, Athlete, Singer, Actor, Political Activist, Rutgers College 1919; Joseph H. Rodriquez, Federal Judge, School of Law-Camden 1958; Junot Diaz, Pulitzer Prize winning author, Rutgers College 1992

ACADEMICS
full-time faculty	2,292
full-time minority faculty	413
student-faculty ratio	14:1
% first-year retention rate	90
% graduation rate (6 yrs)	71

Popular majors Biology/Health Sciences, Business, Communication, Engineering, Fine and Performing Arts

CAMPUS LIFE
% live on campus (% fresh.)	41 (81)

Multicultural student clubs and organizations Fusion: The Rutgers Union of Mixed People; Diversity WORKS; Global Thought Society of Rutgers; Black Student Union; Indian Student Association; Douglas Asian Women Association; Latino Student Council; National Hispanic Business Association (NHBA) - Rutgers NB Chapter; Rutgers Union of Cuban American Students; Association of Philippine Students (Rutgers); Haitian Association; Latin American Student Organization and West Indian Student Organization

Athletics Rutgers-New Brunswick: NCAA Division I, Big East conference; Rutgers-Camden: NCAA Division III; Rutgers-Newark: NCAA Division III

ADMISSIONS
# of applicants	46,340
% accepted	54
# of first-year students enrolled	7,275
SAT Critical Reading range	530-630
SAT Math range	560-670
SAT Writing range	530-640
ACT range	n/a
average HS GPA	n/a

Deadlines
regular decision	12/1
application fee (online)	$65 ($65)
fee waiver for applicants with financial need	yes

COST & AID (2009 - 2010)
tuition	in-state $11,886; out-of-state $22,796
room & board	$10,376
total need-based institutional scholarships/ grants	$44,535,610
% of students apply for need-based aid	65
% of students receive aid	89
% receiving need-based scholarship/ grant aid	63
% receiving aid whose need was fully met	54
average aid package	$17,700
average student loan debt upon graduation	$18,620

Saint Peter's College

Saint Peter's College, founded in 1872, is a Jesuit, Catholic, co-educational, liberal-arts college which seeks to develop the whole person in preparation for a lifetime of learning, leadership and service in a diverse and global society. Committed to academic excellence and individual attention, Saint Peter's College provides education, informed by values, primarily in degree-granting programs in the arts, sciences and business, to resident and commuting students from a variety of backgrounds.

"The advice I would give to the incoming freshman class is to take advantage of all the great opportunities SPC offers. Join as many clubs on campus and do not be afraid to do something new, like going to service trip outside of the U.S.!"

– Barza H., '10
Jersey City, NJ
Accounting

> ACCESS **Summer Scholars**

Each summer Saint Peter's College offers outstanding high school juniors and seniors the opportunity to participate in its Summer Scholars Program. Classes are conducted on a colloquium model: a one-day general scholars meeting and two days of individual class meetings. General scholars meetings include performances and presentations by professionals from the various fields represented in the Summer Scholars Program: the arts, the social sciences and the sciences. At the end of the semester, students work in groups to create presentations that illustrate what they have learned in their classes.

> OPPORTUNITY **Educational Opportunity Fund (EOF)**

In conjunction with the state of New Jersey, Saint Peter's College sponsors the Educational Opportunity Fund. Since its establishment in 1968, the EOF has provided the opportunity for economically and academically disadvantaged students to attend college in New Jersey. This program offers access to higher education to students who meet the academic and financial guidelines established by the State of New Jersey and Saint Peter's College.

> SUCCESS **Academic Success Program (ASP)**

Saint Peter's College's Academic Success Program is a commitment to working with at-risk incoming freshmen to provide necessary academic support and mentoring. ASP provides students with a Summer Academy, where they can earn three credits, a $60 textbook voucher, academic monitoring and counseling, workshops and events, evening study sessions, connections to other campus resources and work-study opportunities.

> SUCCESS **Student Educational Programming for Ultimate Preparation**

These workshops are designed to provide first-year students with information, advice and practical skills that are essential for success. Addressing a wide variety of issues, past workshops included topics such as how to choose a major, leadership skills, career planning, alcohol abuse and study techniques. Workshops are jointly sponsored by the faculty, ASP, Center for the Advancement of Language and Learning, Center for Personal Development, Career Services and the Academic Dean's Office.

Saint Peter's College
Office of Admission
2641 Kennedy Blvd.
Jersey City, NJ 07306
Ph: (201) 761-7100
admissions@spc.edu
www.spc.edu

F A S T F A C T S

STUDENT PROFILE
# of degree-seeking undergraduates	2,436
male/female	48/52
African American	24
American Indian or Alaska Native	<1
Asian or Pacific Islander	11
Hispanic	27
Pell grant recipients	40

First-generation and minority alumni Honorable Robert Menendez

ACADEMICS
full-time faculty	115
full-time minority faculty	n/a
student-faculty ratio	15:1
average class size	22
% first-year retention rate	70
graduation rate (6 years)	46

Popular majors Business Management, Accounting, Elementary Education, Nursing, Pre-Medicine

CAMPUS LIFE
% live on campus (% fresh.)	44 (55)

Multicultural student clubs and organizations Asian American Student Union, Black Action Committee, Indian-Pakistani Culture Club, Latin American Service Organization, Middle Eastern Culture Club, Multicultural Heritage Club, Students of Caribbean Ancestry

Athletics NCAA Division I, Metro Atlantic Athletic Conference (football I-AA)

ADMISSIONS
# of applicants	5,505
% accepted	54
# of first-year students enrolled	544
SAT Critical Reading range	420-510
SAT Math range	420-530
SAT Writing range	420-510
ACT range	n/a
average HS GPA	3.2

Deadlines
regular decision	rolling
application fee (online)	$0 ($0)

COST & AID
tuition	$26,070
room and board	$10,854
total need-based institutional scholarships/grants	n/a
% of students apply for need-based aid	n/a
% of students receive aid	97
% receiving need-based scholarship or grant aid	n/a
% receiving aid whose need was fully met	15
average aid package	$17,330
average student loan debt upon graduation	$19,654

New Mexico Highlands University

New Mexico Highlands University
Office of Admissions
Box 9000
Las Vegas, NM 87701-9000
Ph: (505) 454-3439
admissions@nmhu.edu
www.nmhu.edu

FAST FACTS

STUDENT PROFILE

# of degree-seeking undergraduates	1,514
% male/female	38/62
% African American	5.1
% American Indian	6.4
% Asian	2.1
% Caucasian	23.4
% Hispanic	57.6
% Pell grant recipients	63.5

First-generation and minority alumni Anthony Edwards, professional football player; Reggie Garrett, professional football player; Lionel Taylor, professional football player

ACADEMICS

full-time faculty	76
student-faculty ratio	25:1
average class size	n/a
% first-year retention rate	58
% graduation rate (6 years)	20

Popular majors Business Administration, Social Work, Education

CAMPUS LIFE

% live on campus	n/a

Multicultural student clubs and organizations Bilingual Education Student Organization, Hispanic Cultural and Language Club, International Club, Los Rumberos, Native American Club, NMHU Mariachi, Pre-Law Association del Norte, Sendero, Servicios Especiales, Society of Hispanic Professional Engineers, Umoja

Athletics NCAA Division III, Rocky Mountain Athletic Conference

ADMISSIONS

# of applicants	1,146
% accepted	71
SAT Critical Reading range	n/a*
SAT Math range	n/a*
ACT range	15-19
average HS GPA	3.6

*New Mexico Highlands University is an open-enrollment institution

Deadlines

early decision	1/1
regular decision	8/1
application fee (online)	$15 ($15)

COST & AID

tuition	$3,198
room & board	$5,590
% of students receiving aid	97
% receiving need-based scholarship or grant aid	78
% receiving aid whose need was fully met	19
average aid package	$6,415
average student loan debt upon graduation	$12,147

New Mexico Highlands University is a co-educational, non-denominational, comprehensive public university serving the global community by integrating education, research, public service and economic development while celebrating its distinctive northern New Mexico cultures and traditions. Founded in 1893, New Mexico Highlands University is committed to programs that focus on its multi-ethnic student body with special emphasis on the rich heritage of Hispanic and Native American cultures that are distinctive to the state of New Mexico. The university perceives that its success depends upon an appreciation of the region's cultural and linguistic identities. By reinforcing cultural identity and encouraging the use of these assets, the university empowers students and the region's ethnic populations to achieve full involvement in the activities of society.

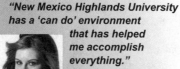

"New Mexico Highlands University has a 'can do' environment that has helped me accomplish everything."
– Tiffany N., '11
Business Management and Music

ACCESS University College Student for a Day

The New Mexico Highlands University's College Student for a Day program is a central part of the university's GEAR UP program. Serving approximately 1,250 seventh graders from 22 northern New Mexico school districts, GEAR UP increases the number of low-income students who will be prepared to enter and succeed in college. Following the New Mexico Regional and State Science Fair competition, GEAR UP students are bused to New Mexico Highlands University for the College Student for a Day program. Students proceed to mini lectures in groups of 20 conducted by university professors in various disciplines, including biology, chemistry, human performance and physics. Hands-on activities are incorporated into the classroom experience. Additionally, university researchers conduct tours of the laboratories and other science facilities.

 ACCESS Student Ambassadors

The New Mexico Highlands University Student Ambassadors are volunteer students who help the recruitment office with outreach into the local community. Ambassadors help recruit underserved students, mentor and encourage local high school students to continue with their education. Ambassador activities include facilitating the University Honors banquet for high school students, organizing career day participants for the local elementary, middle and high school events as well as organizing a "cowboy lunch" for all local high schools. The New Mexico Highlands cosponsored event is held every year and encourages students to attend "College Night," an event allowing prospective students to gather information about the university.

SUCCESS Early and Mid-Term Alert Program

The Early and Mid-Term Alert Program is an early intervention program that aids in identifying students (dual-enrolled, freshmen and sophomores) who are experiencing poor academic performance and excessive absenteeism in any of their introductory level courses. Academic advisers contact the at-risk students via e-mail or telephone, or personally visit their classrooms or residential halls. Advisers discuss their concerns regarding the student's academic performance and work with the students to identify the various services that are available to assist them to be more academically successful.

University of New Mexico

University of New Mexico
Office of Admissions
P.O. Box 4895
Albuquerque, NM 87196-4895
Ph: (800) 225-5866 / (505) 277-2446
apply@unm.edu
www.unm.edu

Founded in 1889, the University of New Mexico offers a unique 600-acre campus along old Route 66 in the heart of Albuquerque. Pueblo Revival architecture is reminiscent of another time and ties the campus to nearby Pueblo Indian villages. Beyond the campus, Albuquerque offers a dynamic community and sense of place defined by mesas, the historic Rio Grande, the Sandia Mountains and a unique blend of cultures. Forty-eight percent of all University of New Mexico students are minorities. Moreover, the university provides a host of programs for supporting and retaining underrepresented students.

> ACCESS **College Enrichment & Outreach Programs**

The College Enrichment & Outreach Programs support students in the development of skills necessary to pursue post-secondary education. The programs provide opportunities through educational, social and cultural experiences designed to recruit, retain and support the development of students in higher education. The programs offer outreach for pre-college students and for the enhancement of community partnerships.

> OPPORTUNITY **Visitation Days**

Admissions and Recruitment collaborates with university ethnic centers (e.g. African American Student Services, American Indian Student Services and El Centro de la Raza) to host campus visits. Minority and first-generation students tour the campus and participate in workshops focusing on the college application process, scholarships and financial aid. These workshops also introduce clubs, organizations, services and other campus opportunities. Visitation programs include Senior Day, American Indian Student Day, African American Student Day and Hispano Student Day.

> SUCCESS **Center for Academic Program Support**

The Center for Academic Program Support is the University of New Mexico's tutoring center. The center offers free academic assistance to all students — from freshmen learning how to study to upperclassmen who just needs additional assistance on a given project. Students can take advantage of the range of services offered to meet the university's diverse needs: individual tutoring, workshops, study groups, language conversation groups, supplemental instruction sessions and online tutoring.

> SUCCESS **NASPA Undergraduate Fellows Program**

The National Association of Student Personnel Administrators (NASPA) Undergraduate Fellows program is a semi-structured mentoring program for undergraduate students wishing to explore the field of student affairs and/or higher education. Students and mentors apply as a pair. The mission of the NASPA Undergraduate Fellows Program is to increase the number of underrepresented persons, persons with disabilities and others in student affairs and higher education. The program includes a host of activities, such as ongoing exchange, attendance to NASPA's annual conference, a paid summer internship and a summer leadership institute.

F A S T   F A C T S

STUDENT PROFILE
# of degree-seeking undergraduates	14,714
% male/female	45/55
% African-American	4
% American Indian or Alaska Native	6
% Asian or Pacific Islander	4
% Hispanic	39
% White	43
% International	1
% Pell grant recipients	n/a

ACADEMICS
full-time faculty	988
full-time minority faculty	296
student-faculty ratio	19:1
average class size	30
% first-year retention rate	77
% graduation rate (6 years)	44

Popular majors Business Administration, Psychology, Biology, Engineering, Fine Arts

CAMPUS LIFE
% live on campus	n/a

Multicultural student clubs and organizations
Afghan Student Association, Club Italiano, Falun Gong Club, Graduate Student Coalition for Diversity, Greek Student Union, Grupo Folklorico Lumbre de UNM, Hellenic Society, Hillel at UNM, Hui O Polynesia, India Students Association, Black Men in Motion, Black Student Union, Brazil Club, Chinese Student Friendship Association

Athletics NCAA Division I (football I-A), Mountain West Athletic Conference

ADMISSIONS
# of applicants	n/a
% accepted	n/a
# of first-year students enrolled	n/a
SAT Critical Reading range	470-610
SAT Math range	460-600
SAT Writing	n/a
ACT range	19-25
average HS GPA	3.3

Deadlines
regular decision application	6/15
application fee (online)	$20 ($20)
fee waiver for applicants with financial need	yes

COST & AID
tuition	in-state: $5,101; out-of-state: $17,254
room & board	$7,738
total need-based institutional scholarships/grants	n/a
% of students apply for need-based aid	58
% of students receive aid	43
% receiving need-based scholarship or grant aid	86
% receiving aid whose need was fully met	17
average aid package	$7,829
average student loan debt upon graduation	$16,595

Adelphi University

Adelphi University
PO Box 701
Garden City, NY, 11530-0701
Ph: (516) 877-3050
admissions@adelphi.edu
www.adelphi.edu

With its main campus in Garden City, Long Island, Adelphi University offers students the benefits of a safe, suburban campus with easy access to a global metropolis. In addition to general coursework options in fields like nursing, education and business, Adelphi also offers tailored academic programs. For example, through its Joint Degree Programs, students can work toward combined or graduate degrees in dentistry, engineering, environmental studies, law, optometry and physical therapy. Students may also participate in the school's unique Levermore Global Scholars Program, a leadership program that allows students across disciplines to learn about global relations.

> ACCESS Adelphi University Alice Hoffman Young Writers Retreat

Through the Young Writers Retreat, the Ruth S. Ammon School of Education in partnership with author alumna Alice Hoffman offers high school students and their teachers the chance to participate in an intensive series of creative writing workshops. The workshops are led by Adelphi faculty, accomplished writers and artists, and English education graduate students. All participants are provided with a full-tuition scholarship.

> OPPORTUNITY General Studies Program

Incoming freshmen whose records and test scores do not meet the admissions standards may participate in the General Studies Program, through which they can complete credit-bearing coursework in the liberal arts while enjoying the benefits of a full academic support system that includes individual tutoring and professional counseling. Upon successful completion of this first-year program, students enter as sophomores and follow an academic program leading to a degree.

> SUCCESS Center for Cross-Cultural Enrichment

The Center for Cross-Cultural Enrichment promotes the acceptance of diversity and encourages students from different ethnic and racial backgrounds to actively participate in campus activities. In addition to providing confidential services to students, the center also assists international students, sponsors workshops on diversity, offers personalized mentoring services and provides leadership training and administrative support to all campus multicultural organizations.

FAST FACTS

STUDENT PROFILE

# of degree-seeking undergraduates	4,225
% male/female	31/69
% African American	15
% American Indian or Alaska Native	<1
% Asian or Pacific Islander	7
% Hispanic	8
% White	61
% International	4
% Pell grant recipients	24.7

First-generation and minority alumni Chuck D, hip-hop artist; Bob Beamon, Olympic long-jumper; Angelina Martinez, M.S.W., founder, Utopia Home Care

ACADEMICS

full-time faculty	295
full-time minority faculty	58
student-faculty ratio	9:1
average class size	n/a
% first-year retention rate	78
% graduation rate (6 years)	63

Popular majors Business Administration/Management, Education, Nursing, Psychology

CAMPUS LIFE

% live on campus (% fresh.)	23 (41)

Multicultural student clubs and organizations African-American Peoples Organization, Korean Student Association, Association of Students from Taiwan, Afrika Unbound, La Union Latina, Asian Student Association, International Student Society

Athletics NCAA Division II, Northeast-10 Conference

ADMISSIONS

# of applicants	6,865
% accepted	66
# of first-year students enrolled	964
SAT Critical Reading range	470-580
SAT Math range	500-590
SAT Writing range	470-580
ACT range	20-26
average HS GPA	3.34

Deadlines

early action	12/1
regular decision	rolling
application fee (online)	$35 ($35)
fee waiver for applicants with financial need	yes

COST & AID

tuition	$24,020
room & board	$10,000
total need-based institutional scholarships/grants	$15,215,525
% of students apply for need-based aid	79
% of students receive aid	88
% receiving need-based scholarship or grant aid	71
% receiving aid whose need was fully met	2
average aid package	$16,500
average student loan debt upon graduation	$27,399

Columbia University

One of the oldest universities in the country, Columbia University offers students the benefits of an Ivy League education as well as access to one of the world's most vibrant, dynamic cities. The university is also proud to be among the schools that have recently revamped their financial aid policies in order to make attending the university possible for low- and middle-income families. Columbia continues to have the highest percentage of Pell grant recipients among any Ivy League school and one of the most socio-economically, racially, ethnically, and religiously diverse student bodies in the country.

"Ever since I was young, it was my dream to attend Columbia. Then I realized that choosing a college was not only about the school you liked, but it was also about affordability. I was ecstatic when I discovered my financial need was met for all four years!"

– Fayette C.
Bronx, NY
Latino Studies and History

> ACCESS Double Discovery Center

A department of Columbia College, the Double Discovery Center began in the 1960s and today serves over 1,000 low-income and first generation college-bound New York City youth each year through its Talent Search and Upward Bound programs. Students learn about colleges and careers, improve their academic work, and participate in personal development activities.

> ACCESS College Access Outreach

The Office of Undergraduate Admissions collaborates with more than 500 non-profit/community-based organizations nationwide, such as QuestBridge and College Horizons, to improve college access and opportunity. The Multicultural Recruitment Committee (MRC), a student volunteer group, assists Admissions to recruit a vibrant and dynamic first-year class.

> ACCESS Multicultural Fly-In Program

The Columbia Engineering Experience (CE²) invites applications from under-represented students nationwide to attend a funded, 3-day overnight program exposing them to The Fu Foundation School of Engineering and Applied Science.

> OPPORTUNITY Columbia is Affordable

Columbia meets 100% of the demonstrated financial need for all students, for all four years of study. Columbia has eliminated loans for all students receiving financial aid, whatever their family income, and replaced them with university grants. Students whose parents' calculated incomes are below $60,000 (with typical assets) are not expected to contribute any of their income or assets to tuition, room, board or mandatory fees, while families with calculated incomes between $60,000 and $100,000 and typical assets have a significantly reduced parent contribution. Students may also apply for additional funding to support study abroad, research, internship and community service opportunities.

> SUCCESS Academic Success Programs (ASP)

Through a network of comprehensive programs and services, ASP provides transitional programming, tutoring, skill-building seminars, educational and personal advising and mentoring to students. Academic Success Programs include Opportunity Programs, The Higher Education Opportunity Program (HEOP), National Opportunity Program (NOP) and the Ronald E. McNair Post-Baccalaureate Achievement Program (McNair Fellows Program), among others.

> SUCCESS Office of Multicultural Affairs (OMA)

Responding to the needs of its diverse undergraduate student body, OMA oversees programming in the areas of critical intellectual inquiry, mentoring, advocacy, social justice and intercultural programming, leadership development and training, diversity education and training and cultural and identity-based student organization advising. Of particular note are the heritage months that this office helps to run, which provide awareness campaigns focused on the Latino, African-American, Native American and Asian Pacific communities.

Columbia University
212 Hamilton Hall, MC 2807
1120 Amsterdam Avenue
New York, NY 10027
Ph: (212) 854-2522
ugrad-ask@columbia.edu
www.columbia.edu

F A S T F A C T S

STUDENT PROFILE

# of degree-seeking undergraduates	5,766
% male/female	52/48
% African American	11
% American Indian or Alaska Native	1
% Asian or Pacific Islander	18
% Hispanic	13
% White	36
% International	10
% Pell grant recipients	15

First-generation and minority alumni Barack Obama, President of the United States; Constance Baker Motley, first African-American woman elected to New York State Senate; David Paterson, governor, New York; Kiran Desai, Booker-Prize winning author; Langston Hughes, poet; Ben Jealous, youngest President and CEO of the National Association for the Advancement of Colored People (NAACP)

ACADEMICS

full-time faculty	791
full-time minority faculty	n/a
student-faculty ratio	6:1
average class size	10-19
% first-year retention rate	99
% graduation rate (6 years)	95

Popular majors Political Science, Economics, Engineering, English, History, Biology

CAMPUS LIFE

% live on campus (% fresh.)	95 (99)

Multicultural student clubs and organizations Accion Boricua, African Students Association, Arab Students' Organization (Turath), Black Students Organization, Caribbean Students Association, Chicano Caucus, Chinese Students and Scholars Association, Korean Students Association, Native American Council, Organization of Pakistani Students, Taiwanese American Students Association, United Students of Color Council, Vietnamese Student Association

Athletics NCAA Division I, ECAC, Ivy League

ADMISSIONS

# of applicants	25,427
% accepted	10
# of first-year students enrolled	1,391
SAT Critical Reading range	680-770
SAT Math range	690-780
SAT Writing	680-770
ACT range	31-34
average HS GPA	n/a

Deadlines

early decision	11/1
regular decision	1/1
application fee	$80
fee waiver for applicants with financial need	yes

COST & AID

tuition	$39,296
room & board	$10,228
total need-based institutional scholarships/grants	$92,000,000
% of students apply for need-based aid	50
% of students receive aid	60
% receiving need-based scholarship or grant aid	49
% receiving aid whose need was fully met	100
average aid package	$35,092
average student loan debt upon graduation	$18,420

Concordia College – New York

Concordia College – New York, a member of the national Concordia University system, offers students an intimate educational environment where students won't get lost in the shuffle. At the same time, students are able to take advantage of the resources offered at 10 sister schools, either by taking courses via video conference or by attending them as visiting students. Located in the college town of Bronxville, Concordia benefits from its proximity to New York City, which is a short train ride away. This is the best of both worlds, especially for the college's 30 percent first-generation student population. The opportunities are endless and are all woven within *The Concordia Experience*. Another unique opportunity at the college is the Concordia Connections program, which helps students with disabilities succeed in college by offering co-curricular support programs. The program is limited to 10 new students a year.

> **ACCESS College For Every Student (CFES) Partnership**

Through College For Every Student (formerly the Foundation for Excellent Schools), Concordia helps Bronx high school students through the college admissions process, providing them with college mentoring throughout their high school careers. Additionally, Concordia is exploring the opportunity to forge more mentoring programs through this program.

> **OPPORTUNITY Financial Aid Seminars / Need-Based Scholarships**

Concordia-NY helps area high school students understand the financial aid process by offering them access to financial aid seminars in the fall and spring. Between these two events, attendees gain access to information about institutional funds, loans, grace periods and interest rates, as well as learn how to fill out the FAFSA (Free Application for Federal Student Aid). Need-based scholarships are also available to many students who attend the college.

> **OPPORTUNITY Destination Concordia**

Prospective students can visit Concordia-NY during Destination Concordia, a campus visitation event that demystifies the college experience for underrepresented students. Student panels are featured and include discussions on the challenges facing first-generation college students. Also, middle school-aged children can visit campus and learn about college life. Financial aid is also an important issue for first-generation college students and sessions are featured covering the financial aid process, aid packages available and how to apply for these programs.

> **SUCCESS Fall Orientation**

During Fall Orientation, new students meet faculty, staff and advisers, attend presentations and discussions and participate in social activities and trips into New York City. Academic testing also occurs during this time, providing administrators and faculty with information about students' educational background, interests and abilities, helping them to address students' needs.

> **SUCCESS Freshman Seminar**

This unique seminar is mandatory for all entering freshmen and lasts eight weeks. Faculty members engage new students and learn the academic profile of each one, allowing for the development of strong support systems to provide for success at Concordia College. The Freshman Seminar is designed to foster relationships between faculty and students and between students themselves. The consequences of various important choices that must be made as freshmen are explored and a range of topics and issues are addressed.

Concordia College NY
171 White Plains Road
Bronxville, NY 10708
Ph: (800) 937-2655 / (914) 337-9300
admission@concordia-ny.edu
www.concordia-ny.edu

F A S T   F A C T S

STUDENT PROFILE

# of degree-seeking undergraduates	748
% male/female	43/57
% African-American	10
% American Indian or Alaska Native	<1
% Asian or Pacific Islander	<1
% Hispanic	8
% White	46
% International	9
% Pell grant recipients	21

ACADEMICS

full-time faculty	33
full-time minority faculty	n/a
student-faculty ratio	n/a
average class size	n/a
% first-year retention rate	73
% graduation rate (6 years)	52

Popular majors Business Administration/ Management, Education, Biology

CAMPUS LIFE

% live on campus	65

Multicultural student clubs and organizations African-Latin Heritage Club, Gospel Choir, International Club, Step Club, Greek Life and Housing

Athletics NCAA Division II, East Coast Conference

ADMISSIONS

# of applicants	682
% accepted	67
# of first-year students enrolled	128
SAT Critical Reading range	410-490
SAT Math range	410-500
SAT Writing	470
ACT range	16-20
average HS GPA	2.7

Deadlines

early action application	11/15
regular admission	3/15
application fee (online)	$50 ($50)
fee waiver for applicants with financial need	yes

COST & AID

tuition	$24,700
room & board	$9,125
total need-based institutional scholarships/grants	n/a
% of students apply for need-based aid	83
% of students receive aid	70
% receiving need-based scholarship or grant aid	70
% receiving aid whose need was fully met	20
average aid package	$22,309
average student loan debt upon graduation	$24,153

Cornell University

Founded in 1865 as both a private, co-educational university and the land-grant institution of New York State, Cornell University has a history of egalitarian excellence and diversity. Cornell educates leaders of tomorrow and extends the frontiers of knowledge in order to serve society. The university community fosters personal discovery, growth, scholarship and creativity, and engages men and women from every segment of society. Valuing enrichment of the mind, Cornell pursues understanding and knowledge beyond the barriers of ideology and disciplinary structure.

> ACCESS **Encourage Young Engineers and Scientists (EYES)**

Encourage Young Engineers & Scientists is a community-service organization committed to promoting engineering and the sciences as career fields and to increasing the math and science skills of elementary, middle and high school students. Each year, teams of Cornell students create exciting, project-based math and science lessons and experiments that are taught at local schools and after-school programs. These programs encourage local youth to pursue academic success.

> ACCESS **Let's Get Ready!**

Cornell's "Let's Get Ready!" program mobilizes those who live and work around disadvantaged students to actively support education. It provides free SAT preparation courses and college/financial aid advising to underserved high school students, and it involves families, schools, churches and businesses in offering these services. College students from surrounding communities run the programs and serve as instructors, role models and mentors to the students, helping them to navigate the college admissions process.

> OPPORTUNITY **Diversity Hosting**

To encourage multicultural students to matriculate to Cornell, the University sponsors Diversity Hosting. This admitted student program occurs throughout April to offer students the chance to "get to know" Cornell. Diversity Hosting provides limited transportation to participants and families are welcome.

> OPPORTUNITY **Higher Education Opportunity Program (HEOP)**

Cornell offers both a Higher Education Opportunity Program and an Education Opportunity Program. Both are programs for New York State residents who possess neither the traditional academic profile nor the financial means to afford college, but who do have the potential for success in a competitive academic environment. Students accepted under the EOP/HEOP programs receive academic counseling, assistance completing the financial aid application, and a financial aid package to for affordable education.

> SUCCESS **Office of Minority Educational Affairs (OMEA)**

Cornell's Office of Minority Educational Affairs facilitates academic and personal adjustment to Cornell for the minority community. It encourages institutional change, when necessary, to ensure that the University embraces its diverse student population. The Office also offers referrals to campus-wide services, announcements of events and scholarships, and a student-produced yearbook.

> SUCCESS **The Learning Strategies Center**

Providing tutoring and supplemental courses in biology, chemistry, economics, mathematics and physics, the Learning Strategies Center is the central academic support unit for Cornell students. Semester long courses, workshops, individual consultations and Web site resources offer assistance in improving general study skills. From time management to exam preparation, the center is a vital resource in helping students to develop effective learning strategies.

Cornell University
Undergraduate Admissions Office
410 Thurston Ave.
Ithaca, NY 14850-2488
Ph: (607) 255-5241
admissions@cornell.edu
www.cornell.edu

F A S T   F A C T S

STUDENT PROFILE

# of degree-seeking undergraduates	13,931
% male/female	51/49
% African American	5
% American Indian or Alaska Native	1
% Asian or Pacific Islander	17
% Hispanic	6
% White	46
% International	9
% Pell grant recipients	15

First-generation and minority alumni
Toni Morrison, winner, Nobel Prize for Literature; Jimmy Smits, actor; Mae Jamisen M.D., astronaut; Ed Lu, astronaut; Derrick Harmon, professional football player

ACADEMICS

full-time faculty	1,639
full-time minority faculty	248
student-faculty ratio	9:1
average class size	n/a
% first-year retention rate	97
% graduation rate (6 years)	93

Popular majors Biological Sciences, Economics, Business, English, Engineering

CAMPUS LIFE

% live on campus (% fresh.)	45 (100)

Multicultural student clubs and organizations
African, Latino, Asian, Native American Programming Board (ALANA), Alpha Kappa Alpha, Asian & Asian-American Forum, Asian Pacific Americans for Action, Association of Students of Color, Baraka Kwa Wimbo Gospel Ensemble, The Black Cornellian Woman, Black Students United Caribbean Students Association, Chinese Student Association, Delta Sigma Theta, Filipino Association, Ghanaians at Cornell, Haitian Students Association, Kappa Alpha Psi, Lambda Pi Chi, Lambda Theta Alpha, Lambda Theta Phi, Men of Color Council, Mexican Students Association at Cornell, Minorities in Agriculture, Minority Business Students Association, Minority Industrial and Labor Relations Student Organization

Athletics NCAA Division I, Ivy League, Eastern College Athletic Conference (football I-AA), Eastern Intercollegiate Wrestling Association

ADMISSIONS

# of applicants	34,371
% accepted	19
# of first-year students enrolled	3,181
SAT Critical Reading range	630-730
SAT Math range	670-770
SAT Writing	n/a
ACT range	29-33
average HS GPA	n/a

Deadlines

early decision	11/1
regular decision	1/2
application fee (online)	$70 ($70)
fee waiver for applicants with financial need	yes

COST & AID

tuition	in-state $23,526; out-of-state $39,666
room & board	$12,160
total need-based institutional scholarships/grants	$145,500,000
% of students apply for need-based aid	45
% of students receive aid	61
% receiving need-based scholarship or grant aid	41
% receiving aid whose need was fully met	100
average aid package	$29,621
average student loan debt upon graduation	$23,485

Dowling College

Dowling College is an independent comprehensive educational institution in the liberal arts tradition whose mission is to provide students with a well-rounded education based upon innovative teaching, informed and engaging research, and a commitment to democratic citizenship with a community service component. Dowling's Schools of Arts and Sciences, Aviation, Business, and Education emphasize excellence in teaching. They offer a challenging curriculum where students and teachers actively engage one another in developing ideas and bringing them to fruition. Dowling's campus promotes individualism and celebrates diversity with a wealth of international students.

> **OPPORTUNITY Higher Education Opportunity Program (HEOP)**

The HEOP has a thirty year longevity and has as its goal the provision of educational opportunity for students who are New York State residents and do not meet the traditional academic profile nor have the economic ability to meet educational expenses. This support services program that offers tutoring, financial literacy, and personal counseling coupled with the student's desire to excel is the perfect combination for potential success.

"The one-on-one interaction with faculty and staff truly helped me navigate my way to success!"
– Jessica Nicasico, '08 Queens, NY Communications

> **SUCCESS Academic Support Service Center (ASSC)**

The mission of the ASSC is to provide a network of academic resources and programs that assist the student through the rigors of academic coursework, thereby maximizing success. This office has oversight of several retention strategies designed to give students accurate and frequent feedback regarding academic progress. Coupled with the Office of Student Services, students are mentored and guided by the liaison between staff and faculty.

> **SUCCESS Student Support Services (SSS)**

Student Support Services (SSS) is a federally funded support services program designed to offer educational opportunity to first generation students. SSS offers an array of services including academic counseling, career counseling, academic advising, financial aid services, and cultural enrichment in an environment that is confidential, professional, supportive, friendly and caring.

> **SUCCESS Center for Minority Teacher Development and Training (CMTDT)**

The CMTDT is a preparation program for high school and college students desiring a career in the teaching profession. Specifically, the Center seeks to identify minority students who are interested in teaching, increase the number of minority teachers locally, regionally and nationally and enhance the quality and effectiveness of instruction for diverse student populations.

Dowling College
150 Idle Hour Blvd.
Oakdale, NY 11769
Ph: (800) 369-5464 (DOWLING)
admissions@dowling.edu
www.dowling.edu

FAST FACTS

STUDENT PROFILE

# of degree-seeking undergraduates	3.351
% male/female	45/55
% African-American	8
% American Indian or Alaska Native	<1
% Asian or Pacific Islander	3
% Hispanic	9
% White	56
% International	4
% Pell grant recipients	n/a

First-generation and minority alumni Sandra J. Brewster-Walker '72, President, L & P International and CEO, Caretakers; Dr. Kevin Bedell '71, Vice Provost for Research and John H. Rourke Professor of Physics, Boston College; Kevin R. Bland '03, Special Agent, Air Force Office of Special Investigations; Gerald J. Curtin '71, CEO, Statewide Roofing, Inc.; Rosalind O'Neal '06, Founder and CEO, African-American/Caribbean Education Associates, Inc.

ACADEMICS

full-time faculty	119
full-time minority faculty	14
student-faculty ratio	17:1
average class size	15
% first-year retention rate	67
% graduation rate (6 years)	36

Popular majors Education, Aviation, Business, Psychology

CAMPUS LIFE

% live on campus (% freshmen)	7 (11)

Multicultural student clubs and organizations International Club, Students Taking a New Direction, La Familia, Overdrive Dance Project, Humanitarian Club

Athletics NCAA Division II, East Coast Conference

ADMISSIONS

# of applicants	2,164
% accepted	86
# of first-year students enrolled	544
SAT Critical Reading range	390-510
SAT Math range	400-530
SAT Writing range	n/a
ACT range	n/a
average HS GPA	2.67

Deadlines

regular decision	rolling
application fee	$35
fee waiver for applicants with financial need	yes

COST & AID

tuition	$20,860
room & board	$10,200
total need-based institutional scholarships/grants	n/a
% of students apply for need-based aid	73
% receiving need-based scholarship or grant aid	96
% receiving aid whose need was fully met	n/a
average aid package	$15,077
average student loan debt upon graduation	n/a

Fordham University

Founded in 1841, Fordham University is an independent university in the Jesuit tradition. Fordham's undergraduate student body reflects the diversity of the metropolitan area in which the university is located. Students from around the world are attracted to New York's cosmopolitan culture. Whether educated at the Rose Hill campus in the Bronx or the Lincoln Center campus in Manhattan, Fordham students benefit from close contact with a distinguished faculty who teach at the undergraduate, graduate and professional levels. At Fordham, students will acquire the knowledge, skills, confidence and experience to succeed in their chosen fields. Fordham offers a firm foundation and a competitive advantage that makes Fordham students leaders at work and successful in life.

> ACCESS **Federal TRiO programs**

Fordham participates in three federally funded TRiO programs—Upward Bound, Talent Search and Student Support Services—that are designed to increase access and success for low-income, first-generation and underserved college students.

> OPPORTUNITY **Merit Scholarships**

The UPS Foundation/Lafarge Endowed Fellowships assist resident students from underrepresented populations who show leadership and academic competence as well as financial need. Candidates are selected by an admissions review committee and receive an average annual award of $7,000 for four years. The Metro Grant is a $6,000 grant awarded to incoming freshmen commuting to Fordham from their permanent residence in New York City or the surrounding areas. It is renewable up to four years for eligible students who continue to commute and maintain satisfactory progress toward their degree. National Merit, Achievement and Hispanic Recognition finalists and semi-finalists who are also in the top 10 percent of their high school classes are considered for a full-tuition award for all four years.

> OPPORTUNITY **The Higher Education Opportunity Program (HEOP)**

The Higher Education Opportunity Program (HEOP) provides economically and educationally disadvantaged students from New York state with the possibility of a Fordham education. The HEOP programs at Rose Hill and Lincoln Center provide support services for all incoming, pre-freshmen and continuing students enrolled in the program, including a pre-freshman summer program; tutorial services; academic advisement; career, personal, and financial aid counseling; developmental reading; and selected workshops in various academic and non-academic areas.

> SUCCESS **Internship Program and Diversity Networking Career Fair**

The professional achievements of Fordham's graduates arise, in part, from the University's extensive internship program. This highly successful program offers students the opportunity to intern with more than 2,600 of New York's most prestigious employers. More than 600 students participate in internships each year. The Office of Career Services hosts the Diversity Networking Banquet each fall for graduating seniors to connect with employers seeking greater diversity in their workplace. Career Services also supports all undergraduate students and alumni with individual counseling, mock interviews, resume-writing workshops, and advice on graduate school preparation, dining etiquette and other useful skills.

"I chose Fordham for its fabulous media department, study abroad opportunities and New York City location, all of which opened many doors of discovery for me. Fordham scholarships and the generosity of people who believe in students like me have given me experiences I could only dream about."

– Lana B., '09
Washington, DC
Communication and Media Studies

Fordham University
441 East Fordham Road
Bronx, NY 10458
Ph: (718) 817-4000
enroll@fordham.edu
www.fordham.edu

FAST FACTS

STUDENT PROFILE
# of degree-seeking undergraduates	7,875
% male/female	45/55
% African American	5
% American Indian or Alaska Native	<1
% Asian or Pacific Islander	8
% Hispanic	13
% Pell grant recipients	25.4

First-generation and minority alumni Denzel Washington, Academy Award-winning actor; Vince Lombardi, NFL Hall of Fame coach; Mary Higgins Clark, bestselling author

ACADEMICS
full-time faculty	723
full-time minority faculty	145
student-faculty ratio	13:1
average class size	22
% first-year retention rate	92
% graduation rate (6 years)	79

Popular majors Business, Communications, Psychology, Political Science, Biology, Pre-Professional Programs

CAMPUS LIFE
% live on campus (% fresh.)	55 (76)

Multicultural Student Clubs and Organizations Office of Multicultural Affairs, African Diaspora, Asian Cultural Exchange, International Students Association, Academia Hispana, *El Grito de Lares*
Athletics NCAA Division I, Atlantic 10 Conference, Patriot League

ADMISSIONS
# of applicants	24,557
% accepted	50
# of first-year students enrolled	1,835
SAT Critical Reading range	570-670
SAT Math range	570-670
SAT Writing range	570-670
ACT range	26-30
average HS GPA	3.54

Deadlines
early action	11/1
regular decision	1/15
application fee (online)	$50 ($50)
fee waiver for applicants with financial need	yes

COST & AID
tuition	$35,825
room & board	$13,716
total need-based institutional scholarships/grants	$50,591,708
% of students apply for need-based aid	81
% of students receive aid	76
% receiving need-based scholarship or grant aid	73
% receiving aid whose need was fully met	20
average aid package	$23,597
average student loan debt upon graduation	$31,300

Hamilton College

Originally founded in 1793 as the Hamilton-Oneida Academy, Hamilton has grown to become one of the nation's most highly regarded colleges. The open curriculum gives students the freedom to shape their own liberal arts education within a research and writing-intensive framework. Hamilton believes that its community will confront and engage most rewardingly with the issue of diversity when it is pursued not just as a social issue, but also as an intellectual one. Diversity thereby expands the breadth and augments the rigor of the intellectual life of the college. Woven throughout Hamilton's curriculum is the study of the world's races, cultures, religions and ideologies. Ultimately, the college wants to continue fostering an intellectual atmosphere that reflects its commitment to exploring and acknowledging the significance of different ideas and perspectives. For more information regarding diversity opportunities or resources, please visit www.hamilton.edu/diversity.

> ACCESS Study Buddies

Study Buddies matches Hamilton volunteers with 7-12th grade students from Utica for lunch, academic tutoring, and on-campus activities tailored to the needs and interests of the students. The friendly mentoring relationship established during the semester's seven Saturday sessions reach beyond the program and its specific academic focus to include exposure and guidance to the college planning process, discovery of new interests, and breakdown of socioeconomic barriers.

"Hamilton College has given me incredible opportunities to cultivate my curiosity, allowing me to pursue my passions and learn about myself in a new and changing world. It truly is an experience of a lifetime."

*– Ngoc N., '11
Utica, NY
Government*

> OPPORTUNITY HEOP and Hamilton College Scholars Program

The Arthur O. Eve Higher Education Opportunity Program, established by the New York State Legislature in 1969, provides access to independent colleges and universities for economically and educationally disadvantaged students. Students enrolled in this program are top performers in their high schools, but are inadmissible under Hamilton's normal admission profile. The Hamilton Scholars Program assists students who are ineligible for HEOP due to economic or residential factors but have similar profiles. Students attend summer classes before freshman year and receive support services throughout their time at Hamilton.

> OPPORTUNITY Posse Foundation

Hamilton participates in the Posse Foundation, a program that brings talented inner-city youth to campus to pursue their academics and to help promote cross-cultural communication. Posse students are nominated by their high school to the program and share a collaborative support system with a special mentor to adjust to campus and college life. Hamilton's Posse Scholars hail from Boston and Miami.

> SUCCESS The ACCESS Project

The ACCESS Project is dedicated to providing parents who are low-income, first generation college students all the support necessary to thrive in an academic community and to successfully enter the career field. The program offers qualified students assistance and support in entering and completing degree programs, and assures career placement that provides economic security and professional fulfillment.

> SUCCESS Residential Engagement in Academic Life (REAL)

Residential Engagement in Academic Life is a unique housing option open to 40 freshmen every year. Students live together in Wertimer House and take one of their four courses in a Wertimer House seminar room with one of Hamilton's best teachers. Because the faculty members who teach in the hall also are academic advisors for the program, there are increased opportunities for interaction with faculty and classmates on a regular basis, strengthening the connection between intellectual and social pursuits during the first year of college.

Hamilton College
Office of Admission
198 College Hill Road
Clinton, NY 13323
Ph: (800) 843-2655
admission@hamilton.edu
www.hamilton.edu

F A S T   F A C T S

STUDENT PROFILE (FOR 2008-2009)

# of degree-seeking undergraduates	1,834
% male/female	48/52
% African American	4
% American Indian or Alaska Native	1
% Asian or Pacific Islander	7
% Hispanic	5
% White	70
% International	5
% Pell grant recipients	11

First-generation and minority alumni Mason Ashe, President, Ashe Sports and Entertainment Consulting; Drew S. Days III, Professor of Law, Yale University, and former Solicitor General of the United States; Fabio Freyre, Group Vice President, Corporate Sales and Marketing, Time Inc., former Publisher, *Sports Illustrated*; Robert P. Moses, Leader, Civil Rights Movement, and founder of The Algebra Project, Kamila N. Shamsie, award-winning author

ACADEMICS

full-time faculty	173
full-time minority faculty	37
student-faculty ratio	10:1
average class size	75% have less than 20
% first-year retention rate	96
% graduation rate (6 years)	91

Popular majors Economics, Government, Mathematics, Psychology, Biology and English

CAMPUS LIFE

% live on campus	97

Multicultural student clubs and organizations Asian Culture Society, Black and Latino Student Union, Brothers Organization, International Students Association, Sistah Girls, West Indian and African Alliance

Athletics NCAA Division III, New England Small College Athletic Conference

ADMISSIONS
(BASED ON FALL 2008 APPLICATIONS)

# of applicants	5,073
% accepted	28
# of first-year students enrolled	467
SAT Critical Reading range	650-730
SAT Math range	650-720
SAT Writing range	640-730
ACT range	n/a
average HS GPA	n/a

Deadlines

early decision	11/15
regular decision	1/1
application fee (online)	$75 ($0)
fee waiver for applicants with financial need	yes

COST & AID (FOR 2009-2010)

tuition	$39,370
room & board	$10,100
total need-based institutional scholarships/grants	$24,600,000
% of students apply for need-based aid	n/a
% of students receive aid	50
% receiving need-based scholarship or grant aid	50
% receiving aid whose need was fully met	100
average aid package	$32,580
average student loan debt upon graduation	$14,000

Hartwick College

The defining characteristics of Hartwick College are its beautiful hillside location overlooking Oneonta, N.Y. and its "Connecting the Classroom to the World" experiential learning emphasis, which forms partnerships between motivated students and experienced faculty. The college is recognized for its January Term, during which students take innovative on-campus courses or participate in internships and programs around the globe. Hartwick is also known for its technology integration, which places a laptop in the hands of every student.

> ACCESS **Beyond Boundaries**

Civic engagement is a central tenet of Hartwick College. Beyond Boundaries, the college's student-led service organization, offers a number of service opportunities in the greater community. These include many youth-focused service sites like the OCAY (Oneonta Community Alliance for Youth), the Oneonta Boys & Girls Club and the Oneonta City School District.

> ACCESS **Foundation for Excellent Schools (FES)**

Hartwick College is part of the Leatherstocking Consortium of the Foundation for Excellent Schools, which is a partnership that serves first-generation, low-income and other underserved students.

> OPPORTUNITY **Hartwick Overnight Program (HOP)**

Hartwick offers peer-to-peer matches for visiting prospective students to fully experience campus life. In addition to the tour and admissions interview, students have the option to stay overnight with host students who share common cultural, club, academic majors and athletic interests.

> OPPORTUNITY **QUEST Gold Loan**

Hartwick College is the only school in New York State to offer the QUEST (Quality Undergraduate Education with Sensible Terms) Gold Loan. This loan allows families to pay their tuition expenses on a monthly basis, rather than in lump sums in fall and spring. The loan is interest-free while the student is in college, and it functions like a "value-added" Federal PLUS Loan. The QUEST Gold Loan also offers post-graduation repayment benefits, no pre-payment penalty and low interest rates after graduation.

> SUCCESS **U.S. Pluralism Programs**

Hartwick College hosts a number of diversity programs under the auspices of its U.S. Pluralism Programs Office. The Pluralism Associates League for Students (PALS) assists students with the transition to college, the Heritage and Leadership Forum examines the role heritage plays in one's leadership style and the Harriet Tubman Mentoring Project explores the self-awareness of personal histories, values and beliefs.

Hartwick College
Box 4022
Oneonta, NY 13820-4022
Ph: (888) 427-8942 / (607) 431-4150
admissions@hartwick.edu
www.hartwick.edu

FAST FACTS

STUDENT PROFILE

# of degree-seeking undergraduates	1,493
% male/female	43/57
% African-American	4
% American Indian or Alaska Native	<1
% Asian or Pacific Islander	2
% Hispanic	4
% White	61
% International	4
% Pell grant recipients	24

First-generation and minority alumni Isaac Newton Arnold, Illinois congressman, introduced resolution to amend the Constitution to prohibit slavery, 1864; Scott Adams, creator of *Dilbert*

ACADEMICS

full-time faculty	111
full-time minority faculty	n/a
student-faculty ratio	11:1
average class size	18
% first-year retention rate	70
% graduation rate (6 years)	57

Popular majors Business, Political Science, English, Nursing, Psychology

CAMPUS LIFE

% live on campus (% freshmen)	78 (97)

Multicultural student clubs and organizations BiGala+, International Club, P.A.L.S. (Pluralism Associates League for Students), Society of Sisters United and Brothers United, Women's Center, Amnesty International, Fair Trade Club

Athletics NCAA Division III, Empire Eight; Division I Mid-American Soccer Conference (m soccer); Division I Collegiate Water Polo Association (w water polo); Division III IHSA (w equestrian)

ADMISSIONS

# of applicants	2,532
% accepted	83
# of first-year students enrolled	444
SAT Critical Reading range	490-590
SAT Math range	500-500
SAT Writing range	n/a
ACT range	22-26
average HS GPA	3.1

Deadlines

early decision I	11/15
early decision II	1/15
regular admission	rolling
application fee (online)	$35 ($0)
fee waiver for applicants with financial need	yes

COST & AID

tuition	$33,330
room & board	$9,075
total need-based institutional scholarships/grants	n/a
% of students apply for need-based aid	90
% of students receive aid	73
% receiving need-based scholarship or grant aid	73
% receiving aid whose need was fully met	14
average aid package	$22,955
average student loan debt upon graduation	$30,802

Iona College

Iona College
715 North Ave.
New Rochelle, NY 10801
Ph: (914) 633-2502
admissions@iona.edu
www.iona.edu

Dedicated to academic excellence in the tradition of the Christian Brothers, Iona College is a private, Catholic, liberal-arts college located in suburban Westchester County, just minutes north of New York City. At Iona, differences and diversity are viewed as valuable resources. The College is home to various multicultural groups and hosts annual events such as Hispanic Heritage Month Festivities, Black History Month Festivities and Heritage Week. In the rich heritage of the Christian Brothers, Iona College fosters intellectual inquiry and the values of justice, peace and service.

> ACCESS Gaining Early Awareness and Readiness for Undergraduate Programs (GEAR UP)

This program aims to significantly increase the number of pre-collegiate low-income students who are prepared to enter and succeed in post-secondary education through academic enhancement, cultural enrichment, social awareness, and parental involvement.

> ACCESS The Success Center

Iona students serve as college mentors to elementary and middle school students in this after-school homework help program. The Success Center provides a positive atmosphere that encourages achievement.

> ACCESS Science and Technology Entry Program (STEP)

The Science and Technology Entry Program enhances the math, science and technology skills of minority and low-income regional high school students. Its goal is to encourage participating students to continue their education after graduation in the fields of mathematics, science, technology and/or the licensed professions where minorities are traditionally underrepresented.

> OPPORTUNITY Today's Students Tomorrow's Teachers (TSTT)

Iona College, in cooperation with Today's Students Tomorrow's Teachers, seeks to attract students from heavily diverse populations in the tri-state area into the teaching profession. Iona offers a half-tuition scholarship to any students who fulfill program requirements during their four years of high school and who gain admission to Iona as education majors.

> SUCCESS The Rudin Center

The Rudin Center is an academic support center that provides students at Iona College with a wide array of support services to enable them to become independent self-learners. Working one-on-one or in small groups, the professional staff, graduate assistants and undergraduate tutors help students acquire, improve, review and strengthen skills. The center stresses academic support in areas related to the college core: reading, composition, mathematics, and computer science.

"College is important to me because it affords me opportunities to succeed in what I love to do and shine in an increasingly competitive world. The intellectual growth I have experienced at college has not only prepared me for the working world post-graduation, but has enriched my life as a whole. I chose to earn my degree at Iona College because of its intimate size and opportunity for hands-on assistance, its close proximity to New York City, and its ACEJMC-accredited journalism program"

– Alana R., '10, Warwick, NY Mass Communications/ Journalism

FAST FACTS

STUDENT PROFILE

# of degree seeking undergraduates	3,314
male/female	44/56
African-American	5.3
American Indian/Alaskan Native	<1
Asian/Pacific Islander	1.7
Hispanic	11.6
White	67.1
% Pell grant recipients	23.2

ACADEMICS

full time faculty	183
average class size	18
first-year retention rate	85
% graduation rate (6 yr)	62

Popular majors Mass Communication, Accounting, Psychology, Finance, Education, Marketing

CAMPUS LIFE

% live on campus	64

Multicultural student clubs and organizations Council of Multicultural Leaders, Hispanic Organization for Latin Awareness (HOLA), Students of Caribbean Ancestry, Iona College Diversity Collaborative

Athletics NCAA Division I, MAAC

ADMISSIONS

# of applicants	7,313
% accepted	58
# of first-year students enrolled	792
SAT Reading range	540-640
SAT Math range	550-660
SAT Writing range	n/a
ACT average	23
avg. H.S. GPA	3.5

Deadlines

early action	12/1
regular decision	2/15
application fee (online)	$50 ($50)
fee waiver for applicants with financial need	yes

COST & AID

tuition	$28,850
room & board	$11,800
total need-based institutional scholarships/grants	$4,227,251
% of students apply for need-based aid	97
% of students receive aid	75
% receiving need-based scholarship or grant aid	49
% receiving aid whose need was fully met	29
average aid package	$18,067
average student loan debt upon graduation	$24,213

Ithaca College

Located in a small city that boasts an impressive range of cultural activities against a stunning backdrop of waterfalls and gorges, Ithaca is a private, residential college that unites tradition with a dynamic living and learning environment. Resting on the south hill of Ithaca, N.Y., this former music conservatory offers a compelling blend of a liberal arts and professional degree programs. Students may select from among more than 100 degree programs within the college's five schools and its Division of Interdisciplinary and International Studies. From classes taught by expert faculty to exciting internships, co-curricular activities and study abroad, students will find all the opportunities and facilities of a large university on Ithaca's vibrant campus of 6,400 students.

> ACCESS **Ithaca College – Frederick Douglass Academy Partnership**

Through an ambitious access program, Ithaca College and Frederick Douglass Academy, a public middle and high school located in Harlem, N.Y., have forged a productive partnership that focuses on cross-cultural communication and understanding of the educational challenges facing inner-city youth. This partnership provides Ithaca's teacher education students with hands-on teaching experience and encourages them to pursue future careers in urban settings. In turn, the college provides practical support for students with college-bound goals.

> OPPORTUNITY **Martin Luther King Jr. Scholar Program**

Exceptional minority students may apply to Ithaca College's Martin Luther King Jr. Scholar program. Much more than a financial award, this dynamic learning community develops future leaders who are committed to promoting King's legacy of social justice and equality in their personal and professional lives. Scholars engage in an array of seminars, interact with distinguished guests and lecturers and take part in funded international and domestic travel and research. Selected participants receive up to full tuition in aid, with a minimum merit-based scholarship of $18,000.

> OPPORTUNITY **African, Latino, and Native American (ALANA) Merit Scholarships**

These scholarships recognize superior academic achievement and are presented to select entering undergraduate students who are members of an underrepresented group, regardless of their financial need. Scholarships range from $2,000 to $7,000 and may be renewed annually so long as the recipient maintains full-time enrollment, a minimum GPA of 3.0 and satisfactory progress toward a degree. ALANA scholarships are reserved for undergraduate students.

> SUCCESS **Ithaca Achievement Program (IAP)**

Participants in this program are committed to personal and academic success. Underrepresented students who elect to join the Ithaca Achievement Program receive support in both academic and career development. Students may join the program in their first, second, or third year; participants are involved in a broad range of activities to help support their academic goals. Those students in the first year of the program attend the summer institute sponsored by Academic Enrichment Services.

> SUCCESS **Housing Offering a Multicultural Experience (HOME)**

This residential program presents an opportunity for new and returning students to live in a culturally diverse environment. The program offers an excellent residential option for students preparing to study abroad as well as for international students who are living in the United States for the first time.

Ithaca College
953 Danby Road
Ithaca, NY 14850-7000
Ph: (607) 274-3124
admisssions@ithaca.edu
www.ithaca.edu

FAST FACTS

STUDENT PROFILE

# of degree-seeking undergraduates	5,968
% male/female	44/56
% African American	3
% American Indian or Alaska Native	<1
% Asian or Pacific Islander	4
% Hispanic	4
% White	75
% International	2
% Pell grant recipients	17.2

First-generation and minority alumni Sandra Pinckney, host of Food Finds, Food Network; CCH Pounder, Emmy-nominated actress, star of The Shield; Erica Reynolds, president/CEO of Moka Marketing, LLC; Edgardo Rivera, investment advisor at Gold State Capital LLC and former vice president of marketing, J Records

ACADEMICS

full-time faculty	463
full-time minority faculty	39
student-faculty ratio	12:1
average class size	17
% first-year retention rate	84
% graduation rate (6 years)	77

Popular majors Business Administration, Communications, Health Sciences and Human Performance, Music, Theater Arts

CAMPUS LIFE

% live on campus (% fresh.)	70 (99)

Multicultural student clubs and organizations African-Latino Society, Amani Gospel Singers, Asian Culture Club, Brothers For Brothers, Ithaca Achievement Program, KUUMBA Repertory Theater, Martin Luther King Scholars, Native American Cultural Club, Sister 2 Sister
Athletics NCAA Division III, ECAC Empire 8

ADMISSIONS

# of applicants	12,233
% accepted	66
# of first-year students enrolled	1,441
SAT Critical Reading range	540-640
SAT Math range	550-640
SAT Writing range	540-640
ACT range	n/a
average HS GPA	n/a

Deadlines

early decision	11/1
regular decision	2/1
application fee (online)	$60 ($60)
fee waiver for applicants with financial need	yes

COST & AID

tuition	$32,060
room & board	$11,780
total need-based institutional scholarships/grants	$55,307,516
% of students apply for need-based aid	75
% of students receive aid	100
% receiving need-based scholarship or grant aid	97
% receiving aid whose need was fully met	54
average aid package	$26,655
average student loan debt upon graduation	n/a

Marymount Manhattan College

Marymount Manhattan College
221 East 71 Street
New York, NY 10021
Ph: (212) 517-0430
admissions@mmm.edu
www.mmm.edu

Marymount Manhattan College is an urban, independent, liberal arts college. The mission of the college is to educate a socially and economically diverse student body by fostering intellectual achievement and personal growth and by providing opportunities for career development. Inherent in this mission is the intent to develop an awareness of social, political, cultural and ethnic issues, in the belief that this awareness will lead to concern for, participation in, and improvement of society. To accomplish this mission, the College offers a strong program in the arts and sciences for students of all ages, as well as substantial pre-professional preparation. Central to these efforts is the particular attention given to the individual student. Marymount Manhattan College seeks to be a resource and learning center for the metropolitan community.

> **OPPORTUNITY** Arthur O. Eve Higher Education Opportunity Program (HEOP)

Provides supportive services and supplementary financial assistance to students who demonstrate potential for academic success. The Program has been a part of Marymount Manhattan College since 1969.

> **OPPORTUNITY** Freshman Academic Excellence Awards

These awards are offered to students with a 3.0 or higher GPA and an SAT of 1150 or higher (Critical Reading and Math). There are also various need based programs to assist students who demonstrate financial need.

> **SUCCESS** Jump Start

Jump Start helps students transition smoothly into the college community of Marymount Manhattan College and New York City. Students gain an advantage by experiencing the campus, becoming familiar with academic support services and engaging in a credit-earning course and many cultural activities. In a three-week intensive program of college course work, first-year students earn credit, meet friends, explore cultural offerings of New York City and connect with the Marymount Manhattan College Community.

"When I think of what Marymount has to offer, a quote from Vince Lombardi comes to mind: 'The quality of a person's life is in direct proportion to their commitment to excellence, regardless of their chosen field of endeavor.' This quote is the basic embodiment of what Marymount Manhattan College stands for. Simply put, this school gives us the tools, the help, and the chance to make our lives better no matter what career path we choose."
– Julio R.

FAST FACTS

STUDENT PROFILE
# of degree-seeking undergraduates	2,000
% male/female	24/76
% African-American	11
% American Indian or Alaska Native	<1
% Asian or Pacific Islander	3
% Hispanic	11
% White	72
% International	3
% Pell grant recipients	22

ACADEMICS
full-time faculty	92
full-time minority faculty	11
student-faculty ratio	11:1
average class size	18
% first-year retention rate	64
% graduation rate (6 years)	46

Popular majors Communication Arts, Theatre, Dance, Psychology, Business Management

CAMPUS LIFE
% live on campus (% fresh.)	50 (87)

Multicultural student clubs and organizations Bedford Hills College Program Club, Black & Latino Student Association
Athletics Intramurals and Club Sports

ADMISSIONS
# of applicants	4,000
% accepted	69
# of first-year students enrolled	500
SAT Critical Reading range	430-750
SAT Math range	400-680
SAT Writing	450-650
ACT range	20-31
average HS GPA	3.2

Deadlines
regular decision	rolling
application fee (online)	$60($60)
fee waiver for applicants with financial need	yes

COST & AID
tuition	$23,610
room & board	$13,416
total need-based institutional scholarships/grants	$5,595,877
% of students apply for need-based aid	76
% of students receive aid	85
% receiving need-based scholarship/grant aid	75
% receiving aid whose need was fully met	12
average aid package	$12,334
average student loan debt upon graduation	$16,903

Molloy College

Molloy College, an independent, comprehensive institution, offers a rich and multidimensional educational experience and encourages critical thinking and creative exploration from within a personalized community setting. Moreover, Molloy combines academic excellence and leadership with personal, compassionate mentoring to bring out the best in every student. Molloy College rests on a 30-acre campus in Rockville Centre, Long Island. Established as a women's college in 1955, the institution became co-educational in 1982. Today, Molloy College welcomes men and women diverse in age, race, religious belief and cultural background. In particular, the undergraduate student body, which has grown to nearly 3,000, consists of 58 percent first-generation students and 35 percent minority students.

> ACCESS TRiO Program

This federally funded program highlights Molloy College's commitment to a quality education for all students regardless of race, ethnic background or economic circumstance. The TRiO Program is open to incoming freshmen or transfer students who are first-generation, low-income, physically challenged, or who have learning disabilities. Services offered by the TRiO Program include academic assessments in reading, writing and mathematics, academic and career advisement, academic support and assistance with admission, financial aid and other applicable Molloy College services. Students benefit from professional mentoring and resources regarding grants, scholarships, volunteer placement, internships and other opportunities.

> ACCESS Mentoring Latinas

The Mentoring Latinas Program at Molloy College is a project originally designed for Latina students at Mineola High School but now also includes Uniondale's middle schools. Molloy Latina undergraduates mentor high school young women and provide support, friendship and positive role models. Some of the planned activities include visits to the nursing and language labs, art and music departments, and meeting the dance and athletic teams. This program is jointly administered by Molloy's departments of Social Work, Modern Languages, Service-Learning and Advancement. Molloy students also provide mentoring and guidance to children in the Uniondale school district through another program, Molloy Mentors.

> SUCCESS Academic Enrichment (AcE) Program

AcE helps students achieve their academic potential in mathematics, science and modern languages. The program develops self-confidence and self-esteem, thereby producing rewarding results for the participants, and provides remediation for students with a "C" average in their major course of study. Supplemental help is also provided if a student is passing a course but still needs assistance. Each of the diverse group of professional coaches is either an active or semi-retired teacher certified in the field in which they coach.

> SUCCESS Success Through Expanded Education Program (STEEP)

STEEP provides the academic assistance needed for those with learning disabilities to reach their full potential. Participants find the learning methods that best help them achieve academic success. Learning disability specialists address particular study habits, help prepare for tests, improve class participation and assist with schedule preparation and course selection. Students develop life skills in time management, their most appropriate learning style, critical-thinking skills, goal setting and stress management.

Molloy College
PO Box 5002
Rockville Centre, NY 11571
Ph: (516) 678-5000
admissions@molloy.edu
www.molloy.edu

F A S T   F A C T S

STUDENT PROFILE

# of degree-seeking undergraduates	2,969
% male/female	22/78
% African-American	15
% American Indian or Alaskan Native	<1
% Asian or Pacific Islander	7
% Hispanic	11
% White	63
% International	<1
% Pell Grant Recipients	27

ACADEMICS

full-time faculty	169
full-time minority faculty	14
student-faculty ratio	10:1
average class size	15
% first-year retention rate	87
% graduation rate (6 years)	59

Popular majors Nursing, Education, Business Management, Music Therapy, Criminal Justice, Social Work

CAMPUS LIFE

% live on campus	0

Multicultural student clubs and organizations
African-American Caribbean Organization, Union Hispana de Molloy, Global Learning Office, Asian Cultural Exchange
Athletics NCAA Division II, East Coast Conference

ADMISSIONS

# of applicants	1,803
% accepted	59
# of first-year students enrolled	420
SAT Critical Reading range	390-720
SAT Math range	400-730
SAT writing	380-760
ACT range	n/a
average H.S. GPA	3.35

Deadlines

early action	12/1
regular decision	rolling
application fee (online)	$30 ($30)
fee waiver for applicants with financial need	yes

COST & AID

tuition	$19,970
room & board	n/a
total needs-based institutional scholarships/grants	$11,161,094
% of students apply for need-based aid	97
% of students receive aid	80
% receiving need-based scholarships or grant aid	72
% receiving aid whose need was fully met	14
average aid package	$12,007
average student loan debt upon graduation	$22,754

Nyack College

Nyack College educates students broadly in preparation for advanced study, dynamic careers and civic responsibility. Nyack College is a private, Christian, liberal arts college with a residential campus that overlooks the Hudson River in Nyack, N.Y., and a commuter campus in Manhattan. For 125 years, Nyack has committed to providing an academically excellent education that is socially relevant and personally transforming in an environment that is globally engaged and intentionally diverse. The college serves a diverse student body, of which 45 percent are first-generation students and 64 percent are minority students. Committed to promoting Christian knowledge, moral maturity, and spiritual development in preparation for lives of ministry and service, Nyack College offers traditional and non-traditional undergraduate programs to a co-educational student body.

> ACCESS English Language Institute

The purpose of Nyack's English Language Institute is to prepare students whose first language is not English for college acceptance. This intensive English program held at the commuter campus during the summer months, meets 24 hours a week for eight weeks. Focus is on academic listening and speaking, reading and writing, vocabulary development, attention to pronunciation and introduction to literature. Students attend labs on accent reduction, structure and listening skills. Field trips, activities and conversation partners enrich the students' first-hand experience of English.

> OPPORTUNITY Inter-cultural Ministry Grant

The Inter-cultural Ministry Grant is a $3,000 grant awarded to any student attending the residential campus who is an active member of a U.S. or Canadian Christian Missionary Alliance intercultural ministry. All Christian Missionary Alliance intercultural ministries are listed in the Christian Missionary Alliance Prayer Directory. Qualifying ministries are those that conduct bilingual services or services in a language other than English. The participant must have a Christian Missionary Alliance pastor complete the pastor's reference form on the application. Once awarded, the recipient must maintain a minimum 2.5 cumulative GPA for renewal.

> OPPORTUNITY Higher Education Opportunity Program (HEOP)

The Higher Education Opportunity Program targets students from households with modest incomes who have potential for success at Nyack College, despite poor high school performance. Since 1975, HEOP at Nyack College has had a proven a record of success. Participants have held many campus leadership positions; some have served as student government officers, class presidents, club presidents, resident assistants, been baccalaureate speakers, been named to the Dean's List, received awards and scholarships for academic achievement, earned citations for community service, been inducted into honor societies and graduated with honors. Participants can also travel to such countries as England, Korea, Japan, Kenya and the Philippines.

> SUCCESS College Warm-Up Program

The College Warm-Up Program is a five-week summer program offered at the residential campus by the Division of Academic Support Services at Nyack College. It orients students to college life and assists them in strengthening their basic academic skills. The program features courses in writing, reading, critical thinking and computer applications. Additionally, a variety of workshops and activities are offered.

> SUCCESS English Language Immersion Program

In addition to ESL courses, Korean- and Spanish-speaking students at the commuter campus have the unique opportunity to take core courses in English language immersion designed to help them adjust to college study using English. These courses are taught by fully bilingual professors who lecture in English, discuss the ideas of the course in English, and provide course materials in English, but who also provide specific support for ESL students. Support may include explanation of difficult concepts and supplemental materials in the students' first language, all of which support their academic progress as they gain more confidence in English. Professors are especially sensitive to students' language issues and understand their needs.

Nyack College
1 South Boulevard
Nyack, NY 10960-3698
Ph: (800) 336-9225 / (845) 358-1710
admissions@nyack.edu
www.nyack.edu

F A S T   F A C T S

STUDENT PROFILE
# of degree-seeking undergraduates	2,043
% male/female	42/58
% African-American	34.9
% American Indian or Alaska Native	<1
% Asian or Pacific Islander	7.4
% Hispanic	20.8
% White	28.5
% International	3.8
% Pell grant recipients	40

First-generation and minority alumni Howard Jones, Billy Graham's first African-American evangelist; Andre Thornton, former Major League Baseball player

ACADEMICS
full-time faculty	148
full-time minority faculty	50
student-faculty ratio	19:1
average class size	15
% first-year retention rate	76
% graduation rate (6 years)	40.3

Popular majors Psychology, Business Administration, Education, Music, Bible and Christian Ministry

CAMPUS LIFE
% live on campus (% freshmen)	59 (85)

Multicultural student clubs and organizations Residential campus: African American Association of Cultural Exchange, Asian Nyackers Seeking Revival, Association of Latin American Students, Messianic Jewish Fellowship, International Students Organization, Hallelujiahfest, Cultural Heritage Week; NYC campus: celebration of Hispanic Heritage Week, Black History Month and Korean Lunar New Year

Athletics NCAA Division II, Central Atlantic Collegiate Athletic Conference

ADMISSIONS
# of applicants	n/a
% accepted	n/a
# of first-year students enrolled	n/a
SAT Critical Reading range	420-550
SAT Math range	400-540
SAT Writing	n/a
ACT range	18-26
average HS GPA	n/a

Deadlines
regular decision	9/1
application fee (online)	$25 ($25)
fee waiver for applicants with financial need	yes

COST & AID
tuition	$19,500
room & board	$7,900
total need-based institutional scholarships/grants	n/a
% of students apply for need-based aid	89.8
% of students receive aid	84
% receiving need-based scholarship or grant aid	83.9
% receiving aid whose need was fully met	20.2
average aid package	$16,808
average student loan debt upon graduation	$23,583

Rochester Institute of Technology

Rochester Institute of Technology is one of the world's leading career-oriented, technological institutions. Students are from all 50 states and over 100 countries and have equally as diverse academic interests. Typically, more than one-fifth of entering freshmen come from minority or international student groups. Rochester Institute of Technology's National Technical Institute for the Deaf supports over 1,400 deaf and hard-of-hearing students, adding a social and educational dynamic not found at any other university. The Institute's eight colleges offer more than 90 undergraduate programs in engineering, computing, information technology, engineering technology, photography, business, science, art, design and the liberal arts.

> **ACCESS   The Program for Rochester to Interest Students in Science and Math (PRIS2M)**

This seven-week summer program, focusing on minority high school students in Rochester, is designed to encourage them to pursue science and math in post-secondary education. Under the leadership of math and science coaches, students learn and strengthen science and math skills. The program has achieved a 100 percent college placement rate and Rochester Institute of Technology commits up to five, $8,000 per year renewable scholarships to students who complete the program and are admitted to the Institute as full-time, matriculated students. Preference is given to students who demonstrate financial need and are admitted to programs in engineering, math, sciences and technologies.

> **OPPORTUNITY   Hillside Work-Scholarship Connection (HWSC)**

Hillside Work-Scholarship Connection links urban adolescents to a support network of youth advocates and employers. Rochester Instititue of Technology commits up to five, $10,000 per year renewable scholarships to students who successfully complete the program and enter the Institute as full-time freshmen, and up to five, $10,000 per year renewable scholarships for students who enter as full-time transfer students from Monroe Community College.

> **SUCCESS   The Upstate Louis Stokes Alliance for Minority Participation**

The Upstate Louis Stokes Alliance for Minority Participation (ULSAMP) was formed to attract and maximize the potential of students from underrepresented populations, specifically African-American, Latino American and Native American (AALANA) attending college in Upstate New York who are enrolled in STEM fields. Supported by a grant from the National Science Foundation, the ULSAMP program will work across the alliance of 7 Upstate colleges and universities to increase recruitment and the subsequent graduation rate of both first-time freshmen and transfer students, by enhancing academic experiences and opportunities.

"The Higher Education Opportunity Program (HEOP) program was a critical key to my success at RIT. The program provided me with the academic, social and financial support that enabled me to reach my full potential. It certainly was a cornerstone of my undergraduate career and I am grateful to have been given the opportunity to take advantage of all that RIT has to offer."

– Alvin R., '09
Buffalo, NY
Hospitality and Service Management

> **SUCCESS   North Star Academy**

The North Star Center develops new approaches in minority recruitment, retention and graduation rate improvement including tutoring, mentoring and a college liaison program. College liaisons serve as advisers, advocates and coaches. The center sponsors a textbook assistance fund for low-income students, professional development workshops, a Global Awareness Fair and a multicultural fashion show. North Star Academy, one such program, brings approximately 40 underserved freshmen together for a three-week summer academic enrichment, confidence, and community-building program each year.

Rochester Institute of Technology
60 Lomb Memorial Drive
Rochester, NY 14623-5604
Ph: (585) 475-7424
admissions@rit.edu
www.rit.edu

FAST FACTS

STUDENT PROFILE
# of degree-seeking undergraduates	13,260
% male/female	67/33
% African American	5
% American Indian or Alaska Native	<1
% Asian or Pacific Islander	5
% Hispanic	4
% White	69
% International	10
% Pell grant recipients	25

First-generation and minority alums Dan Loh, Pulitzer Prize winner, photojournalism

ACADEMICS
full-time faculty	945
% full-time minority faculty	18
student-faculty ratio	14:1
average class size	25
% first-year retention rate	89
% graduation rate (6 years)	69

Popular majors Engineering, Computing, Engineering Technology, Business Administration/ Management, Information Technology

CAMPUS LIFE
% live on campus (% fresh.)	68 (95)

Multicultural student clubs and organizations Asian Culture Society, Korean Student Association, Latin American Student Association, Organization of African Students, Organization of the Alliance of Students from the Indian Subcontinent, Taiwanese Student Association, Vietnamese Student Association, Chinese Student Scholar Association
Athletics NCAA Division III, Atlantic Hockey Association (NCAA Division I, m ice hockey only); ECAC West Ice Hockey League (w ice hockey); Patriot League; New York State Women's Collegiate Athletic Association

ADMISSIONS
# of applicants	12,994
% accepted	61
# of first-year students enrolled	2,602
SAT Critical Reading range	540-630
SAT Math range	560-670
SAT Writing range	520-620
ACT range	25-30
average HS GPA	3.5

Deadlines
early decision	12/1
regular decision	rolling
application fee (online)	$50 ($50)
fee waiver for applicants with financial need	yes

COST & AID
tuition	$30,282
room & board	$10,044
total need-based institutional scholarships/grants	$73,972,000
% of students apply for need-based aid	77
% of students receive aid	88
% receiving need-based scholarship or grant aid	83
% receiving aid whose need was fully met	78
average aid package	$19,200
average student loan debt upon graduation	$22,800

St. John Fisher College

An independent, liberal-arts school in the Catholic tradition, St. John Fisher College prides itself on its strong liberal arts curriculum and its emphasis on community. To this end, the school maintains involvement in the city of Rochester, and, through its Office of Multicultural Affairs and Diversity Programs, boasts a number of diversity initiatives. The college offers 31 academic majors in the humanities, social sciences, sciences, business and nursing, as well as 10 pre-professional programs. Fisher also offers 13 graduate programs, including two doctoral programs. Of note, the college offers a unique minor in Peace and Social Justice Studies. Through this program, students take cross-disciplinary coursework that focuses on areas like conflict resolution, poverty and race relations.

> ACCESS Fisher-Jefferson Partnership

St. John Fisher College has a long-standing relationship with Thomas Jefferson High School, an urban public school with a high percentage of first-generation, low-income and minority students. Through this partnership, Fisher students offer mentoring and tutoring to Jefferson students.

> ACCESS Science Outreach Program

Each year, the college hosts three separate regional science competitions — Science Olympiad for middle school students (one day), Science Exploration Days for junior and senior high school students (two days) and Science Congress (two days) for high school students. These programs expose pre-college students to various areas of science, including biology, chemistry and physics. These campus programs are designed to encourage students, especially students of color, to become more involved in science and learn about the college and career opportunities within these disciplines.

> ACCESS College Bound

The College Bound program, an intensive five-day resident program, is intended to familiarize students with the various aspects of the college admission and application process and provide them with the knowledge and skills to successfully search for, apply to and select a college. The program is designed for students who are between their junior and senior year of high school. In addition, students should be considered first-generation, low-income and have a minimum of a B average in high school.

> OPPORTUNITY Accepted Student ALANA Brunch

Before attending Fisher's Accepted Student Open House in the spring, ALANA students can participate in a brunch designed especially for them. During this brunch, students have the opportunity to meet faculty, staff and students, gain additional information about the college and learn about the opportunities and support offered to students of diverse backgrounds. St. John Fisher also presents attending students with certificates celebrating their acceptance.

> OPPORTUNITY First Generation Scholarship Program

This program is designed to provide financial and academic assistance to high school students who exhibit a high degree of motivation and academic potential, and whose parents did not graduate from a post-secondary institution. Each year, up to 36 students are offered the First Generation Scholarship. Recipients receive yearly awards ranging from $5,000 to one-third of resident student cost. Recipients also take part in a freshman learning community designed especially for them.

> OPPORTUNITY Higher Education Opportunity Program (HEOP)

St. John Fisher College participates in HEOP, a New York State program designed to provide academically and economically disadvantaged residents access to independent colleges and universities throughout the state. HEOP students have the potential for and interest in pursuing a college degree, but they typically do not meet the regular admission requirements of a particular college. HEOP students who attend Fisher are required to participate in a five-week orientation program in the summer before their freshman year, pursue their studies on a full-time basis and utilize academic support services such as advising, counseling and tutoring.

St. John Fisher College
3690 East Avenue
Rochester, NY 14618-3597
Ph: (585) 385-8064
admissions@sjfc.edu
www.sjfc.edu

F A S T F A C T S

STUDENT PROFILE
# of degree-seeking undergraduates	2,878
% male/female	41.9/58.1
% African-American	5
% American Indian or Alaska Native	<1
% Asian or Pacific Islander	2
% Hispanic	3
% White	86.6
% International	0.2
% Pell grant recipients	26

First-generation and minority alumni Paul Hewitt '85, head men's basketball coach, Georgia Tech; William Clark '78, president/CEO, Urban League of Rochester; Maria Cino '79, president/CEO, 2008 Republican National Convention; Jackie Peterson, VP of Student Affairs, dean of students, College of the Holy Cross

ACADEMICS
full-time faculty	201
full-time minority faculty	n/a
student-faculty ratio	13:1
average class size	25
% first-year retention rate	84
% graduation rate (6 years)	73

Popular majors Management, Education, Nursing, Communication/Journalism

CAMPUS LIFE
% live on campus (% freshmen)	49 (87)

Multicultural student clubs and organizations Asian Student Union, Black Student Union, Fisher Pride, Gospel Choir, Latino Student Union
Athletics NCAA Division III, Eastern Collegiate Athletic Conference, New York State Association of Intercollegiate Athletics for Women, Empire 8

ADMISSIONS
# of applicants	3,231
% accepted	62
# of first-year students enrolled	569
SAT Critical Reading range	480-570
SAT Math range	510-600
SAT Writing range	470-560
ACT range	22-26
average HS GPA	3.5

Deadlines
early decision	12/1
regular decision	rolling
application fee (online)	$30 ($30)
fee waiver for applicants with financial need	yes

COST & AID
tuition	$24,280
room & board	$10,090
total need-based institutional scholarships/grants	n/a
% of students apply for need-based aid	94
% of students receive aid	81
% receiving need-based scholarship or grant aid	99
% receiving aid whose need was fully met	36
average aid package	$19,951
average student loan debt upon graduation	$29,288

St. John's University

For 140 years, St. John's University has provided access and opportunity for students of diverse economic backgrounds. A Catholic university in the Vincentian tradition of excellence and service, St. John's values the talents of every student. With its New York City location, St. John's also reflects the harmonious diversity of immigrants and minority groups that add to the city's energy. St. John's has three residential New York City campuses; a campus in Oakdale, NY; and campuses in the center of Paris, France and Rome, Italy. More than 95 percent of St. John's students receive in excess of $380 million in financial aid through scholarships, loans, grants and work-study. All new students receive their own wireless laptop computer and benefit from St. John's focus on quality academics, service, global learning, high-tech resources and an outstanding residence life program.

> ACCESS Scholars Program

St. John's prepares qualified high school students for college. To apply, juniors submit to the Admissions Committee their high school transcripts and recommendations from their principal or counselor. Accepted students take two courses during the summer after their junior year. As seniors, they enroll for one fall and spring college-level course.

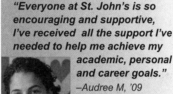

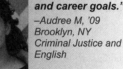

"Everyone at St. John's is so encouraging and supportive, I've received all the support I've needed to help me achieve my academic, personal and career goals."
–Audree M, '09
Brooklyn, NY
Criminal Justice and
English

> ACCESS GEAR-UP Program

With the U.S. Department of Education and Higher Education Services Corporation, St. John's offers academic services for lower-income, first-generation students from local middle and high schools, including college tours, tutoring, mentoring, residential summer camp, parent workshops, SAT/PSAT preparation and summer youth employment through the city's Department of Youth and Community Development.

> ACCESS College Bound: Liberty Partnerships Program

Coordinated with the New York State Department of Education, the program provides support services to middle and senior high school students who demonstrate college potential but need assistance to graduate. Services include counseling, tutoring and enrichment activities.

> OPPORTUNITY Options Program

St. John's provides academic and financial assistance to eligible students at its Staten Island campus. Qualified students are from out-of-state and demonstrate circumstances that would hinder their attending college. Offered through the Division of Special and Opportunity Programs, the program includes tutoring, mentoring and other services.

> SUCCESS College Science and Technology Entry Program (CSTEP)

This program prepares New York State residents from underrepresented backgrounds for careers in science, technology, health-related and licensed professions including pharmacy. Selected as freshmen and sophomores, students enjoy career and academic counseling, tutoring and workshops.

> SUCCESS Ronald E. McNair Scholars Program

Named for the African-American astronaut who perished in the Challenger accident, this Queens-campus program prepares first-generation, low-income students from underrepresented groups for post-baccalaureate and graduate study.

> SUCCESS Mentoring Programs

All students benefit from mentoring. Count On Alumni for Career Help (C.O.A.C.H.) provides alumni mentors. The Alpha Mentoring Program assigns on-campus peer mentors. Through the University Freshman Center, professional counselors guide freshmen to success.

St. John's University
8000 Utopia Parkway
Queens, NY 11439
Ph: (888) 661-1334
admissions@stjohns.edu
www.stjohns.edu/learnmore/01757.stj

F A S T   F A C T S

STUDENT PROFILE

# of degree-seeking undergraduates	14,808
% male/female	42/58
% African American	17
% American Indian or Alaska Native	<1
% Asian or Pacific Islander	18
% Hispanic	15
% White	37
% International	5
% Pell grant recipients (freshman)	48

First-generation and minority alumni Haron A. Amin, '99C, '05G, ambassador to Japan, Afghanistan Embassy; Louis Carnesecca, '05C, '60GEd, '00HON, former head men's basketball coach, St. John's University; Hon. Charles B. Rangel '60L, '83HON, congressman, New York's 15th District, U.S. House of Representatives; Hon. Reinaldo E. Rivera '76L, associate justice, appellate division, Second Judicial Department, New York State Unified Court System

ACADEMICS

full-time faculty	669
full-time minority faculty	134
student-faculty ratio	17:1
average class size	20-29
% first-year retention rate	78
% graduation rate (6 years)	58

Popular majors Pharmacy, Liberal Studies, Finance, Psychology, Accounting

CAMPUS LIFE

% live on campus (% freshmen)	30 (56)

Multicultural student clubs and organizations African Students Association, Albanian American College Club, Arab Students United, Asian Students Association, Caribbean Students Association, Chinese Cultural Association, Guyanese Students Association, Indian Sub-Continent Student Organization, Japanese Cultural Association, Korean Students Association, LASO, Organization of Pakistani Students, Polish Students Association, Taiwanese Students Association, Vietnamese Cultural Organization

Athletics NCAA Division I, Big East Conference

ADMISSIONS

# of applicants	52,980
% accepted	43
# of first-year students enrolled	3,108
SAT Critical Reading range	480-590
SAT Math range	490-620
SAT Writing	n/a
ACT range	n/a
average HS GPA	3.3

Deadlines

regular decision	rolling
application fee (online)	$50 ($0)
fee waiver for applicants with financial need	yes

COST & AID

tuition	$29,350
room & board	$13,140
total need-based institutional scholarships/grants	$50,682,149
% of students apply for need-based aid	87
% of students receive aid	79
% receiving need-based scholarship or grant aid	68
% receiving aid whose need was fully met	8
average aid package	$20,524
average student loan debt upon graduation	$21,793

St. Lawrence University

St. Lawrence University is an independent, private, diverse, liberal-arts learning community of inspiring faculty, serious students and accomplished alumni, guided by tradition and focused on the future. Chartered in 1856, St. Lawrence is New York's oldest continuously co-educational institution of higher learning, evidence of the university's heritage of inclusiveness. The university's expansive 1,000-acre campus, which rests midway between the Adirondacks Mountains and Ottawa, Canada, offers unmatched opportunity for outdoor activities. St. Lawrence students celebrate the multicultural heritage of all Laurentians and are committed to being educated students for responsible global citizenship. The university believes that a campus of people with different histories, experiences and ideas is the richest environment for learning.

> OPPORTUNITY Higher Education Opportunity Program (HEOP)

In partnership between St. Lawrence University and the New York State Education Department, HEOP finds and supports students who are capable and motivated to be successful. In particular, the program provides opportunity for low-income students whose test scores or grades do not meet regular admission standards. HEOP provides comprehensive academic and financial support to those who would otherwise be unable to attend an institution of higher learning.

> OPPORTUNITY Presidential Diversity Scholarship

The $120,000 Presidential Diversity Scholarship is awarded to students of African-American, Asian-American, Hispanic-American and Native American heritage. Winners are awarded $30,000 annually and are offered an all-expenses-paid trip to visit the campus. The visit takes place after the participant's selection as a scholar but before enrollment decisions are due. Applicants must write a 200-500 word essay in which they are asked to "Describe an experience you have had that has led you to value diversity."

> SUCCESS Collegiate Science and Technology Entry Program (CSTEP)

CSTEP is a New York State-funded program for eligible students. The goal is to increase the number of historically underrepresented students who complete programs of study that lead to professional licensure and careers in mathematics, science, technology and health-related fields. The program provides academic advising, internships, networking opportunities, graduate/professional school preparation and career, personal, and financial counseling.

> SUCCESS McNair Scholar Program

Funded by a federal grant to the University, this program is aimed at encouraging students in underrepresented groups to pursue doctoral studies. The program offers a variety of services, including a mentored summer research internship, research opportunities, GRE preparation, monetary support to assist McNair scholars in attending professional conferences and academic personal and career counseling.

"I know that one day I will use everything that St. Lawrence University has given me to improve our world, but it can't end with me."
– Brittany P. '10, Fort Drum, NY Psychology major and McNair Scholar

FAST FACTS

STUDENT PROFILE
# of degree-seeking undergraduates	2,206
% male/female	45/55
% African-American	3
% American Indian or Alaska Native	<1
% Asian or Pacific Islander	2
% Hispanic	3
% White	67.8
% International	5.2
% Pell grant recipients	17

First-generation and minority alumni Joseph Lekuton, member, Kenya Parliament, youngest recipient of Kenya's Order of the Grand Warrior; Derrick Pitts, vice president/chief astronomer, Franklin Institute Science Museum/Fels Planetarium, Philadelphia; Elinor Tatum, publisher, *The Amsterdam News* (oldest continuously published black newspaper in New York City)

ACADEMICS
full-time faculty	173
full-time minority faculty	29
student-faculty ratio	11:1
average class size	18
% first-year retention rate	88
% graduation rate (6 years)	76

Popular majors Economics, Psychology, Environmental Studies, Government, Biology, Mathematics

CAMPUS LIFE
% live on campus (% freshmen)	98 (100)

Multicultural student clubs and organizations Theme Cottages (La Casa Latina, Ray Ross, Black Women's Residence), African Students Union, Black Cultural Center, Black Student Union, Caribbean Latin American Studies (CLAS), International House, Intervarsity Christian Fellowship, Jewish Student Union

Athletics NCAA Division III, Upstate Collegiate Athletic Conference

ADMISSIONS
# of applicants	5,419
% accepted	34
# of first-year students enrolled	639
SAT Critical Reading range	570-640
SAT Math range	570-640
SAT Writing	560-650
ACT range	25-29
average HS GPA	3.6

Deadlines
early decision I	11/15
early decision II	1/15
regular decision	2/1
application fee (online)	$60 ($60)
fee waiver for applicants with financial need	yes

COST & AID
tuition	$39,765
room & board	$10,160
total need-based institutional scholarships/grants	$34,530,884
% of students apply forneed-based aid	70
% of students receive aid	63
% receiving need-based scholarship or grant aid	99
% receiving aid whose need was fully met	52
average aid package	$36,230
average student loan debt upon graduation	$29,941

State University of New York at Geneseo

SUNY Geneseo
1 College Circle
Geneseo, NY, 14454
Ph: (866) 245-5211
admissions@geneseo.edu
www.geneseo.edu

Founded in 1871, the State University of New York at Geneseo is a co-educational, non-denominational, public liberal arts college with selected professional and master's level programs. Part of the State University of New York (SUNY) system, Geneseo combines a rigorous curriculum and a rich co-curricular life to create a learning-centered environment. The entire college community works together to develop socially responsible citizens with skills and values important to the pursuit of an enriched life and success in the world. Geneseo is considered to be the most selective campus of SUNY's Public Honors Colleges.

> OPPORTUNITY **Higher Education Opportunity Program (HEOP)**

The State University of New York at Geneseo's state-sponsored Higher Education Opportunity Program (HEOP) seeks to provide higher education to traditionally bypassed residents of New York State. The program is aimed at students who have the potential to complete a college degree but do not meet the general admission requirements because their academic credentials may have been adversely affected during their high school years by economic factors. HEOP students are subject to several obligations designed to ensure a successful academic experience. All participants are assigned to a personal academic adviser who assists with course selection through the first four semesters at Geneseo. They are also limited to four academic courses during their first semester of study, and must participate in an sponsored summer activity. To this end, SUNY Geneseo allows academically talented, underrepresented students to add their own unique talent to the fabric of the Geneseo community of learners.

> SUCCESS **Transitional Opportunity Program (TOP)**

The Transitional Opportunity Program is a SUNY Geneseo-sponsored program that includes many of the services commonly associated with HEOP. Although the academic standards for admission are the same, TOP applicants are not held to the same firm economic guidelines expected of HEOP applicants. Most students qualify for the program because of the university's interest in and commitment to expanding its student body to include the rich ethnic, racial, economic and age diversity of society. In addition to being assigned a personal academic adviser, TOP pre-freshmen are tested in writing, mathematics and reading. During a summer orientation, they have the opportunity to meet Geneseo's faculty and staff and acquire specific information that could impact their life as a Geneseo student, such as counseling services, financial aid, residence life and co-curricular life.

> SUCCESS **COMPASS**

The primary goal of COMPASS at the State University of New York at Geneseo is to create a system of support for admitted students of African, Latino, Asian or Native American descent. To minimize struggles so that students can achieve early success in their college careers, COMPASS pairs first-year students — "Protégés" — with upperclassmen "Peer Mentors" and faculty "Fellows." In addition, Protégés enroll in a biweekly College Success Seminar taught by the Peer Mentors. Tutoring support to COMPASS Protégés is available.

FAST FACTS

STUDENT PROFILE
# of degree-seeking undergraduates	5,441
% male/female	41/59
% African-American	2
% American Indian or Alaska Native	<1
% Asian or Pacific Islander	6
% Hispanic	4
%White	73
% Pell grant recipients	19

First-generation and minority alumni My Hang V. Hyunh, scientist, recipient, 2007 MacArthur Fellowship

ACADEMICS
full-time faculty	258
full-time minority faculty	40
student-faculty ratio	19:1
average class size	27
% first-year retention rate	91
% graduation rate (6 years)	78

Popular majors Special Education, Psychology

CAMPUS LIFE
% live on campus (% freshmen)	57 (100)

Multicultural student clubs and organizations Black Student Union, Geneseo Chinese Cultural Club, Japanese Culture Club, Korean American Students Association (KASA), Latino Student Association, Liberty in North Korea at Geneseo, Men of Action and Change, Muslim Students and Friends Association, Shakti

Athletics NCAA Division III, State University of New York Athletic Conference

ADMISSIONS
# of applicants	10,588
% accepted	37
# of first-year students enrolled	1,081
SAT Critical Reading range	610-690
SAT Math range	620-690
SAT Writing range	n/a
ACT range	28-30
average HS GPA	3.7

Deadlines
early decision	11/15
regular decision	1/1
application fee (online)	$40 ($40)
fee waiver for applicants with financial need	yes

COST & AID
tuition	in-state: $4,970; out-of-state: $12,870
room & board	$9,070
total need-based institutional scholarships/grants	$7,797,603
% of students apply for need-based aid	99
% of students receive aid	100
% receiving need-based scholarship or grant aid	83
% receiving aid whose need was fully met	75
average aid package	$5,260
average student loan debt upon graduation	$18,700

Union College

Founded in 1795, Union College offers programs in the liberal arts and engineering. Union enjoys a rich history, yet keeps an eye to the future. Converging Technologies — interdisciplinary programs which link engineering and the liberal arts — offer students opportunities for courses, programs and research in an increasing number of fields such as nanotechnology, digital art and entrepreneurship. Union also utilizes Minerva, a unique housing system that allows students to interact with each other and with faculty, and affords them space to work, play and even host parties. International study and community service are other strong tenets of a Union education, prompting students to remain engaged with the outside world.

"Union is a welcoming place. It feels like I'm living in a small village. What I like best are the small classes. I can focus. I'm getting to know my professors, and they know my name."

– Gina C., '11
Brighton, MA
Biochemistry, Spanish

> **ACCESS Science and Technology Entry Program (STEP)**

Co-sponsored by the New York State Department of Education, STEP helps students in grades seven through 12 from underrepresented and low-income backgrounds to prepare for academic programs in scientific, technical, health-related and licensed professions. Participants receive high-quality instruction in math, science and technology, including academic tutoring, college-level courses for enrichment and opportunities to work on research projects. STEP takes place through workshops offered during the school year, as well as through a summer camp program.

> **OPPORTUNITY Multicultural Weekends: Getting to Know "U" (fall) and Represent "U" (spring)**

Prospective students from diverse cultural backgrounds are invited to stay overnight on campus and experience what Union has to offer. The weekends are planned to be informational and to provide hands-on experience with the college process. The programs include cultural and academic-life panel discussions, workshops on applying to college, as well as information on what type of supportive services are offered and should be sought in college.

> **OPPORTUNITY Posse Foundation**

Union College participates in the Posse Foundation, a program that brings talented inner-city youth to campus to pursue their academics and to help promote cross-cultural communication. Posse students are nominated by their high school to the program and share a collaborative support system with a special mentor to adjust to campus and college life. Union's Posse Scholars hail from Boston.

> **OPPORTUNITY AOP/HEOP Program**

The Academic Opportunity Program, an extension of the New York State Higher Education Opportunity Program, brings approximately 20-25 students to the college who are from academically and financially disadvantaged backgrounds. Participants are talented students who benefit from the financial and academic support services offered through the program such as individual advising, tutoring and full-need financial aid packaging.

> **SUCCESS Office of Multicultural Affairs**

In support of the college's strategic plan objectives and institutional goals, the Office of Multicultural Affairs develops and implements diversity leadership programs for the community. Serving as a location for the development and awareness of all campus-wide multicultural programs, the office provides programming assistance for cultural events, LGBTQ programs, religious and multi-faith programs, interdisciplinary studies and other special events.

Union College
Grant Hall, Union College
Schenectady, NY 12308
Ph: (518) 388-6112
admissions@union.edu
www.union.edu

F A S T   F A C T S

STUDENT PROFILE

# of degree-seeking undergraduates	2,199
% male/female	51/49
% African American	4
% American Indian or Alaska Native	<1
% Asian or Pacific Islander	6
% Hispanic	4
% White	82
% International	3
% Pell grant recipients	19.9

First-generation and minority alumni Allen Sessoms, president, University of the District of Columbia; Robert F. Murray, Jr., chief, Division of Medical Genetics, Dept. of Pediatrics and Child Health, professor of medicine and genetics, Howard University School of Medicine; Jennifer Smith Turner, author, poet

ACADEMICS

full-time faculty	197
full-time minority faculty	23
student-faculty ratio	10:1
average class size	19
% first-year retention rate	93
% graduation rate (6 years)	85

Popular majors Political Science and Government, Psychology, Economics, Mechanical Engineering, History

CAMPUS LIFE

% of fresh. live on campus	100

Multicultural student clubs and organizations African and Latino Alliance of Students, Asian Student Union, Black Student Union, Circulo Estudiantil Latino Americano, Middle Eastern Civilization and Culture Association

Athletics Division III, Liberty League

ADMISSIONS

# of applicants	5,271
% accepted	39
# of first-year students enrolled	580
SAT Critical Reading range	570-660
SAT Math range	600-680
SAT Writing range	560-670
ACT range	26-30
average HS GPA	3.50

Deadlines

early decision	11/15
regular decision	1/15
application fee (online)	$50 ($0)
fee waiver for applicants with financial need	yes

COST & AID

tuition (includes room & board)	$50,439
total need-based institutional scholarships/grants	$25,880,127
% of students apply for need-based aid	53
% of students receive aid	100
% receiving need-based scholarship or grant aid	98
% receiving aid whose need was fully met	99
average aid package	$29,188
average student loan debt upon graduation	$14,652

University of Rochester

The University of Rochester, founded in 1850, is one of the nation's leading private, co-educational, nonsectarian universities. Located near downtown Rochester, the campus offers a balance between urban access and spacious comfort, thus creating a comfortable and unique learning environment. This environment no doubt contributes in part to the academic reputation of the institution: In 2007, the University of Rochester was named one of 25 'New Ivies.' The university's 5000 undergraduate students enjoy a well-rounded college experience and 96 percent of freshmen return for their sophomore year. In maximizing retention and success among all community members, the University of Rochester offers a breadth of services targeted to the specific needs of minority and first-generation students.

> **ACCESS National Hispanic Institute (NHI) Lorenzo de Zavala Youth Legislative Session**

The Lorenzo de Zavala Youth Legislative Session is designed for students with college and leadership potential. Students learn to see themselves as leaders, and then learn how to become leaders within the context of electoral politics. Participants create their own government, write and pass legislation and collaborate to support community prosperity.

> **ACCESS Science and Technology Entry Program**

The Science and Technology Entry Program serves students enrolled in high school grades eight through 12. In particular, participants come either from economically disadvantaged backgrounds or from groups that are historically underrepresented in scientific, technical, health-related, and licensed professions. The program works to raise participants' interest in the aforementioned fields, thereby encouraging them to join the professional workforce in medicine and the health care professions.

> **OPPORTUNITY Higher Education Opportunity Program (HEOP) & Early Connection Opportunity (ECO)**

The University of Rochester's HEOP and ECO programs are designed to serve students of diverse racial, ethnic and cultural backgrounds. HEOP addresses the specific needs of students who have had economic or educational challenges in high school. For eligible students, the program provides a strong support network, academic advising, personal counseling, and substantial financial assistance. Meanwhile, ECO is designed to help students positively and appropriately establish themselves within the academic setting. The program prepares students for classes, informs them about services and introduces them to social life on campus.

> **SUCCESS McNair Program**

The objective of the McNair Program is to increase the numbers of low-income, first-generation and underrepresented undergraduates who pursue doctoral degrees and go on to careers in research and teaching at the university level. The program prepares students for the rigors of graduate study by providing the opportunity to conduct research under the guidance of faculty mentors. Students accepted to the program attend a series of colloquia, receive training for the Graduate Record Exam and are trained to present the results of their research at university-sponsored and national academic conferences.

"My time at the University of Rochester has been incredible! Through a liberal arts education I have maximized my academic experience to earn a B.A. in Financial Economics, a minor in German, a Management Studies Certificate in conjunction with the Simon School of Business, and an International Relations Certificate. Personally, I have made many great friends through my undergraduate journey; they are people who have influenced me on many aspects. Additionally, I have complemented my academic experience with three challenging internship opportunities in the banking field: Miami, the Middle East, and Wall Street. Following graduation, I plan to earn an MBA in Finance."

– Edgard D., '09
Pembroke Pines, FL
Financial Economics

University of Rochester
300 Wilson Boulevard
Box 270251
Rochester, NY 14627-0251
Ph: (585) 275-3221
admit@admissions.rochester.edu
www.rochester.edu

F A S T   F A C T S

STUDENT PROFILE

# of degree-seeking undergraduates	5,291
% male/female	50/50
% African American	5.6
% American Indian or Alaska Native	<1
% Asian or Pacific Islander	10
% Hispanic	4.6
% White	59.8
% International	7.7
% Pell grant recipients	18.5

First-generation and minority alumni Dr. Steven Chu, Nobel Prize winner, physics, and current Secretary of Energy; David Satcher, former U.S. Surgeon General; Kathy Waller, VP and chief of internal audit, Coca-Cola; Brian Roseboro, former Under Secretary of the Treasury; Awista Ayub, founder, the Afghan Youth Sports Exchange, winner, 2006 ESPY Arthur Ashe Courage Award

ACADEMICS

full-time faculty	524
full-time minority faculty	73
student-faculty ratio	9:1
average class size	25
% first-year retention rate	96
% graduation rate (6 years)	84

Popular majors Psychology, Political Science, Economics, Biological Sciences, Engineering

CAMPUS LIFE

% live on campus (% fresh.)	86 (100)

Multicultural student clubs and organizations National Society of Black Engineers, Society of Hispanic Professional Engineers, Black Students' Union, Chinese Students' Association, Filipino American Students' Association, Korean American Students' Association, Spanish and Latino Students' Association, Student Assoc for the Dev. of Arab Cultural Awareness

Athletics NCAA Division III, Liberty League; University Athletic Association

ADMISSIONS

# of applicants	12,111
% accepted	39
# of first-year students enrolled	1,087
SAT Critical Reading range	610-720
SAT Math range	650-750
SAT Writing range	620-720
ACT range	28-33
average HS GPA	3.8

Deadlines

early decision	11/1
regular decision	1/1
application fee (online)	$60 ($30)
fee waiver for applicants with financial need	yes

COST & AID

tuition	$39,480
room & board	$11,640
total need-based institutional scholarships/grants	$53,450,841
% of students apply for need-based aid	65
% of students receive aid	88
% receiving need-based scholarship or grant aid	87
% receiving aid whose need was fully met	96
average aid package	$32,203
average student loan debt upon graduation	$27,121

Appalachian State University

Appalachian State University
A.S.U. Box 32004
Boone, NC 28608
Ph: (828) 262-2000
admissions@appstate.edu
www.appstate.edu

Located in the Blue Ridge Mountains of North Carolina, Appalachian State University combines the best attributes of a small liberal arts college with those of a large research institution. This dynamic university features high-quality academics at an affordable price, and an energetic campus life with incredible opportunities for leadership, service-learning and study abroad. The beautiful mountains surrounding campus provide unique opportunities academically, culturally and recreationally. Small classes and close interactions between faculty and students create a strong sense of community, which is an Appalachian hallmark.

> ACCESS GEAR UP

Appalachian encourages young people to have high expectations, stay in school, study hard, and take the right courses to go to college. The main objectives of the GEAR UP program are to ensure that all students have access to rigorous college courses, provide early information about college admission process and offer information to families about the costs of college and the availability of student financial assistance The mission of the GEAR UP initiative is to accelerate the academic achievement of middle and secondary school students, so that increasing numbers will graduate from high school and enroll and succeed in college.

"Through Appalachian's ACCESS program I've been given the opportunity to attend a four year university and have educational opportunities that I didn't think were attainable coming from a low income family. Appalachian has allowed me the gift of education."

– Ivan P., '11 Durham, NC Biology

> ACCESS Western NC Network for Access & Success (WNCNAS)

As a clearinghouse of information and data related to higher education access improvement activities in the state, serving the entire Appalachian region of North Carolina, WNCNAS provides opportunities for high schools to apply for mini-grants to improve high school graduation and post-secondary enrollment.

> ACCESS Upward Bound

At Appalachian, rising seniors who participate in the Upward Bound program take part in the Senior Adventure Group Experience (SAGE), which has been nationally recognized as a model program. Based on the concept of experiential education, the program brings students to sites like the Appalachian Trail, the Biltmore Estate and the Nantahala River in order to experience these environments first-hand. SAGE students also visit colleges, learn about leadership and prepare for college-entrance exams.

> OPPORTUNITY Diversity Scholarships

As part of the university's effort to create a more diverse student body, diversity scholarships are awarded to students who demonstrate and value academic achievement, exhibit strong leadership potential, and eagerly identify ways to implement positive change. Although priority is given to students from underrepresented groups, students from all ethnic backgrounds who can contribute to campus diversity are considered for this award.

FAST FACTS

STUDENT PROFILE

# of undergraduate enrollment	14,872
% male/female	48/52
% African American	3
% American Indian	<1
% Asian	1
% Caucasian	91
% Hispanic	3
% Pell grant recipients	n/a

First-generation and minority alumni Dr. Harry Williams, president, Delaware State University

ACADEMICS

full-time faculty	824
full-time minority faculty	59
student-faculty ratio	17:1
average class size	25
% first-year retention rate	87
% graduation rate (6 years)	64

Popular majors Business Administration/ Management, Communication, Elementary Education, Psychology

CAMPUS LIFE

% live on campus (% freshmen)	36 (97)

Multicultural student clubs and organizations African Student Association, AIESEC, Asian Student Association, ASU Anime Club, Hip Hop Oasis, Hispanic Student Association, International Friendship Association, NOW, Sexuality and Gender Alliance, TransAction

Athletics NCAA Division I, Southern Conference, Northern Pacific Field Hockey Conference

ADMISSIONS

# of applicants	13,039
% accepted	63
# of first-year students enrolled	2,743
SAT Critical Reading range	530-620
SAT Math range	550-630
SAT Writing range	510-600
ACT range	22-26
average HS GPA	3.87

Deadlines

regular admission	rolling
application fee (online)	$50 ($50)
fee waiver for applicants with financial need	yes

COST & AID

tuition	in-state $2,341; out-of-state $12,962
room & board	$6,400
total need-based institutional scholarships/grants	$33,421,119
% of students receiving aid	59
% receiving need-based scholarship or grant aid	65
% receiving aid whose need was fully met	70
average aid package	$7,843
average student loan debt upon graduation	$15,529

Davidson College

Davidson College
Box 7156
Davidson, NC 28035-7156
Ph: (800) 768-0380
admission@davidson.edu
www.davidson.edu

Davidson is a highly selective independent liberal arts college of approximately 1,800 students located 20 minutes north of Charlotte in Davidson, N.C. Since its establishment in 1837, the college has been consistently regarded as one of the top liberal arts colleges in the country. Through The Davidson Trust, the college became the first liberal arts institution in the nation to replace loans with grants in all financial aid packages, giving all students the opportunity to graduate debt-free. The college values diversity in all forms and the role it plays in creating a rich and meaningful experience for all students. Davidson competes in NCAA athletics at the Division I level, and a longstanding Honor Code is central to student life at the college.

> OPPORTUNITY **The Davidson Trust**

Through The Davidson Trust, the college meets 100 percent of demonstrated financial need through grants and students employment. Financial aid counselors are available to help families navigate the financial aid process.

> OPPORTUNITY **Need Blind Admission**

Davidson practices a need-blind admission policy, which means an applicant's character, academic achievement, potential and talents are the factor's considered for admission, not the family's bank balance.

"Davidson College immediately welcomes you with open arms. It is an all around pleasant place that offers many opportunities to expand ones horizons. This can be done in class and by becoming a part of various organizations and clubs on campus."
– Claudia R., '11
Chicago, IL
Sociology

> SUCCESS **Leadership Development**

Through the office of leadership development, mentoring and other programs, Davidson prepares students for the challenges and opportunities that come with a first class education.

> SUCCESS **Exchange Programs**

Davidson College has cooperative arrangements with Howard University and Morehouse College which provide students opportunities for study at campuses with significant African-American student, faculty and staff populations. Study may be arranged for a year or a semester.

> SUCCESS **Students Together Reaching for Individual Development & Education (STRIDE)**

STRIDE is a support program purposed to assist first year ethnic minority students with their adjustment to Davidson College. A series of designed experiences offer academic, cultural, and social support as well as vital information to aid students in understanding and working effectively within the college community.

> SUCCESS **The Emerging Professionals Group (EPG)**

The EPG works to prepare black students for the challenges of people of color in corporate America through education, exposure, and empowerment in career and professional development. The group meets monthly and focuses on resume writing, corporate culture, business etiquette, and interviews.

FAST FACTS

STUDENT PROFILE
# of degree-seeking undergraduates	1,661
% male/female	49/51
% African-American	6
% American Indian or Alaska Native	1
% Asian or Pacific Islander	4
% Hispanic	4
% White	74
% International	4
% Pell grant recipients	6.8

First-generation and minority alumni Ketan Bulsara, professor of neurosurgery, Yale University School of Medicine; Anthony Foxx, attorney, community leader; Jana Mashonee, recording artist; Rosie Molinary, writer, author

ACADEMICS
full-time faculty	168
full-time minority faculty	26
student-faculty ratio	10:1
average class size	12-15
% first-year retention rate	96
% graduation rate (6 years)	94

Popular majors Biology, Chemistry, Political Science, History, Economics

CAMPUS LIFE
% live on campus (% fresh.)	94 (100)

Multicultural student clubs and organizations Black Student Coalition, Davidson International Association, Organization of Latin American Students, Asian Cultural Awareness Association, Davidson African Students Association, Middle Eastern Cross-Cultural Association, Muslim Students Association, Sistahs of Essence, United Community Action

Athletics NCAA Division I, Southern Conference, Pioneer League

ADMISSIONS
# of applicants	4,412
% accepted	26
# of first-year student enrolled	482
SAT Critical Reading range	630-730
SAT Math range	640-730
SAT Writing range	630-730
ACT range	28-32

Deadlines
early decision	11/15
regular decision	1/2
application fee (online)	$50 ($50)
fee waiver for applicants with financial need	yes

COST & AID
tuition	$36,683
room & board	$10,346
total need-based institutional scholarships/grants	$10,290,965
% of students apply for need-based aid	47
% of students receive aid	99
% receiving need-based scholarship or grant aid	97
% receiving aid whose need was fully met	99
average aid package	$21,506
average student loan debt upon graduation	$13,410

Johnson C. Smith University

Ranked among the best historically black colleges and universities, and the first to give a laptop to every student, Johnson C. Smith has a lot to offer. Its location in the "Queen City" of Charlotte, N.C., is also a boon — the city offers its students the amenities of a metropolitan hub, as well as relative proximity to the beaches and mountains. Students can also take advantage of joint-enrollment opportunities at more than 20 colleges and universities in the area, further increasing the locale's value.

> ACCESS Service Learning

Service learning is an integral part of the Smith experience, combining academics and community service. In fact, all students must participate in service learning before they graduate. Many of the service-learning programs partner with organizations that support children, including the Charlotte Mecklenburg School District, Right Moves for Youth and Communities in Schools, among others.

> OPPORTUNITY Scholarship Information

While 89 percent of Smith students receive financial aid, the school nevertheless encourages students to seek outside funding as well. To this end, it maintains a comprehensive list of scholarships, many of which are earmarked for minority students. In addition, the university offers an Honors College for high-achieving minority students.

> SUCCESS Freshman Academy/Learning Communities and IBM ThinkPad Initiative

All freshmen at Johnson C. Smith participate in the Freshman Academy/Learning Communities Program. In this program, students engage in integrated assignments, co-curricular activities, and active learning. With all students participating in IBM's ThinkPad University program, each student receives a fully-loaded laptop. Smith was the first historically black college to offer laptops to all students, and it remains one of the few schools nationwide to do so.

> SUCCESS Student Support Services (SSS)

First-generation students, including low-income and disabled students, participate in a program that promotes academic and social engagement activities. The program provides tutoring and peer mentoring support.

> SUCCESS HBCU-UP

The Historically Black Colleges and Universities Undergraduate Program provides support for students majoring in STEM (science, technology, engineering, and mathematics) disciplines. Students may enhance their experience within the program by serving as peer mentors. Participating students also have numerous research and internship opportunities.

Johnson C. Smith University
100 Beatties Ford Road
Charlotte, NC 28216-5398
Ph: (800) 782-7303 / (704) 378-1010
admissions@jcsu.edu
www.jcsu.edu

F A S T   F A C T S

STUDENT PROFILE
# of degree-seeking undergraduates	1,571
% male/female	37/63
% African-American	99
% American Indian or Alaska Native	<1
% Asian or Pacific Islander	<1
% Hispanic	<1
% White	<1
% International	<1
% Pell grant recipients	62

First-generation and minority alumni
Dr. Dorothy Cowser Yancy, 12th (first female) president, Johnson C. Smith University; Eva M. Clayton, congresswoman; Don Pullen, jazz musician; Clarence F. Stephens, ninth African-American to receive a Ph.D. in mathematics; Fred "Curley" Neal, Harlem Globetrotter legend; Judge Sandra Lynn Townes, U.S. District Court, eastern district of New York

ACADEMICS
full-time faculty	103
full-time minority faculty	65
student-faculty ratio	14:1
average class size	25
% first-year retention rate	63
% graduation rate (6 years)	38

Popular majors Business Administration, Communication Arts, Computer Science/Information Systems, Computer Science, Computer Engineering, Criminology

CAMPUS LIFE
% live on campus (% freshmen)	73 (97)

Multicultural student clubs and organizations
Muslim Students Association, Caribbean and International Student Association, NAACP, National Association of Black Accountants (NABA), National Association of Black Engineers
Athletics NCAA Division II, Central Intercollegiate Athletic Association

ADMISSIONS
# of applicants	5,049
% accepted	49
# of first-year students enrolled	726
SAT Critical Reading range	380-460
SAT Math range	370-490
SAT Writing range	380-460
ACT range	17-18
average HS GPA	3.0

Deadlines
regular admission	rolling
application fee (online)	$25 ($25)
fee waiver for applicants with financial need	yes

COST & AID
tuition	$15,754
room & board	$6,132
total need-based institutional scholarships/grants	n/a
% of students apply for need-based aid	85
% of students receive aid	80
% receiving need-based scholarship or grant aid	73
% receiving aid whose need was fully met	1
average aid package	$14,800
average student loan debt upon graduation	$34,308

Meredith College

Meredith College
3800 Hillsborough Street
Raleigh, NC 27607
919-760-8581
admissions@meredith.edu
www.meredith.edu/admissions

Meredith College has grown to become one of the largest independent private women's colleges in the U.S. They offer a comprehensive liberal arts undergraduate education, with a focus on leadership, experiential learning and individual attention. In addition to welcoming students and faculty from 27 states and 37 countries, Meredith College enjoys a strong population of first generation college students. Meredith College is also a partner with the Zawadi Africa Education Fund and the Initiative to Educate Afghan Women.

"I never imagined that I would attend one of the best women's colleges in the nation. I am the first member of my family to go to college. I am well prepared because Meredith College, my family, my professors and friends have given me the tools I needed."
– Nayely Perez-Huerta, '09
Community Organizer
El Pueblo, Inc.

F A S T   F A C T S

STUDENT PROFILE
# of degree-seeking undergraduates	1,765
% male/female	0/100
% African-American	11
% American Indian or Alaska Native	<1
% Asian or Pacific Islander	2
% Hispanic	2
% White	76
% International	2
% Pell grant recipients	n/a

First-generation and minority alumni
C.C. Wiggins, '76, first woman and first African American officer in command and support roles in the Chaplain Corps

ACADEMICS
full-time faculty	147
full-time minority faculty	14
student-faculty ratio	10:1
average class size	16
% first-year retention rate	74
% graduation rate (6 years)	66

Popular majors Psychology, Biology, Interior Design, Business

CAMPUS LIFE
% live on campus (% fresh.)	60 (93)

Multicultural student clubs and organizations
Association of Cultural Awareness, Meredith International Association, Meredith "N" Harmony, SGA Unity Council, Diversity Council, Meredith Hues

Athletics NCAA Division III, USA South Conference

ADMISSIONS
# of applicants	1,615
% accepted	65
# of first-year student enrolled	478
SAT Critical Reading range	450-560
SAT Math range	470-570
SAT Writing range	n/a
ACT range	19-24
average HS GPA	3.2

Deadlines
regular decision	2/15
application fee (online)	$40 ($40)
fee waiver for applicants with financial need	yes

COST & AID
tuition	$24,490
room & board	$7,020
total need-based institutional scholarships/grants	$9,441,647
% of students apply for need-based aid	82
% receiving need-based scholarship or grant aid	70
% receiving aid whose need was fully met	14.5
average aid package	$18,638
average student loan debt upon graduation	$21,002

> ACCESS ¡Levántate, North Carolina! College Fair

This college fair, which highlights colleges and scholarship organizations, is hosted by Meredith College for the Hispanic population of Central and Eastern North Carolina. The fair is set up to assist Latino high school students and their families in understanding the importance of going to college. Students have the opportunity to meet representatives from more than 40 colleges and scholarship organizations.

> ACCESS Meredith Hues Program

The Meredith Hues Program is a student group run through the Office of Admissions that allows multicultural freshmen the opportunity to assist in the recruitment of new multicultural students.

> OPPORTUNITY Meredith Promise Scholarships

In recognition of academic ability, intellectual promise and leadership skills, Meredith College has established the Meredith Promise Scholarship for students from underrepresented groups. The scholarship is renewable up to a total of four years, provided the recipient remains in good standing, is a full-time student, and maintains a 2.5 quality point ratio on all courses taken at Meredith.

> SUCCESS The First Year Experience Class

The FYE Class is a one-hour credit class taught by a variety of faculty and staff across campus. This class is designed to help students make a successful transition into college. Topics covered include: effective study skills for college, time management, communicating with professors and academic dialogue, critical thinking skills, diversity, learning about Raleigh and dealing with homesickness. Because the class is small and interactive, it also provides a support group for new students, as well as the chance to develop a strong relationship with a faculty/staff member.

> SUCCESS The Learning Center

The Learning Center is a free academic support program for all Meredith College students staffed by students who are trained to assist their peers. The Learning Center offers subject specific tutoring in 100 and 200 level courses, including English, writing, grammar, mathematics and other subjects that vary by semester. Writing tutors work with students writing papers for any course, regardless of level.

> SUCCESS Summer Symposium

Meredith College's Summer Syposium is a two-day educational and transitional experience to foster a sense of community among incoming first-year and transfer multicultural students.

St. Andrews Presbyterian College

St. Andrews Presbyterian College
1700 Dogwood Mile
Laurinburg, NC 28352-5598
Ph: (910) 277-5555
admissions@sapc.edu
www.sapc.edu

FAST FACTS

STUDENT PROFILE

# of degree-seeking undergraduates	623
% male/female	39/ 61
% African-American	10
% American Indian or Alaska Native	<1
% Asian or Pacific Islander	<1
% Hispanic	3
% White	84.3
% International	1.6
% Pell grant recipients	24

ACADEMICS

full-time faculty	40
full-time minority faculty	n/a
student-faculty ratio	n/a
average class size	17
% first-year retention rate	62
% graduation rate (6 years)	54

Popular majors Business Administration/
Management, Equestrian-related degrees, Forensic
Science, Creative Writing

CAMPUS LIFE

% live on campus (fresh.)	81 (99)

Multicultural student clubs and organizations
Black Student Union
Athletics Division II, Carolinas-Virginia Athletic
Conference

ADMISSIONS

# of applicants	845
% accepted	78
# of first-year students enrolled	181
SAT Critical Reading range	440-560
SAT Math range	430-530
SAT Writing	430-530
ACT range	18-23
average HS GPA	3.1

Deadlines

regular decision	rolling
application fee (online)	$30 ($30)
fee waiver for applicants with financial need	yes

COST & AID

tuition	$21,190
room & board	$8,762
total need-based institutional scholarships/grants	n/a
% of students apply for need-based aid	85
% of students receive aid	80
% receiving need-based scholarship or grant aid	99
% receiving aid whose need was fully met	31
average aid package	$14,424
average student loan debt upon graduation	$17,341

St. Andrews educates its students to be knowledgeable and imaginative servant-leaders well prepared for a lifetime of learning, leadership and service in an ever-changing and interdependent world. The college's scenic lakeside environment provides a beautiful and unique setting that propels students toward success. Students take advantage of state-of-the-art "smart" classrooms, a science lab the size of an sports arena, a state-of-the-art Electronic Fine Arts Lab and study abroad opportunities. Moreover, this experience is affordable — the *US News & World Report* continually places St. Andrews in the top 20 colleges for having graduates with the lowest debt, as well as naming it one of the top liberal arts colleges for over a decade.

> ACCESS Educational and Athletic Mentoring

St. Andrews has a longstanding relationship with the local educational community. Student teaching and tutoring are part of the teacher education program, the therapeutic horsemanship program and the athletic program's community service component. St. Andrews students are locally active in schools, non-profit organizations and churches, creating wonderful opportunities for mentoring.

> OPPORTUNITY Open House / Scholarships

Students interested in St. Andrews are encouraged to attend an Open House and schedule a personal visit to explore the various aspects of the college. This also allows for discussion of the many scholarship opportunities available, including awards based on scholastic achievement and community involvement. Specialty scholarships are available for athletics, choir, bagpipe band, honors and equestrian programs. Need-based grants and work-study are available to further encourage students to attend the college.

> SUCCESS St. Andrews General Education (SAGE)

The St. Andrews General Education program teaches and supports its community of learners with a rigorous, interdisciplinary pursuit of knowledge and perspectives. This critical exploration takes place within a community rooted in Christian traditions and engaged in a dialogue with other spiritual traditions. The program fosters self-understanding, respect for the dignity of all persons and responsibility toward both natural and social environments. General education at St. Andrews prepares students for a lifetime of learning, leadership and service. The organizing theme for SAGE is a set of questions central to the liberal arts and sciences. The intention of the program is not to provide standard answers to the guiding questions, but rather to use tradition to explore afresh the source and scope of ideas. The SAGE courses in particular, and the St. Andrews curriculum broadly, challenge a variety of perspectives.

University of North Carolina at Asheville

University of North Carolina at Asheville
One University Heights
Asheville, NC 28804-8502
www.unca.edu/admissions
Ph: (828) 251-6481
admissions@unca.edu

The University of North Carolina at Asheville is a co-educational, public liberal arts university. Since 1927, the University of North Carolina at Asheville has offered a superior liberal arts education for well-prepared students who are committed to learning and personal growth. Its education is liberating, promoting the free and rigorous pursuit of truth, respect for differing points of view and heritage and an understanding that values play a role in thought and action. Through this education, the university aims to develop students of broad perspective who think critically and creatively, communicate effectively and participate actively in their communities.

"I wanted a small private school experience at a reasonable public school price. UNC Asheville offered me a unique community where I could thrive as both a student and a leader. Part of what I enjoy as an upper classman is taking part in mentoring and advising students who are thinking about college through our campus's access opportunities like AVID and GEAR UP. It's great to be a role model!"

*– Ashley P., '09
Literature and Language,
9-12 English Licensure*

> ### ACCESS Advancement Via Individual Determination (AVID) Program

The University of North Carolina at Asheville partners with Asheville City Schools to provide tutors for the AVID program. Through AVID, college students work with 250 students in sixth to 12th grade from Asheville Middle, Asheville High School and SILSA (School of Inquiry and Life Sciences Asheville). AVID targets students with a GPA between 2.0 and 3.5 and considers first-generation college, low-income, historically underserved and special-circumstance students.

> ### OPPORTUNITY Minority Presence Grant Program

The University of North Carolina funds the Minority Presence Grant Program, allocating money to historically white and historically black institutions to aid them in recruiting financially needy North Carolina students who would be minority presence students at the respective institutions by enabling the institutions to offer relatively more aid for minority presence students in the form of grants rather than loans.

> ### SUCCESS Summer Opportunity for Academic Success (SOAR)

This intensive six-week program invites a hand-selected group of recent high school graduates to campus to ensure a smoother transition to college. During SOAR, students are exposed to UNC Asheville's academic expectations through Math and Liberal Studies writing courses, which are taught by dedicated faculty with a commitment to the development of each student. Additional support from SOAR Mentors and math and writing tutors provide assistance in and out of the classroom and they become familiar with the cultures of our campus and the greater Asheville community through a variety of on and off-campus programs and trips. In the fall semester, SOAR students continue to interact with each other and SOAR faculty and staff and since they are well-established on campus, they become campus leaders and role models for their peers.

> ### SUCCESS The Center for Diversity Education

The Center for Diversity Education at UNC Asheville celebrates and teaches diversity in order to foster conversation and respect among cultures. Each year the Center works with over 15,000 students and teachers in school districts throughout Western North Carolina with Road Shows, Exhibits, Staff Development and a lending library. Students at UNC Asheville are integral to those programs as interns, volunteers and researchers. To learn more about the Center visit www.diversityed.org.

FAST FACTS

STUDENT PROFILE
# of degree-seeking undergraduates	2,873
% male/female	42/58
% African-American	3
% American Indian or Alaska Native	<1
% Asian or Pacific Islander	<1
% Hispanic	2
% White	88
% International	<1
% Pell grant recipients	29

First-generation and minority alumni Ty Wigginton, Second/Third Baseman, Baltimore Orioles; Ann B. Ross ('84),10-time *NY Times* Best Selling Author; Michael Cogdill ('84), Emmy Award-Winning News Anchor; Wilma Dykeman ('38), Author, Environmental Activist; Roy A. Taylor ('29), Member of Congress, 1959-1976; Michael Gugino ('01), Musician, Steep Canyon Rangers

ACADEMICS
full-time faculty	207
full-time minority faculty	26
student-faculty ratio	13:1
average class size	19
% first-year retention rate	82
% graduation rate (6 years)	54

Popular majors Psychology, Management, Environmental Studies, Biology, Art, Literature

CAMPUS LIFE
% live on campus (% freshmen)	35 (95)

Multicultural student clubs and organizations Africana Club, Alliance, Asian Students in Asheville (ASIA), Black Student Association (BSA), EPEC (Hispanic), Hispanic Outreach for Learning Awareness (HOLA), Hillel, International Students Association, Student Diversity Association, N.U.E. Noize Step Team

Athletics NCAA Division I, Big South Conference

ADMISSIONS
# of applicants	2,530
% accepted	75
# of first-year students enrolled	572
SAT Critical Reading range	540-640
SAT Math range	520-620
SAT Writing	510-620
ACT range	22-26
average HS GPA	3.9

Deadlines
regular admission	2/15
application fee (online)	$50
fee waiver for applicants with financial need	yes

COST & AID
tuition, fees, room, board and meal plan in-state: $12,662; out-of-state: $24,378	
total need-based institutional scholarships/grants	$4,981,962
% of students apply for need-based aid	63
% of students receive aid	64
% receiving need-based scholarship or grant aid	36
% receiving aid whose need was fully met	29
average aid package	$8,703
average student loan debt upon graduation	$15,972

University of North Carolina at Chapel Hill

Founded in 1795, the University of North Carolina at Chapel Hill is a public, co-educational, research university, and the oldest institution in the University of North Carolina System — in fact, it was the only public university in the United States to graduate students in the 18th century. The university seeks to serve all as a center for scholarship and creative endeavor. Teaching students at all levels in an environment of research, free inquiry and personal responsibility, the University of North Carolina at Chapel Hill strives to expand the body of knowledge, improve the condition of human life through service and publication and to enrich culture.

> ACCESS Camp Carolina Scholars

The University of North Carolina at Chapel Hill's Camp Carolina Scholars brings talented high school freshmen and sophomores, with a special emphasis on first-generation, minority, low-income, rural and disadvantaged students, to campus to experience residential college life. Students spend three days on campus living in a residence hall, learning about academic and extra-curricular preparation for selective admissions and scholarship opportunities. Sessions include information on admissions, financial aid and scholarship, time management, study habits, test preparation and other important skills needed for high school and college success.

> ACCESS National College Advising Corps (NCAC)

Headquartered at the Office of Undergraduate Admissions at Chapel Hill, the National College Advising Corps (NCAC) places college advisers in high schools with low college-going rates to assist existing guidance efforts. NCAC recruits dynamic recent college graduates to serve in a one- to two-year commitment, similar to programs such as the Peace Corps and Teach for America. Advisers spend two to three days per week in each of two assigned high schools. Their work supplements, not competes with, the work of guidance counselors already present in member-schools. Not only does NCAC increase college recruitment and retention rates for traditionally underserved students, but it also creates a generation of young public servants who will remain informed and committed to these issues over a lifetime.

> OPPORTUNITY Carolina Covenant

The Carolina Covenant is a college financing commitment between the University of North Carolina at Chapel Hill and historically low-income youth throughout the nation. The covenant pledges that the university will meet 100 percent of an admitted, eligible student's financial need with a combination of grants, scholarships and a reasonable amount of federal work-study. This combination of financial aid, together with the amount the family is expected to pay, gives students who qualify and who work 10 to 12 hours per week in a work-study job, the opportunity to earn a baccalaureate degree at Chapel Hill without having to borrow to meet their financial need.

> SUCCESS The Learning Center

The Learning Center at the University of North Carolina at Chapel Hill aims to help students become self-confident, self-directed learners. While the immediate goal of the Learning Center is improving students' abilities to learn, remember and solve problems, the center's ultimate goal is increasing student achievement, retention and graduation from the university. The center's programs include one-on-one academic counseling, laboratories that teach effective reading and learning strategies, guided study groups and peer tutoring.

University of North Carolina at Chapel Hill
CB# 2200, Jackson Hall
Chapel Hill, NC 27599-2200
Ph: (919) 966-3621
unchelp@admissions.unc.edu
www.unc.edu

FAST FACTS

STUDENT PROFILE
# of degree-seeking undergraduates	16,587
% male/female	41/59
% African-American	11
% American Indian or Alaska Native	1
% Asian or Pacific Islander	7
% Hispanic	4
% White	72
% Pell grant recipients	14

First-generation and minority alumni Stuart Scott, anchor, ESPN; Karen Leslie Stevenson '79, first black female Rhodes Scholar; Rachel Mazyck '05, Rhodes Scholars; Randall Kenan, writer; Ken Jeong, actor

ACADEMICS
full-time faculty	1,600
full-time minority faculty	314
student-faculty ratio	14:1
average class size	n/a
% first-year retention rate	97
% graduation rate (6 years)	97

Popular majors Biology, Chemistry, Mass Communications/Media Studies, Psychology

CAMPUS LIFE
% live on campus (% fresh.)	42 (82)

Multicultural student clubs and organizations Black Student Movement, Carolina Hispanic Association, Hellenic Student Association, Carolina Indian Circle, Korean-American Student Association, South Asian Awareness Organization, Association of International Students, African Student Association, Asian Student Association
Athletics NCAA Division I, Atlantic Coast Conference

ADMISSIONS
# of applicants	21,543
% accepted	34
# of first-year students enrolled	3,865
SAT Critical Reading range	590-690
SAT Math range	620-700
SAT Writing range	590-690
ACT range	26-31
average HS GPA	4.4

Deadlines
regular decision	1/15
application fee (online)	$70 ($70)
fee waiver for applicants with financial need	yes

COST & AID
tuition	in-state $3,705; out-of-state $20,603
room & board	$7,334
total need-based institutional scholarships/grants	$52,020,355
% of students apply for need-based aid	56
% of students receive aid	43
% receiving need-based scholarship or grant aid	32
% receiving aid whose need was fully met	4
average aid package	$11,678
average student loan debt upon graduation	$14,936

University of North Carolina Wilmington

Founded in 1946, the University of North Carolina Wilmington is a co-educational, non-denominational, comprehensive public university. The College of Arts and Sciences, the professional schools and the graduate school seek to stimulate intellectual curiosity, imagination, critical thinking and thoughtful expression in a broad range of disciplines and professional fields. Encouraging public access to its educational programs, the university is committed to diversity, international perspectives and regional service. The Wilmington campus community strives to create a safe, supportive and technologically progressive environment in which students, faculty and staff work together to develop their interests, skills and talents to the fullest extent. The university seeks to celebrate and study the heritage and environment of the coastal region, and to enrich its quality of life, economy and education.

> ACCESS GEAR UP SUMMER INSTITUTE

The GEAR UP Summer Institute is a 5-day, 4-night residential program for 9th grade students, who reside on campus and experience college life first-hand during the summer months. The program includes sessions led by UNCW faculty, staff and students. There are opportunities for exploratory, hands-on, and themed-based experiences that connect students with academic disciplines, and encourage them to pursue post secondary education. Enrichment experiences are also built into the residential program and allow for teamwork, social interaction and problem solving. Students also participate in sessions for college exploration and admissions.

> OPPORTUNITY Success Opportunities Aid and Responsibilities (SOAR)

The SOAR program is a financial assistance program that facilitates continued academic success and graduation for low-income students while limiting their accrual of student loan debt. A minimum GPA of 2.5 enables participation in the program, but increased financial awards are awarded at the start of each academic year to recipients that achieve higher GPAs. Students utilize a host of campus resources that lead to individual success and gains for the university community. To qualify, a student must be a North Carolina resident, enrolled full-time, have a combined family income of less than 200% of the federal poverty level and provide the required documentation to demonstrate they meet criteria.

> SUCCESS The Global Perspectives Initiative

The Global Perspectives Initiative is designed to enhance student's world view through education, service, leadership and cultural understanding. It serves as a support program for first-generation college students, single parent, low socio-economic status and students referred by and admissions counselor. This dynamic learning experience provides students with the knowledge and the opportunity to become community leaders and engaged citizens. Through civic engagement activities, students have the opportunity to learn while making a positive impact in the local community. During the fall semester students are enrolled in a learning community which includes common courses surrounding the global perspectives theme and are required to participate in extracurricular activities.

"I chose to attend UNC Wilmington because I knew it had a rigorous chemistry program with professors who go above and beyond their expectations. The campus environment is enticing and provides a home-like feeling. It provides the feeling of a small university on a big campus, a rare find indeed!"

*– Montwaun Y. '10
Greensboro, NC
Chemistry*

University of North Carolina Wilmington
Office of Admissions
601 S. College Rd.
Wilmington, NC 28403
Ph: (910) 962-3000
admissions@uncw.edu
www.uncw.edu

F A S T   F A C T S

STUDENT PROFILE
# of degree-seeking undergraduates	10,761
% male/female	42/58
% African American	4
% American Indian or Alaska Native	1
% Asian or Pacific Islander	2
% Hispanic	4
% White	84
% International	<1
% Pell grant recipients	19.6

First-generation and minority alumni Ernest Fullwood, Senior Resident Superior Court Judge

ACADEMICS
full-time faculty	587
full-time minority faculty	79
student-faculty ratio	16:1
average class size	21
% first-year retention rate	85
% graduation rate (6 years)	65

Popular majors Management and Leadership, Marine Biology, Nursing, Psychology and Education

CAMPUS LIFE
% live on campus (% freshmen)	34 (94)

Multicultural student clubs and organizations Black Student Union, NAACP, Mi Gente, International Student Organization
Athletics NCAA Division I, Colonial Athletic Association

ADMISSIONS
# of applicants	10,507
% accepted	52
# of first-year students enrolled	1,950
SAT Critical Reading range	540-610
SAT Math range	550-620
SAT Writing	520-600
ACT range	22-26
average HS GPA	3.79

Deadlines
early action	11/1
regular decision	2/1
application fee (online)	$60($60)
fee waiver for applicants with financial need	yes

COST & AID
tuition	in-state $2,765; out-of-state $13,647
room & board	$7,608
total need-based institutional scholarships/grants	n/a
% of students apply for need-based aid	76
% of students receive aid	n/a
% receiving need-based scholarship or grant aid	n/a
% receiving aid whose need was fully met	40
average aid package	$9,038
average student loan debt upon graduation	$16,115

Western Carolina University

Western Carolina University is a co-educational public university associated with the University of North Carolina System. Founded in 1889, the University offers an environment in which students, faculty and staff jointly assume responsibility for learning and in which high standards of scholarship prevail. Valuing critical thinking, effective communication, problem solving, the responsible use of information and technology, as well as the creative and performing arts, Western Carolina University is committed to personal growth and life-long learning.

Western Carolina University
Office of Admissions
102 Camp Building
Cullowhee, NC 28723
Ph: (822-928-4968) / (828) 227-7211
admiss@email.wcu.edu
www.wcu.edu

> ACCESS Legislators' School for Youth Leadership Development (LSYLD)

This is a summer residential leadership program for rising 8th through 11th graders. Legislators' School helps these students to develop their skills in thinking, communication and leadership while participating in community service. They also attend informational sessions focused on choosing a college, admissions processes, and scholarship initiatives.

> ACCESS Pre-College Program (PCP)

The Western Carolina University-sponsored North Carolina Mathematics and Science Education Network Pre-College Program seeks to broaden the pool of students graduating from high school with sufficient preparation to pursue mathematics and science programs at the university level and to move into careers in those fields. To achieve these goals, the program offers enrichment classes and activities in science and mathematics to traditionally underserved middle and high school students. Saturday Academies and Summer Scholars programs comprise the core curriculum and include career awareness, leadership training, academic advising and tutoring, academic competitions and hands-on laboratory experiences.

"Western Carolina University and the Office for Teacher Education Recruitment provide for college access through the Teachers of Tomorrow Program. I am currently a Birth-Kindergarten major and enjoy participating in the Teachers of Tomorrow conference. Teacher recruitment and college access are critical to students in North Carolina."
– Brynn J., '10
Bryson City, NC
Birth to Kindergarten

> ACCESS Teachers of Tomorrow (TOT) Programs

Teachers of Tomorrow is a program held on the Western Carolina University campus for middle and high school students who are interested in exploring teaching as a career. Regional high school students attend an on-campus program each October; regional middle school students attend each February. Professional educators and speakers lead breakout sessions presenting information on topics related to college access, scholarships and financial aid, teaching in a diverse world, admissions processes, campus tours, and how to choose a college or university.

> OPPORTUNITY Experience Western

Experience Western is a program designed to introduce prospective minority students to Western Carolina University resources and to promote a supportive and educational experience at the University. Students who attend Experience Western get a preview of life on campus over the course of two days, and arrive in Cullowhee for their freshman year already connected to the University. Participants tour the campus and interact with current Western students and staff during panel discussions, information sessions, and social activities, and they also have the chance to stay in the residence halls.

> SUCCESS Project C.A.R.E. (Committed to African-American Retention in Education)

Project C.A.R.E. is a combination of programs that seek to improve the academic performance and retention of Western Carolina University's African-American student population. A fall retreat for African-American first-year and transfer students takes place the first weekend after classes begin. The retreat is designed as an extension of the orientation process. The primary focus is to address specific questions and concerns about life as an African-American student at Western Carolina University. Students meet peer counselors, other entering freshmen and African-American faculty and staff, and develop friendships that help them through their undergraduate years and beyond.

FAST FACTS

STUDENT PROFILE
# of degree-seeking undergraduates	7,006
% male/female	47/53
% African-American	5
% American Indian or Alaska Native	1
% Asian or Pacific Islander	1
% Hispanic	1
% White	85
% International	5
% Pell grant recipients	27

First-generation and minority alumni Kevin Martin, professional basketball player; Joyce Dugan, first woman chief, Eastern Band – Cherokee Indians

ACADEMICS
full-time faculty	494
full-time minority faculty	42
student-faculty ratio	13:1
average class-size	13
% first-year retention rate	67
% graduation rate (6 yr)	47

Popular majors Elementary Education, Marketing, Nursing

CAMPUS LIFE
% live on campus (% fresh.)	45 (95)

Multicultural student clubs and organizations Organization of Ebony Students, Cultures in Asia, Black Theater Ensemble, International Club, La Voz Latina, National Pan-Hellenic Council (Historical African American Fraternities & Sororities), Native American Student Awareness Society, Di Ga Li I, Western's B.E.S.T. (Black Educational Support Team), Black Student Fellowship

Athletics NCAA Division I, Southern Conference

ADMISSIONS
# of applicants	4,792
% accepted	68
# of first-year students enrolled	1,259
SAT Critical Reading range	450-550
SAT Math range	470-560
SAT Writing range	430-530
ACT range	18-23
average HS GPA	3.35

Deadlines
early action	10/15
early decision	10/15
regular decision	4/1
application fee (online)	$40 ($0)
fee waiver for applicants with financial need	yes

COST & AID
tuition	in-state $2,078; out-of-state $11,661
room & board	$5,462
total need-based institutional scholarships/ grants	$1,927,126
% of students apply for need-based aid	69
% of students receive aid	97
% receiving need-based scholarship/grant aid	96
% receiving aid whose need was fully met	58
average aid package	$8,114
average student loan debt upon graduation	$11,285

Winston-Salem State University

Winston-Salem State University offers a quality baccalaureate program in a traditional, residential setting as well as flexible weekend, evening, and online courses to accommodate students in the workforce. As a comprehensive, historically black constituent of the University of North Carolina, Winston-Salem State University contributes to the social, cultural, intellectual and economic vitality of the Triad region and the state. Students find easy access to their professors, who have a long history of working closely with their students to ensure their success. Campus life pulses with the energy of student organizations, a full roster of men's and women's athletics, and a wealth of internship and volunteer options are available to enrich students' experiences and give them a leg up in the knowledge-based economy.

> **OPPORTUNITY** **Financial Aid Office**

WSSU offers scholarships to admitted students who have at least a 3.5 GPA and a total SAT score of 1100 or an ACT composite score of 24. In addition, the Financial Aid Office works with students to ensure they have taken all necessary steps to secure financial assistance. Approximately 89% of students receive some type of financial assistance.

> **OPPORTUNITY** **Open House**

WSSU hosts an Open House each Fall and Spring to showcase academics, organizations, campus life, students and faculty. Prospective students and their families are encouraged to schedule a campus visit.

> **SUCCESS** **The STEM Scholars Program**

The Science, Technology, Engineering and Mathematics (STEM) Scholars Program offers an academically and culturally enriched undergraduate experience that will prepare historically underrepresented students interested in STEM fields to earn a Ph.D. degree. There is a Summer Bridge Program component that is designed to assist with making the transition from high school to college and provides students with a foundation for a successful undergraduate experience. It includes course work, educational seminars, career exploration, and assessment. To be considered for the program, students must have a GPA of 3.5 or higher, SAT score of 1100 or higher or ACT score of 24 or higher, submit an essay about career aspirations and reasons for interests in the program, and participate in an interview with WSSU faculty and administrators.

> **SUCCESS** **University College**

University College (UC) is the academic home of all new students at Winston-Salem State University until they complete the requirements necessary to declare a major. Services include academic advising (including registration, major selection advice, and all other academic concerns), learning support, supplemental instruction, tutoring, and more. UC advisors, instructors, and tutors effectively and accurately communicate university-wide regulations, procedures, and expectations, provide services designed to promote student achievement, and work to ensure that all freshmen meet their common core requirements and successfully prepare for their intended majors. They help students help themselves, through computerized and individual academic support.

"From the time I was a toddler, my mother instilled in me the importance of academics.

But I knew she wouldn't be able to afford my tuition as a single parent. I am so appreciative of my scholarship, and the opportunity I've had to combine athletics with helping people."

– Shaun T., '10
Exercise Science major, School of Education and Human Performance, Chancellor's Scholar

---

Winston-Salem State University
601 S. Martin Luther King Jr. Drive
Winston-Salem, NC 27110
Ph: (336) 750-2070
admissions@wssu.edu
www.wssu.edu

F A S T   F A C T S

STUDENT PROFILE

# of degree-seeking undergraduates	5,975
% male/female	30/70
% African-American	83
% American Indian or Alaska Native	<1
% Asian or Pacific Islander	1
% Hispanic	1
% White	12
% Pell grant recipients	48

First-generation and minority alumni Lorraine Hairston '38, Mayor of Evanston, Ill.; Elias Gilbert '60, World Class Olympic Hurdler; Earl "The Pearl" Monroe '68, selected one of NBA's Top 50 greatest players in league history; Joseph Johnson '73, listed as one of the top African-American attorneys in the U.S. by *Black Enterprise Magazine*; Stephen A. Smith, '92, sports writer, talk show host, and NBA commentator

ACADEMICS

full-time faculty	419
full-time minority faculty	269
student-faculty ratio	16:1
average class size	n/a
% first-year retention rate	73
% graduation rate (6 years)	43

Popular majors Nursing, Education, Mass Communications, Business, Computer Science

CAMPUS LIFE

% live on campus	37.8

Multicultural student clubs and organizations Black Men for Change, Black Women for Change, Club Latino, Gay-Straight Student Alliance, Justice Studies Club, NAACP, National Black MBA Association, Nontraditional Adult Student Organization

Athletics NCAA Division II, Central Intercollegiate Athletics Association (CIAA)

ADMISSIONS

# of applicants	4,069
% accepted	53
# of first-year students enrolled	1,357
average SAT Critical Reading	432
average SAT Math	442
average ACT score	17
average HS GPA	2.93

Deadlines

early decision	11/15
regular decision	3/1
application fee (online)	$50 ($50)
fee waiver for applicants with financial need	yes

COST & AID

tuition	in-state $1,985; out-of-state $6,478
room & board	$3,181
total need-based institutional scholarships/grants	n/a
% of students apply for need-based aid	76
% of students receive aid	89
% receiving need-based scholarship or grant aid	64
% receiving aid whose need was fully met	77
average aid package	$6,522
average student loan debt upon graduation	$10,500

Baldwin-Wallace College

Baldwin-Wallace College
Bonds Hall, 275 Eastland Road
Berea, OH 44017-2088
Ph: (877) BWAPPLY / (440) 826-2222
admission@bw.edu
www.bw.edu

One of the first colleges to admit students without regard to race or gender, Baldwin-Wallace College retains that spirit of inclusiveness and innovation today. Founded in 1845, the College offers liberal arts education in a small college setting with excellent teaching and personalized instruction with a 15:1 student-to-faculty ratio and an average class size of 19 to 23 students. Students may choose from more than 50 academic programs, with an emphasis on pursuing personal and professional excellence.

> ACCESS Baldwin-Wallace Scholars Program

The Baldwin-Wallace Scholars Program provides young urban males with the confidence, skills and knowledge to enter college on a level equivalent to that of their peers from surrounding high schools. Scholars participate in a 12-month schedule of academic enrichment, mentoring, leadership development, an intensive summer program and targeted support over four years from the Cleveland Municipal School District and Baldwin-Wallace College.

> OPPORTUNITY Student Transfer Enrichment Program (STEP)

The STEP program builds upon Baldwin-Wallace and Cuyahoga Community College's dual admission and cross-registration programs. The new program provides students accepted into STEP with campus housing and special residential programming at Baldwin-Wallace, transportation between the two schools, and support services in advising, mentoring, and career development. STEP allows the opportunity for students who begin their postsecondary education at Cuyahoga Community College to build a firm academic foundation and to be successful at Baldwin-Wallace.

> SUCCESS Heritage Scholarship

Heritage Scholarships are $4,000 awards given to admitted students who will enrich the college's cultural diversity. Eligible students must rank in the top 25 percent of their class and have a minimum 3.3 GPA.

> SUCCESS Jacket Link

Jacket Link is a multicultural student retention program focused on two primary goals: increased retention of multicultural students between the freshman and sophomore years and improved overall satisfaction of first-year multicultural students with their initial college experience. Each fall, students participate in a leadership retreat and participate in workshops throughout the academic year on topics including academic, social and vocational issues. Additionally, Jacket Link supports a multicultural peer mentoring program that assigns an upperclassman student to a first-year student mentee.

> SUCCESS Single Parents Reaching Out for Unassisted Tomorrows

Single parents are supported at Baldwin-Wallace through Single Parents Reaching Out for Unassisted Tomorrows (SPROUT), a comprehensive residential program for single parents, ages 18 to 23, and their children. Founded at the college in 1990 to improve the retention rate of single parents, SPROUT allows parents to overcome the many obstacles that otherwise would limit their educational aspirations. Each mother and child has a private room on campus and shares group living space such as living rooms, study areas and dining facilities. SPROUT also assists parents in securing funds from social welfare programs, grants, and scholarships to offset costs for childcare and provides professional development and academic support throughout the year.

FAST FACTS

STUDENT PROFILE
# of degree-seeking undergraduates	3,110
% male/female	44/56
% African-American	7
% American Indian or Alaska Native	<1
% Asian or Pacific Islander	1
% Hispanic	3
% White	90
% International	1
% Pell grant recipients	24

First-generation and minority alumni David Byrd, M.D., first African-American president of the National Medical Association; James Lawson, civil rights leader and minister; Hazel Mountain Walker, among the first African-American lawyers in the State of Ohio

ACADEMICS
full-time faculty	164
full-time minority faculty	15
student-faculty ratio	15:1
average class size	18
% first-year retention rate	83
% graduation rate (6 years)	68

Popular major Psychology, Visual Arts, Business, Marketing, Education

CAMPUS LIFE
% live on campus (fresh.)	60 (84)

Multicultural student clubs and organizations Black Student Alliance, Hispanic-American Student Association, Middle Eastern Student Alliance, Native American Student Association, People of Color United, World Student Association
Athletics NCAA Division III, Ohio Athletic Conference

ADMISSIONS
# of applicants	3,321
% accepted	66
# of first-year students enrolled	738
SAT Critical Reading range	500-610
SAT Math range	490-600
SAT Writing range	490-600
ACT range	21-26
average HS GPA	3.5

Deadlines
regular decision	5/1
application fee (online)	$25 ($25)
fee waiver for applicants with financial need	yes

COST & AID
tuition	$24,230
room & board	$7,960
total need-based institutional scholarships/grants	$28,800,551
% of students apply for need-based aid	89
% of students receive aid	85
% receiving need-based scholarship or grant aid	76
% receiving aid whose need was fully met	56
average aid package	$20,222
average student loan debt upon graduation	$19,586

Case Western Reserve University

Case Western Reserve University is a private, four-year, comprehensive university located in the heart of Cleveland, Ohio's cultural and intellectual district. The campus offers an intimate collegiate setting within a city bustling with activity in health care, law and business. The university is home to four colleges offering undergraduate and graduate programs (arts and sciences, engineering, management and nursing) as well as six professional schools (medicine, dentistry, law, management, nursing and applied social sciences). As a major research university, there are many opportunities for students to get involved with a faculty member's research, and faculty members are deeply involved with students and their scholarship. A Case education pairs classroom learning with hands-on experience throughout all four years. Case is dedicated to the support, retention and success of all students, with additional offices, programs and resources dedicated to addressing the needs of students from underrepresented groups.

"As a student who is attending college without any financial assistance from my family, I have found the financial aid office at Case Western Reserve University to be especially sensitive to the unique barriers that many minority students encounter in their pursuit of higher education."

*– Sean H., '11
Cleveland, OH
Philosophy and
Biochemistry*

> ACCESS **Upward Bound**

Local high school students who come from low-income families in which neither parent holds a bachelor's degree can benefit from Case Western Reserve University's Upward Bound, a pre-college program that provides a group of students with the right tools to pursue their dreams of earning a college degree. Students benefit from weekly tutoring, field trips, workshops, and a six-week summer enrichment program at Case.

> ACCESS **Pre-College Scholars Program**

Case's Pre-College Scholars Program allows highly motivated and able high school students to enroll in college courses at Case during either the summer or the academic year. Pre-College Scholars attend classes with Case undergraduates for a first-hand college experience.

> OPPORTUNITY **Diversity Scholarships**

Provost's Special Scholarships are partial tuition awards granted to promising applicants who will add to the diversity and the value of the education offered by Case. Congressional Black Caucus (CBC) Foundation Scholarships are full-tuition scholarships awarded to students nominated by members of the Congressional Black Caucus. High school curriculum and academic performance, extracurricular involvement, standardized test results and leadership are factors considered for both scholarships. For the CBC Foundation Scholarship, preference is given to competitive students who are economically and/or educationally disadvantaged.

> SUCCESS **The Office of Multicultural Affairs (OMA)**

The Office of Multicultural Affairs encourages, supports and facilitates the success of students by providing opportunities for diverse interactions and cultural education that occur outside of the classroom. While the primary goal of the OMA is to assist students in being academically successful during their college career at Case, it also provides students with professional networking and mentoring opportunities, skill-building workshops and job and internship opportunities, in collaboration with the Career Center. Additional programming and resources include book vouchers, a freshman retreat, and 3.0 and Up Club, which recognizes academic achievement.

> SUCCESS **Case/Cleveland Scholarship Program (CSP) Partnership**

The Case/CSP Partnership supports underrepresented, low-income and first-generation students through programs that prepare students to transition from high school to college, acclimate to university life and develop academic skills and habits that will ensure academic success. Participants are further supported with academic advising, tutoring, mentoring, career coaching and additional financial aid.

Case Western Reserve University
10900 Euclid Avenue
Cleveland, OH 44106-7055
Ph: (216) 368-4450
admission.case.edu
www.case.edu

F A S T   F A C T S

STUDENT PROFILE

# of degree-seeking undergraduates	4,267
% male/female	56/44
% African American	6
% American Indian or Alaska Native	<1
% Asian or Pacific Islander	17
% Hispanic	2
% White	57
% International	3
% Pell grant recipients	16.5

First-generation and minority alumni Dr. David Satcher, 16th U.S. Surgeon General; Hon. Louis Stokes, first African American member of Congress, Ohio; Stephanie Tubbs-Jones, first Ohio African-American woman elected to the House of Representatives; Fred Gray, attorney, friend of Dr. Martin Luther King Jr., defended Rosa Parks

ACADEMICS

full-time faculty	737
full-time minority faculty	111
student-faculty ratio	10:1
average class size	n/a
% first-year retention rate	92
% graduation rate (6 years)	81

Popular majors Biology, Management, Psychology, Engineering, Nursing

CAMPUS LIFE

% live on campus (% fresh.)	78 (97)

Multicultural student clubs and organizations African Students Association, Asian American Alliance, Black Greek Council, Black Women's Society, Undergraduate Indian Student Association, Intercultural Dialogue Group, Korean Student Association, La Alianza, Middle Eastern Club, Muslim Student Association, National Association of Black Accountants, National Society of Black Engineers, Society of Hispanic Professional Engineers

Athletics NCAA Division III, University Athletic Association

ADMISSIONS

# of applicants	7,351
% accepted	73
# of first-year students enrolled	1,026
SAT Critical Reading range	590-690
SAT Math range	620-720
SAT Writing	580-680
ACT range	26-32
average H.S. GPA	n/a

Deadlines

early action	11/1
regular decision	1/15
application fee (online)	$0 ($0)

COST & AID

tuition	$35,900
room & board	$10,890
total need-based institutional scholarships/grants	$48,936,931
% of students apply for need-based aid	72
% of students receive aid	100
% receiving need-based scholarship or grant aid	99
% receiving aid whose need was fully met	91
average aid package	$20,966
average student loan debt upon graduation	$37,892

College of Mount St. Joseph

The College of Mount St. Joseph is a Catholic, four-year college that provides more than 2,200 students with a liberal arts and professional education. The Mount's goals are to assist students in becoming leaders in their professions and in their communities, and to prepare them for their life journey equipped with values, integrity and a sense of social responsibility. Smaller class sizes, individual attention, career preparation, and service learning opportunities support students' development and success. In addition to nearly 40 undergraduate degree programs, the Mount offers graduate and associate degrees as well a certificates and licensure programs. The College is a close-knit campus community that includes a newly renovated residence hall, athletic facilities, theatre, daycare center, state-of-the-art computer centers, and WI-FI access.

> ACCESS Summer Collegiate Orientation Program and Enrichment (Project SCOPE)

Through this program African-American high school sophomores from the Greater Cincinnati area reside on the Mount's campus and attend classes for one to two weeks. Classes improve skills in sciences, computer literacy, psychology and spoken word. Students attend workshops about the college admission process, library research, financial aid and study skills. The program is offered for three consecutive years, culminating in college preparedness and six transferable college credits for high school seniors.

> ACCESS Upward Bound

Local high school students who come from low-income families in which neither parent holds a bachelor's degree can benefit from the College of Mount St. Joseph's Upward Bound, a pre-college program that provides a group of students with the right tools to pursue their dreams of earning a college degree. Students benefit from weekly tutoring, field trips, workshops, and a six-week summer enrichment program at the Mount.

"My advice to other first-generation students is to join any club or organization or sports team, take charge and put energy into it. It will only benefit you because when you're involved, you're connected. Us at the Mount, we're a big family and that's how it should be."

– Sondra W., '10 Cincinnati, OH Communications Studies

> OPPORTUNITY Discovery Days/Get Acquainted Days (GAD)

Discovery Days and Get Acquainted Days allow potential Mount students the opportunity to explore academic programs and tour the campus as well as learn about financial aid and other support services at the college. Students enjoy lunch with faculty and current Mount students. Representatives from all academic majors and support services are on-hand to provide additional information.

> SUCCESS Office of Multicultural Affairs

The Office of Multicultural Affairs at the College is committed to an on-campus environment that values and respects all of its students, faculty and staff, regardless of gender, age, race, sexual preference, cultural background, religion, nationality, or beliefs. Through diversity awareness and multicultural education, a safe environment is supported on campus and in the Greater Cincinnati area. The office also oversees on-campus cultural events, the Black Student Union, and the International Student Association among other services and organizations.

College of Mount St. Joseph
5701 Delhi Road
Cincinnati, OH 45233-1670
Ph: (513) 244-4531
admission@mail.msj.edu
www.msj.edu

F A S T   F A C T S

STUDENT PROFILE
# of degree-seeking undergraduates	1,852
% male/female	37/63
% African American	11
% American Indian or Alaska Native	0
% Asian or Pacific Islander	<1
% Hispanic	1
% White	83
% International	4
% Pell grant recipients	31.5

First-generation and minority alumni Bernadette Coutain Plair, life-long wildlife conservationist

ACADEMICS
full-time faculty	116
full-time minority faculty	4
student-faculty ratio	12:1
average class size	n/a
% first-year retention rate	72
% graduation rate (6 years)	55

Popular majors Nursing, Business Administration, Sport Management, Graphic Design, Athletic Training, Criminology/Sociology

CAMPUS LIFE
% live on campus	24

Multicultural student clubs and organizations Office of Multicultural Affairs, Black Student Union, International Student Association

Athletics NCAA Division III, Heartland Collegiate Athletic Conference

ADMISSIONS
# of applicants	1,417
% accepted	70
# of first-year students enrolled	368
SAT Critical Reading range	n/a
SAT Math range	440-560
SAT Writing	n/a
ACT range	19-24
average HS GPA	3.19

Deadlines
regular decision	rolling to 8/15
application fee (online)	$25 ($25)
fee waiver for applicants with financial need	yes

COST & AID
tuition	$22,000
room & board	$7,152
total need-based institutional scholarships/grants	$9,864,763
% of students apply for need-based aid	80
% of students receive aid	21
% receiving need-based scholarship or grant aid	67.5
% receiving aid whose need was fully met	13.1
average aid package	$13,535
average student loan debt upon graduation	$21,302

The College of Wooster

College of Wooster
847 College Avenue
Wooster, OH 44691-2363
Ph: (330) 263-2322
admissions@wooster.edu
www.wooster.edu

The College of Wooster is nationally recognized for its emphasis on mentored independent research. Each Wooster senior creates an original research project, written work, performance or exhibit of artwork on a topic of his or her choosing, supported one-on-one by a faculty adviser. If the project requires travel or special equipment, to study the lives of West African immigrants in Paris or produce a documentary on survivors of Hiroshima, for example, significant grant funding is available. This independent study project, combined with a strong liberal arts curriculum, fosters creativity, resourcefulness, critical thinking, and communication skills in every Wooster student. Generations can attest to the life-changing quality of a Wooster education.

"Coming to college is a big step and can be very scary, but the Emerging Wooster Scholars program helped to ease some of my butterflies and concerns. During the program we had an opportunity to meet professors, deans, and other faculty members who showed us the various resources that are offered here at The College of Wooster. The Writing Center, Math Center and Learning Center all help students individually to improve a particular skill and assist in becoming a better students and critical thinker"
– Carmen G., '12 Oakwood Village, OH

> ### ACCESS **Youngstown Early Intervention Program**

Select students from Youngstown, Ohio can participate in the Youngstown Early Intervention Program, which brings students to campus for two-week summer programs. During the summer sessions, students take math and English courses, as well as enrichment offerings in theater, science, college advising and other areas.

> ### ACCESS **Emerging Wooster Scholars Program**

The Emerging Scholars program consists of a select group of students who represent an array of backgrounds who will benefit from the opportunity to enhance their foundation of academic skills. Students stay in a campus residence hall for three weeks and attend a tuition-free class, sessions on important college success skills, and earn money through an on-campus job.

> ### OPPORTUNITY **Multicultural and Underrepresented Scholarships**

The College of Wooster awards several merit-based scholarships to deserving multicultural and underrepresented students. These include the Clarence Beecher Allen Scholarship, named for the first African-American student at The College of Wooster, and Making a Difference Scholarships, awarded to students committed to promoting diversity awareness. Awards range from $2,000 to two-thirds tuition and are renewable each year for four years.

> ### OPPORTUNITY **Posse Foundation**

Wooster participates in the Posse Foundation, a program that brings talented inner-city youth to campus to pursue their academics and to help promote cross-cultural communication. Posse students are nominated by their high school to the program and share a collaborative support system with a special mentor to adjust to campus and college life. Wooster's Posse Scholars hail from Atlanta.

> ### SUCCESS **Summer Early Engage Research**

The Summer Early Engaged Research (SEER) program will provide fellowships to underrepresented graduating high school seniors interested in the sciences to participate in a four week summer research experience, under the guidance of a faculty member and an upper class student mentor.

FAST FACTS

STUDENT PROFILE

# of degree-seeking undergraduates	1,815
% male/female	47/53
% African American	6
% American Indian or Alaska Native	<1
% Asian or Pacific Islander	2
% Hispanic	3
% White	70
% International	5
% Pell grant recipients	16

First-generation and minority alumni Solomon Oliver, U.S. District Court judge; Lance Mason, Ohio state senator; Dr. April Sorrell-Taylor, pediatric oncologist; June Millikan, sculptor, artist

ACADEMICS

full-time faculty	131
full-time minority faculty	17
student-faculty ratio	11:1
average class size	17
% first-year retention rate	88
% graduation rate (6 years)	75

Popular majors English, History, Psychology, Philosophy, Biology, Political Science

CAMPUS LIFE

% live on campus (% fresh.)	97 (96)

Multicultural student clubs and organizations Babcock International Hall, Black Students' Association, Chinese Culture Club, Dene House, DREAM Program, Women of IMAGES, International Student Association, Men of Harambee, Proyecto Latino, Pueblo de Esperanza, South East Asia Committee, UJAMAA

Athletics NCAA Division III, North Coast Athletic Conference

ADMISSIONS

# of applicants	4,752
% accepted	58
# of first-year students enrolled	482
SAT Critical Reading range	540-660
SAT Math range	540-650
SAT Writing range	540-660
ACT range	23-29
average HS GPA	3.51

Deadlines

early decision	11/15
early action	12/15
regular decision	2/15
application fee (online)	$40 ($0)
fee waiver for applicants with financial need	yes

COST & AID

tuition	$36,598
room & board	$9,070
total need-based institutional scholarships/grants	n/a
% of students apply for need-based aid	80
% of students receive aid	78
% receiving need-based scholarship or grant aid	97
% receiving aid whose need was fully met	46
average aid package	$28,225
average student loan debt upon graduation	$25,140

Denison University

With its multicultural student enrollment over 20 percent, Denison University maintains a deep-rooted commitment to diversity, defining itself as an "intercultural university that values each member for his or her uniqueness while building on common strengths." The university provides numerous unique opportunities for its students, such as an innovative summer research program that gives selected students a stipend and free housing while they pursue collaborative research projects with professors. Denison also offers substantial service opportunities for its students.

> ACCESS Denison Community Association/Service Learning

The Denison Community Association oversees 25 volunteer service programs such as the After School Mentoring and Tutoring program through which Denison students work with elementary and middle school students from nearby Newark to provide tutoring, literacy-related activities, and educational games. Denison also has a comprehensive service-learning program. One program of note is "Hispanic Culture Service," which brings students into local Hispanic communities.

> OPPORTUNITY Merit Scholarships

Denison has a number of merit scholarships available, including the Bob and Nancy Good, Tyree/Parajon and Hla/Fisher Scholarships, all of which are awarded to students who can help diversify the university community. Underrepresented students can also benefit from the Upward Bound Scholarship, which is awarded to outstanding participants in the Upward Bound program.

> OPPORTUNITY Posse Foundation

Denison University participates in the Posse Foundation, a program that brings talented inner-city youths to campus to pursue their academics and to help promote cross-cultural communication. Posse students are nominated by their high school to the program and share a collaborative support system with a special mentor to adjust to campus and college life. Denison's Posse Scholars hail from Chicago and Boston.

> SUCCESS Sustained Dialogue

An outgrowth of a program started at Princeton University, Denison University houses one of approximately 15 to 20 college-based Sustained Dialogue programs, which facilitate discussions about issues of race and diversity on campus. Students must apply to be a part of the group, which meets bi-monthly and is led by two moderators.

"Sustained Dialogue at Denison is unlike any organization I've ever been in. It makes people open their minds and talk about issues in a meaningful way. SD has shown me that after college I want to do something that will make an impact on people and change lives."

*– LaForce B., '10
Chicago, IL
Communication*

Denison University
100 West College Street
Granville, OH 43023
Ph: (800) DENISON
admissions@denison.edu
www.denison.edu

FAST FACTS

STUDENT PROFILE

# of degree-seeking undergraduates	2,240
% male/female	44/56
% African-American	5.7
% American Indian or Alaska Native	4
% Asian or Pacific Islander	2.4
% Hispanic	2.9
% White	79.4
% International	5.5
% Pell grant recipients	11

First-generation and minority alumni Jose Rivera '77, first Puerto Rican screenwriter nominated for an Oscar; Alberto J. Verme '79, managing director and head of Global Energy and Power of Salomon Smith Barney Investment Banking; Kelly Brown Douglas '79, Episcopal priest, professor of theology, Howard University

ACADEMICS

full-time faculty	195
full-time minority faculty	30
student-faculty ratio	10:1
average class size	18
% first-year retention rate	90
% graduation rate (6 years)	83

Popular majors Economics. Biology, Communication, Psychology, Political Science, History

CAMPUS LIFE

% live on campus (% fresh.)	98 (100)

Multicultural student clubs and organizations Asian Culture Club, Black Student Union, Denison International Student Association, Denison Muslim Student Association, La Fuerza Latina, Asian-American Student Union, Outlook, Sustained Dialogue

Athletics NCAA Division III, North Coast Athletic Conference

ADMISSIONS

# of applicants	5,002
% accepted	2,509
# of first-year students enrolled	649
SAT Critical Reading range	580-690
SAT Math range	570-680
SAT Writing range	n/a
ACT range	25-30
average HS GPA	3.6

Deadlines

early decision	12/1
regular decision	1/15
application fee (online)	$40 ($40)
fee waiver for applicants with financial need	yes

COST & AID

tuition	$35,650
room & board	$8,690
total need-based institutional scholarships/grants	$21,607,791
% of students apply for need-based aid	52.1
% of students receive aid	81.9
% receiving need-based scholarship or grant aid	42.5
% receiving aid whose need was fully met	60.9
average aid package	$30,099
average student loan debt upon graduation	$14,775

Hiram College

The 1,200 undergraduates who attend Hiram College full-time chose it for many reasons, most often because of its pristine environment and location, small class sizes and close, mentoring relationships with faculty. With a student-to-faculty ratio of 12:1, there are plenty of opportunities for students to interact with their professors. Whether it is by recommending internship opportunities, potential career paths or summer learning experiences, Hiram College faculty members are involved. From their first days on campus, Hiram students realize they will not be anonymous.

> OPPORTUNITY Tuition Guarantee

A challenge for many families when looking for the perfect college is the overall "sticker price" and how it can be minimized. Hiram offers scholarships that recognize students' academic, co-curricular accomplishments and financial need. The college works with each individual student to recognize multiple attributes and talents. Students who demonstrate outstanding academic promise are rewarded for their achievements. Prestigious awards such as the James A. Garfield Award and the Hiram College Grant are renewable for all four years of schooling. The Hiram College Tuition Guarantee ensures students that their annual cost for tuition will not increase at any point between their first and senior years.

> SUCCESS The Hiram Plan

Most colleges and universities offer international study experiences, internships and undergraduate research opportunities with a professor. Hiram College has a unique way to create these experiences and many others with a rare academic calendar called the Hiram Plan. Each semester at Hiram College is divided into two sessions — a 12-week session when students take three or four academic courses and a three-week session where students can choose to study abroad, intern, work off-campus or take an intensive academic course. This semester breakdown happens twice a year, each year.

> SUCCESS New Student Orientation

Because 40 percent of students in Hiram College's incoming class are first-generation, the college does everything it can to ease them into their college experience. At New Student Orientation, students come away with a better understanding of the many aspects of life at Hiram College and a renewed sense of excitement to return in August. Hiram's orientation program is designed to accomplish several goals, including aiding new students in their academic and social transition to Hiram College, assisting new students in making friendships with their future classmates and fostering an understanding of the college's academic and institutional opportunities, expectations and values. New Student Orientation also creates an awareness of the diverse extracurricular opportunities, resources and people at Hiram, and enhances parents' awareness of the issues facing college students and understanding of the Hiram College environment and services.

Hiram College
PO Box 67
Hiram, OH 44234
Ph: (330) 569-3211
admission@hiram.edu
www.hiram.edu

FAST FACTS

STUDENT PROFILE
# of degree-seeking undergraduates	1,335
% male/female	46.1/53.9
% African-American	10.7
% American Indian or Alaska Native	0.5
% Asian or Pacific Islander	1.1
% Hispanic	1.6
% White	65.8
% International	5.4
% Pell grant recipients	31.9

ACADEMICS
full-time faculty	74
full-time minority faculty	n/a
student-faculty ratio	12:1
average class size	16
% first-year retention rate	80
% graduation rate (6 years)	62

Popular majors Biology/Biological Sciences, Business/Commerce, Education

CAMPUS LIFE
% live on campus (% freshmen)	85 (94)

Multicultural student clubs and organizations
African American Student Union, Black Professionals Organization, GAIA, PRYSM, Interfaith Council, Islamic Society, United Voices of Hiram Gospel Choir

Athletics NCAA Division III, North Coast Athletic Conference

ADMISSIONS
# of applicants	1,513
% accepted	75
# of first-year students enrolled	339
SAT Critical Reading range	480-610
SAT Math range	470-590
SAT Writing range	n/a
ACT range	20-26
average HS GPA	3.3

Deadlines
regular decision	rolling
application fee (online)	$0 ($0)
fee waiver for applicants with financial need	yes

COST & AID
tuition	$27,135
room & board	$9,010
total need-based institutional scholarships/grants	n/a
% of students apply for need-based aid	90.8
% of students receive aid	100
% receiving need-based scholarship or grant aid	100
% receiving aid whose need was fully met	94.9
average aid package	$17,172
average student loan debt upon graduation	$17,125

John Carroll University

John Carroll University is a Jesuit Catholic university founded in 1886. Known for its rigorous and highly regarded undergraduate curriculum, John Carroll offers degree programs in more than 30 major fields of the natural sciences, education, arts, the social sciences and business. The 60-acre suburban campus consists of 26 buildings located in University Heights, just 10 miles east of downtown Cleveland. The region is a cultural mecca boasting the country's second largest performing arts complex (Playhouse Square), the world-renowned Cleveland Symphony Orchestra and a metro-park system with a combined 52,000 acres and over 275 biking trails across Northeast Ohio.

> ACCESS Early Awareness

John Carroll helps families start planning for the goal of a college degree early. Annually, middle and high school students spend a day on the university campus. Participants come from public and parochial schools in Greater Cleveland, Lorain, Akron and Canton. They experience a true day in the life, meet with admission and financial aid staff, the Office of Multicultural Affairs staff and John Carroll students of color, tour the campus, eat lunch and have a recreation period. Students are informed of the importance of a college education and how to prepare for success in college.

"I chose John Carroll specifically for the Ohio Access Initiative. The financial support in exchange for a commitment to service is such a unique program. To be honest, I never thought I would be at such a great school. The people here are helpful and caring. I don't know where I'd be without the OAI Program."

– Jennylee G., '12
Cleveland, OH
Biology

> OPPORTUNITY Ohio Access Initiative

The commitment to keeping private education affordable is quite visible at John Carroll. The Ohio Access Initiative is the newest financial aid program at the school, making it possible for qualified Ohio families with annual incomes below $40,000 to enroll their incoming freshmen tuition-free. Students are expected to participate in 30 hours of service through the university's Center for Service and Social Action.

> OPPORTUNITY Pathways to Success Scholarship Program

Pathways to Success focuses on providing support tools to help students explore majors and career options, obtain internships, and prepare for the work world. In addition to a $1,000 award, Pathways to Success provides an orientation session, resume writing workshop, resume and cover letter review, interview training and attendance at a career fair. The scholarship is renewable for up to four years.

> SUCCESS Pathways to Success

In an effort to help students of color successfully transition from high school to college, John Carroll University offers a distinct first year program focused on the first year adjustment to John Carroll, designed to prepare students academically and socially for their college experience. It is an excellent opportunity for incoming students to become acquainted with the campus and university services and establish bonds with other incoming students. Some benefits to participating in the Pathways to Success Program include free participation, up to $500 for textbooks in both the fall and spring semesters, valuable information from JCU faculty and administrators about effective study and time management skills. The Pathways program enables students to develop relationships with other incoming students of color. These relationships often serve as important support systems for students during the academic year.

John Carroll University
20700 N. Park Boulevard
University Heights, OH 44118
Ph: (215) 397-4294
admission@jcu.edu
www.jcu.edu

F A S T   F A C T S

STUDENT PROFILE

# of degree-seeking undergraduates	3,135
% male/female	48/52
% African American	6
% American Indian or Alaska Native	<1
% Asian or Pacific Islander	2
% Hispanic	3
% White	79
% International	0
% Pell grant recipients	16.6

First-generation and minority alumni Dr. Evelyn Jenkins Gunn, Carnegie Scholar & Fellow (NBCT), National Academy (Carnegie Academy for the Advancement of Teaching & Learning); Annette L. Haile, vice president, IBM; Ric Harris, executive vice president and general manager, Digital Media & Strategic Marketing, NBC Universal; London Fletcher, NFL linebacker, Washington Redskins; Dr. Monique Ogletree, Ph.D., cardiovascular researcher, Baylor College of Medicine and Texas Children's Hospital; Tim Russert, moderator, Meet the Press, senior vice president and Washington bureau chief, NBC News

ACADEMICS

full-time faculty	210
full-time minority faculty	23
student-faculty ratio	15:1
average class size	17
% first-year retention rate	90
% graduation rate (6 years)	74

Popular majors Communications, Biology, Education, Business, Psychology, Political Science

CAMPUS LIFE

% live on campus (% freshmen)	58 (93)

Multicultural student clubs and organizations Black Student Union, International Student Union, African American Alliance, Asian Cultural Organization, Hip Hop Dance Club, Japan Society, Latin American Student Association (LASA), Middle Eastern Student Association

Athletics NCAA Division III, Ohio Athletic Conference

ADMISSIONS

# of applicants	3,481
% accepted	80
# of first-year students enrolled	792
SAT Critical Reading range	490-590
SAT Math range	490-600
SAT Writing range	480-590
ACT range	21-26
average HS GPA	3.34

Deadlines

regular decision	2/1
application fee (online)	$0 ($0)
fee waiver for applicants with financial need	n/a

COST & AID

tuition	$27,940
room & board	$8,330
total need-based institutional scholarships/grants	$14,919,323
% of students apply for need-based aid	80
% of students receive aid	100
% receiving need-based scholarship or grant aid	100
% receiving aid whose need was fully met	24
average aid package	$21,262
average student loan debt upon graduation	$19,079

Kent State University

Kent State University- Kent Campus
161 Schwartz Center
Kent, OH 44242
Ph: (330) 672-2444 / (800) 988-5368
admissions@kent.edu
www.kent.edu

F A S T   F A C T S

STUDENT PROFILE

# of degree-seeking undergraduates	19,337
% male/female	42/58
% African American	9
% American Indian or Alaska Native	<1
% Asian or Pacific Islander	2
% Hispanic	2
% White	83
% International	1
% Pell grant recipients	43

First-generation and minority alumni Bertice B. Berry, Ph D., Comedian, Speaker and Writer; Robert L. Billingslea, Corporate Director of Urban Affairs, Disney Worldwide Services; Edmund D. Cooke, Jr., Attorney, Partner Drinker Biddle & Reath LLP; Albert "Al" Fitzpatrick, Retired executive and editor, Knight Ridder; Arsenio Hall, Entertainer

ACADEMICS

full-time faculty	888
full-time minority faculty	155
student-faculty ratio	20:1
average class size	32
% first-year retention rate	78
% graduation rate (6 years)	50.1

Popular majors Architecture, Business, Education, Journalism, Nursing

CAMPUS LIFE

% live on campus (% fresh.)	36 (84)

Multicultural student clubs and organizations Association of International Students, Black Greek Council, Black United Studies, Harambee, Indian Student Association, Native American Student Association, Spanish and Latino Student Association

Athletics Division I, Mid-American Athletic Conference

ADMISSIONS

# of applicants	14,933
% accepted	72
# of first-year students enrolled	4,151
SAT Critical Reading range	460-560
SAT Math range	460-580
SAT Writing	440-560
ACT range	20-25
average HS GPA	3.19

Deadlines

regular decision	rolling to 8/1
application fee (online)	$40 ($40)
fee waiver for applicants with financial need	yes

COST & AID

tuition in-state: $8,726; out-of-state:	$16,418
room & board	$7,940
total need-based institutional scholarships/grants	$13,718,897
% of students apply for need-based aid	70
% of students receive aid	100
% receiving need-based scholarship or grant aid	69
% receiving aid whose need was fully met	49
average aid package	$7,895
average student loan debt upon graduation	$23,957

Located in Kent, Ohio, Kent State University features nearly 900 acres and 24 residence halls and enrolls more than 38,000 students across eight campuses. Kent State offers over 280 academic programs at the undergraduate level and engages students in diverse learning environments that expand their intellectual horizons and encourage them to become responsible citizens. The University provides a supportive community devoted to teaching excellence, first-tier scholarship, and academic freedom.

> SUCCESS **Student Multicultural Center**

The Student Multicultural Center seeks to ensure the successful enrollment, retention and graduation of underrepresented students. The Center develops and implements holistic retention programs and encourages mutual respect through cultural, educational and social programming.

> SUCCESS **Department of Pan-African Studies**

The Department of Pan-African Studies encompasses the Center for Pan-African Culture and the Institute for African-American affairs. Its mission is to offer an Afrocentric academic curriculum grounded in the cultural traditions and experiences of people of African descent. Providing a major and minor that span the humanities, fine arts, and social sciences, the Department fosters tolerance for cultural diversity on campus and throughout the surrounding community. This is implemented through its African Community Theatre and Outreach Programs.

> SUCCESS **Academic STARS (Students Achieving and Reaching for Success)**

Academic STARS is a freshman year transition and retention program for African-American freshman students who want to enhance their opportunity for academic success, to develop leadership, and to enrich their college experience. The program kicks off with a seven-week summer program during which participants can earn seven credit hours to be applied toward graduation. Students also learn success strategies and skills through advising and workshops throughout the school year.

"Kent State has made me a well-rounded person. My favorite class, honors writing, was basically a roundtable discussion on books and novels. There were only 20 of us, and Professor Cutti encouraged us to think critically about storytelling, so our conversations were always interesting."

– Miranda M., '10 Columbus, OH Nursing

> SUCCESS **Kupita/Transiciones**

Kupita/Transiciones is a four-day holistic enrollment management, orientation and retention program for newly admitted African American, Latino, American Indian freshmen and transfer students. It includes academic success workshops a week before the start the start of the semester.

> SUCCESS **The University Mentoring Program**

This program is a transition and retention support program designed to enhance the college and life-management skills of under-represented students by building a community of support around the freshman student.

Miami University

Miami University encourages students to become citizen leaders, infused with the desire to learn and think critically. Dedicated to grounding students in a liberal arts education, Miami consistently places among the top public universities in national college guides and is specifically cited by *U.S. News and World Report* for academic programs that lead to student success. Miami students graduate at a rate above the national average, due largely to the personal attention and support they receive from their professors. Through the Miami Access Initiative, which guarantees complete funding of tuition for eligible Ohio students, Miami University is accessible to all of Ohio's academically qualified students, regardless of income.

> OPPORTUNITY BRIDGES: A Plan for Excellence

The BRIDGES Program serves outstanding underrepresented students who are interested in studying at Miami University. BRIDGES recruits high-school seniors who maintain at least a 3.0 cumulative GPA in a college preparatory curriculum, who are active in extracurricular activities, and who demonstrate leadership. The program offers an all-expenses-paid overnight visit to the Oxford campus. Students participate in activities that prepare them for college, the admission process, and offer financial aid information. Students completing this program receive a four year renewable scholarship upon enrollment at Miami.

> OPPORTUNITY Miami Access Initiative

The Miami Access Initiative guarantees that eligible Ohio students receive scholarship/grant funding that meets or exceeds the cost of tuition and academic fees at Miami University. The majority of the program's scholars are first-generation college students. All Ohio residents entering the Miami University Oxford campus as first-time, full-time freshmen are considered. Dependent students relocating to Oxford from the Hamilton or Middletown campuses are also eligible.

> SUCCESS MADE@Miami

MADE@Miami, MU's Pre-First Year Institute, comprises qualities valued by the University community – Mentoring, Achievement, Diversity, and Excellence. This program provides a diverse group of academically ambitious first- year students the opportunity to engage in workshops to ease their transition to the University community, contribute to their academic success, and stimulate thinking related to their common experience.

> SUCCESS Rinella Learning Center

The Rinella Learning Center offers individual and group tutoring, a learning disabilities program, and help with study skills. The mission of the Bernard B. Rinella, Jr. Learning Center is to help students reach their individual academic goals by empowering them with skills needed to be independent and successful learners and to provide academic support through various programs and services with the help of the center's staff.

> SUCCESS Connection Coaches Peer Mentor Program

The Office of Diversity Affairs (ODA) Connection Coaches Peer Mentor Program is designed to pair first-year students with a trained peer coach, or mentor, who can help new students feel more connected and comfortable at the university by helping with transition difficulties often faced in the first year. Whether helping students navigate the university community by referring them to resources, acting as a sounding board, or introducing students to athletic and cultural events, these mentors will offer assistance, motivation and support to achieve success.

"Ever since I was young, I wanted to be an inventor. I'm in the Scholastic Enhancement Program, and I'm paired with an engineering professor to learn how to do research. We built a robot, and it's been a great experience. I also received a Miami Access Initiative scholarship, which helps."
–Justinn E., '11 Cleveland, OH Mechanical Engineering

Miami University
301 S. Campus Avenue
Oxford, OH 45056
Ph: (513) 529-2531
admission@muohio.edu
www.muohio.edu

F A S T   F A C T S

STUDENT PROFILE
# of degree-seeking undergraduates	14,699
% male/female	46/54
% African American	5
% American Indian or Alaska Native	1
% Asian or Pacific Islander	3
% Hispanic	2
% White	84
% International	3
% Pell grant recipients	14

First-generation and minority alumni Rita Dove '73, former U.S. poet laureate (first African American and youngest); Wil Haygood '76, journalist, *The Washington Post*; Marilyn Gaston '60, former assistant surgeon general

ACADEMICS
full-time faculty	867
full-time minority faculty	135
student-faculty ratio	17:1
average class size	31
% first-year retention rate	90
% graduation rate (6 yr.)	82

Popular majors Zoology, Psychology, Marketing, Finance, Education

CAMPUS LIFE
% live on campus (% fresh.)	46 (98)

Multicultural student clubs and organizations Historically Black and Latino-interest Greek Fraternities and Sororities, Hillel, Spectrum, Miami Ambassadors Advocating for Diversity, Indian Student Association, International Club, Japanese Culture and Language Club, Muslim Student Association, Love you Like a Sista, Miami University Gospel Singers, Minority Health Association, Association of Latino and American Students, Chinese Student and Scholars Friendship Association, Asian American Association, Diwali, National Association for the Advancement of Colored People, Minority Business Association, Black Student Action Association, GLTBQ Alliance
Athletics NCAA Division I, Mid-America Conference

ADMISSIONS
# of applicants	16,800
% accepted	75
# of first-year students enrolled	3,250
SAT Critical Reading range	540-640
SAT Math range	560-650
ACT range	24-29
average HS GPA	3.66

Deadlines
early action	12/1
early decision	11/1
regular decision	2/1
application fee (online)	$50 (50)
fee waiver for applicants with financial need	yes

COST & AID
tuition in-state: $11,442; out-of-state	$26,202
room & board	$9,458
total need-based institutional scholarships & grants	$11,386,112
% of students apply for need-based aid	57
% of students receive aid	98
% receiving need-based scholarship or grant aid	57
% receiving aid whose need was fully met	17
average aid package	$10,137
average student loan debt upon graduation	$26,798

Mount Vernon Nazarene University

Founded in 1968, Mount Vernon Nazarene University is characterized by an engaging environment where diversity is embraced and differences in ethnicity, denomination, gender and economic level are celebrated. Students of every denomination are welcomed and encouraged to join the dynamic MVNU community, in which over 40 other Christian denominations are represented. Students are challenged to live up to their utmost potential through a wide variety of degree programs and various opportunities for service, both on- and off-campus. Faculty, staff and administrators nurture and empower students with caring relationships, preparing them to be life-long learners and leaders in the professional world. "To seek to learn is to seek to serve," the University motto, encourages students to involve themselves in the local and international community and view learning with a global vision.

"As an International student from Germany, I have been attending Mount Vernon Nazarene University for three years. This has been a great cross-cultural experience at an American University meeting new friends and having professors that care. I've even had the opportunity to travel to Papua New Guinea and Belize through mission trips and meet people from other countries. Coming to MVNU has been global and life changing for me."

– Inga C., '10, Germany Biology

> ACCESS **Project Recruit**

Project Recruit is a recruitment initiative designed to identify, select and recruit potential minority and urban students from four targeted Ohio urban public high schools. The program's goal is to provide collaborative recruitment strategies, including events and activities to give students the opportunity to prepare for college and hopefully gain admission to Mount Vernon Nazarene University. Past events included ACT/SAT prep sessions.

> OPPORTUNITY **Diversity Leadership Scholars Award**

Diversity Leadership Scholars are admitted students who are committed and willing to make an impact on- and off-campus through leadership, academic talent, and service. Students receive an award ranging from $2,000 to $5,000 per year, and eligibility for renewal of the scholarship is based on maintaining at least a 2.8 GPA and participation in service and leadership activities. In addition to the financial advantages, scholars are assigned a faculty advisor and a student mentor, attend bi-monthly leadership luncheons and benefit from intensive service experiences off-campus in urban and rural settings. Leadership Scholars serve as stewards in recruiting the next generation of leaders to MVNU, hosting new multicultural prospects at multicultural visitation days.

> SUCCESS **AIM for Excellence Program**

The AIM for Excellence Program serves international students, missionary students and students of color. The program, from the Multicultural Affairs Office, has a goal to recruit and serve students with diverse ethnic and cultural backgrounds. In support of MVNU's mission to offer a supportive and inspiring environment to students of all backgrounds, the AIM for Excellence Program helps students get involved through a variety of activities, clubs and organizations.

> SUCCESS **AIM Student Mentoring Program**

This mentoring program provides first-year students with a dedicated and knowledgeable Mount Vernon Nazarene faculty/staff mentor for the fall semester. The program is designed to provide strong academic, cultural, and social experiences for students. The goal of the program is to prepare students for success in college, helping them to develop the skills, attitudes and motivation that they will need for this important journey. Referral services to campus and academic resources and career guidance help students to succeed. The program is associated with the Diversity Leaders Scholarship Program, but mentoring services are available to all first-year students at Mount Vernon Nazarene University.

Mount Vernon Nazarene University
Office of Admissions
800 Martinsburg Road
Mount Vernon, OH 43050
Ph: (866) 462-6868
admissions@mvnu.edu
www.mvnu.edu

F A S T   F A C T S

STUDENT PROFILE
# of degree-seeking undergraduates	2,090
% male/female	37/63
% African American	5
% American Indian or Alaska Native	<1
% Asian or Pacific Islander	1
% Hispanic	1
% Pell grant recipients	26

First-generation and minority alumni Reverend Josephus Foster '04, (Master's degree) Pastor, Fountain of Hope Church of the Nazarene Trustee, Mount Vernon Nazarene University

ACADEMICS
full-time faculty	119
full-time minority faculty	6
student-faculty ratio	14:1
average class size	15
% first-year retention rate	75
% graduation rate (6 years)	56

Popular majors Biology, Business, Education, Nursing, Religion

CAMPUS LIFE
% live on campus (% freshmen)	50 (95)

Multicultural student clubs and organizations Cross Cultural Club, International Student Organization, Diversity Scholars

Athletics NCAA Division II, NAIA, NCCAA, AMC

ADMISSIONS
# of applicants	813
% accepted	79
# of first-year students enrolled	368
SAT Critical Reading range	500-610
SAT Math range	450-580
SAT Writing range	n/a
ACT range	23-27
average HS GPA	3.3

Deadlines
priority application	3/15
regular decision	7/15
application fee (online)	$25 ($25)
fee waiver for applicants with financial need	yes

COST & AID
tuition	$19,730
room and board	$5,890
total need-based institutional scholarships/grants	$11,221,034
% of students received aid	99
% receiving need-based scholarship or grant aid	94
% receiving aid whose need was fully met	71
average aid package	$16,171
average student loan debt upon graduation	$32,791

Oberlin College

Oberlin College, founded in 1833, is a four-year, highly selective liberal arts college and home to America's oldest continuously operating music conservatory. From its founding, Oberlin has been a community of thinkers, scholars, scientists, musicians, athletes, activists and artists. Students are united by a commitment to social justice and a willingness to confront social issues that many would prefer to ignore. Oberlin invented coeducation in 1837 and made interracial education central to its mission in 1835. Oberlin offers 47 majors and 42 minors and areas of concentration. Students pursue studies in the College of Arts and Sciences, the Conservatory of Music or both divisions through a distinctive five-year double-degree program. More Oberlin graduates have gone on to earn a Ph.D. than those at any other American college.

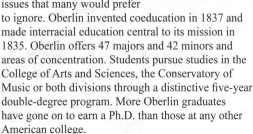

"When I started researching Oberlin I fell in love with its history of change and progressive activism... Students here are just as active and committed as they have ever been. Their continued commitment to changing the world, social justice, and environmental sustainability were all things that drew me to Oberlin."

– Justin B., '09
Cincinnati, OH
Politics, Psychology

> ACCESS Ninde Scholars Program

An outgrowth of Oberlin College's community-based Writing Program, the Ninde Scholars Program pairs Oberlin rhetoric and composition students with Oberlin High School students who are low-income, first-generation and/or from underrepresented minority groups in post-secondary education. Ninde Scholars receive support in navigating the college process while building writing and research skills as necessary tools for college success.

> OPPORTUNITY Multicultural Visit Program

Six times each year, Oberlin's Office of Admissions sponsors a Multicultural Visit Program, an all-expenses-paid campus visit for minority students interested in a liberal arts education.

> OPPORTUNITY Oberlin Access Initiative

The Oberlin Access Initiative allows Oberlin to maintain its historic leadership in providing access to a diversity of individuals. It ensures that any qualified student who wishes to attend Oberlin College will be able to do so, regardless of his or her ability to pay. Students who are eligible to receive the federally funded Pell Grant will receive loan-free financial aid packages.

> OPPORTUNITY Posse Foundation

Oberlin participates in the Posse Foundation, a program that brings talented public school youth to campus to pursue their academics and to help promote cross-cultural communication. Posse students are nominated by their high school to the program and share a collaborative support system with a special mentor to adjust to campus and college life. Oberlin's Posse Scholars hail from Chicago.

> OPPORTUNITY QuestBridge

Oberlin partners with QuestBridge, a national program that links bright, motivated, low-income students to some of the nation's best colleges. The target is to "match," a process similar to early decision, approximately five students with Oberlin annually. Approximately 70 percent of QuestBridge scholars are minority students and come from households with annual incomes under $29,000.

> OPPORTUNITY Office of Undergraduate Research

Each year the Office of Undergraduate Research selects ten Oberlin College Research Fellows and five Mellon Mays Undergraduate Fellows from low-income families, first-generation students, and students underrepresented in graduate studies to encourage them to pursue Ph.D.s. Fellows are mentored by faculty during the academic year and participate in intensive research projects for two summers.

Oberlin College
101 North Professor St
Oberlin, OH 44074
Ph: (440) 775-8411
college.admissions@oberlin.edu
www.oberlin.edu

F A S T   F A C T S

STUDENT PROFILE
# of degree-seeking undergraduates	2,839
% male/female	45/55
% African American	6
% American Indian or Alaska Native	<1
% Asian or Pacific Islander	7
% Hispanic	5
% White	75
% International	6
% Pell grant recipients	13.3

First-generation and minority alumni Ishmael Beah, author, *A Long Way Gone: Memoirs of a Boy Soldier*; Johnnetta Betsch Cole, first African-American to serve as chair of the Board of the United Way of America, first African-American woman to serve as president of Spelman College; Chris Broussard, NBA reporter, ESPN's SportsCenter, columnist, *ESPN the Magazine*; Adrian Fenty, mayor of Washington, D.C.; James McBride, author, *The Color of Water*; Eduardo Mondlane, the father of modern Mozambique; Carl Rowan, prominent African-American journalist; Anthony Stallion, chairman, Diversity Councils for Cleveland Clinic hospitals; Moses Fleetwood Walker, first African-American to play major league baseball, member of Toledo Blue Stockings

ACADEMICS
full-time faculty	285
full-time minority faculty	31
student-faculty ratio	9:1
average class size	19
% first-year retention rate	94
% graduation rate (6 years)	83

Popular majors Biology/Biological Science, English Language and Literature, History, Environmental Studies, Music, East Asian Studies

CAMPUS LIFE
% live on campus (% freshmen)	88 (100)

Multicultural student clubs and organizations Asian American Alliance, African Student Association, Chinese Student Association, Filipino American Student Association, La Alianza Latina, Middle Eastern Students Association, Oberlin Korean Students Association

Athletics NCAA Division III, NCAC

ADMISSIONS
# of applicants	7,006
% accepted	33
# of first-year students enrolled	768
SAT Critical Reading range	640-740
SAT Math range	620-710
SAT Writing range	640-730
ACT range	27-32
average HS GPA	3.60

Deadlines
early decision	11/15
regular decision	1/2
application fee (online)	$35 ($35)
fee waiver for applicants with financial need	yes

COST & AID
tuition	$40,000
room & board	$9,870
total need-based institutional scholarships/grants	$35,904,591
% of students apply for need-based aid	60
% of students receive aid	67
% receiving need-based scholarship or grant aid	52
% receiving aid whose need was fully met	100
average aid package	$31,257
average student loan debt upon graduation	$17,579

Ohio Northern University

Ohio Northern University
525 South Main Street
Ada, OH 45810
Ph: (888) 408-4ONU (4668)
admissions-ug@onu.edu
www.onu.edu

When many colleges were debating whether to admit women, Ohio Northern University had been doing it since its inception in 1871. A private, independent school located in the rural community of Ada, Ohio and affiliated with the United Methodist Church, this former teaching institution was built from the ground up by local educator Henry Solomon Lehr. Today, Ohio Northern boasts five colleges, including a law school, a robust curriculum, and a range of organizations and activities, including 21 varsity sports for men and women.

> ACCESS **Catch-A-Ride (CAR)**

Catch-A-Ride is a program for high school seniors of color in Cincinnati, Cleveland, Columbus, Dayton and the surrounding areas. During the fall of the senior year, a bus is sent out to these major cities for students to "catch-a-ride" to the Ohio Northern campus. At no cost to the student, CAR provides an opportunity for these seniors to experience a day in the life of an ONU student by attending classes and interacting with deans, faculty, and students. After students have been accepted to Ohio Northern, they have the opportunity to return to campus in the spring for an overnight visit to learn more about life outside of the classroom at Ohio Northern.

"As a student of color, Ohio Northern has provided me with opportunities to learn and grow with the resources I need to be successful. Being here has allowed me to interact with and learn from students from different cultural backgrounds, which will prepare me to pursue a career in the field of business."

— Terryn T., '12 Lima, OH Business Management

> OPPORTUNITY **Dimension Award**

The Dimension Award financially assists accepted students from underrepresented ethnic backgrounds. Award amounts may be up to $10,000 in gift aid. Accepted students who apply for the Dimension Award are encouraged to file the FAFSA to ensure maximum assistance. The award is coordinated with other financial aid programs and awards. The Dimension Award is available to new full-time undergraduate students (four years for pharmacy) and transfer students.

> SUCCESS **Office of Multicultural Development**

The Office of Multicultural Development offers a seven-step series as a part of an aggressive initiative to acknowledge, retain, and embrace its multicultural student population. The office opened in 1991 and has sponsored a wealth of programs and events to celebrate diversity. The components include activities and programs that serve both academic and social objectives that educate the entire campus community.

> SUCCESS **Finding U at ONU**

Finding U at ONU, conducted by the Office of Multicultural Development, works to help multicultural students adjust to life at Ohio Northern University. Through peer mentoring and staff involvement, select first-year multicultural students are encouraged to participate in a host of events and activities that address their history, background, and interests.

F A S T   F A C T S

STUDENT PROFILE
# of degree-seeking undergraduates	2,445
% male/female	52/48
% African American	4
% American Indian or Alaska Native	<1
% Asian or Pacific Islander	1.5
% Hispanic	1.5
% White	92
% International	2
% Pell grant recipients (2009)	28

ACADEMICS
full-time faculty	242
full-time minority faculty	26
student-faculty ratio	12:1
average class size	23
% first-year retention rate	83
% graduation rate (6 yr)	67

Popular majors Business, Management, Marketing, Education, Engineering, Pharmacy, Biology

CAMPUS LIFE
% live on campus (% fresh.)	68 (96)

Multicultural student clubs and organizations Black Student Union, Asian American Student Union, Indian Student Association, Open Doors, Latino Student Union, Men of Distinction, Sister Circle, World Student Organization

Athletics NCAA Division III, Ohio Athletic Conference

ADMISSIONS
# of applicants	2,896
% accepted	89
# first-year students enrolled	641
SAT Critical Reading range	510-630
SAT Math range	560-650
SAT Writing range	510-620
ACT Range	23-29
Average HS GPA	3.64

Deadlines
regular decision	rolling to 8/15
application fee (online)	$30 ($30)
fee waiver for applicants with financial need	yes

COST & AID
tuition	$32,859
room & board	$9,072
total need-based institutional scholarships/grants	$29,941,287
% of students apply for need-based aid	96
% of students receive aid	96
% receiving need-based scholarship or grant aid	78
% receiving aid whose need was fully met	12
average aid package	$25,576
average student loan debt upon graduation	$45,902

The Ohio State University

The Ohio State University is a co-educational, non-denominational, public research university. The university was founded in 1870 as a land-grant university and is currently among the largest universities in the United States. With an overarching goal of advancing the well-being of the people of Ohio and the global community through the creation and dissemination of knowledge, Ohio State strives to pursue knowledge for its own sake, ignite in its students a lifelong love of learning, produce discoveries that make the world a better place, celebrate and learn from its diversity and "open the world" to its students.

> ACCESS Blueprint: College

The Ohio State University's free series of college planning workshops is designed especially for the parents of children enrolled in local elementary schools. The program has two main goals: to provide first-generation, low-income and/or minority parents with tips on how to prepare their children for college and to relay the importance of college to their children. The program begins with a kick-off dinner in the spring and is then held weekly for five weeks. Two Saturday campus visits also occur. Dinner, transportation and childcare are provided by the university.

> *"Growing up, I realized how hard it was for my mother to support me and my two brothers. Though she always pushed for me to go to college, we both knew our family could not afford it. But I was determined to go! When I applied to Ohio State, I filled out the FAFSA and OSU gave me many scholarships and grants. Keeping my grades up so that I can continue to go to school for free is the least I can do."*
>
> *– Tacoi S., '13*
> *Columbus, OH*
> *Math*

> ACCESS Economic Access Initiative

The Economic Access Initiative ensures that qualified students who lack financial resources and information about the college process are not denied the opportunity to attend Ohio State. The university has developed initiatives throughout the state for educating low-income students and their parents about available financial aid resources and programs.

> OPPORTUNITY Land Grant Opportunity Scholarship

The Land Grant Opportunity Scholarship program was established to help high-ability, low-income students enroll at Ohio State. Through the program, the full in-state cost of education at Ohio State is covered via a combination of scholarships, grants, and work-study opportunities for one or more qualified students from each of Ohio's 88 counties.

> OPPORTUNITY Morrill Scholars Program (MSP)

This is a merit scholarship program for students who contribute to diversity at Ohio State. The Office of Minority Affairs offers this program to promote diversity, multiculturalism and leadership and to enrich the educational experiences of all Ohio State students so they will be prepared for optimum success in the world community. Eligible students include racial and ethnic minorities, Ohio Appalachian, first-generation and low-income students. Nearly 600 students were offered an MSP scholarship for fall 2008, with the minimum award being full in-state tuition.

> SUCCESS First-Year Success Series

The First-Year Success Series helps to promote success by offering short courses on the common concerns and questions first-year students have during their transition to university life. The very first week of sessions focuses on issues related to financial literacy and understanding financial aid, covering topics including managing a checking account, credit card debt and "Financial Aid 101." Additional topics include study skills, procrastination, leadership, health and wellness, sexual health, drugs and alcohol awareness and diversity issues. First-year students are required by their academic adviser to attend two to four of these sessions.

The Ohio State University
Undergraduate Admissions and First
Year Experience
110 Enarson Hall, 154 W. 12th Ave.
Columbus, OH 43210
Ph: (614) 292-3980
askabuckeye@osu.edu
www.osu.edu

FAST FACTS

STUDENT PROFILE
# of degree-seeking undergraduates	40,178
% male/female	54/46
% African American	7
% American Indian or Alaska Native	<1
% Asian or Pacific Islander	5
% Hispanic	3
% White	79
% International	4
% Pell grant recipients	30.6

First-generation and minority alumni Samella Lewis, artist; Chester Himes, writer; Aimee Nezhukumatathil, poet; Manu Mehta, CEO, Matabyte Networks, Inc.; Phuthuma Nhleko, CEO, MTN Group; Yang Huiyan, China's wealthiest person in 2007; Ruby Elzy, opera singer; Ljubica Acevska, diplomat of the Republic of Macedonia to the United States; Amodou Ba, Diplomat Senegal Ambassador; Chester Crocker, former undersecretary of state for African Affairs; Jayaprakash Narayan, Indian freedom fighter; Ken Nnamani, senate president, Nigeria; Roberto Sanchez Vilella, former governor of Puerto Rico; Jesse Brown, first African-American Navy pilot; P. Chungmoo Auh, president, Korean Institute of Energy Research; Robert Henry Lawrence, Jr., first African-American NASA astronaut; Esther Takeuchi, inventor; Michael White, former mayor, Cleveland

ACADEMICS
full-time faculty	3,310
full-time minority faculty	675
student-faculty ratio	13:1
average class size	26
% first-year retention rate	93
% graduation rate (6 years)	75

Popular majors Biology, Finance, Political Science, English, Accounting, Marketing, Communication, Psychology

CAMPUS LIFE
% live on campus (% fresh.)	24(91)

Multicultural student clubs and organizations African-American Media Organization, Afrikan Student Union, American Indian Council, Asian-American Association, Black Law Student Association, Hispanic groups, Indian-American Student Association, NAACP; African, Asian, Chinese, Egyptian, Indian, Indonesian, Japanese, Korean, Laotian, Malaysian, Pakistani, Singaporean, Taiwanese, Thai, Turkish and International student associations
Athletics NCAA Division I, Big Ten Conference (football I-A), Central Collegiate Hockey Association, Great Western Lacrosse League, Midwestern Intercollegiate Volleyball Association, Western Collegiate Hockey Association

ADMISSIONS
# of applicants	18,256
% accepted	76
# of first-year students enrolled	6,739
SAT Critical Reading range	540-650
SAT Math range	580-690
SAT Writing range	540-640
ACT range	25-30
average HS GPA	n/a
Deadlines	
regular decision	2/1
application fee (online)	$40 ($40)
fee waiver for applicants with financial need	yes

COST & AID
tuition	in-state: $8,706; out-of-state: $22,278
room & board	$2,800
total need-based institutional scholarships/grants	$57,054,742
% of students apply for need-based aid	69
% of students receive aid	99
% receiving need-based scholarship or grant aid	60
% receiving aid whose need was fully met	17
average aid package	$10,752
average student loan debt upon graduation	$18,425

Ohio Wesleyan University

In 1842, Ohio residents Adam Poe and Charles Elliott decided to establish a university "of the highest order" in central Ohio. Today, with several support programs at Ohio Wesleyan University for pre-college, first-generation, underserved students, the university continues to be a leader in cultural diversity and international education in all its forms. For example, the President's Commission on Racial and Cultural Diversity issues an annual report with recommendations and concerns about the state of racial and cultural diversity at Ohio Wesleyan. Also, the school offers on-campus housing options focusing on multicultural issues, including the House of Black Culture as one of the University's small living units.

"OWU does a great job of incorporating all students. I've been to El Salvador and New Orleans on mission trips and have studied in Spain. The more I engage myself, the more I feel a real sense of belonging here. It can be a life-changing experience."
– *Alfonso T. '11, Oakland, CA International Business and Spanish*

> ACCESS **Upward Bound**

Upward Bound is one of six national federally funded TRIO Programs. The mission is to provide high school students (low-income and potential-first-generation college students) with the skills and motivation needed to enter and complete a college or university of their choice. Over the past 40 years, the program has served hundreds of Columbus-area families. OWU Upward Bound has a 100 percent college-placement rate and a 64 percent college graduation rate.

> OPPORTUNITY **Campus Visit Cost Assistance**

To enable multicultural and first-generation students to visit campus, Ohio Wesleyan assists with transportation arrangements and costs.

> OPPORTUNITY **Branch Rickey Scholarships**

In recognition of the importance of cultural diversity in its student body, these awards are made in the amount of $7,000 to $14,000. This award can be renewed at the same value for up to three years of full-time enrollment if students attain the required level of academic performance and maintain it each year.

> SUCCESS **Multicultural and First-Generation Pre-Orientation**

Multicultural and first-generation students arrive for orientation two days prior to other first-year students. This pre-orientation program provides an opportunity for students to connect individually with their advisers and administrators. In addition, they familiarize themselves with the campus, the facilities and the community. Most importantly, these students begin relationships with others who have the same feelings and fears that they have.

> SUCCESS **Student Advising Registration and Testing (StART)**

First-year students (and parents) are invited to connect to Ohio Wesleyan academically by attending one of several sessions to register for the fall semester, learning about distribution requirements and taking language placement exams. Individual advising regarding course selections and other support services is available.

> SUCCESS **Office of Multicultural Affairs**

The Office of Multicultural Student Affairs at Ohio Wesleyan provides extensive programming and support for multicultural students from academic, social, personal and cultural perspectives. Some of the events sponsored by the office include Hispanic Awareness Week, Cultural Minifest, Asian Heritage Month, Kushinda, Rafiki Wa Afrika African Festival, Black History Month, Kwanzaa celebration, SUBA Step Show, and Women of Color Month.

Ohio Wesleyan University
75 South Sandusky Street
Delaware, OH 43015-2398
Ph: (740) 368-3020
owuadmit@owu.edu
www.owu.edu

FAST FACTS

STUDENT PROFILE

# of degree-seeking undergraduates	1,880
% male/female	46/54
% African American	5
% American Indian or Alaska Native	<1
% Asian or Pacific Islander	2
% Hispanic	2
% White	80
% International	9
% Pell grant recipients	20.7

First-generation and minority alumni Byron Pitts, chief national correspondent, CBS News, Contributor, *60 Minutes*; Greg Moore, managing editor, *Boston Globe*, editor, *Denver Post*; Barbranda Lumpkins Walls, former travel editor at *USA Today*, features editor at *AARP Bulletin*, author, *Soul Sanctuary: Images of the African American Worship Experience*

ACADEMICS

full-time faculty	138
full-time minority faculty	9
student-faculty ratio	11:1
average class size	16.4
% first-year retention rate	81
% graduation rate (6 years)	59

Popular majors Psychology, Economics, Education, Pre-Med, Zoology

CAMPUS LIFE

% live on campus (% fresh.)	81 (97)

Multicultural student clubs and organizations SUBA (Student Union on Black Awareness), Black Men of the Future, Sisters United, VIVA (recognizes Latin American cultures), Rafiki Wa Afrika, Black Presidents Council, S.T.R.I.D.E. (Standing Together to Reduce Intolerance and Develop Equality), Muslim Students Association, SANGAM (recognizes East Asian cultures), Chinese Culture Club

Athletics NCAA Division III, North Coast Athletic Conference (NCAC)

ADMISSIONS

# of applicants	4,210
% accepted	64
# of first-year students enrolled	498
SAT Critical Reading range	520-660
SAT Math range	520-660
ACT range	23-29
average HS GPA	3.46

Deadlines

early action I	11/30
early action II	1/15
regular decision	3/1
application fee (online)	$35 ($0)
fee waiver for applicants with financial need	yes

COST & AID

tuition	$35,918
room & board	$9,276
total need-based institutional scholarships/grants	$6,000,000
% of students apply for need-based aid	66
% of students receive aid	96
% receiving need-based scholarship or grant aid	95
% receiving aid whose need was fully met	25
average aid package	$27,000
average student loan debt upon graduation	$26,000

The University of Findlay

The University of Findlay is a mid-size private, comprehensive university affiliated with the Church of God. Findlay is the largest and most diverse private school in northwest Ohio and is located within two hours of Columbus and Cleveland. The university offers a solid academic curriculum with a liberal arts foundation and students may choose from over 60 majors. Findlay emphasizes career preparation and experience with campus-sponsored service projects and internships. Many of these internships can be found in the surrounding city of Findlay, where the school also creates outreach partnerships with local high schools and volunteer campaigns for community growth.

> ## > OPPORTUNITY Desmond V. Buford "One Race, One People, One World" Memorial Scholarship

The Desmond V. Buford Scholarship is in memory of a University of Findlay graduate who was passionate about educating others in diversity. The scholarship is awarded to a sophomore, junior or senior student who demonstrates leadership on campus and adheres to Buford's "One race, one people, one world" ideology. The recipient must have a GPA of 3.0 or higher.

> ## > OPPORTUNITY Heritage Scholarships for African-American Students

Established through the generosity of Janet Mrvosh Taylor, this scholarship is awarded to sophomore and junior students of African-American descent, who must have maintained at least a cumulative 2.8 GPA or above through two semesters of the previous academic year.

> ## > OPPORTUNITY Gift of Hope Hispanic Scholarship

Established by the undergraduate language and culture program at The University of Findlay, this scholarship is awarded to a Hispanic or Latino student who is a permanent resident of the United States, is a natural citizen of the United States or is enrolled in an approved major with a major or minor in a foreign language or with an endorsement in TESOL or bilingual/multicultural studies and at least a 2.0 GPA.

> ## > OPPORTUNITY Whirlpool Scholarship for Women and Minorities

The Whirlpool Foundation Scholarship for Women and Minorities is funded through Whirlpool's Findlay Division and is awarded to a junior-year student majoring in environmental, safety and occupational health management who has at least a 2.75 GPA and demonstrated financial need.

> ## > SUCCESS Assisting Student's Progress in Reaching Educational Goals (ASPIRE) Program

Established by the Office of Intercultural Student Services, the ASPIRE Mentoring Program provides academic and social mentoring to at-risk students. ASPIRE selects qualified junior or senior Findlay students to serve as mentors to freshmen and sophomores who need encouragement to succeed and to graduate. The partnership requires students to meet on a weekly basis to help younger students adjust to the Findlay college experience with success.

> ## > SUCCESS Intercultural Student Services

The Office of Intercultural Student Services is committed to providing a socially and culturally well-rounded educational experience. Each and every student of The University of Findlay has an opportunity to engage in activities, events and educational programs that are diverse in nature. This office also plays an active role in preparing students for an intercultural workforce upon graduation.

University of Findlay
1000 North Main Street
Findlay, OH 45840-3695
Ph: (419) 422-8313
admissions@findlay.edu
www.findlay.edu

F A S T   F A C T S

STUDENT PROFILE

# of degree-seeking undergraduates	4,210
% male/female	n/a
% African-American	3
% American Indian or Alaska Native	<1
% Asian or Pacific Islander	1
% Hispanic	1
% White	n/a
% Pell grant recipients	24

ACADEMICS

full-time faculty	190
full-time minority faculty	n/a
student-faculty ratio	17:1
average class size	17
% first-year retention rate	76
% graduation rate (6 years)	53

Popular majors Health Professions and Related Sciences, Business/Marketing, Education

CAMPUS LIFE

% live on campus (% fresh.)	40 (86)

Multicultural student clubs and organizations Black Student Union, Indian Student Association, Japanese Culture Club, Spanish Club
Athletics NCAA Division II, Great Lakes Intercollegiate Athletic Conference, Intercollegiate Horse Show Association

ADMISSIONS

# of applicants	2,914
% accepted	68
# of first-year students enrolled	817
SAT Critical Reading range	460-570
SAT Math range	480-590
SAT Writing range	480-580
ACT range	20-26
average HS GPA	3.4

Deadlines

regular decision	rolling
application fee (online)	$0 ($0)

COST & AID

tuition	$25,774
room & board	$8,554
total need-based institutional scholarships/grants	$28,400,000
% of students apply for need-based aid	91
% of students receive aid	71
% receiving need-based scholarship or grant aid	89
% receiving aid whose need was fully met	10
average aid package	$19,003
average student loan debt upon graduation	$32,659

University of Mount Union

University of Mount Union is one of the top colleges in the Midwest according to *U.S. News and World Report*, and it is grounded in the traditions of the liberal arts education but provides a practical experience. The college's vigorous academic program prepares students for success with a liberal-arts education, critical thinking and communication skills, and a global understanding. To maintain the comfort of the students' experience graduate programs are currently being developed at Mount Union. The college offered the first graduate program, Physician's Assistant in the summer of 2009. Mount Union's population of first-generation students exceeds 40 percent of the student body and the college offers many support services for these students and their families. The college's Office of Multicultural Student Affairs serves as a resource for minorities in academic, social, cultural issues, as well as promoting well-being and diversity on campus.

 ACCESS Council Attracting Prospective Educators Program (CAPE)

The Council Attracting Prospective Educators Program's original goal was to attract minority students to the teaching profession, and has been expanded to encourage minority students to consider a college education in general. University of Mount Union was instrumental in implementing this change and now works with local school districts to recruit students for the program's Summer Academy. The Summer Academy and other events, such as "College Visitation Day," are aimed at middle school students in the northeast Ohio area. Students tour the Mount Union campus and are introduced to college application information such as application timelines, the admission process, financial aid and academic preparation.

> *"I would definitely choose Mount Union all over again. The professors are kind, supportive and encouraging, and I felt comfortable here from the moment I stepped on campus. Being a first generation student, I want to do well and inspire the rest of my family to attend college, too."*
>
> *– Tiffany Ormiston, '11 Minerva, OH Middle Childhood Education*

 ACCESS Dowling Mentor Program

The Dowling Mentor Program targets local, underserved students who are uncertain if a college education is in their future. These students are paired with Mount Union students in middle school and the relationship continues through high school so the students receive sustained academic and personal mentoring, college application assistance and friendship. The Dowling Mentor Program includes group activities and engagement with students' parents as well.

 OPPORTUNITY Minority Achievement Award

University of Mount Union annually sponsors a Minority Achievement Award competition. The award is open to all minority students who wish to apply to Mount Union. The competition involves an on-campus interview and an essay, and brings multicultural students onto the Mount Union campus to experience the school firsthand. This visit determines the results of the award program and introduces students and their families to minority faculty, staff and students at the college. The Minority Achievement Award ranges up to $10,000 depending on students' application and academics.

SUCCESS Kaleidoscope Program

Mount Union's Kaleidoscope Program is a voluntary orientation program geared toward minorities to ease their transition from high school to college. Kaleidoscope's orientation program is tailored to address the specific needs of minority students at Mount Union. Program sessions cover Support Services, Expectations of Professors, Diversity at University of Mount Union, Counseling Services and more. A welcome dinner for parents and students with various members of the college community and returning minority students is also included in the Kaleidoscope Program.

University of Mount Union
1972 Clark Avenue
Alliance, OH 44601-3993
Ph: (330) 823-2590
admission@muc.edu
www.mountunion.edu

F A S T F A C T S

STUDENT PROFILE

# of degree-seeking undergraduates	2,138
% male/female	52/48
% African American	4
% American Indian or Alaska Native	<1
% Asian or Pacific Islander	<1
% Hispanic	1
% White	87
% International	1
% Pell grant recipients	26.4

First-generation and minority alumni Ralph Regula, U. S. Representative, 16th Congressional District; Vincent G. Marotta, president, Marotta Corp., inventor, Mr. Coffee; Lee Ann (Johnston) Thorn, consultant, chair, University of Mount Union Board of Trustees; Sylvester Green, retired CEO and chairman, e2Value, Inc., managing director and executive vice president, Chubb & Son, Inc., chairman of the board, INROADS; Napoleon A. Bell, 45-year career as a successful attorney; Anita Richmond Bunkley, speaker, author of numerous books

ACADEMICS

full-time faculty	120
full-time minority faculty	13
student-faculty ratio	13:1
average class size	18
% first-year retention rate	76
% graduation rate (6 years)	65

Popular majors Business Administration, Education (Early and Middle), Sport Business, Exercise Science

CAMPUS LIFE

% live on campus (% fresh.)	71 (93)

Multicultural student clubs and organizations Association for International Students, Black Student Union, Women of Color United
Athletics NCAA Division III, Ohio Athletic Conference

ADMISSIONS

# of applicants	2,178
% accepted	1,697
# of first-year students enrolled	593
The 25 to 75 percentile:	
SAT Critical Reading range	420-550
SAT Math range	450-570
ACT range	19-24
average HS GPA	3.22
Deadlines	
regular decision	rolling
application fee (online)	$0 ($0)
fee waiver for applicants with financial need	n/a

COST & AID

tuition	$23,120
room & board	$7,050
total amount of need-based institutional grants awarded	$8,765,947
total amount of institutional gift aid awarded	$20,663,462
total amount of gift aid awarded (institutional, federal, state, and outside)	$26,574,082
average aid package graduation	$17,370
% of students who rec'd need-based grants	73
% of students who rec'd institutional gift aid awards	94
% of students awarded gift aid (institutional, federal, state, and outside)	97
average student loan debt upon graduation (08-09)	$14,408 (Staff & Perkins)

Oklahoma Christian University

Oklahoma Christian University, associated with the churches of Christ, takes its fellowship seriously. Many students, faculty and staff spend thousands of hours each semester in local, national and world volunteer work, including supporting an at-risk school, Western Village Elementary, a few miles from the campus. Oklahoma Christian's respect for faith-based roots does not impede its vision, however. The institution consistently produces students who perform highly on graduate, medical and law school entrance exams. Alumni are highly sought by businesses and other institutions for their high moral and ethical behavior. Also, Oklahoma Christian was one of the first universities to provide laptops and a wireless campus, and the university maintains its commitment to technological innovation.

> ACCESS **Backpack Program**

In conjunction with the local community group G.O.A.L.S. (Greater Oklahomans Achieving Lifelong Success), Oklahoma Christian's Alumni Office recently provided 1,000 backpacks to underprivileged children living in a nearby, inner-city district. The university plans to make the outreach an annual event.

> ACCESS **Outreach to African American Churches of Christ**

Oklahoma Christian was founded by members of the churches of Christ and continues to maintain strong ties with its faith group. In support of these ties, an Oklahoma Christian admissions counselor serves student families at 15 historically African American churches of Christ in the region, educating them about the college application process.

> ACCESS **Regional and National Youth Conferences**

Oklahoma Christian sponsors and attends a series of regional and national conferences targeted to African American Church of Christ youth. The university is similarly involved in the National Youth Worker Conference, an event that provides education for youth ministers, mentors and volunteers — all of whom work with youth members of African-American Church of Christ congregations.

> OPPORTUNITY **Southwestern Christian College Scholarship**

Oklahoma Christian University partners with Southwestern Christian College to attract Southwestern Christian College graduates who want to complete four-year degrees not offered by Southwestern. Southwestern Christian College is a historically African American institution associated with the churches of Christ. Students who complete an associate's degree at Southwestern Christian College receive scholarship support to attend Oklahoma Christian.

> SUCCESS **BRIDGE Program**

Underrepresented students whose secondary education has not fully prepared them for college can benefit from this program. The BRIDGE Program provides these students with special tutoring, developmental classes, instruction in time management and study skills, career counseling, guidance and mentoring.

> SUCCESS **Campus-Wide Retention Program**

Oklahoma Christian University's Student Life Office partners with academic leaders to quickly identify students at risk of not returning to the institution. Advisers reach out to students displaying risk factors, which include low grades, excessive class absences and financial difficulties. They are referred to Student Life for follow-up and support.

Oklahoma Christian University
PO Box 11000
Oklahoma City, OK 73136-1100
Ph: (405) 425-5050
admissions1@oc.edu
www.oc.edu

F A S T   F A C T S

STUDENT PROFILE
# of degree-seeking undergraduates	1,904
% male/female	49/51
% African-American	4
% American Indian or Alaska Native	<1
% Asian or Pacific Islander	2
% Hispanic	3
% White	77.5
% International	5.6
% Pell grant recipients	35

ACADEMICS
full-time faculty	103
full-time minority faculty	n/a
student-faculty ratio	15:1
average class size	27
% first-year retention rate	70
% graduation rate (6 years)	44

Popular majors Business Administration/ Management, Engineering, Biology/Pre-Medical Programs, Education

CAMPUS LIFE
% live on campus (% freshmen)	80 (96)

Multicultural student clubs and organizations Spanish Club, Multicultural Student Association, International Student Club
Athletics NAIA Division I, Sooner Athletic Conference

ADMISSIONS
# of applicants	1,472
% accepted	49
# of first-year students enrolled	436
SAT Critical Reading range	450-600
SAT Math range	460-620
SAT Writing range	n/a
ACT range	19-26
average HS GPA	3.4
Deadlines	
regular decision	rolling
application fee (online)	$25 ($25)
fee waiver for applicants with financial need	yes

COST & AID
tuition	$16,366
room & board	$6,630
total need-based institutional scholarships/grants	$14,711,652
% of students apply for need-based aid	98
% of students receive aid	99
% receiving need-based scholarship or grant aid	52
% receiving aid whose need was fully met	24
average aid package	$15,445
average student loan debt upon graduation	$24,377

Oklahoma City University

Founded in partnership with the United Methodist church in 1904, Oklahoma City University offers academic rigor and unique access to a vibrant metropolitan community. Beyond its proximity to Oklahoma City, the university offers an educational experience unique in both priority and population. Oklahoma City University prides itself in providing personal attention to

each of the undergraduate students, of which nearly half are minority or international students. The university prepares students to become effective community leaders by offering a rigorous curriculum focused on intellectual, moral andspiritual development.

> OPPORTUNITY **Clara Luper Scholarship Program**

The Clara Luper Scholarship Program helps thirty recipients from underserved populations to realize the dream of a private college education. Each year, five of the recipients of the Luper Scholarship are also awarded internships with Oklahoma City-based company Devon Energy. After all available state aid, federal aid, tribal aid and/or external scholarships received have been applied, the Clara Luper Scholarship pays the remaining balance for tuition, applicable fees, room and board, and provides a $200 per-semester book allowance. Applicants must be first-time, entering freshmen and complete a separate application in addition to the regular undergraduate application for admission.

> OPPORTUNITY **American Indian Scholarship Program**

Oklahoma City University is committed to investing in the future of Oklahoma's American Indian people. The American Indian Scholarship Program helps to provide a private college education to well-deserving American Indian students who may not otherwise have the opportunity. Each year, the university awards 15 scholarships to incoming American Indian students. After all available state aid, federal aid, tribal aid and/or other external scholarships have been applied, the American Indian Scholarship pays the remaining balance for tuition, applicable fees, room and board, and provides a $200 per semester book allowance. Additionally, the American Indian Scholarship Program provides support services dedicated to the growth, welfare and success of each student. Scholarship candidates must be admitted to Oklahoma City University, submit a scholarship application, provide an essay and an activity/volunteer resume and complete an interview.

> OPPORTUNITY **OCU V.I.P.**

Oklahoma City University aspires to provide prospective students personal attention and make them feel like they are already a part of the OCU community. Being an OCU V.I.P. will allow you to learn more about campus life, programs of study, financial aid and the admissions process. You will receive emails from professors, invitations to events, financial aid announcements, scholarship awards and campus events. Visit www.okcu.edu/vip to sign up.

"The Honors Program experience has been a breath of fresh air. Not only do my fellow students have the same drive and motivation as I do, but the 'Pizza with a Professor' Thursdays are always fun and a learning experience."
– Ainsley L., '12
Tulsa, OK
World Religions

> SUCCESS **Department of Multicultural Student Affairs**

The Department of Multicultural Student Affairs promotes cultural diversity, fosters positive human relations, and addresses the needs of those who are historically underrepresented or undeserved in the campus setting. The department provides vision, leadership, coordination and long-range planning for the university's comprehensive diversity program. The department actively supports diversity workshops, student leadership development, student career development, the Clara Luper Scholarship program, the American Indian Scholarship Program, the Multicultural Student Association and other cultural campus organizations.

Oklahoma City University
2501 North Blackwelder
Oklahoma City, OK 73106
Ph: (405) 208-5050
uadmissions@okcu.edu
www.okcu.edu

F A S T   F A C T S

STUDENT PROFILE

# of desgree-seeking undergraduates	1,945
% male/female	41/59
% African American	9
% American Indian	5
% Asian American	4
% Hispanic/Latino	6
% Caucasian	66
% International	7
% Other/Unknown	3
Pell grant recipients	24.8

First-generation and minority alumni Jacqueline Miller '85, '91, '92, Judge, Oklahoma Corporation Commission; Rana Husseini '90, '93, Human Rights Activist, Middle East; Freddy Sanchez '00, Second Base, San Francisco Giants; Marquita Lister '85, Opera Singer, Various Companies

ACADEMICS

full-time faculty	198
full-time minority faculty	n/a
student-faculty ratio	11:1
Average class size	17
%first-year retention rate	76
%graduation rate	51

Popular majors Nursing, Acting, Dance, Business Administration, Music Theatre

CAMPUS LIFE

% live on campus (% freshmen)	69 (94)

Multicultural student clubs and organizations President's Advisory Council on Diversity, Black Student Association, Hispanic Student Association, Indian Student Association, Multicultural Student Association, Thai Student Association, S.A.A.S. (Sisterhood of African American Students), Amnesty International, Korean Student Association, Black History Month, Latino Youth Leadership Conference, FACES Program

Athletics NAIA, Sooner Athletic Conference

ADMISSIONS

# of applicants	1,184
% accepted	78
# of first-year students enrolled	404
SAT Critical Reading range	510-620
SAT Math range	510-620
SAT Writing range	490-600
ACT range	23-27
average HS GPA	3.51

Deadlines

early decision	11/15
regular decision	3/1
application fee (online)	$40
fee waiver for applicants with financial need	yes

COST & AID

tuition	$24,350
room & board	$7,160
total need-based institutional scholarships/grants	n/a
% of students apply for need-based aid	n/a
% of students receive aid	84.2
% receiving need-based scholarship or grant aid	85.4
% receiving aid whose need was fully met	78
average aid package	$21,998
average student loan debt upon graduation	$28,680

Lewis & Clark College

Lewis & Clark College rests on a 137-acre campus in the southwest hills of Portland. This private institution is known for its academic rigor and a focus on community involvement, having earned recognition as "A Best Western College" and "A College with a Conscience" by the *Princeton Review*. The student body — more than a third of which consists of first-generation students — can choose from among 27 academic majors and study abroad options in nearly two dozen countries to build their academic experience.

> ACCESS Oregon Independent Colleges Foundation

As a member of the Oregon Independent Colleges Foundation, Lewis & Clark partners with local community-based organizations to give local students insight into life at the college. Each year the program brings to Lewis & Clark more than 100 middle and high school students from Self-Enhancement, Inc. and the Native American Youth Association.

> OPPORTUNITY Lewis & Clark Fly-in Program

Each year, Lewis & Clark College invites approximately 50 newly admitted students to visit campus at the expense of the college. These selected students of color and first-generation college-goers learn about life and academics at Lewis & Clark through a series of activities. They attend classes, meet faculty and staff, spend time with current students and experience life in the residence halls.

> SUCCESS Lewis & Clark Intercultural Network for Connecting Students (LINCS)

LINCS is a peer-mentorship program that focuses on diversity and retention. The program helps incoming students of diverse ethnic and cultural backgrounds adjust to college, and all entering students are invited to participate in the program. Successful returning students connect new students to resources on campus and help them as they develop relationships with Lewis & Clark faculty, staff and peers.

> SUCCESS Ray Warren Multicultural Symposium

The Ray Warren Multicultural Symposium is a three-day annual event to increase the college's awareness of cultural history, ethnic identity and knowledge of social issues that impact minority communities, both locally and nationally. Named for the late Ray Warren, it is one of four student-planned academic symposia held each year on campus. All events are free and open to the public.

> SUCCESS Multicultural Residence Hall

Students from diverse backgrounds come to Akin Hall to live with and learn from one another. Here the residents educate themselves through the celebration and exploration of diverse cultural identities. They promote understanding of ethnic and racial diversity and contribute to Lewis & Clark's awareness of international and multicultural issues. Toward this end, the residence hall sponsors diversity-focused programs such as the annual Cultural and International Fairs.

Lewis & Clark College
0615 SW Palatine Hill Road
Portland, OR 97219-7899
Ph: (503) 768-7040
admissions@lclark.edu
www.lclark.edu

F A S T   F A C T S

STUDENT PROFILE
# of degree-seeking undergraduates	1,999
% male/female	39.1/60.9
% African-American	2
% American Indian or Alaska Native	0.8
% Asian or Pacific Islander	5.8
% Hispanic	4.5
% White	58.3
% International	7.8
% Pell grant recipients	14.8

First-generation and minority alumni Serena Cruz Walsh '89, former commissioner, Multnomah County; Sandra Osawa '64, Native American independent filmmaker; Adam Bradley '96, assistant professor; Sagala Ratnayaka '93, member, Sri Lankan Parliament; Linda Castaneda '98, Cat Ambassador Program, Cincinnati Zoo; Randy Massengale '78, president, Spinoza Technologies; Shahzeb Jillani '94, radio editor, BBC Urdu

ACADEMICS
full-time faculty	222
full-time minority faculty	n/a
student-faculty ratio	12:1
average class size	19
% first-year retention rate	86
% graduation rate (6 years)	71

Popular majors Psychology, English, Biology, International Affairs, Studio Art

CAMPUS LIFE
% live on campus (% freshmen)	66 (99)

Multicultural student clubs and organizations Office of Multicultural Affairs, Lewis & Clark Intercultural Network for Connecting Students (LINCS), Multicultural Themed Residence Hall (Akin), Interdisciplinary minor in Ethnic Studies offered, Asian Student Union, Black Student Union, Gente Latina Unida, Hawai'i Club, Native Student Union, International Students of Lewis & Clark, Interfaith Council, Jewish Student Union, United Sexualities, Music Ensembles (African Marimba, African Rhythm & Dance, Gamelan, and West African Rhythms)

Athletics NCAA Division III, Northwest Conference

ADMISSIONS
# of applicants	5,551
% accepted	58
# of first-year students enrolled	585
SAT Critical Reading range	630-720
SAT Math range	590-680
SAT Writing	610-700
ACT range	27-31
average HS GPA	3.72

Deadlines
regular decision	2/1
application fee (online)	$50 (reduced)
fee waiver for applicants with financial need	yes

COST & AID
tuition	$35,233
room & board	$9,006
total need-based institutional scholarships/grants	n/a
% of students apply for need-based aid	70.9
% of students receive aid	100
% receiving need-based scholarship or grant aid	99.3
% receiving aid whose need was fully met	36.7
average aid package	$26,741
average student loan debt upon graduation	$20,611

Linfield College

Linfield College
900 SE Baker Street
McMinnville, OR 97128-6894
Ph: (503) 883-2213
admission@linfield.edu
www.linfield.edu

Linfield College, a private, comprehensive, undergraduate institution located in the Pacific Northwest, connects learning, life and community through collaborative and experiential education opportunities. Recognizing the importance of diversity in its student body, Linfield College offers both financial and academic support to attract and retain minority students. With Linfield's challenging and exciting academic program, featuring a broad liberal arts core, it is nationally recognized for its strong faculty, outstanding academic programs and distinctive international emphasis. Over half of Linfield students study internationally and approximately 90 percent are in a job or graduate school within one year of graduation.

"When I talk to my friends at larger institutions, they have never even talked to their professors, and that's kind of strange to me because I always make it a priority to meet with my professors outside of class. Everyone here is willing to help. That has really helped me reach my academic goals."
– Graciela G., '09
McMinnville, OR
Elementary Education

> ACCESS Upward Bound

Linfield College is home to one of Oregon's Upward Bound programs. Funded through the U.S. Department of Education, Upward Bound is a college preparatory program designed to assist high school students with building the skills and motivation necessary for success in post-secondary education. Linfield's program serves over 60 area high school students throughout the academic year.

> ACCESS College Information Nights

Linfield hosts an annual College Night for Yamhill County high school juniors and seniors along with their parents. Information about Linfield's academic programs, international study, and student life is presented, along with an overview of the application and financial aid process. There are Spanish-speaking faculty members present to better serve local families.

> OPPORTUNITY Linfield Diversity Grant

Students of color who are likely to make a significant contribution to the Linfield community are eligible for an award of $1,000 to $6,000, determined by financial need and other factors. Recommendations for the grant are made to the Director of Multicultural Programs in consultation with the Director of Financial Aid and the Director of Admission.

> SUCCESS Colloquium

Groups of 20 incoming students are each assigned a faculty advisor and peer advisor. Advisors stay in contact with new students over the summer; groups meet daily during new student Orientation and weekly for 10 weeks in the fall semester. Topics such as academic advising, academic resources, academic expectations and time management are discussed.

> SUCCESS Office of Learning Support Services

The Office of Learning Support Services coordinates the peer tutoring program and academic department study sessions. The office offers a Learning Skills course every semester, dealing with topics like time management, test-taking, and memory enhancement. The office also works individually with students who have documented learning differences.

FAST FACTS

STUDENT PROFILE
# of degree-seeking undergraduates	1,677
% male/female	43/57
% African American	2
% American Indian or Alaska Native	2
% Asian or Pacific Islander	9
% Hispanic	5
% White	66
% International	6
% Pell grant recipients	24

First-generation and minority alumni Baruti Artharee, Director of Diversity Program, Providence Health System; Gale Castillo, Executive Director, Hispanic Chamber of Commerce; Leroy Fails, Vice President, The College Board; Jose Gaitan, Owner, Gaitan Group; Sandra Thompson, Judge, Los Angeles Superior Court

ACADEMICS
full-time faculty	118
full-time minority faculty	8
student-faculty ratio	12:1
average class size	17
% first-year retention rate	81
% graduation rate (6 years)	71

Popular majors Business Administration, Elementary Education, Mass Communications, Nursing

CAMPUS LIFE
% live on campus (% fresh.)	76 (100)

Multicultural student clubs and organizations Office of Multicultural Programs, Hawaiian Club, Multicultural Student Club, Asian Culture Club, International Club

Athletics NCAA Division III, Northwest Conference

ADMISSIONS
# of applicants	1,692
% accepted	82
# of first-year students enrolled	430
SAT Critical Reading range	490-610
SAT Math range	500-610
SAT Writing	490-590
ACT range	21-27
HS GPA range	3.36-3.85

Deadlines
early action	11/15
regular decision (priority)	2/15
application fee (online)	$0 ($0)
fee waiver for applicants with financial need	yes

COST & AID
tuition	$30,300
room & board	$8,560
total need-based institutional scholarships/grants	$17,767,383
% of students apply for need-based aid	63
% of students receive aid	100
% receiving need-based scholarship or grant aid	92
% of need met for students receiving aid	85
average aid package	$18,274
average student loan debt upon graduation	$27,140

Willamette University

Willamette University
900 State Street
Salem, OR 97301-3931
Ph: (503) 370-6303
libarts@willamette.edu
www.willamette.edu

Willamette University was founded in 1842 as a forward-thinking, co-educational institution — its first graduate was a woman. The 81-acre campus is located in the center of Salem, across the street from the Oregon State Capitol building. This proximity has given generations of Willamette students the opportunity to participate in the important social and political issues of their day through internships and other direct action. The university motto, "Not Unto Ourselves Alone Are We Born," provides the underpinnings for a campus culture that is committed to service and making a difference in the world. Among the campus organizations that reflect this commitment are the Council for Diversity and Social Justice and the Council for Sustainability.

> ACCESS Willamette Academy

Willamette University sponsors the Willamette Academy, an experiential, academic enrichment program for underrepresented and ethnically diverse seventh graders from the local community. The five-year commitment of the participants and their families helps them prepare for higher education by enhancing critical thinking skills, developing leadership skills and inspiring their love of learning.

> OPPORTUNITY Financial Aid Programs

Approximately 20 percent of Willamette undergraduates receive federal Pell grants. The university's comprehensive, need-based financial aid program is supplemented by a generous, merit-based scholarship program. More than 90 percent of the student body is receiving some financial assistance to put a Willamette education within reach.

> OPPORTUNITY Black United Fund Partnership Scholarship / Scholarship for Oregon Latinos (SOL)

The Black United Fund Partnership Scholarship provides $15,000 for two African-American students from Oregon who demonstrate academic strength and community and school leadership. The Scholarship for Oregon Latinos provides up to $15,000 for Latin-American students from Oregon who demonstrate school and community leadership and an excellent academic record.

> SUCCESS Ohana Pre-Orientation Program

Ohana, the Hawaiian word for "family," is the theme of a four-day retreat for new students of color at Willamette. Student leaders of campus multicultural organizations welcome new students and help orient them through outdoor activities, service projects and a "Cultural Food and Shop Tour" of Salem and Portland, ensuring that new students begin their first day of class already familiarized with their new home.

> SUCCESS Committee for Academic Success

This is a standing faculty committee that monitors student progress and offers direct support and intervention to students who are struggling academically.

> SUCCESS Office of Multicultural Affairs

The Office of Multicultural Affairs promotes diversity throughout the campus community through education, enrichment and support. It also serves the campus community as a clearinghouse for the various multicultural resources that Salem has to offer.

FAST FACTS

STUDENT PROFILE
# of degree-seeking undergraduates	1,864
% male/female	46/54
% African-American	2
% American Indian or Alaska Native	1
% Asian or Pacific Islander	8
% Hispanic	4
% White	56
% Pell grant recipients	18

First-generation and minority alumni Lin Sue Glass Cooley, evening news anchor, KPNX-TV; Ricardo Baez, vice president for marketing and sales, partner, Puentes Brothers Inc. / Don Pancho Authentic Mexican Foods; Harold Sublett, Jr., commercial banker, Wells Fargo Bank; Danny Santos, labor policy adviser to the governor, Oregon; Carmen Bendixon-Noe, former fellow and staffer, Congressional Hispanic Caucus Institute, Sen. Barbara Boxer (D-Calif.)

ACADEMICS
full-time faculty	207
full-time minority faculty	29
student-faculty ratio	10:1
average class size	14
% first-year retention rate	86
% graduation rate (6 years)	71

Popular majors Biology, Economics, English

CAMPUS LIFE
% live on campus	72 (98)

Multicultural student clubs and organizations Alianza, Hawaii Club, Native American Enlightenment Association, Black Student Organization, Unidos por Fin

Athletics NCAA Division III, Northwest Conference

ADMISSIONS
# of applicants	3,501
% accepted	76
# of first-year students enrolled	509
SAT Critical Reading range	570-680
SAT Math range	550-660
SAT Writing range	550-660
ACT range	25-29
average HS GPA	3.7

Deadlines
regular decision	2/1
application fee (online)	$50 ($50)
fee waiver for applicants with financial need	yes

COST & AID
tuition	$35,610
room & board	$8,350
total need-based institutional scholarships/grants	$23,564,675
% of students apply for need-based aid	77
% of students receive aid	75
% receiving need-based scholarship or grant aid	
% receiving aid whose need was fully met	23
average aid package	$27,374
average student loan debt upon graduation	$24,465

Bryn Mawr College

Bryn Mawr College is a private, women's liberal arts college located just outside of Philadelphia and only two hours by train from New York City and Washington, D.C. Because of its unique academic history, Bryn Mawr students may take classes at nearby Haverford and Swarthmore Colleges, as well as the University of Pennsylvania. Providing a rigorous education and encouraging the pursuit of knowledge in preparation for life and work, Bryn Mawr College has taught and valued critical, creative and independent habits of thought and expression since 1885. Bryn Mawr's dedication to sustaining a community diverse in nature and democratic in practice is guided by an overarching belief — it is only through considering many perspectives that individuals can gain a deeper understanding of each other and the world. Bryn Mawr women share an intense intellectual commitment, a purposeful vision of their lives and a desire to make a meaningful contribution to the world.

"Bryn Mawr is a place where you will be challenged, both academically and socially. Your professors will challenge your mind and ways of thinking while Mawrters will challenge your values and beliefs. At Bryn Mawr, I have come to acknowledge the power of my voice and the strength of my actions."
— Arielle H., '11

> OPPORTUNITY **Travel Scholar Information**

Bryn Mawr College is dedicated to cultivating young women as leaders, intellectuals and barrier breakers and will award travel scholarships to deserving high school seniors. Students must be U.S. citizens living in the U.S. or in U.S.territories who want to visit and experience the College first-hand. Because the scholarship is competitive, students are asked to submit both a high school transcript and standardized test scores in addition to the travel scholar application.

> OPPORTUNITY **Standardized Testing**

Bryn Mawr College has adopted a new testing policy that will give students greater flexibility in applying to the college and is more in line with current research regarding the role standardized tests should play in the admissions process. The policy sets a new precedent for the use of Advanced Placement (AP) tests in the admissions process and allows for an option that focuses exclusively on subject mastery.

> SUCCESS **Customs Week**

The College and the Bryn Mawr-Haverford Customs Week Committee provide orientation for first-year and transfer students, who take residence before the College is opened to upperclass students. Faculty members are available for consultation, and all incoming students have appointments with a dean or other adviser to plan their academic programs for the fall semester. Undergraduate organizations at Bryn Mawr and Haverford Colleges acquaint new students with other aspects of college life.

> SUCCESS **The Emily Balch Seminar**

The Balch Seminars introduce all first-year students at Bryn Mawr to a critical, probing, thoughtful approach to the world and our roles in it. These challenging seminars are taught by scholar/teachers of distinction within their fields and across academic disciplines. They facilitate the seminars as active discussions among students, not lectures. Through intensive reading and writing, the thought-provoking Balch Seminars challenge students to think about complex, wide-ranging issues from a variety of perspectives.

> SUCCESS **The Undergraduate Deans**

The Undergraduate Dean's Office promotes the academic and personal growth of undergraduates at the College. They work with students through their educational and personal Bryn Mawr journey. Bryn Mawr help students learn about available opportunities and resources and make decisions about when and how to take advantage of them.

Bryn Mawr College
Office of Admissions
101 North Merion Avenue
Bryn Mawr, PA 19010
Ph: (610) 526-5152
admissions@brynmawr.edu
www.brynmawr.edu

F A S T F A C T S

STUDENT PROFILE

# of degree-seeking undergraduates	1,300
% male/female	0/100

PROFILE OF THE CLASS OF 2013

% African American	6
% American Indian	1
% Asian	17
% Caucasian	33
% Hispanic	11
% International	21

First-generation and minority alumni Maya Ajmera, founder, The Global Fund for Children; Sarmila Bose, journalist; Ana Patrica Botin, CEO, Banesto; Salima Ikram, Egyptologist; Frederica de Laguna, anthropologist; Rosemarie Said Zahlan, historian, writer; Kaity Tong, journalist; Neda Ulaby, NPR reporter; Betty Peh T'i Wei, historian; Mai Yamani, anthropologist, activist

ACADEMICS

full-time faculty	153
student-faculty ratio	8:1
average class size	n/a
% first-year retention rate	94
% graduation rate (6 years)	84

Popular majors Growth and Structure of Cities, Political Science, Biology, Math, Psychology

CAMPUS LIFE

% live on campus (% fresh.)	95 (100)

Multicultural student clubs and organizations Asian Students Association, Association of International Students, Bryn Mawr Caribbean and African Student Organization, Bahai Club Barkada, Coming to Racial Understanding Through Community Involvement, Action and Learning, Ethnic Studies Committee, Mujeres, Muslim Students Association, Rainbow Alliance, Sisterhood, South Asian Society, Vietnamese Culture Club, Women's Center, Zami

Athletics NCAA Division III, Centennial Conference

ADMISSIONS

# of applicants	2,276
% accepted	49
SAT Critical Reading range	600-700
SAT Math range	580-690
SAT Writing	610-710
ACT Median	28
average HS GPA	n/a

Deadlines

early decision I	11/15
early decision II	1/1
regular admission	1/15
rolling	no
application fee (online)	$50 ($0)
fee waiver for applicants with financial need	yes

COST & AID

tuition	$37,120
room & board	$12,000
% of students receiving aid	62
% receiving need-based scholarship or grant aid	56
% receiving aid whose need was fully met	100
average aid package	$33,086
average student loan debt upon graduation	$19,049

Bucknell University

Bucknell University is home to exceptionally talented students from across the U.S. and around the world. With academic programs in the arts, engineering, humanities, management, and social and natural sciences, and broad learning opportunities outside of class, the University prepares students for success in an increasingly complex and interconnected global society. Its 3,500 undergraduates can choose from more than 50 majors and 60 minors. Students can build robots, write and perform in their own plays or debate solutions to the crisis in Sudan. Engineers can make art, artists can analyze DNA and philosophers can make music. Each student chooses his or her own pathway, but what unites everyone is a shared passion for learning and a desire to achieve deeper levels of understanding about life and the world.

> ACCESS Issues for the 21st Century

Each year, up to 200 high school seniors attend a weekend summit exploring a theme or topic connected to pressing global concerns. Participants discuss aspects of the topic with each other, current students and University professors. Recent themes include Darfur, food, Hurricane Katrina, money and navigating divisive issues in society.

> OPPORTUNITY Community College Scholars Program

The Bucknell Community College Scholars Program serves high-achieving, low to moderate-income community college students at five partner schools. The program provides financial and administrative support to help scholars experience the full scope of academic and campus life at Bucknell. During a six-week summer program, students take courses co-taught by Bucknell and community college professors and explore campus life, library and technology, and facilities. Upon successful completion of the summer program and receipt of an associate's degree, students can apply for enrollment at Bucknell. Accepted Community College Scholars receive full tuition scholarships.

"I transferred to Bucknell from a community college. As I look back on how far I've come, the best part is the overall life experience, being a part of the Bucknell family, and the community that I have learned to appreciate so much."

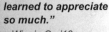

– Winnie O., '10
Whitehall, PA
Civil and Environmental Engineering

> OPPORTUNITY Posse Foundation

Bucknell University participates in the Posse Foundation, a program that brings talented inner-city youth to campus to pursue their academics and to help promote cross-cultural communication. Posse students are nominated by their high school to the program and share a collaborative support system with a special mentor to adjust to campus and college life. Bucknell University's Posse Scholars hail from Washington D.C., Boston and Los Angeles.

> SUCCESS Civic Engagement

The Office of Civic Engagement and Service Learning connects academic coursework with experiences that fulfill a community need. Service learning enhances classroom learning, builds camaraderie among students and faculty, and is often considered by participants to be a life-changing experience. Examples include a week-long service trip to Nicaragua, tutoring in local schools, and working with the Katrina Recovery Team.

> SUCCESS Career Development Center

The Career Development Center helps students create career action plans and assists them in exploring internship and job opportunities and in preparing job search materials. Services include counseling and advising, self-assessment tools, resume and cover letter writing workshops, interviewing essentials, mock interviews, resume critiques, internship search workshops, career networking events, alumni career conversations, and on- and off-campus fairs. Bucknell's placement rate is high: Of the past few classes graduating from Bucknell, 93 to 97 percent have secured jobs or entered graduate school within nine months of graduation.

Bucknell University
Freas Hall
Lewisburg, PA 17837
Ph: (570) 577-1101
admissions@bucknell.edu
www.bucknell.edu

FAST FACTS

STUDENT PROFILE

# of degree-seeking undergraduates	3,500
% male/female	47/53
% African American	3
% American Indian or Alaska Native	<1
% Asian or Pacific Islander	6
% Hispanic	4
% White	81
% International	3
% Pell grant recipients	10.9

First-generation and minority alumni Gbenga Akinnagbe, actor; Michael E. Flowers, first African American selected chair of the Business Law Section, American Bar Association; Edward McKinley Robinson, former member of the senior staff and vice president for development, Colin Powell's America's Promise Alliance; Gerald Purnell, judge; Maria Lopez, human resources manager, Morgan Stanley in Hong Kong

ACADEMICS

full-time faculty	345
full-time minority faculty	46
student-faculty ratio	10:1
average class size	20
% first-year retention rate	94
% graduation rate (6 years)	90

Popular majors Engineering, BSBA/Management, Economics, Psychology, Biology

CAMPUS LIFE

% live on campus (% fresh.)	87 (99)

Multicultural student clubs and organizations Black Student Union, Bucknell African Students Association, Common Ground (student-led diversity immersion retreat program), Greeks for the Advancement of Multicultural Education, Jelani (African American Cultural Dance Group), Multicultural Council of Presidents (leadership council for promoting diversity), National Society of Black Engineers, OHLAS (Latino/Hispanic club)

Athletics NCAA Division I, Patriot League

ADMISSIONS

# of applicants	7,572
% accepted	29.87
# of first-year students enrolled	920
SAT Critical Reading range	600-680
SAT Math range	630-720
ACT range	27-31
average HS GPA	3.61

Deadlines

early decision	11/15
regular decision	1/15
application fee (online)	$60 ($60)
fee waiver for applicants with financial need	yes

COST & AID

tuition	$42,112
room & board	$9,938
total need-based institutional scholarships/grants	$40,000,000 +
% of students apply for need-based aid	57.8
% of students receive aid	62
% receiving need-based scholarship or grant aid	50
% receiving aid whose need was fully met	95
average aid package	$25,000
average student loan debt upon graduation	$19,000

Dickinson College

Dickinson College, founded in 1783, is a highly selective, private, liberal arts college known for its innovative curriculum. Its mission is to offer students a useful education in the arts and sciences that will prepare them for lives as engaged citizens and leaders. Dickinson fosters a community that thrives on the collegial exchange of differing opinions. It promotes individual expression and encourages the celebration of disparate backgrounds and experiences. Dickinson is committed to bringing the world to campus. But it's the students — their beliefs, ideals and passions — who bring the greatest enlightenment to campus diversity.

> OPPORTUNITY Posse and Other Foundations

Dickinson participates in the Posse Foundation, a program that brings talented inner-city youth to campus to pursue their academics and to help promote cross-cultural communication. Posse students are nominated by their high school to the program and share a collaborative support system with a special mentor to adjust to campus and college life. Dickinson's Posse Scholars hail from New York City and Los Angeles. Other foundations also help to select and prepare talented inner-city students for college. In addition to Posse, Dickinson partners with Philadelphia Futures, the Wight Foundation (Newark, N.J.), CollegeBound (Baltimore) and DC-CAP (Washington, D.C.).

> SUCCESS Office of Diversity Initiatives

The office of Diversity Initiatives (ODI) at Dickinson College is a resource center charged with advancing Dickinson's commitment to broadening the understanding of and building a pluralistic society that promotes equality and integrity on the campus, within the community and in the world. The office provides individuals with the opportunity to enrich their cultural experiences through participation in diversity programs and training workshops. The office encourages and facilitates activities that allow students to voice their opinions, serve the community and advocate for making Dickinson a place that welcomes difference and individuality.

> SUCCESS Office of Academic Resource Services

The Office of Academic Resource Services offers individual and group programming which supports the intellectual development of Dickinson students. Programming includes evening workshops to assist students in developing skills in time management, note-taking and exam preparation, library research skills and stress management.

> SUCCESS Mosaic: Learning by Living

The Community Studies Center encourages joint student and faculty fieldwork and community-oriented research through the American and Global Mosaic programs. During a semester of fieldwork immersion, Mosaic students interview a community's residents, listen to their histories and learn from their experiences. Through this cross-cultural program, students make connections between theory and practice, among people and ideas, across academic disciplines and around the world. They also set off on a journey of personal discovery — learning much about their own lives as they listen to the lives of others.

> SUCCESS Crossing Borders

The Crossing Borders program allows students to study in several locations in one year. Recently, the program has been conducted as a joint venture with Dillard and Xavier universities, two historically black institutions in New Orleans. In the summer, students from Dickinson, Dillard and Xavier travel to Dickinson's study center in Cameroon, West Africa, where they are immersed in local culture — learning first-hand about the traditions, beliefs and culture of West Africa. The next planned Crossing Borders is a Comparative Black Liberation Mosaic. Students go to South Africa in the summer, spend the fall at Dickinson with a trip to the Mississippi Delta, and then go either to Dillard or Morehouse University in the spring.

Dickinson College
P.O. Box 1773
Carlisle, PA 17013-2896
Ph: (800) 644-1773 / (717) 245-1231
admit@dickinson.edu
www.dickinson.edu

F A S T   F A C T S

STUDENT PROFILE

# of degree-seeking undergraduates	2,388
% male/female	44/56
% African-American	5
% American Indian or Alaska Native	<1
% Asian or Pacific Islander	5
% Hispanic	5
% White	77
% International	5
% Pell grant recipients	9

ACADEMICS

full-time faculty	194
full-time minority faculty	27
student-faculty ratio	10:1
average class size	17
% first-year retention rate	94
% graduation rate (6 years)	82

Popular majors Biology, English, History, International Business & Management, Political Science, Psychology

CAMPUS LIFE

% live on campus (% fresh.)	91 (100)

Multicultural Student Clubs and Organizations African-American Society, ABOLISH, Active Minds, Amnesty International, Asian Social Interest Association, Club Afrique, Delta Sigma Theta, Dickinson Christian Fellowship, Dickinson Desi Association, Hillel, Latin American Club, Middle Eastern Club, Muslim Student Association, Newman Club, Spectrum, Students for Social Action, Sustained Dialogue, Third Degree Steppers, Umoja, Zatae Longsdorff Center for Women
Athletics NCAA Division III, ECAC

ADMISSIONS

# of applicants	5,282
% accepted	44
# of first-year students enrolled	628
SAT Critical Reading range	620-720
SAT Math range	620-700
SAT Writing range	n/a
ACT range	26-31
average HS GPA	n/a

Deadlines

early decision I	11/15
early decision II	1/15
regular application	2/1
application fee (online)	$65 ($65)
fee waiver for applicants with financial need	yes

COST & AID

tuition	$39,780
room & board	$10,080
total need-based institutional scholarships/grants	$29,000,000
% of students apply for need-based aid	56
% of students receive aid	48
% receiving need-based scholarship or grant aid	95
% receiving aid whose need was fully met	72
average aid package	$31,165
average student loan debt upon graduation	$21,924

Gettysburg College

Gettysburg College, a historic institution with a reputation for academic excellence, provides students with a liberal arts education characterized by academic intensity and learning by getting involved. Founded in 1832 by anti-slavery theologian Samuel Simon Schmucker, Gettysburg College prides itself on an 11:1 student-faculty ratio that fosters close relationships and spirited class discussions. A champion for independent thinking and public action, Gettysburg students graduate with a love of learning, knowledge and skills they need for success and new insight into the world, their place in it, and their obligations to it. Gettysburg College engages highly motivated students in a comprehensive educational experience that prepares them for lives of personal fulfillment, career success, and responsible, engaged citizenship.

> *"Whether it's faculty or alumni, if you're willing to put in the effort, somebody at Gettysburg will help you accomplish your goal. At Gettysburg, if you can dream it up, you get there."*
>
> *– Lawrese B., '10*
> *East Orange, NJ*
> *Interdisciplinary Major—Writing for Public Policy*

> OPPORTUNITY **Making College Affordable for All Students**

Gettysburg College is committed to working with students and their families to ensure that one's ability to pay not become an obstacle to a Gettysburg education. Approximately 75 percent of all students receive some form of financial aid, and the average aid package exceeds $30,000 a year. Most aid is awarded based on financial need, but academic merit and music scholarships are also available. Gettysburg College awarded $37 million in scholarships and grants for the 2009-2010 academic year. Merit-based scholarships range from $7,000 to $15,000 per year.

> SUCCESS **Intercultural Resource Center**

The Intercultural Resource Center celebrates Gettysburg's diversity by providing a warm and affirming home on campus for students from all backgrounds and by sponsoring activities that build mutual respect and understanding. The IRC brings speakers to campus who address topics related to diversity, provides services such as tutoring and mentoring, runs discussion groups to foster open conversation on important issues, hosts meals with ethnic themes, and offers a variety of other services to create a welcoming atmosphere on campus. The IRC encourages involvement in its activities from all students at Gettysburg. It has a particular commitment to the academic and personal development of African American, Asian American, Latino and American Indian students on campus.

> SUCCESS **First-Year Residential College Program**

First year students' residence hall assignments are linked to First-Year Seminar and College Writing courses, which helps extend class discussions into the less-formal arena of the living environment and promotes the open exchange of ideas. The program benefits new students by easing their transition to the college life, introducing them to the kind of thoughtful conversation that is characteristic of a good liberal arts education, enriching their learning and serving as a kind of academic ice-breaker, helping them to build relationships with hallmates. The First-Year Residential College also offers opportunities for peer tutoring, faculty counseling and mentoring with upper-class students.

Gettysburg College
300 N. Washington St.
Gettysburg, PA 17325
Ph: (800) 431-0803
admiss@gettysburg.edu
www.gettysburg.edu

F A S T   F A C T S

STUDENT PROFILE
# of degree-seeking undergraduates	2,516
% male/female	47/53
% African American	4
% American Indian or Alaska Native	5
% Asian or Pacific Islander	2
% Hispanic	2
% White	87
% International	2
% Pell grant recipients	11

First-generation and minority alumni Bruce Gordon '68, former NAACP president and CEO

ACADEMICS
full-time faculty	209
full-time minority faculty	28
student-faculty ratio	11:1
average class size	18
% first-year retention rate	90
% graduation rate (6 years)	82

Popular majors Management, History, English, Psychology, Political Science, Biology

CAMPUS LIFE
% live on campus (fresh.)	94 (100)

Multicultural student clubs and organizations Black Student Union, Diaspora House, Intercultural Resource Center, Muslim Student Association, NAACP, Office of Intercultural Advancement, SALSA (Spanish and Latino Students' Association)
Athletics NCAA Division III, Centennial Conference

ADMISSIONS
# of applicants	5,448
% accepted	40
# of first-year students enrolled	739
SAT Critical Reading range	610-690
SAT Math range	610-690
SAT Writing	n/a
ACT range	n/a
average HS GPA	n/a

Deadlines
early decision I	11/15
early decision II	1/15
regular decision	2/1
application fee (online)	$55 ($55)
fee waiver for applicants with financial need	yes

COST & AID
tuition	$41,070
room and board	$9,810
total need-based institutional scholarships/grants	$37,745,071
% of students who applied for need-based aid	64
% of students receive aid	83
% receiving need-based scholarship or grant aid	83
% receiving aid whose need was fully met	100
average aid package	$30,027
average student loan debt upon graduation	$23,258

Haverford College

Haverford College
370 Lancaster Avenue
Haverford, PA, 19041
Ph: (610) 896-1350
admission@haverford.edu
www.haverford.edu

Haverford is a coeducational, residential liberal arts college located 8 miles west of center city Philadelphia. Haverford's 1,200 students represent an exceptional diversity of interests, backgrounds, and talents, with individuals hailing from nearly all 50 states, DC, Puerto Rico, and more than 40 countries around the world. The Haverford experience revolves around opportunities for students to be directly engaged with their education – through strong personal relationships with faculty and peers, through small, seminar-based classes, and through tremendous opportunities for research and independent scholarship. The Haverford Honor Code, affirmed by the student body each year, embodies the community values and philosophy of conduct within the College: students are expected to maintain a strong sense of individual responsibility as well as intellectual integrity, honesty, and genuine concern for others.

> OPPORTUNITY Commitment to Financial Aid

Haverford has a long-standing commitment to making college affordable, meeting 100 percent of the demonstrated need of all students for the full four years of undergraduate study. Beginning with the Haverford Class of 2012 financial aid awards are loan-free, with this portion of the award replaced by additional scholarship funds.

> OPPORTUNITY Haverford Summer Science Institute

The Summer Science Institute is an intensive, residential, five-week introduction to college-level science study for incoming first-year students who come from groups traditionally underrepresented in the sciences or who come from families with little or no college experience. With the help of over 15 Haverford professors, administrators, and staff members, HSSI students participate in seminar-like courses and lab modules in Chemistry, Biology, Mathematics, Physics, Psychology, and Writing.

> OPPORTUNITY QuestBridge

Haverford partners with QuestBridge, a non-profit program that links bright, motivated low-income students with educational and scholarship opportunities at some of the nation's best colleges. Through QuestBridge, Haverford has been able to reach out to and enroll many students who may not have otherwise considered Haverford, providing greater opportunities for these students and enriching the Haverford student body.

> SUCCESS Multicultural Scholars Program

The Multicultural Scholars Program offers a series of workshops to enhance students' academic success, peer tutoring and mentoring, and opportunities for research during the summer and academic year. The program provides guidance, support, and a variety of opportunities to Haverford minority students, helping students to succeed academically in their four years at Haverford and fostering future success in graduate school and career plans.

> SUCCESS The Office of Multicultural Affairs (OMA)

The OMA provides a comprehensive program to ensure that historically under-represented groups in particular, and all Haverford students in general, will have rich learning experiences in and outside the classroom. The OMA provides opportunities for cultural exploration, dialogue, personal reflection, and leadership development, and supports student cultural organizations such as the Black Student's League, the Alliance of Latin American Students, and the Asian Students Association.

FAST FACTS

STUDENT PROFILE
# of degree-seeking undergraduates	1,169
% male/female	47/53
% African-American	8.4
% American Indian or Alaska Native	1
% Asian or Pacific Islander	10.4
% Hispanic	9
% White	66
% International	6.1
% Pell grant recipients	10.2

ACADEMICS
full-time faculty	132
full-time minority faculty	35
student-faculty ratio	8:1
average class size	14
% first-year retention rate	98
% graduation rate (6 years)	92

Popular majors Biology, Economics, English, Chemistry, Political Science, Psychology

CAMPUS LIFE
% live on campus (% fresh.)	99 (100)

Multicultural student clubs and organizations
Alliance of Latin American Students, Asian Students Association, Japanese Culture Club, Korean Students Association, Black Students League, Caribbean Essence Organization, Committee on International Initiatives, Hellenic Club, Indian Fusion Dance Team, International Students Association, Jewish Student Union, Muslim Students Association, Queer Discussion Group, Re-Mix Multiracial Students Organization, Sons of Africa, South Asian Society, Women of Color

ADMISSIONS
# of applicants	3,403
% accepted	25
# of first-year students enrolled	323
SAT Critical Reading range	660-740
SAT Math range	640-740
SAT Writing range	660-750
ACT range	n/a
average HS GPA	n/a

Deadlines
early action	11/15
regular decision	1/15
application fee (online)	$60 ($60)
fee waiver for applicants with financial need	yes

COST & AID
tuition	$38,375
room & board	$11,890
total need-based institutional scholarships/grants	$24,600,000
% of students apply for need-based aid	48
% of students receive aid	100
% receiving need-based scholarship or grant aid	n/a
% receiving aid whose need was fully met	100
average aid package	$31,701
average student loan debt upon graduation	$17,125

Indiana University of Pennsylvania

Just an hour outside of Pittsburgh, Indiana University of Pennsylvania offers students proximity to a city along with the benefits of the great outdoors. The Student Cooperative Association even runs its own recreational park near campus, and other outdoor destinations are also nearby. Attending Indiana University is not all about play however; the university takes students' academic success seriously, offering for-credit classes in study skills, personal time management, career exploration and a student-focused Academic Recovery Program. Students are also expected to apply their skills in jobs and internships in the community, as the school's students have always done — historically, home economics students were once required to borrow orphaned children and care for them. Indiana University of Pennsylvania alumni have established outstanding careers in business and nonprofit organizations. Highly valued by employers, graduates often demonstrate personal passion, innovation and professional achievement.

> ACCESS **Benjamin Wiley Program Partnership**

Indiana University of Pennsylvania participates in the multi-year Benjamin Wiley Program Partnership, which helps urban high school students attain post-secondary education. Through the program, for which financial assistance is offered, students work with university staff and faculty to develop the academic and social skills needed to succeed in college. Program graduates who attend the program must also enroll in the College Undergraduate Success Program, an early-entrance freshman experience for first-year students.

> OPPORTUNITY **Minority Campus Visits**

During the Latino Exploration Day Program, high-achieving Latino students from the Philadelphia area spend two days on campus learning about the university. Minority students from four Pittsburgh School District high schools can also visit during Reaching New Heights, a similar visitation program that allows participants to talk with professors, tour the campus, meet with representatives from Admissions and Financial Aid and talk to current students.

> OPPORTUNITY **Board of Governors Scholarship**

The Board of Governors Scholarship provides full in-state tuition to admitted students who meet certain admissions requirements. A mailing informs students from over 300 state high schools about the scholarship and provides ongoing information about admissions. Counselors from these schools also receive from the university a list of over 180 minority scholarships nationwide.

> SUCCESS **Project ROCS (Retaining Our College Students)**

A program of the African American Cultural Center, Project ROCS is a voluntary program that helps African American freshmen by providing them with academic, cultural, social and personal support services in their first year of school. Each student receives individual attention, being paired with a peer outreach assistant and assigned a Caseload Adviser. Sample exams and course syllabi are available for student use, and nearly 50 faculty members and administrators have volunteered to work with the programs. Enrollment is limited but open to any freshman who feels he or she can benefit from the various services provided by the program.

Indiana University of Pennsylvania
1011 South Drive
Suite 117 Sutton Hall
Indiana, PA 15705
Ph: (724) 357-2100
admissions-inquiry@iup.edu
www.iup.edu

FAST FACTS

STUDENT PROFILE
# of degree-seeking undergraduates	8,778
% male/female	47/53
% African-American	11
% American Indian or Alaska Native	<1
% Asian or Pacific Islander	1
% Hispanic	2
% White	80
% International	2
% Pell grant recipients	34

First-generation and minority alumni William E. Powell '69, vice president of Industry Dealer Affairs, General Motors North America; Dr. Charlene Mickens Dukes '80, president, Prince George's Community College; Leland Hardy '84, founder/managing director, No Limit; Davie Huddleston '68, vice president of Human Resources, director of Strategic Talent Acquisition, PNC Financial Services Group; Gary Jefferson '67, vice president of Public Affairs, United Airlines, Inc.

ACADEMICS
full-time faculty	648
full-time minority faculty	84
student-faculty ratio	16:1
average class size	27
% first-year retention rate	73
% graduation rate (6 years)	51

Popular majors Communications Studies/Speech Communication and Rhetoric, Criminology, Elementary Education, Teaching

CAMPUS LIFE
% live on campus (% fresh.)	35 (84)

Multicultural student clubs and organizations Latino Student Organization, Black Emphasis Committee, Black Student League, NAACP, National Panhellenic Council, Voices of Joy, African American Dance Ensemble, Pan African Student Association, Women's Studies Center, Korean Student Association, Japanese Student Association, Chinese Student Association

Athletics NCAA Division II, Pennsylvania State Athletic Conference

ADMISSIONS
# of applicants	11,030
% accepted	64
# of first-year students enrolled	4,470
SAT Critical Reading range	440-540
SAT Math range	440-540
SAT Writing range	430-520
ACT range	n/a

Deadlines
regular admission	rolling
application fee (online)	$35 ($35)
fee waiver for applicants with financial need	yes

COST & AID
tuition	in-state: $7,225; out-of-state: $15,557
room & board	$6,278
total need-based institutional scholarships/grants	$25,065,464
% of students apply for need-based aid	83
% of students receive aid	66
% receiving need-based scholarship or grant aid	73
% receiving aid whose need was fully met	9
average aid package	$9,002
average student loan debt upon graduation	$23,265

Juniata College

Juniata College
Office of Admissions
1700 Moore Street
Huntingdon, PA 16652
Ph: (877) JUNIATA
admissions@juniata.edu
www.juniata.edu

Juniata College is a small, private, liberal arts college located in the Allegheny Mountains of central Pennsylvania. The vast majority of pre-college students in Juniata's surrounding area, should they attend college, would be first-generation college students, and Juniata's outreach programs create a college-bound culture in area school districts and offer college-level coursework to local high school students. Juniata's distinctive Program of Emphasis (POE) is an approach to learning that gives each student the opportunity to integrate his or her diverse interests into a concentrated program of study. Because it encourages students to personalize their education, the POE system creates an engaged student body committed to academic success.

> ACCESS Dual Enrollment Program

Juniata College's Dual Enrollment Program allows a broad range of local high school students to experience post-secondary coursework on the Juniata campus. Through state grants, the college is able to significantly discount the per-credit-hour fees to make this program affordable to all local families and school districts.

> ACCESS Science in Motion and Language in Motion

Science in Motion is a nationally recognized program at Juniata that reaches out to rural, underrepresented local school districts to provide the opportunity for science instruction with state-of-the-art laboratory equipment to which students would not otherwise have access. Similarly, Juniata's Language in Motion program promotes exposure to world languages among area schools and assists teachers in efforts to improve cultural awareness and language fluency among underrepresented students.

> OPPORTUNITY Heritage Awards

Juniata College awards Heritage Scholarships annually to students committed to leadership, community service, diversity and academic excellence. Renewable scholarships ranging in value from $2,000 to $6,000 are targeted at minority students who have shown a commitment to diversity in their high school years. Heritage Scholars are encouraged to be involved in the Juniata College community and to promote diversity awareness on campus throughout their four years.

> OPPORTUNITY Plexus Orientation

Plexus is a week-long, pre-orientation event open to any Juniata student with concerns about diversity inclusion. New students with concerns about multiculturalism on campus meet other new and returning students and offer their friendship, support and guidance in a safe and relaxing atmosphere. Plexus gives students insight into how diversity is integrated into Juniata campus life and highlights opportunities for multicultural experiences and student services available on campus and in surrounding communities.

FAST FACTS

STUDENT PROFILE

# of degree-seeking undergraduates	1,402
% male/female	44/56
% African-American	1
% American Indian or Alaska Native	<1
% Asian or Pacific Islander	2
% Hispanic	2
% Pell grant recipients	17

First-generation and minority alumni Harriet Michel, president, National Minority Supplier Development Council; Sammy K. Buo, deputy director, Africa II Division, United Nations; Martin A. Ewi, consultant on terrorism and security, African Union, Addis-Ababa, Ethiopia; Maurice C. Taylor, dean, graduate school, Morgan State University; John Kuriyan, chancellor's professor of chemistry, UC Berkeley; Rosalie Rodriguez, assistant to the president, director of Diversity & Inclusion, Juniata College; Dr. Eugene C. Baten, professor, Central Connecticut University; Richard Ikeda, retired, DuPont; Heng Lim, M.D., cardiologist; Hang Du Kim, retired project manager, IBM; Linda Cheng Pu, Trans Global Logistics Taiwan Ltd.

ACADEMICS

full-time faculty	103
full-time minority faculty	5
student-faculty ratio	12:1
average class size	17
% first-year retention rate	84
% graduation rate (6 years)	80

Popular majors Biology, Education, Business and Accounting

CAMPUS LIFE

% live on campus (% fresh.)	82 (96)

Multicultural student clubs and organizations African-American Student Alliance, All Ways of Loving (LGBTA), Asian Sensations United, Chinese Club, Club International, Club Mediterrano, Discover India, French Club, International Club, Japanese Club, Russian Club, Spanish Club, United Cultures of Juniata College

Athletics NCAA Division I, Eastern Intercollegiate Volleyball Association, NCAA Division III Commonwealth Conference, Middle Atlantic States Collegiate Athletic Conference

ADMISSIONS

# of applicants	2,349
% accepted	69
# of first-year students enrolled	n/a
SAT Critical Reading range	550-650
SAT Math range	550-640
SAT Writing range	n/a
ACT range	n/a
average HS GPA	3.8

Deadlines

early decision	12/1
regular decision	3/15
application fee (online)	$30 ($30)
fee waiver for applicants with financial need	yes

COST & AID

tuition	$31,550
room & board	$8,650
total need-based institutional scholarships/grants	$17,798,510
% of students apply for need-based aid	81
% of students receive aid	n/a
% receiving need-based scholarship or grant aid	99
% receiving aid whose need was fully met	54
average aid package	$22,440
average student loan debt upon graduation	$21,343

King's College

King's College
Office of Admission
133 North River Street
Wilkes-Barre, PA 18711
Ph: (570) 208-5858
admissions@kings.edu
www.kings.edu

King's College is a Catholic liberal arts college founded in 1946 by the Congregation of Holy Cross from the University of Notre Dame. The college is located on a small urban campus in Wilkes-Barre, Pa. King's aims for its students to be success-oriented, and provides them with top-notch faculty, technology and facilities. The college has a nationally recognized CORE curriculum and career placement program that prides itself on helping all King's students and graduates find meaningful employment. The campus is service-oriented, with faculty, staff and students coming together for volunteer projects on and off campus. The Office of College Diversity assists in making the campus inclusive and tolerant. King's students describe the campus as friendly and warm, with a strong sense of community.

"The highlight of my time here is the relationships with the members of the community, and the impression and impact I have had on first-year students. While involved with the Hispanic Outreach Program I was able to see myself as a role model for young students of my background and ethnicity. "

*– Milva V., '09
Hazleton, PA
Business Administration,
Human Resources
Management*

> ACCESS **College Discovery Program**

Gifted local high school students may take introductory college courses during the academic year and summer at King's College. The purpose of these course offerings is to challenge talented high school students, to orient them to the college environment, and to encourage a local college-bound culture.

> ACCESS **McGowan Hispanic Outreach Program**

King's College is dedicated to its McGowan Hispanic Outreach Program, which consists of outreach programs to the local Hispanic population, a mentorship program for Hispanic King's students, and hosting Hispanic cultural events and conferences on campus.

> OPPORTUNITY **Diversity Award and Presidential Scholarships**

The Diversity Award is a need-based award granted to multicultural first-year applicants to the college who are enrolled in a college preparatory curriculum. The award amount varies. Eight to 12 full-tuition Presidential Scholarships are given to students demonstrating the highest level of academic achievement. Students must be in the top 5 percent of their high school class, have a minimum SAT score of 1870 (ACT 28), a minimum GPA of 3.5, and a campus interview.

> SUCCESS **College Entry Program**

The College Entry Program is a pre-orientation summer program that prepares students for the challenges of college life at King's. The program allows students to earn up to six college credits in King's CORE curriculum with the advantage of smaller class sizes and academic support staff on hand. Career planning professionals meet with students to assist with career planning strategies. College Entry Program students also receive priority advisement, may plan their fall schedule ahead of time and consistently achieve grades equal to or surpassing classmates in later semesters at King's.

FAST FACTS

STUDENT PROFILE

# of degree-seeking undergraduates	1,966
% male/female	52/48
% African American	2
% American Indian or Alaska Native	<1
% Asian or Pacific Islander	1
% Hispanic	4
%White	82
% Pell grant recipients	29

First-generation and minority alumni William G. McGowan, founder, MCI; Santo Loquasto, Academy Award winner, Tony Award winner; Patrick J. Murphy, U.S. Congressman

ACADEMICS

full-time faculty	119
full-time minority faculty	6
student-faculty ratio	3:1
average class size	18
% first-year retention rate	78
% graduation rate (6 years)	70

Popular majors Business Administration, Physician Assistant, Biology, Education, Accounting

CAMPUS LIFE

% live on campus (% fresh.)	50 (72)

Multicultural student clubs and organizations Multicultural/International Club
Athletics NCAA Division III, Freedom Conference, Middle Atlantic States Collegiate Athletic Conference

ADMISSIONS

# of applicants	2,172
% accepted	75
# of first-year students enrolled	496
SAT Critical Reading range	460-550
SAT Math range	470-560
SAT Writing range	450-550
ACT range	19-24
average HS GPA	3.3

Deadlines

regular decision	rolling
application fee (online)	$30 ($0)
fee waiver for applicants with financial need	yes

COST & AID

tuition	$25,644
room & board	$10,138
total need-based institutional scholarships/grants	$15,264,400
% of students apply for need-based aid	90
% of students receive aid	94
% receiving need-based scholarship or grant aid	80
% receiving aid whose need was fully met	13
average aid package	$18,300
average student loan debt upon graduation	$28,145

Lafayette College

Lafayette College is committed to maintaining and supports diversity through the understanding that awareness, a deeper sense of cultural knowledge, and the ability to operate in a pluralistic community are essential to an undergraduate education. Lafayette is uniquely positioned among America's leading colleges for its strictly undergraduate focus that offers the best in liberal arts and engineering programs. Through active learning experiences in small-group seminars, student-centered team projects, independent study, student-faculty research, study abroad, and internships, students have the opportunity to cross academic boundaries in the arts, sciences, and engineering. An independent, coeducational, residential, undergraduate institution, Lafayette maintains a growing faculty of distinction.

> OPPORTUNITY **Multicultural Student Visit Opportunities**

Each November, prospective students of color experience campus life on Multicultural Visit Day. In April Lafayette hosts admitted students from multicultural backgrounds for Prologue, a day-long campus program. The college flies a number of these students to campus and hosts many students of color who visit through the activities of community-based organizations, including TORCH, Prep for Prep, and the Princeton University Pre-Collegiate Program.

> OPPORTUNITY **Posse Foundation**

Lafayette participates in the Posse Foundation, a program that brings talented inner-city youth to campus to pursue their academics and to help promote cross-cultural communication. Posse students are nominated to the program by their high school and share a collaborative support system with a special mentor to adjust to campus and college life. Lafayette's Posse Scholars hail from New York City and Washington DC.

"I have really started to love this school. Lafayette is a purely undergraduate school, and you are getting introductory courses by senior professors. We are really lucky as undergraduates to be able to do research with these professors and to really feel like you're the number one on campus."

– Fairouz F., '11
Washington, DC
Music, Africana Studies

> SUCCESS **Office of Intercultural Development (OID)**

The Office of Intercultural Development affirms that the presence of diversity and cultural richness is an essential component of student learning and enhancing students' cultural experience. It provides the community with intercultural programming and cross-cultural dialogue, as well as information, advice, and services to African, Latino/a, Asian and Native American (ALANA) students and the wider Lafayette community.

> SUCCESS **Portlock Black Cultural Center**

An integral part of the College's effort to provide multicultural education to the campus community, the Portlock Center provides a way to assess the educational and social experiences of ALANA students and to initiate and improve programs. It features an art gallery, seminar and meeting room, social spaces, and a library on issues of cultural diversity and social justice. Activities include exhibits, workshops, alumni events, guest lectures, classes, receptions and film showings. The center works with community organizations to increase cultural awareness, support community-wide programs, and provide a forum for networking.

> SUCCESS **Lafayette Intercultural Networking Council (LINC)**

The Lafayette Intercultural Networking Council promotes intercultural exchange with dialogue and collaborative efforts among student groups and organizations, administration offices, and faculty/academic departments.

Lafayette College
118 Markle Hall
Easton, PA 18042
Ph: (610) 330-5100
admissions@lafayette.edu
www.lafayette.edu

F A S T   F A C T S

STUDENT PROFILE
# of degree-seeking undergraduates	2,352
% male/female	54/46
% African American	5
% American Indian or Alaska Native	<1
% Asian or Pacific Islander	4
% Hispanic	5
% White	71
% International	7
% Pell grant recipients	9

First-generation and minority alumni David Kearney McDonogh, Lafayette's first African American graduate and perhaps the first person with legal status as a slave to receive a college degree, physician (Harlem's first hospital named for him); Riley K. Temple, founder, Temple Strategies, Washington, D.C.; Darlyne Bailey, assistant to the president, University of Minnesota; Marcia Bloom Bernicat, U.S. Ambassador to Senegal and Guinea-Bissau; Winston Thompson, physician, Department of Obstetrics and Gynecology, Morehouse School of Medicine, Atlanta, Ga.

ACADEMICS
full-time faculty	197
full-time minority faculty	20
student-faculty ratio	11:1
average class size	18
% first-year retention rate	94
% graduation rate (6 years)	89

Popular majors Economics, English, Engineering, Government and Law, Biology, Art, Psychology

CAMPUS LIFE
% live on campus (% fresh.)	94 (100)

Multicultural student clubs and organizations African and Caribbean Students Association, Asian Culture Association, Association of Black Collegians, Brothers of Lafayette, Heritage of Latin America, Hispanic Society, International Students Association, NIA (multicultural women's group)

Athletics NCAA Division I, Patriot League

ADMISSIONS
# of applicants	6,357
% accepted	37
# of first-year students enrolled	601
SAT Critical Reading range	580-670
SAT Math range	610-700
SAT Writing range	590-680
ACT range	26-30
average HS GPA	3.53

Deadlines
early decision	1/1
regular decision	1/1
application fee (online)	$60 ($60)
fee waiver for applicants with financial need	yes

COST & AID
tuition	$37,520
room & board	$11,799
total need-based institutional scholarships/grants	$25,187,534
% of students apply for need-based aid	60
% of students receive aid	93
% receiving need-based scholarship or grant aid	86
% receiving aid whose need was fully met	93
average aid package	$29,246
average student loan debt upon graduation	$18,747

Lebanon Valley College

Lebanon Valley College
Office of Admission
101 North College Avenue
Annville, PA 17003
Ph: (866) LVC-4ADM / (717) 867-6181
admission@lvc.edu
www.lvc.edu

Lebanon Valley College is a private, co-educational college associated with the United Methodist Church. Founded in 1866, Lebanon Valley seeks to provide an education that affords students the knowledge, skills, attitudes and values necessary to live and work in a changing, diverse, and fragile world. Furthermore, the college cultivates a welcoming environment: Lebanon Valley College is like a big family that provides camaraderie and support to all students throughout their undergraduate years.

> ACCESS Lebanon Valley Education Partnership

The Lebanon Valley Education Partnership between Lebanon Valley College and the Lebanon School District encourages children in the city of Lebanon to study, stay in school, and aspire to attend college. Beginning in the eighth grade, the partnership identifies academic high achievers who face circumstances that may prevent them from attending college. These students are matched with current Lebanon Valley students who serve as mentors throughout the students' high school years. Students who enroll in college preparatory classes and maintain good academic standing in high school become eligible for a tuition scholarship at Lebanon Valley.

> ACCESS Project Forward Leap

Project Forward Leap assists Pennsylvania's academically promising but economically and socially disadvantaged children. As participants of this program, Pennsylvania middle school students live and study for five weeks on participating college campuses for three consecutive summers. Students take courses in mathematics, language arts, science and Latin, and all courses are taught by experienced instructors. Residential supervision is provided by faculty and assistants, usually current college students.

> OPPORTUNITY The Multicultural Fellowship

To support diversity, Lebanon Valley offers the Multicultural Fellowship. Limited to high school seniors identifying most closely with African-American, Asian-American, Hispanic-American and/or Native American racial and ethnic groups, the fellowships provide multicultural students with much financial support. Annual awards range from $2,000 to $12,000.

> SUCCESS Multicultural Mentors

Multicultural Mentors are upperclassmen who have either received Multicultural Fellowships or who have positively contributed to the multicultural programs and initiatives at Lebanon Valley College. Mentors are responsible for assisting first-year students in meeting the fellowship requirements and providing academic, social, cultural and personal support.

> SUCCESS Office of Multicultural Affairs

The Office of Multicultural Affairs provides the campus community with opportunities to develop cross-cultural understanding. Multicultural Affairs supports the academic mission of the college: "to free students (and college community) from ignorance, prejudice and narrowness of vision." From its annual Martin Luther King Day lecture to film screenings, multicultural leadership roundtables to musical performances, Multicultural Affairs provides ample opportunity for students to share a wide range of multicultural events and activities.

FAST FACTS

STUDENT PROFILE

# of degree-seeking undergraduates	1,600
% male/female	46/54
% African-American	1
% American Indian or Alaska Native	<1
% Asian or Pacific Islander	2
% Hispanic	2
% Pell grant recipients	15

ACADEMICS

full-time faculty	99
full-time minority faculty	6
student-faculty ratio	13:1
average class size	17
% first-year retention rate	81
% graduation rate (6 years)	68

Popular majors Music, Business Management, Elementary Education, Psychology, Physical Therapy

CAMPUS LIFE

% live on campus (% fresh.)	74 (89)

Multicultural student clubs and organizations Council for International Affairs, Iota Phi Theta, Multicultural Leadership Roundtable, Leading Educational Awareness for Diversity

Athletics NCAA Division III, Commonwealth Conference, Middle Atlantic States Collegiate Athletic Conference

ADMISSIONS

# of applicants	1,885
% accepted	73
# of first-year students enrolled	467
SAT Critical Reading range	490-600
SAT Math range	510-610
SAT Writing range	490-600
ACT range	20-27
average HS GPA	n/a

Deadlines

regular decision	rolling
early decision	no
application fee (online)	$30 ($30)
fee waiver for applicants with financial need	yes

COST & AID

tuition	$30,490
room & board	$8,080
total need-based institutional scholarships/grants	n/a
% of students apply for need-based aid	88
% of students receive aid	100
% receiving need-based scholarship or grant aid	100
% receiving aid whose need was fully met	25
average aid package	$21,978
average student loan debt upon graduation	$32,437

Lehigh University

Lehigh University
27 Memorial Drive West
Bethlehem, PA 18015
Ph: (610) 758-3100
admissions@lehigh.edu
www.lehigh.edu

A selective private school in Bethlehem, Pa., Lehigh University is noted for both its strong academic programs and picturesque campus, located within 100 miles of both New York City and Philadelphia. While Lehigh offers many broad academic programs, the university prides itself on the personal connection that professors have with their students. Lehigh's 4,800+ undergraduate students and 2,100 graduate students can experience interesting, independent research and work closely with faculty who offer their time and attention to projects, internships, and innovative studies. With more than 90 majors in the liberal arts, business, education, engineering and the sciences, students are able to customize their college experience. Academic support, career services, and other departments work closely with faculty to ensure that students, and their families have access to an open door that allows students to take advantage of all resources designed for their success both in the classroom and after graduation.

> *"Choosing to attend Lehigh was one of the best decisions I have ever made and I believe the rewards of a Lehigh University education will never cease. Now that I am going into my junior year, I am still discovering more and more opportunities that Lehigh has to offer. If you are looking for an institution that will work just as hard for you as you work for it; then Lehigh University is your best choice."*
> – Adrienne L., '11
> Bucks County, PA
> Molecular Biology

> ACCESS Students That Are Ready (STAR) Academies

A partnership between Lehigh University and local schools, businesses, and parents, the Students That Are Ready Academies provide local middle and high school aged students with access to two unique programs: a year-long academic success and mentoring program for students in sixth through twelfth grades, and a three-week summer program in math, science and technology for students entering sixth through ninth grades. STAR also offers a Summer Eighth Grade Experience (SEE) that helps current academy students transition into high school. The fundamental mission of the academy is to enable students to develop intellectually, socially, spiritually and emotionally so that they will become productive citizens.

> ACCESS March for Education

Founded by the National Society of Black Engineers, the March for Education brings Lehigh students, faculty and staff, along with local community college members and members from the community at large into the homes of local families to talk about the importance of higher education. Information is presented regarding SAT preparation and local testing centers, as well as information about local colleges and universities in the area.

> OPPORTUNITY Diversity Recruitment and Accepted Student Programs

Throughout the year, any student interested in visiting Lehigh can meet with the Director or Assistant Director of Diversity Recruitment to discuss some of the unique challenges that may face individual families. Personalized attention, follow through, and support are what makes the Diversity Recruitment aspect of Lehigh's admissions process so special. Accepted students have the opportunity to visit at Lehigh's cost for the April Diversity Life Weekend, where students attend classes, stay with current Lehigh students, and experience the range of academic and social opportunities available.

FAST FACTS

STUDENT PROFILE
# of degree-seeking undergraduates	4,746
% male/female	58/42
% African American	3.6
% American Indian or Alaska Native	<1
% Asian or Pacific Islander	6.3
% Hispanic	6.3
% White	71
% International	3.8
% Pell grant recipients	9.4

First-generation and minority alumni Pongpol Adireksarn, Thai politician; Ali Al-Naimi, oil minister, Saudi Arabia; Dr. Ron Williams, vice president, College Board in Washington, D.C.; Dr. Frank Douglas, MD, Ph.D., executive director, Center for Biomedical Innovation at MIT

ACADEMICS
full-time faculty	443
full-time minority faculty	74
student-faculty ratio	9:1
average class size	25-30
% first-year retention rate	94
% graduation rate (6 years)	85

Popular majors Accounting, Biology, Finance, Mechanical Engineering, Psychology

CAMPUS LIFE
% live on campus (% fresh.)	68 (99)

Multicultural student clubs and organizations African-Caribbean Cultural, Anime Eki Animation, Asian Cultural Society, Association of International Students, Bhangra, Black Students Union, Chinese Cultural, Hispanic Union of Business Students, Indian Students Association, Korean Students, Mariachi, National Society of Black Engineers, Society of Hispanic Engineers, South American and Latino Students Alliance, Thai Students at Lehigh

Athletics NCAA Division I (football – championship subdivision), Eastern Intercollegiate Wrestling Association, Patriot League

ADMISSIONS
# of applicants	10,333
% accepted	37
# of first-year students enrolled	1,170
SAT Critical Reading range	620-710
SAT Math range	640-720
SAT Writing range	660-740
ACT range	28-32
average HS GPA	B+ - A-

Deadlines
early decision	11/15
regular decision	1/1
application fee (online)	$70 ($70)
fee waiver for applicants with financial need	yes

COST & AID
tuition	$39,480
room & board	$10,520
total need-based institutional scholarships/grants	$47,811,683
% of students apply for need-based aid	51
% of students receive aid	100
% receiving need-based scholarship or grant aid	97
% receiving aid whose need was fully met	68
average aid package	$31,611
average student loan debt upon graduation	$29,756

Muhlenberg College

Founded in 1848, Muhlenberg College is an independent, undergraduate, co-educational institution that provides challenging academics and passionate teaching within a warm and caring community environment. Committed to educating the whole person through experiences within and beyond the classroom, the college's curriculum integrates the traditional liberal arts with selected pre-professional studies. Muhlenberg College faculty are passionate about teaching, value close relationships with students and are active scholars. Honoring its historical heritage from the Lutheran Church and its continuing connection with the Evangelical Lutheran Church in America, Muhlenberg welcomes and celebrates a variety of faith traditions on campus and encourages members of the college community to value spiritual life.

> ACCESS Community Service

Muhlenberg's Community Service Office is designed to promote, facilitate and support positive interaction among students, faculty and community members. The office provides leadership opportunities for students through community outreach projects and coordinating volunteer programs. By linking social action with reflection, Muhlenberg service opportunities strive to prepare students for their roles as citizens and leaders while addressing the needs of the surrounding community. Jefferson Field Day introduces local elementary students to Muhlenberg and its students by inviting them to campus for a fun-filled day of activities. The college reaches out to local high school students through programs such as IMPACT, a mentoring program for teens facing difficulties.

> OPPORTUNITY Advising Days

To help ease the transition from high school into college life, Muhlenberg College offers many opportunities for students to get to know each other and the campus. In mid-May, incoming Muhlenberg first-year students are assigned an "Advising Day" to come to campus for an individual advising session with a faculty member. At this event, students meet fellow first-year students and current students during panel discussions and social events, including a special luncheon in the Garden Room, the college's student dining facility. The day concludes with a reception at the home of Muhlenberg's president.

> SUCCESS Multicultural Center

All are welcome at Muhlenberg College's Multicultural Center, whose aim is to provide a supportive and safe space on campus for multicultural students, faculty and staff. The center strives to nurture and promote the academic success and leadership development of multicultural students at Muhlenberg, and is committed to promoting and sustaining an inclusive atmosphere that fosters and enriches multicultural understanding among all members of the Muhlenberg and Lehigh Valley communities. Its mission is to serve as a campus-wide resource for facilitating and promoting a learning community of multicultural understanding and exchange through collaboration, dialogue and action. Housing the Office of Multicultural Life and the Office of International Programs – Study Abroad, the Multicultural Center contains a seminar room for classes, plus a living room, dining room, kitchen and finished basement. Students enjoy spending social time in the center, along with hosting cultural events, panel discussions and dinner parties there.

> SUCCESS Peer Tutoring

The Peer Tutoring program at Muhlenberg College seeks to assist students' efforts to successfully navigate the challenges of competitive higher education. Working collaboratively with tutors, faculty and staff, the program helps a diverse population develop higher level critical thinking skills, better course performance and more adaptive, independent learning strategies. Most importantly, the program works hard to foster student engagement in the learning process.

Muhlenberg College
Office of Admission
2400 Chew Street
Allentown, PA 18104
Ph: (484) 664-3200
admission@muhlenberg.edu
www.muhlenberg.edu

F A S T   F A C T S

STUDENT PROFILE
# of degree-seeking undergraduates	2,149
% male/female	42/58
% African American	2
% American Indian	<1
% Asian	2
% Hispanic	4
% Pell grant recipients	7

First-generation and minority alumni Lt. Gen. Julius W. Becton, Jr., first black army officer to attain the rank of lieutenant general and command a corps; Kam-Kam Cheng, Broadway actress

ACADEMICS
full-time faculty	161
student-faculty ratio	12:1
average class size	19
% first-year retention rate	93
% graduation rate (6 years)	86

Popular majors Biology, Psychology, Business Administration, Theater/Dance, English

CAMPUS LIFE
% live on campus (% freshmen)	92 (99)

Multicultural student clubs and organizations Asian Students Association, Black Students Association, Comunidad Latina, Soul Sound Steppers

Athletics NCAA Division III, Centennial Conference

ADMISSIONS
# of applicants	4,703
% accepted	37
SAT Critical Reading range	550-650
SAT Math range	560-660
SAT Writing range	560-660
ACT range	26-29
average HS GPA	3.4

Deadlines
early decision	2/1
regular decision	2/15
application fee (online)	$50 ($50)
fee waiver for applicants with financial need	yes

COST & AID
tuition	$36,990
room & board	$8,060
total need-based institutional scholarships/grants	n/a
% applying for aid	57
% of students receiving aid	45
% receiving need-based scholarship or grant aid	96
% receiving aid whose need was fully met	92
average aid package	$18,166
average student loan debt upon graduation	$18,000

Rosemont College

Rosemont College
1400 Montgomery Avenue
Rosemont, PA 19010
Ph: (610) 527-0200
admissions@rosemont.edu
www.rosemont.edu

At Rosemont College you will gain knowledge, develop critical skills, and grow as a person of character. Located in suburban Philadelphia, Rosemont College offers students an exceptional and comprehensive coeducational learning experience. With 23 undergraduate majors; seven graduate programs; 10 pre-professional, certification, and dual-degrees programs; 13 varsity sport teams; and numerous clubs, Rosemont develops your unique talents emphasizing what you're best at and remains connected to what you want to do.

> ACCESS Bridge to Success Program

Rosemont conducts the Bridge to Success Program each August for incoming students. Bridge is a pre-orientation program which offers: academic support emphasizing writing and reading, college readiness, and study skills, individual mentoring, and team-building to a selected group of students. Under the guidance of a Bridge Coordinator, and with the instructional expertise of two Rosemont professors, students attend four days of classes prior to the start of the academic year. During the course of the year both the Coordinator and the staff of Student Academic Support will "touch base" with each student regularly, as well as with the student mentors.

> OPPORTUNITY Rosemont Scholarship

Rosemont College seeks to provide an affordable college education to all students, regardless of family income, who demonstrate the potential for academic success. In order to promote academic excellence while providing opportunities to students of all backgrounds the College offers both merit based awards, Rosemont Scholarships, and need based awards, Rosemont Grants.

> *"The responsibility to succeed is on me, but I feel as though the faculty and my friends are constantly encouraging me to do my best, and to achieve my dreams and goals."*
> – Chris P.,
> Philadelphia, PA
> Sociology

> SUCCESS Mission Plan

Within the first few days at Rosemont, students take a number of surveys that identify their personal and academic strengths, career interest, and learning styles. This information helps them work more efficiently and helps others be better teachers and mentors. Students will also work closely with professors and advisors to draft their personalized Mission Plan, a four year road map for their Rosemont experience. The Mission Plan guides students' intellectual and extracurricular lives, helps them develop leadership skills and strength of character and ensure that all the things they do in college work together to prepare for their future.

FAST FACTS

STUDENT PROFILE

# of degree-seeking undergraduates	422
% male/female	18/82
% African-American	49
% American Indian or Alaska Native	0
% Asian or Pacific Islander	n/a
% Hispanic	8
% White	31
% International	1
% Pell grant recipients	52

First-generation and minority alumni
Mari Carmen Aponte, executive director, Puerto Rico Federal Affairs Administration; Yvonne Chism-Peace, educator, award-winning author; Gwen Owens, multiple Emmy Award-nominated news veteran and news anchor; Varsovia Fernandez, executive director, Greater Philadelphia Hispanic Chamber of Commerce.

ACADEMICS

full-time faculty	28
full-time minority faculty	0
student-faculty ratio	10:1
average class size	12
% first-year retention rate	64
% graduation rate (6 years)	63

Popular majors English, Psychology, Business

CAMPUS LIFE

% live on campus (% fresh.)	60.5 (60)

Multicultural student clubs and organizations Association of Latin American Students, French Club, International Club, Irish Heritage Society, Italian Club, Muslim Student Association, Organization of African American Students
Athletics NCAA Division III, Colonial States Athletic Association (CSAC)

ADMISSIONS

# of applicants	1,119
% accepted	54
# of first-year students enrolled	181
SAT Critical Reading range	400-510
SAT Math range	400-490
SAT Writing range	380-500
ACT range	17-20
average HS GPA	3.05

Deadlines

regular decision	rolling
application fee (online)	$35 ($0)
fee waiver for applicants with financial need	yes

COST & AID

tuition	$26,230
room & board	$10,580
total need-based institutional scholarships/grants	n/a
% of students apply for need-based aid	93
% of students receive aid	80
% receiving need-based scholarship or grant aid	84
% receiving aid whose need was fully met	15
average aid package	$25,237
average student loan debt upon graduation	$22,619

Saint Francis University

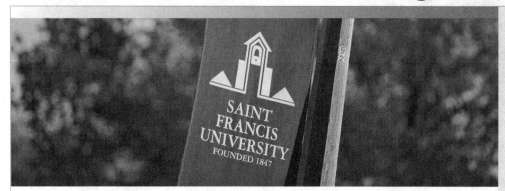

As a Franciscan institution located in rural Pennsylvania, Saint Francis University strives to imbue its students with "a mind for excellence, a spirit for peace and justice [and] a mind for service." To this end, the university has opened the state-of-the-art DiSepio Institute for Rural Health and Wellness, an education and research center featuring physical training, conference, clinical, human performance laboratory and meditation spaces. It is used both to foster the science and health programs at the university and to help the school serve those suffering from illnesses common to rural areas. The oldest Franciscan institution of higher learning in the United States, Saint Francis University offers 25 undergraduate majors to nearly 2,000 students, and is an inclusive community that welcomes all people. By emphasizing values, skills and knowledge, each of its academic programs provides an understanding of Franciscan heritage, values and traditions.

> ACCESS Upward Bound

Saint Francis University participates in the federally funded Upward Bound program, a federal TRIO program funded through the U.S. Department of Education, which has prepared over 1,500 disadvantaged high school students for the rigors of postsecondary education since 1966. Provided at no cost to participants, the program offers a wide variety of academic, career, cultural, and social development activities for high school students from Blair and Cambria counties. Each participant must come from a low-income family and/or be a potential first-generation college student. From September through May, the students participate in follow-ups held on campus and tutorials held after-school in their communities. Additional academic year activities include college visits, SAT sessions, and college fairs. During a six-week residential summer program, students attend academic classes each day and participate in a wide variety of cultural and recreational activities. Each summer Upward Bound Bridge students take Saint Francis University courses for credit.

> OPPORTUNITY Scholarship Opportunities

Saint Francis University believes every person who desires higher education has the right to pursue it. The university offers a variety of awards to supplement families' funds whenever possible, and aggressively seeks financial aid for those demonstrating need. The university offers a comprehensive program of merit-based scholarships, institutional grants, loans, part-time employment and federal and state financial assistance.

> SUCCESS Opportunities for Academic Success in Studies Program

Students are expected to meet with their counselor on a monthly basis through the Opportunities for Academic Success in Studies program, which is designed to assist first-year students who have not yet fully developed their academic potential. The program provides academic assistance and support services to enhance student growth, success, and persistence towards attaining a college degree. Although the support programming and services are important factors for success, the motivation to take advantage of these workshops and tutorials comes from within the student.

Saint Francis University
P.O. Box 600
117 Evergreen Drive
Loretto, PA 15940
Ph: (814) 472-3100
admissions@francis.edu
www.francis.edu

FAST FACTS

STUDENT PROFILE
# of degree-seeking undergraduates	1,571
% male/female	40/60
% African American	5
% American Indian or Alaska Native	<1
% Asian or Pacific Islander	1
% Hispanic	1
% Pell grant recipients	16

First-generation and minority alumni Maurice Stokes, Norm van Lier, Kevin Porter Former, former basketball players

ACADEMICS
full-time faculty	105
full-time minority faculty	3
student-faculty ratio	14:1
average class size	17
% first-year retention rate	84
% graduation rate (6 years)	56

Popular majors Business Administration/Management, Natural Science, Occupational Therapy, Physical Therapy and Physician Assistant Science

CAMPUS LIFE
% live on campus (% freshmen)	70 (85)

Multicultural student clubs and organizations Office of Multicultural Affairs, Multicultural Awareness Society, Multicultural Awareness Living and Learning Center, Center for International Education and Outreach, Student Government Association, Student Activities Organization
Athletics NCAA Division I, Eastern Intercollegiate Volleyball Association, Northeast Conference

ADMISSIONS
# of applicants	1,700
% accepted	75
# of first-year students enrolled	433
SAT Critical Reading range	470-570
SAT Math range	470-590
SAT Writing range	n/a
ACT range	21-27
average HS GPA	3.5

Deadlines
regular decision	1/15
application fee (online)	$30 ($30)
fee waiver for applicants with financial need	yes

COST & AID
tuition	$25,484
room & board	$9,006
total need-based institutional scholarships/grants	$14,247,945
% of students apply for need-based aid	92
% of students receive aid	83
% receiving need-based scholarship or grant aid	81
% receiving aid whose need was fully met	16
average aid package	$17,053
average student loan debt upon graduation	$10,762

Saint Vincent College

Saint Vincent College
300 Fraser Purchase Road
Latrobe, PA 15650-2690
Ph: (742) 805-2500
admission@stvincent.edu
www.stvincent.edu

Saint Vincent College is a private, co-educational, liberal arts college with an educational tradition that dates back to 1846. Rooted in the tradition of the Catholic faith, the heritage of Benedictine monasticism, and a liberal approach to life and learning, Saint Vincent encourages students to pursue their intellectual gifts, professional aptitudes, and personal aspirations. With a welcoming hospitality and an attention to individual needs, Saint Vincent teaches students to integrate their professional aims with the broader purposes of human life.

> ACCESS The Challenge Program

The Challenge Program at Saint Vincent College is designed for gifted, creative, or talented students, grades six through 12. The school offers exciting daytime courses in subjects like computers, history, and the humanities for highly motivated youth who seek opportunities to explore new interests and develop their creativity and talents. In addition to the classroom experience, Challenge also includes evening recreation and social interaction.

> ACCESS Pathways to Success

Pathways to Success empowers underserved local middle school and high school students. Saint Vincent students act as mentors during the year-round program and provide participants with support structures and on-going educational opportunities. With special attention to academic development, cultural awareness, community service, and personal development, the program tailors educational content and methods to complement both the goals of cooperating schools and Pennsylvania's academic standards. Thus, learning experiences adapt to changing needs as students progress from middle school through high school.

> OPPORTUNITY Special Admission Policy

The Opportunity SVC/ACT 101 Program is a statewide academic support system funded, in part, by the Commonwealth of Pennsylvania through Act 101. Placement in the program is determined after the Admission Committee evaluates the applicant's grades, test scores, and recommendations. Although each candidate is evaluated according to individual merits and potential, academic and financial eligibility requirements may be taken into consideration in accordance with Act 101 state guidelines. The Opportunity staff provides ongoing academic support and counseling to the student throughout his or her college years. In addition, a fall transitional semester is an added benefit of the program.

> SUCCESS Office of Multicultural and International Student Life

The Office of Multicultural and International Student Life is the "connective tissue" for the many national, ethnic and cultural groups of the Saint Vincent College community. The office not only seeks to ensure a diverse environment at both the curricular and co-curricular levels, but also works to ensure everyone at Saint Vincent feels comfortable, valued, and connected. The office offers special programming, activities, on-campus employment opportunities, and a special multicultural orientation.

"I chose Saint Vincent College because I was looking for a college close to home that provided a good education. The faculty and staff here are friendly, intelligent and always willing to help students. They are very approachable."
– Nettisha H., '09
Gibsonia, PA
Communications

FAST FACTS

STUDENT PROFILE
# of degree-seeking undergraduates	1,680
% male/female	49/51
% African American	7
% American Indian or Alaska Native	<1
% Asian or Pacific Islander	3
% Hispanic	4
% White	90
% International	1
% Pell grant recipients	28.4

First-generation and minority alums Ramon Martin, M.D., Ph.D., Physician, Brigham and Women's Hospital, Harvard Medical School, Boston; Warner Johnson, Director of Alumni, Robert Morris University; James Overton, Chief Financial Officer, United Way of Allegheny County; Dr. Willette Stinson, Ph.D.; Bryan K. Ulishney, Vice President Finance and Operations, A Second Chance Inc.; Christina Domasky, Bridal Consultant, Nemacolin Woodlands Resort and Spa; Antoine D. Terrar, Program Manager, Pearson Peacekeeping Centre

ACADEMICS
full-time faculty	208
full-time minority faculty	5
student-faculty ratio	14:1
average class size	20
% first-year retention rate	82
% graduation rate (6 years)	72

Popular majors Business Administration, Biology, Communication, Environmental Studies, Psychology/Education

CAMPUS LIFE
% live on campus (% fresh.)	83 (90)

Multicultural student clubs and organizations Minority Student Coalition, Italian Club, International Student Union
Athletics NCAA Division III, Presidents' Athletic Conference

ADMISSIONS
# of applicants	1,843
% accepted	65
# of first-year students enrolled	447
SAT Critical Reading range	470-570
SAT Math range	480-590
SAT Writing range	460-570
ACT range	19-24
average HS GPA	3.57
Deadlines	
regular decision	4/1
application fee (online)	$25 ($0)
fee waiver for applicants with financial need	yes

COST & AID
tuition	$26,350
room & board	$8,754
total need-based institutional scholarships/grants	$14,528,589
% of students apply for need-based aid	97
% of students receive aid	100
% receiving need-based scholarship or grant aid	100
% receiving aid whose need was fully met	28
average aid package	$20,563
average student loan debt upon graduation	$17,500

Seton Hill University

Seton Hill University
Seton Hill Drive
Greensburg, PA 15601
Ph: (724) 838-4255
admit@setonhill.edu
www.setonhill.edu

A Catholic, liberal arts university, Seton Hill University offers students a range of academic and co-curricular options. Potential education majors might be particularly well-served by Seton Hill, which boasts a strong education division with an emphasis on special education. The school also houses a Child Development Center and a kindergarten, where education students can research and practice in their focus areas. Seton Hill is also the home of the National Education Center for Women in Business and the National Catholic Center for Holocaust Education, both of which offer supplemental programming for many majors.

> ACCESS Community Service Program

As a Catholic university, Seton Hill promotes community-wide service. In the fall semester, students can participate in Labor of Love, which sends them to various service sites ranging from the Westmoreland County Food Bank to Habitat for Humanity. A similar program — Martin Luther King Jr. Take the Day On — occurs during the spring; a week of educational programs on issues of peace and justice follows this. Finally, Seton Hill organizes Operation Christmas Basket, through which students make and sell baked goods as a fundraiser to support the Greensburg community.

> OPPORTUNITY Opportunity Program

Select incoming students with low tests scores and/or GPAs, or whose previous grades do not reflect their potential, can participate in the Opportunity Program, a summer residential program designed to help students acclimate to school. The Opportunity Program provides basic skill development in reading, writing, and critical thinking, as well as career and educational planning, among other services. Participants also attend "Faculty Forums," a series of lectures given by Seton Hill faculty, and they take part in social and cultural activities.

> SUCCESS C.A.P.S. Program

The C.A.P.S. Program oversees a variety of academic and personal support services, including tutoring, counseling, course instruction, study skills and writing and computer assistance. C.A.P.S. also oversees Act 101, a state-sponsored program that provides assistance to students who are financially disadvantaged and educationally under-prepared and Student Support Services, a federally sponsored program that provides support to a similar demographic of students.

F A S T F A C T S

STUDENT PROFILE

# of degree-seeking undergraduates	1,666
% male/female	38.7/ 61.3
% African-American	8
% American Indian or Alaska Native	<1
% Asian or Pacific Islander	1
% Hispanic	2
% White	84
% International	n/a
% Pell grant recipients	24

ACADEMICS

full-time faculty	75
full-time minority faculty	3
student-faculty ratio	14:1
average class size	17
% first-year retention rate	81
% graduation rate (6 years)	60

Popular majors Business Administration/ Management, Fine/Studio Arts

CAMPUS LIFE

% live on campus (% freshmen)	61 (89)

Multicultural student clubs and organizations Intercultural Student Association, NAACP, Spanish Club

Athletics NCAA Division II, West Virginia Intercollegiate Athletic Conference

ADMISSIONS

# of applicants	1,754
% accepted	64
# of first-year students enrolled	475
SAT Critical Reading range	440-560
SAT Math range	440-570
SAT Writing	n/a
ACT range	n/a
average HS GPA	3.4

Deadlines

regular decision	rolling
application fee (online)	$35 ($35)
fee waiver for applicants with financial need	yes

COST & AID

tuition	$26,622
room & board	$8,550
total need-based institutional scholarships/grants	n/a
% of students apply for need-based aid	92
% of students receive aid	84
% receiving need-based scholarship or grant aid	99
% receiving aid whose need was fully met	17
average aid package	$21,103
average student loan debt upon graduation	$27,120

Susquehanna University

Susquehanna University
Office of Admissions
514 University Avenue
Selinsgrove, PA 17870-1164
Ph: (800) 326-9672 / (570) 372-4260
suadmiss@susqu.edu
www.susqu.edu

Susquehanna University, located in Pennsylvania's scenic Susquehanna River Valley, is continually ranked among the top 110 liberal arts colleges in the country. The school's focus on community creates a close-knit group of teachers and learners who are dedicated to learning, school pride, achievement and service. Susquehanna's involvement in its region includes outreach programs like SU4U, geared toward local first-generation and minority students, and volunteer service through the school's 15 service-learning courses. The school values every student's academic success through continual preparation and monitoring and highly engaged professors and staff. Susquehanna's distinctive central curriculum allows students to incorporate internships and explore other cultures into their learning and prepare themselves for life in a diverse and interconnected world.

> ACCESS **SU4U**

The Degenstein Foundation and Susquehanna University have partnered to develop SU4U, a program to encourage middle school students in regional Pennsylvania students and their families in pursuit of higher education. The mentoring and scholarship program targets students with substantial financial need who are in the first generation of their families to consider college. SU4U provides scholarships to five graduating high school seniors each year; preference is given to graduates of regional high schools and first-generation students. In addition to scholarships, the program consists of an outreach effort designed for middle school grade students to make going to college a feasible goal. This program shows students and their families that if they work hard and plan ahead, finances need not be an obstacle to obtaining a college education.

> OPPORTUNITY **Richard R. Green Memorial Scholarships**

Richard R. Green Memorial Scholarships are annually renewable merit awards of up to $15,000 ($60,000 over four years) depending on academic ability. These scholarships are offered by the school to academically talented students within groups traditionally underrepresented in higher education.

> SUCCESS **Academic Advancement Services (AAP)**

Members of the Tutorial Services staff work with participants in the Susquehanna University Academic Advancement Program. AAP helps selected students make the transition to college life within the Susquehanna University community. Students enrolled in AAP are required to work with tutors in subject relevant to their coursework at least seven times each semester and meet with an assigned academic mentor on a weekly basis during fall semester. Meetings during spring semester are scheduled based on first semester performance.

FAST FACTS

STUDENT PROFILE

# of degree-seeking undergraduates	2,079
% male/female	47/53
% African-American	3
% American Indian or Alaska Native	<1
% Asian or Pacific Islander	2
% Hispanic	2
% Pell grant recipients	15

First-generation and minority alumni Michael Ozlanksi '05, founder, Susquehanna's Students in Free Enterprise (SIFE) team, accountant, PricewaterhouseCoopers; Michael Collins '73, senior vice president, Federal Reserve Bank of Philadelphia

ACADEMICS

full-time faculty	128
full-time minority faculty	19
student-faculty ratio	13:1
average class size	18
% first-year retention rate	85
% graduation rate (6 years)	82

Popular majors Business Administration/ Management, Communications Studies/Speech Communication and Rhetoric

CAMPUS LIFE

% live on campus (% freshmen)	75 (97)

Multicultural student clubs and organizations Asian Student Coalition, Black Student Union, Gay/Straight Alliance, Hispanic Organization for Latino Awareness, Diversity Council, Peer Diversity Trainers, R.E.A.L. Conversations (Relationships, Ethnicity, Activism, Life), SU Roots Project

Athletics NCAA Division III, Commonwealth Conference, Middle Atlantic States Collegiate Athletic Conference

ADMISSIONS

# of applicants	2,777
% accepted	73
# of first-year students enrolled	632
SAT Critical Reading range	500-610
SAT Math range	520-600
SAT Writing	500-610
ACT range	21-26
average HS GPA	3.2

Deadlines

early decision	11/15
regular decision	3/1
application fee (online)	$35 ($35)
fee waiver for applicants with financial need	yes

COST & AID

tuition	$32,450
room & board	$8,800
total need-based institutional scholarships/grants	n/a
% of students apply for need-based aid	75
% of students receive aid	65
% receiving need-based scholarship or grant aid	90
% receiving aid whose need was fully met	39
average aid package	$22,907
average student loan debt upon graduation	$17,222

Swarthmore College

Swarthmore, founded by Quakers in 1864, is a nonsectarian, liberal arts college and a forward-thinking school that encourages students to discuss and embrace their passion, whether it's ending genocide, singing in a gospel choir or building a robot. The lush campus facility, with its outstanding resources and distinguished faculty, promises students a memorable and rewarding college life. One of the many compelling features of Swarthmore is its size. As a highly-regarded private Pennsylvania college with about 1,500 students, the college basks in the positives of being small, yet consistently competitive. Located on a 399-acre campus, Swarthmore boasts an 8:1 student-to-faculty ratio, allowing rich academic relationships to develop between students and faculty.

> ACCESS Chester Children's Chorus

Children living in the Chester-Upland School District are given the opportunity to expand their intellectual and cultural horizons through the Chester Children's Chorus. The rigorous musical training includes school year and summer rehearsals, a full day Summer Learning Program with two to three hours of music daily plus reading, science, art and African Dance and Drumming, all taking place at Swarthmore College in the state-of-the-art Lang Music Building.

> ACCESS Science for Kids (SFK)

The Science for Kids program, held on campus during the summer, exposes elementary school children from Chester, PA to a variety of experiences in science and math. The SFK program is one of several innovations in science education supported by a $1.6 million grant from the Howard Hughes Medical Institute (HHMI) designed to foster diversity and interdisciplinary thinking and teaching. Since 2004, the five-week summer program has had students participating in science workshops taught by Swarthmore faculty, instructors and undergraduate SFK counselors.

> OPPORTUNITY Discover Swarthmore!

Discover Swarthmore! is a weekend overnight program for prospective students of color. High school seniors accepted to the program will receive an all-expenses-paid trip to campus to experience a lot of what Swarthmore has to offer. Discover Swarthmore! events include student hosted social events, financial aid workshops, panel discussions on the value of a liberal arts education, lunch and dinner with faculty, deans and students, the opportunity to attend classes, campus tours, and an overnight in the dorms hosted by a current Swarthmore student.

> SUCCESS Tri-College Summer Institute

The Tri-College Summer Institute Program is sponsored by Bryn Mawr, Haverford, and Swarthmore Colleges for first-year students who are interested in exploring issues of multicultural identity and leadership, especially relating to race, class, and gender. The program consists of a series of interactive workshops and seminars led by administrators and Student Resource Persons (SRPs) from each of the three colleges.

> SUCCESS Swarthmore's Externship Program

Swarthmore's Externship Program enables students to spend a week immersed in the activities and work life in a career of their interest by providing shadowing opportunities with college alumni. Currently, programs are available in New York, Philadelphia, Washington, D.C., San Francisco and Boston.

Swarthmore College
500 College Avenue
Swarthmore, PA 19081
Ph: (800) 667-3110 / (610) 328-8300
admissions@swarthmore.edu
www.swarthmore.edu

F A S T   F A C T S

STUDENT PROFILE
# of degree-seeking undergraduates	1,505
% male/female	48/52
% African American	10
% American Indian or Alaska Native	1
% Asian or Pacific Islander	16
% Hispanic	11
% White	45
% International	7
% Pell grant recipients	14

ACADEMICS
full-time faculty	173
full-time minority faculty	30
student-faculty ratio	8:1
average class size	15
% first-year retention rate	99
% graduation rate (6 years)	93

Popular majors Biology, Engineering, Political Science, English, Economics

CAMPUS LIFE
% live on campus (% fresh.)	95 (100)

Multicultural student clubs and organizations ENLACE (Latino Student Organization), MULTI (Multicultural Student Organization), Students of Caribbean Ancestry, Swarthmore African Student Association, Native American Student Association, COLORS, Deshi (South Asian Student Organization), Han (Korean Student Organization), Swarthmore Asian Organization, Swarthmore African American Student Society, Intercultural Center, Black Cultural Center
Athletics NCAA Division III, Centennial Conference, Eastern College Athletic Conference

ADMISSIONS
# of applicants (class of 2013)	5,575
% accepted	17
# of first-year students enrolled	394
SAT Critical Reading range	670-770
SAT Math range	670-770
SAT Writing range	670-770
ACT range	29-33
average HS GPA	n/a

Deadlines
early decision	11/15
regular decision	1/2
application fee (online)	$60 ($60)
fee waiver for applicants with financial need	yes

COST & AID
tuition	$39,260
room & board	$11,900
total need-based institutional scholarships/grants	$23,400,000
% of students apply for need-based aid	78
% of students receive aid	50
% receiving need-based scholarship or grant aid	100
% receiving aid whose need was fully met	100
average aid package	$35,238
average student loan debt upon graduation	$0

Temple University

Temple University attracts the nation's brightest and most motivated minds from all 50 states and 130 foreign countries. Offering a combination of large-school resources and a small-school feel, Temple has something for every kind of student. Students choose between suburban and city campuses. Temple University instills a sense of global perspective in their students and offers the ability to study at their campuses in Rome, Italy and Tokyo, Japan. With an average class-size of just 27, students have the access they need to thrive within the classroom. Temple is renowned in areas such as Business, Communications, Education, Art, Music, Science, and the Health Professions. With a campus that is home to 20,000 students, activities are as diverse as the student body. In addition to cultural, athletic, and social events on campus, students always have the nation's 6th largest city at their fingertips.

> ## OPPORTUNITY **Philidelphia Diamond Scholars Program**

The Temple University Philadelphia Diamond Scholars program, or PhDS for short, is a mentoring program administered by the Center for Social Justice and Multicultural Education of the Office of Multicultural Affairs to improve the retention and graduation rates of Temple University students from Philadelphia. Scholars receive support from a wide array of student leaders, as well as administrators and alumni who participate in various program activities. The program is open to any incoming new or first year transfer student who is committed to being academically successful at Temple by participating in a variety of academic, social and professional development activities.

> ## SUCCESS **First Year Seminar I and II**

First Year Seminar I is a 1-credit academic course that introduces first-year students to the opportunities and rigors of higher education, as well as to the skills needed to use academic resources successfully in college. The topics covered in the seminar help first year students articulate and reach their academic goals. Seminar II is a 1-credit course that introduces first-year students discovering major interests through applied learning and other career-oriented experiences. The course exposes students to career paths and encourages major exploration through discussions with faculty, informational interviews, reading, and opportunities to practice skills needed to be a more efficient student.

> ## SUCCESS **Academic Resource Center**

The Academic Resource Center offers University Studies students a place to explore majors and career options. They can find information on Temple majors ("checksheets"), reference their career library, or pick up a test that can help you learn about your career interests.

> ## SUCCESS **University Writing Center**

The Writing Center offers a variety of services designed to support Temple students in their writing. The most important of these services is one-on-one tutoring, and it is available to undergraduate and graduate students across the curriculum. Tutoring is available on a drop-in basis or by appointment, and e-mail tutoring is available through the Web site. In addition, the Writing Center offers in-class writing workshops.

Temple University
1801 North Broad St.
Philadelphia, PA 19122
Ph: (888) 340-2222 / (215) 204-7200
tuadm@temple.edu
www.temple.edu

FAST FACTS

STUDENT PROFILE

# of degree-seeking undergraduates	25,598
% male/female	46/54
% African-American	16.8
% American Indian or Alaska Native	0.3
% Asian or Pacific Islander	10.1
% Hispanic	3.7
% White	57.8
% International	2.7
% Pell grant recipients	32

ACADEMICS

full-time faculty	1,384
full-time minority faculty	216
student-faculty ratio	17:1
average class size	27
% first-year retention rate	88
% graduation rate (6 years)	67

Popular majors Biology, Psychology, Elementary Education, Accounting, Marketing

CAMPUS LIFE

% live on campus (% fresh.)	19 (79)

Multicultural student clubs and organizations Asian Student Association, Asociacion de Estudiantes Latinos, Black Public Relations Society, Black Student Union, Esencia Latina, National Association of Black Accountants, National Society of Black Engineers, Organization of African Students, Society of Emerging African Leaders, Student Organization for Caribbean Awareness

Athletics NCAA Division I, Atlantic-10 Conference

ADMISSIONS

# of freshman applicants	18,574
% accepted	61
# of first-year students enrolled	4,203
SAT Critical Reading range	490-600
SAT Math range	510-610
SAT Writing	500-600
ACT range	21-26
average HS GPA	3.41

Deadlines

regular decision	3/1
application fee (online)	$50 ($25)
fee waiver for applicants with financial need	yes

COST & AID

tuition	in-state: $11,174; out-of-state: $20,454
room & board	$9,198
total need-based institutional scholarships/grants	$81,734,533
% of students apply for need-based aid	89
% of students receive aid	77
% receiving need-based scholarship or grant aid	64
% receiving aid whose need was fully met	27
average aid package	$15,110
average student loan debt upon graduation	$29,900

University of Pennsylvania

Founded by Benjamin Franklin in 1740, the University of Pennsylvania is the nation's oldest university and a member of the Ivy League. The university offers undergraduate programs in the College of Arts & Sciences, the School of Engineering & Applied Science, the School of Nursing, and the Wharton School (Business). Penn's beautiful Philadelphia campus combines the best elements of a traditional collegiate experience with the excitement and energy of city living. The University of Pennsylvania is a popular choice among high achieving students who are the first in their families to attend college. Family income is not considered in the admissions process — the university is "need-blind" and committed to meeting 100 percent of demonstrated financial need. More than 260 years after its founding, it remains faithful to Franklin's philosophy of clear-headed practicality and limitless intellectual inquiry.

> ### ACCESS QuestBridge College Prep Scholarship

QuestBridge has partnered with the University of Pennsylvania to offer students a unique opportunity to take college-level courses on a top-tier university campus while residing in a dormitory with peers from across the country and the world. These scholarships offer outstanding low-income students a special chance to experience life beyond high school and to see first-hand what to expect from attending a selective university.

> ### OPPORTUNITY Loan-Free Aid for Qualifying Students

All undergraduate students eligible for financial aid receive loan-free aid packages, regardless of family income level, making it possible for students from a broad range of economic backgrounds to graduate debt-free. This initiative will ensure that talented, high-achieving students can chart their educational path without regard to financial resources. Typical students from families with income less than $40,000 will pay no tuition, fees, room or board (receiving aid of approximately $53,000). Students from typical families with incomes less than $90,000 will pay no tuition and fees (receiving aid of approximately $38,000).

> ### SUCCESS Pre-Freshman Program (PFP) and Pennsylvania College Achievement Program (PENNCAP)

The Pre-Freshman Program, a four-week summer academic experience, helps students become acclimated to the university. Through PENNCAP, academically talented students, many from low-income or educationally disadvantaged backgrounds, receive coaching, counseling, academic support and assistance in identifying personal priorities, clarifying career objectives and developing a financial plan.

> ### SUCCESS Cultural Resource Centers

Cultural resource centers are important part of the Penn community. Student leaders and staff mentors inspire involvement and facilitate communication among groups across campus, creating a network of personal and academic support communities. Centers serve as meeting places for many cultural groups, and include the Greenfield Intercultural Center, La Casa Latina, the Lesbian Gay Bisexual Transgender Center, Makuu: The Black Student Cultural Center, and the Pan Asian American Community House.

"Coming from a family of Penn alums, I grew up not too far from Philadelphia, but it wasn't until I came to Penn that I really had the chance to explore everything that Philly has to offer. One of the things that I love about Penn is that it really feels like Philadelphia is an extension of the campus. You can walk right off the campus and experience everything that Philadelphia has to offer. I'll go downtown and look at the architecture, or to the art museum to see a new exhibit. As a student, there's just something about Philadelphia that just draws you in makes you want to stay."

– Bryce S., '10 Bristol, PA Chemical and Biomolecular Engineering (concentration: Pharmaceutics and Biotechnology)

University of Pennsylvania
Office of Undergraduate Admissions
1 College Hall, Room 1
Philadelphia, PA 19104-6376
Ph: (215) 898-7507
info@admissions.upenn.edu
www.admissions.upenn.edu

F A S T   F A C T S

STUDENT PROFILE
# of degree-seeking undergraduates	9,490
% male/female	49.1/50.9
% African-American	8.0
% American Indian or Alaska Native	0.5
% Asian or Pacific Islander	18.8
% Hispanic	6.5
% White	40.0
% International	10.3
% Race/ethnicity unknown	16.0

First-generation and minority alumni Harold Ford Jr., former U.S. Representative from Tennessee, current chairman of the Democratic Leadership Council; John Legend, five-time Grammy Award-winning recording artist; William Thaddeus Coleman Jr., first African-American Supreme Court law clerk and co-author of NAACP brief on Brown v. Board of Education; Sadie Tanner Mossell Alexander, first African-American woman to earn a Ph.D. (economics)

ACADEMICS
full-time faculty	2,549
student-faculty ratio	6:1
average class size	<25
% first-year retention rate	98
% graduation rate (6 years)	95

Popular majors Business, Bioengineering, History, Economics, Nursing

CAMPUS LIFE
% live on campus (% fresh.)	62 (100)

Multicultural student clubs and organizations United Minorities Council Alliance and Understanding, Asian Pacific Student Coalition, Black Student League, Brazilian Club, Canadians at Penn, Caribbean-American Student Association, Chinese Students and Scholars, Chinese Students Association, Club Singapore, Dessalines Haitian Students Association, Hellenic Association, Hong Kong Student Association, Japan Student Association, Korean Student Association, Lambda Alliance, Mexico@Penn, Muslim Students Association, Onda Latina, Program for Awareness in Cultural Education, Penn African Students Association, Pakistan Society, Penn Arab Students Society, Penn Philippine Association, Penn Polish Society

Athletics NCAA Division I, Ivy League

ADMISSIONS (ENTERING FALL 2009)
# of applicants	22,808
% accepted	17.6
# of first-year students enrolled	2,477
SAT Critical Reading range	660-750
SAT Math range	690-780
SAT Writing range	670-760
ACT range	30-35

Deadlines
early decision	11/1
regular admission	1/1
application fee (online)	$75
fee waiver for applicants with financial need	yes

COST & AID
tuition	$40,514
room & board	$11,430
total need-based institutional scholarships/grants	>$130,000,000
% of students receive aid	60
% receiving need-based grant aid	40
% receiving aid whose need was fully met	100
average aid package	$34,435
average student loan debt upon graduation	$19,085

Ursinus College

Ursinus College
Box 1000, Main Street
Collegeville, PA 19426-1000
Ph: (610) 409-3200
admissions@ursinus.edu
www.ursinus.edu

Ursinus College is a small, private, liberal arts college dedicated to enabling students to become independent, responsible and thoughtful individuals and leaders. Ursinus is especially well-known for its first-year program, which includes a two-semester seminar, the Common Intellectual Experience, or CIE. This innovative-yet-traditional class is designed and taught by professors from all academic disciplines. Ursinus is strongly linked with science and technology — the college boasts several outstanding alumni in the field and all Ursinus students are issued laptop computers upon arrival. Ursinus has a strong reputation for its close faculty mentoring and faculty-student collaboration in research as well as its robust study-abroad program. Diversity at Ursinus is supported by Multicultural Services, an institutional commitment to cultural diversity and minority success at the college. The Ursinus Bridge Program assists minority students in adjusting to college life with academic and personal support.

> ACCESS Regional Partnerships

Ursinus College has a summer collaboration with local schools that brings 40 underserved middle school students to the Ursinus campus for computer technology training and a pre-college orientation. Each year, Ursinus hosts several groups for tours of campus and college awareness information sessions.

> OPPORTUNITY Tower Scholarships

African-American and Latino applicants to Ursinus who plan to pursue graduate academic work or professional school after college may be considered for the Tower Scholarship. The Tower Scholarship is an award of $27,500, renewable for four years, given to students who demonstrate superior academic and multicultural leadership achievement throughout high school.

> SUCCESS The Bridge Program

Ursinus College sponsors a three-week, pre-orientation summer program designed to help incoming first-year students of underrepresented groups make a successful transition to college. The Bridge Program utilizes a combination of college courses, necessary skill-building and social orientation. Each Bridge Program student completes a four-credit course that introduces him or her to academics at Ursinus in a small, supportive atmosphere. Students meet with a faculty member weekly to monitor progress throughout the summer and into the academic year. Bridge Program students enter their first year of college at Ursinus in good academic standing, a head start with classes and a boost in self confidence.

F A S T   F A C T S

STUDENT PROFILE

# of degree-seeking undergraduates	1,680
% male/female	48/ 52
% African-American	6
% American Indian or Alaska Native	<1
% Asian or Pacific Islander	4
% Hispanic	3
% White	73
% Pell grant recipients	18

First-generation and minority alumni Hon. Joseph Melrose, former U.S. Ambassador to Sierra Leone, senior advisor, U.S. Mission to the United Nations; Odessia Joyner, magistrate, Ninth Judicial District, Orlando, Fla.; W. Robert Crigler, Ph.D., president, Penny Lane

ACADEMICS

full-time faculty	123
full-time minority faculty	13
student-faculty ratio	12:1
average class size	16
% first-year retention rate	88
% graduation rate (6 years)	76

Popular majors Biology, Business and Economics, Psychology, English

CAMPUS LIFE

% live on campus (% fresh.)	95 (98)

Multicultural student clubs and organizations Arab Language and Culture Club, Association of Latinos Motivated to Achieve, Sankofa Umoja Nia, Southeast Asian Student Association
Athletics NCAA Division III, Centennial Conference

ADMISSIONS

# of applicants	6,192
% accepted	55
# of first-year students enrolled	548
SAT Critical Reading range	570-680
SAT Math range	570-670
SAT Writing range	560-660
ACT range	25-29
average HS GPA	3.7

Deadlines

early decision	1/15
regular decision	2/15
application fee (online)	$50 ($50)
fee waiver for applicants with financial need	yes

COST & AID

tuition	$38,670
room & board	$9,250
total need-based institutional scholarships/grants	n/a
% of students apply for need-based aid	84
% of students receive aid	100
% receiving need-based scholarship or grant aid	99
% receiving aid whose need was fully met	27
average aid package	$25,675
average student loan debt upon graduation	$21,171

York College of Pennsylvania

York College of Pennsylvania is a mid-sized, four-year, private, liberal arts college founded in 1787. The college cultivates a teaching and learning environment characterized by individual attention to students, high-quality classroom instruction, thoughtful application of relevant technology, encouragement of life-long learning, attention to critical thinking skills, and strict adherence to principles of academic honesty. Moreover, York College is committed to attracting applicants from a variety of social, economic and geographic backgrounds. Additionally, the college plays a special role in addressing the higher education aspirations of the people of York County.

> **ACCESS** **York College Community Opportunity Scholarship Program**

The York College Community Opportunity Scholarship Program identifies and prepares York City youth as future business and professional leaders for the York community. The York College Community Opportunity Scholarship Program provides select high school students with additional enrichment and support services that lead them to successful high school completion and college readiness. Upon high school graduation these students receive full scholarships to attend York College of Pennsylvania.

> **OPPORTUNITY** **Prospective Student Programs**

York College of Pennsylvania offers prospective students with a variety of programs to introduce them to college life and meet with faculty and students, including senior open house, sophomore and junior open house, multicultural overnight and class visits for accepted students.

> **OPPORTUNITY** **WHTF Tim Drayer Scholarship Fund**

York College of Pennsylvania's WHTF Tim Drayer Scholarship Fund was established as a permanent source of scholarship funds for African-American and Hispanic students pursuing an education at York. Scholarships may be awarded to freshman students who have attained a satisfactory secondary school average and show promise for achievement and to full-time upperclassmen who have maintained a minimum GPA of 2.0.

> **OPPORTUNITY** **Rehmeyer Minority Opportunity Scholarship Fund**

York College of Pennsylvania established the Herbert M. Rehmeyer Minority Opportunity Scholarship Fund through a grant from the H. M. Rehmeyer trust. The fund is available to African-American and Hispanic residents of York County who matriculate at York College of Pennsylvania. Scholarships may be awarded to entering freshman students who show promise for achievement and to returning students who have maintained a minimum GPA of 2.0.

> **SUCCESS** **Student Affairs Office**

The York Student Affairs Office serves all students. The department sponsors many events on campus, including multicultural celebrations, with a goal of enriching the overall educational experience for York College of Pennsylvania students. Committed to education within a diverse setting, the Multicultural Affairs Office helps to prepare students to become understanding and culturally aware of other individuals different from themselves in society, and recognize and celebrate their similarities.

> **SUCCESS** **Academic Affairs Department**

The York College Academic Affairs Department provides students with academic support services through the Learning Resource Center and the Academic Advising Office. The Learning Resources Center offers tutoring services and houses the Writing Center. Every student at York College is assigned an academic adviser to guide the student in academic matters.

York College of Pennsylvania
441 Country Club Road
York, PA 17403-3651
Ph: (800) 455-8018 / (717) 849-1600
admissions@ycp.edu
www.ycp.edu

FAST FACTS

STUDENT PROFILE
# of degree-seeking undergraduates	5,126
% male/female	47/53
% African-American	3
% American Indian or Alaska Native	<1
% Asian or Pacific Islander	1
% Hispanic	2
% White	89
% Pell grant recipients	14

ACADEMICS
full-time faculty	154
full-time minority faculty	8
student-faculty ratio	15:1
average class size	21
% first-year retention rate	78
% graduation rate (6 years)	65

Popular majors Nursing, Business Administration, Sport Management, Elementary Education, Criminal Justice, Biology, Accounting, Psychology, Mechanical Engineering

CAMPUS LIFE
% live on campus (% fresh.)	39 (71)

Multicultural student clubs and organizations Hispanic Cultural Society, International Students Club, Unity Club, Multicultural Affairs Council
Athletics NCAA Division III, Capital Athletic Conference

ADMISSIONS
# of applicants	7,395
% accepted	60
# of first-year students enrolled	1,582
SAT Critical Reading range	490-570
SAT Math range	500-590
SAT Writing range	480-570
ACT range	21-25
average HS GPA	3.5

Deadlines
regular decision	rolling
application fee (online)	$30 ($30)
fee waiver for applicants with financial need	yes

COST & AID
tuition	$14,460
room & board	$8,080
total need-based institutional scholarships/grants	n/a
% of students apply for need-based aid	79
% of students receive aid	49
% receiving need-based scholarship or grant aid	69
% receiving aid whose need was fully met	28
average aid package	$10,204
average student loan debt upon graduation	$20,625

Brown University

Brown University is a leading Ivy League institution located in Providence, Rhode Island — three hours northeast of New York City and one hour south of Boston. Brown is proud of its distinctive undergraduate program, world-class faculty, and tradition of innovative and multi-disciplinary study. Students at Brown are distinguished by their academic excellence, self-direction, and collaborative style of learning. As the architects of their own education, undergraduates work closely with advisors to design a curriculum that allows them to maximize their education goals. Brown faculty are preeminent in their fields, deeply committed to teaching undergraduates, and are leaders in advancing knowledge. With over 80 fields of concentration (majors), myriad research and individualized study opportunities, and numerous study abroad options, Brown University provides a wealth of resources to its students.

> ACCESS Outreach Efforts

Through its own outreach efforts and partnerships with community based organizations and schools Brown University participates in a variety of programs designed to assist students of underrepresented groups in the college application process as well as fostering success for students once they attend college.

> OPPORTUNITY Fall Open House

A day-long program is held each Fall on the Brown campus which is particularly tailored towards the interests of underrepresented minority students.

> OPPORTUNITY Admissions

Brown University admissions is "need-blind," meaning that decisions regarding admission are made without consideration of the applicant's financial need. All admitted student will be awarded the financial aid necessary for them to attend Brown. The typical financial aid package allows students whose family income is less than $100,000 per year to graduate with no debt when they graduate from Brown.

> SUCCESS Multicultural Center

Brown's Multicultural Center is the heart of the community for students of color. It is designed to serve their needs in particular, as well as to promote racial and ethnic pluralism on campus.

> SUCCESS Fall Pre-Orientation Programs

An intensive, five-day seminar program is offered to selected incoming students who would benefit from additional orientation to Brown's academic culture. The program includes five classes taught by distinguished Brown professors from a range of academic disciplines. Students complete reading and writing assignments and work with staff at Brown's Writing Center. Social programming helps students build community and learn about Brown's campus. Brown's Multicultural Center hosts a community-building event for entering students that promotes interracial understanding. The program helps all students identify and increase their awareness of issues encountered by minority students at Brown. During the weekend following the first several days of fall classes, students may participate in a program which helps students build community and leadership skills through dialogue, interaction, and outreach across cultural experiences and group identities, including race, ethnicity, class, gender, sexual identity, ability, and religious affiliation.

> SUCCESS A Variety of Academic Enhancement Programs

The Dean of the College office provides a variety of academic support programs such as tutoring and study skills workshops. It also offers advising to students regarding research opportunities and the planning of independent study projects which encourage and facilitate the optimal use of the academic resources at Brown.

"As a Hmong student, my involvement in Southeast Asian Heritage Week gave me a comfortable space to explore my identity and its politics. The experience was not only personally and culturally meaningful, but also academically enriching."

– Teng Y., '11
Milwaukee, WI

Brown University
45 Prospect Street
PO Box 1876
Providence, RI 02912
Ph: (401) 863-2378
admission_undergraduate@brown.edu
www.brown.edu

FAST FACTS

STUDENT PROFILE

# of degree-seeking undergraduates	5,800
% male/female	52/48
% African American	7
% American Indian or Alaska Native	1
% Asian or Pacific Islander	16
% Hispanic	9
% White	40
% International	9
% Pell grant recipients	11

ACADEMICS

full-time faculty	700
full-time minority faculty	105
student-faculty ratio	9:1
average class size	<20
% first-year retention rate	97
% graduation rate (6 years)	95

Popular majors Biological Sciences, Economics, International Relations, History, Neuroscience

CAMPUS LIFE

% live on campus	79

Multicultural student clubs and organizations 40+

Athetics NCAA Division I, Ivy League

ADMISSIONS

# of applicants	24,988
% accepted	10.8
SAT Critical Reading range (middle 50%)	670-770
SAT Math range (middle 50%)	680-780
ACT range (middle 50%)	26-32
average HS GPA	n/a

Deadlines

early decision	11/1
regular decision	1/1
application fee	$75 ($75)
fee waiver for applicants with financial need	yes

COST & AID

tuition	$38,048
room & board	$10,280
total need-based institutional scholarships/grants	$3,313,882
% of students apply for need-based aid	57
% of students receive aid	n/a
% receiving need-based scholarship or grant aid	41
% receiving aid whose need was fully met	100
average aid package	$33,226
average student loan debt upon graduation	$19,390

Providence College

Founded in 1917, Providence College is a four-year, private, Catholic, co-educational liberal arts college. Providence is the only college in the United States under the stewardship of the Dominican Friars, a Roman Catholic order which emphasizes quality teaching and scholarship. As a result, Providence actively cultivates aesthetic values within the context of the Judeo-Christian heritage. Encouraging the deepest respect for the essential dignity, freedom and equality of every person, Providence welcomes qualified students from all religious, racial, and ethnic backgrounds.

> ACCESS The Feinstein Institute for Public Service (FIPS)

Founded in 1993, the Feinstein Institute for Public Service seeks to provide students with an understanding of how to be thoughtful and productive citizens in a democratic society, stimulate an understanding of — and appreciation for — community, and make positive contributions to the larger community by providing students with opportunities for learning through community service. For example, Providence students may tutor and/or volunteer at Times2 Academy, a K-12 school that helps to prepare multicultural and first-generation students for careers in mathematics, engineering and science.

> OPPORTUNITY Multicultural Scholarship Program (MSP)

Providence College's Multicultural Scholarship Program is a unique system of mentoring, with opportunities designed to support the recipients of select multicultural scholarships. In line with Providence's holistic Catholic and Dominican mission, MSP scholars receive academic advising, transitional guidance, professional development and mentorship from the MSP program director. In return, MSP scholars are expected to share their culture through leadership activities, to serve with varying student clubs and organizations specific to their majors and to their general social interest.

> OPPORTUNITY Martin Luther King, Jr. Scholarship

The Martin Luther King, Jr. Scholarship assists undergraduate racial and ethnic minority students and others who demonstrate a desire and ability to contribute to the college's diversity. Successful applicants demonstrate solid academic achievement, outstanding leadership and community service activities, strong personal qualities and financial need.

> OPPORTUNITY Cunningham Scholarship

Recruiting and maintaining a diverse student body is central to Providence's mission. In response to the growing population of Southeast Asians in Rhode Island, Providence established the Cunningham Scholarship in 1985. Available to qualified students who demonstrate financial need, this scholarship provides full tuition renewable annually for four years. Recipients meet regularly with an adviser who monitors their progress and arranges support services as necessary.

> OPPORTUNITY Supplemental Educational Opportunity Grants (SEOG)

Supplemental Educational Opportunity Grants are awarded to undergraduate students with exceptional need. Priority awarding of the SEOG by Providence College is given to students who have demonstrated Pell eligibility. Awards ranged from $250 to $4,000 in the 2006-2007 academic year. These awards allow Providence College to attract a more socio-economically varied group of students, enhancing both the lives of recipients as well as the lives of the Providence community at large.

> SUCCESS Balfour Center for Multicultural Affairs (BCMA)

The Balfour Center for Multicultural Affairs provides the resources and support needed to increase cross-cultural appreciation and understanding between students, faculty and staff. To achieve this mission, the center sponsors numerous events, programs, trainings, seminars and workshops throughout the campus. Student volunteers in the Peer Mentors program help freshmen make a successful transition to higher education. Mentors offer support, tutoring and information on social gatherings and academic and career opportunities.

Providence College
Harkins Hall 222
549 River Avenue
Providence, RI 02918-0001
Ph: (800) 721-6444 / (401) 865-1000
admissions@providence.edu
www.providence.edu

F A S T   F A C T S

STUDENT PROFILE
# of degree-seeking undergraduates	3,850
% male/female	44/56
% African American	2
% American Indian	0
% Asian	2
% Caucasian	84
% Hispanic	2
% Pell grant recipients	8

First-generation and minority alumni Otis Thorpe '84, former NBA player

ACADEMICS
full-time faculty	295
student-faculty ratio	12:1
average class size	22
% first-year retention rate	92
% graduation rate (6 years)	86

Popular majors Special/Elementary Education, Marketing, Management, Biology, English, Political Science

CAMPUS LIFE
% live on campus (% freshmen)	80 (97)

Multicultural student clubs and organizations African American Society, Middle Eastern Student Association (MESA), Amigos Unidos, Asian American Club, Board of Multicultural Student Affairs (BMSA), Circolo Italiano, Clube Portugues, Eastern European Union, French Club, Gaelic Society, The Society Organized Against Racism (SOAR)

Athletics NCAA Division I, Big East Conference, Hockey East Association, Metro Atlantic Athletic Conference

ADMISSIONS
# of applicants	9,802
% accepted	42
SAT Critical Reading range	530-640
SAT Math range	540-650
ACT range	23-28
average HS GPA	3.47 unweighted

Deadlines
early decision application	11/1
regular admission	1/15
application fee (online)	$50 ($50)

COST & AID
tuition	$28,920
room & board	$10,335
% of students receiving aid	87
% receiving need-based scholarship or grant aid	96
% receiving aid whose need was fully met	17
average aid package	$17,906
average student loan debt upon graduation	$20,362

Roger Williams University

Roger Williams University is a 54-year-old independent, coeducational liberal arts university that has quickly established itself as a leader in higher education. A dynamic educational environment in which students live and learn to be global citizens, the university is committed to its mantra of learning to bridge the world. With 42 academic programs and a robust array of co-curricular activities available on its waterfront campus in historic Bristol, RI, the University looks to a set of core values in fulfilling its mission to prepare students for life as 21st century citizen-scholars. Following in the footsteps of the institution's namesake, it is dedicated to the principles Roger Williams advocated – education, freedom and tolerance. Roger Williams University places particular emphasis on the value of civil discourse and is home to an array of initiatives designed to bring to campus individuals from a tremendous variety of backgrounds and perspectives.

> ACCESS Discovery Series

Each year, the University hosts a series of college discovery events for students from local school districts, many of whom are first-generation and from underrepresented communities. Annual events include 5th Grade Day, a program that brings local fifth-graders to campus for tours and student presentations; the FIRST LEGO League Robotics Competition, which brings young minds to campus to inspire their curiosity in technology and engineering; and GRRL Tech, a collaborative, interactive technology exposition for outstanding young women interested in science and technology education. RWU also hosts Junior Jumpstart, a program aimed at high school students and their parents who wish to learn how to navigate the college application process, annually.

"In high school, I did Bridge to Success for four years. Every Wednesday I came to campus and just absolutely fell in love with RWU. I applied to all of the schools in the area, but I definitely knew this was my first choice. When I got the Intercultural Leadership Award, it sealed the deal."

*– Melisa C., '11
Newport, RI
Anthropology, Sociology*

> ACCESS Bridge to Success

The University's Bridge to Success Program (BTS), founded in 1993 through a grant from the Balfour Foundation, partners with select Newport and Providence high schools and service organizations to promote the development of academic, social and emotional support systems for high school students in under-resourced communities. BTS provides academic tutoring, student-to-student mentoring, intensive college prep, and parental outreach to hundreds of high school students throughout Rhode Island so that they may achieve academic success toward admission into RWU or any other four-year college/university.

> OPPORTUNITY The Intercultural Leadership Award (ILA)

Established in 2007, the Intercultural Leadership Award program at Roger Williams provides financial and programmatic support to high-achieving students who are proven community leaders and who have overcome a significant life challenge while meeting at least one of the following three criteria: first-generation college student, ethnic diversity, or English as the second language spoken at home. In its initial 2007-08 cycle Roger Williams welcomed 13 ILA students, granting them $26,000 scholarships and organizing a structured series of co-curricular learning opportunities.

> SUCCESS The Intercultural Center

A landing zone for international students, spiritual life, LGBT student advocacy, the Multicultural Student Union, and Bridge to Success, the university's Intercultural Center is a nexus of different social identities. At its essence, the center provides a welcoming environment for all students in which ideas concerning personal identity and diversity are discussed freely. The Intercultural Center sponsors a wide range of cultural programming at RWU, all of which encourage an open dialogue on diversity, social justice and global citizenship.

Roger Williams University
Office of Admission
1 Old Ferry Road
Bristol, RI 02809
Ph: (401) 254-3500
admit@rwu.edu
www.rwu.edu

F A S T   F A C T S

STUDENT PROFILE
# of degree-seeking undergraduates	4,267
% male/female	51/49
% African American	2
% American Indian or Alaska Native	<1
% Asian or Pacific Islander	1
% Hispanic	4
% White	87
% International	2
% Pell grant recipients	11

ACADEMICS
full-time faculty	210
full-time minority faculty	30
student-faculty ratio	12:1
average class size	10-19
% first-year retention rate	82
% graduation rate (6 years)	58

Popular majors Architecture, Business/Commerce, Psychology

CAMPUS LIFE
% live on campus	66

Multicultural student clubs and organizations
Multicultural Student Union

ADMISSIONS
# of applicants	8,220
% accepted	77
# of first-year students enrolled	954
SAT Critical Reading range	500-580
SAT Math range	510-600
SAT Writing range	480-580
ACT range	21-25
average HS GPA	3.17

Deadlines
early action	11/1
regular decision	2/1
application fee (online)	$50 ($50)
fee waiver for applicants with financial need	yes

COST & AID
tuition	$27,840
room & board	$12,740
total need-based institutional scholarships/grants	$23,792,788
% of students apply for need-based aid	72
% of students receive aid	84
% receiving need-based scholarship or grant aid	35
% receiving aid whose need was fully met	4
average aid package	$17,017
average student loan debt upon graduation	$32,856

Anderson University

Anderson University is a comprehensive, private, co-educational, liberal arts university offering a high-quality education in a Christian environment. Anderson University encourages faculty-student interaction, and Anderson faculty members are committed to helping students develop and grow intellectually, physically, socially, morally and spiritually. Anderson offers an intimate, welcoming campus environment in which students can mature in their own unique way while having fun. A Christ-centered education provides opportunities for personal growth through emphasis of service to others. In addition to hosting many civic events that bring students and the local community together, more than 50 percent of Anderson students participate in community service projects.

> ACCESS Minorities Involved in Change (MIC)

Minorities Involved in Change, a campus organization, seeks to unite Anderson University and the community through campus and community projects, including assisting with youth activities at Fusion Warehouse, a safe, positive environment where students can gain vocational skills. MIC students also work with after-school programs at selected elementary schools and assist in the clean-up of community parks. A primary focus of MIC is to benefit minority students academically, spiritually, culturally and financially through scholarships.

> OPPORTUNITY Diversity Scholarships

Anderson University offers three different scholarship opportunities to students from diverse backgrounds, including international students. The Diversity Scholarship is awarded in the amount of $1,000 to students with a minimum of 3.0 GPA, 950 SAT and 19 ACT. The William A. Floyd Scholarship, in the amount of $2,000, is offered to boarding students with a minimum of 3.5 GPA, 1050 SAT and 21 ACT. The Diversity Education Scholarship is awarded in the amount of $1,000 to education majors with a 3.0 GPA, 950 SAT and 19 ACT. All applicants must submit an essay on their role in adding to diversity at the university.

> SUCCESS AUTS Program

Anderson University Transforming Students (AUTS) is a program designed to allow entering students to achieve academically, develop socially and grow spiritually. Through the AUTS Program, all first-year students are provided a personal support mentoring program that is structured to help students make a successful transition from high school to college. In addition, students complete an extensive academic and social skills inventory during orientation, which provides important information to academic advisers and freshmen mentors.

> SUCCESS The Journey

The Journey, a unique Anderson University program, has been created to provide students with opportunities to gain knowledge and grow through a wide range of learning experiences such as workshops, short courses, lectures, plays and musical events, as well as weekly community worship. Students are required to attend 12 Journey events during each semester; eight of the 12 must be Campus Worship services. The other four must be part of a cultural experience and focus on personal achievement, college survival or career preparation.

Anderson University
316 Boulevard
Anderson, SC 29621-4035
Ph: (864) 231-2030
admissions@andersonuniversity.edu
www.andersonuniversity.edu

F A S T   F A C T S

STUDENT PROFILE

# of degree-seeking undergraduates	1,977
% male/female	36/64
% African-American	10.8
% American Indian or Alaska Native	<1
% Asian or Pacific Islander	1.2
% Hispanic	2
% White	83.2
% International	2
% Pell grant recipients	33.5

First-generation and minority alumni Marian Chapman Robinson, community liaison with College of Health, Education & Human Dev., Clemson University; Dr. Cacia Soares Welch, endocrinologist; Michael Henri Thompson, information technology officer; Natasha K. Freeman Armfield, senior sales representative for Eli Lilly and Company; Shawn Williams Clinkscales, director of human resources, SC School District, Edgefield Co.; Alphaeus B. Anderson, founder/owner of ABA Ministries, Music2ChangeU Productions

ACADEMICS

full-time faculty	76
full-time minority faculty	n/a
student-faculty ratio	17:1
average class size	n/a
% first-year retention rate	61.9
% graduation rate (6 years)	48.0

Popular majors Education, Business, Fine Arts (especially Graphic Design), Psychology

CAMPUS LIFE

% live on campus (% fresh.)	57 (86)

Multicultural student clubs and organizations Minorities Involved in Change, International Club
Athletics NCAA Division II, Carolinas Conference

ADMISSIONS

# of applicants	1,296
% accepted	78
# of first-year students enrolled	835
SAT Critical Reading range	410-560
SAT Math range	480-560
SAT Writing range	448-570
ACT range	18-24
average HS GPA	3.3
Deadlines	
regular decision	7/1
application fee (online)	$25 ($25)
fee waiver for applicants with financial need	yes

COST & AID

tuition	$19,212
room & board	$7,600
total need-based institutional scholarships/grants	n/a
% of students apply for need-based aid	83.2
% of students receive aid	100
% receiving need-based scholarship or grant aid	100
% receiving aid whose need was fully met	83.1
average aid package	$17,200
average student loan debt upon graduation	$15,125

Claflin University

Claflin University is a small, private, historically black, liberal arts institution affiliated with the United Methodist Church. At the undergraduate level, the university emphasizes a broad, liberal arts education designed to produce graduates who understand themselves and the historical and social forces that impact the world around them, which includes religious and aesthetic values. Central to the university's success is the unique Freshman College, a program in which new students are introduced to college life in a supportive learning environment for a full year. Half of Claflin students are first-generation students and the university strongly encourages first-generation and minority outreach through a variety of student services.

> ACCESS **GEAR UP**

The Claflin University GEAR UP Program (CUGU) aims to provide academic support to local at-risk middle school students and encourages their participation and success in post-secondary education. The partnership between Claflin University and local public schools emphasizes disadvantaged students' academic achievement, college goals and parental involvement and sets high expectations for success. CUGU meets these goals through increased test scores, high school graduation rates, college enrollment rates and financial aid assistance. CUGU also provides professional development for local teachers and staff. Claflin University was the first Historically Black College and University GEAR UP grantee in the nation.

> OPPORTUNITY **Dean's Scholarships**

Claflin's Dean's Scholarships were established to consider the need of diversity and first-generation students who wish to attend the university. In addition, Diversity Scholarships are funded by the university to meet overall diversity needs. Claflin is currently seeking external funds to establish more endowed scholarships as part of its ongoing Capital Campaign.

> SUCCESS **The Freshman College**

The Freshman College is a unique and integral strategy to the success of all Claflin University students. Separate from upperclassmen, freshmen at Claflin are supported by the Freshman College, a coordination of freshman life including placement, orientation, advisement, counseling, tutoring and mentoring. The university implements an "Early Warning" system through the Freshman College to track at-risk students and give them the individual attention they need to succeed. Freshman College courses are designed to assure retention and build skills necessary for academic success. At the end of the year, students' families are invited to attend a "Parting Ceremony," marking students' graduation to sophomore year.

> SUCCESS **The SOAR Center**

The SOAR Center (Student Outreach for Academic Retention) assists Claflin students in reaching their academic and personal potentials. The SOAR Center is comprised of a coordination of all of Claflin's various student support services, including TRIO Programs, GEAR UP, and the Claflin Counseling Center. The SOAR Center also assists with discipline programs such as "Call Me MISTER," a national model for recruitment, retention and graduation of minority male teachers.

Claflin University
400 Magnolia Street
Orangebury, SC 29115
Ph: (803) 535-5404
admissions@claflin.edu
www.claflin.edu

F A S T   F A C T S

STUDENT PROFILE
# of degree-seeking undergraduates	1,657
% male/female	32/68
% African-American	94.4
% American Indian or Alaska Native	<1
% Asian or Pacific Islander	<1
% Hispanic	<1
% White	1.3
% International	3
% Pell grant recipients	85

First-generation and minority alumni Dr. Henry N. Tisdale; Arthur E. Rose; Dr. James S. Thomas; Dr. Nathaniel Middelton; Justice Ernest A. Finney. Jr

ACADEMICS
full-time faculty	104
full-time minority faculty	74
student-faculty ratio	14:1
average class size	23
% first-year retention rate	50
% graduation rate (6 years)	51

Popular majors Biology, Business Administration, Sociology

CAMPUS LIFE
% live on campus (% freshmen)	85 (90)

Multicultural student clubs and organizations
International Student Association, Ladies of Black and Gold, Ladies of Essence, NAACP, National Pre Alumni Council of the College Fund

Athletics Southern Intercollegiate Athletic Conference (SIAC)

ADMISSIONS
# of applicants	4,008
% accepted	36
# of first-year students enrolled	634
SAT Critical Reading range	400-500
SAT Math range	400-500
SAT Writing range	n/a
ACT range	n/a
average HS GPA	3.0

Deadlines
priority application	4/15
regular admission	6/30
application fee (online)	$20
fee waiver for applicants with financial need	yes

COST & AID
tuition	$12,768
room & board	$6,806
total need-based institutional scholarships/grants	$16,124,084
% of students apply for need-based aid	98
% of students receive aid	96
% receiving need-based scholarship or grant aid	88
% receiving aid whose need was fully met	18
average aid package	$15,635
average student loan debt upon graduation	$3,403

College of Charleston

Founded in 1770, the College of Charleston is a nationally recognized, public liberal arts and sciences university located in the heart of historic Charleston, S.C. Students from 50 states and territories and nearly 70 countries choose the College for its small-college feel blended with the advantages and diversity of an urban, mid-sized university. The College provides a creative and intellectually stimulating environment where students are challenged by a committed and caring faculty of distinguished teacher-scholars. The city of Charleston serves students as a learning laboratory for experiences in business, science, teaching, the humanities, languages and the arts. For multicultural and first-generation college students, the College of Charleston is a particularly strong match. The College is intimately involved with these populations and offers a number of programs catered to them.

> **ACCESS Call Me MISTER Program**

In an effort to address the critical shortage of African American male teachers, particularly in South Carolina's lowest performing schools, the School of Education, Health, and Human Performance's Call Me MISTER program selects students from among underrepresented, underserved, socio-economically disadvantaged, and educationally at-risk communities, and provides them with tuition assistance for certain approved programs of study, as well as academic, social and cultural support.

> **OPPORTUNITY Bonner Leaders Grant**

Bonner Leaders are outstanding students who commit themselves to leadership through service and making positive change across campus and in the Charleston community. This four-year, service-based scholarship program allows students to apply theory to practice through real-life work experience at area nonprofit organizations. The program also facilitates students' transition from being volunteers to becoming leaders in their community through powerful leadership-development training and education. Grant recipients receive up to $2,000 each year.

> **OPPORTUNITY Avery Scholars**

The College's Avery Research Center for African American History and Culture collects, preserves and documents the history and culture of African American's in Charleston and the South Carolina Lowcountry. The Avery Research Scholarship helps underrepresented freshman and transfer students fund their college education while also gaining valuable skills through undergraduate research.

> **SUCCESS Speedy Consolidation and Transition Program (SPECTRA)**

Through the Office of Multicultural Student Programs and Services (MSPS), the College offers a challenging transitional summer academic program, SPECTRA, for first-generation students and students from underrepresented populations who will attend the College full-time in the fall. During a five-week, on-campus experience, students learn to develop successful academic and social networks; bridge the gap between traditional, stereotypical barriers that students of color face on predominantly white campuses; and understand the academic rigors of college life. Students are further supported throughout the school year, receiving academic advising, peer mentoring, workshops, financial aid advising and special seminars.

> **SUCCESS South Carolina Alliance for Minority Participation (SCAMP)**

Another MSPS program, SCAMP, funded by the National Science Foundation, provides mentoring and summer-research opportunities to African American, Hispanic and Native American students who want to pursue a degree in the sciences, engineering or mathematics. Qualified students may receive an annual $500-$1,000 scholarship.

"College of Charleston's Multicultural Student Programs and Services has a great program for incoming minority and first-generation students. The program is called SPECTRA and I attribute much of my success at the College to the program. Because of this opportunity I was able to establish networks on campus and grow as a student."

– Katreena M., '12 Lane, SC Communication with Media Studies concentration

College of Charleston
66 George Street
Charleston, SC 29424
Ph: (843) 953-5670
admissions@cofc.edu
www.cofc.edu

FAST FACTS

STUDENT PROFILE
# of degree-seeking undergraduates	9,736
% male/female	34/66
% African American	5.4
% American Indian or Alaska Native	0.4
% Asian or Pacific Islander	2
% Hispanic	2.3
% White	82.8
% International	0.6
% Pell grant recipients	18.2

First-generation and minority alumni Kevin Summers, CIO, Whirlpool; Jon Bryant, Secret Service agent, on president's detail; Michelle Cooper, president, Institute of Higher Education Policy; Anthony Johnson, NBA player

ACADEMICS
full-time faculty	523
full-time minority faculty	53
student-faculty ratio	16:1
average class size	26.3
% first-year retention rate	82.9
% graduation rate (6 years)	64

Popular majors Biology, Communication, Business Administration, Psychology, and Political Science

CAMPUS LIFE
% live on campus (% fresh.)	33.6 (92.2)

Multicultural student clubs and organizations Black Student Union, Student Union for Multicultural Affairs, Aya Hwe M', Alpha Phi Omega Business Service Fraternity, Student Government Association: Campus Diversity Committee, Global Citizens Council, Color of We: All Power to the People, South Carolina Diversity Council, Coalition of Minority Leaders In Higher Education, Asian Student Association, Association of Black Accountants
Athletics NCAA Division I, Southern Conference

ADMISSIONS
# of applicants	11,083
% accepted	69.5
# of first-year students enrolled	2,143
SAT Critical Reading range	560-650
SAT Math range	560-640
SAT Writing	n/a
ACT range	23-27
average HS GPA	3.89

Deadlines
early action	11/1
regular decision	rolling to 4/01
application fee (online)	$50 ($50)
fee waiver for applicants with financial need	yes

COST & AID
tuition	in-state: $8,988; out-of-state:$21,846
room & board	$9,411
total need-based institutional scholarships/grants	$3,152,375
% of students apply for need-based aid	54
% of students receive aid	96
% receiving need-based scholarship or grant aid	64
% receiving aid whose need was fully met	32
average aid package	$12,697
average student loan debt upon graduation	$17,139

Furman University

Founded in 1826, Furman University is a private, coeducational institution providing engaged learning to students at the undergraduate and graduate levels. Grounded in the humanities, arts and sciences, the University has gained a national reputation for its innovative program of engaged learning, an experience-based approach to liberal arts that encourages students to actively participate in internships, service learning, study abroad and research. Furman's heritage is rooted in the Baptist tradition, and faculty and students are encouraged to foster a sense of social justice and civic responsibility. Furman is fully committed to sustainability.

> ACCESS Bridges to a Brighter Future

Bridges to a Brighter Future is a three-year enrichment program for Greenville County high-achieving high school students who come from backgrounds with limiting factors to their academic growth. The program provides students with education opportunities, tools for graduating high school, and college guidance. Students begin the program the summer before the 10th grade, and if they successfully maintain a 3.0 GPA they may continue participation through senior year. Students attend an annual four-week summer college at Furman University where they take liberal-arts and scientific classes taught by Greenville County teachers. During the academic year, weekend services include tutoring, success workshops, and mentoring programs.

"Bridges placed a lens before my eyes, making the image of my prospective self clearer. Stepping back into my reality, I was well aware of the fact that my circumstances remained the same, but the lenses subsisted, and my vision was forever transformed and no longer conformed to those circumstances."

– Cierra R., '12
Greenville, SC
Law, Communication

> SUCCESS The Office of Multicultural Affairs

The Office of Multicultural Affairs works to enhance the quality of life of minority students, to increase recruitment of minorities and to promote an inclusive environment for students of all backgrounds. The office sponsors several programs to promote understanding of different cultures. There is a one-day workshop available, where cultural stereotypes are dispelled and participants learn skills to break down barriers between groups. Black Awareness, International, Asian History, and Hispanic Heritage months are all celebrated through the Office of Multicultural Affairs.

> SUCCESS The Office of Academic Assistance

The Office of Academic Assistance provides students with academic assistance and general support services. Tutoring services are offered to all students free of charge. Office staff is available to advise and inform students about academic tools and resources to improve their study skills. Resources include online resources on time management, test taking, scheduling assistance and contact information for all Furman University professors. The Office of Academic Assistance Staff is dedicated to retaining students.

Furman University
Office of Admissions
3300 Poinsett Highway
Greenville, SC 29613
Ph: (864) 294-2034
admissions@furman.edu
www.furman.edu

FAST FACTS

STUDENT PROFILE
# of degree-seeking undergraduates	2,634
% male/female	43/57
% African American	7
% American Indian or Alaska Native	<1
% Asian or Pacific Islander	3
% Hispanic	2
% White	83
% International	2
% Pell grant recipients	14

ACADEMICS
full-time faculty	234
full-time minority faculty	29
student-faculty ratio	11:1
average class size	18
% first-year retention rate	92
% graduation rate (6 years)	86

Popular majors Political Science, Business Administration, History, Communication Studies

CAMPUS LIFE
% live on campus (% fresh.)	96 (98)

Multicultural student clubs and organizations Asia Club, NAACP, International Students Association, Hispanic Organization of Learning and Awareness, Student League for Black Culture, Minority Association of Pre-Medical Students
Athletics NCAA Division I, Southern Conference

ADMISSIONS
# of applicants	4,600
% accepted	68
# of first-year students enrolled	656
SAT Critical Reading range	580-690
SAT Math range	600-680
SAT Writing range	580-680
ACT range	25-30
average HS GPA	3.8

Deadlines
early decision	11/15
regular decision	1/15
application fee (online)	$50 ($0)
fee waiver for applicants with financial need	yes

COST & AID
tuition	$37,728
room & board	$9,572
total need-based institutional scholarships/ grants	$18,174,854
% of students apply for need-based aid	56
% of students receive aid	83
% receiving need based scholarship/grant aid	38
% receiving aid whose need was fully met	43
average aid package	$28,495
average student loan debt upon graduation	$27,373

University of South Carolina

The University of South Carolina is a comprehensive research institution serving the needs of more than 28,000 students. Undergraduate students benefit from a friendly campus atmosphere where faculty and students form communities that encourage successful learning and personal growth. The campus embraces diversity and offers many programs designed to increase multicultural awareness and foster respect for each member of the Carolina community. USC's Student Success Center provides outreach and academic support, while the nationally-acclaimed University 101 course for new students eases their transition to college. USC's Gamecock Guarantee program keeps the college dream alive for South Carolina's underprivileged and/or first generation students. This past year, USC awarded $1.2 million worth of need-based aid to its undergraduate students via three different grant categories.

> ACCESS TRIO Programs

USC's access programs include TRIO Programs, Upward Bound, Talent Search, and the Bridge Program. Upward Bound provides comprehensive educational support to prepare high school students for college. Talent Search provides long-term guidance on the college search process to students from middle school, through high school graduation, and up until college placement. The Bridge Program is designed for recent high-school graduates who are SC residents and who plan to attend a South Carolina technical college before transferring to USC. It provides pre-college guidance to ease the complex transfer process.

> *"I am thrilled that, because of the Gamecock Guarantee program, I do not have to add any financial or emotional burdens on my mother. I can continue my dream of being at USC and continue to make my mom proud by accomplishing all that she has always told me that I could."*
>
> *– Jordan A., '13*
> *Goose Creek, SC*
> *Social Work*

> OPPORTUNITY The University's Gamecock Guarantee Program

The University's Gamecock Guarantee Program ensures that South Carolina residents who are admitted to USC, who are most in need financially, and who meet specific eligibility requirements do not have to pay out-of-pocket for their USC tuition or technology fees. Gamecock Guarantee recipients receive a minimum award of $2,500 each year for up to four years. If tuition and technology fees exceed the value of a student's total financial aid/scholarship package, the Gamecock Guarantee makes up the difference.

> SUCCESS The Opportunity Scholars Program

The Opportunity Scholars Program assists first-generation college students who come from low-income families. The program is structured as a learning community and includes a curriculum of six freshman-level courses, support services designed to help students adjust to the campus environment, and financial assistance through the University's Gamecock Guarantee.

> SUCCESS The Office of Multicultural Student Affairs

The Office of Multicultural Student Affairs promotes appreciation for the University's culturally diverse populations. It sponsors annual Minority Welcome receptions, as well as the Minority Assistance Peer Program, which provides outreach to freshmen by trained peer counselors. The African American Male Institute motivates its student members to pursue academic and personal success through leadership training.

University of South Carolina
Undergraduate Admissions
Columbia, SC 29208
Ph: (803) 777-7700
admissions-ugrad@sc.edu
www.sc.edu/admissions

FAST FACTS

STUDENT PROFILE

# of degree-seeking undergraduates	20,494
% male/female	46/54
% African-American	11
% American Indian or Alaska Native	<1
% Asian or Pacific Islander	3
% Hispanic	3
% White	77
% International	2
% Pell grant recipients	23

First-generation and minority alumni James Bennett, Sierra Carter, Dean Lemuel W. Watson, Attorney Tom Bellinger, Attorney Moses Boyd, Lonnie Randolph, Rev. Ronnie Brailsford

ACADEMICS

full-time faculty	1,142
full-time minority faculty	179
student-faculty ratio	18:1
average class size	28
% first-year retention rate	87
% graduation rate (6 years)	69

Popular majors Business, Biology, Nursing, Pharmacy, Sport and Entertainment Management, Exercise Science, Psychology

CAMPUS LIFE

% live on campus (% fresh.)	36 (96)

Multicultural student clubs and organizations Association of African American Students, Brothers of Nubian Descent, International Student Association, National Student Exchange Association, Students Associated for Latin America, SAVVY (multicultural organization for women), Study Abroad Returnee Association, Women for a Multicultural Tomorrow

Athletics NCAA Division I, Southeastern Conference

ADMISSIONS

# of applicants	17,694
% accepted	64
# of first-year students enrolled	3,917
SAT Critical Reading range	530-640
SAT Math range	560-650
SAT Writing	n/a
ACT range	24-29
average HS GPA	3.9

Deadlines

regular decision	12/1
application fee	$50
fee waiver for applicants with financial need	yes

COST & AID

tuition	$8,756
room & board	$7,328
total need-based institutional scholarships/grants	$1,200,000
% of students apply for need-based aid	63
% receiving need-based scholarship or grant aid	22
% receiving aid whose need was fully met	26
average aid package	$12,016
average student loan debt upon graduation	$17,800

Augustana College

Augustana College is a private, residential, comprehensive college of the Evangelical Lutheran Church in America. Augustana strives to provide students with an education of enduring worth that challenges the intellect, fosters integrity and integrates faith with learning and service in a diverse world. As such, Augustana embraces and celebrates five shared core values: Christian, liberal arts, excellence, community and service.

Augustana College
Office of Admission
2001 S. Summit Avenue
Sioux Falls, SD 57197
Ph: (800) 727-2844 / (605) 274-5516
admission@augie.edu
www.augie.edu

F A S T   F A C T S

STUDENT PROFILE
# of degree-seeking undergraduates	2,512
% male/female	43/57
% African-American	2
% American Indian or Alaska Native	<1
% Asian or Pacific Islander	2
% Hispanic	3
% White	82
% Pell grant recipients	14

ACADEMICS
full-time faculty	181
full-time minority faculty	15
student-faculty ratio	12:1
average class size	17
% first-year retention rate	87
% graduation rate (6 years)	76

Popular majors Business Administration, Nursing, Biology

CAMPUS LIFE
% live on campus (% freshmen)	71 (95)

Multicultural student clubs and organizations
International Student Club
Athletics NCAA Division III, College Conference of Illinois and Wisconsin

ADMISSIONS
# of applicants	3,413
% accepted	69
# of first-year students enrolled	639
SAT Critical Reading range	520-610
SAT Math range	500-620
SAT Writing range	n/a
ACT range	22-28
average HS GPA	3.6

Deadlines
regular decision	rolling
application fee (online)	$35 ($35)
fee waiver for applicants with financial need	yes

COST & AID
tuition	$31,326
room & board	$7,950
total need-based institutional scholarships/grants	$20,291,779
% of students apply for need-based aid	79
% of students receive aid	67
% receiving need-based scholarship or grant aid	67
% receiving aid whose need was fully met	41
average aid package	n/a
average student loan debt upon graduation	n/a

> **ACCESS** **School-Based Mentor Program**

Augustana participates in the Lutheran Social Services School-Based Mentor Program, providing positive role models to local youth. Through the program, Augustana students are matched with an elementary or middle school student from the Sioux Falls Public School District. In addition to increased self-esteem, a heightened sense of character and more confidence, the program helps students to improve their academic skills and provides them with a greater awareness of the importance of education. Mentors and students enjoy a variety of activities, such as working in the computer lab, playing board games, reading, playing basketball or simply eating lunch together and talking.

> **ACCESS** **Augie Reads**

Augustana Reads is an after-school literacy program for English Language Learners that maximizes student learning by increasing engagement in the reading and writing process. This Sioux Empire United Way funded program is a collaborative effort among Augustana, the Multicultural Center and the Sioux Falls School District.

> **OPPORTUNITY** **Admission Possible**

Augustana has partnered with Admission Possible, a non-profit organization focused on providing low-income high school students from the Twin Cities with access to higher education. The college organizes several campus visits for these students throughout the year. These visits include a campus tour, panel presentation by Augustana students, campus dining experiences and opportunities for classroom observation. Some include an overnight in the residence halls.

> **OPPORTUNITY** **Upward Bound Visit Program**

Augustana hosts a summer visit program for Upward Bound, a federally funded program that assists low-income and first-generation high school students. The visit events include a campus tour, panel presentation by Augustana students, a campus dining experience and the opportunity to meet college faculty and staff.

> **OPPORTUNITY** **Circle of Courage Scholarship**

This renewable scholarship is awarded to full-time students who are members of a minority ethnic group. The amount varies and is contingent upon financial need.

> **SUCCESS** **The Writing Center**

Staffed by nationally certified peer tutors, the Writing Center promotes writing across the curriculum by offering workshops, presentations and tutoring services. Tutors help students complete writing assignments (not just in English), develop ideas, organize and plan papers and suggest editing and proofreading strategies.

> **SUCCESS** **A.S.A.P.**

The Academic Success Achievement Program (A.S.A.P.) resides in first-year residence halls, creating opportunities that support first-year students in their academic success and in gaining greater understanding of themselves as learners. The program includes evening workshops on time management, editing papers, test-taking skills, and career exploration. Tutoring is available four nights a week. In addition, Study Cafés are held prior to exams in popular first-year general education courses. These study groups help students identify main points, review the information and clarify any areas of confusion. Study Cafés also provide a quiet, relaxing environment for study or reading.

The University of South Dakota

The University of South Dakota is a comprehensive, co-educational, non-denominational, public liberal arts university offering undergraduate, graduate and professional programs within the South Dakota System of Higher Education. Founded in 1862, the university is the state's oldest and the only liberal arts university. The University of South Dakota is home to the state's only law and medical schools as well as the College of Fine Arts, School of Health Sciences and Beacom School of Business. The school provides opportunities for involvement in music, theatre and a wide range of additional recreational, cultural, social and professional activities and organizations. The university seeks to provide graduate and undergraduate programs in the liberal arts and sciences and in professional education, to promote excellence in teaching and learning, to support research, scholarly and creative activities and to provide service to South Dakota and the region.

> ## ACCESS Math and Science Initiative Program (MSIP)

Funded by the U.S. Department of Education, MSIP at The University of South Dakota provides high school students with an enriched math and science curriculum beyond what most high schools are able to offer. Each year, MSIP provides 40 rural South Dakota high school students an opportunity to experience college life through an intensive six-week summer program under the instruction and supervision of summer staff. Three separate components — Summer, Academic Year, and Bridge — expose students to math and science-based topics, courses of study and careers.

> ## OPPORTUNITY The Ullyot Endowment

The University of South Dakota's Ullyot Endowment provides a select number of American Indian student scholarships each year. The Ullyot Scholarships will encourage and support students to pursue their dreams at The University of South Dakota. Applicants must be members of a federally recognized American Indian tribe from within the United States and enrolled or accepted at the university as full-time students in good standing. Entering first-year, returning undergraduate and graduate students receive full in-state (South Dakota) tuition, fees and book allowance. Scholarships may be renewed based upon student performance.

> ## SUCCESS Student Support Services

Student Support Services offers academic services including tutoring, improvement of study skills, counseling and academic advising. Student Support Services is a grant-funded project supported by the U.S. Department of Education. The primary purpose of the program is to improve the retention and graduation rates of students from "disadvantaged" backgrounds.

> ## SUCCESS Tiospaye Council

The University of South Dakota Tiospaye Council was established to assist Native American students in adjusting to the college environment and to encourage their pursuit of higher education. In addition, the council works to promote a better understanding of the Native American culture by the university community and the Vermillion community. These undertakings are reflected in the council's efforts to provide an environment of cultural development, spiritual growth and social interaction by developing an extended community of resource people. Council-sponsored activities include the Wawokiya Mentoring Program, poetry readings, book signings, traditional music (drum practice and singing) and the annual spring pow-wow.

The University of South Dakota
414 East Clark
Vermillion, SD 57069
Ph: (605) 677-5434
admissions@usd.edu
www.usd.edu

FAST FACTS

STUDENT PROFILE
# of degree-seeking undergraduates	6,046
% male/female	41/59
% African-American	1
% American Indian or Alaska Native	2
% Asian or Pacific Islander	1
% Hispanic	1
% White	85
% International	1
% Pell grant recipients	33

ACADEMICS
full-time faculty	366
full-time minority faculty	39
student-faculty ratio	14:1
average class size	18
% first-year retention rate	72
% graduation rate (6 years)	48

Popular majors Psychology, Business Management, Pre-Medicine, Education, Criminal Justice, Fine Arts

CAMPUS LIFE
% live on campus (% fresh.)	30 (82)

Multicultural student clubs and organizations Black Student Union, Tiospaye U, American Indian Science & Engineering Society, American Indian Business Leaders, International Students Club, Manga Sei'iki, Spanish Club, Taiwanese Student Association
Athletics NCAA Division I, Great West Conference

ADMISSIONS
# of applicants	3,499
% accepted	80
# of first-year students enrolled	1,178
SAT Critical Reading range	420-540
SAT Math range	490-590
SAT Writing	n/a
ACT range	20-25
average HS GPA	n/a

Deadlines
regular decision	rolling
application fee (online)	$20 ($20)
fee waiver for applicants with financial need	no

COST & AID
tuition	in-state $6,468; out-of-state $7,841
room & board	$5,174
total need-based institutional scholarships/grants	n/a
% of students apply for need-based aid	81
% of students receive aid	61
% receiving need-based scholarship or grant aid	48
% receiving aid whose need was fully met	28
average aid package	$5,660
average student loan debt upon graduation	$22,781

Belmont University

Belmont University
1900 Belmont Boulevard
Nashville, TN 37212-3757
Ph: (615) 460-6785
buadmission@mail.belmont.edu
www.belmont.edu

Belmont University, a private, coeducational university in Nashville at the heart of Music Row, offers its students an atmosphere of warmth, acceptance, and possibility within a student-centered, Christian community. Founded in 1891, Belmont offers undergraduate degrees in more than 75 major areas of study and is a great choice for students who intend to pursue a career in the entertainment and/or music business. Belmont boasts the only College of Entertainment and Music Business in the world, and it sends hundreds of students each year to work in every facet of the music industry, from publicists, to industry record labels, to law firms. Belmont is the largest Christian university in Tennessee.

> *"Coming from a small town, Belmont was a place that felt like home to me. The faculty and staff and the helpfulness that they showed to students pleased me. I knew that I was going to need that; moving away from home and to a new place, and I wanted that guidance that you get from a student professor relationship. Belmont's small size helped with that."*
>
> *– Ameshia C., '09*
> *Political Science and Journalism*

> ACCESS **Hispanic Achievers**

Belmont students can devote their Saturdays to Belmont-YMCA Hispanic Achievers, a program designed to empower Hispanic youth through activities and mentoring specific to their career goals. Hispanic Achievers promotes professionalism and higher education among Hispanic youth in the Nashville area. The program takes place at Belmont University and is a free service to the community. Belmont students help specifically with skills in mathematics, speech and writing in English and Spanish, and offer vocational orientation in interests such as Business, Law, and Engineering. For high school youth, the program offers preparation for the SAT and ACT exams, information on the college application process, and a tour of Belmont University.

> OPPORTUNITY **Merit Scholarships**

Belmont offers several substantial merit scholarships in addition to generous need-based aid. The William Randolph Hearst Endowed Scholarship is offered annually to an incoming freshman from a diverse background with outstanding academic and leadership records. It covers full tuition, room, board, books, and fees. The Ingram Diversity Leadership Scholarship, offered to four incoming freshmen with diverse backgrounds from the Nashville area, covers the full amount of tuition and is awarded based on outstanding academic and leadership records.

> OPPORTUNITY **Towering Traditions New Student Orientation**

The Towering Traditions Orientation Program, founded more than 20 years ago, is designed to welcome new students to Belmont University. The program includes Summer Orientation, Summer Experiences, and Welcome Week. Summer Orientation includes academic orientation, institutional orientation and registration sessions. Students have the opportunity to meet administration, faculty, and fellow students in preparation for their first days on campus in August.

> OPPORTUNITY **Black Student Association (BSA)**

Belmont's Black Student Association promotes cultural awareness through campus events and forums. Open to students of all races, BSA strives to reach out to the Belmont and Nashville community through its involvement in the university's Martin Luther King Week, and community service projects in the Metro Nashville area.

F A S T   F A C T S

STUDENT PROFILE

# of degree-seeking undergraduates	4,378
% male/female	41/59
% African American	5
% American Indian or Alaska Native	<1
% Asian or Pacific Islander	3
% Hispanic	2
% White	84
% International	1
% Pell grant recipients	17

First-generation and minority alumni Melinda Doolittle, American Idol contestant; Kimberly Locke, American Idol contestant; Rachel Smith, Miss USA

ACADEMICS

full-time faculty	269
full-time minority faculty	30
student-faculty ratio	12:1
average class size	n/a
% first-year retention rate	82
% graduation rate (6 years)	68

Popular majors Music Business, Nursing, Business Administration, Music, Biology

CAMPUS LIFE

% live on campus (% fresh.)	27 (96)

Multicultural student clubs and organizations Black Student Association, International Student Association

Athletics NCAA Division I, Atlantic Sun Conference

ADMISSIONS

# of applicants	3,227
% accepted	77
# of first-year students enrolled	996
SAT Critical Reading range	540-630
SAT Math range	530-640
SAT Writing range	n/a
ACT range	23-29
average HS GPA	3.53

Deadlines

regular decision	rolling to 8/1
application fee (online)	$50 (50)
fee waiver for applicants with financial need	yes, if received ACT/SAT waiver

COST & AID

tuition	$22,360
room & board	$8,590
total need-based institutional scholarships/grants	$4,709,225
% of students apply for need-based aid	89
% of students receive aid	70
% receiving need-based scholarship or grant aid	62
% receiving aid whose need was fully met	21
average aid package	$10,781
average student loan debt upon graduation	$16,898

Rhodes College

With 17 of its buildings and gateways listed on the National Register of Historic Places, Rhodes College can certainly boast of its classic and historic architecture. Founded in 1848, Rhodes has much more than a pretty face, however — it has been recognized in numerous publications for offering one of the best educational deals and it was a *CosmoGIRL* "Best College" because of its prominent female student leaders and faculty members and strong women's sports programs. Rhodes students also benefit from its location in Memphis, commonly known as the home of soul and barbeque.

> *"Being in a city like Memphis makes my experience at Rhodes even more diverse. Lots of private, liberal arts schools are far away from any kind of urban center—but to be in the heart of a city with so much cultural history, from the Civil Rights movement to the start of rock & roll, it only makes being a student here that much more enlightening."*
> – Jarrett T., '11
> Atlanta, GA
> English

> ACCESS **Kinney Program**

Approximately 100 service programs operate under the auspices of the Kinney program, an initiative of the school's chaplaincy. Through the program, in which over 80 percent of graduating students participate, students can either help with one-time service drives or make an ongoing commitment to a particular service project. Furthermore, Kinney sponsors voter-registration drives, educational events on social issues, service training and reflection opportunities, social activism and advocacy, and works with faculty to develop service-learning courses and community-based research projects.

> SUCCESS **ALANA Orientation Dinner / Mentoring and Support**

This activity provides African American, Latino/a, Asian and Native American students with important information to help facilitate their transition to college life at Rhodes. First-year ALANA students are assigned upperclassmen mentors who can help them acclimate to the campus experience. The mentoring program also offers structured monthly group meetings and workshops/programs to supplement the needs of students. Additionally, students can participate in two optional support groups — Brothers With Purpose (BWP) and African-American Women Speaking Our Minds on Empowerment (AWSOME) — that exist to promote connections between students, faculty, staff and alumni.

> SUCCESS **Office of Multicultural Affairs / Multicultural Resource Center**

The Office of Multicultural Affairs has a unique role in offering programs & services that enhance the overall quality of life for students of color. All of the cultural organizations reside under the Office of Multicultural Affairs. These organizations are open to all faculty, staff and students. Also under the direction of the Office of Multicultural Affairs is the Multicultural Resource Center where faculty, staff and students can facilitate dialogue in a small, intimate and safe place about diversity-related issues, and conduct tutoring or study groups.

Rhodes College
2000 N. Parkway
Memphis, TN 38112
Ph: (901) 843-3000
adminfo@rhodes.edu
www.rhodes.edu

FAST FACTS

STUDENT PROFILE
# of degree-seeking undergraduates	1,675
% male/female	42/58
% African American	7
% American Indian	<1
% Asian	5
% Caucasian	75
% Hispanic	2
% Pell grant recipients	9

First-generation and minority alums Charles Holt, Broadway and film actor; Willie Hulon, executive assistant director, National Security Branch, Federal Bureau of Investigation; Vicki Gilmore Palmer, executive vice president, Coca-Cola Enterprises

ACADEMICS
full-time faculty	161
full-time minority faculty	17
student-faculty ratio	10:1
average class size	13
% first-year retention rate	88
% graduation rate (6 years)	82

Popular majors Biology, Business, English, History, Political Science, Psychology

CAMPUS LIFE
% live on campus	75

Multicultural student clubs and organizations ASIA (All Students Interested in Asia), Black Student Association, Gay Straight Alliance, HOLA (Hispanic Organization for Language and Activities), RICE (Rhodes Indian Cultural Exchange)
Athletics NCAA Division III, Southern Collegiate Athletic Conference

ADMISSIONS
# of applicants	5,039
% accepted	42
SAT Critical Reading range	570-680
SAT Math range	580-700
SAT Writing range	580-680
ACT range	26-30
average HS GPA	3.8

Deadlines
early decision	11/1
early action	11/15
regular decision(for Fall enrollment)	1/15
regular decision(for Spring enrollment)	11/1
application fee (online)	$45 ($0)
fee waiver for applicants with financial need	yes

COST & AID
tuition	$33,400
room & board	$8,314
total need-based institutional scholarships/grants	$15,483,353
% of students receiving aid	85
% receiving need-based scholarship or grant aid	47
% Freshmen receiving aid whose need was fully met	25
average aid package (scholarship and grants)	$16,967
average student loan debt upon graduation	$25,000

Union University

Union University is a four-year co-educational Christian institution and is heir to some of the oldest schools in the country. Affiliated with the Tennessee Baptist Convention, Union has received national recognition for its commitment to community service. Its largest event is the annual "Campus and Community: A Day of Remembrance and Service," in which the university sends out more than 50 teams across Jackson and West Tennessee for various service projects. The school, founded in 1823, is a union of several different schools. In addition to the main campus located in Jackson, the university also offers graduate and adult programs on its Germantown campus, in suburban Memphis.

> ACCESS Rising High School Senior Program

Union University offers an available Rising High School Senior Program to high school students who have already completed their junior year. This program offers academic classes at a discounted rate. In addition, the student life team provides leadership, career counseling and service opportunities for students involved in this program. Minority students involved in this program receive special attention from the assistant dean of students. In addition, all enrollment counselors receive training in the advising and recruitment of first-generation college students, in order to more fully educate the student and family on the college process.

> OPPORTUNITY Minority Student Scholarship

Two specific scholarships are offered for minority students, the African American Scholarship and Minority Student Scholarship. Awards range from $1,000 to $2,000 annually and are in addition to other institutional assistance.

> OPPORTUNITY Minority Preview Days

Union also offers targeted minority preview days. Union's enrollment office also helps coordinate transportation from inner-city Memphis high schools to allow students to visit the campus during these days.

> SUCCESS The Hundley Center for Academic Enrichment

The Hundley Center for Academic Enrichment is one of Union's initiatives to provide academic help to students. Peer tutoring is offered in more than 13 disciplines at no charge to the student. The program's director is also on hand to meet one-on-one with students who struggle with courses or time management.

> SUCCESS The Keystone Program

Union also sponsors The Keystone Program where specific students facing serious academic uncertainties receive specialized help. The program also provides a select number of incoming students who are at higher academic risk a special opportunity for success. These students work with the full-time director of The Keystone Program, meeting weekly and following guidelines that provide a strong springboard for academic achievement.

> SUCCESS Minority Student Resources

In an effort to build community and social support, minority student social support programs are offered, including TGI Friday's, African American Women's Bible Study Group, Minority Men's Bible Study Group, Mosaic Student Group and Open Mic Night. Black History Month Programming and the orientation "Dinner and Dialogue" are offered to all students and create conversations among student cultures.

Union University
1050 Union University Drive
Jackson, TN 38305-3697
Ph: (731) 661-5000
info@uu.edu
www.uu.edu

F A S T   F A C T S

STUDENT PROFILE
# of degree-seeking undergraduates	2,574
% male/female	41/ 59
% African-American	11
% American Indian or Alaska Native	<1
% Asian or Pacific Islander	1
% Hispanic	1
% White	81
% Pell grant recipients	24

First-generation and minority alumni Luis Ortiz, professional baseball player

ACADEMICS
full-time faculty	177
full-time minority faculty	n/a
student-faculty ratio	12:1
average class size	17
% first-year retention rate	93
% graduation rate (6 years)	76

Popular majors Elementary Education, Nursing, Christian Studies, Communication Arts

CAMPUS LIFE
% live on campus (% freshmen)	42 (86)

Multicultural student clubs and organizations Mosaic Student Group, Mu Kappa, International Student Organization, Common Ground
Athletics NAIA, TranSouth Athletic Conference

ADMISSIONS
# of applicants	1,164
% accepted	82
# of first-year students enrolled	547
SAT Critical Reading range	510-650
SAT Math range	510-640
SAT Writing range	n/a
ACT range	21-29
average HS GPA	3.5

Deadlines
regular decision	rolling
application fee (online)	$35 ($35)
fee waiver for applicants with financial need	yes

COST & AID
tuition	$20,940
room & board	$6,930
total need-based institutional scholarships/grants	n/a
% of students apply for need-based aid	96
% of students receive aid	64
% receiving need-based scholarship or grant aid	73
% receiving aid whose need was fully met	25
average aid package	$15,036
average student loan debt upon graduation	$21,543

Vanderbilt University

Vanderbilt University
2305 West End Avenue
Nashville, TN 37203-1727
Ph: (800) 288-0432 or (615) 322-2561
admissions@vanderbilt.edu
http://admissions.vanderbilt.edu

Founded in 1873, Vanderbilt University is a private, nonsectarian, co-educational research university. Vanderbilt is a center for research, dedicated to service to the community and society at large. Cultivating an atmosphere that prizes scholarship, the dissemination of knowledge through teaching and outreach, and the creative experimentation of ideas, the University supports intellectual freedom, open inquiry, equality, compassion and excellence in all endeavors.

> **ACCESS** **YMCA Mentor Program**

Run by Vanderbilt's Black Cultural Center, the YMCA mentor program provides disadvantaged low-income and minority junior high and high school students from the Nashville area with free tutoring, mentoring and training in important life skills.

> **ACCESS** **PAVE Program**

Vanderbilt University's PAVE Program is a six-week summer course designed to strengthen the academic skills of high school juniors and seniors who are planning to enter a college engineering, pre-medical, science or technology program. PAVE participants can improve their problem solving skills, technical writing skills, computer application skills and laboratory skills by performing experiments in the sciences, pre-med and engineering disciplines.

> **ACCESS** **Vanderbilt Summer Academy (VSA)**

VSA invites highly talented students (grades 7-12) to a residential summer program on campus. Vanderbilt Summer Academy offers engaging and challenging curricula in math, science, and the humanities. The program integrates resources from the university's many research programs directly into the classroom experience.

> **OPPORTUNITY** **Vandy Fan for a Day**

Vandy Fan for a Day provides high school sophomores and juniors of diverse socioeconomic backgrounds with information about the selective college admissions process and Vanderbilt's need-based aid, and a chance to enjoy an SEC football game. High school counselors nominate students for this program held in the fall each year.

> **OPPORTUNITY** **Diverse VU**

DiverseVU is a program held annually at Vanderbilt University in mid-November that attracts approximately 200 minority students from around the country. The program features academic sessions highlighting each of Vanderbilt's four colleges, an admissions session, a multicultural student panel, campus tours, and an activities fair with student organizations. In addition, financial assistance for travel is provided to needy students.

> **OPPORTUNITY** **MOSAIC Weekend**

Held in mid-March, Vanderbilt University's MOSAIC Weekend invites minority students admitted to Vanderbilt to campus. The students receive early notice of their admission to Vanderbilt and a MOSAIC letter invitation. The weekend features ice-breaker exercises, academic sessions, student activities, performances and tickets to the annual Vanderbilt Step Show.

"Vanderbilt offers ample opportunities for any student to get involved – it's a place where so many people mix together that you never know what's going to happen."

– Ben C., '11
Kansas City, MO
Computer Engineering, Math

FAST FACTS

STUDENT PROFILE
# of degree-seeking undergraduates	6,704
% male/female	48/52
% African-American	8
% American Indian or Alaska Native	1
% Asian or Pacific Islander	10
% Hispanic	9
% White	52
% International	4
% Pell grant recipients	11.9

First-generation and minority alumni Jamie Duncan, Shelton Quarles, Jamie Winborn, Corey Chavous, Jimmy Williams, Perry Wallace, professional basketball players; Joey Cora, professional baseball player; Muhammad Yunus, Economist

ACADEMICS
full-time faculty	1,029
full-time minority faculty	168
ftudent-faculty ratio	8:1
average class size	n/a
% first-year retention rate	96
% graduation rate (6 years)	91

Popular majors Human and Organizational Development, Economics, English, Biomedical Engineering, and Political Science

CAMPUS LIFE
% live on campus (% freshmen)	90 (100)

Multicultural student clubs and organizations African Students Union, Asian American Students Association, Black Student Alliance, Vanderbilt Association of Hispanic Students, Multicultural Student Leadership Council, MOSAIC Executive Committee, Alliance for Cultural Diversity in Research

Athletics NCAA Division I, Southeastern Conference (football I-A)

ADMISSIONS
# of applicants	19,353
% accepted	20
# of first-year students enrolled	1,599
SAT Critical Reading range	660-750
SAT Math range	690-770
SAT Writing range	660-750
ACT range	30-34
average HS GPA	3.71

Deadlines
early decision	11/1
regular decision	1/3
application fee	$50
fee waiver for applicants with financial need	yes

COST & AID (ESTIMATED 2010/2011)
tuition	$38,952
room & board	$13,068

AID (2009/2010)
total need-based institutional scholarships/grants	$92,092,632
% of students apply for need-based aid	47
% of students receive aid from any source regardless of need	61
% of students with demonstrated need who receive financial assistance	100
% of students receiving need-based scholarship/grant aid	41
% receiving aid whose need was fully met	100
average aid package	$41,002
average student debt upon graduation	$19,142

Abilene Christian University

Founded in 1906, Abilene Christian University is a private, coeducational institution offering undergraduate and graduate degrees. ACU's outstanding faculty members are committed to high-quality teaching, scholarship and service. The university also offers state-of-the-art facilities and innovative uses of mobile technology. The mission of the university is to educate students for Christian service and leadership throughout the world. Education is grounded in core Christian values, but the Abilene community is an inclusive environment for students from a variety of religious, ethnic, social, cultural and geographical backgrounds.

> ACCESS ACU en Español

Abilene Christian University is dedicated to diversity and inclusion of other cultures, especially Hispanic students. The university provides a Spanish version of its Web site to ensure that Spanish-speaking students get any information they might need about ACU.

> OPPORTUNITY First-Generation and Diversity Scholarships

Recognizing the roadblocks many minority students face in succeeding at institutions of higher learning, Abilene Christian University provides scholarships designed to attract multicultural students. For example, the Hispanic Leadership Council/Abilene Christian University Partnership Scholarship provides full tuition for four years to admit students who qualify. The Cultures of ACU scholarships provide awards for students of any ethnicity whose experience and perspective can help promote diversity at ACU. Admissions counselors are dedicated to aiding students in making their educational goals a reality. They can provide information on scholarships from many private organizations offering assistance to multicultural students.

"ACU has given me so many experiences that have helped me grow, as well as the knowledge to teach children and become a master teacher. Community with other students and community with faculty and staff - this community is always there to help you in academics and in faith."

– Geraldine C., '10 Abilene, TX Education

> SUCCESS Keystone

Members of this student group at Abilene Christian University are student leaders selected by the director of the Office of Multicultural Enrichment to serve the greater Abilene community and provide advising, mentoring and on-campus support to their peers among the campus body.

> SUCCESS The Office of Multicultural Enrichment

The Office of Multicultural Enrichment oversees student groups at Abilene Christian University that are focused on multicultural diversity. Many student-led groups, each with their own cultural focus, meet on a monthly or bi-monthly basis. Each year, the number of diversity groups on campus increases.

Abilene Christian University
Office of Admissions
ACU Box 29000
Abilene, TX 79699-9000
Ph: (800) 460-6228
info@admissions.acu.edu
www.acu.edu

FAST FACTS

STUDENT PROFILE

# of degree-seeking undergraduates	4,800
% male/female	45/55
% African American	6
% American Indian	1
% Asian American	1
% Hispanic/Latino	7
% Caucasian	78
% International	4
% Pell grant recipients	25.8

First generation and minority alumni Dr. Billy Curl, '66, ACU trustee and minister, Crenshaw Church of Christ, Los Angeles, Calif. Wilbert Montgomery, '77, former NFL all-pro running back, assistant coach, Baltimore Ravens Football Club, Baltimore, Md. Hubert Pickett, '77, ACU trustee and director of personnel, Abilene Independent School District, Abilene, Texas Marcela Gutierrez, '06, accounts analyst for PFSweb, Dallas, Texas Fabiola Leon, '08, elementary school teacher in Plano Independent School District, Plano, Texas

ACADEMICS

full-time faculty	368
full-time minority faculty	n/a
student-faculty ratio	16:1
average class size	n/a
% first-year retention rate	74
% graduation rate (6 years)	58

Popular majors Business, Education, Psychology, Biology, Journalism and Mass Communication

CAMPUS LIFE

% live on campus (% fresh.)	41 (96)

Multicultural student clubs and organizations Essence of Ebony, Hispanos Unidos, International Students Association, Milonga (Latin), Shades Step Squad, Virtuous African Heritage Sisterhood
Athletics NCAA Division II, Lone Star Conference

ADMISSIONS

# of applicants	4,622
% accepted	n/a
# of first-year students enrolled	1,135
SAT Critical Reading range	490-610
SAT Math range	490-620
SAT Writing	n/a
ACT range	21-27
average HS GPA	3.51

Deadlines

early decision	11/1
regular decision	1/15
application fee	$50
fee waiver for applicants with financial need	n/a

COST & AID

tuition	$19,200
room & board	$6,226
total need-based institutional scholarships/grants	$57,000,000
% of students apply for need-based aid	n/a
% of students receive aid	92
% receiving need-based scholarship or grant aid	n/a
% receiving aid whose need was fully met	n/a
average aid package	$12,000
average student loan debt upon graduation	n/a

Hardin-Simmons University

Hardin-Simmons University
2200 Hickory, HSU Box 16050
Abilene, TX 79698
Ph: (877) GOHSUTX
enroll@hsutx.edu
www.hsutx.edu

With liberal arts and sciences, music, nursing and education classes offered, Hardin-Simmons University provides a range of academic opportunities to undergraduates, all while affording them a true Texas experience in the Old West town of Abilene. In addition to these offerings, Hardin-Simmons hosts special programs, such as the Center for Missionary Education, which provides continuing education opportunities to missionaries. In the Southern spirit, Hardin-Simmons also takes its athletic program seriously, but not to the detriment of its academics — the school strives for its students to be strong academic and social leaders.

> ACCESS Baptist Student Ministries

Through the Baptist Student Ministries, students can participate in a number of service opportunities, including Christmas break projects, 10-week summer missions, two-week impact teams and study-abroad missions, as well as semester positions. Students reach out to the campus and community through campus Bible studies, a nursing home ministry, prayer meetings, care groups and children's outreach.

> ACCESS Hardin-Simmons University Community Renewal Program

Hardin-Simmons' community renewal program works to rebuild houses, literacy and hope in the neighborhood around campus. Students participate in the program through a recycling center, winterization program, Bible studies, after-school care and tutoring, a Habitat for Humanity chapter and GED obtainment and assistance.

> OPPORTUNITY Campus Visits

Interested students have a variety of ways to visit the Hardin-Simmons campus, all of which offer their own features. During Cowboy Fridays, for example, students can attend classes, participate in tours and take residual ACT exams, which can only be used at Hardin-Simmons, but which can be scored within the week. During Spring Round-Up, students can stay on campus overnight, as well as register for fall classes. In addition to these special visit opportunities, students can also schedule a personalized campus visit any day of the week.

> SUCCESS Student Success Seminar / New Student Orientation

Hardin-Simmons offers a nationally recognized Student Success Seminar, which helps students transition into college life. This three-credit, cooperatively taught (by a faculty member, staff member and student leader) course covers such diverse subjects as note-taking, relationship issues and diversity. The New Student Orientation, where new students are placed in upperclassmen-lead teams, also provides support for students.

> SUCCESS Free Tutoring and Counseling

Students at Hardin-Simmons can take advantage of both free tutoring and counseling. Tutoring is offered through the Advising Center, which employs academically successful undergraduates as peer tutors, while counseling is offered through the Department of Psychology, which employs graduate interns in the field.

FAST FACTS

STUDENT PROFILE

# of degree-seeking undergraduates	1,882
% male/female	48/51
% African American	6.8
% American Indian or Alaska Native	1.2
% Asian or Pacific Islander	<1
% Hispanic	6.4
% Pell grant recipients	34

First-generation and minority alumni Stedman Graham, nationally known author, speaker and founder of Athletes Against Drugs; Victor Carrillo, Chairman of the Texas Railroad Commission; Harvey Catchings, former NBA star, Former President Harvey Catchings Promotions, former Director of Player Programs National Basketball Association, current Sr. Tax Consultant Tax Masters, Inc.; Alex Vasquez, associate general counsel in the Office of the General Counsel of Wal-Mart Stores, Inc.; Consuelo Castillo Kickbusch, Lieutenant Colonel, U.S. Army (retired), Founder & President of Educational Achievement Services, Inc., author, motivational speaker, educator

ACADEMICS

full-time faculty	136
full-time minority faculty	3
student-faculty ratio	14:1
average class size	17
% first-year retention rate	71
% graduation rate (6 years)	50

Popular majors Pre-Med, Business, Education, Physical Therapy, Nursing

CAMPUS LIFE

% live on campus (% fresh.)	92

Multicultural student clubs and organizations M.E.S.H., Unity Group, International Student Fellowship

Athletics NCAA Division III, American Southwest Conference

ADMISSIONS

# of applicants	2,354
% accepted	38.6
SAT Verbal average	510
SAT Math average	540
SAT composite average (excluding writing)	1050
ACT composite average	22.4
average HS GPA	3.56

Deadlines

regular admission	rolling
application fee (online)	$50 ($50)
fee waiver for applicants with financial need	yes

COST & AID

tuition	$18,750
room & board	$5,180
total need-based institutional scholarships/grants	$7,763,656
% of students apply for need-based aid	96
% of students receive aid	95
% receiving need-based scholarship or grant aid	49
% receiving aid whose need was fully met	69
average aid package	$16,930
average student loan debt upon graduation	$35,429

Howard Payne University

Howard Payne University
1000 Fisk Street
Brownwood, TX 76801-2715
Ph: (800) 880-3478 or (325) 649-8020
enroll@hputx.edu
www.hputx.edu

Co-founded by a Baptist minister and a Texas blacksmith, Howard Payne University retains much of the principles upon which it was founded in 1889. A Christian, co-educational school, Howard Payne is located in Brownwood, Texas, a close-knit town of 20,000 residents who embrace the university's students. Howard Payne offers more than 50 majors, minors and pre-professional programs offered throughout its six schools. Howard Payne University is at the forefront of leadership development and encourages students to incorporate such activities into their academic life. As an example, S.W.A.R.M. Day (Serving With A Right Motive) is an annual campus event that provides opportunities for students to volunteer for community service projects.

> ACCESS Sigues Tú

This three-day program, in its fourth year, connects Howard Payne students with Hispanic middle school students in scheduled weekend events. Campus volunteers spend time with the young students exposing them to college life as well as encouraging them to pursue college after high school. One of the popular activities is climbing the university's infamous rock wall in the Outdoor Recreation Complex.

> OPPORTUNITY Financial Aid Opportunities

In addition to generous merit scholarship packages offered by the institution to help make college affordable, there are a variety of other scholarships, grants and work programs available to assist in covering college costs. In addition to institutional aid, Howard Payne students receive outside assistance through the state and federal sources. Over the past several years, over one-third of the Howard Payne University student population has qualified to receive the federal Pell grant. The combination of these sources has assisted in opening educational opportunities for many students to take part in a quality education in a Christian environment.

> SUCCESS Center for Academic and Personal Success

The Center for Academic and Personal Success (CAPS) offers a variety of support mechanisms in place to help students reach their goals. From Tutoring and Career Services to Seminars and Success Inventories, the center is designed to facilitate students' achievement and success. Under Success Inventories, there are 11 workshops and seminars students can take to sharpen skills for academic and career preparation: The Art of Note Taking, Study Skills, Test-Taking Strategies, Tips for Personal Health and Wellness, Budgeting Now for Wealth Later, Essential Interview Skills, Secrets of Banking, Resume Writing and How to Build Your GPA.

> SUCCESS Jacket Journey

Jacket Journey is a unique new student orientation week designed to encourage students to experience and develop school spirit and to understand the social and academic expectations of the university. Students become a vital part of the Howard Payne University family by building relationships with peers, faculty and staff. During Jacket Journey, students also become acquainted with the university's facilities, resources and services.

FAST FACTS

STUDENT PROFILE
# of degree-seeking undergraduates	1,371
% male/female	52/48
% African-American	7
% American Indian or Alaska Native	1
% Asian or Pacific Islander	1
% Hispanic	15
% White	74
% Pell grant recipients	36

ACADEMICS
full-time faculty	76
full-time minority faculty	n/a
student-faculty ratio	12:1
average class size	n/a
% first-year retention rate	55
% graduation rate (6 years)	35

Popular majors Bible/Biblical Studies, Business Administration/Management

CAMPUS LIFE
% live on campus (% freshmen)	46 (91)

Multicultural Student Clubs and Organizations Black Student Alliance (BSA), Global Interest Association, Spanish Club

Athletics NCAA Division III, American Southwest Conference

ADMISSIONS
# of applicants	874
% accepted	65
# of first-year students enrolled	415
SAT Critical Reading range	420-550
SAT Math range	450-560
SAT Writing	n/a
ACT range	17-24
average HS GPA	3.4

Deadlines
regular decision	rolling
application fee (online)	$25 ($25)
fee waiver for applicants with financial need	yes

COST & AID
tuition	$18,650
room & board	$5,588
total need-based institutional scholarships/grants	n/a
% of students apply for need-based aid	88
% of students receive aid	77
% receiving need-based scholarship or grant aid	97
% receiving aid whose need was fully met	26.5
average aid package	$13,599
average student loan debt upon graduation	$18,960

Jarvis Christian College

A small, historically black college located in Hawkins, Texas, Jarvis Christian College provides students with both a strong liberal arts education and the support structure to be successful. Its size makes it particularly equipped to reach students on an individual level; in fact, the school's motto is "The College With The Personal Touch." Academically motivated students, especially those in STEM (science, technology, engineering and mathematics) disciplines, can especially benefit from a Jarvis education, as the school has special programs for all of these constituencies.

> ACCESS **Upward Bound**

Jarvis Christian College participates in the federally funded Upward Bound program, serving high school students from the East Texas area. In addition to its year-long academic program, the Jarvis Upward Bound program also includes a six-week summer residential component and a pre-college Bridge experience.

> OPPORTUNITY **STEM Scholar Initiative**

Students in the STEM fields can benefit from Jarvis Christian's "Creating Windows of Opportunity for Success in the Sciences" initiative. A Historically Black Colleges and Universities Undergraduate Program (HBCU-UP), this program addresses the historical under-representation of minorities by allowing select undergraduates to participate in research under the guidance of experienced faculty mentors in each of the targeted disciplines. The HBCU-UP program for the STEM Scholars has been funded by the National Science Foundation since 2000.

> SUCCESS **The Ronald L. Hay Mentoring Program**

Students facing academic or personal hardship may be referred to the Ronald L. Hay Mentoring Program, which provides them with a trained mentor. Mentors help students to enhance their skills and face challenges while improving school-wide attrition rates.

> SUCCESS **Advanced Summer Enrichment Program**

Incoming Jarvis freshmen have the opportunity to participate in the Advanced Summer Enrichment Program, a 10-day residential program during which they can earn college credits and engage in cultural and social activities. Financial aid beyond the registration fee is available.

> SUCCESS **Honors Program**

In order to meet the needs of high-achieving students, Jarvis Christian provides an honors program designed to challenge gifted and talented students. Rather than function as a separate degree program, the Honors program enhances students' individual academic programs by providing opportunities for creative and scholarly work, and exposing them to cultural events and internships programs.

Jarvis Christian College
PO Box 1470
Hawkins, TX 75765-1470
Ph: (903) 769-5734
recruiter@jarvis.edu
www.jarvis.edu

F A S T   F A C T S

STUDENT PROFILE
# of degree-seeking undergraduates	727
% male/female	n/a
% African-American	95
% American Indian or Alaska Native	<1
% Asian or Pacific Islander	0
% Hispanic	<1
% White	n/a
% International	n/a
% Pell grant recipients	99.2

ACADEMICS
full-time faculty	35
full-time minority faculty	n/a
student-faculty ratio	n/a
average class size	23
% first-year retention rate	50
% graduation rate (6 years)	17

Popular majors Computer and Information Sciences, Criminal Justice/Law Enforcement Administration, Education

CAMPUS LIFE
% live on campus (% fresh.)	80 (93)

Multicultural student clubs and organizations Gospel Choir, National Association of Black Accountants, Concert Choir
Athletics NAIA, Red River Athletic Conference

ADMISSIONS
# of applicants	662
% accepted	22
# of first-year students enrolled	4,470
SAT Critical Reading range	390-400
SAT Math range	380-400
SAT Writing range	340-420
ACT range	17-18
average HS GPA	2.5

Deadlines
regular admission	rolling
application fee (online)	$25 ($25)
fee waiver for applicants with financial need	yes

COST & AID
tuition	$8,208
room & board	$4,954
total need-based institutional scholarships/grants	n/a
% of students apply for need-based aid	96
% of students receive aid	100
% receiving need-based scholarship or grant aid	85
% receiving aid whose need was fully met	76
average aid package	$10,263
average student loan debt upon graduation	$19,000

Prairie View A&M University

Founded in 1876, Prairie View A&M University is a historically black, co-educational, non-denominational, comprehensive, public university and the second-oldest public institution of higher learning in the state of Texas. With an established reputation for producing engineers, nurses and educators and a member of The Texas A&M University System, the university is dedicated to fulfilling its land-grant mission of achieving excellence in teaching, research and service. Prairie View is also known for its specialized programs and services in juvenile justice, architecture, teacher education, social work and agricultural and natural resource sciences.

> ACCESS Institute for Pre-College Enrichment (PCI)

The Prairie View A&M University sponsored Institute for Pre-College Enrichment (PCI) is a two-week residential summer program for talented high school students. The mission of PCI is to help prepare high school students for the new school year and to assist them in making early plans to pursue a college education in an area that interests them most. Students entering 12th grade receive emphasis on essay writing, college application, funding for college, scholarship awareness and leadership.

> OPPORTUNITY Academy for Collegiate Excellence and Student Success (ACCESS) Program

Prairie View A&M University's "bridge to college" program is designed to improve students' academic performance and assist in their transition from high school to college. ACCESS students participate in a seven-week residential, academic summer program that provides instruction in mathematics, reading comprehension, writing, critical thinking and problem solving. Complementing the weekly classroom instruction are off-campus field experiences designed to enhance and bring relevance to the academic studies. These activities are critical in the development of leadership, personal, social and cultural enrichment skills needed for success in college and in the world of work. In the fall, ACCESS students who attend Prairie View enter into the second component, University College, a structured, academically focused environment that seeks to make the freshman year a successful one by providing support services and a residential learning community.

"On Prairie View A&M University's Seal it reads "Teaching, Research, and Service" but to thousands of other students and me, it is that and so much more. Prairie View A&M University is a stairway to a higher education and higher achievements. PV is the place to be."
– Chelsee H., '10
Miss Prairie View A&M University 2009-2010
The Woodlands, TX
Psychology

> SUCCESS University College

Prairie View A&M University's University College program is committed to improving matriculation, retention and graduation rates, increasing student success in academics and facilitating a smooth transition to the world of higher education for first-year students. Within University College each student belongs to a University College Academic Team (UCAT) consisting of approximately 100 to 125 students, a professional adviser, a learning community manager, two community assistants and a faculty fellow. The staff, faculty and older students on each team provide the support services/referrals, the sense of community and the concerned "others" a freshman needs to flourish in the college environment.

Prairie View A&M University
Office of Undergraduate Admissions
P.O. Box 519, Mail Stop 1009
Prairie View, TX 77446
Ph: (936) 261-1000
admissions@pvamu.edu
www.pvamu.edu

FAST FACTS

STUDENT PROFILE
# of degree-seeking undergraduates	6,118
% male/female	38/62
% African American	89
% American Indian	0
% Asian	1
% Caucasian	4
% Hispanic	4
% Pell grant recipients	54.5

First-generation and minority alumni Lafayette Collins, special agent, U.S. Secret Service; Charles Brown, singer; Dave Webster, professional football player; Craig Washington, former United States congressman; Frederick Douglass Patterson, founder, United Negro College Fund

ACADEMICS
full-time faculty	359
student-faculty ratio	17:1
average class size	18
% first-year retention rate	75.7
% graduation rate (6 years)	39.1

Popular majors Business, Agriculture, Nursing, Engineering, Education

CAMPUS LIFE
% live on campus (% fresh.)	60 (95)

Multicultural student clubs and organizations African Student Association, Muslim Student Association. League of United Latin American Citizens (LULAC), National Association for the Advancement of Colored People (NAACP)
Athletics NCAA Division I, Southwestern Athletic Conference

ADMISSIONS
# of applicants	4,049
% accepted	56.8
SAT Critical Reading range	370-460
SAT Math range	370-470
ACT range	17-20
average HS GPA	2.94

Deadlines
regular admission	5/1
application fee	$25

COST & AID
tuition	in-state $6,046; out-of-state $15,406
room & board	$6,477
% of students receiving aid	62
% receiving need-based scholarship or grant aid	77
% receiving aid whose need was fully met	76
average aid package	$10,903
average student loan debt upon graduation	$20,000

Schreiner University

Schreiner University has a tagline: "Learning by Heart." This motto underscores its commitment to continuously, holistically, educating students both inside and outside of the classroom. It also refers to the faculty's commitment to ensuring each student's success. With a student body of 1,084, small class sizes and student-to-teacher ratio of 13:1, it isn't hard for every professor to know each of his or her students. Primarily undergraduate, the university offers liberal arts, science and pre-professional majors and programs. Minorities comprise 26 percent of Schreiner's student body and 41 percent are the first in their families to attend college. Schreiner is related to the Presbyterian Church (USA), but welcomes students, faculty and staff of all faiths.

> ACCESS **Schreiner Energizers**

The Schreiner Energizers, a motivational student organization, is associated with the Campus Ministry program and is available to lead interactive exercises for youth groups and provide information about college.

> ACCESS **Past is Prologue (PIP)**

Schreiner's Center for Innovative Learning houses PIP, a U.S. Department of Education-validated program that draws on traditional Native American thinking and stories to foster child development. Schreiner provides information and workshops about PIP, which Native American author Paula Underwood founded.

> OPPORTUNITY **Financial Aid**

Schreiner University is committed to being accessible to qualified students, regardless of their families' financial means. Ninety percent of Schreiner students receive some sort of financial aid and the average financial aid package is $13,230. Financial aid counselors volunteer to visit schools and talk with students and parents about college expenses and financial aid options. Parents of students considering Schreiner may sign up for Schreiner's future parents' e-newsletter for more information about how to apply, how to get financial aid and what to expect.

> SUCCESS **Program for Academic Success**

The Program for Academic Success, which is reserved for students who may need extra assistance in the transition process from high school to college, allows students to receive faculty assistance in special sections of the Freshman Seminar. These faculty mentors also monitor grades and provide early intervention when necessary.

> SUCCESS **Free Tutoring and Full-Time Retention Counselor**

Free peer tutoring is available to all Schreiner students through the university's Faskin Teaching and Learning Center and its Writing Center. Schreiner also employs a full-time "advocate" who is available to help any student who may be getting behind in their academic work but is hesitant to go to their professors or academic advisers.

> SUCCESS **Christian Vocations Internship Program (CVIP)**

Schreiner also offers a Christian Vocations Internship Program, which helps students, regardless of denomination, to prepare for faith-based vocations such as youth ministry. In fact, Catholic and Baptist students currently outnumber Presbyterians and the vibrant Campus Ministry program supports the spiritual needs of all.

"Schreiner has given me many opportunities to grow and succeed as a college student. The financial aid office is very friendly and we've become close friends. They're always looking out for scholarships that pertain to me. My advice to everyone is to get involved in campus organizations that interest you."
– Matthew M., '11
San Antonio, TX
Mathematics

Schreiner University
2100 Memorial Blvd.
Kerrville, Texas 78028
Ph: (800) 343.4919 / (830) 792-7217
admissions@schreiner.edu
www.schreiner.edu

FAST FACTS

STUDENT PROFILE
# of degree-seeking undergraduates	1,013
% male/female	44/56
% African American	4
% American Indian	2
% Asian	<1
% Caucasian	72
% Hispanic	22
% Pell grant recipients	37

First-generation and minority alumni Hossein "Hagi" Hagigholam, owner, Texas restaurant chain

ACADEMICS
full-time faculty	61
full-time minority faculty	5
student-faculty ratio	14:1
average class size	19
% first-year retention rate	68
% graduation rate (6 years)	42

Popular majors Business, Biological/ Life Sciences, Teacher Education, Exercise Science, Graphic Design

CAMPUS LIFE
% live on campus (% fresh.)	69 (86)

Athletics NCAA Division III, American Southwest Conference

ADMISSIONS
# of applicants	991
% accepted	62
# of first-year students enrolled	290
SAT Critical Reading range	440-550
SAT Math range	440-570
SAT Writing range	420-530
ACT range	18-23
average HS GPA	3.54

Deadlines
regular decision	8/1
application fee (online)	$25 ($25)
fee waiver for applicants with financial need	yes

COST & AID
tuition	$18,131
room & board	$8,726
total need-based institutional scholarships/grants	$7,210,080
% of students apply for need-based aid	88
% of students receiving aid	86
% receiving need-based scholarship or grant aid	76
% receiving aid whose need was fully met	14
average aid package	$14,453
average student loan debt upon graduation	$27,986

Southern Methodist University

Southern Methodist University, a private university of 11,000 students, is a caring academic community in the heart of the vibrant city of Dallas, Texas. Students come from all 50 states and nearly 90 foreign countries and represent diverse economic, ethnic, and religious backgrounds. SMU offers an academic experience that prepares students for success in and out of the classroom. Academic advisers give students the framework and guidance needed to make and execute a successful academic plan. Internship opportunities and career advising give SMU students the edge needed in today's competitive job market and nearly 180 student organizations allow students to be involved and make a difference. SMU offers an environment that fosters a sense of belonging, promotes physical and emotional well-being, and supports intellectual, cultural, moral and spiritual growth. SMU is a great place for the education of your life.

> ACCESS Hispanic Youth Symposium

The Hispanic Youth Symposium is a four day, three night summer program that will bring more than 200 local Hispanic high school students and 100 community volunteers to SMU. The program is a life-changing event that inspires Hispanic high school students to achieve a college education, pursue a professional career, and invest in their community. Following the summer symposium, students participate in a yearlong institute which consists of mentoring and tutoring by SMU students, as well as activities at local businesses and internships.

> ACCESS Upward Bound

SMU participates in the federally funded Upward Bound program, which serves first generation, low income high school students in Dallas County. The program provides a yearlong college preparation program in addition to a six week residential summer program where students are exposed to the college experience, as well as take academic and test preparation courses.

> OPPORTUNITY Multicultural Recruitment Conference

Each year the Department of Student Activities and Multicultural Student Affairs collaborates with the Undergraduate Admission Office to host a Multicultural Recruitment Conference. Hundreds of local high school students are invited to campus to learn about the college admission and financial aid process, hear inspirational speakers on the importance of attending college, and interact with current students from various backgrounds.

> OPPORTUNITY A Different View of SMU

A Different View of SMU is a targeted multicultural student preview day held at SMU in the fall. The program features sessions on SMU's academic programs, a presentation on admission and financial aid, multicultural faculty and student panels, a campus tour, as well as an activities fair featuring our student organizations and academic resources.

> SUCCESS Department of Multicultural Student Affairs/Minority Student Resources

The Department of Multicultural Student Affairs works to recognize, educate, and celebrate diversity on the SMU campus. Within the department there is an African American, Hispanic, and Asian American coordinator who assist' with providing leadership development in addition to academic and social support services for multicultural students. Some of the events sponsored by this office include the annual Multicultural Student Retreat, the Association of Black Students Fish Fry, MLK week, the Hispanic Issues Forum, the Asian Arts and Dance Festival, Hispanic Heritage Month, and the Soul Food Dinner.

> SUCCESS CONNECT Mentorship Program

The CONNECT mentorship program is geared towards first year and transfer multicultural students to support their transition to SMU. Each new student is matched with an upper-class student who serves as a friend on campus, as well as a resource helping them to identify key resources for their academic and social success.

Southern Methodist University
P.O. Box 750181
Dallas, Texas 75275
Ph: (214) 768-2000
enroll_serv@smu.edu
www.smu.edu

F A S T   F A C T S

STUDENT PROFILE

# of degree-seeking undergraduates	6,172
% male/female	47/53
% African American	4.7
% American Indian or Alaska Native	<1
% Asian or Pacific Islander	6
% Hispanic	8
% White	74
% International	6
% Pell grant recipients	15.7

First-generation and minority alumni Jerry LeVias, '69, College Football Hall of Fame, President of LeVias Enterprises, Inc.; John W. Nieto, '59, Internationally renowned artist; Regina Taylor, '81, Actress, playwright, director; Richie L. Butler, '93, Founding senior Pastor of Union Cathedral community and Partner with CityView; Tony Garza, '83, Ambassador to Mexico

ACADEMICS

full-time faculty	656
full-time minority faculty	111
student-faculty ratio	12:1
average class size	25
% first-year retention rate	89
% graduation rate (6 years)	71

Popular majors Finance, Political Science, Economics, Psychology, and Business

CAMPUS LIFE

% live on campus (% fresh.)	31 (95)

Multicultural student clubs and organizations Association of Black Students, College Hispanic American Students, Asian Council, Black Men Emerging, Sisters Supporting Sisters, The League of United Latin American Citizens, Voices of Inspiration Gospel Choir, Multicultural Greek Council, Asian-American Leadership and Educational Conference, Student Initiative to Promote Unity, Education, Determination, Empowerment, and Spirituality

Athletics NCAA Division I, Conference USA

ADMISSIONS

# of applicants	8,270
% accepted	50
# of first-year students enrolled	1,398
SAT Critical Reading range	560-660
SAT Math range	590-680
SAT Writing range	560-660
ACT range	25-30
average HS GPA	3.57

Deadlines

early decision	1/15
regular decision	3/15
application fee (online)	$60
fee waiver for applicants with financial need	no

COST & AID

tuition	$31,200
room & board	$12,445
total need-based institutional scholarships/grants	$39,319,687
% of students apply for need-based aid	40
% of students receive aid	81
% receiving need-based scholarship or grant aid	27
% receiving aid whose need was fully met	26
average aid package	$28,129
average student loan debt upon graduation	$20,883

Texas State University

Texas State values diversity in its classrooms, residence halls, dining venues and recreational events. The university offers 100 undergraduate programs in a supportive, academically challenging environment. Bobcats hail from across Texas and across the United States, as well as from countries as far away as India, China and Israel. No matter where they come from, students find countless campus organizations that serve as enclaves of activity and support for those searching for familiar faces and customs — or wanting to discover new ones. Approximately one-third of the university's 26,000 undergraduates are ethnic minorities; of these, approximately 25 percent are Hispanic/Latino. This diversity contributes to the richness of the Bobcat experience. Texas State's investment in students results in freshman-to-sophomore retention and graduation rates that rank near the highest in the state.

"I know that all the assistance I need is on campus and that everyone here will help me accomplish my goal of graduating from Texas State University. Support is always available through organizations such as Latinas Unidas, Student Support Services and others."

– Isaura M., '12
Austin, TX
Psychology and International Studies

> ACCESS Bobcat Days and Bobcat Trails

Bobcat Days is a day for prospective students to visit and explore the academic and cultural environment of Texas State University. During the tour students can speak with faculty and staff about majors and coursework, speak with students from the Student Panel about campus life, take a campus tour, and dine at the university's student food court. Representatives from Multicultural Student Affairs are also available to visit with first-generation students. Bobcat Trails offers bus trips originating out of a select group of cities to bring prospective students to campus for Bobcat Days.

> OPPORTUNITY LBJ Achievement Scholarship

This $2,000 scholarship is offered to incoming freshmen each year who are full-time students, ranked in the top quarter of their high school graduating classes, and are either first-generation college students or current/past participants in one of the following programs: College Assistance Migrant Program (CAMP), Educational Opportunity Center Program High School Equivalency Program (HEP), Ronald E. McNair Post Baccalaureate Achievement Program, Subsidized High School Lunch Program, Summer Enrichment Program (SEP), Student Support Services Program, Talent Search, and/or Upward Bound.

> OPPORTUNITY National Hispanic Scholarship

The National Hispanic Scholarship is an $8,000 scholarship awarded over four years to eligible incoming freshmen. The scholarship applicants must be National Hispanic Scholars, received a score of 1200 or more on a single SAT test or a score of 27 or more on the ACT, and is ranked in the top 15% of his or her class or received an IB diploma.

> SUCCESS Student Support Services

This program assists eligible first-generation college students, low-income students and students with disabilities from all racial and ethnic backgrounds who have a need for academic and other support services in order to successfully complete their college education.

> SUCCESS The Foster Care Alumni Program

The Foster Care Alumni Program works with students who are alumni of the foster care system to build a support community and provide helpful resources. The mentorship program allows students to get help from trained faculty/staff or peer/student mentors with academic and social activities during their first year at Texas State University.

Texas State University- San Marcos
429 N. Guadalupe Street
San Marcos, TX 78666
Ph: (512) 245-8044
admissions@txstate.edu
www.txstate.edu

F A S T   F A C T S

STUDENT PROFILE
# of degree-seeking undergraduates	26,002
% male/female	45/55
% African American	6
% American Indian or Alaska Native	1
% Asian or Pacific Islander	2
% Hispanic	24
% Caucasian	66
% International	1
% Pell grant recipients	18

First-generation and minority alumni Tomás Rivera, '58 and '64, former chancellor, University of California-Riverside; Jerry Fields, '69, chief executive officer, J.D. Fields & Co.; Eugene Lee, '74, actor and playwright; Thomas Carter, '74, Emmy-winning director, producer and actor; Charles Austin, '91, Olympic gold medalist, owner of So High Sports and Fitness; Nina Vaca-Humrichouse, '94, chief executive officer, Pinnacle Technical Resources

ACADEMICS
full-time faculty	1,017
full-time minority faculty	274
student-faculty ratio	20:1
average class size	20-29
% first-year retention rate	79
% graduation rate (6 years)	56

Popular majors Education, Business (Management and Accounting), Psychology, Criminal Justice, and Communication Studies

CAMPUS LIFE
% live on campus (% fresh.)	24 (89)

Multicultural student clubs and organizations African Student Organization, Latino Student Organization, South Asian Student Association, First Generation Student Organization, Indian Student Association, Japanese Language & Culture, League of United Latin American Citizens, Native American Student Association, International Student Association, Bobcat Equality Alliance
Athletics NCAA Division I, Southland Conference

ADMISSIONS
# of applicants	12,172
% accepted	76
# of first-year students enrolled	3,667
SAT Critical Reading range	480-570
SAT Math range	490-590
SAT Writing range	460-550
ACT range	21-25

Deadlines
regular decision	5/1
application fee (online)	$60 ($60)
fee waiver for applicants with financial need	yes

COST & AID
tuition	in-state: $7,838; out-of-state: $17,138
room & board	$6,392
total need-based institutional scholarships/grants	$50,923,610
% of students apply for need-based aid	68
% receiving need-based scholarship or grant aid	38
% receiving aid whose need was fully met	4
average aid package	$13,769
average student loan debt upon graduation	$19,691

University of Houston

University of Houston
122 E. Cullen Building
Houston, TX 77204-2023
Ph: (713) 743-1010
admissions@uh.edu
www.uh.edu

Students chose the University of Houston for the diversity of its student body and the unlimited opportunities offered by UH's dynamic campus life. In fact, the reasons to choose UH are as diverse as the individuals on campus. Students choose from more than 100 undergraduate majors, several of which rank among the nation's best. The University of Houston's faculty members win awards, earn international acclaim and work closely with students as individuals. Students can take on internships at the largest medical center in the world or learn about the energy industry first-hand: professional opportunities are around every corner in Houston, the nation's fourth-largest city and a hub of international business. The University of Houston's graduates are CEOs, astronauts, judges, educators, Olympic athletes, actors, artists, and more. Across the world, UH alumni are fulfilling their dreams and making things happen.

> OPPORTUNITY Urban Experience Program

The multifaceted components of the Urban Experience Program promote scholarship, community service, and personal and professional development. Opportunities include internships, community service, tutoring, mentoring, cultural enrichment activities, on-campus housing, academic success workshops, career development activities, personal development workshops, and monitoring to insure academic success. Participants are selected on the basis of demonstrated or potential ability for campus leadership, community service, and academic achievement. The selection process includes an application, an essay, interviews with candidates and their parents, demonstrated financial need, and exceptional life challenges in pursuing higher education.

> SUCCESS Challenger Program

The Challenger Program seeks to help students develop positive academic and personal goals through offering an array of educationally and intellectually enriching programs. Tutors are available to assist students in a wide variety of academic subjects, along with academic and personal counseling services to address specific needs on an individual or group basis. A reading, writing, and study skills college course is available to provide academic support toward strengthening basic learning skills. The Challenger Program staff help students meet their financial needs, enabling them to continue to pursue post-secondary education. Additionally, the program supports campus social gatherings and cultural events.

"I chose the University of Houston because of its location to the Texas Med Center – I want to be a doctor. My sister was in the hospital at 9 months old and I felt like the doctors were really knowledgeable and able to give her reassurance. I want to give others that reassurance and go into pediatrics."
– Ashley L., '14
Pasadena, TX
Biology - Pre Medicine

> SUCCESS University of Houston Wellness

University of Houston Wellness, a campus-wide education and prevention program, promotes healthier choices and a healthier, safer learning environment. Goals include outreach programs on wellness topics, peer involvement in promoting health and wellness, consultation to students, faculty, and staff, and providing a clearinghouse of information on health and wellness. UH Wellness offers outreach and educational programs for the campus and community, along with referral information and resources on a wide range of health related topics including stress management, alcohol, drugs, and sexual health. The department co-sponsors large-scale prevention campaigns including Alcohol Awareness Month, the Texans' War on Drugs, Red Ribbon Week, Safer Sex Awareness Week, Eating Disorders Awareness Day, the Great American Smokeout, and the Safe Spring Break Campaign.

FAST FACTS

STUDENT PROFILE
# of degree-seeking undergraduates	28,056
% male/female	49/51
% African American	13
% American Indian or Alaska Native	<1
% Asian or Pacific Islander	20
% Hispanic	21
% White	35
% International	9
% Pell grant recipients	34.4

First-generation and minority alumni Clyde Drexler, former NBA player; Carl Lewis, track and field legend/US Olympian; Loretta Devine, actress; Master P, hip hop artist; Henry Cuellar, US/Texas State Representative; Raul Gonzales, former Texas Supreme Court Justice

ACADEMICS
full-time faculty	1,256
full-time minority faculty	288
student-faculty ratio	22:1
average class size	20-29
% first-year retention rate	79
% graduation rate (6 years)	41

Popular majors Liberal Arts and Social Sciences, Business, Natural Sciences and Mathematics

CAMPUS LIFE
% live on campus (% fresh.)	13 (34)

Multicultural student clubs and organizations Caribbean Student Organization, Chinese Student Association, Colombian Students Association, Houston Bridges, Indian Students Association, League of United Latin American Citizens, Nigerian Students Association, Pakistan Students Association, The Houston Suitcase Theater (THST), Vietnamese Students Association
Athletics NCAA Division I, Conference USA

ADMISSIONS
# of applicants	11,393
% accepted	70
# of first-year students enrolled	3,295
SAT Critical Reading range	470-570
SAT Math range	500-620
SAT Writing range	n/a
ACT range	20-25
average HS GPA	4.59

Deadlines
regular decision	4/1
application fee (online)	$50 ($50)
fee waiver for applicants with financial need	yes

COST & AID
tuition	$6,921 in-state; $13,569 out-of-state
room & board	$7,164
total need-based institutional scholarships/grants	$20,714,828
% of students apply for need-based aid	63
% of students receive aid	85
% receiving need-based scholarship or grant aid	62
% receiving aid whose need was fully met	25
average aid package	$11,660
average student loan debt upon graduation	$13,000

University of the Incarnate Word

The University of the Incarnate Word is a co-educational, private, Catholic, liberal arts university committed to educational excellence in a context of faith. The University of the Incarnate Word curriculum offers students an integrated program of liberal-arts and professional studies that includes a global perspective and an emphasis on social justice and community service. Promoting life-long learning and fostering the development of the whole person, the University of the Incarnate Word welcomes persons of diverse backgrounds in the belief that their respectful interaction advances the discovery of truth, mutual understanding, self-realization and the common good.

 ACCESS   UIW Summer Institute

To motivate local students to contribute to service and research professions in the San Antonio region, the University of the Incarnate Word sponsors the UIW Summer Institute, an overnight summer program for high school students. During the two-week camp, students experience university-level research and enjoy personal time with university faculty and students. Participants also visit area hospitals and science and research labs to gain first-hand knowledge of the valuable real-life applications of the health sciences. Moreover, the on-campus experience and seminars on college career success and personal growth bring participants meaningful insights on how to survive and succeed in college and in life. It remains the city's only overnight college-based program for high-performing high schoolers focused specifically on health care and health science.

 OPPORTUNITY   Multicultural Scholars in Nutrition

The University of the Incarnate Word Multicultural Scholars in Nutrition Program is designed to reward academically successful high school students and community college students with scholarships to the university's undergraduate Nutrition Program. Nominated by faculty or recruited through brochures and/or admissions advisers, multicultural scholars are first-generation college students demonstrating high academic and leadership potential. Scholars are assigned to University of the Incarnate Word student mentors and career mentors from the local San Antonio community. In addition, tutors are available to assist with scholars' class work, study skills and time management. Among other tasks, scholars develop nutrition education projects in groups for specific audiences, requiring the students to research nutrition topics and utilize and transform their knowledge to create a creative, engaging curriculum for an audience other than college students.

 SUCCESS   Student Success Program

The Student Success Program is a federally funded program for students who are first-generation college students. With a goal of increasing retention and graduation rates of its participants, the program provides both academic resources and non-academic support services tailored to assist each individual participant from the time he or she enters the University of the Incarnate Word through graduation from the university. The program participants receive free writing and math assistance, a peer mentor and academic tutoring.

 SUCCESS   First Year Engagement Office (FYE)

The University of the Incarnate Word's First Year Engagement Office works directly with first-year students to promote the success of first-year students by enhancing student engagement. To do so, FYE helps students to identify the appropriate resources for their academic success including assistance in major selection, study skills, time management skills, campus involvement and accessing campus resources.

University of the Incarnate Word
4301 Broadway
San Antonio, TX 78209-6397
Ph: (210) 829-6005
admis@uiwtx.edu
www.uiw.edu

F A S T   F A C T S

STUDENT PROFILE
# of degree-seeking undergraduates	5,110
% male/female	31/ 69
% African-American	n/a
% American Indian or Alaska Native	<1
% Asian or Pacific Islander	7
% Hispanic	57
% White	24
% Pell grant recipients	40

First-generation and minority alums Jesse Borrego, actor

ACADEMICS
full-time faculty	200
full-time minority faculty	46
student-faculty ratio	14:1
average class size	20-29
% first-year retention rate	63
% graduation rate (6 years)	38

Popular majors General Business, Applied Arts/ Sciences, Nutrition

CAMPUS LIFE
% live on campus (% fresh.)	20 (50)

Multicultural student clubs and organizations Hispanic Latino Association, Black Student Association, Vietnamese Student Association, International Student Association, Multicultural Greek Alliance, Taiwanese Student/Sports Association

Athletics NCAA Division II, Heartland Conference

ADMISSIONS
# of applicants	3,390
% accepted	67
# of first-year students enrolled	1,348
SAT Critical Reading range	420-530
SAT Math range	430-540
SAT Writing range	420-520
ACT range	17-22
average HS GPA	3.5

Deadlines
regular application	rolling
application fee (online)	$20
fee waiver for applicants with financial need	yes

COST & AID
tuition	$21,290
room & board	$8,780
total need-based institutional scholarships/grants	n/a
% of students apply for need-based aid	98
% of students receive aid	n/a
% receiving need-based scholarship or grant aid	79
% receiving aid whose need was fully met	33
average aid package	$15,033
average student loan debt upon graduation	$39,985

University of Mary Hardin-Baylor

The University of Mary Hardin-Baylor has an academic history tracing back to its charter as a co-educational institution by the Republic of Texas in 1845. Founded on Christian values, the university offers a solid undergraduate liberal arts program based in academic rigor. The University of Mary Hardin-Baylor is located in Belton, Texas, rests in proximity to recreational lakes and lively cities and offers a scenic setting within which to pursue a baccalaureate degree. The University of Mary Hardin-Baylor embraces diversity of all types as seen in the make-up of the student body — 25 percent of all students are minority students, and another 36 percent are first-generation college students.

> ACCESS "College 101" Seminars and Other Events

The University of Mary Hardin-Baylor offers a range of events for first-generation students and their parents, including College 101 presentations at local churches and schools to educate participants and their families about the higher education process, lingo and opportunities. The university takes part in college fairs across the state providing information to first-generation and minority students. Financial aid assistance is provided at several events throughout February to promote financial aid awareness. The University of Mary Hardin-Baylor also hosts "Super Goal Saturdays," held at local area high schools, to provide financial aid packets as well as personal support with completing the FAFSA. In addition, the university presents at dozens of evening events held in area high schools to educate students and parents about state and federal financial aid processes.

> OPPORTUNITY Mary Hill Davis Ethnic / Minority Scholarship Program

This scholarship program is offered by the Texas Baptists, who are concerned about ensuring higher education takes place in a Christian atmosphere. The program provides grants to help worthy, capable, young, minority students receiving a Christian education, and are funded through the Mary Hill Davis Offering for Texas Missions, sponsored annually by Woman's Missionary Union of Texas. The Mary Hill Davis Ethnic/Minority Scholarship Program strengthens Texas Baptist churches by providing scholarships to Baptist students from minority backgrounds planning to attend a Texas Baptist university. All grants are for a maximum award of $6,400 over a four-year period.

> OPPORTUNITY Rudy and Micaela Camacho Scholarship

The Hispanic Baptist Convention of Texas offers the Rudy and Micaela Camacho Scholarship for the purpose of developing leadership in Hispanic Baptist churches in Texas. Each year, one or two undergraduate students are selected to receive a scholarship of $1,000 per semester, renewable up to four years. Applications must be submitted to the Institutional Ministries Office of the Baptist General Convention of Texas. Applications are reviewed and processed by the Christian Education Committee of the Hispanic Baptist General Convention of Texas.

> OPPORTUNITY Transfer Honor Scholarship

Many transfer students are first-generation college students or minority students, and the University of Mary Hardin-Baylor helps meet the needs of these groups by offering the Transfer Honor Scholarship. The scholarship of $2,000 per year is awarded to entering transfer students with a minimum of 24 transferable hours from a regionally accredited college and a minimum 3.5 cumulative GPA. The award is renewable for up to six consecutive semesters and renewal is based on a cumulative GPA of 3.25 or above. The award may be limited to the first 50 qualifying students. All scholarship recipients must meet the following requirements — graduate from an accredited high school if award is based on class rank, maintain full-time status of 12 or more hours each fall and spring semester and have official, final transcripts filed by July 1 for the fall semester or November 1 for the spring semester.

> SUCCESS The Center for Academic Excellence

The Center for Academic Excellence works individually with students to support them in their efforts to become strategic learners. The Success in Academics class gives participants skills in time management, note-taking, reading textbooks, test preparation and taking final exams. Each freshman is assigned an Academic Support Counselor for weekly meetings that offer guidance and ensure the student is successful. Free tutoring is also available for all freshman-level courses.

University of Mary Hardin-Baylor
Admissions Office
900 College Street, UMHB Box 8004
Belton, TX 76513
Ph: (800) 727-8642 or (254) 295-4520
admission@umhb.edu
www.umhb.edu

F A S T   F A C T S

STUDENT PROFILE
# of degree-seeking undergraduates	2,206
% male/female	49/ 51
% African-American	12
% American Indian or Alaska Native	<1
% Asian or Pacific Islander	2
% Hispanic	13
% White	71
% Pell grant recipients	35

First-generation and minority alumni Robert Dominguez '80, president and CEO, Belton, Texas-based business, named 2004 Hispanic Business Entrepreneur of the Year, featured on cover of *Hispanic Business* magazine; Freddie Mattox '80, one of 47 of American Institute for Public Service's Jefferson Award winners; Dr. George Martinez '82, physician, Central Texas Veteran's Healthcare System; Derrick Wright '82, pastor, first African-American to serve as district superintendent, North Texas Conference of the United Methodist Church; Dr. Shaylon Rettig '95, pediatrician, San Antonio; Bill Braxton '00, associate hedge fund manager, Merrill Lynch; Byron Wilkerson '01, general manager, CenTex Barracudas, Texas indoor football team

ACADEMICS
full-time faculty	143
full-time minority faculty	17
student-faculty ratio	15:1
average class size	25
% first-year retention rate	63
% graduation rate (6 years)	43

Popular majors Elementary Education, Nursing, Business

CAMPUS LIFE
% live on campus (% fresh.)	48 (90)

Multicultural student clubs and organizations African American Outreach, Cross Cultural Cru, International Student Services Office

Athletics NCAA Division III, American Southwest Athletic Conference

ADMISSIONS
# of applicants	3,612
% accepted	42
# of first-year students enrolled	755
SAT Critical Reading range	410-610
SAT Math range	420-620
SAT Writing range	400-610
ACT range	18-27
average HS GPA	n/a

Deadlines
regular decision	rolling
application fee (online)	$35 ($35)
fee waiver for applicants with financial need	yes

COST & AID
tuition	$20,650
room & board	$5,350
total need-based institutional scholarships/grants	n/a
% of students apply for need-based aid	91
% of students receive aid	n/a
% receiving need-based scholarship or grant aid	n/a
% receiving aid whose need was fully met	22
average aid package	$11,206
average student loan debt upon graduation	$17,500

University of St. Thomas

Founded in 1947, the University of St. Thomas is a small, private, coeducational institution located in Houston, Texas – allowing for many venues to pursue cultural and career-related experiences within an urban environment. With over half of the student body coming from traditionally underserved backgrounds, there is a strong commitment to diversity and a desire for students to achieve more in their academic, personal, and spiritual lives than they ever imagined possible. The average financial aid package covers more than two-thirds of tuition, and a wide variety of merit and need-based scholarships are available to offset costs.

> OPPORTUNITY **V.J. Guinan Full Tuition Presidential Scholarship**

Academically strong freshman with SAT scores of 1350 (30 ACT) or above, and a 3.5 GPA or higher are invited to apply for the V.J. Guinan Full Tuition Presidential Scholarship. Candidates file an additional application along with the Application for Undergraduate Admission. Students also write a 500-word essay about 1) a modern challenge young Catholics face in today's society that impedes their ability to live a faithful Catholic life.; or 2) an impact you believe attending a Catholic university, rather than a secular university, will have on your life.

> SUCCESS **Mendenhall Summer Institute**

The Mendenhall Summer Institute is a five-week summer program for 50 incoming freshman to get a head start academically at the University of St. Thomas. Ideal candidates will have a combined SAT score of 1020 and a high school GPA of 2.5, as well as a demonstrated commitment to earning a college degree. Attending the Mendenhall Summer Institute costs $500, but financial aid is available for students demonstrating need. Moreover, completing the program qualifies students for a $2,000 grant toward tuition.

> SUCCESS **Science and Math Summer Institute**

With a goal to increase the number of Hispanic and low-income students earning degrees in mathematics and science-related fields, the Science and Math Summer Institute (funded by the Department of Education's College Cost Reduction Access Act/ Hispanic-Serving Institution program) is a five-week summer program available to all students at the University of St. Thomas. Although the program costs $500, financial aid opportunities are available to those who qualify.

"The Mendenhall Summer Institute at the University of St. Thomas helped me become more acclimated to the campus, its services, teachers, and buildings. I also gained a better idea of what to expect from my future college courses, and found my own niche before the semester started. Career services provided the support to help me decide what I wanted to do with my life."
– Alexandria H., '12
Pasadena, TX
Psychology

> SUCCESS **Odyssey**

This one-credit, first-semester course is designed to ease transition for incoming freshmen as they become acquainted with university life and to develop social, personal, and academic skills contributing to a successful collegiate experience. As the bulk of the semester will be dedicated to reading and discussing literature within a small group setting, the course will encourage students to acquire strategies to improve reading, writing, and research competencies.

> SUCCESS **Creating and Educating Leaders of Tomorrow (CELTs)**

This comprehensive four-year leadership program assists emerging student leaders as they begin their journeys at University of St. Thomas. With a strong emphasis on mentoring, this program is aimed for students to understand the "big picture of leadership" and encourages them to work effectively as team members through off-campus retreats and meals within a group setting.

University of St. Thomas
3800 Montrose Blvd
Houston, TX 77006-4696
Ph: (713) 525-3500
admissions@stthom.edu
www.stthom.edu

F A S T   F A C T S

STUDENT PROFILE

# of degree-seeking undergraduates	1,609
% male/female	39/61
% African American	5
% American Indian or Alaska Native	1
% Asian or Pacific Islander	11
% Hispanic	29
% White	38
% International	4
% Pell grant recipients	30.1

First-generation and minority alumni Laura Avila, ABC KXXV, News Channel 25 in Waco, Texas, Paula Henao, Revenue Agent, IRS

ACADEMICS

full-time faculty	131
full-time minority faculty	17
student-faculty ratio	12:1
average class size	17
% first-year retention rate	68
% graduation rate (6 years)	55

Popular majors Psychology, Biology, Accounting, International Studies, Communication

CAMPUS LIFE

% fresh. live on campus	44

Multicultural student clubs and organizations Al'Nadi Cultural Society, Black Student Union, Chinese Student Union, El Club Hispanico, Filipino Student Association, Hispanic Business Student Association, Student Organization of Latinos, Vietnamese Student Association

Athletics NAIA

ADMISSIONS

# of applicants	861
% accepted	84
# of first-year students enrolled	294
SAT Critical Reading range	510-630
SAT Math range	530-630
SAT Writing range	510-610
ACT range	21-27
average HS GPA	3.41

Deadlines

regular decision	rolling
application fee (online)	$25 ($25)
fee waiver for applicants with financial need	yes

COST & AID

tuition	$18,900
room & board	$7,300
total need-based institutional scholarships/grants	$4,130,594
% of students apply for need-based aid	64
% of students receive aid	46
% receiving need-based scholarship or grant aid	97
% receiving aid whose need was fully met	14
average aid package	$14,934
average student loan debt upon graduation	$21,780

The University of Texas at Austin

A major co-educational, nondenominational, public research university, the University of Texas at Austin is the flagship institution of The University of Texas System. Since 1883, the University of Texas at Austin has been dedicated to improving the quality of life of the people of Texas and the United States. As an enduring symbol of the spirit of Texas — big, ambitious and bold — the university drives economic and social progress in Texas and serves the nation as a leading center of knowledge and creativity. The University of Texas at Austin strives to transform lives for the benefit of society by encouraging learning, discovery, freedom, leadership, individual opportunity and responsibility in all of its students.

> ACCESS The Neighborhood Longhorns Program (NLP)

The University of Texas at Austin's Neighborhood Longhorns Program is an educational incentive program operated in partnership with local elementary and middle schools. The program helps disadvantaged youth in grades two through eight improve overall grade performance in reading, math, science and language arts skills. The program also provides scholarships for students to obtain a college education.

> ACCESS University Outreach Centers

The University Outreach Centers provide a five-year college preparatory program for students in grades 8-12. Group and individual services are designed to enhance students' success academically and to ensure they are college admissible upon graduation from high school. Staff assist students with potential barriers and equip them with the tools they need to successfully negotiate the college admissions process.

> OPPORTUNITY Longhorn Opportunity Scholarships/Longhorn Scholars Program

Longhorn Opportunity Scholarships are awarded to students in economically disadvantaged and historically underserved Texas communities. The scholarships provide $5,000 per year up to four years. Once on campus, all recipients become part of a four-year comprehensive academic community, the Longhorn Scholars Program. Students benefit from interaction with program advisors, support from peer mentors and opportunities to make connections across disciplines that integrate classroom, research and internship experiences.

> OPPORTUNITY Gateway Scholars Program

The University of Texas at Austin's Gateway Scholars Program seeks to maximize the academic success and social connections of new first-generation and underrepresented students. The program includes UTransition, a learning community for first generation and underrepresented transfer students, the Achieving College Excellence (ACE) Program, a service for students who seek additional academic assistance, and the Welcome Program, a diversity education program for incoming first-year students. In addition, scholars attend small-size classes in many math and science courses, receive coursework in critical thinking and college life skills, professional academic advising, individual counseling, peer advising, registration assistance and priority registration and tutoring, and participate in a variety of social, cultural and recreational activities.

"Coming to The University of Texas is an accomplishment that I am most proud of. In high school, I could have never imagined the experiences and changes I would go through that led me to where I am today. The prestige, honor, and culture that this school entails allows me to believe that everyday I spend on campus will truly fulfill our motto of 'What starts here changes the world."

– Claudio A., '09 Cedar Hill, TX Nursing

The University of Texas at Austin
Office of Admissions
P.O. Box 8058
Austin, TX 78713-8058
Ph: (512) 475-7440
askadmit@austin.utexas.edu
www.utexas.edu

F A S T   F A C T S

STUDENT PROFILE
# of degree-seeking undergraduates	36,711
% male/female	48/52
% African American	5
% American Indian or Alaska Native	<1
% Asian or Pacific Islander	18
% Hispanic	18
% White	54
% International	4
% Pell grant recipients	22.1

First-generation and minority alumni Kevin Alejandro, actor; Rodney Ellis, Texas senator; Charles Gonzalez, U.S. Congressman; Juliet Villarreal Garcia, president, UT Brownsville; Billy Ray Hunter, Jr., Principal Trumpet NY Metropolitan Opera Orchestra; Ron Kirk, U.S. Trade Representative; Robert Rodriguez, filmmaker; Moushaumi Robinson, Sanya Richards, Olympic Gold Medalists; Cedric Benson, Earl Campbell, Michael Huff, Leonard Davis, Derrick Johnson, Mike Williams, Ricky Williams, Roy Williams, DeAndre De Wayne Lewis, Shaun Rogers, NFL players; Kevin Durant, Maurice Evans, Daniel Gibson, James Thomas, NBA players; Betty Nguyen, anchor, CNN; Ricardo Romo, President, UT San Antonio; Stephanie Wilson, NASA astronaut; Judith Zaffirini, Texas senator

ACADEMICS
full-time faculty	2,687
full-time minority faculty	515
student-faculty ratio	17:1
average class size	n/a
% first-year retention rate	91
% graduation rate (6 years)	78

Popular majors Biology/Biological Sciences, Liberal Arts, Business, Government

CAMPUS LIFE
% live on campus (% freshmen)	20 (59)

Multicultural student clubs and organizations Afrikan American Affairs, Asian/Desi/Pacific Islander American Collective, Black Student Alliance, Latino Leadership Council, Longhorn American Indian Council, Student African American Brotherhood, Students for Equity and Diversity, Umoja, Vietnamese Student Association

Athletics NCAA Division I (football I-A), Big 12 Conference

ADMISSIONS
# of applicants	29,501
% accepted	44
# of first-year students enrolled	6,718
SAT Critical Reading range	540-660
SAT Math range	570-690
SAT Writing range	540-670
ACT range	24-30
average HS GPA	n/a

Deadlines
regular decision	rolling from 10/15
application fee (online)	$60 ($60)
fee waiver for applicants with financial need	yes

COST & AID
tuition	in-state: $8,532; out-of-state: $27,760
room & board	$9,246
total need-based institutional scholarships/grants	$50,500,000
% of students apply for need-based aid	74
% of students receive aid	95
% receiving need-based scholarship or grant aid	77
% receiving aid whose need was fully met	82
average aid package	$10,500
average student loan debt upon graduation	$17,000

University of Texas at El Paso

University of Texas at El Paso
500 West University Ave
El Paso, Texas 79968
Ph: (915) 747-5000
futureminer@utep.edu
www.utep.edu

Founded in 1914, the University of Texas at El Paso is a co-educational, non-denominational public research university. A Hispanic-Serving Institution committed to the ideals of access and excellence, the university is the only major research university in the country whose students are predominantly Mexican-American. The university works to capitalize on its bi-national location to create and maintain multicultural, inter-American educational and research collaborations among students, faculty, institutions and industries, especially in northern Mexico. As a public institution, the university seeks to extend the greatest possible educational access to a region which has been geographically isolated with limited economic and educational opportunities for many of its people.

> ACCESS The College Readiness Initiative (CRI)

The University of Texas at El Paso-sponsored College Readiness Initiative was established to increase students' college readiness and decrease the large number of entering students at the university who require one or more developmental courses. A major strategy of the CRI is to administer the ACCUPLACER, the exam used for math, reading and writing placement at the university, to students while they are still in high school and to provide interventions followed by a re-test for those students who place at the developmental level. CRI components include an orientation at least two weeks prior to the administration of the exam to explain the exam's purpose and design and to provide a list of resources for pre-test review; completion of a admissions application to the university or a local community college; testing during students' junior or senior year; interventions for students whose scores indicate developmental placement; and ACCUPLACER re-testing of students after interventions.

> OPPORTUNITY UTEP Promise and the Guaranteed Tuition Program

The UTEP Promise is a scholarship program that covers all tuition and fees for low-income Texans. Awarded to new freshmen who qualify for Texas resident tuition with an annual family income of $25,000 or less, the UTEP Promise covers all tuition and mandatory fees for 30 credit hours each year. The university's Guaranteed Tuition Plan also caters to low-income students. Helping students and their parents plan better financially for college, the program offers financial stability and predictability. To do so, the plan guarantees that students' tuition and mandatory fees will not increase for four consecutive years from the date of initial enrollment.

> SUCCESS The Entering Student Program (ESP)

This is a program that assists the university's freshmen population to transition into the university environment. The first component of ESP, the "University 1301 First-Year Seminar," is a three-hour core curriculum course for incoming freshmen. This class provides freshmen with critical thinking, academic research and academic success skills. The second component of the ESP is "learning communities." Through these communities, students take linked courses that allow them to form friendships, develop study groups and ultimately help each other succeed. Finally, the third ESP component, CircLES, is designed to provide an academic home for pre-science and pre-engineering students. CircLES helps to introduce these students to their major, provides developmental academic advising by a professional staff and links courses that the students take together.

FAST FACTS

STUDENT PROFILE
# of degree-seeking undergraduates	11,112
% male/female	45/55
% African-American	3
% American Indian or Alaska Native	0
% Asian or Pacific Islander	1
% Hispanic	77
% White	9
% Pell grant recipients	60

First-generation and minority alumni Olapade Adeniken, Adriana Pirtea, Obadele Thompson, professional runners; Ana Alicia Ortiz, actress; Bob Beamer, Suleiman Nyambui, professional track and field athletes

ACADEMICS
full-time faculty	662
full-time minority faculty	128
student-faculty ratio	20:1
average class size	n/a
% first-year retention rate	68
% graduation rate (6 years)	31

Popular majors Interdisciplinary Studies, Criminal Justice, Psychology, Biology, History, Nursing

CAMPUS LIFE
% live on campus (% fresh.)	n/a

Multicultural student clubs and organizations Black Student Coalition, Movimiento Estudiantil Chicana/o de Aztlan, National Association for Chicana/Chicano Studies, National Society of Black Engineers, Society of Mexican American Engineers and Scientists, Society of Hispanic Professionals, Union of African Students, Quartier Francais, Chicano/a Pre-Law Society, United Muslim Student Association

Athletics NCAA Division I, Conference USA

ADMISSIONS
# of applicants	5,147
% accepted	99
# of first-year students enrolled	2,309
SAT Critical Reading range	420-530
SAT Math range	410-530
SAT Writing range	n/a
ACT range	18-23
average HS GPA	3.12

Deadlines
regular decision application	7/31
application fee	$0

COST & AID
tuition	in-state: $6,224; out-of-state: $14,534
room & board	$7,616
total need-based institutional scholarships/grants	$44,005,514
% of students apply for need-based aid	66
% of students receive aid	78
% receiving need-based scholarship or grant aid	50
% receiving aid whose need was fully met	29
average aid package	$6,502
average student loan debt upon graduation	$23,807

University of Texas at San Antonio

University of Texas at San Antonio
One UTSA Circle
San Antonio, TX 78249-0617
Ph: (210) 458-4599
prospects@utsa.edu
www.utsa.edu

Founded by the Texas Legislature in 1969 to become a "university of the first class", UTSA has exceeded those expectations by becoming one of the most diverse, dynamic, and largest public universities in the state. The second largest of the UT System, UTSA has remained true to its mission of being an institution of access and excellence, serving as a center for intellectual and creative resources as well as a catalyst for socioeconomic development for Texas, the nation, and the world. UTSA ranks third overall in the total number of undergraduate degrees awarded to Hispanics in the country. It represents the San Antonio community with all the benefits of a big city and hospitality, personal attention, and feel of a small town.

> ACCESS **After School All Stars Tutoring Program**

UTSA employs UTSA students as tutors in the after school program, and staffing for the summer enrichment program. UTSA tutors provide mentoring, as well as basic tutoring services to all students enrolled in the After School All Stars Program.

> OPPORTUNITY **UTSAccess**

To help make higher education affordable, accessible, and provide financial support to students and families of Texas, UTSA has established UTSAccess (Undergradaute Tuition, Support, Access.) UTSA students who are first-time Freshmen as well as Texas residents with a family income of $30,000 or less can qualify for grants and/or scholarships to cover tuition and mandatory fess for four years under the UTSAccess program. Work-study funds and low interest loans can also be identified to help cover the cost of room and board and other educational expenses.

> SUCCESS **Tomas Rivera Center for Student Success**

The Tomás Rivera Center (TRC) is a comprehensive academic support center for students. Services offered at the TRC include; tutoring in quantitative subjects, academic coaching and study strategies, Supplemental Instruction (SI) to accompany difficult courses, Math Assistance Program, Online Study Skills Resources, and Learning Communities.

> SUCCESS **Academic Advising**

UTSA academic advisors offer academic advising and guidance to empower students to realize their full potential. There are dedicated advisors who work exclusively with first year students to help assure a successful transition into the core curriculum. Each of the colleges has an extensive Advising Center that continues with the students once they move into their major field.

> SUCCESS **Business Scholars Program**

The Business Scholars Program is a mentoring program for first generation college students pursuing careers in business. Established by the College of Business in 2002, the program is designed to help students make a smooth transition from high school to college and on to graduation. It is open to College of Business freshmen, sophomores and transfer students at the Downtown Campus. Currently, there are 100 students enrolled in the program.

> SUCCESS **Center for Excellence in Engineering Education**

The Center of Excellence for Engineering Education (CE[3]) provides a holistic approach for improving the quality of engineering education at The University of Texas at San Antonio. The center strives to improve the preparedness and marketability of the students in the College of Engineering for challenging and rewarding careers.

F A S T   F A C T S

STUDENT PROFILE

# of degree-seeking undergraduates	24,308
% male/female	49/51
% African American	8
% American Indian or Alaska Native	<1
% Asian or Pacific Islander	7
% Hispanic	43
% White	39
% International	2
% Pell grant recipients	42.8

First-generation and minority alumni Maria Berriozabal, first elected Latina on San Antonio City Council, and past president of the National League of Cities

ACADEMICS

full-time faculty	976
full-time minority faculty	344
student-faculty ratio	22:1
average class size	n/a
% first-year retention rate	59
% graduation rate (6 years)	28

Popular majors Business/marketing, Interdisciplinary Studies, Biological/life sciences, Psychology, Social Sciences, Engineering

CAMPUS LIFE

% live on campus (% fresh.)	43(12)

Multicultural student clubs and organizations African Student Association, Chinese Student and Scholar Association, Filipino Student Association, Hispanic Student Association, Indian Cultural Association, Mexican Americans Studies Student Organization, Association of Latino Professionals in Finance and Accounting, National Society of Black Engineers, Society of Mexican-American Engineers and Scientists

Athletics NCAA Division III, Southland Conference

ADMISSIONS

# of applicants	12,442
% accepted	88
# of first-year students enrolled	4,858
SAT Critical Reading range	450-560
SAT Math range	465-580
SAT Writing range	430-540
ACT range	19-24
average HS GPA	n/a

Deadlines

regular decision	rolling to 7/1
application fee (online)	$40 ($40)
fee waiver for applicants with financial need	yes

COST & AID

tuition	in-state: $7,527; out-of-state: $15,837
room & board	$8,937
total need-based institutional scholarships/grants	n/a
% of students apply for need-based aid	82
% of students receive aid	96
% receiving need-based scholarship or grant aid	79
% receiving aid whose need was fully met	23
average aid package	$7,856
average student loan debt upon graduation	$18,790

Westminster College

Westminster is a nationally recognized, comprehensive liberal arts college. With a broad array of graduate and undergraduate programs, Westminster is distinguished by its unique environment for learning. Westminster prepares students for success through active and engaged learning, real world experiences, and its vibrant campus community. Westminster's unique location, adjacent to the Rocky Mountains and to the dynamic city of Salt Lake, further enriches the college experience.

> ACCESS Access to Success

Westminster recently partnered with a local high school to provide English Language Learners (ELL) and/or members of underrepresented groups with weekly opportunities to play sports and practice English language skills with college-level athletes. The Access to Success program offered students from the same high school summer field trips to Westminster that included campus tours and small group discussions between high school and college students who shared their experiences of what college is like.

> OPPORTUNITY Exemplary Achievement Scholarship

Annual scholarships of $20,000 are awarded to 10 students who have demonstrated ability to overcome significant personal hardships and achieve academic excellence. Applicants are evaluated based on a personal statement or essay; resume of activities, awards, and achievements; and at least two letters of recommendation. Also considered are achievements outside of the normal academic setting including athletics and community service. Selection of recipients is based on character, background, excellence in any field, and whether a student has overcome significant difficulties. Eligible applicants must have a minimum of a 3.0 GPA.

> SUCCESS The Diversity & International Center

Through mentoring, programming, and collaboration with students, the Diversity Center strives to foster student learning, leadership and identity development; build genuine community among and within diverse groups; and advocate for and provide safe, inclusive learning environments for all students.

> SUCCESS First-Year Orientation, Mentoring and Learning Communities

Westminster's first-year student orientation includes a session specifically focusing on first-generation college students, and all first-year students are assigned to a faculty or administrator mentor to guide and support them through their first and second years of college. In addition, all first-year students are enrolled in a learning community, to connect with each other, faculty and the college community once they arrive on campus.

> *"Westminster has given me many tools to succeed and grow as a student and as a person by giving me opportunities to be involved in many activities while feeding my thirst for knowledge. Through the Latino Club and Allies Coalition, I took an active role in shaping the programming and culture of Westminster. In the Diversity Center, I found mentors and friends. Through these and other experiences, I have learned to be open and appreciate different points of view."*
> — *Princess G., '10, West Jordan, UT Pre-Law/Justice Studies,*

Westminster College
Office of Admissions
1840 South 1300 East
Salt Lake City, UT 84105
Ph: (800) 748-4753
admission@westminstercollege.edu
www.westminstercollege.edu

F A S T   F A C T S

STUDENT PROFILE

# of degree-seeking undergraduates	1,959
% male/female	43/57
% African American	<1
% American Indian	<1
% Asian	3.5
% Caucasian	77.9
% Hispanic	5.5
% Pell grant recipients	28.9

First-generation and minority alumni Silvia Thomas, Utah Hispanic/Latino Affairs Director; Forrest Cuch, Executive Director, Utah Division of Indian Affairs; Rev. France Davis, Pastor, Calvary Baptist Church

ACADEMICS

full-time faculty	119
student-faculty ratio	11:1
average class size	n/a
% first-year retention rate	79
% graduation rate (6 years)	59

Popular majors Nursing, Psychology, Economics, Accounting, Communications

CAMPUS LIFE

% live on campus (% freshmen)	27 (55)

Multicultural student clubs and organizations International Student Association, Latin@ Westminster, African American Intellectual Union, Alphabet Soup, Students Promoting Pacific Islander and Asian Mentoring at Westminster, Spanish Club, Multicultural Club, French Club, Chinese Club

Athletics NAIA, Frontier Conference

ADMISSIONS

# of applicants	1,182
% accepted	79
SAT Critical Reading range	490-632
SAT Math range	480-610
ACT range	21-27
average HS GPA	3.5

Deadlines

rolling	yes
application fee	$40

COST & AID

tuition	$21,984
room & board	$6,354
% of students receiving aid	n/a
% receiving need-based scholarship or grant aid	95
% receiving aid whose need was fully met	46
average aid package	$19,406
average student loan debt upon graduation	$16,200

Champlain College

Champlain College
163 South Willard St
P.O. Box 670
Burlington, VT 05402
Ph: (802) 860-2727
admission@champlain.edu
www.champlain.edu

Founded in 1878, Champlain College is a private, baccalaureate college offering professionally focused programs balanced by an interdisciplinary core curriculum. Champlain is a leader in educating students to become skilled practitioners, effective professionals and global citizens. Students are strongly encouraged to participate in the college's extensive internship program, while the distinctive BYOBiz program helps student entrepreneurs in any major build a business while they earn their college degree. The college has created innovative initiatives to reach out to and support the success of students from diverse backgrounds. Programming includes outreach, mentoring and scholarships.

> ACCESS **Outreach to Underserved Populations**

Champlain College works closely with TRIO, Upward Bound and GEAR UP programs to provide outreach and support to first-generation college students. Partnerships with high school technical centers allow for college credit for technical school students, while a matriculation agreement with Vermont Community College eases transfers into Champlain's four-year program. In another outreach program, Champlain students mentor at-risk middle school students over the Internet and in person — with the goal of breaking down educational barriers. Students also tutor and mentor refugee students in nearby schools for improved academic success.

> OPPORTUNITY **Vermont First and New American Scholarships**

Champlain's Vermont First Scholarship program offers need-based scholarships that broaden access to a bachelor's degree for Vermonters who are first-generation college students. The New American Student Scholarship program is a need-based scholarship program that helps Vermont's refugee and asylum students earn a college degree. This program was highlighted by the *Chronicle of Higher Education* for addressing the educational dreams of refugees. For both of these scholarships, applicants must qualify for admission to Champlain College, plan to enroll as a full-time, undergraduate student and be eligible for the Pell grant program.

> SUCCESS **Single Parents Program**

The college's long-time Single Parents Program and Scholarship offers mentoring and logistical support to single parents who want to climb out of a cycle of poverty. More than 500 students have been served by the Single Parents Program in 20 years.

> SUCCESS **Access and Success Coordinator**

This staff member works with students, admissions, the Center for Service and Civic Engagement, and the Office of Student Diversity and Inclusion to build systems, programs and support for new American students and first-generation college students. The coordinator serves as an ally and mentor to the students.

> SUCCESS **Office of Student Diversity and Inclusion**

The Office of Student Diversity and Inclusion helps Champlain College's increasingly diverse campus include and support underrepresented students on campus. Staff members implement inclusive practices in the classroom and throughout the campus and provide collaboration and support to increase diversity and cultural awareness on the Champlain campus and in the greater community.

F A S T   F A C T S

STUDENT PROFILE

# of degree-seeking undergraduates	2,618
% male/female	59/41
% African-American	1
% American Indian or Alaska Native	1
% Asian or Pacific Islander	2
% Hispanic	65
% Pell grant recipients	17

ACADEMICS

full-time faculty	88
full-time minority faculty	n/a
student-faculty ratio	15:1
average class size	22
% first-year retention rate	74
% graduation rate (6 years)	72

Popular majors Business, Graphic Design & Digital Media, Electronic Game & Interactive Development

CAMPUS LIFE

% live on campus (% freshmen)	40 (90)

Multicultural student clubs and organizations Multicultural Affairs Committee, International Club, URGE (Underrepresented Groups for Equality), Include/LBGTQA, Spirituality Committee
Athletics No varsity athletics; wide variety of intramural and club programs

ADMISSIONS

# of applicants	2,980
% accepted	74
# of first-year students enrolled	871
SAT Critical Reading range	500-600
SAT Math range	510-600
SAT Writing range	n/a
ACT range	20-25
average HS GPA	n/a

Deadlines

early admission	11/15, 1/15
regular admission	1/31
application fee (online)	$50 ($0)
fee waiver for applicants with financial need	yes

COST & AID

tuition	$25,900
room & board	$11,670
total need-based institutional scholarships/grants	n/a
% of students apply for need-based aid	90
% of students receive aid	100
% receiving need-based scholarship or grant aid	87
% receiving aid whose need was fully met	4
average aid package	$13,850
average student loan debt upon graduation	n/a

Marlboro College

Tucked away in the Green Mountains of southern Vermont is Marlboro College, a small, co-educational New England college that offers students unbridled independence and, with that, a responsibility to be an active participant in their educational development and academic success. As many colleges strategize for expansions and growth, this is a school that delights in its size.

> **OPPORTUNITY** **Financial Aid Through Institutional Scholarships**

Marlboro is committed to helping every student who qualifies for financial aid, in addition to rewarding merits of leadership potential, academic success and humanitarian efforts via institutional scholarships. More than 90 percent of all Marlboro students receive financial assistance, and the decision to seek financial aid does not affect a candidate's chances for admission.

> **SUCCESS** **Woods Orientation Trip**

The Woods Orientation Trip gives new students the chance to get to know each other through small group trips. Annually, students plan six trips spanning three to five days. The Woods Orientation Trips offer new students opportunities to get to know each other in small team environments. The expeditions are as diverse as the students themselves, with trips from kayaking to working in the college organic garden. In previous years, trips have included backpacking on the Long Trail, mountain biking in the Berkshires, sea kayaking on Lake Champlain and a tour of art museums and music in western New England.

> **SUCCESS** **Sophomore Review and Preliminary Plan Application**

The Sophomore Review and Preliminary Plan Application is a planning and review tool used by students together with their advisor to help map their education. Under this review, students reflect on their coursework and extracurricular activities as they address the following four areas: broad study, the development of a global perspective, continued work towards clear writing and the preparation for a Plan of Concentration.

> **SUCCESS** **Plan of Concentration**

The Plan of Concentration is an in-depth, self-designed exploration of a field or fields of each student's choosing. By the end of their senior year, each student completes this major independent project which involves research, one-to-one study with faculty in tutorials and a two- to three-hour oral examination with Marlboro faculty and an outside evaluator who is an expert in the student's field.

> **SUCCESS** **Dedicated Hour**

Advising at Marlboro is an important aspect of academic life at the college. The Dedicated Hour is one of the advising mechanisms by which students and advisors meet on a regular basis on Wednesdays. Advising groups, which contain students from each class year, may discuss academic matters and issues of community import and/or engage in context-related activities. Peer writing tutors are available in an academic support center, along with a professional academic support director.

> **SUCCESS** **Town Meeting**

Marlboro has a self-governing environment with 330 students and 115 faculty and staff members. Town Meeting is a regularly held assembly of the entire community that makes important, campus-wide decisions. Each student, faculty and staff member has an equal say and an equal vote at Town Meeting, which has in recent semesters tackled such issues as land use planning, smoking policy and the allotment of tens of thousands of dollars in project funding.

Marlboro College
PO Box A, South Road
Marlboro, VT 05344
Ph: (802) 258-9236
admissions@marlboro.edu
www.marlboro.edu

FAST FACTS

STUDENT PROFILE
# of degree-seeking undergraduates	329
% male/female	43/47
% African-American	<1
% American Indian or Alaska Native	<1
% Asian or Pacific Islander	3.6
% Hispanic	3
% White	88
% Pell grant recipients	30.7

ACADEMICS
full-time faculty	41
full-time minority faculty	4
student-faculty ratio	8:1
average class size	10
% first-year retention rate	82
% graduation rate (6 years)	60

Popular majors Interdisciplinary, Visual Arts, Political Science, Environmental Studies

CAMPUS LIFE
% live on campus (% freshmen)	80 (98)

Multicultural student clubs and organizations Gay-Straight Alliance, Feminist Club, International Student Club

Athletics No varsity sports

ADMISSIONS
# of applicants	447
% accepted	64
# of first-year students enrolled	91
SAT Critical Reading range	590-690
SAT Math range	510-650
SAT Writing range	640-720
ACT range	23-27
average HS GPA	3.2

Deadlines
early decision	12/1
regular decision	2/1
application fee (online)	$50 ($50)
fee waiver for applicants with financial need	yes

COST & AID
tuition	$32,550
room & board	$9,220
total need-based institutional scholarships/grants	n/a
% of students apply for need-based aid	87
% of students receive aid	80
% receiving need-based scholarship or grant aid	65
% receiving aid whose need was fully met	n/a
average aid package	$19,062
average student loan debt upon graduation	$19,482

Middlebury College

Students who attend Middlebury College receive an education at one of the United States' top liberal arts colleges. Founded in 1800, Middlebury's campus is located in Champlain Valley of Vermont, surrounded by forests and mountains. Middlebury's 2,350 undergraduate students enjoy a broad curriculum that embraces humanities, arts, literature, foreign languages and sciences in addition to a historic commitment to internationalism. Middlebury seeks to bring together a community of distinct individuals that will share their many talents and experiences. This richness of backgrounds and melding together of ideas challenges students daily and happens in an environment where respect and honest discourse dominate and personal growth and ample learning opportunities abound.

"The 21st Century Atlanta Scholars is a program that encourages students from Atlanta Public Schools to consider New England colleges. This program helped me find Middlebury, and Middlebury helped me find myself. Now, I truly see the world surrounding me--it's not black or white, it's a rainbow of colors."

– Conetrise H., '10 Atlanta, GA

> ACCESS **Discover Middlebury**

Each year, Discover Middlebury brings more than 60 seniors from traditionally underrepresented groups to campus to spend two days living the life of a college student. Students sleep in residence halls, attend classes, and interact with current undergraduates. The program was developed to give students a taste of the academic and social rewards of college with the hope that they will seriously consider higher education.

> OPPORTUNITY **Community-Based Organizations**

Middlebury works closely with a number of community-based organizations in order to reach out to a variety of students. These organizations include the Posse Foundation (New York), 21st Century Atlanta Scholars, Bright Prospect (Pomona, Calif.), College Match (Los Angeles), Harlem Educational Activities Fund (New York), Leadership Enterprise for a Diverse America (New York), National Hispanic Institute (Maxwell, Texas), One Voice (Santa Monica, Calif.) and Prep for Prep (New York).

> SUCCESS **Office for Institutional Planning and Diversity (OIPD)**

By collaborating with many other departments on campus, the Office for Institutional Planning and Diversity develops events and programming throughout the year that strive to encourage dialogue and provide diverse programming that helps to enhance an appreciation for difference in the Middlebury College community. OIPD is responsible for, among many other things, the Cafecito Hour Lecture Series, dinner discussions at the PALANA Academic Interest House and support of the many cultural organizations on campus.

> SUCCESS **Center for Teaching, Learning and Research (CTLR)**

The educational mission of Middlebury College is served by the Center for Teaching, Learning and Research, where students can use tools developed to enhance scholastic performance. Staff at CTLR work with other departments across campus to offer workshops, study groups and one-on-one educational sessions which focus on oral presentation skills, effective note-taking, reading skills enhancement, test-taking preparation and time and workload management to develop skills for success inside and outside the classroom. CTLR also prepares students for leadership roles as mentors via Students for Academic Excellence and Study Group Leader programs, and implements prevention and intervention initiatives for students who are at academic risk or who face challenges related to learning styles or disabilities.

Middlebury College
Emma Willard House
Middlebury, VT 05753
Ph: (802) 443-3000
admissions@middlebury.edu
www.middlebury.edu

F A S T   F A C T S

STUDENT PROFILE
# of degree-seeking undergraduates	2,422
% male/female	50/50
% African American	3
% American Indian or Alaska Native	1
% Asian or Pacific Islander	9
% Hispanic	6
% White	64
% International	10
% Pell grant recipients	8.9

First-generation and minority alumni Julia Alvarez, Middlebury's writer-in-residence, author, acclaimed books *How the Garcia Girls Lost Their Accents, In the Time of Butterflies*; Ron Brown, former chairman, Democratic National Committee, Secretary of Commerce under first Clinton administration, first African-American head of a national political party, first African-American Secretary of Commerce; Alexander Twilight, first African-American to earn a degree at an American college or university, first African-American member of the Vermont General Assembly

ACADEMICS
full-time faculty	249
full-time minority faculty	30
student-faculty ratio	9:1
average class size	16
% first-year retention rate	95
% graduation rate (6 years)	93

Popular majors Economics, English Language and Literature, Psychology, International Studies, Environmental Studies

CAMPUS LIFE
% live on campus (% fresh.)	97(100)

Multicultural student clubs and organizations African American Alliance, African Issues Awareness Club, Alianza Latinoamericana y Caribeña, Arabesque, Distinguished Men of Color, International Students Organization, Korea Town, Mediterranean Society, Middlebury Asian Students Organization, MIX Club, Pan-Caribbean Student Organization, Russian and Eastern European Society, Scandinavian Society, South Asian Association, Umoja, Voices of Indigenous People
Athletics NCAA Division III, New England Small College Athletic Conference

ADMISSIONS
# of applicants	7,823
% accepted	17
# of first-year students enrolled	576
SAT Critical Reading range	630-740
SAT Math range	640-740
SAT Writing range	640-740
ACT range	29-33
average HS GPA	3.73

Deadlines
early decision	11/1
regular decision	1/1
application fee (online)	$65($65)
fee waiver for applicants with financial need	yes

COST & AID
tuition (includes room and board)	$50,780
total need-based institutional scholarships/grants	$28,462,149
% of students apply for need-based aid	52
% of students receive aid	100
% receiving need-based scholarship or grant aid	100
% receiving aid whose need was fully met	100
average aid package	$32,896
average student loan debt upon graduation	$19,981

Saint Michael's College

Saint Michael's College, a vibrant, Catholic, liberal arts college, is located in Colchester, Vermont, just five minutes from Lake Champlain and three miles from Burlington, Vermont's largest city and a metropolitan college town. Saint Michael's offers an abundance of ways to explore the liberal arts, with 30 majors, and provides financial aid to nearly all admitted students. Founded by the Society of Saint Edmund over 100 years ago, Saint Michael's is the only Edmundite college in the world. The Edmundites are known for their commitment to social justice and remembered for their role in helping Dr. Martin Luther King Jr. lead desegregation efforts in Selma, Alabama. Saint Michael's honors the Edmundite tradition with a strong residential campus community, a commitment to the liberal arts and a passion for social justice.

> *"The multicultural recruiter arranged a campus visit for me and my mother that convinced us: even if we had to borrow most of the cost to attend, it was a sacrifice my family was willing to make. Then a great financial package ended up covering most expenses."*
>
> *– Manuel F., '13*
> *Tucson, AZ*
> *Political Science*

> ACCESS Mobilization of Volunteer Efforts (MOVE)

Mobilization of Volunteer Efforts meets local needs directly, helping to build strong connections between the college and the town. These are mainly geared toward youth, education and college mentoring. Programs include Woodside Tutoring program, where Saint Michael's students act as role models and serve as tutors for young adults at the Woodside Juvenile Rehabilitation Center; Middle School Mentor program, where Saint Michael's students mentor middle school girls in the neighboring Winooski school system; and America Reads, a nationwide program designed to improve literacy among children.

> SUCCESS Office of Multicultural Student Affairs (MSA)

The Office of Multicultural Student Affairs supports and assists students from diverse racial, linguistic and cultural backgrounds in their pursuit of academic success, community involvement, personal development and intellectual engagement. The office is active in recruiting and retaining students from diverse backgrounds, and also provides leadership opportunities and training to students around issues of diversity and multiculturalism. Programs include Peer Diversity Educators, First-Year Transition Program, Faculty Staff Mentors and Peer Mentors.

> SUCCESS Diversity Coalition

The Diversity Coalition at Saint Michael's promotes awareness of issues such as gender, race, religion and ethnicity and hosts many events on issues of diversity and social justice. Diversity Coalition also invites well-known speakers to campus to address relevant campus and societal issues. The coalition, which meets regularly twice a month, organizes one of Saint Michael's most well-attended and successful events: the International Festival.

> SUCCESS Martin Luther King, Jr. Society

The Martin Luther King, Jr. Society encourages students to examine the content of their own character, regardless of skin color, and to be honest about whether or not their actions are in accordance with their principles. The society organizes two of the largest events on campus, the MLK Talent Show and the MLK Convocation. In addition, the society invites at least four speakers a year to address issues affecting our society.

> SUCCESS Alianza

The Alianza Society celebrates Latino culture and experience through programs, workshops and lectures that focus on Latino heritage, address socio-political issues that impact the Latino community and raises awareness about issues of tolerance.

Saint Michael's College
One Winooski Park
Colchester, VT 05439
Ph: (802) 654-3000
admission@smcvt.edu
www.smcvt.edu

FAST FACTS

STUDENT PROFILE
# of degree-seeking undergraduates	1,900
% male/female	48/52
% African American	1
% American Indian or Alaska Native	<1
% Asian or Pacific Islander	1
% Hispanic	1
% White	94
% International	1
% Pell grant recipients	14.5

First-generation and minority alumni Loung Ung, nationally acclaimed author, *First They Killed My Father: A Daughter of Cambodia Remembers*, spokesperson, Campaign for A Landmine-Free World; Alex Okosi, senior vice president and general manager, MTV Africa; Most Reverend Moses Anderson, auxiliary bishop, Archdiocese of Detroit; Jason Curry, president/director of operations, Big Apple Basketball, Inc.; Jamila Headly, Rhodes Scholar, Oxford University

ACADEMICS
full-time faculty	151
full-time minority faculty	13
student-faculty ratio	12:1
average class size	18-20
% first-year retention rate	89
% graduation rate (6 years)	80

Popular majors Business Administration/Management, English Language and Literature, Psychology, Journalism and Mass Communication, and Education

CAMPUS LIFE
% live on campus (% fresh.)	98 (99)

Multicultural student clubs and organizations Alianza, Diversity Coalition, Martin Luther King, Jr. Society

Athletics NCAA Division II, Northeast-10 Conference and East Collegiate Athletic Conference

ADMISSIONS
# of applicants	3,228
% accepted	70
# of first-year students enrolled	475
SAT Critical Reading range	520-630
SAT Math range	520-630
SAT Writing	530-620
ACT range	22-26
average HS GPA	3.4
Deadlines	
early action	11/1
regular decision	2/1
application fee (online)	$50 ($50)
fee waiver for applicants with financial need	yes

COST & AID
comprehensive fee	$43,530
total need-based institutional scholarships/grants	$22,279,117
% of students apply for need-based aid	83
% of students receive aid	68
% receiving need-based scholarship or grant aid	88
% receiving aid whose need was fully met	27
average aid package	$22,625
average student loan debt upon graduation	$27,000

Southern Vermont College

Southern Vermont College
982 Mansion Drive
Bennington, VT 05201
Ph: (802) 447-6304
admis@svc.edu
www.svc.edu

Located on a mountainside campus overlooking Bennington, VT, Southern Vermont College is a model of an enlightened educational community: diverse, supportive, environmentally respectful and socially responsible. Through its career-enhancing liberal-arts curriculum, Southern Vermont College endeavors to transform students into engaged citizens with a broad perspective of an ever-changing society. Whether students find themselves drawn to Criminal Justice, Nursing, Business, Humanities or Social Services, the college seeks to immerse students in the concept of becoming life-long and dynamic learners. At the same time, Southern Vermont College encourages students to combine classroom learning with real-life, real-world experiences, through internships and learn-by-doing service projects. In short, Southern Vermont College may be small in size, but is most assuredly not small in the skills and self-confidence it strives to give its students.

"Southern Vermont College encourages students to stray from the normal and leave a trail. Students even have the option of designing a major that is tailored to meet their future career goals. It's a great place."
– Zach G., '09
Natick, MA
Political Science

> SUCCESS **Build the Enterprise**

"Build the Enterprise" is an entrepreneurship program which provides an opportunity for students to research, create and run a real business over the course of their Southern Vermont College education. Businesses of all kinds can be created — in retail, computer software, healthcare or whatever most interests students. The most successful ideas are funded through a college-created Venture Fund with $100,000 in assets. The program has four phases: Teams of students research business opportunities, finalize a plan of operation, manage their own enterprise — learning first-hand what it takes to run a business — and, upon graduation, can take it as a first job or sell it, with funds used to repay the Venture Fund.

> SUCCESS **Quest for Success**

A required course for incoming freshmen enrolled in a degree program, "Quest for Success" combines academics with service-learning to acclimate students to the expectations of college-level education. During the course, students plan, implement and assess a project in the community, and through that project gain skills in teamwork, organization, problem-solving, decision-making and budgeting. "Quest for Success" has earned national and state recognition as one of the most effective and successful programs for creatively addressing first-year students.

> SUCCESS **Service-Learning Initiatives**

Service-learning and civic engagement are central to the college's curriculum and its sense of community and social responsibility. At any one time, 40 percent of Southern Vermont College students are engaged in service-learning activities.

> SUCCESS **The Success Center**

The "Success Center" is a student support services center. Funded in part by a TRIO grant, it provides personalized academic planning and support. Its services include counseling and career-counseling, special courses in composition and math, the Learning Differences Support Program and the Learning Cooperative, a peer-tutoring program. The Success Center is open and available to all students free of charge.

FAST FACTS

STUDENT PROFILE
# of degree-seeking undergraduates	481
% male/female	36/64
% African American	15
% American Indian or Alaska Native	<1
% Asian or Pacific Islander	<1
% Hispanic	3
% Pell grant recipients	37

ACADEMICS
full-time faculty	24
full-time minority faculty	n/a
student-faculty ratio	13:1
average class size	16
% first-year retention rate	65
% graduation rate (6 years)	42

Popular majors Business, Criminal Justice, Nursing, Psychology, Radiologic Technology

CAMPUS LIFE
% live on campus (% fresh.)	58 (92)

Multicultural student clubs and organizations
Diversity Club
Athletics NCAA Division III, New England Collegiate Conference

ADMISSIONS
# of applicants	383
% accepted	86
# of first-year students enrolled	125
SAT Critical Reading range	420-500
SAT Math range	400-480
SAT Writing range	n/a
ACT range	15-20
average HS GPA	2.7

Deadlines
regular decision	rolling
application fee (online)	$30 ($0)
fee waiver for applicants with financial need	yes

COST & AID
tuition	$18,690
room & board	$8,840
total need-based institutional scholarships/grants	$2,400,000
% of students apply for need-based aid	97
% of students receive aid	97
% receiving need-based scholarship or grant aid	94
% receiving aid whose need was fully met	10
average aid package	$13,900
average student loan debt upon graduation	$20,244

University of Vermont

The University of Vermont, founded in 1791, is the fifth-oldest university in New England (following Brown, Dartmouth, Harvard and Yale) and is one of the 20 oldest institutions of higher education in the United States. Also known as UVM, an abbreviation for its Latin name, Universitas Viridis Montis, the university is a public, co-educational, liberal arts university that offers the best of both worlds — a research university's intellectual resources and breadth of opportunity and the student attention that's typical of a smaller college. UVM prepares students to lead productive, responsible and creative lives. University of Vermont students succeed after graduation. A recent study shows that more than 88 percent were employed and 22 percent enrolled in graduate school within a year of receiving their UVM degree.

> ACCESS Summer Happening Program

The University of Vermont partners with the Abenaki community to sponsor the Summer Happening Program, which brings Abenaki middle school students to the university for three days to experience on-campus life. The goal is to convince participants that a college education is feasible. Participants get assistance with course selection and financial aid and gain valuable exposure to university programs, faculty and cultural activities. Past highlights of the Summer Happening Program have included an orienteering workshop and a dinner featuring authentic native foods.

> ACCESS Columbus Campus-University of Vermont Partnership

The Christopher Columbus Campus-University of Vermont Partnership encourages greater diversity at the university. Christopher Columbus Campus is an urban, multicultural setting for several high schools in the Bronx. The partnership seeks to "catch" students from Columbus High School, Pelham Prep Academy and Collegiate Institute for Math and Science during their freshman and sophomore years to provide them with an "early awareness" of the college process. Participants attend workshops, sponsored by the University of Vermont, on topics such as college admissions and financial aid. In addition, participants may also receive fully paid trips to UVM campus to experience college life first-hand.

> SUCCESS ALANA Peer Mentoring

The University of Vermont's ALANA (African-American, Latino, Asian, Native American) Peer Mentoring program pairs incoming first-year ALANA students with outstanding upperclassmen. These upperclassmen act as mentors, both academically and socially. Mentors help ALANA freshmen strive for academic excellence, directing them to tutors and/or other learning aids. The program also fosters a sense of community by sponsoring a series of social events including intergalactic bowling, skiing, free tickets to sporting events and the theater, pizza parties and apple picking. In addition, the program offers funds for mentors and mentees to engage in fun activities on their own, such as a night out at the movies or coffee at a local café.

> SUCCESS Summer Enrichment Scholarship

The Summer Enrichment Scholarship at the University of Vermont is a bridge program sponsored by and administered through the ALANA Student Center. The program introduces incoming first-year ALANA, first-generation and low-income students to university life before the challenges of the first year formally begin. Participants earn credit for two classes (at no cost), a paid campus job, free room and board and a $500 stipend at the successful completion of the program. More importantly, participants build relationships with other students, enjoy a variety of recreational activities in the Vermont area (such as camping and a ropes course) and develop valuable leadership skills.

University of Vermont
Undergraduate Admissions Office
194 South Prospect St.
Burlington, VT 05401
Ph: (802) 656-3370
admissions@uvm.edu
www.uvm.edu

F A S T   F A C T S

STUDENT PROFILE

# of undergraduate enrollment	10,937
% male/female	44/56
% African American	1
% American Indian	<1
% Asian	2
% Hispanic	2
% Pell grant recipients	17

First-generation and minority alumni Pedro Albizu Campos, Puerto Rican political leader

ACADEMICS

full-time faculty	609
minority faculty	84
student-faculty ratio	15:1
average class size	24
% first-year retention rate	86
% graduation rate (6 years)	71

Popular majors Business Administration, English, Psychology

CAMPUS LIFE

% live on campus (% freshmen)	53 (97)

Multicultural student clubs and organizations Alianza Latina, Black Student Union, Asian-American Student Union, Council for Unity, Muslim Student Association

Athletics NCAA Division I, American East Conference, Hockey East Association

ADMISSIONS

# of applicants	21,062
% accepted	65
# enrolled	2,778
SAT Critical Reading range	540-640
SAT Math range	550-650
SAT Writing	540-640
ACT range	23-28
average HS GPA	n/a

Deadlines

early action	11/1
regular decision	1/15
application fee	$55
fee waiver for applicants with financial need	yes

COST & AID

tuition	in-state: $13,554; out-of-state: $31,410
room & board	$8,996
total need-based institutional scholarships/grants	$54,790,440
% applying for aid	66
% of students receiving aid	54
% receiving need-based scholarship or grant aid	90
% receiving aid whose need was fully met	24
average aid package	$17,576
average student loan debt upon graduation	$25,599

Hollins University

Hollins University
P.O. Box 9707
Roanoke, VA 24020
Ph: (540) 362-6401
huadm@hollins.edu
www.hollins.edu

Recognized as one of the top women's colleges in country, Hollins provides students with a personalized education that stresses critical thinking and interdisciplinary study. Hollins has also been recognized for its art, dance and creative writing programs, and it channels this creativity across the curriculum. Hollins graduates — many of whom take advantage of the university's extensive internship and study abroad programs — may also earn a certificate in leadership studies through the university's Batten Leadership Institute, poising them for success in the job market. Founded in 1842, Hollins University is a private liberal arts school for women.

> ## ACCESS **Hollinsummer**

Hollinsummer is a two-week summer program that gives high school girls a taste of college life through living together in dorms, eating in the dining hall and taking their choice of two classes. Courses are taught by Hollins professors and include creative writing, modern dance, photography, leadership, forensic chemistry, pottery, literature and psychology.

> ## OPPORTUNITY **Minority and High-Need Scholarships**

Hollins provides students with information on a variety of aid sources, including many scholarships that may benefit minority and high-need students. Among these are the Martin Luther King Memorial Scholarship, preference for which is given to African-American students and the Cecelia M. Long '70 Endowed Scholarship, awarded to outstanding African-American women whose records of community service and achievement in high school reveal promise for high achievement at Hollins. The Willie Mae Jackson, Sue Jackson and Thomas Bain scholarships are all reserved for students with high financial need. In addition, Hollins offers generous merit scholarships for academic performance, leadership and creative talent.

> ## OPPORTUNITY **Horizon Program**

Students who have been out of high school for five to six years, even if they are transferring from a community college, can take advantage of the Hollins Horizon Program, which caters to nontraditional students. Program participants ultimately earn the same degree as other graduates — in any field of their choosing — but they do so with the added benefit of a special advisor and a strong support network of other program participants. Horizon students may apply for regular financial aid, as well as for special Horizon scholarships.

> ## SUCCESS **Cultural and Community Engagement**

Through the Office of Cultural and Community Engagement, Hollins offers a variety of programs geared to support underrepresented students. For example, students are invited to a special, early orientation, the Early Transition Program, where they interact with peer mentors and receive information about their impending university experience. The office also coordinates academic outreach for these underserved students, houses intercultural organizations and trainings, and acts as the clearinghouse for multicultural programming.

"Hollins is preparing me for the writing future I've always wanted. The classes are an experience like no other, and budding writers are everywhere. There's always someone to laugh at your bad jokes or to cry over your tragic heroine and offer advice on how to make your writing better."

*– Deirdra S., '12
Hillsville, VA
English*

FAST FACTS

STUDENT PROFILE

# of degree-seeking undergraduates	785
% male/female	0/100
% African-American	7.8
% American Indian or Alaska Native	0.6
% Asian or Pacific Islander	1.8
% Hispanic	3.1
% White	81.9
% International	4.8
% Pell grant recipients	34.8

First-generation and minority alumni Kiran Desai, novelist

ACADEMICS

full-time faculty	73
full-time minority faculty	7
student-faculty ratio	10:1
average class size	13
% first-year retention rate	74
% graduation rate (6 years)	61

Popular majors Art, Business, Communication Studies, English and Creative Writing, Psychology

CAMPUS LIFE

% live on campus (% fresh.)	73 (94)

Multicultural student clubs and organizations Bell, Book and Candle (Pagan), Black Student Alliance (BSA), OUTloud (LGBTQ), French Club, Global Interest Association, Spanish Club, Spiritual and Religious Life Association

Athletics NCAA Division III, Old Dominion Athletic Conference

ADMISSIONS

# of applicants	658
% accepted	87.1
# of first-year students enrolled	209
SAT Critical Reading range	540-650
SAT Math range	490-590
SAT Writing	n/a
ACT range	n/a
average HS GPA	3.52

Deadlines

early decision	12/1
application fee (online)	$35 ($35)
fee waiver for applicants with financial need	yes

COST & AID

tuition	$26,500
room & board	$9,650
total need-based institutional scholarships/grants	$7,498,811
% of students apply for need-based aid	79.7
% of students receive aid	82.9
% receiving need-based scholarship or grant aid	66
% receiving aid whose need was fully met	13.5
average aid package	$21,407
average student loan debt upon graduation	$22,161

Marymount University

Marymount is a comprehensive, co-educational Catholic university. With approximately 3,600 students from more than 40 states and 70 countries, Marymount offers a student-centered learning community that values diversity and focuses on the education of the whole person. The university offers a wide range of undergraduate and graduate programs through its four schools: Arts and Sciences, Business Administration, Education and Human Services and Health Professions. The resources of Washington, D.C. enrich the learning experience, and the region's government, business and nonprofit organizations offer exciting opportunities for internships and employment. Undergraduate programs combine a liberal arts foundation with career preparation. Scholarship, leadership, service and ethics are hallmarks of a Marymount education.

> OPPORTUNITY Grant and Scholarship Information

Marymount is committed to making private higher education accessible and affordable for qualified students from diverse backgrounds. Many Marymount undergraduates benefit from the Marymount Tuition Assistance Grant. In addition, a variety of need- and merit-based scholarships are available. Some scholarships are linked to specific programs, like business administration, communications, interior design or nursing. The university's Spirit of Service Scholarship recognizes individuals with a strong record of community service. Finally, through a grant from the National Science Foundation, Marymount awards scholarship funds through the S-STEM Program (Scholarships in Science, Technology, Engineering, and Mathematics), to students interested in these disciplines who are academically talented and can demonstrate financial need.

> SUCCESS Internships

Marymount students in every discipline gain hands-on experience through a required internship. Business students intern at international corporations like Morgan Stanley and Ernst & Young. Nursing students train in some of the most prestigious health care facilities in the nation, including Walter Reed Army Medical Center and Children's National Medical Center. Criminal justice majors in the forensic science track spend time interning with government agencies such as the FBI and the Department of Homeland Security. Fashion merchandising majors work with companies like Burberry and Saks Fifth Avenue. Politics majors intern on Capitol Hill and at the White House. Other popular internship sites include Gannett/USA Today, local television stations, the National Institutes of Health, and the Smithsonian Institution.

> SUCCESS Peer Mentor Program and Academic Success Center

Marymount's Peer Mentor Program pairs upperclassmen with first-year students to help them make the transition to college. Peer mentors introduce new students to campus and community activities and resources, and they are always available to answer questions. The university's Academic Success Center, Learning Resource Center and Counseling Center also contribute to a campus atmosphere that promotes students' academic success and personal well-being.

Marymount University
2807 North Glebe Road
Arlington, VA 22207
Ph: (800) 548-7638 or (703) 284-1500
admissions@marymount.edu
www.marymount.edu

FAST FACTS

STUDENT PROFILE
# of degree-seeking undergraduates	2,224
% male/female	24/76
% African-American	15
% American Indian or Alaska Native	<1
% Asian or Pacific Islander	7
% Hispanic	10
% White	48
% International	8
% Pell grant recipients	18

First-generation and minority alums W. Geovanni Munoz, JD '03, attorney, Chandler Law Group; Shingai Mavengere '02, accountant/consultant, Ernst & Young, LLP; Bill Johnson '95, furniture and interior designer, featured in *The Washington Post*, *Washington Times*, *The New York Times* and *Elle* magazine

ACADEMICS
full-time faculty	138
full-time minority faculty	6
student-faculty ratio	14:1
average class size	21
% first-year retention rate	70
% graduation rate (6 years)	48

Popular majors Business Administration, Nursing, Psychology, Fashion Merchandising, Interior Design

CAMPUS LIFE
% live on campus (% freshmen)	34 (69)

Multicultural Student Clubs and Organizations Black Student Alliance, Hispanic Student Association, International Club, Muslim Student Organization, Saudi Student Society, Vietnamese Student Association

Athletics NCAA Division III, Capital Athletic Conference

ADMISSIONS
# of applicants	1,766
% accepted	84
# of first-year students enrolled	597
SAT Critical Reading range	440-540
SAT Math range	440-540
SAT Writing range	440-540
ACT average	14
average HS GPA	3.02
Deadlines	
regular decision	rolling
application fee (online)	$40 ($40)
fee waiver for applicants with financial need	yes

COST & AID
tuition	$22,370
room & board	$9,745
total need-based institutional scholarships/grants	$2,637,442
% of students apply for need-based aid	72
% of students receive aid	83
% receiving need-based scholarship or grant aid	65
% receiving aid whose need was fully met	14
average aid package	$14,935
average student loan debt upon graduation	$22,993

Norfolk State University

Norfolk State University
700 Park Avenue
Norfolk, Virginia 23504
Ph: (800) 274-1821
www.nsu.edu/admissions

Norfolk State University is one of the nation's largest historically black universities. The university has evolved from a modest teachers' college to a doctoral-granting institution with a solid track record of producing outstanding graduates in every field of human endeavor. Norfolk State University's mission is to provide an affordable high-quality education for an ethnically and culturally diverse student population, equipping its students with the capability to become productive citizens who continuously contribute to a global and rapidly changing society. Strategic imperatives involve high-quality academic instruction, efficient management and a solid fiscal foundation.

> ACCESS **Techno-Scholars Program**

The Techno-Scholars Program is designed to aid targeted male students who live in Norfolk (ages 12 to 16) become goal-oriented and community-conscious. This intervention is provided to inspire and prepare students for college and/or career success, thereby reducing their likelihood of falling prey to risk factors that affect African-American males. Participants will meet on-site at least five hours a week and/or via webcam and be matched with three different mentors. Community Mentors will provide positive guidance, academic assistance, life skills and male development sessions, and join students in social, cultural and educational field trips. Additionally, Career Professional Mentors will expose participants to their respective careers via workplace shadowing, panel discussions, career fairs and technical periodicals. Collegiate Mentors will provide academic tutoring, homework assistance and exposure to their respective technology studies and campus environments via classroom visits, related student programs and activities.

> OPPORTUNITY **Financial Aid Awareness Month**

February is Financial Aid Awareness Month. During this month, the Financial Aid Office at Norfolk State hosts a number of events designed to improve financial literacy, deliver financial aid and scholarship information and provide personalized assistance to both current and prospective students. Parents and student are encouraged to participate in these activities. Some of the events are as follows: FAFSA Workshop, Financial Literacy Workshop and Scholarship Essay Writing Workshop. These activities attract new and prospective students as well as currently enrolled students.

> SUCCESS **UNI 101**

UNI 101 is a course designed to help first-year undergraduate students adjust to the university, develop a better understanding of the college environment and acquire essential academic success skills. Common themes include Norfolk State's mission and history, orientation to campus services, students' rights and responsibilities and an appreciation of service-learning civic engagement. Students gain an overview of their learning strengths and weaknesses, and understand their learning style to learn more effectively and accomplish their goals.

> SUCCESS **The Academy for Collegiate Excellence and Student Success (ACCESS)**

Norfolk State University's Academy for Collegiate Excellence and Student Success has been designed to prepare admitted freshmen for study at the college-level. Participants normally demonstrate academic achievement in high school, but have lower college examination (SAT/ACT) scores than are required for regular admission. Through intensive course work in areas such as communication skills and mathematics and through a required University Orientation course that stresses study skills and adjustment to college, these students are successful by the end of the freshman year.

FAST FACTS

STUDENT PROFILE

# of degree-seeking undergraduates	5,194
% male/female	38/62
% African-American	85
% American Indian or Alaska Native	<1
% Asian or Pacific Islander	1
% Hispanic	1.5
% White	5
% International	n/a
% Pell grant recipients	55

First-generation and minority alums Nathan McCall, best-selling author, former reporter, The *Washington Post*; Rear Admiral (retired) Evelyn J. Fields, former director NOAA Corps (first woman/African-American to hold this position); Derek Dingle, executive editor of *Black Enterprise Magazine*

ACADEMICS

full-time faculty	272
full-time minority faculty	n/a
student-faculty ratio	18:1
average class size	18
% first-year retention rate	72
% graduation rate (6 years)	31

Popular majors Business, Nursing, Interdisciplinary Studies, Psychology, Mass Communications

CAMPUS LIFE

% live on campus (% freshmen)	43 (75)

Multicultural student clubs and organizations Caribbean Students Association, Gospel Choir/Voices of Inspiration, NAACP, National Society of Black Engineers, National Society of Minorities in Hospitality, Spanish Club

Athletics NCAA Division I, Mid-Eastern Athletic Conference

ADMISSIONS

# of applicants	4,748
% accepted	68
# of first-year students enrolled	n/a
SAT Critical Reading range	n/a
SAT Math range	n/a
SAT Writing	n/a
ACT range	n/a
average HS GPA	2.71

Deadlines

regular admission	n/a
application fee (online)	$35 ($25)
fee waiver for applicants with financial need	yes

COST & AID

tuition	in-state: $5,872; out-of-state: $17,931
room & board	$7,329
total need-based institutional scholarships/grants	n/a
% of students apply for need-based aid	92.5
% of students receive aid	98.7
% receiving need-based scholarship or grant aid	89.9
% receiving aid whose need was fully met	8.6
average aid package	$8,834
average student loan debt upon graduation	$15,467

Old Dominion University

Old Dominion University expects its students to thrive in the modern world, seek possibility around every corner, and know that knowledge and experience lead to success. With more than 160 mind-expanding programs, including 70 undergraduate degrees, and internships in every imaginable field, students are able to bring their thoughts to life at ODU. Students are a part of a vibrant, diverse, learning community and are encouraged to take advantage of the campus environment to understand and develop an appreciation of the different cultures, traditions and lifestyles in which they will encounter during and after their undergraduate experience at ODU.

"I chose ODU because I wanted diversity and ODU made me feel at home and comfortable. Out of the many schools that I looked into ODU made me feel like I was getting the true college experience."
– Brittany S., '10
Goodview, VA
Communications

> ACCESS Upward Bound

Located on the campus of Old Dominion University, the Upward Bound Program has two phases, a summer residential phase and an academic year phase. During the summer, students reside on campus for six weeks and receive intensive classroom instructions to prepare them for the upcoming school year. During the academic year phase, students attend sessions on Saturdays and receive individualized tutorial instructions designed to enrich their performance in high school classes. The Program is offered to ninth through twelfth grade students who reside in Norfolk and Portsmouth. Selected students shall show potential for success in a two or four-year college, but because of inadequate educational preparation, admission to such an institute would be difficult without the benefit of Upward Bound.

> OPPORTUNITY Career Advantage Program (CAP)

Old Dominion University's partnership with employers, alumni, mentors, and the community provides a wealth of experience opportunities for students through student employment, internships, cooperative education, employer events and career fairs. The Career Advantage Program (CAP) incorporates a wide variety of career related activities and *guarantees* all undergraduate students a credit bearing, practical work experience related to their major. At last count, there were more than 4,665 internships and career-relevant experiences available to students.

> SUCCESS Student Support Services (SSS)

Student Support Services is a comprehensive program designed to promote retention and academic success in college. It provides participants with academic and support services in a caring environment that seeks to ensure their successful completion of a baccalaureate degree at Old Dominion University, and to help students make the transition from one level of higher education to the next. These services are offered free of charge to participants and include tutoring, academic and financial advising, counseling, mentoring, workshops, and cultural enrichment trips.

Old Dominion University
108 Rollins Hall
5115 Hampton Boulevard
Norfolk, VA 23529
Ph: (757) 683- 3685
admit@odu.edu
www.odu.edu

FAST FACTS

STUDENT PROFILE
# of degree-seeking undergraduates	18,253
% male/female	46/54
% African American	23
% American Indian or Alaska Native	<1
% Asian or Pacific Islander	5
% Hispanic	4
% White	61
% International	2
% Pell grant recipients	25.7

ACADEMICS
full-time faculty	697
full-time minority faculty	154
student-faculty ratio	17:1
average class size	25
% first-year retention rate	80
% graduation rate (6 years)	47

Popular majors Criminal Justice, Business Administration, Education, Nursing, Engineering

CAMPUS LIFE
% live on campus (% fresh.)	29 (66)

Multicultural student clubs and organizations
Black Student Alliance, Global Student Friendship, Latino Student Alliance, Society of Hispanic Professional Engineers, The F.O.R.E.I.G.N.E.R's, T.R.U.S.T, Xeqtion, African Caribbean Association, 3D, D.E.S.T.I.N.E.D
Athletics NCAA Division I, Colonial Athletic Association

ADMISSIONS
# of applicants	9,878
% accepted	72
# of first-year students enrolled	2,755
SAT Critical Reading range	480-570
SAT Math range	490-590
SAT Writing range	470-570
ACT range	18-23
average HS GPA	3.3

Deadlines
early action	12/1
regular decision	2/1
application fee (online)	$50 ($50)
fee waiver for applicants with financial need	yes

COST & AID
tuition	in-state $7,470; out-of-state $20,910
room & board	$8,000
total need-based institutional scholarships/grants	$27,957,171
% of students apply for need-based aid	71
% of students receive aid	95
% receiving need-based scholarship or grant aid	48
% receiving aid whose need was fully met	51
average aid package	$7,597
average student loan debt upon graduation	$17,250

Sweet Briar College

Sweet Briar College
PO Box B
Sweet Briar, VA, 24595
Ph: (800) 381-6142
admissions@sbc.edu
www.sbc.edu

Sweet Briar College, a premier liberal arts and sciences college for women, offers its students the opportunity to take on leadership roles both inside the classroom — the college ranked 13th on the Princeton Review's "Class Discussion Encouraged" list — and out. In fact, the college even offers a leadership certificate program. Sweet Briar students, many of whom have had extensive resume and cover-letter writing training from the exceptional staff in the Career Services Center (ranked No. 5 on the Princeton Review's "Best Career/Job Placement Services" list), are particularly poised to enter the job market, particularly if they seek to enter traditionally male-dominated fields, such as the sciences and government. In the end, Sweet Briar is all about women's empowerment, which is why so many students design their own majors.

> ACCESS Local Community Partnerships

Sweet Briar has partnerships with several local community organizations to help encourage racial and ethnic minority students to pursue higher education. The college is dedicated to having a diverse student body and works actively to promote the importance of higher education, and specifically women's education, to students from all backgrounds. Sweet Briar has a generous merit scholarship program and need-based assistance policy.

> OPPORTUNITY Admissions Office Open Houses

Sweet Briar encourages any student who wishes to explore the opportunities at the college to visit campus. Sweet Briar hosts two open house programs in the fall (one in October and one in November) that provide students the opportunity to stay in a residence hall with a current student, visit classes of interest, and meet with faculty and staff members at the college who will help guide the student's academic and co-curricular program. There is also a one-day open house program in the spring for juniors and sophomores just beginning the college search to be introduced to the programs and opportunities for student success at Sweet Briar. Students are also welcome to visit campus at a time that is convenient for them by calling the Admissions Office.

> SUCCESS First Year Experience (FYE)

All Sweet Briar students benefit from the college's nationally recognized first-year program, the First Year Experience. FYE is an intentionally designed, comprehensive curricular and co-curricular initiative that provides new students with opportunities and resources for making meaningful connections to the campus community. This program goes far beyond the standard, brief orientation in the fall to offer ongoing programs and support services throughout the year that aid in the adjustment to college life and to Sweet Briar. Collectively, FYE activities provide students with a greater sense of self-knowledge, a heightened appreciation for others and a broader scope of thought.

FAST FACTS

STUDENT PROFILE

# of degree-seeking undergraduates	813
% male/female	0/100
% African-American	3
% American Indian or Alaska Native	<1
% Asian or Pacific Islander	<1
% Hispanic	3
% White	87
% Pell grant recipients	15

ACADEMICS

full-time faculty	65
full-time minority faculty	3
student-faculty ratio	9:1
average class size	13
% first-year retention rate	71
% graduation rate (6 years)	72

Popular majors Biology, Government, Business, Psychology, Education

CAMPUS LIFE

% live on campus (% freshmen)	90 (95)

Multicultural student clubs and organizations French Club, German Club, Italian Club, ONYX
Athletics NCAA Division III, Old Dominion Athletic Conference

ADMISSIONS

# of applicants	629
% accepted	83
# of first-year students enrolled	212
SAT Critical Reading range	510-630
SAT Math range	470-600
SAT Writing	n/a
ACT range	20-26
average HS GPA	3.5

Deadlines

early decision	12/1
regular decision	2/1
application fee (online)	$40 ($40)
fee waiver for applicants with financial need	yes

COST & AID

tuition	$29,335
room & board	$10,460
total need-based institutional scholarships/grants	$5,264,464
% of students apply for need-based aid	67
% of students receive aid	64
% receiving need-based scholarship or grant aid	83
% receiving aid whose need was fully met	88
average aid package	$13,633
average student loan debt upon graduation	$20,118

University of Mary Washington

University of Mary Washington
1301 College Avenue
Fredericksburg, VA 22401
Ph: (540) 654-2000
admit@umw.edu
www.umw.edu

The University of Mary Washington is a mid-sized, public college that combines rich history and tradition with academic achievement. Nationally ranked as one of the top liberal arts colleges in the country, Mary Washington's academic program is rigorous, focusing on preparing students for success after college. The university's focus on diversity outreach is noteworthy, especially with the introduction of the Rappahannock Scholars Program, a program aimed at college preparation and guaranteed admission for local high school students of underrepresented groups. The University of Mary Washington campus is located in the picturesque, culturally active city of Fredericksburg, Va., only a short drive from Washington, D.C. and Richmond, Va.

> ACCESS Rappahannock Scholars Program

In participation with local high schools in the Northern Neck region of Virginia, the Rappahannock Scholars Program guarantees admission to the University of Mary Washington when program criteria are met. The Rappahannock Scholars Program also provides support, guidance and encouragement throughout high school for prospective students to prepare for success in college. Students who attend participating high schools and exhibit promising academic, economic and leadership characteristics may be nominated by guidance counselors for the Rappahannock Scholars Program. Preference is given to students of underrepresented groups who will add cultural diversity to the university campus, first-generation students and students from economically disadvantaged backgrounds.

> OPPORTUNITY Summer Orientation Program

Summer Orientation Program begins five days prior to the beginning of classes, new students arrive on-campus and partake in various programs and activities designed to help them get to know each other, and to prepare for a successful first year at the University.

> SUCCESS James Farmer Multicultural Center

The University of Mary Washington's James Farmer Multicultural Center facilitates student learning and personal development, particularly that of underrepresented groups, by increasing students' awareness and knowledge of diversity issues. Of particular note is the Student Transition Program, a three-week summer enrichment program for accepted students from underrepresented groups.

> SUCCESS Study Skills Workshop

Mary Washington's Office of Academic Services offers a series of workshops that provide important strategies for academic success. Study Skills Workshops are original because they are developed and presented by Mary Washington students themselves. Workshop topics include Time Management, Preparation for the Perfect Paper, Test Preparation and Taking and more. Study Skills Tutorials are also available online.

"My career goal is to become a successful businessman. Being team leader for the Service Learning Project at UMW has made me cognizant of the critical components needed to become an effective leader. "
– Charles R., '11
Jersey City, NJ
Business Administration

FAST FACTS

STUDENT PROFILE
# of degree-seeking undergraduates	4,258
% male/female	34/66
% African American	5
% American Indian or Alaska Native	<1
% Asian or Pacific Islander	4
% Hispanic	4
% White	60
% International	<1
% Pell grant recipients	8.4

ACADEMICS
full-time faculty	242
full-time minority faculty	31
student-faculty ratio	16:1
average class size	n/a
% first-year retention rate	83
% graduation rate (6 years)	76

Popular majors Business Administration, Psychology, Biology, Education

CAMPUS LIFE
% live on campus (% fresh.)	57 (93)

Multicultural student clubs and organizations Black Student Association, Brothers of a New Direction, Citizens of the World, Hispanic Group Women of Color

Athletics NCAA Division III, Capital Athletic Conference

ADMISSIONS
# of applicants	4,761
% accepted	74
# of first-year students enrolled	963
SAT Critical Reading range	540-650
SAT Math range	520-620
SAT Writing	530-640
ACT range	24-28
average HS GPA	3.6

Deadlines
early action	1/15
regular decision	2/1
application fee (online)	$50 ($50)

COST & AID
tuition	in-state: $3,900; out-of-state: $16,810
room & board	$8,200
total need-based institutional scholarships/grants	n/a
% of students apply for need-based aid	50
% of students receive aid	26
% receiving need-based scholarship or grant aid	24
% receiving aid whose need was fully met	5
average aid package	$7,540
average student loan debt upon graduation	$14,500

University of Virginia

University of Virginia
Box 400160
Charlottesville, VA 22904-4160
Ph: (434) 924-3587
undergradadmission@virginia.edu
www.virginia.edu

Founded by Thomas Jefferson, the University of Virginia has three core standards when admitting students: access, diversity and affordability. The University is committed to meeting the financial needs of every single student who qualifies for admission, regardless of economic circumstance, and its 13,600 undergraduate students come from every state, more than 100 nations, and every imaginable background. As a research university, the University of Virginia values the liberal arts and boasts strong undergraduate programs in engineering, nursing, architecture, leadership and public policy, commerce and education, as well as the liberal arts and sciences. Students are encouraged to take ownership of the University community and to become leaders not just at the University of Virginia, but in the world.

> OPPORTUNITY Access UVA

Access UVa is a comprehensive financial aid plan that includes a new commitment to eliminate need-based loans with grants that low-income students do not have to repay as part of their financial aid package. For other students, the University caps the amount of need-based loans offered so that no student is left with an excessive amount of debt upon graduation. University of Virginia has pledged to meet 100 percent of demonstrated financial need for all undergraduate students, and will provide comprehensive financial education to prospective and current students and their families.

"Getting this wonderful education would have been impossible if someone hadn't encouraged me to come to this school. I want to be an example for younger students who never dreamed that they could afford higher education."

– Chalais M., '09
Ashburn, VA
Sociology, Spanish

> OPPORTUNITY The Outreach Office

The Outreach Office is a unit within the Office of Admission created specifically to work with minority, first generation, and low income students. The office oversees multicultural weekends, assisting students and families with visitations to the University, offers college counseling, and works with the financial aid office and scholarships programs specifically to encourage diversity.

> SUCCESS Transition Programs

The College of Arts and Sciences Transition Program assists students accepted into the College with the college transition through academic and social programs. The School of Engineering Bridge Program supports students entering in the field of Engineering through academic programs and research. The Rainey Scholars Program is specifically for entering low income students and offers them academic and social support.

> SUCCESS Peer and Faculty Mentor Programs

There are Peer and Faculty Mentor Programs specifically for minorities and low income students coming to the University. The Office of African American Affairs has established a Parent Organization that works together on behalf of African American students' experiences at the University.

FAST FACTS

STUDENT PROFILE
# of degree-seeking undergraduates	13,869
% male/female	44/56
% African-American	9
% American Indian or Alaska Native	<1
% Asian or Pacific Islander	11
% Hispanic	4
% White	63
% International	5
% Pell grant recipients	7.8

First-generation and minority alumni Sean Patrick Thomas, actor, "Save the Last. Dance", "Courage Under Fire", "Barbershop", "The District"; Thomas Jones, pro-football player for the New York Jets; Helen Elizabeth, Assistant Secretary for Tax Policy at the Department of Treasury in Obama Administration; Dawn Staley, professionally in the WNBA/ head basketball coach at Temple University/ won three Olympic gold medals as a member of U.S. women's basketball teams

ACADEMICS
full-time faculty	1,267
full-time minority faculty	n/a
student-faculty ratio	n/a
average class size	n/a
% first year retention rate	97
% graduation rate (6 years)	93

Popular majors Psychology, History, English, Biology, Government and International Affairs

CAMPUS LIFE
% live on campus (% fresh.)	43 (100)

Multicultural student clubs and organizations Black Student Alliance, Asian Pacific American Leadership Training Institute (APALTI), Latino Student Alliance, American Indian Student Union, Brothers United Celebrating Knowledge and Success (BUCKS), Association of African and Caribbean Cultures, National Society of Black Engineers (NSBE) and Hispanic Engineers (NSHE)

Athletics NCAA Division I, ACC

ADMISSIONS
# of applicants	18,363
% accepted	37
# of first-year students enrolled	3,535
SAT Critical Reading range	600-710
SAT Math range	620-730
SAT Writing	610-730
ACT range	27-32
average HS GPA	n/a

Deadlines
regular decision	1/1
application fee (online)	$60 ($60)
fee waiver for students with financial need	yes

COST & AID
tuition	in-state: $9,672; out-of-state: $31,230
room & board	$8,290
total need-based institutional scholarships/grants	n/a
% of students apply for need-based aid	61
% of students receive aid	44
% receiving need-based scholarship/grant aid	n/a
% receiving aid whose need was fully met	100
average aid package	$17,742
average student loan debt upon graduation	$19,016

Virginia Commonwealth University

Situated in Richmond, Virginia's capital city since 1779, Virginia Commonwealth University (VCU) continues to grow in size, programs and students. With more than 32,000 undergraduate, graduate and professional students, the university offers prestigious programs that have developed the university into an institution with an international reputation. VCU is one of the nation's top research universities, ranking among the top universities in the country in sponsored research. The university enrolls students in 208 certificate and degree programs in the arts, sciences and humanities. Sixty-five of the programs are unique in Virginia, many of them crossing the disciplines of Virginia Commonwealth University's 15 schools and one college. Since its founding, the university has combined the traditional and nontraditional, creating diversity in our academic programs, campus events, students, faculty and staff.

> ACCESS Primeros Pasos (First Steps)

This one-day program, designed to motivate and encourage Latino high school students to attend college, showcases all that the university has to offer. Virginia Commonwealth University students, parents, administrators, faculty and alumni participate throughout the day sharing their experiences. Activities include a bilingual workshop for parents regarding financial aid and scholarships, a panel discussion with university students from the Latino community, conversations with undergraduate admissions counselors, and campus tours.

> OPPORTUNITY Acceleration Program

Students admitted into this program begin college with an on-campus, four-week summer enrichment program where they are exposed to a pre-health-specific math and science curriculum. Students participate in internships in various clinical health service provider settings and receive a stipend. Students are expected to commit to 50 hours of volunteer work per year in community health provider settings and receive specialized, career-related academic advising and support services throughout the program.

> SUCCESS University College (UC)

The VCU University College is a central home for university-wide programs and resources that help to enhance students' undergraduate academic experience. Through academic advising, tutoring, writing assistance, group study sessions, orientation programs and courses introducing students to the demands of a university education, the University College provides opportunities for students to achieve greater levels of academic success.

> SUCCESS Office of Multicultural Student Affairs (OMSA)

A resource for students, faculty and staff, the primary mission of the VCU Office of Multicultural Student Affairs is to assist traditionally underserved and/or underrepresented student populations (i.e. race, ethnicity, sexual orientation, and gender) through advising, support, program development, retention, and mentoring, as well as by promoting an appreciation of diversity throughout the campus community.

"Adjusting to the academic demands and college life was made easier thanks to the advising provided through the University College. My advisors have always been helpful in regards to classes, financial aid and school. I always receive encouraging words and motivation from them that give me the boost I need to continue."

– Moises E., '11
Alexandria, VA
Clinical Exercise
Science, Spanish

Virginia Commonwealth University
821 West Franklin Street
Richmond, VA 23284
Ph: (804) 828-1222
ugrad@vcu.edu
www.vcu.edu

FAST FACTS

STUDENT PROFILE
# of degree-seeking undergraduates	21,500
% male/female	43/57
% African American	20
% American Indian or Alaska Native	1
% Asian or Pacific Islander	11
% Hispanic	4
% White	52
% International	3
% Pell grant recipients	18

ACADEMICS
full-time faculty	1,919
full-time minority faculty	390
student-faculty ratio	18:1
average class size	28
% first-year retention rate	84
% graduation rate (6 years)	51

Popular majors Biology, Psychology, Mass Communications, Business, and Criminal Justice

CAMPUS LIFE
% live on campus (% fresh.)	22 (79)

Multicultural student clubs and organizations
African Student Union, Black Caucus, Filipino Americans Coming Together (FACT), Indian Student Association, Latino Student Association, NAACP at VCU, Vietnamese Student Association, Persian American Students, Caribbean Student Organization, and many more

Athletics NCAA Division I, Colonial Athletic Association

ADMISSIONS
# of applicants	16,915
% accepted	59
# of first-year students enrolled	3,665

For middle 50% of admitted students:
SAT Critical Reading range	500-600
SAT Math range	500-610
SAT Writing range	490-600
ACT range	21-26
Middle 50% range HS GPA	3.17-3.81

Deadlines
scholarship consideration	12/1
recommended freshman deadline	1/15
application fee (online)	$50($40)
fee waiver for applicants with financial need	yes

COST & AID
tuition	in-state: $7,117; out-of-state: $20,549
room & board	$8,231
% of students apply for need-based aid	59
% of students receive aid	47
% receiving need-based scholarship or grant aid	35
% receiving aid whose need was fully met	16
average aid package	$8,381
average student loan debt upon graduation	$22,610

Washington and Lee University

Founded in 1749, Washington and Lee University is the nation's ninth-oldest institution of higher learning. The university was the first in the U.S. to offer courses in business and journalism, and continues as the only institution ranked in the nation's top 20 liberal arts schools to have accredited schools of both business and journalism. As a national institution with teacher-scholars committed to teaching in small classes, Washington and Lee's 40 undergraduate majors are augmented by numerous study abroad opportunities and interdisciplinary courses and programs. The student-run Honor System defines a community of trust in which exams are unproctored and facilities are open 24/7. The university's strengths include the Speaking Tradition and the widely regarded quadrennial Mock Presidential Convention. Washington and Lee's students routinely win prestigious fellowships, including the Fulbright, Luce and Goldwater.

> ## OPPORTUNITY **Diversity Open Houses**

It is nearly impossible to know if a university is the right "fit" unless you visit campus. Through a series of three day, all-expenses-paid diversity open houses at Washington & Lee, multicultural, low-income and first-generation students come to campus to meet current students, sit in on classes, and experience historic Lexington, Virginia for themselves.

> ## OPPORTUNITY **Questbridge**

Washington and Lee University partners with Questbridge, a national program that connects bright, motivated, low-income students to 26 of the top colleges in the country. By centralizing information for both applicants and universities, this program makes the distance between intelligent, disadvantaged students and higher education much shorter and smoother. Questbridge not only prepares applicants for the transition to college, but for success throughout college and beyond.

> ## OPPORTUNITY **Johnson Scholarship Program in Leadership and Integrity**

An unprecedented gift of $100 million is allowing Washington and Lee University to invest in students of exceptional academic and personal promise by giving them the opportunity to graduate free of debt. Two hundred finalists — selected for their academic achievements and leadership potential — are invited to interview on campus each year. Ultimately, 44 Johnson scholars are named for each enrolling class, and they all receive scholarships in the amount of at least tuition, room and board.

> ## OPPORTUNITY **H.J. Heinz Scholarship**

The H.J. Heinz Scholarship provides full tuition, room and board, plus a stipend for books and personal expenses for disadvantaged students who are interested in pursuing a career in business. Award winners also benefit from paid summer internships with the Heinz Corporation.

> ## SUCCESS **The Bonner Leader and Shepherd Poverty Program**

These programs both engage students in service within the Lexington community and beyond. The Bonner Leader program provides scholarship assistance to students who commit to 900 hours of community service over two years. The Shepherd Poverty Program integrates academics with community service through interdisciplinary academic courses and an eight-week summer internship program.

"As a first-generation college student and the oldest of seven children, I have been the first to experience 'college life.' I knew that I wanted to go to a small school where I could really get a feel for what the students and faculty stood for, and where no one could say that their voice would not be heard. "

– Regina M., '09
Warrenton, VA
English, Sociology, Anthropology

Washington and Lee University
204 West Washington Street
Lexington, VA 24450
Ph: (540) 458-8710
admissions@wlu.edu
www.wlu.edu

FAST FACTS

STUDENT PROFILE
# of degree-seeking undergraduates	1,749
% male/female	50/50
% African American	4
% American Indian or Alaska Native	<1
% Asian or Pacific Islander	3
% Hispanic	2
% White	86
% International	4
% Pell grant recipients	4.2

First-generation and minority alumni Dr. Kenneth P. Ruscio, president, Washington and Lee University; Dr. Theodore C. DeLaney, head, history department, Washington and Lee University; William Thornton, senior vice president, SunTrust Bank; William B. Hill, Jr., former associate judge, George State Supreme Court

ACADEMICS
full-time faculty	187
full-time minority faculty	23
student-faculty ratio	8:1
average class size	15
% first-year retention rate	94
% graduation rate (6 years)	89

Popular majors Business Administration, Economics, Journalism, History, English

CAMPUS LIFE
% live on campus (% fresh.)	58 (100)

Multicultural student clubs and organizations International House, International Relations Association, Multicultural Student Association, Onyx, Pan Asian Association Cultural Exchange, Caribbean Society

Athletics NCAA Division III, Old Dominion Conference

ADMISSIONS
# of applicants	6,386
% accepted	17
# of first-year students enrolled	454
SAT Critical Reading range	660-740
SAT Math range	660-740
SAT Writing range	660-730
ACT range	29-31

Deadlines
early decision	11/15 and 1/3
regular decision	1/3
Johnson scholarship	12/1
application fee (online)	$50 ($50)
fee waiver for applicants with financial need	yes

COST & AID
tuition	$39,500
room & board	$10,243
total need-based institutional scholarships/grants	$15,344,522
% of students apply for need-based aid	46
% of students with need to receive aid	100
% receiving aid whose need was fully met	86
average aid package	$32,977
average student loan debt upon graduation	$23,616

The Evergreen State College

The Evergreen State College is particularly committed to issues of social justice; it houses several public service centers, two of which serve local Native American communities, and the college offers extensive counseling and support to veterans who enroll in the school. Evergreen approaches learning in a dynamic, unique way. Students enroll in interdisciplinary, theme-based 'programs,' rather than in individual courses. Also, they receive narrative evaluations from their professors, rather than letter grades.

> ACCESS College Success Foundation/Achievers Programs

Evergreen State works with the College Success Foundation, a non-profit organization that provides college scholarships and mentoring to low-income, high-potential students. The college supports the Achievers College Experience, which provides Achievers Scholarship Candidates with a college-readiness experience.

> ACCESS Boys & Girls Club Partnership

The Office of Admissions sustains relationships with the Boys & Girls Club at 11 sites in Washington State and four in Portland, Oregon. Mentoring, high school course advising, college search counseling, and scholarship/financial aid assistance is provided.

> ACCESS Gaining Early Awareness and Readiness for Undergraduate Programs (GEAR UP)

Low-income middle and high school students are encouraged through this program to stay in school, study hard, have high expectations, and go to college. Evergreen works in partnership with a number of national, state and local organizations to provide services to 1,200 Washington state students at 3 schools.

> ACCESS Upward Bound

Evergreen serves 90 low-income students needing academic support who live in Tacoma and the Reservation of the Puyallup (Indian) Nation. The students are provided with tutoring, counseling, mentoring, cultural enrichment, and work-study programs in their preparation for college entrance.

> *"I love the education that I received at Evergreen! I felt out of place my first year, and there will be times you might feel lost and alone too. But since I got involved in the campus community, my experiences here at Evergreen have been amazing. When times are rough, there will be people around you that genuinely care about your success and are here to help you."*
>
> *– Natasha C., '09*
> *Portland, OR*
> *Interdisciplinary Studies, Sociology*

> OPPORTUNITY Multicultural Services

First Peoples' Advising Services provides students of color with comprehensive academic, social and personal advising, as well as referral services to campus and community resources. Evergreen also offers a First Peoples' Scholars program, which offers students of color a chance to get acclimated to Evergreen by visiting in small groups.

> SUCCESS Gateways for Incarcerated Youth

This academic program is dedicated to helping incarcerated youth develop self-esteem, achieve academic success, and increase their cultural awareness. Evergreen students are given the opportunity to be peer learners with incarcerated young men, held in two maximum-security institutions. Both groups of students address issues of diversity, equality and critical thinking.

> SUCCESS Keep Enhancing Yourself (KEY) Student Services

Evergreen State offers this federally-funded program to students who meet eligibility requirements. Participants benefit from a comprehensive support system designed to increase graduation rates, including the assistance of a personal mentor. The campus also hosts a number of workshops and social events for participating students.

> SUCCESS Washington TRIO Expansion Program (WaTEP)

Program staff strive to increase the retention, academic achievement and graduation rates of students by providing comprehensive academic needs assessment, academic and career planning, tutoring services and financial aid guidance. Eligible students must be first generation, low income, or have a documented physical or learning disability.

The Evergreen State College
2700 Evergreen Parkway NW
Olympia, WA 98505
Ph: (360) 867-6170
admissions@evergreen.edu
www.evergreen.edu

FAST FACTS

STUDENT PROFILE

# of degree-seeking undergraduates	4,108
% male/female	45/55
% African American	5
% American Indian or Alaska Native	4
% Asian or Pacific Islander	5
% Hispanic	5
% White	70
% International	<1
% Pell grant recipients	40

First-generation and minority alumni Sharon Tomiko Santos, Washington Representative

ACADEMICS

full-time faculty	169
full-time minority faculty	40
student-faculty ratio	23:1
average class size	40
% first-year retention rate	70
% graduation rate (6 years)	63

Popular areas of study Culture & Language, Social Sciences, Liberal Arts/Interdisciplinary Studies, Expressive Arts, Environmental Studies

CAMPUS LIFE

% live on campus (% fresh.)	22 (79)

Multicultural student clubs and organizations Black Student Union, Committee in Solidarity with the People of El Salvador (CISPES), Iraqi Solidarity Committee, MEChA, Women of Color Coalition
Athletics NAIA, Cascade Collegiate Conference (CCC)

ADMISSIONS

# of applicants	1,769
% accepted	96
# of first-year students enrolled	577
SAT Critical Reading range	500-640
SAT Math range	460-590
SAT Writing	480-600
ACT range	20-26
average HS GPA	3.05

Deadlines

regular decision	rolling
application fee (online)	$50 ($50)
fee waiver for applicants with financial need	yes

COST & AID

tuition	in-state: $4,797; out-of-state: $15,657
room & board	$8,052
total need-based institutional scholarships/grants	$719,250
% of students apply for need-based aid	68
% of students receive aid	95
% receiving need-based scholarship or grant aid	80
% receiving aid whose need was fully met	11
average aid package	$7,369
average student loan debt upon graduation	$15,371

Gonzaga University

Gonzaga University
502 East Boone Avenue
Spokane, WA 99258
Ph: (509) 313-6572
www.gonzaga.edu

Gonzaga University is a medium-sized, private, four-year university founded in the Jesuit Catholic tradition. Gonzaga's educational philosophy is based on the Ignation model and aims to educate the mind, body and spirit through an integration of science, art, faith, reason, action and contemplation. This focus on the individual is at the core of Gonzaga's emphasis on academic success, community service and student involvement. Gonzaga's ongoing outreach into its local community includes diversity education and the installation of a college-bound culture in neighboring Yakima Valley.

> OPPORTUNITY Act Six

Act Six, open to Spokane-area high school seniors, provides four-year, full-tuition, full-need scholarships to attend Gonzaga University. Act Six trains and prepares a small group of students in the year prior to college, equipping them to support each other, succeed academically, and grow as service-minded leaders and agents of transformation. The rigorous selection process seeks to identify student leaders who are passionate about learning, eager to foster intercultural relationships, willing to step out of their comfort zones, committed to serving those around them, and ready to make a difference on campus and at home. The selection process also places high value on applicants' teamwork, critical thinking and communication skills, and academic potential. While ethnicity and family income are factors in selecting an intentionally diverse group of scholars, there are no income restrictions, and students from all ethnic backgrounds are encouraged to apply. The deadline to apply for this competitive program is November 1.

> OPPORTUNITY Gonzaga University Community Scholarship

The Gonzaga University Community Scholarship is a $20,000 award over four years for outstanding students who are first-generation college bound, from an under-represented cultural background or whose unique life experiences would contribute to the diversity of the Gonzaga community. Scholarship recipients should demonstrate significant contributions to school or community in promoting cultural awareness and exhibit intercultural leadership qualities. Students are automatically considered for the award upon admission to the university.

> SUCCESS Academic Cultural Excellence (ACE) Student Leadership Program

The ACE program prepares African American, Hispanic, Asian and Native American students to assume leadership roles in diversity education and training for the purpose of promoting cross-cultural understanding and improving race relations within the Gonzaga campus and Spokane community. Students gain an understanding of servant leadership, develop facilitation skills in diversity training and create opportunities to serve others in pursuit of multicultural competency. Applications for the program are available through the Office of Intercultural Relations.

> SUCCESS Building Relationships in Diverse Gonzaga Environments

The Summer BRIDGE Program (Building Relationships in Diverse Gonzaga Environments) is a pre-orientation program designed to support students of color as they enter Gonzaga University in the fall. The program complements the university's general Student Orientation Program by introducing students to diverse Gonzaga faculty, staff and students. Personal relationships are built and stories are shared as new students bond with each other and the Gonzaga campus.

FAST FACTS

STUDENT PROFILE

# of degree-seeking undergraduates	4,517
% male/female	45/55
% African-American	2
% American Indian or Alaska Native	<1
% Asian or Pacific Islander	5
% Hispanic	4
% White	77
% Pell grant recipients	15

First-generation and minority alumni Frank Burgess, U.S. federal magistrate; Carl Maxey (deceased), Spokane attorney and civil rights leader; Steven Meneses, president and founder, Continental Financial; Ed Taylor, vice provost, University of Washington

ACADEMICS

full-time faculty	372
full-time minority faculty	30
student-faculty ratio	11:1
average class size	17
% first-year retention rate	92
% graduation rate (6 years)	80

Popular majors Business Administration, Communications, Engineering, Biology, Psychology

CAMPUS LIFE

% live on campus (% freshmen)	57 (95)

Multicultural student clubs and organizations Black Student Union, Chinese Club, Filipino American Student Union, First Nations Student Association, Hawaii Pacific Islanders Club, International Student Union, Japanese Club, La Raza Latina, NAACP – GU Student Chapter, Taiwanese Student Association

Athletics NCAA Division I, West Coast Conference

ADMISSIONS

# of applicants	5,026
% accepted	78
# of first-year students enrolled	1,297
SAT Critical Reading range	540-630
SAT Math range	550-650
SAT Writing range	n/a
ACT range	24-29
average HS GPA	3.6

Deadlines

regular decision	2/1
application fee (online)	$50 ($50)
fee waiver for applicants with financial need	yes

COST & AID

tuition	$29,675
room & board	$7,976
total need-based institutional scholarships/grants	n/a
% of students apply for need-based aid	76
% of students receive aid	58
% receiving need-based scholarship or grant aid	98
% receiving aid whose need was fully met	37
average aid package	$20,630
average student loan debt upon graduation	$24,094

Heritage University

Heritage University is a private, co-educational, non-denominational, four-year, non-residential institution of higher education. Its mission is to provide quality, accessible higher education to multicultural populations that have been educationally isolated. Within its liberal-arts curriculum, Heritage offers strong professional and career-oriented programs designed to enrich the quality of life for students and their communities.

> ### ACCESS **HEP Alliance**

The High School Equivalency Program (HEP Alliance) helps seasonal agriculture workers earn a GED so that they can be placed in a career, military service, post-secondary education or another training program. Participants in the program receive computer training, tutorial assistance, academic and vocational counseling, as well as paid tuition, books, testing fees and supplies. Bilingual Spanish and English instructors are available.

> ### OPPORTUNITY **The College Assistance Migrant Program (CAMP)**

This program helps students from migrant and seasonal farm-working backgrounds succeed in college. CAMP offers pre-college transition and first-year support services to help students develop the skills they need to stay in school and successfully graduate from college. For pre-college students, CAMP provides help with admissions and financial aid. Once in the program, students are eligible for financial assistance in the form of stipends or tuition payments, mentoring, tutoring, academic advising, career planning and other support programs.

> ### OPPORTUNITY **EAGLES Program**

Heritage University provides resources and support to students that may enhance their academic pursuits through the EAGLES Program. Programming includes career services, scholarships, internships and work-study assistance to students. Additionally, it hosts college success workshops and houses the Associated Student Body and student clubs.

> ### SUCCESS **The Presidential Fellows Program**

The Presidential Fellows Program at Heritage University offers students a number of activities designed to foster their leadership development. It includes activities such as a six-week leadership training, exposure to community leaders, job-shadowing of university administrators and experience in volunteerism.

> ### SUCCESS **STEP-UP**

Heritage University's STEP-UP initiative provides scholarships, child-care subsidies and specialized training to university students in exchange for their services as parent educators and outreach workers. As parent educators and outreach workers, the students provide supportive services to families with small children that include literacy training for parents, teaching parents to keep track of records affecting their child's development and establishing parent support groups.

"The first day I stepped foot on Heritage University soil I knew it was where I wanted to be. Heritage has helped me grow and discover the skills and confidence I need to be successful. I attend class everyday excited to learn something new."

– Laura A., '12
Sunnyside, WA
Mathematics

Heritage University
Admissions Office
3240 Fort Road
Toppenish, WA 98948
Ph: (509) 865-8508
admissions@heritage.edu
www.heritage.edu

F A S T   F A C T S

STUDENT PROFILE
# of degree-seeking undergraduates	823
% male/female	24/76
% African American	1
% American Indian or Alaska Native	9
% Asian or Pacific Islander	1
% Hispanic	55
% White	31
% International	0
% Pell grant recipients	83.4

ACADEMICS
full-time faculty	51
full-time minority faculty	12
student-faculty ratio	8:1
average class size	15
% first-year retention rate	62
% graduation rate (6 years)	6

Popular majors Business Administration/ Management, Elementary Education and Teaching, Social Work

CAMPUS LIFE
% live on campus	n/a

Multicultural student clubs and organizations Native American Club, Students in Free Enterprise, Social Work Student Association, Education Club

Athletics Club sports

ADMISSIONS
# of applicants	341
% accepted	48
# of first-year students enrolled	108
SAT Critical Reading range	n/a
SAT Math range	n/a
SAT Writing range	n/a
ACT range	n/a
average HS GPA	n/a

Deadlines
early decision	3/15
regular decision	rolling
application fee (online)	$0 ($0)

COST & AID
tuition	$7,080
room & board	$0
total need-based institutional scholarships/grants	$489,893
% of students apply for need-based aid	100
% of students receive aid	90
% receiving need-based scholarship or grant aid	93
% receiving aid whose need was fully met	3
average aid package	$9,516
average student loan debt upon graduation	$11,509

Saint Martin's University

Founded in 1895, Saint Martin's University is a private, four-year, liberal arts university affiliated with the Benedictine order of the Catholic Church. Saint Martin's offers 21 majors and six graduate programs that span the liberal arts, business, education and engineering. Saint Martin's embraces holistic education and diversity, warmly welcoming 1,250 students from many ethnic and religious backgrounds to its main campus and 650 more to five extension campuses. Guided by its Catholic heritage, Saint Martin's retains a strong commitment to public service and community.

> ACCESS Community Service Major

In accordance with Saint Martin's commitment to service learning, the university offers a baccalaureate degree program in Community Services. Extensive field internships are especially important as they provide students with work experience that can reduce the need for prolonged on-the-job training after college. In one past field internship, Saint Martin's students had the opportunity to work at a local high school. Working with the ninth through 12th grades, Community Service majors tutored bilingual students in English while gaining valuable experience in a classroom setting. The Community Services program combines classroom study with the field internships to allow students to develop both personally and professionally.

"Diversity is not about how we differ here at Saint Martin's; diversity is about embracing one another's uniqueness."
– Andrew A., '11 Dupont, WA Psychology

> OPPORTUNITY John D. Ishii Scholarship

A need-based scholarship of $2,250, the John D. Ishii Scholarship is awarded to students who have demonstrated significant leadership in their ethnic or cultural community. Priority is given to students whose continuing cultural involvement will also increase the diversity of the Saint Martin's community. This scholarship is part of Saint Martin's generous financial assistance package, which annually provides 95 percent of the student body scholarships and grants.

> SUCCESS Summer Bridge

To better integrate first-generation and low-income students into college life, Saint Martin's developed the Summer "Bridge to Success!" program. A nine-day transitional program held in July, Summer Bridge offers students the opportunity to improve academic skills in writing and critical thinking, become acquainted with faculty and staff, meet other students, develop leadership skills and become better acquainted with the university.

> SUCCESS Office of Intercultural Initiatives (OII)

The Office of Intercultural Initiatives promotes respect and appreciation for cultural difference and provides support for multicultural issues through programming, activities, resources and education. All students, faculty and staff gather to work toward greater cultural understanding, as the office serves as the university's cultural resource center. Nurturing diversity awareness at Saint Martin's is viewed as a way for students to access the broader issues of social justice and democratic citizenship.

> SUCCESS Academic Support Services

Saint Martin's University provides a variety of personal and academic support programs for first-generation and underserved students, including tutoring, academic counseling, career guidance and a computer resource center. The Learning and Writing Center is one of Saint Martin's most successful academic support programs. It provides academic learning resources to help students strengthen study skills and employ new learning strategies. Services are free and include tutoring, individual consultations, study skills information, computer assisted learning inventories, disability support services and test proctoring.

Saint Martin's University
5300 Pacific Ave SE
Lacey, WA 98503-7500
Ph: (360) 438-4596
admissions@stmartin.edu
www.stmartin.edu

F A S T   F A C T S

STUDENT PROFILE

# of degree-seeking undergraduates	1,296
% male/female	45/55
% African American	7
% American Indian or Alaska Native	2
% Asian or Pacific Islander	11
% Hispanic	6
% White	61
% International	7
% Pell grant recipients	34

ACADEMICS

full-time faculty	79
full-time minority faculty	10
student-faculty ratio	10:1
average class size	14
% first-year retention rate	72
% graduation rate (6 years)	54

Popular majors Business Administration, Psychology, Education (Secondary, Elementary and Special), Engineering (Civil and Mechanical), Biology.

CAMPUS LIFE

% live on campus (% fresh.)	33 (72)

Multicultural student clubs and organizations International Club, Black Student Union, Minorities in Action, Filipino Heritage Club, Hui O Hawaii Club, Japanese Neko, Pacific Islander Connection Club

Athletics NCAA Division II, Great Northwest Athletic Conference (GNAC)

ADMISSIONS

# of applicants	624
% accepted	84
# of first-year students enrolled	204
SAT Critical Reading range	420-550
SAT Math range	430-570
SAT Writing	410-540
ACT range	17-23
average HS GPA	3.21

Deadlines

regular decision	rolling
application fee (online)	$35 ($35)
fee waiver for applicants with financial need	yes

COST & AID

tuition	$24,880
room & board	$8,360
total need-based institutional scholarships/grants	$4,603,876
% of students apply for need-based aid	93
% of students receive aid	100
% receiving need-based scholarship or grant aid	98
% receiving aid whose need was fully met	16
average aid package	$16,369
average student loan debt upon graduation	$27,264

University of Puget Sound

Located in the pristine Pacific Northwest, the University of Puget Sound offers students both the urban amenities of local Tacoma and nearby Seattle, as well as access to a variety of outdoor activities, such as kayaking and hiking. Puget Sound might further appeal to those interested in environmental activism, as it supports a campus-wide sustainability program. Within this dynamic context, the college provides its students a broad-based, liberal arts education that focuses on critical thinking and writing skills. Students also benefit from the School of Music and the School of Business. Puget Sound seeks to create a diverse and welcoming campus community that will cultivate "effective citizen-leaders for a pluralistic world." The mission of the University is to develop in its students the capacities for critical analysis, aesthetic appreciation, sound judgment, and apt expression that will sustain a lifetime of intellectual curiosity, active inquiry, and reasoned independence. A Puget Sound education, both academic and co-curricular, encourages a rich knowledge of self and others, an appreciation of commonality and difference, the full, open, and civil discussion of ideas, thoughtful moral discourse, and the integration of learning, preparing the University's graduates to meet the highest tests of democratic citizenship. The University of Puget Sound is an independent, four-year liberal arts college founded in 1888 and located in Tacoma, Washington.

> ACCESS **Access Programs**

Access Programs, sponsored by Puget Sound, specifically focus on students traditionally underrepresented in higher education. Through a partnership with the Tacoma Public Schools, the program provides day-long sessions, mentoring, tutoring and other programs such as the "Summer Academic Challenge" to participating students. Students in the program are recruited from Tacoma Public middle and high schools and are accepted into the program based on several criteria, including test scores, classroom performance, study habits, attendance patterns and social behavior.

> OPPORTUNITY **Students of Color Open House**

Annually prospective students are invited to participate in a campus event introducing them to the academic and co-curricular opportunities they will experience as enrolled students. Typically scheduled around events in the arts and athletics, the Students of Color Open House enables students to see Puget Sound in action through several settings.

> SUCCESS **Student Diversity Center**

Seeking to support historically underrepresented groups on college campuses, the Student Diversity Center serves as a resource library, study space and meeting space for the many multicultural groups on campus, which range from the Community for Hispanic Awareness to Hui-O-Hawai'i, a group representing native Hawaiians or those seeking to learn more about this culture. The Student Diversity Center also sponsors student programming, maintains a monthly calendar of multicultural events, and fosters communication between campus and Tacoma community groups. The center works with the University to publish an annual Cultural Resource Guide, which apprises students of relevant organizations and services that address culture-specific needs both on campus and in the Tacoma area.

> SUCCESS **Diversity Theme Year**

For 16 years running, the University of Puget Sound sponsors a Diversity Theme Year. The theme year program included lectures, art events and student activities that highlight issues of visibility and invisibility, economic inequality and justice, religious conviction and acceptance of differences. The theme year program has proven successful in highlighting issues of identity and cultural awareness, in strengthening student affinity groups and coalitions, and in giving visibility to many groups that are underrepresented on campus.

University of Puget Sound
1500 N. Warner St.
Tacoma, WA 98416
Ph: (253) 879-3211
admission@pugetsound.edu
www.pugetsound.edu

F A S T   F A C T S

STUDENT PROFILE

# of degree-seeking undergraduates	2,499
% male/female	42/58
% African-American	3
% American Indian or Alaska Native	1
% Asian or Pacific Islander	9
% Hispanic	4
% White	74
% International	<1
% Pell grant recipients	14

First-generation and minority alumni Thomas Dixon '71, founder, Tacoma Urban League; Jill Nishi '89, program manager, U.S. Libraries Initiative, Bill and Melinda Gates Foundation; George Obiozor '69, Nigerian Ambassador to the United States; Seema Sueko '94, founder, Mo'olelo Performing Arts Company

ACADEMICS

full-time faculty	228
full-time minority faculty	n/a
student-faculty ratio	11:1
average class size	n/a
% first-year retention rate	86
% graduation rate (6 years)	77

Popular majors Business Administration/Management, Psychology, English Language and Literature, Biology, International Political Economy

CAMPUS LIFE

% live on campus (% fresh.)	60 (98)

Multicultural student clubs and organizations Asian and Pacific American Student Union, B-GLAD, Black Student Union, Community for Hispanic Awareness, First Nations, Hui-O-Hawai'i, International Club, Jewish Students Organization, Muslim Student Alliance, Pagan Student Alliance, Religious Organizations Council, Vox
Athletics NCAA Division III, Northwest Conference

ADMISSIONS

# of applicants	5580
% accepted	65
# of first-year students enrolled	676
SAT Critical Reading range	570-675
SAT Math range	570-665
SAT Writing	560-660
ACT range	25-29
average HS GPA	3.5

Deadlines

early decision I	11/15
early decision II	1/2
regular decision	2/15
application fee (online)	$50
fee waiver for applicants with financial need	yes

COST & AID

tuition	$35,440
room & board	$9,190
total need-based institutional scholarships/grants	$30,195,815
% of students apply for need-based aid	68
% of students receive aid	80
% receiving need-based scholarship or grant aid	98
% receiving aid whose need was fully met	28
average aid package	$26,047
average student loan debt upon graduation	$27,648

Washington State University

Washington State University is a public, co-educational, land-grant research institution that offers a premier undergraduate experience. The university is known for world-class research, scholarship and arts; the exemplary working and learning environment fosters student engagement. The university works hard to embody a set of core values: inquiry and knowledge, engagement and application, leadership, diversity, character, stewardship and teamwork. Toward this end, the university fosters learning, inquiry and engagement. Washington State University enhances the intellectual, creative and practical abilities of individuals, institutions and communities.

> ACCESS GEAR UP Program / Educational Talent Search / Upward Bound

The GEAR UP Program prepares middle and high school students for success in higher education. Serving low-income, migrant and rural students, the program provides tutoring, an enriched curriculum, visits to the Washington State campus, motivational speakers, and a limited number of scholarships to the university. The Educational Talent Search is designed to assist middle school and high school students, along with high school dropouts, with the necessary understanding, knowledge, skills and self-esteem to continue in, and graduate from, high school. This program also helps students that have been traditionally underrepresented to explore training and educational options, and enroll in post-secondary institutions. Upward Bound prepares and motivates low-income, first-generation high school students to pursue a college education. The federally funded program offers tutorial services, monthly workshops, a summer residential program, local and extended college visitations, career advising and assistance in researching and applying for financial aid and college admission.

> ACCESS Imagine U at WSU

A number of presenters (professors, graduate students, deans) are brought into underrepresented high schools for hands-on classes and discussion on the various fields of research. Presenters teach an interactive class, demonstration or workshop for different classes in grades seven to 12. This interaction enlightens them to the kinds of careers available to them, inspires the students and gives them motivation to pursue higher education. In the evening, there is a dinner meeting for parents allowing Washington State to develop a relationship with the entire family.

> OPPORTUNITY Future Cougars of Color (FCOC)

Washington State University offers the FCOC scholarship and visitation program for high-achieving high school seniors of color from across the state of Washington. The campus visit gives them insight into the academic environment and student life at the university. Participants who enroll at Washington State are eligible for scholarships of $1,000 to $10,000.

> SUCCESS College Assistance Migrant Program (CAMP) / Student Support Services / Ronald E. McNair Achievement Program

CAMP is designed to support students from migrant and seasonal farm worker backgrounds during their freshman year in college. The program provides students with both financial and academic support. CAMP is specifically designed to identify, recruit and monitor the academic achievement and retention of migrant students. Student Support Services is a college academic assistance program (TRIO) that has been at Washington State since 2001. Its purpose is to assist 160 eligible students per year by providing the academic assistance each student needs to help meet their educational goals. The McNair Achievement Program prepares qualified undergraduates for their future doctoral studies. The goal of the program is to increase the number of underrepresented students in Ph.D programs and to provide undergraduates with opportunities to participate in research activities.

> SUCCESS Future Teachers and Leaders of Color (FTLOC)

Future Teachers and Leaders of Color offers faculty mentoring, career guidance, student support services and scholarship assistance to select undergraduate and graduate students providing opportunities in becoming teachers, principals and educational administrators.

Washington State University
PO Box 641067
Pullman, WA 99164-1067
Ph: (888) 468-6978
admiss2@wsu.edu
www.wsu.edu

F A S T   F A C T S

STUDENT PROFILE
# of degree-seeking undergraduates	21,149
% male/female	49/51
% African-American	2
% American Indian or Alaska Native	1
% Asian or Pacific Islander	6
% Hispanic	5
% White	74
% Pell grant recipients	26

First-generation and minority alumni Sherman J. Alexie Jr., award-winning poet, author, screenwriter, film director; Phyllis J. Campbell, president/CEO, Seattle Foundation; James E. Blackwell, sociologist, scholar in the areas of minorities in higher education, social movement in black communities; William Julius Wilson, sociologist, author; Matsuyo Omori Yamamoto, first chief of the Rural Home-Living Improvement section, Japan's agricultural extension

ACADEMICS
full-time faculty	1,204
full-time minority faculty	n/a
student-faculty ratio	14:1
average class size	17
% first-year retention rate	82
% graduation rate (6 years)	67

Popular majors Business/Marketing, Social Sciences, Communication, Education, Health Professions

CAMPUS LIFE
% live on campus (% freshmen)	36 (99)

Multicultural student clubs and organizations There are clubs that represent African-American, American Indian, Chicano/a, Chinese, Hawaiian/Pacific Islander, Japanese, Muslim, Russian, Latino/a, Filipino, Indian, Korean, Middle Eastern, Indonesian, Persian, Sikh, Somalian, Taiwanese, Thai and Vietnamese cultures
Athletics NCAA Division I, Pacific-10 Conference

ADMISSIONS
# of applicants	11,983
% accepted	72
# of first-year students enrolled	6,414
SAT Critical Reading range	490-600
SAT Math range	510-610
SAT Writing range	n/a
ACT range	24-29
average HS GPA	3.5

Deadlines
regular decision	rolling
application fee (online)	$50 ($50)
fee waiver for applicants with financial need	yes

COST & AID
tuition	in-state: $8,489; out-of-state: $19,565
room & board	$9,330
total need-based institutional scholarships/grants	n/a
% of students apply for need-based aid	65
% of students receive aid	98
% receiving need-based scholarship or grant aid	69
% receiving aid whose need was fully met	37
average aid package	$10,366
average student loan debt upon graduation	n/a

Western Washington University

With 13,700 students, an increasingly multicultural community, an esteemed Honors Program, and a commitment to the empowerment of undergrads, Western Washington University is a premier choice for driven scholars looking to thrive as young professionals. By offering small classes and faculty mentorship, Western offers the type of individual attention one might only expect from a small private school. Additionally, Western is nationally recognized for environmental leadership, as well as vehicle research and design. *U.S. News & World Report* has ranked Western No. 1 among public, master's-granting universities in the Pacific Northwest and No. 2 in the western United States. Students enjoy a first-rate education, direct access to faculty, a tight-knit community, and an empowering experience at a prominent institution. At Western Washington University, administrators are preparing tomorrow's leaders one student at a time. This is the Western tradition, and for many, a fast track to lifelong success.

> ## ACCESS **Encounter Youth Conference**

The annual Encounter Youth Conference is organized and staffed by students of Western's Ethnic Student Center (ESC), and attended by high school students from around the state. This event is aimed at encouraging minority youth to pursue higher education while developing leadership skills and learning to feel comfortable in a university setting. Workshops topics include media awareness, leadership, and community activism. Academic advising, financial aid, and college admissions guidance is also provided. The most empowering and poignant highlight is always the student panel; current Western students share their experiences, trials, and triumphs with younger students working hard to follow in their footsteps.

> ## ACCESS **HANDS - Helping Admit New and Diverse Students**

Helping Admit New and Diverse Students (HANDS) recruits and retains today's top leaders from multicultural backgrounds. Based out of the Office of Admissions, HANDS is a taskforce of current students who provide personalized mentoring relationships with prospective students. The HANDS team uses their own student experiences to connect with first generation, low-income, and students of color while providing college admissions guidance. From community outreach to reviewing personal essays, HANDS team members provide access to resources that many underrepresented students may otherwise not have.

"My professors care about me as a person and that definitely has helped me be a much better student. It is amazing—the more confident I feel in my academics, the more I'm able to take on leadership roles that help me model the way for others."

– Abraham R., '10
Bellevue, WA
American Cultural Studies and Spanish

> ## OPPORTUNITY **The Multicultural Achievement Program (MAP)**

Through the MAP program, incoming freshmen and transfer students who have demonstrated an ongoing commitment to multiculturalism and/or diversity in their community are eligible for scholarships ranging from $500 to $2,000. There are additional two-year, $1,000 awards available in the form of on-campus meal plans for incoming freshmen living in the residence halls.

> ## SUCCESS **Student Outreach Services (SOS)**

SOS serves underrepresented, non-traditional, and multicultural students by offering personalized advising on class selection, registration, and major declaration. SOS especially advises Washington State Achievers, Governor's Scholars, and Western's Access program, and plans the Women of Color & Empowerment Dinner and Strategies for Success. SOS's main role is to facilitate a smooth transition to university life and increase retention rates for groups with less historical access and fewer generational ties to higher education.

Western Washington University
WWU Office of Admissions
516 High Street
Bellingham, WA 98225-9009
Ph: (360) 650-3440
admit@wwu.edu
www.wwu.edu

FAST FACTS

STUDENT PROFILE

# of degree-seeking undergraduates	13,236
% male/female	45/55
% African-American	3
% American Indian or Alaska Native	2.5
% Asian or Pacific Islander	8.8
% Hispanic	4.4
% White	77

First-generation and minority alumni Joyce Taylor, '84, news anchor, Seattle King 5 News; Jesse Moore, '05, Special Assistant for Public Affairs to the Administration for Children and Families (Presidential appointment), U.S. Department of Health and Human Services; Bill Wright, '60, first African-American USGA Champion (1959)

ACADEMICS

full-time faculty	629
full-time minority faculty	74
student-faculty ratio	19:1
average class size	10-19
% first-year retention rate	84
% graduation rate (6 years)	69

Popular majors Business, Social Sciences, English, Psychology

CAMPUS LIFE

% live on campus	32 (92)

Multicultural student clubs and organizations African Caribbean Club, Black Student Union, Brown Pride, Calling All Colors, Filipino American Student Association, Hui 'O Hawaii, La Mesa Espanola, mEChA (Movimiento Estudiantil Chicano/a de Aztlan), Mixed Identity Student Organization (MISO), MOSAIC, Native American Mentoring Program (NAMP), Native American Student Union, Ritmo Latino, South Asian Student Association, Taiwanese Student Association, Vietnamese Student Association, Western Sister Cities Association

Athletics NCAA Division II, Great Northwest Athletic Conference

ADMISSIONS

# of applicants	9,518
% accepted	71
# of first-year students enrolled	2,697
SAT Critical Reading range	500-620
SAT Math range	500-610
SAT Writing range	490-590
ACT range	21-27
average HS GPA	3.5

Deadlines

regular decision	3/1
application fee (online)	$50 ($50)
fee waiver for applicants with financial need	yes

COST & AID

tuition	in-state: $4,890; out-of-state: $15,921
room & board	$8,393
total need-based institutional scholarships/grants	$22,807,813
% of students apply for need-based aid	58
% of students receive aid	37
% receiving need-based scholarship or grant aid	29
% receiving aid whose need was fully met	13
average aid package	$10,032
average student loan debt upon graduation	$15,560

Whitman College

Whitman College
345 Boyer Avenue
Walla Walla, WA 99362
Ph: (509) 527-5176
admission@whitman.edu
www.whitman.edu

Founded in 1882, Whitman College is a private, co-educational liberal arts institution. Located in Walla Walla, Wash., four hours southeast of Seattle, Whitman offers an ideal setting for rigorous learning and scholarship and encourages creativity, character, and responsibility. Through the study of humanities, arts and social and natural sciences, Whitman's students develop capacities to analyze, interpret, criticize, communicate and engage. A concentration on basic disciplines, in combination with a supportive residential life program that encourages personal and social development, is intended to foster intellectual vitality, confidence, leadership and the flexibility to succeed in a changing technological, multicultural world.

> ACCESS **Continuing Relationships**

Whitman works collaboratively with a variety of community-based organizations to provide access to more students. Admission officers meet with organization leaders, recruit and counsel students, help arrange campus visits, and assist in scholarship application reading for the organizations. Partners include: One Voice, Bright Prospects, Admission Possible, Summer Search, GEAR-UP, College Horizons, the Achievers Program, and more.

> ACCESS **College Horizons**

Whitman College participates annually in College Horizons, a five day pre-college workshop for Native American, Native Hawaiian and Alaska Native high school juniors and seniors. Students work one on one with experienced college guidance counselors and admission officers to prepare for the college admission and financial aid process. Whitman College has hosted the College Horizons program three times in the past 10 years, the most of any participating institution.

> ACCESS **Whitman Institute for Summer Enrichment (WISE)**

WISE is an all-expenses-paid, pre-college program for local middle school students who show academic promise and are from first-generation, minority, or low-income families.

> OPPORTUNITY **Visit Scholarship Program (VSP)**

Approximately 85 high school seniors from underrepresented socioeconomic, racial, and cultural backgrounds are invited for an expenses-paid visit to Whitman during the fall or spring semester. Visiting students stay with an overnight host in a residence hall, eat in campus dining halls, visit up to two classes, meet with coaches, faculty, staff and student leaders, and interview with an admission officer. The Visit Scholarship Program was created in an effort to increase socioeconomic and multicultural diversity at Whitman College.

> OPPORTUNITY **Lomen-Douglas Scholarships**

Students whose backgrounds and experiences demonstrate the ability to contribute to increasing socioeconomic, racial or ethnic diversity awareness at Whitman are chosen to receive these scholarships. Lomen-Douglas scholarships range from $2,000 to $43,000 and vary depending on achievement and financial need.

"The college has done a great job in their efforts to enhance multicultural diversity recruitment programs. With these types of programs, support is available to all students regardless of their cultural background or economic status. The Visit Scholarship Program in particular really gives students a sense for what it would be like to be a Whittie."

– Thanh V., '11
Kent, WA
Biochemistry, Biophysics, and Molecular Biology

F A S T   F A C T S

STUDENT PROFILE
# of degree-seeking undergraduates	1,450
% male/female	43/57
% African American	2
% American Indian or Alaska Native	1
% Asian or Pacific Islander	12
% Hispanic	6
% White	67
% International	3
% Pell grant recipients	11.1

First-generation and minority alumni Danielle Garbe, Woodrow Wilson fellow, State Department; Ana Hernandez, President, Luna Textiles; Sarah Wang, College Overseer, Partner in Marr, Jones, & Wang; Bishop Othal Lakey, Presiding Prelate of the Sixth Episcopal District of the Christian Methodist Episcopal (CME) Church

ACADEMICS
full-time faculty	130
full-time minority faculty	22
student-faculty ratio	10:1
average class size	15
% first-year retention rate	93
% graduation rate (6 years)	92

Popular majors Biology, English, History, Environmental Studies, Psychology

CAMPUS LIFE
% live on campus (% fresh.)	61(100)

Multicultural student clubs and organizations American Indian Association, Asian Cultural Association, Black Student Union, Club Latino, First-Generation/Working-Class Students, Hui Aloha, International Students and Friends Club, South Asian Students Association, Vietnamese Club
Athletics NCAA Division III, Northwest Conference

ADMISSIONS
# of applicants	3,436
% accepted	43.8
# of first-year students enrolled	400
SAT Critical Reading range	630-730
SAT Math range	610-700
SAT Writing range	610-710
ACT range	29-33
average HS GPA	3.84

Deadlines
early decision	11/15
regular decision	1/15
application fee (online)	$50 ($50)
fee waiver for applicants with financial need	yes

COST & AID
tuition	$38,450
room & board	$9,720
total need-based institutional scholarships/grants	$20,500,000
% of students apply for need-based aid	70
% of students receive aid	81
% receiving need-based scholarship or grant aid	45
% receiving aid whose need was fully met	90
average aid package	$31,406
average student loan debt upon graduation	$17,956

Whitworth University

Whitworth University is a private, residential, liberal arts institution affiliated with the Presbyterian Church. Founded in 1890, Whitworth enrolls 2,500 students in 53 undergraduate and degree programs. Seeking to provide its diverse student body with "an education of mind and heart," Whitworth stresses open and rigorous intellectual inquiry. This mission is carried out by a community of Christian scholars committed to excellent teaching and to the integration of faith and learning.

> OPPORTUNITY Act Six Leadership and Scholarship Initiative

The Act Six Leadership and Scholarship Initiative reflects Whitworth University's devotion to faith and diversity. Act Six scholarships ensure scholars receive financial aid packages that cover all billable costs without loan or work for a time period sufficient to obtain an undergraduate degree. Whitworth's Act Six scholars represent six continents and speak 13 native languages. More than 67 percent are first-generation college students and 79 percent are from low-income families. Examples of Act Six scholars' recent activities include authoring a discussion guide for the film *Crash* for cultural diversity advocates on campus, participating in a leadership exchange program with partner institutions in rural Chang Mail, Thailand and serving as volunteer instructors for steel drum groups at local high schools. Connecting urban ministries and faith-based colleges, Act Six equips emerging urban leaders to engage the university campus and their university campus at home.

> SUCCESS Center for Service Learning (CSL)

The Center for Service Learning provides Whitworth students with the opportunity to incorporate community service into academic learning. Service learning is a teaching approach integrating academic instruction with community service that engages students in civic responsibility, critical and creative thinking and structured reflection. Classes sponsored by the CSL embrace participative learning in which students work in and learn from the local community. From planting trees to conducting a sociological survey for an inner-city neighborhood to leading drama workshops for mentally ill adults, students are able to experience service learning first-hand. These experiences enhance their academic experience and provide a way to live out Whitworth's commitment to community service.

> SUCCESS Multicultural Advocacy Council (MAC)

The Multicultural Advocacy Council was established to emphasize Whitworth's cultural activities and events and to support and be a voice for the cultural clubs already established on campus. Striving to produce cultural awareness through unity and creative collaboration, MAC seeks to provide and facilitate open dialogue concerning issues on race relations, diversity and underrepresented voices on campus. The council sponsors Multicultural Awareness Week, an event that focuses on raising awareness of racial and diversity issues at Whitworth and the surrounding community. Events include interactive lectures, film screenings, performance art and an international banquet.

> SUCCESS Educational Support Services

Committed to providing education support to students, Whitworth Educational Support Services works with students on an individual basis to assist each in becoming an integral part of the campus community. Resources available to students include admission assistance, academic planning, career exploration, individual counseling, assistance with disability issues, tutoring and study-skills assistance and financial aid. As resources tailored to individual needs, these support services provide a specialized and stable support system available to all students.

Whitworth University
300 West Hawthorne Road
Spokane, WA 99251-0002
Ph: (800) 533-4668 or (509) 777-4786
admissions@whitworth.edu
www.whitworth.edu

FAST FACTS

STUDENT PROFILE
# of degree-seeking undergraduates	2,365
% male/female	47/53
% African-American	2
% American Indian or Alaska Native	1
% Asian or Pacific Islander	3
% Hispanic	5
% White	84
% Pell grant recipients	20

First-generation and minority alumni Frank Hernandez '93, internationally known opera singer; Dr. Saisuree Chutikul, Ph.D '56, secretary general, National Youth Bureau of Thailand, former adviser to the Prime Minister; Noel Castellanos '82, associate executive director, Christian Community Development Association, president, Latino Leadership Foundation

ACADEMICS
full-time faculty	126
full-time minority faculty	6
student-faculty ratio	12:1
average class size	17
% first-year retention rate	87
% graduation rate (6 years)	74

Popular majors Business Management, Communications

CAMPUS LIFE
% live on campus (% freshmen)	63 (96)

Multicultural student clubs and organizations Black Student Union, Four Directions Native Club, Hawaiian Club, International Club, Latin America Club

Athletics NCAA Division III, Northwest Conference

ADMISSIONS
# of applicants	5,863
% accepted	53
# of first-year students enrolled	570
SAT Critical Reading range	550-650
SAT Math range	560-650
SAT Writing range	540-640
ACT range	25-29
average HS GPA	3.7

Deadlines
regular decision	3/1
application fee (online)	$0 ($0)

COST & AID
tuition	$28,650
room & board	$8,120
total need-based institutional scholarships/grants	n/a
% of students apply for need-based aid	73
% of students receive aid	63
% receiving need-based scholarship or grant aid	63
% receiving aid whose need was fully met	14
average aid package	$13,298
average student loan debt upon graduation	$19,305

Concord University

Concord University
PO Box 1000
Athens, WV 24712-1000
Ph: (888) 384-5249 or (304) 384-5248
admissions@concord.edu
www.concord.edu

Concord University, with its 123-acre campus and beautiful architecture, has the look, feel and academic excellence of a private school — all with the accessibility of a public institution state school. In 1872, the university was founded with a mission to train teachers. Concord now offers more than 80 majors, minors and programs of study to a student body that is culturally, regionally and socio-economically diverse. Men and women have come from 22 countries and 27 states to study at Concord, and 55 percent of all those enrolled are first-generation college students. The vibrant community continues beyond the boundaries of the Concord University campus to surrounding Mercer County, which was designated "One of the Best 100 Communities for Young People."

> ACCESS Upward Bound

Each year, Upward Bound helps 90 low-income or first-generation students as they strive to complete high school, enter college, and earn a baccalaureate degree. The program includes a ten-month academic year program and a six-week residential component. Students receive instruction in composition, foreign languages, literature, mathematics, laboratory science, computer science, study skills, career exploration and multicultural awareness. Activities focusing on life skills, tutoring and counseling also help prepare the participants for college entry.

> ACCESS Mountain Lion Open House Programs

The Mountain Lion Open House gives college-bound students a sound overview of many aspects of college life and offers insight into the general level of academic rigor at Concord University. Prospective students and their parents take part in a host of activities, including a tour of the campus and residence halls, face-to-face interaction with professors in the student's areas of interest, direct financial aid counseling, interaction with campus clubs and organizations, lunch in the university cafeteria and free SAT preparation assistance. To ensure individual needs are met, Concord students assist the visitors throughout the day.

> OPPORTUNITY Bonner Scholars Program

Concord University is the nation's only public institution with the Bonner Scholars program. The program helps transform students' lives and helps transform communities. Each year the Bonner Scholars Program provides four-year community-service scholarships to approximately 1,500 students. The scholarship helps meet the needs of individuals who have significant financial need and a demonstrated commitment to service. The scholarship furthers students' service work and helps give them the tools, knowledge, and perspective necessary to comprehend the significance of their service.

> SUCCESS Student Support Services

In 2001, Concord University's Student Support Services program scored 100 percent in a nationwide assessment of colleges and universities. This placed the program in the 10th percentile of Student Support Services programs and earned it considerable federal grants. The office offers a breadth of services including instruction in basic study skills; tutorial services; academic, financial, and personal counseling; financial aid for enrollment in graduate school; career information; and mentoring to lower-income, first-generation and disabled students.

FAST FACTS

STUDENT PROFILE

# of degree-seeking undergraduates	2,740
% male/female	41/59
% African-American	6
% American Indian or Alaska Native	<1
% Asian or Pacific Islander	2
% Hispanic	<1
% White	92
% International	4
% Pell grant recipients	41.7

ACADEMICS

full-time faculty	104
full-time minority faculty	n/a
student-faculty ratio	n/a
average class size	19
% first-year retention rate	63
% graduation rate (6 years)	n/a

Popular majors Accounting, Advertising & Graphic Design, Athletic Training, Biology, Business Administration, Computer Science, Pre-law, Management, Pre-med, Psychology, Recreation & Tourism Management, Social Work, Sociology and Teacher Education

CAMPUS LIFE

% live on campus	39

Multicultural student clubs and organizations Office of Multicultural Office, International Student Organization, Black Student Union, Bonner Scholars

Athletics NCAA Division II, West Virginia Intercollegiate Athletic Conference

ADMISSIONS

# of applicants	2,167
% accepted	73
# of first-year students enrolled	721
SAT Critical Reading range	400-540
SAT Math range	400-540
SAT Writing range	n/a
ACT range	17 - 24
average HS GPA	n/a

Deadlines

regular admission	rolling
application fee (online)	no fee required

COST & AID

tuition	in-state: $4,974; out-of-state: $11,050
room & board	$6,766
total need-based institutional scholarships/grants	$21,000,000
% of students apply for need-based aid	88
% of students receive aid	69
% receiving need-based scholarship or grant aid	82
% receiving aid whose need was fully met	38
average aid package	$8,934
average student loan debt upon graduation	$13,713

West Virginia Wesleyan College

With over 70 campus activities and access to state parks, ski resorts and other outdoor-adventure destinations, West Virginia Wesleyan College offers students a range of opportunities both on campus and off. Wesleyan also offers a number of programs designed to help students support and tailor their academic experience, including a variety of freshmen seminars. Wesleyan is affiliated with the United Methodist Church, and it offers both weekly chapel services — during which no classes are offered — and access to the Dean of the Chapel, who functions as a pastoral caregiver.

> ACCESS Leadership and Service

Students at Wesleyan are encouraged to participate in community service programming, whether through the Bonner Scholars program, newly formed service learning courses, work-study placements, or housing initiatives. Examples of service opportunities of which Wesleyan students take advantage include Project ISAAC (Increasing Student Achievement Advancing Communities), Upshur County Head Start, Big Brothers/Big Sisters, Valley Green Learning Center, and many more. Additionally, a first-year seminar course titled Community Engagement: Recipes for Success introduces students to community service opportunities and leadership development.

"Wesleyan strives to assist in the transition from high school to college, specifically through its housing department. As a Resident Assistant, I know the importance of "community building" and its contribution to a student's overall college experience. Wesleyan, as an institution, upholds this idea of community and it's undoubtedly evident when interacting with faculty, staff, and other students alike."
– Keith B., '10
Upshur County, WV

> OPPORTUNITY Academic Advising

During the first semester of the freshman year, students are advised by their Freshman Seminar instructor. Following the first year of study, students are assigned to a faculty advisor in their particular field of study, or in a related field. If, after the first year, students are still undecided about their major, they are assigned to a faculty advisor who helps them to explore their personal and academic interests and work toward setting their educational goals. In addition to faculty advisors, members of the Academic & Career Office staff are available to assist students and provide guidance to those who are undeclared, in-between majors, or have unique advising needs.

> SUCCESS The Office of Intercultural Relations

The Office of Intercultural Relations, an integral part of the Student Affairs division at Wesleyan, serves as a primary resource for multicultural education, information, and training. While serving the needs of underrepresented students continues to be at the core of its mission, the Office of Intercultural Relations is committed to initiatives designed to enhance Wesleyan student, faculty, and staff consciousness about issues of social justice and equality. Each year, the Office of Intercultural Relations sponsors an International Student Organization Banquet where students provide cuisine and entertainment from their native countries, and also provides numerous programs during Black History Month aimed at educating the campus on diversity issues. A daily trivia contest allows students the opportunity to conduct research on various cultural issues and win a variety of campus prizes.

> SUCCESS Student Academic Support Services

Tutoring is available in all subjects through Student Academic Support Services, an office dedicated to supporting students with all aspects of their academic challenges. In addition to tutoring, the office will work with students to develop their study skills, time-management abilities, goal setting skills, and other productive habits. Students with specific disabilities are also supported through this office.

West Virginia Wesleyan College
59 College Avenue
Buckhannon, WV 26201-2998
Ph: (304) 473-8510
admission@wvwc.edu
www.wvwc.edu

FAST FACTS

STUDENT PROFILE
# of degree-seeking undergraduates	1,193
% male/female	46/54
% African American	3
% American Indian or Alaska Native	<1
% Asian or Pacific Islander	<1
% Hispanic	1
% Pell grant recipients	31

First-generation and minority alumni Sir John Swan, former premier of Bermuda, owner, John W. Swan Limited in Bermuda; Dr. Alfred Moye, independent consultant, former director of university relationships for Hewlett-Packard Company, worked in the Carter administration; William Stanley Norman, former president and CEO, Travel Industry Association of America

ACADEMICS
full-time faculty	76
full-time minority faculty	n/a
student-faculty ratio	12:1
average class size	18
% first-year retention rate	74
% graduation rate (6 years)	59

Popular majors Athletic Training, Biology, Business, Education, Nursing

CAMPUS LIFE
% live on campus (% fresh.)	76 (90)

Multicultural student clubs and organizations Black Business Student Association, Black Student Union, International Student Organization
Athetics NCAA Division II, West Virginia Intercollegiate Athletic Conference

ADMISSIONS
# of applicants	1,428
% accepted	72
# of first-year students enrolled	426
SAT Critical Reading range	450-560
SAT Math range	430-560
SAT Writing range	410-550
ACT range	20-26
average HS GPA	3.4

Deadlines
early decision	3/1
regular decision	rolling
application fee (online)	$35 ($0)
fee waiver for applicants with financial need	yes

COST & AID
tuition	$22,080
room & board	$6,470
total need-based institutional scholarships/grants	$1,280,000
% of students apply for need-based aid	84
% of students receive aid	75
% receiving need-based scholarship or grant aid	100
% receiving aid whose need was fully met	38
average aid package	$25,479
average student loan debt upon graduation	$19,750

Lawrence University

Lawrence University
Office of Admissions
711 E. Boldt Way, SPC 29
Appleton, WI 54911
Ph: (920) 832-6500
excel@lawrence.edu
www.lawrence.edu

Lawrence University, one of the nation's first coeducational institutions, is the nation's only liberal arts college and conservatory of music both devoted exclusively to undergraduate education. Ranking among the nation's best, small private colleges, Lawrence is featured in the book *Colleges That Change Lives: 40 Schools That Will Change the Way You Think About College*. With a picturesque, residential campus nestled on the banks of the Fox River in Appleton, Wisconsin (metro pop. 225,000), Lawrence draws its 1,400 students from 43 states and more than 50 countries. One of the most internationally diverse campuses in the country, Lawrence attracts students from a wide variety of geographic, ethnic, socioeconomic and experiential backgrounds.

> ACCESS College Readiness 21

Lawrence co-sponsors a northeast Wisconsin pre-college program called College Readiness 21. The initiative provides college visits, tutoring, personal and life-skills development, mentoring and college admissions coaching to low-income, minority and first-generation students. College Readiness 21 served 40 freshmen and sophomores from six northeast Wisconsin communities in its first year alone — all were the first in their families to aspire to go to college.

> *"Lawrence professors facilitate an environment of community. Their attitude is, "We're here to learn from each other."*
>
> *– Isake S., '11
> Brooklyn, NY
> Psychology*

> ACCESS The Partners Reaching Youth in Science and Math (PRYSM)

Through a one-to-one tutoring program between female Lawrence undergraduates who study math and science and seventh and eighth grade girls at Roosevelt Middle School in Appleton, Lawrence University's PRYSM program helps encourage girls to increase their skills and confidence in these fields. Lawrence has also hosted a GEMS (Girls Exploring Math and Science) Day on campus, where these students attended hands-on math and science workshops.

> ACCESS Posse Foundation

Lawrence University participates in the Posse Foundation, a program that brings talented inner-city youth to campus to pursue their academics and to help promote cross-cultural communication. Posse students are nominated by their high school to the program and share a collaborative support system with a special mentor to adjust to campus and college life. Lawrence's Posse Scholars hail from New York City.

> ACCESS Multicultural Affairs Office and Diversity Center

The staff of the Multicultural Affairs Office works to provide diversity resources through its various academic, social and cultural areas. By collaborating with university departments, student organizations and student services, the office aids various campus constituencies in developing large-scale events for the community inside and outside Lawrence University, such as the yearly Identity Forum, Women's Heritage Forum and many cultural celebrations. Nearby, the Diversity Center houses many multicultural groups, ranging from the Downer Feminist Council to the Latin American Students Organization.

> OPPORTUNITY Scholarships

Lawrence University strives to make it financially viable for all admitted students to enroll, including offering a variety of scholarships recognizing student achievement. For more information about scholarships and other financial aid, visit the Lawrence University admissions website.

FAST FACTS

STUDENT PROFILE
# of degree-seeking undergraduates	1,452
% male/female	46/54
% African American	2
% American Indian or Alaska Native	<1
% Asian or Pacific Islander	3
% Hispanic	2
% White	72
% International	8
% Pell grant recipients	17.8

First-generation and minority alums Cory L. Nettles, managing director at Generation Growth Capital Inc. and former secretary of the Wisconsin Department of Commerce; Dr. Crystal Cash, Family Practice Department Chair at Provident Hospital; Elijah Brewer III, Associate Professor of Finance at DePaul University; Michael Martino, vice president of Morgan Stanley

ACADEMICS
full-time faculty	155
full-time minority faculty	17
student-faculty ratio	9:1
average class size	15
% first-year retention rate	90
% graduation rate (6 years)	76

Popular majors Music Performance, Biology, Chemistry, Physics, Psychology, Geology

CAMPUS LIFE
% live on campus (% fresh.)	97 (99)

Multicultural Student Clubs and Organizations Amnesty International, Black Organization of Students, Latin American Students Organization, ¡Viva! (Spanish/Hispanic Student group), LUNA (Lawrence University Native Americans), Muslim Student Association, Hillel
Athletics Division III, Midwest Conference

ADMISSIONS
# of applicants	2,618
% accepted	59
# of first-year students enrolled	360
SAT Critical Reading range	590-720
SAT Math range	610-700
SAT Writing range	610-690
ACT range	27-31
average HS GPA	3.62

Deadlines
early decision	11/15
early action	12/1
regular decision	1/15
application fee (online)	$40 ($40)
fee waiver for applicants with financial need	yes

COST & AID
tuition	$34,596
room & board	$7,053
total need-based institutional scholarships/grants	$14,913,931
% of students apply for need-based aid	71
% of students receive aid	93
% receiving need-based scholarship or grant aid	93
% receiving aid whose need was fully met	62
average aid package	$26,800
average student loan debt upon graduation	$26,054

Marquette University

Marquette University
P.O. Box 1881
Milwaukee, WI 53201-1881
Ph: (414) 288-7302
admissions@marquette.edu
www.marquette.edu/explore

Marquette University is a mid-sized, private, four-year, comprehensive university affiliated with the Society of Jesus (Jesuits) of the Catholic Church. Marquette is dedicated to fostering excellence, faith, leadership and service in all of its students and offers strong support to first-generation and underserved students. The university runs four unique programs under The Educational Opportunity Program (EOP) in addition to an institutionally funded college transition program. Marquette's Multicultural Center works hard to promote diversity awareness and cultural inclusiveness within the diverse student body and the Office of Student Services supports every individual student's educational goals. With an urban campus located in downtown Milwaukee, Marquette students take advantage of the many educational, cultural and social outlets the city has to offer.

> ACCESS Upward Bound Math and Science

Local high school students who come from low-income families in which neither parent holds a bachelor's degree can benefit from Marquette's Upward Bound Math and Science, a pre-college program that provides a group of students with the right tools to pursue their dreams of earning a college degree. This program is intended for students with a strong interest in math, science, computer technology, or engineering. Students benefit from weekly tutoring, field trips, workshops, and a six-week summer enrichment program.

> OPPORTUNITY Urban Scholars Scholarship Program

Marquette's Urban Scholars Program provides 10 full-tuition awards to low-income students, including undocumented students, who show great academic promise. The award guarantees that a student's federal, state, and Marquette gift assistance cover tuition costs for a four-year undergraduate program, provided the student maintains a 2.0 GPA. Students are selected for this award based on academic merit, leadership and financial need. The 10 awards are granted to graduates from Milwaukee area high schools and the Cristo Rey High School network.

> OPPORTUNITY Goizueta Foundation Scholarship Award

The Goizueta Foundation Scholarship Award is for Hispanic/Latino high school seniors who demonstrate financial need. The award covers one-half of the Marquette tuition.

> OPPORTUNITY Boys & Girls Club Scholarship

Marquette University is proud to announce its new national partnership with the Boys & Girls Clubs of America (BGCA), targeting the Clubs' Youth of the Year (YOY) winners for three full-tuition scholarships to Marquette.

> SUCCESS Multicultural Center

The Multicultural Center was established as a focal point for the interaction and activities of students of colors. Through training, programming, and advising, the goal of the Multicultural Center is to educate and work with students from a variety of cultural backgrounds as well as the community to create a campus environment supportive of their educational goals.

"Both the Educational Opportunity and the Ronald E. McNair Program have been great blessings in my life. They have provided me with a strong personal example of the benefits one can receive if they make a decision in their mind to achieve despite circumstance."
– James B., '09
Milwaukee, WI
History

FAST FACTS

STUDENT PROFILE
# of degree-seeking undergraduates	7,821
% male/female	48/52
% African American	6
% American Indian or Alaska Native	<1
% Asian or Pacific Islander	4
% Hispanic	6
% White	82
% International	1
% Pell grant recipients	21.7

ACADEMICS
full-time faculty	622
full-time minority faculty	94
student-faculty ratio	15:1
average class size	28
% first-year retention rate	91
% graduation rate (6 years)	80

Popular majors Nursing, Marketing, Engineering, Psychology, Business Administration

CAMPUS LIFE
% live on campus	95

Multicultural student clubs and organizations
African Students Association, Arab Student Association, Bayanihan Student Association, Black Student Council, Chinese Student Association, Cuban American Student Association, Global Village, Indian Student Association, Indonesian Student Association, Latin American Student Organization, Malaysian Student Organization, Pacific Islands Student Organization, Society of Caribbean Ambassadors.
Athletics NCAA Division I, Big East Conference

ADMISSIONS
# of applicants	20,000
% accepted	52
# of first-year students enrolled	1,900
SAT Critical Reading range	520-640
SAT Math range	540-650
SAT Writing range	530-630
ACT range	24-30
average HS GPA	3.5 (on 4.0 unweighted)

Deadlines
regular decision	12/1
application fee (online)	$30 ($0)
fee waiver for applicants with financial need	yes

COST & AID
tuition	$30,040
room & board	$9,860
total need-based institutional scholarships/grants	$50,000,000
% of students apply for need-based aid	69
% of students receive aid	99
% receiving need-based scholarship or grant aid	96
% receiving aid whose need was fully met	29
average aid package	$22,000
average student loan debt upon graduation	$31,000

St. Norbert College

Intellectually, spiritually and personally challenging, St. Norbert is a private liberal arts college founded by the Norbertines, a Catholic order committed to community and service. St. Norbert offers small class sizes, individual attention, and faculty members who make student success their top priority. Students have 40-plus programs to choose from, and a multitude of internship opportunities. Students can study abroad at 75 program sites on six continents and undergraduates regularly experience graduate-level collaborative research with faculty. Academic advisers guide students throughout their college careers, and an active alumni community provides valuable career networking.

> ACCESS Women's Center Eighth Grade Mentoring Program

St. Norbert's Women's Center Eighth Grade Mentoring Program embodies the college's commitment to social justice and diversity. St. Norbert students work with first-generation, eighth-grade students on a variety of academic and social issues. The eighth graders have the opportunity to spend a day on the St. Norbert campus, experiencing college living and socializing.

> ACCESS Upward Bound

Upward Bound is a pre-college program funded by the Department of Education to serve and assist low-income, first generation college and disabled students. The program provides the support and resources to help students develop the skills and motivation necessary to pursue and succeed in college, offering cultural and social activities, career and educational opportunities, and other hands-on experiences.

"I didn't realize what an impact being a First Year Experience and Multicultural Student Services Mentor would have on my life. I was able to influence the first year students and they changed my perception of what a community is."

– Avery G., '11
Kewaunee, WI
International Studies,
Spanish

> OPPORTUNITY Diversity Leadership Award

St. Norbert offers a Diversity Leadership Award that recognizes students who are committed to diversity and actively involved in bringing awareness to their community. This award is distributed on an annual basis in amounts ranging from $1,000 to $6,000. Recipients of the award are required to assist in at least two diversity-focused campus activities, thereby ensuring continued multicultural community involvement.

> OPPORTUNITY Red Carpet Program

To increase minority enrollment, St. Norbert College instituted the Red Carpet Program. High school juniors and seniors visit the St. Norbert campus, meet with current students and faculty and obtain information about financial aid and admission requirements.

> SUCCESS Academic Enhancement Program

The Academic Enhancement Program is a one-semester program offering freshmen the opportunity to learn and practice academic habits associated with success in college. Support services include study skills, time management skills, note-taking skills and good academic habits.

> SUCCESS Mission and Heritage Diversity Initiative

The Mission and Heritage Diversity Initiative is St. Norbert College's way of celebrating diversity of faith. The initiative is composed of a variety of strategies and programs to serve the needs of students from different religious backgrounds.

St. Norbert College
Office of Admission
100 Grant Street
De Pere, WI 54115
Ph: (800) 236-4878 / (920) 403-3005
admit@snc.edu
www.snc.edu

F A S T   F A C T S

STUDENT PROFILE

# of degree-seeking undergraduates	2,045
% male/female	43/57
% African-American	<1
% American Indian or Alaska Native	1
% Asian or Pacific Islander	1
% Hispanic	3
% White	90
% International	3
% Pell grant recipients	15.5

First-generation and minority alums Tadashi Yamamoto, president, Japan Center for International Exchange

ACADEMICS

full-time faculty	109
full-time minority faculty	7
student-faculty ratio	14:1
average class size	21
% first-year retention rate	85
% graduation rate (6 yr)	70

Popular majors Business Administration, Elementary Education, Communication and Media Studies

CAMPUS LIFE

% live on campus (% fresh.)	74 (96)

Multicultural student clubs and organizations Discoveries International, Beyond Borders, Japan Club, Viva Espanol

Athletics NCAA Division III, Midwest Conference

ADMISSIONS

# of applicants	2,116
% accepted	81
# of first-year students enrolled	543
SAT Critical Reading range	n/a
SAT math range	n/a
SAT Writing range	n/a
ACT range	22-27
average HS GPA	3.52

Deadlines

regular decision	rolling
application fee (online)	$25 ($0)
fee waiver for applicants with financial need	yes

COST & AID

tuition	$24, 253
room & board	$6,579
total need-based institutional scholarships/grants	$12,164,263
% of students apply for need-based aid	78
% of students receive aid	100
% receiving need-based scholarship or grant aid	97
% receiving aid whose need was fully met	35
average aid package	$17,025
average student loan debt upon graduation	$27,207

University of Wisconsin – Platteville

University of Wisconsin – Platteville
1 University Plaza
Platteville, Wisconsin 53818
Ph: 877-UWPLATT
admit@uwplatt.edu
www.uwplatt.edu

The University of Wisconsin – Platteville is a four-year comprehensive public institution, located 20 miles east of the Mississippi River. The campus is a leader in the University of Wisconsin system with diversity and access issues. Faculty, staff and students attend diversity training and workshops addressing topics such as comprehensive racism, campus climate, and cultural awareness. The university strives to demonstrate leadership, creativity and vision in supporting the continuing development of racial competence. Faculty and staff are focused on student success and dedicate time not only for meetings with students during office hours but also for participating in special help sessions. Classes are taught by professors, not teaching assistants. Coursework includes practical demonstrations, group work, and field experience. There are numerous opportunities for students to participate in scholarly research projects with their professors. Additionally, students have the opportunity to practice the skills they learn in the classroom and develop leadership capacity through involvement in more than 220 student clubs and organizations.

> ACCESS Pre-College Program

The pre-college program serves 6th-12th grade low-income and disadvantaged students through weekly and bi-weekly summer camps that are designed to teach skills that will help close the educational achievement gap between disadvantaged and advantaged students in Wisconsin.

> ACCESS Paths to Platteville

Paths to Platteville enables underserved high school students to visit college campuses in Wisconsin. Every year about 500 students learn about the admissions and financial aid process in addition to touring college campuses and interacting with current first-generation and minority students.

"The Multicultural Educational Resource Center at UWP provides support systems for interested students on multiple levels. Study tables are set up in the center with tutors from a variety of majors available to assist. The staff motivates students to excel academically and socially."

– Brittany D., '11
Milwaukee, WI
Elementary Education

> OPPORTUNITY Alliant Energy 5x5x5 Diversity Scholarship

The Alliant Energy 5x5x5 Diversity Scholarship is a $1,000 awarded to five students annually. To qualify, students must be entering their freshman year, have a high school GPA of a 3.0 or better, belong to a historically-underrepresented group and major in accounting, agricultural education, agri-business, business administration, communication technologies, comprehensive business, computer science, or engineering.

> SUCCESS Multicultural Educational Resource Center (MERC)

The purpose of the Multicultural Educational Resource Center is to enhance the visibility and awareness of racial diversity at UW-Platteville. The center is dedicated to promoting positive racial identity development for all students. Advisors are available to assist students in the areas of academic, personal and social concerns.

> SUCCESS Mentoring and Academic Advising

The Multicultural Educational Resource Center offers a Peer Mentor Group and Multicultural Advisors to assist students. The Peer Mentor Group pairs upperclassmen with freshman to help new students adjust to college life and become acclimated to campus, while the Multicultural Advisors assist with academic counseling, class selection, and retention.

FAST FACTS

STUDENT PROFILE
# of degree-seeking undergraduates	6,856
% male/female	60/40
% African-American	2
% American Indian or Alaska Native	1
% Asian or Pacific Islander	1
% Hispanic	1
% White	92
% Pell grant recipients	25

First-generation and minority alumni Robert Jeter III, Head Men's Basketball Coach for UW-Milwaukee, 2005 Outstanding Alumni Recipient and 2006 Athletic Hall of Fame Recipient; Dr. Eduardo Manual, Senior Director, Development Chicago Region and Diversity, University of Wisconsin-Madison Foundation, CASE (council for Advancement and Support of Education) District V board of directors; Patricia Gomez, 2005 (MSED), Producer and Host for Milwaukee Public Television production, ¡Adelante!; Artanya M. Wesley, 2006 and 2008, Student Service Coordinator for the Department of Student Affairs, University of Wisconsin-Platteville, 2009 Outstanding Woman of Color Award

ACADEMICS
full-time faculty	290
full-time minority faculty	50
student-faculty ratio	26:1
average class size	27
% first-year retention rate	75
% graduation rate (6 years)	57

Popular majors Agriculture, Biology, Business, Criminal Justice, Education, Engineering, Industrial Technology

CAMPUS LIFE
% live on campus (% fresh.)	40 (92)

Multicultural student clubs and organizations Black Student Union (BSU), Hmong Club, InterTribal Council, Student Organization of Latinos (SOL), Multicultural Educational Resource Center (MERC)

Athletics NCAA Division III, Wisconsin Intercollegiate Athletic Conference (WIAC)

ADMISSIONS
# of applicants	3,661
% accepted	80
# of first-year students enrolled	1,518
SAT Critical Reading range	450-550
SAT Math range	450-550
SAT Writing	n/a
ACT range	20-25
average HS GPA	2.75

Deadlines
regular decision	rolling
application fee (online)	$44 ($44)
fee waiver for applicants with financial need	yes

COST & AID
tuition	in-state $6,456; MN resident $6,725
	Tri-State Initiative $10,456; out-of-state $14,029
room & board	$5,651
total need-based institutional scholarships/grants	n/a
% of students apply for need-based aid	n/a
% of students receive aid	75
% receiving need-based scholarship or grant aid	36
% receiving aid whose need was fully met	n/a
average aid package	$9,086
average student loan debt upon graduation	$17,250

University of Wisconsin – River Falls

Established in 1874, the University of Wisconsin – River Falls is a public, co-educational, four-year liberal arts university. Situated in a community of 12,500 in scenic western Wisconsin, the campus is 24 miles from the heart of the metropolitan area of Minneapolis and St. Paul, Minn. The university strives to maintain an environment of mutual respect, academic freedom and appreciation of individual and cultural differences. A primary mission of the University of Wisconsin — River Falls is to help students learn so that they are successful as productive, creative, ethical, engaged citizens and leaders with an informed global perspective. International study and travel opportunities and service-learning projects and collaborative relationships in communities both in the U.S. and abroad are encouraged. The University of Wisconsin — River Falls promises to encourage and support all members of the campus community as they discover their own potential and the richness and complexity of a multifaceted world.

> ACCESS Pre-College Programs

A variety of programs, funded by state and federal agencies, as well as by regional, not-for-profit organizations, are made available thoughout the year to students entering grades nine through 12. Designed to help with college readiness and career exploration, first-generation or low-income future college students experience campus life while participating in academic courses, career exploration exercises and health and wellness activities. Annually, approximately 550 secondary school students participate in the year-round Upward Bound and GEAR UP/Get Ready programs, the College Camp program and the Milwaukee Vincent High School Enviomental Studies Collaborative offered during the summer months.

> ACCESS Falcon Tutors Program

Falcon Tutors is a University of Wisconsin – River Falls service-learning and field experience program. The collaborative initiative — with active partners from AmericorpsVISTA, the Corporation for National and Community Service and the university's Upward Bound Program — has made tutors available at multiple public school sites in St. Paul, Minn. to provide classroom assistance, observe urban classrooms and participate in after-school individual or small group tutoring sessions. Falcon Tutors receive valuable experiences in urban classrooms and multicultural education settings. Since 2004, Falcon Tutors have provided over 18,000 hours of service to St. Paul Public Schools.

> OPPORTUNITY Scholarships

The University of Wisconsin – River Falls is very proud of its scholarship program, which has grown considerably in recent years. In 2007-08, more than 530 scholarships, in excess of $460,000 were awarded to new and continuing students. Factors that influence eligibility for scholarships are academic achievement, financial need, high school activity and community service record. Complete scholarship information, including eligibility and application instructions, can be found on the university's Web site.

> OPPORTUNITY Multicultural Scholars Program

Administered by the College of Agriculture, Food and Environmental Sciences (CAFES), and funded by the U.S. Department of Agriculture, this program provides renewable scholarships for incoming freshman students. In addition to full-tuition funding, Multicultural Scholars participate in paid internships, undergraduate student-faculty research projects, professional development activities, and employment through the university's pilot plants, greenhouses and farm enterprises. Intensive mentoring and advising by CAFES faculty ensure student success.

> SUCCESS Academic Services Center (ASC)

The Academic Services Center provides a broad range of support services to the entire campus community, and serves as "home base" for all campus undergraduate TRIO programs. In adition to housing the Multicultural Services Office, the center also provides pre-major advising for the undecided student, tutoring for all students free of charge and Disability Services. The I AM Series highlights various issues of relevance to students through interactive discussion workshops.

University of Wisconsin- River Falls
410 South Third Street
River Falls, WI 54022-5001
Ph: (715) 425-3500
admit@uwrf.edu
www.uwrf.edu

F A S T   F A C T S

STUDENT PROFILE

# of degree-seeking undergraduates	6,050
% male/female	41/ 59
% African-American	1
% American Indian or Alaska Native	<1
% Asian or Pacific Islander	3
% Hispanic	1
% White	91
% Pell grant recipients	23

First-generation and minority alumni Dan Brandenstein '65, Astronaut, NASA Program Director, US Astronaut Hall of Fame inductee; Sigurd Hanson '75, International Humanitarian and Author, with three decades of relief work in the Third World; Congressman Bruce Vento '65, Minnesota's 4th District for 24 years, national advocate for the environment and the homeless; How Man Wong '76, International Explorer and Photojournalist

ACADEMICS

full-time faculty	236
full-time minority faculty	n/a
student-faculty ratio	20:1
average class size	20-29
% first-year retention rate	74
% graduation rate (6 years)	55

Popular majors Business Administration, Elementary Education, Animal Science

CAMPUS LIFE

% live on campus (% freshmen)	48 (90)

Multicultural student clubs and organizations Asian Americans, Black Student Union, Diversity Awareness, Native American Council, International Student Association

Athletics NCAA Division III, Wisconsin Intercollegiate Athletic Conference

ADMISSIONS

# of applicants	2,959
% accepted	89
# of first-year students enrolled	1,744
SAT Critical Reading range	n/a
SAT Math range	n/a
SAT Writing range	n/a
ACT range	20-24
average HS GPA	3.3

Deadlines

regular decision	rolling
application fee (online)	$44 ($44)
fee waiver for applicants with financial need	yes

COST & AID

tuition	in-state: $6,390; out-of-state: $13,963
room & board	$5,330
total need-based institutional scholarships/grants	n/a
% of students apply for need-based aid	77
% of students receive aid	58
% receiving need-based scholarship or grant aid	62
% receiving aid whose need was fully met	64
average aid package	$3,764
average student loan debt upon graduation	$12,500

University of Wisconsin – Whitewater

The University of Wisconsin-Whitewater desires a reputation as an institution that truly values and nurtures diverse intellectual, cultural, creative, and service opportunities. To accomplish that, it must promote its image as a diverse, respected and empowering institution of higher learning. The university attracts and supports students from all parts of the region, nation and world, sustaining optimum enrollment, retention and graduation rates for all student populations. Wisconsin-Whitewater will create and maintain programs for intercultural or international study, research and service in every department along with developing, attracting, and retaining a diverse faculty and staff.

> OPPORTUNITY King/Chavez Scholars

The King/Chavez Scholars program is designed to complement the array of multicultural/disadvantaged programs at UW-Whitewater that serve the interests and needs of first generation/low income TRIO students. The King Chavez Scholars program is designed to attract and retain scholars for the McNair Scholars Program, University Honors Program and Undergraduate Research. Students receive a scholarship during their freshman year.

> SUCCESS Academic Network

Academic Network targets multicultural/disadvantaged students who are not designated users of Minority Business/Teacher Preparation Program, EOP, Latino Student Programs, the McNair Program, Native American Support Services, or Southeast Asian Support Services. Academic Network provides advising and referrals to academic services.

> SUCCESS McNair Scholars Program

McNair Scholars Program prepares first-generation and multicultural students for doctoral study and eventually careers as college professors. The program matches each student with a faculty mentor in their major; provides resources for undergraduate research projects; enhances students' quantitative computer, test taking, research methods, and critical thinking skills; provides students with opportunities to present research findings at regional and national conferences; provides stipends for on-campus and external summer research internships.

> SUCCESS Minority Business/Teacher Preparation Program (MB/TPP)

Minority Business/Teacher Preparation Program provides support for targeted students majoring in business and education. The program is located in the College of Business & Economics and College of Education.

> SUCCESS Minority Student Support Programs

Latino Student Programs, Native American Support Services (NASS), and Southeast Asian Student Services (SASS) foster the retention and graduation of Latino, Native American and Southeast Asian students through: academic advising, multicultural/ globalized programming, scholarships and study abroad experiences.

"Attending the University of Wisconsin-Whitewater has been an incredible experience. I am a member of a few student organizations and I feel like I'm an important part of the campus community. My classes have been challenging, but the academic support resources have helped me perform at a high level."
– Shanika T., '12
Milwaukee, WI
Social Work

University of Wisconsin- Whitewater
Office of Admissions
800 West Main Street
Whitewater, WI 52190-1790
Ph: (262) 472-1440
uwwadmit@uww.edu
www.uww.edu

F A S T   F A C T S

STUDENT PROFILE
# of degree-seeking undergraduates	9,409
% male/female	51/49
% African American	2
% American Indian or Alaska Native	<1
% Asian or Pacific Islander	2
% Hispanic	2
% White	89
% International	1
% Pell grant recipients	19.9

First-generation and minority alumni David Hill, Chief State Affairs Officer-Government Relations Legal Department, Assurant Health

ACADEMICS
full-time faculty	403
full-time minority faculty	76
student-faculty ratio	22:1
average class size	22
% first-year retention rate	76
% graduation rate (6 years)	56

Popular majors Accounting\Finance, Biology\Chemistry, Communications (Broadcast and Print Journalism), Education, Management Computer Systems

CAMPUS LIFE
% live on campus (% fresh.)	40 (90)

Multicultural student clubs and organizations Black Student Union, Latinos Unidos, Native Aboriginal Cultural Awareness Association, Southeast Asian Organization, National Association of Black Accountants, National Association of Black Journalists

Athletics NCAA Division III, Wisconsin Intercollegiate Athletic Conference

ADMISSIONS
# of applicants	6,805
% accepted	73
# of first-year students enrolled	2,154
SAT Critical Reading range	n/a
SAT Math range	n/a
SAT Writing range	n/a
ACT range	20-24
average HS GPA	3.20

Deadlines
regular decision	rolling to 8/1
application fee (online)	$44 ($44)
fee waiver for applicants with financial need	yes

COST & AID
tuition	in-state: $6,496; out-of-state: $14,068
room & board	$4,980
total need-based institutional scholarships/grants	$10,550,000
% of students apply for need-based aid	69
% of students receive aid	97
% receiving need-based scholarship or grant aid	45
% receiving aid whose need was fully met	64
average aid package	$7,280
average student loan debt upon graduation	$17,869

University of Wyoming

Wyoming's only four-year educational institution, the University of Wyoming is a co-educational, public university. Founded in 1887, the University of Wyoming combines big-university benefits and small-school advantages, offering students the opportunity to stand at the forefront in the exploration of emerging technologies and concepts, while at the same time, providing students with hands-on involvement and one-on-one attention.

> ACCESS I'm Going to College!

This is a program designed to familiarize ethnic minority and first-generation elementary and middle-school students with a college campus. Providing students and their parents with a taste of college life, "I'm Going to College!" seeks to introduce a philosophy of expected attendance into the early school careers of underrepresented students. Academic stations on campus illustrate the avenues of study and potential career areas available to those individuals who obtain a college degree. Additionally, parents participate in sessions about motivating children and financing higher education.

> ACCESS Experimental Program to Stimulate Competitive Research

This program provides a seven-week summer research apprentice program serving over 20 underrepresented high school students (grades 10 to 12) who are interested in pursuing a career in the sciences. Students are paired with research teams led by a Wyoming faculty member, and they present their research at a research symposium at the end of the summer program. Throughout the program, college preparation activities are held while the students live on the university campus. The university's program prides itself on its high rate of college attendees and graduation rates.

> ACCESS Shadows of Success

This program provides an individualized opportunity for ethnic minority students to obtain a real-life college experience. Through the Shadows of Success program, high school students are paired up with current minority students on campus and have the opportunity to "shadow" that student through a day of college life. Students who participate can have their admission application fees waived.

> OPPORTUNITY American Indian Scholarships

Given that Wyoming is home to two tribal governments, the Northern Arapaho Nation and the Eastern Shoshone Tribe, the university provides several scholarships for American Indian students. These include the Northern Arapaho Endowment, the Chief Washakie Scholarship, McCarthy Scholarship, Winner Scholarship, and Thorpe Scholarship. Additionally, the Office of Multicultural Affairs has received two bequests for American Indian students that will be offered in the future. These scholarships ensure the school's commitment to community involvement and multiculturalism.

> SUCCESS Student Success Services (SSS)

The Student Success Services program provides a host of student-support services and information designed to increase the persistence, good academic standing, and graduation rates of first-generation, low-income students and students with disabilities. From study skill development to personal budgeting and money management assistance, these services are delivered individually through one-on-one structured advising or in small-group settings. Each participant meets regularly with her/his adviser to identify academic, financial, personal, social, career and major needs and to devise an individualized educational action plan to meet those needs.

University of Wyoming
1000 E. University Avenue
Laramie, WY 82070
Ph: (307) 766-5160
why-wyo@uwyo.edu
www.uwyo.edu/

FAST FACTS

STUDENT PROFILE

# of degree-seeking undergraduates	9,544
% male/female	50/50
% African-American	1
% American Indian or Alaska Native	1
% Asian or Pacific Islander	1
% Hispanic	4
% White	82
% Pell grant recipients	24

First-generation and minority alumni Sol Trujillo '73, businessman; Gene Huey '71, NFL coach

ACADEMICS

full-time faculty	715
full-time minority faculty	60
student-faculty ratio	14:1
average class size	27
% first-year retention rate	73
% graduation rate (6 years)	57

Popular majors Elementary Education and Teaching, Nursing

CAMPUS LIFE

% live on campus (% fresh.)	28 (88)

Multicultural student clubs and organizations Asian American Pacific Islander Student Organization, MILAAP (Indian Students Organization), Students for Campus and Community Chicana Awareness, Turkish Student Organization, Wyoming African Students Association, American Indian Studies Alliance, Association of Black Student Leaders, Chinese Students & Scholars Association, Korean Student Association, Muslim Student Association

Athletics NCAA Division I (football I-A), Mountain West Conference

ADMISSIONS

# of applicants	3,589
% accepted	96
# of first-year students enrolled	49
SAT Critical Reading range	470-610
SAT Math range	500-640
SAT Writing range	n/a
ACT range	21-27
average HS GPA	3.5

Deadlines

regular decision	rolling
application fee (online)	$40($40)
fee waiver for applicants with financial need	yes

COST & AID

tuition	in-state: $15,980; out-of-state: $23,900
room & board	$8,006
total need-based institutional scholarships/grants	$7,858,476
% of students apply for need-based aid	74
% of students receive aid	98
% receiving need-based scholarship or grant aid	50
% receiving aid whose need was fully met	27
average aid package	$7,612
average student loan debt upon graduation	$12,500

Notes

Notes

Notes

Notes

Notes

Notes

Notes